# Object Model Notation
# Advanced Concepts

**Abstract Operation:**

| Superclass |
| --- |
| |
| operation {abstract} |

Operation is abstract in the superclass.

| Subclass-1 | Subclass-2 |
| --- | --- |
| | |
| operation | operation |

Subclasses must provide concrete implementations of operation.

**Association as Class:**

| Class-1 |    | Class-2 |

| Association Name |
| --- |
| link attribute |
| ... |
| link operation |
| ... |

**Generalization Properties:**

| Superclass |
| --- |

| Subclass-1 | Subclass-2 | ...

More subclasses exist.

| Superclass |
| --- |

| Subclass-1 | Subclass-2 |

Subclasses have overlapping (nondisjoint) membership.

**Multiple Inheritance:**

| Superclass-1 | Superclass-2 |

...   | Subclass |   ...

| Superclass |
| --- |

**discriminator**

| Subclass-1 | Subclass-2 |

Discriminator is an attribute whose value differentiates between subclasses.

**Class Attributes and Class Operations:**

| Class Name |
| --- |
| $attribute |
| $operation |

**Derived Attribute:**

| Class Name |
| --- |
| /attribute |

**Derived Class:**

| Class Name |

**Propagation of Operations:**

| Class-1 |
| --- |
| operation |

operation →

| Class-2 |
| --- |
| operation |

**Derived Association:**

| Class-1 |  /  | Class-2 |

**Constraints on Objects:**

| Class-1 |
| --- |
| attrib-1 |
| attrib-2 |

{ attrib-1 ≥ 0 }

**Constraint between Associations:**

| Class-1 |    *A1*    | Class-2 |

{subset}

*A2*

This page may be freely copied without obtaining permission from the publisher.

# Object-Oriented Modeling and Design

James Rumbaugh
Michael Blaha
William Premerlani
Frederick Eddy
William Lorensen

General Electric Research and Development Center
Schenectady, New York

Prentice-Hall International, Inc.

©1991 by Prentice-Hall, Inc.
**A Division of Simon & Schuster**
**Englewood Cliffs, New Jersey 07632**

Apple, LaserWriter, and MacAPP are registered trademarks of Apple Computer, Inc.
DEC and VAX are registered trademarks of Digital Equipment Corporation.
Eiffel is a registered trademark of Interactive Software Engineering, Inc.
FrameMaker is a registered trademark of Frame Technology Corporation.
GemStone is a registered trademark of Servio Logic.
INGRES is a trademark of Ingres Corporation.
Interleaf is a trademark of Interleaf, Inc.
Linotronic is a registered trademark of Allied Corporation.
MS-DOS is a trademark of Microsoft Corporation.
MacDraw is a registered trademark of Claris Corporation.
NeWS, Sun Workstation, and Sun View are registered trademarks of Sun Microsystems,Inc.
Objective-C is a registered trademark of Stepstone Corporation.
ONTOS is a trademark of Ontologic, Inc.
ORACLE is a registered trademark of Oracle Corporation.
PostScript is a registered trademark of Adobe Systems, Inc.
Smalltalk-80 is a trademark of ParcPlace Systems.
Statemate is a registered trademark of i-Logix, Inc.
UNIX is a trademark of AT & T Bell Laboratories.
X Window System is a trademark of Massachusetts Institute of Technology.

Printed in the United States of America

20 19 18 17 16 15 14

ISBN 0-13-630054-5

Prentice-Hall International (UK) Limited, *London*
Prentice-Hall of Australia Pty. Limited, *Sydney*
Prentice-Hall Canada Inc., *Toronto*
Prentice-Hall Hispanoamericana, S.A., *Mexico*
Prentice-Hall of India Private Limited, *New Delhi*
Prentice-Hall of Japan, Inc., *Tokyo*
Simon & Schuster (Asia) Pte. Ltd., *Singapore*
Editora Prentice-Hall do Brasil, Ltda., *Rio de Janeiro*
Prentice-Hall, Inc, Englewood Cliffs, *New Jersey*

# Contents

# Preface

This book presents an object-oriented approach to software development based on *modeling objects* from the real world and then using the model to build a language-independent *design* organized around those objects. Object-oriented modeling and design promote better understanding of requirements, cleaner designs, and more maintainable systems. We describe a set of object-oriented concepts and a language-independent graphical notation, the Object Modeling Technique, that can be used to analyze problem requirements, design a solution to the problem, and then implement the solution in a programming language or database. Our approach allows the same concepts and notation to be used throughout the entire software development process. The software developer does not need to translate into a new notation at each development stage as is required by many other methodologies.

We show how to use object-oriented concepts throughout the entire software life cycle, from analysis through design to implementation. The book is not primarily about object-oriented languages or coding. Instead we stress that coding is the last stage in a process of development that includes stating a problem, understanding its requirements, planning a solution, and implementing a program in a particular language. A good design technique defers implementation details until later stages of design to preserve flexibility. Mistakes in the front of the development process have a large impact on the ultimate product and on the time needed to finish. We describe the implementation of object-oriented designs in object-oriented languages, non-object-oriented languages, and relational databases.

The book emphasizes that object-oriented technology is more than just a way of programming. Most importantly, it is a way of thinking abstractly about a problem using real-world concepts, rather than computer concepts. This may be a difficult transition for some people because older programming languages force one to think in terms of the computer and not in terms of the application. Books that emphasize object-oriented programming often fail to help the programmer learn to think abstractly without using programming constructs. We have found that the graphical notation that we describe helps the software developer visualize a problem without prematurely resorting to implementation.

We show that object-oriented technology provides a practical, productive way to develop software for most applications, regardless of the final implementation language. We take an informal approach in this book; there are no proofs or formal definitions with Greek letters. We attempt to foster a pragmatic approach to problem solving drawing upon the intuitive sense that object-oriented technology captures and by providing a notation and methodology for using it systematically on real problems. We provide tips and examples of good and bad design to help the software developer avoid common pitfalls. To illustrate the pragmatic nature of these concepts, we describe several real applications developed by the authors using object-oriented techniques.

This book is intended for both software professionals and students. The reader will learn how to apply object-oriented concepts to all stages of the software development life cycle. At present, there are few, if any, object-oriented books covering the entire life cycle, as opposed to programming or analysis alone. In fact, there are few textbooks on object-oriented technology of any kind. Although object-oriented technology is currently a "hot" topic, most readers have limited experience with it, so we do not assume any prior knowledge of object-oriented concepts. We do assume that the reader is familiar with basic computing concepts, but an extensive formal background is not required. Even existing object-oriented programmers will benefit from learning how to design programs systematically; they may be surprised to discover that certain common object-oriented coding practices violate principles of good design.

The database designer will find much of interest here. Although object-oriented programming languages have previously received the most attention, object-oriented design of databases is perhaps even more compelling and immediately practical. We include an entire chapter describing how to implement an object-oriented design using existing relational database management systems.

This book can be used as a textbook for a graduate or advanced undergraduate course on software engineering or object-oriented technology. It can be used as a supplementary text for courses on databases or programming languages. Prerequisites include exposure to modern structured programming languages and a knowledge of basic computer science terms and concepts, such as syntax, semantics, recursion, set, procedure, graph, and state; a detailed formal background is not required. Exercises of varying difficulty are included in each chapter along with selected answers at the back of the book.

Many object-oriented books primarily discuss programming issues, usually from the point of view of a single language. The best of them discuss design issues, but they are nevertheless mainly about programming. Fewer books address object-oriented analysis or design. We show that object-oriented concepts can and should be applied throughout the entire software life cycle. Recently books on object-oriented methodology have begun to appear. Our book is compatible with other books on object-oriented analysis and design, and we feel that it is complementary to them in content.

Several existing books on software methodology discuss the entire life cycle from a procedural viewpoint. The traditional data flow methodologies of DeMarco, Yourdon, and others are based mainly on functional decomposition, although recent revisions have been
influenced by object-oriented concepts. Even Jackson's methodology, which superficially
seems to be based on objects, quickly reverts to procedural issues.

Our emphasis differs in some respects from the majority of the object-oriented programming community but is in accord with the information modeling and design methodology
communities. We place a much greater emphasis on object-oriented constructs as models of
real things, rather than as techniques for programming. We elevate interobject relationships
to the same semantic level as classes, rather than hiding them as pointers inside objects. We
place somewhat less importance on inheritance and methods. We downplay fine details of
inheritance mechanisms. We come down strongly in favor of typing, classes, modeling, and
advance planning. We use terminology that is universally accepted when possible, otherwise
we try to choose the best terms among various alternatives. There is as yet no commonly accepted graphical notation for object-oriented constructs, so despite concerns about introducing "yet another notation" we use our own Object Modeling Technique notation, which we
have used extensively on real problems and which has been successfully adopted by others.
In any case, the object-oriented concepts themselves are the most important thing, not the
shape of the symbols used to represent them. We also show how to apply object-oriented
concepts to state machines.

The book contains four parts. Part 1 presents object-oriented concepts in a high-level,
language-independent manner. These concepts are fundamental to the rest of the book, although advanced material can be skipped initially. The Object Modeling Technique notation
is introduced in Part 1 and used throughout the book to show examples. Part 2 describes a
step-by-step object-oriented methodology of software development from problem statement
through analysis, system design, and object design. All but the final stages of the methodology are language-independent; even object design is concerned mostly with issues independent of any particular language. Part 3 describes the implementation of object-oriented
designs in various target environments, including object-oriented languages, non-object-oriented languages, and relational databases. It describes the considerations applicable to different environments, although it is not intended to replace books on object-oriented
programming. Part 4 presents case studies of actual object-oriented applications developed
by the authors at the General Electric Research and Development Center. The problems cover a range of application domains and implementation targets.

The authors have used object-oriented analysis, design, programming, and database
modeling for several years on a variety of applications. We have also implemented an object-
oriented language, developed an object-oriented notation and methodology, and developed
object-oriented support tools, so we are familiar with both theoretical and pragmatic issues
of implementing and using object-oriented technology. We are enthusiastic about the object-
oriented approach and have found that it is applicable to almost any kind of application. We
have found that the use of object-oriented concepts, together with a graphical notation and a
development methodology, can greatly increase the quality, flexibility, and understandability
of software. We hope that this book can help to get that message across.

## ACKNOWLEDGMENTS

We wish to thank the many individuals who have made this book possible. We especially want to thank GE and our management at the Research and Development Center for their foresight in giving us the opportunity to develop the ideas presented here by working on object-oriented technology when it was still a new and unproven field as well as for their support, encouragement, and facilities in writing the book. We also wish to thank our colleagues at GE who worked with us in exploring this exciting new field. We acknowledge the important contribution of Mary Loomis and Ashwin Shah, who participated in the original development of the Object Modeling Technique notation.

Many individuals helped in the review of the manuscript, but in particular we wish to thank David Hentchel, Mark Kornfein, and Marc Laymon for their thorough reviews and perceptive comments.

Finally and most importantly we wish to thank our wives and families for their patience and encouragement during the many long weekends and evenings that went into the writing of this book.

## Production Note

The manuscript of this book was prepared by the authors on SUN workstations using the FrameMaker document preparation system. We drew the diagrams using the FrameMaker system. We created most object diagrams using our OMTool editor and converted them to FrameMaker format. We performed detailed page layout, made the index, and generated the table of contents using the FrameMaker system. Proof copies of the complete document were printed on Apple LaserWriter Plus printers. We generated PostScript page description files from the final document, copied them onto a Unix *tar* tape, and sent the tape to the publisher for generation of the camera copy on a Linotronic 202 typesetter. The publisher prepared and set the title and copyright pages.

# 1

---

# Introduction

*Object-oriented modeling and design* is a new way of thinking about problems using models organized around real-world concepts. The fundamental construct is the object, which combines both data structure and behavior in a single entity. Object-oriented models are useful for understanding problems, communicating with application experts, modeling enterprises, preparing documentation, and designing programs and databases. This book presents an object-oriented software development methodology, the Object Modeling Technique (OMT), which extends from analysis through design to implementation. First an analysis model is built to abstract essential aspects of the application domain without regard for eventual implementation. This model contains objects found in the application domain, including a description of the properties of the objects and their behavior. Then design decisions are made and details are added to the model to describe and optimize the implementation. The application-domain objects form the framework of the design model, but they are implemented in terms of computer-domain objects. Finally the design model is implemented in a programming language, database, or hardware.

We describe a graphical notation for expressing object-oriented models. Application-domain and computer-domain objects can be modeled, designed, and implemented using the same object-oriented concepts and notation. The same seamless notation is used from analysis to design to implementation so that information added in one stage of development need not be lost or translated for the next stage.

## 1.1  WHAT IS OBJECT-ORIENTED?

Superficially the term "object-oriented" means that we organize software as a collection of discrete objects that incorporate both data structure and behavior. This is in contrast to conventional programming in which data structure and behavior are only loosely connected. There is some dispute about exactly what characteristics are required by an object-oriented approach, but they generally include four aspects: identity, classification, polymorphism, and inheritance.

1

### 1.1.1 Characteristics of Objects

*Identity* means that data is quantized into discrete, distinguishable entities called *objects*. A *paragraph in a document*, a *window on my workstation*, and the *white queen in a chess game* are examples of objects. Figure 1.1 shows some additional objects. Objects can be concrete, such as a *file* in a file system, or conceptual, such as a *scheduling policy* in a multiprocessing operating system. Each object has its own inherent identity. In other words, two objects are distinct even if all their attribute values (such as name and size) are identical.

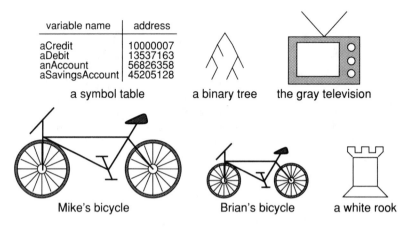

**Figure 1.1** Objects

In the real world an object simply exists, but within a programming language each object has a unique *handle* by which it can be uniquely referenced. The handle may be implemented in various ways, such as an address, array index, or unique value of an attribute. Object references are uniform and independent of the contents of the objects, permitting mixed collections of objects to be created, such as a file system directory that contains both files and subdirectories.

*Classification* means that objects with the same data structure (*attributes*) and behavior (*operations*) are grouped into a *class*. *Paragraph*, *Window*, and *ChessPiece* are examples of classes. A *class* is an abstraction that describes properties important to an application and ignores the rest. Any choice of classes is arbitrary and depends on the application.

Each class describes a possibly infinite set of individual objects. Each object is said to be an *instance* of its class. Each instance of the class has its own value for each attribute but shares the attribute names and operations with other instances of the class. Figure 1.2 shows two classes and some of their respective instance objects. An object contains an implicit reference to its own class; it "knows what kind of thing it is."

*Polymorphism* means that the same operation may behave differently on different classes. The *move* operation, for example, may behave differently on the *Window* and *ChessPiece* classes. An *operation* is an action or transformation that an object performs or is subject to. *Right-justify*, *display*, and *move* are examples of operations. A specific implementation of an

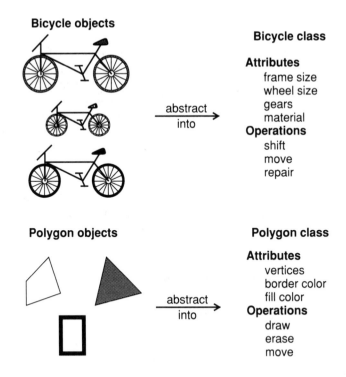

**Figure 1.2** Objects and classes

operation by a certain class is called a *method*. Because an object-oriented operator is polymorphic, it may have more than one method implementing it.

In the real world, an operation is simply an abstraction of analogous behavior across different kinds of objects. Each object "knows how" to perform its own operations. In an object-oriented programming language, however, the language automatically selects the correct method to implement an operation based on the name of the operation and the class of the object being operated on. The user of an operation need not be aware of how many methods exist to implement a given polymorphic operation. New classes can be added without changing existing code, provided methods are provided for each applicable operation on the new classes.

*Inheritance* is the sharing of attributes and operations among classes based on a hierarchical relationship. A class can be defined broadly and then refined into successively finer *subclasses*. Each subclass incorporates, or *inherits,* all of the properties of its *superclass* and adds its own unique properties. The properties of the superclass need not be repeated in each subclass. For example, *ScrollingWindow* and *FixedWindow* are subclasses of *Window*. Both subclasses inherit the properties of *Window,* such as a visible region on the screen. *ScrollingWindow* adds a scroll bar and an offset. The ability to factor out common properties of several classes into a common superclass and to inherit the properties from the superclass can greatly reduce repetition within designs and programs and is one of the main advantages of an object-oriented system.

## 1.2 WHAT IS OBJECT-ORIENTED DEVELOPMENT?

This book is about *object-oriented development* as a new way of thinking about software based on abstractions that exist in the real world. In this context *development* refers to the front portion of the software life cycle: analysis, design, and implementation. The essence of object-oriented development is the identification and organization of application-domain concepts, rather than their final representation in a programming language, object-oriented or not. Brooks observes that the hard part of software development is the manipulation of its *essence* due to the inherent complexity of the problem, rather than the *accidents* of its mapping into a particular language which are due to temporary imperfections in our tools that are rapidly being corrected [Brooks-87].

This book does not explicitly address integration, maintenance, and enhancement, but a cleaner design in a precise notation facilitates these stages of the entire software life cycle. The same object-oriented concepts and notation used to express a design provide useful documentation during these stages.

### 1.2.1 Modeling Concepts, Not Implementation

Most of the effort to date in the object-oriented community has been focused on programming language issues. The current emphasis in the literature is on implementation rather than analysis and design. Object-oriented programming languages are useful in removing restrictions due to the inflexibility of traditional programming languages. In a sense, however, this emphasis is a step backwards for software engineering by focusing excessively on implementation mechanisms, rather than the underlying thought process that they support.

The real payoff comes from addressing front-end conceptual issues, rather than back-end implementation issues. Design flaws that surface during implementation are more costly to fix than those that are found earlier. Focusing on implementation issues too early restricts design choices and often leads to an inferior product. An object-oriented development approach encourages software developers to work and think in terms of the application domain through most of the software engineering life cycle. It is only when the inherent concepts of the application are identified, organized, and understood that the details of data structures and functions can be addressed effectively.

Object-oriented development is a conceptual process independent of a programming language until the final stages. Object-oriented development is fundamentally a new way of thinking and not a programming technique. Its greatest benefits come from helping specifiers, developers, and customers express abstract concepts clearly and communicate them to each other. It can serve as a medium for specification, analysis, documentation, and interfacing, as well as for programming. Even as a programming tool, it can have various targets, including conventional programming languages and databases as well as object-oriented languages.

### 1.2.2 Object-Oriented Methodology

We present a methodology for object-oriented development and a graphical notation for representing object-oriented concepts. The methodology consists of building a *model* of an application domain and then adding implementation details to it during the *design* of a system. We call this approach the Object Modeling Technique (OMT). The methodology has the following stages:

1. *Analysis*: Starting from a statement of the problem, the analyst builds a model of the real-world situation showing its important properties. The analyst must work with the requestor to understand the problem because problem statements are rarely complete or correct. The analysis model is a concise, precise abstraction of *what* the desired system must do, not *how* it will be done. The objects in the model should be application-domain concepts and not computer implementation concepts such as data structures. A good model can be understood and criticized by application experts who are not programmers. The analysis model should not contain any implementation decisions. For example, a *Window* class in a workstation windowing system would be described in terms of the attributes and operations visible to a user. Analysis is described in Chapter 8.

2. *System design*: The system designer makes high-level decisions about the overall architecture. During system design, the target system is organized into subsystems based on both the analysis structure and the proposed architecture. The system designer must decide what performance characteristics to optimize, choose a strategy of attacking the problem, and make tentative resource allocations. For example, the system designer might decide that changes to the workstation screen must be fast and smooth even when windows are moved or erased, and choose an appropriate communications protocol and memory buffering strategy. System design is described in Chapter 9.

3. *Object design*: The object designer builds a design model based on the analysis model but containing implementation details. The designer adds details to the design model in accordance with the strategy established during system design. The focus of object design is the data structures and algorithms needed to implement each class. The object classes from analysis are still meaningful, but they are augmented with computer-domain data structures and algorithms chosen to optimize important performance measures. Both the application-domain objects and the computer-domain objects are described using the same object-oriented concepts and notation, although they exist on different conceptual planes. For example, the *Window* class operations are now specified in terms of the underlying hardware and operating system. Object design is described in Chapter 10.

4. *Implementation*: The object classes and relationships developed during object design are finally translated into a particular programming language, database, or hardware implementation. Programming should be a relatively minor and mechanical part of the development cycle, because all of the hard decisions should be made during design. The target language influences design decisions to some extent, but the design should not depend on fine details of a programming language. During implementation, it is important to follow good software engineering practice so that traceability to the design is straightforward and so that the implemented system remains flexible and extensible. For example, the *Window* class would be coded in a programming language, using calls to the underlying graphics system on the workstation. Implementation is described in Part 3 according to the target vehicle.

Object-oriented concepts can be applied throughout the system development life cycle, from analysis through design to implementation. The same classes can be carried from stage to stage without a change of notation, although they gain additional implementation details in the later stages. Although the analysis view and the implementation view of *Window* are both correct, they serve different purposes and represent a different level of abstraction. The same object-oriented concepts of identity, classification, polymorphism, and inheritance apply through the entire development cycle.

Some classes are not part of analysis but are introduced as part of the design or implementation. For example, data structures such as *trees, hash tables,* and *linked lists* are rarely present in the real world. They are introduced to support particular algorithms during design. Such data structure objects are used to implement real-world objects within a computer and do not derive their properties directly from the real world.

### 1.2.3 Three Models

The OMT methodology uses three kinds of models to describe a system: the *object model,* describing the objects in the system and their relationships; the *dynamic model,* describing the interactions among objects in the system; and the *functional model,* describing the data transformations of the system. Each model is applicable during all stages of development and acquires implementation detail as development progresses. A complete description of a system requires all three models.

The *object model* describes the static structure of the objects in a system and their relationships. The object model contains object diagrams. An *object diagram* is a graph whose nodes are object *classes* and whose arcs are *relationships* among classes. The object model is described in Chapters 3 and 4.

The *dynamic model* describes the aspects of a system that change over time. The dynamic model is used to specify and implement the *control* aspects of a system. The dynamic model contains state diagrams. A *state diagram* is a graph whose nodes are *states* and whose arcs are *transitions* between states caused by *events*. The dynamic model is described in Chapter 5.

The *functional model* describes the data value transformations within a system. The functional model contains data flow diagrams. A data flow diagram represents a computation. A *data flow diagram* is a graph whose nodes are *processes* and whose arcs are *data flows*. The functional model is described in Chapter 6.

The three models are orthogonal parts of the description of a complete system and are cross-linked. The object model is most fundamental, however, because it is necessary to describe *what* is changing or transforming before describing *when* or *how* it changes.

### 1.2.4 Differences from Functional Methodology

Object-oriented development inverts the previous function-oriented methodology, as exemplified by the methodologies of Yourdon [Yourdon-89] and DeMarco [DeMarco-79]. In these methodologies, primary emphasis is placed on specifying and decomposing system functionality. Such an approach might seem the most direct way of implementing a desired goal, but the resulting system can be fragile. If the requirements change, a system based on decomposing functionality may require massive restructuring. (To be fair, these methodologies are more complex than this. See Chapter 12 for more details.)

By contrast, the object-oriented approach focuses first on identifying objects from the application domain, then fitting procedures around them. Although this may seem more indirect, object-oriented software holds up better as requirements evolve, because it is based on the underlying framework of the application domain itself, rather than the ad-hoc functional requirements of a single problem.

## 1.3 OBJECT-ORIENTED THEMES

There are several themes underlying object-oriented technology. Although these themes are not unique to object-oriented systems, they are particularly well supported in object-oriented systems.

### 1.3.1 Abstraction

*Abstraction* consists of focusing on the essential, inherent aspects of an entity and ignoring its accidental properties. In system development, this means focusing on what an object is and does, before deciding how it should be implemented. Use of abstraction preserves the freedom to make decisions as long as possible by avoiding premature commitments to details. Most modern languages provide data abstraction, but the ability to use inheritance and polymorphism provides additional power. Use of abstraction during analysis means dealing only with application-domain concepts, not making design and implementation decisions before the problem is understood. Proper use of abstraction allows the same model to be used for analysis, high-level design, program structure, database structure, and documentation. A language-independent style of design defers programming details until the final, relatively mechanical stage of development.

### 1.3.2 Encapsulation

*Encapsulation* (also *information hiding*) consists of separating the external aspects of an object, which are accessible to other objects, from the internal implementation details of the object, which are hidden from other objects. Encapsulation prevents a program from becoming so interdependent that a small change has massive ripple effects. The implementation of an object can be changed without affecting the applications that use it. One may want to change the implementation of an object to improve performance, fix a bug, consolidate code, or for porting. Encapsulation is not unique to object-oriented languages, but the ability to combine data structure and behavior in a single entity makes encapsulation cleaner and more powerful than in conventional languages that separate data structure and behavior.

### 1.3.3 Combining Data and Behavior

The caller of an operation need not consider how many implementations of a given operation exist. Operator polymorphism shifts the burden of deciding what implementation to use from the calling code to the class hierarchy. For example, non-object-oriented code to display the contents of a window must distinguish the type of each figure, such as polygon, circle, or text, and call the appropriate procedure to display it. An object-oriented program would simply invoke the *draw* operation on each figure; the decision of which procedure to use is made implicitly by each object, based on its class. It is unnecessary to repeat the choice of procedure every time the operation is called in the application program. Maintenance is easier, because the calling code need not be modified when a new class is added. In an object-oriented system, the data structure hierarchy is identical to the operation inheritance hierarchy (Figure 1.3).

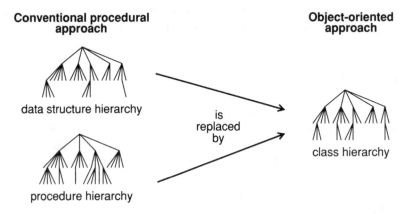

**Figure 1.3**  An object-oriented approach has one unified hierarchy

### 1.3.4 Sharing

Object-oriented techniques promote sharing at several different levels. Inheritance of both data structure and behavior allows common structure to be shared among several similar subclasses without redundancy. The sharing of code using inheritance is one of the main advantages of object-oriented languages. More important than the savings in code is the conceptual clarity from recognizing that different operations are all really the same thing. This reduces the number of distinct cases that must be understood and analyzed.

Object-oriented development not only allows information to be shared within an application, but also offers the prospect of reusing designs and code on future projects. Although this possibility has been overemphasized as a justification for object-oriented technology, object-oriented development provides the tools, such as abstraction, encapsulation, and inheritance, to build libraries of reusable components. Object-orientation is not a magic formula to ensure reusability, however. Reuse does not just happen; it must be planned by thinking beyond the immediate application and investing extra effort in a more general design.

### 1.3.5 Emphasis on Object Structure, Not Procedure Structure

Object-oriented technology stresses specifying what an object *is*, rather than how it is *used*. The uses of an object depend highly on the details of the application and frequently change during development. As requirements evolve, the features supplied by an object are much more stable than the ways it is used, hence software systems built on object structure are more stable in the long run [Booch-86]. Object-oriented development places a greater emphasis on data structure and a lesser emphasis on procedure structure than traditional functional-decomposition methodologies. In this respect, object-oriented development is similar to information modeling techniques used in database design, although object-oriented development adds the concept of class-dependent behavior.

### 1.3.6 Synergy

Identity, classification, polymorphism, and inheritance characterize mainstream object-oriented languages. Each of these concepts can be used in isolation, but together they complement each other synergistically. The benefits of an object-oriented approach are greater than they might seem at first. The greater emphasis on the essential properties of an object forces the software developer to think more carefully and more deeply about what an object is and does, with the result that the system is usually cleaner, more general, and more robust than it would be if the emphasis were only on the use of data and operations. According to Thomas, these various features come together to create a different style of programming [Thomas-89]. Cox claims that encapsulation is the foundation for the object-oriented approach, shifting emphasis from coding technique to packaging, while inheritance builds on encapsulation to make reuse of code practical [Cox-86].

### 1.4 EVIDENCE FOR USEFULNESS OF OBJECT-ORIENTED DEVELOPMENT

We have been actively using object-oriented development in internal applications at the General Electric Research and Development Center (GE R&D). We have used object-oriented techniques for developing compilers (Chapter 18), graphics (Chapter 19), user interfaces (Chapter 20), databases [Blaha-89], an object-oriented language [Shah-89], CAD systems, simulations, meta models, control systems, and other applications. We have used object-oriented models to document existing programs that are ill-structured and difficult to understand. Our implementation targets have ranged from object-oriented languages to non-object-oriented languages to relational databases. We have successfully taught this approach to others and have used it to communicate with application experts.

We are enthusiastic supporters of object-oriented development and see no reason it should not be used on most software projects. The main benefit is not reduced development time; object-oriented development may take more time than conventional development, because it is intended to promote future reuse and reduce downstream errors and maintenance. The time until code is first completed is probably about the same as, or slightly greater than, using a conventional approach. However, subsequent iterations of an object-oriented development are easier and faster than with conventional development because revisions are more localized. Furthermore, fewer iterations are usually needed because more problems are uncovered and corrected during development.

The annual OOPSLA (Object-Oriented Programming Systems, Languages, and Applications) and ECOOP (European Conference on Object-Oriented Programming) conferences are the most important forums for disseminating new object-oriented ideas and application results. OOPSLA and ECOOP proceedings describe many applications that have benefited from an object-oriented approach. [Russo-88] describes a project that used C++ as the target language for implementing an operating system. [Kerr-87] presents the results of using Flavors to implement a program for statistical analysis. [Jacky-86] describes a large medical application that was designed with object-oriented techniques and implemented in Pascal. [Piersol-86] summarizes the results of using Smalltalk-80 to implement an advanced spreadsheet package. [Barry-89] describes the implementation of a signal processor prototype using Smalltalk. We should note that most of the object-oriented literature to date has been concerned with implementation and languages. We hope that this book will encourage more emphasis on object-oriented development.

Many persons have heard of object-oriented technology but think of it as inefficient. This attitude is due to the early object-oriented languages, such as Smalltalk, that were interpreted and were inefficient compared to C or Fortran. Subsequent object-oriented languages, such as C++, can be used in an efficient manner, and compiler designers are improving the efficiency of even the "pure" object-oriented languages [Chambers-89]. In any case, object-oriented design is broader than object-oriented programming and provides logical benefits regardless of the choice of implementation language.

## 1.5 ORGANIZATION OF THIS BOOK

The remainder of this book is organized into four parts: modeling concepts, methodology, implementation, and application case studies. Appendices summarize the OMT notation and provide a glossary of object-oriented terms.

Part 1 explains object-oriented concepts and presents a graphical notation for expressing them. It does not discuss the process of developing object-oriented models, which is the subject of Part 2. Chapter 2 introduces our Object Modeling Technique (OMT) notation. The OMT consists of three orthogonal views: the object model, dynamic model, and functional model. Chapters 3 and 4 describe the object model, which deals with the structural "data" aspects of a system. Chapter 3 presents basic object modeling concepts. Even readers familiar with object-oriented programming should read this chapter, as we introduce modeling concepts not found in most object-oriented languages. Chapter 4 presents advanced object modeling concepts; this chapter may be skipped on a first reading of the book. Chapter 5 describes the dynamic model, which deals with states and events and models the control aspects of a system. Readers familiar with state machines may skim the beginning of the chapter, but the remainder of the chapter describes some state machine structuring concepts that are not widely taught. Chapter 6 describes the functional model, which captures functions, values, constraints and derived information. Readers who know conventional functionally-oriented methodologies will find this material familiar. Part 1 of the book deals with concepts that permeate the software development cycle, applying equally to analysis, design, and implementation. The notation described in Part 1 is used throughout the book.

Part 2 shows how to develop an object-oriented model and use it to develop a system using our OMT methodology. Chapter 7 provides an overview of the OMT methodology. Chapter 8 discusses analysis, the process of describing and understanding the application domain without imposing implementation decisions. Analysis begins with a problem statement from the customer. The analyst incorporates customer interviews and application domain knowledge to construct an object model, a dynamic model, and a functional model. Chapter 9 addresses high-level system design, which is primarily a task of partitioning a system into subsystems and making policy decisions. Chapter 10 discusses object design, the augmentation of the analysis model with design decisions. These decisions include the specification of algorithms, assigning functionality to objects, introduction of internal objects to avoid recomputation, and optimization. Chapter 11 summarizes the methodology presented in Chapters 8 through 10. Chapter 12 compares object-oriented methodologies with other popular methodologies, including conventional software engineering approaches and information modeling notations from the database world.

Part 3 addresses implementation issues dependent on the target language. Chapter 13 provides an overview of implementation. Chapter 14 discusses guidelines for enhancing readability, reusability, and maintainability using good object-oriented programming style. Chapter 15 discusses problems of implementing object-oriented designs using object-oriented languages, including varying degrees of support for different concepts by various languages. The chapter includes a brief survey of several commercially-available languages and describes current work on integrating object-oriented languages with databases. Chapter 16 describes how to implement an object-oriented design with a non-object-oriented language, such as C or Ada. Chapter 17 shows how to implement an OMT design using a relational database. Chapter 17 contains a small amount of introductory material for readers unfamiliar with database concepts.

Part 4 presents several case studies from our work at the GE R&D Center. These are substantial applications that we developed using the OMT methodology. Chapter 18 describes a compiler for object diagrams. The compiler accepts an object diagram as input and generates a relational database schema as output. This compiler was part of a bill-of-materials application and helped motivate a successor project to generate declarations for object-oriented languages and for Ada. Chapter 19 describes a three-dimensional computer animation system that was implemented in C, using conventions on the definition and use of C structures to obtain object-oriented behavior. The computer animation system produces high quality video sequences illustrating the results of scientific calculations and experiments. Chapter 20 discusses a computer-aided design tool for electrical power distribution. This chapter illustrates some of the dynamic modeling concepts presented in the book.

All chapters contain exercises. Selected exercises are answered in the back of the book. We suggest that you try to work the exercises as you read this book, even if you are not a student. The exercises bring out many subtle points that are only touched upon in the text. The exercises provide practice in using the OMT methodology and serve as a stepping stone to real applications.

| abstraction | functional model | object design |
| analysis | identity | object-oriented |
| classification | implementation | Object Modeling Technique (OMT) |
| dynamic model | inheritance | polymorphism |
| encapsulation | object model | system design |

**Figure 1.4** Key concepts for Chapter 1

## BIBLIOGRAPHIC NOTES

Dave Thomas and Peter Wegner have published readable and informative articles on object-oriented concepts in the March 1989 issue of *BYTE* magazine. The references listed below by Grady Booch, Brad Cox, and Bertrand Meyer are particularly good sources of information. However, Cox and to a lesser extent Meyer emphasize the language aspects, although they do devote some space to design issues. Shlaer and Mellor discuss object-oriented analysis and database implementation.

## REFERENCES

[Barry-89] Brian M. Barry. Prototyping a real-time embedded system in Smalltalk. *OOPSLA'89* as *ACM SIGPLAN 24*, 10 (Oct. 1989), 255-265.

[Blaha-89] Michael R. Blaha, Nancy L. Eastman, Malcolm M. Hall. An extensible AE&C database model. *Computers and Chemical Engineering 13*, 7 (July 1989) 753-766.

[Booch-86] Grady Booch. Object-oriented development. *IEEE Transactions on Software Engineering SE-12*, 2 (Feb. 1986), 211-221.

[Booch-91] Grady Booch. *Object-Oriented Design*. Redwood City, Calif.: Benjamin/Cummings, 1991.

[Brooks-87] Frederick P. Brooks. No silver bullet—essence and accidents of software engineering. *IEEE Computer* (April 1987), 10-19.

[Chambers-89] Craig Chambers, David Ungar, Elgin Lee. An efficient implementation of SELF, a dynamically-typed object-oriented language based on prototypes. *OOPSLA'89* as *ACM SIGPLAN 24*, 10 (Oct. 1989), 49-70.

[Cox-86] Brad J. Cox. *Object-Oriented Programming*. Reading, Massachusetts: Addison-Wesley, 1986.

[DeMarco-79] Tom DeMarco. *Structured Analysis and Systems Specification*. Englewood Cliffs, New Jersey: Prentice Hall, 1979.

[Jacky-86] Jonathan Jacky, Ira Kalet. An object-oriented approach to a large scientific application. *OOPSLA'86* as *ACM SIGPLAN 21*, 11 (Nov. 1986), 368-376.

[Kerr-87] R.K. Kerr, D.B. Percival. Use of object-oriented programming in a time series analysis system. *OOPSLA'87* as *ACM SIGPLAN 22*, 12 (Dec. 1987), 1-10.

[Meyer-88] Bertrand Meyer. *Object-Oriented Software Construction*. Hertfordshire, England: Prentice Hall International, 1988.

[Piersol-86] Kurt W. Piersol. Object-oriented spreadsheets: the analytic spreadsheet package. *OOPSLA'86* as *ACM SIGPLAN 21*, 11 (Nov. 1986), 385-390.

[Russo-88] Vincent Russo, Gary Johnston, Roy Campbell. Process management and exception handling in multiprocessor operating systems using object-oriented design techniques. *OOPSLA'88* as *ACM SIGPLAN 23*, 11 (Nov. 1988), 248-258.

[Shah-89] Ashwin Shah, James Rumbaugh, Jung Hamel, Renee Borsari. DSM: an object-relationship modeling language. *OOPSLA'89* as *ACM SIGPLAN 24*, 11 (Nov. 1989), 191-202.

[Shlaer-88] Sally Shlaer, Stephen J. Mellor. *Object-Oriented Systems Analysis: Modeling the World in Data*. Englewood Cliffs, New Jersey: Yourdon Press, 1988.

[Thomas-89] Dave Thomas. What's in an object? *BYTE 14*, 3 (March 1989), 231-240.

[Wegner-89] Peter Wegner. Learning the language. *BYTE 14*, 3 (March 1989), 245-253.

[Yourdon-89] Edward Yourdon. *Modern Structured Analysis*. Englewood Cliffs, New Jersey: Yourdon Press, 1989.

## EXERCISES

The number in parentheses next to each exercise indicates the difficulty, from 1 (easy) to 10 (very difficult). The word "(Project)" in front of an exercise means that the problem statement for the exercise is taken from the literature or that the exercise requires extensive work.

**1.1** (2) What major problems have you encountered during past software projects? Estimate what percentage of your time you spend on analysis, design, coding, and testing/debugging/fixing. How do you go about estimating how much effort a project will require?

**1.2** (3) Recall a system that you created on your own in the past. Briefly describe the system. What obstacles did you encounter in the design? What software engineering methodology, if any, did you use? What were your reasons for choosing or not choosing a methodology? Are you satisfied with the system as it exists? How difficult is it to add new features to the system? Is it maintainable?

**1.3** (4) Describe a large software system that was supposed to be created in the last five years that was behind schedule, over budget, or failed to perform as expected. What factors were blamed? How could the failure have been avoided?

**1.4** (3) From a user's point of view, criticize a hardware or software system that has a flaw that particularly annoys you. For example, some cars require the bumper to be removed to replace a tail light. Describe the system, the flaw, how it was overlooked, and how it could have been avoided with a bit more thought during design.

**1.5** (5) All objects have identity and are distinguishable. However, for large collections of objects, it may not be a trivial matter to devise a scheme to distinguish them. Furthermore, a scheme may depend on the purpose of the distinction. For each of the following collections of objects, describe how they could be distinguished:

a. All persons in the world for the purpose of sending mail.
b. All persons in the world for the purpose of criminal investigations.
c. All customers with safe deposit boxes in a given bank.
d. All telephones in the world for making telephone calls.
e. All customers of a telephone company for billing purposes.
f. All electronic mail addresses throughout the world.
g. All employees of a company to restrict access for security reasons.

**1.6**    (4) Prepare a list of objects that you would expect each of the following systems to handle:

a.  a program for laying out a newspaper

b.  a program to compute and store bowling scores

c.  a telephone answering machine

d.  a controller for a video cassette recorder

e.  a catalog store order entry system

**1.7**    (6) There are two lists below. The first is a list of classes that describe implementation objects. The second is a list of operations. For each class, select the operations that make sense for objects in that class. Discuss the behavior of each operation listed for each class.

Classes:

variable length array — ordered collection of objects, indexed by an integer, whose size can vary at run-time

symbol table — a table that maps text keywords into descriptors

set — unordered collection of objects with no duplicates

Operations:

append — add an object to the end of a collection

copy — make a copy of a collection

count — return the number of elements in a collection

delete — remove a member from a collection

index — retrieve an object from a collection at a given position

intersect — determine the common members of two collections

insert — place an object into a collection at a given position

update — add a member to a collection, writing over whatever is already there

**1.8**    (4) Discuss what the objects in each of the following lists have in common. You may add more classes to each list.

a.  scanning electron microscope, eyeglasses, telescope, bomb sight, binoculars

b.  pipe, check valve, faucet, filter, pressure gauge

c.  bicycle, sailboat, car, truck, airplane, glider, motorcycle, horse

d.  nail, screw, bolt, rivet

e.  tent, cave, shed, garage, barn, house, skyscraper

f.  square root, exponential, sine, cosine

# PART 1: MODELING CONCEPTS

# 2

# Modeling as a Design Technique

A model is an abstraction of something for the purpose of understanding it before building it. Because a model omits nonessential details, it is easier to manipulate than the original entity. Abstraction is a fundamental human capability that permits us to deal with complexity. Engineers, artists, and craftsmen have built models for thousands of years to try out designs before executing them. Development of hardware and software systems is no exception. To build complex systems, the developer must abstract different views of the system, build models using precise notations, verify that the models satisfy the requirements of the system, and gradually add detail to transform the models into an implementation.

Part 1 of the book describes the concepts and notations involved in object-oriented modeling. These concepts are applied to analysis, design, and implementation in Parts 2 and 3 of the book. This chapter discusses modeling in general and then introduces the three kinds of object-oriented models composing the Object Modeling Technique: the object model, which describes static structure; the dynamic model, which describes temporal relationships; and the functional model, which describes functional relationships among values.

## 2.1 MODELING

Designers build many kinds of models for various purposes before constructing things. Examples include architectural models to show customers, airplane scale models for wind-tunnel tests, pencil sketches for composition of oil paintings, blueprints of machine parts, storyboards of advertisements, and outlines of books. Models serve several purposes:

• *Testing a physical entity before building it.* The medieval masons did not know modern physics, but they built scale models of the Gothic cathedrals to test the forces on the structure. Scale models of airplanes, cars, and boats have been tested in wind tunnels and water tanks to improve their aerodynamics. Recent advances in computation permit the simulation of many physical structures without having to build physical models. Not only is simulation cheaper, but it provides information that is too fleeting or inaccessible to be measured from a physical model. Both physical models and computer models are usually cheaper than building a complete system and enable flaws to be corrected early.

• *Communication with customers.* Architects and product designers build models to show their customers. Mock-ups are demonstration products that imitate some or all of the external behavior of a system.

• *Visualization.* Storyboards of movies, television shows, and advertisements allow the writers to see how their ideas flow. Awkward transitions, dangling ends, and unnecessary segments can be modified before detailed writing begins. Artists' sketches allow them to block out their ideas and make changes before committing them to oil or stone.

• *Reduction of complexity.* Perhaps the main reason for modeling, which incorporates all the previous reasons, is to deal with systems that are too complex to understand directly. The human mind can cope with only a limited amount of information at one time. Models reduce complexity by separating out a small number of important things to deal with at a time.

### 2.1.1 Abstraction

Abstraction is the selective examination of certain aspects of a problem. The goal of abstraction is to isolate those aspects that are important for some purpose and suppress those aspects that are unimportant. Abstraction must always be for some purpose, because the purpose determines what is and is not important. Many different abstractions of the same thing are possible, depending on the purpose for which they are made.

All abstractions are incomplete and inaccurate. Reality is a seamless web. Anything we say about it, any description of it, is an abridgement. All human words and language are abstractions—incomplete descriptions of the real world. This does not destroy their usefulness. The purpose of an abstraction is to limit the universe so we can do things. In building models, therefore, you must not search for absolute truth but for adequacy for some purpose. There is no single "correct" model of a situation, only adequate and inadequate ones.

A good model captures the crucial aspects of a problem and omits the others. Most computer languages, for example, are poor vehicles for modeling algorithms because they force the specification of implementation details that are irrelevant to the algorithm. A model that contains extraneous detail unnecessarily limits your choice of design decisions and diverts attention from the real issues.

### 2.2 THE OBJECT MODELING TECHNIQUE

We find it useful to model a system from three related but different viewpoints, each capturing important aspects of the system, but all required for a complete description. The Object

Modeling Technique (OMT) is our name for the methodology that combines these three views of modeling systems. The *object model* represents the static, structural, "data" aspects of a system. The *dynamic model* represents the temporal, behavioral, "control" aspects of a system. The *functional model* represents the transformational, "function" aspects of a system. A typical software procedure incorporates all three aspects: It uses data structures (object model), it sequences operations in time (dynamic model), and it transforms values (functional model). Each model contains references to entities in other models. For example, operations are attached to objects in the object model but more fully expanded in the functional model.

The three kinds of models separate a system into orthogonal views that can be represented and manipulated with a uniform notation. The different models are not completely independent—a system is more than a collection of independent parts—but each model can be examined and understood by itself to a large extent. The interconnections between the different models are limited and explicit. Of course, it is always possible to create bad designs in which the three models are so intertwined that they cannot be separated, but a good design isolates the different aspects of a system and limits the coupling between them.

Each of the three models evolves during the development cycle. During analysis, a model of the application domain is constructed without regard for eventual implementation. During design, solution-domain constructs are added to the model. During implementation, both application-domain and solution-domain constructs are coded. The word *model* has two dimensions—a view of a system (object model, dynamic model, or functional model) and a stage of development (analysis, design, or implementation). The meaning is generally clear from context.

### 2.2.1 Object Model

The *object model* describes the structure of objects in a system—their identity, their relationships to other objects, their attributes, and their operations. The object model provides the essential framework into which the dynamic and functional models can be placed. Changes and transformations are meaningless unless there is something to be changed or transformed. Objects are the units into which we divide the world, the molecules of our models.

Our goal in constructing an object model is to capture those concepts from the real world that are important to an application. In modeling an engineering problem, the object model should contain terms familiar to engineers; in modeling a business problem, terms from the business; in modeling a user interface, terms from the application domain. An analysis model should not contain computer constructs unless the application being modeled is inherently a computer problem, such as a compiler or an operating system. The design model describes how to solve a problem and may contain computer constructs.

The object model is represented graphically with object diagrams containing object classes. Classes are arranged into hierarchies sharing common structure and behavior and are associated with other classes. Classes define the attribute values carried by each object instance and the operations which each object performs or undergoes.

### 2.2.2 Dynamic Model

The *dynamic model* describes those aspects of a system concerned with time and the sequencing of operations—events that mark changes, sequences of events, states that define the context for events, and the organization of events and states. The dynamic model captures *control*, that aspect of a system that describes the sequences of operations that occur, without regard for what the operations do, what they operate on, or how they are implemented.

The dynamic model is represented graphically with state diagrams. Each state diagram shows the state and event sequences permitted in a system for one class of objects. State diagrams also refer to the other models. Actions in the state diagrams correspond to functions from the functional model; events in a state diagram become operations on objects in the object model.

### 2.2.3 Functional Model

The *functional model* describes those aspects of a system concerned with transformations of values—functions, mappings, constraints, and functional dependencies. The functional model captures what a system does, without regard for how or when it is done.

The functional model is represented with data flow diagrams. Data flow diagrams show the dependencies between values and the computation of output values from input values and functions, without regard for when or if the functions are executed. Traditional computing concepts such as expression trees are examples of functional models, as are less traditional concepts such as spreadsheets. Functions are invoked as actions in the dynamic model and are shown as operations on objects in the object model.

### 2.2.4 Relationship among Models

Each model describes one aspect of the system but contains references to the other models. The object model describes data structure that the dynamic and functional models operate on. The operations in the object model correspond to events in the dynamic model and functions in the functional model. The dynamic model describes the control structure of objects. It shows decisions which depend on object values and which cause actions that change object values and invoke functions. The functional model describes functions invoked by operations in the object model and actions in the dynamic model. Functions operate on data values specified by the object model. The functional model also shows constraints on object values.

There are occasional ambiguities about which model should contain a piece of information. This is natural, because any abstraction is only a rough cut at reality; something will inevitably straddle the boundaries. Some properties of a system may be poorly represented by the models. This is also normal, because no abstraction can capture everything; the goal is to simplify the system description without loading down the model with so many constructs that it becomes a burden and not a help. For those things that the model does not adequately capture, natural language or application-specific notation is still a perfectly acceptable tool.

## 2.3 CHAPTER SUMMARY

Models are abstractions built to understand a problem before implementing a solution. All abstractions are subsets of reality selected for a particular purpose.

The Object Modeling Technique (OMT) consists of three kinds of models. The object model describes the static structure of a system in terms of objects and relationships corresponding to real-world entities. The dynamic model describes the control structure of a system in terms of events and states. The functional model describes the computational structure of a system in terms of values and functions. Different problems place different emphasis on the three kinds of models, but all three are necessary for any large system.

| | |
|---|---|
| abstraction | modeling |
| dynamic model | object model |
| functional model | relationship among models |

**Figure 2.1** Key concepts for Chapter 2

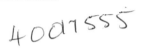

## EXERCISES

**2.1**   (1) Some characteristics of a tire are its size, material, internal construction (bias ply, steel belted, for example), tread design, cost, expected life, and weight. Which factors are important in deciding whether or not to buy a tire for your car? Which ones might be relevant to someone simulating the performance of a computerized anti-skid system for cars? Which ones are important to someone constructing a swing for a child?

**2.2**   (2) Suppose your bathroom sink is clogged and you have decided to try to unclog it by pushing a wire into the drain. You have several types of wire available around the house, some insulated and some not. Which of the following wire characteristics would you need to consider in selecting a wire for the job? Explain your answers.
   a. Immunity to electrical noise
   b. Color of the insulation
   c. Resistance of the insulation to saltwater
   d. Resistance of the insulation to fire
   e. Cost
   f. Stiffness
   g. Ease of stripping the insulation
   h. Weight
   i. Availability
   j. Strength
   k. Resistance to high temperatures
   l. Resistance to stretching

**2.3** (3) Wire is used in the following applications. For each application, prepare a list of wire characteristics that are relevant and explain why each characteristic is important for the application.
  a. Selecting wire for a transatlantic cable
  b. Choosing wire that you will use to create colorful artwork
  c. Designing the electrical system for an airplane
  d. Hanging a bird feeder from a tree
  e. Designing a piano
  f. Designing the filament for a light bulb

**2.4** (3) If you were designing a protocol for transferring computer files from one computer to another over telephone lines, which of the following details would you select as relevant? Explain how your selected details are relevant:
  a. Electrical noise on the communication lines
  b. The speed at which serial data is transmitted, typically 300, 1200, 2400, 4800, or 9600 bits per second
  c. Availability of a relational database
  d. Availability of a good full screen editor
  e. Buffering and flow control such as an XON/XOFF protocol to regulate an incoming stream of data
  f. Number of tracks and sectors on the hard and/or floppy disk drive
  g. Character interpretation such as special handling of control characters
  h. File organization, linear stream of bytes versus record-oriented, for example
  i. Math co-processor

**2.5** (2) There are several models used in the analysis and design of electrical motors. An electrical model is concerned with voltages, currents, electromagnetic fields, inductance, and resistance. A mechanical model considers stiffness, density, motion, forces, and torques. A thermal model is concerned with heat dissipation and heat transfer. A fluid model describes the flow of cooling air. Which model(s) should be considered to answer the following questions? Discuss your conclusions:
  a. How much electrical energy is required to run a motor? How much of it is wasted as heat?
  b. How much does a motor weigh?
  c. How hot does a motor get?
  d. How much vibration does a motor create?
  e. How long will it take for the bearings of a motor to wear out?

**2.6** (3) Decide which model(s) (object, dynamic, functional) are relevant for the following aspects of a computer chess player. The board and pieces will be displayed graphically on a video display. Human moves will be indicated via a cursor controlled by a mouse. Of course, in some cases, more than one category may apply. Defend your answers:
  a. User interface which displays computer moves and accepts human moves
  b. Representation of a configuration of pieces on the board
  c. Consideration of a sequence of possible legal moves
  d. Validation of a move requested by the human player

# 3

---

# Object Modeling

An *object model* captures the static structure of a system by showing the objects in the system, relationships between the objects, and the attributes and operations that characterize each class of objects. The object model is the most important of the three models. We emphasize building a system around objects rather than around functionality, because an object-oriented model more closely corresponds to the real world and is consequently more resilient with respect to change. Object models provide an intuitive graphic representation of a system and are valuable for communicating with customers and documenting the structure of a system.

Chapter 3 discusses basic object modeling concepts that will be used throughout the book. For each concept, we discuss the logical meaning, present the corresponding OMT notation, and provide examples. Some important concepts that we consider are object, class, link, association, generalization, and inheritance. You should master the material in this chapter before proceeding in the book.

## 3.1 OBJECTS AND CLASSES

### 3.1.1 Objects

The purpose of object modeling is to describe objects. For example, *Joe Smith, Simplex company, Lassie, process number 7648*, and *the top window* are objects. An object is simply something that makes sense in an application context.

We define an *object* as a concept, abstraction, or thing with crisp boundaries and meaning for the problem at hand. Objects serve two purposes: They promote understanding of the real world and provide a practical basis for computer implementation. Decomposition of a problem into objects depends on judgment and the nature of the problem. There is no one correct representation.

All objects have identity and are distinguishable. Two apples with the same color, shape, and texture are still individual apples; a person can eat one and then eat the other. Similarly, identical twins are two distinct persons, even though they may look the same. The term *identity* means that objects are distinguished by their inherent existence and not by descriptive properties that they may have.

The word *object* is often vaguely used in the literature. Sometimes *object* means a single thing, other times it refers to a group of similar things. Usually the context resolves any ambiguity. When we want to be precise and refer to exactly one thing, we will use the phrase *object instance*. We will use the phrase *object class* to refer to a group of similar things.

## 3.1.2 Classes

An *object class* describes a group of objects with similar properties (attributes), common behavior (operations), common relationships to other objects, and common semantics. *Person*, *company*, *animal*, *process*, and *window* are all object classes. Each person has an age, IQ, and may work at a job. Each process has an owner, priority, and list of required resources. Objects and object classes often appear as nouns in problem descriptions.

The abbreviation *class* is often used instead of *object class*. Objects in a class have the same attributes and behavior patterns. Most objects derive their individuality from differences in their attribute values and relationships to other objects. However, objects with identical attribute values and relationships are possible.

The objects in a class share a common semantic purpose, above and beyond the requirement of common attributes and behavior. Thus even though a barn and a horse both have a cost and age, they may belong to different classes. If barn and horse were regarded as purely financial assets, they may belong to the same class. If the developer took into consideration that a person paints a barn and feeds a horse, they would be modeled as distinct classes. The interpretation of semantics depends on the purpose of each application and is a matter of judgment.

Each object "knows" its class. Most object-oriented programming languages can determine an object's class at run time. An object's class is an implicit property of the object.

If objects are the focus of object modeling, why bother with classes? The notion of abstraction is at the heart of the matter. By grouping objects into classes, we abstract a problem. Abstraction gives modeling its power and ability to generalize from a few specific cases to a host of similar cases. Common definitions (such as class name and attribute names) are stored once per class rather than once per instance. Operations can be written once for each class, so that all the objects in the class benefit from code reuse. For example, all ellipses share the same procedures to draw them, compute their areas, or test for intersection with a line; polygons would have a separate set of procedures. Even special cases, such as circles and squares, can use the general procedures, though more efficient procedures are possible.

## 3.1.3 Object Diagrams

We began this chapter by discussing some basic modeling concepts, specifically *object* and *class*. We have described these concepts with examples and prose. Since this approach is vague for more complex topics, we need a formalism for expressing object models that is coherent, precise, and easy to formulate.

*Object diagrams* provide a formal graphic notation for modeling objects, classes, and their relationships to one another. Object diagrams are useful both for abstract modeling and for designing actual programs. Object diagrams are concise, easy to understand, and work well in practice. We use object diagrams throughout this book. New concepts are illustrated by object diagrams to introduce the notation and clarify our explanation of concepts. There are two types of object diagrams: class diagrams and instance diagrams.

A *class diagram* is a schema, pattern, or template for describing many possible instances of data. A class diagram describes object classes.

An *instance diagram* describes how a particular set of objects relate to each other. An instance diagram describes object instances. Instance diagrams are useful for documenting test cases (especially scenarios) and discussing examples. A given class diagram corresponds to an infinite set of instance diagrams.

Figure 3.1 shows a class diagram (left) and one possible instance diagram (right) described by it. Objects *Joe Smith*, *Mary Sharp*, and an anonymous person are instances of class *Person*. The OMT symbol for an object instance is a rounded box. The class name in parentheses is at the top of the object box in boldface. Object names are listed in normal font. The OMT symbol for a class is a box with class name in boldface.

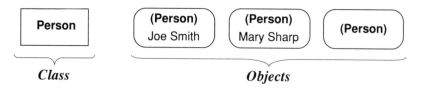

**Figure 3.1** Class and objects

Class diagrams describe the general case in modeling a system. Instance diagrams are used mainly to show examples to help to clarify a complex class diagram. The distinction between class diagrams and instance diagrams is in fact artificial; classes and instances can appear on the same object diagram, but in general it is not useful to mix classes and instances. (The exception is metadata, discussed in Section 4.5.)

### 3.1.4 Attributes

An *attribute* is a data value held by the objects in a class. *Name*, *age*, and *weight* are attributes of *Person* objects. *Color*, *weight*, and *model-year* are attributes of *Car* objects. Each attribute has a value for each object instance. For example, attribute *age* has value "24" in object *Joe Smith*. Paraphrasing, Joe Smith is 24 years old. Different object instances may have the same or different values for a given attribute. Each attribute name is unique within a class (as opposed to being unique across all classes). Thus class *Person* and class *Company* may each have an attribute called *address*.

An attribute should be a pure data value, not an object. Unlike objects, pure data values do not have identity. For example, all occurrences of the integer "17" are indistinguishable, as are all occurrences of the string "Canada." The country Canada is an object, whose *name* attribute has the value "Canada" (the string). The capital of Canada is a city object and should not be modeled as an attribute, but rather as an association between a country object and a city object (explained in Section 3.2). The *name* of this city object is "Ottawa" (the string).

Attributes are listed in the second part of the class box. Each attribute name may be followed by optional details, such as type and default value. The type is preceded by a colon. The default value is preceded by an equal sign. At times, you may choose to omit showing attributes in class boxes. It depends on the level of detail desired in the object model. Class boxes have a line drawn between the class name and attributes. Object boxes do not have this line in order to further differentiate them from class boxes.

Figure 3.2 shows object modeling notation. Class *Person* has attributes *name* and *age*. *Name* is a string and *age* is an integer. One object in class *Person* has the value *Joe Smith* for name and the value *24* for age. Another object has name *Mary Sharp* and age *52*.

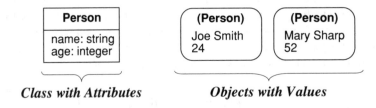

*Class with Attributes*          *Objects with Values*

**Figure 3.2**  Attributes and values

Some implementation media, such as many databases, require an object to have a unique identifier that identifies each object. Explicit object identifiers are not required in an object model. Each object has its own unique identity. Most object-oriented languages automatically generate implicit identifiers with which to reference objects. You need not and should not explicitly list identifiers. Figure 3.3 emphasizes this point. Identifiers are a computer artifact and have no intrinsic meaning beyond identifying an object.

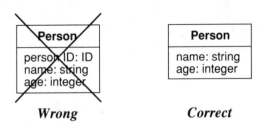

*Wrong*                          *Correct*

**Figure 3.3**  Do not explicitly list object identifiers

Do not confuse internal identifiers with real-world attributes. Internal identifiers are purely an implementation convenience and have no meaning in the problem domain. For example, social security number, license plate number, and telephone number are not internal identifiers because they have meaning in the real world. Social security number, license plate number, and telephone number are legitimate attributes.

### 3.1.5 Operations and Methods

An *operation* is a function or transformation that may be applied to or by objects in a class. *Hire, fire,* and *pay-dividend* are operations on class *Company. Open, close, hide,* and *redisplay* are operations on class *Window.* All objects in a class share the same operations.

Each operation has a target object as an implicit argument. The behavior of the operation depends on the class of its target. An object "knows" its class, and hence the right implementation of the operation.

The same operation may apply to many different classes. Such an operation is *polymorphic;* that is, the same operation takes on different forms in different classes. A *method* is the implementation of an operation for a class. For example, the class *File* may have an operation *print.* Different methods could be implemented to print ASCII files, print binary files, and print digitized picture files. All these methods logically perform the same task—printing a file; thus you may refer to them by the generic operation *print.* However, each method may be implemented by a different piece of code.

An operation may have arguments in addition to its target object. Such arguments parameterize the operation but do not affect the choice of method. The method depends only on the class of the target object. (A few object-oriented languages, notably CLOS, permit the choice of method to depend on any number of arguments, but such generality leads to considerable semantic complexity, which we shall not explore.)

When an operation has methods on several classes, it is important that the methods all have the same *signature*—the number and types of arguments and the type of result value. For example, *print* should not have *file-name* as an argument for one method and *file-pointer* for another. The behavior of all methods for an operation should have a consistent intent. It is best to avoid using the same name for two operations that are semantically different, even if they apply to distinct sets of classes. For example, it would be unwise to use the name *invert* to describe both a matrix inversion and turning a geometric figure upside-down. In a very large project, some form of name scoping may be necessary to accommodate accidental name clashes, but it is best to avoid any possibility of confusion.

Operations are listed in the lower third of the class box. Each operation name may be followed by optional details, such as argument list and result type. An argument list is written in parentheses following the name; the arguments are separated by commas. The name and type of each argument may be given. The result type is preceded by a colon and should not be omitted, because it is important to distinguish operations that return values from those that do not. An empty argument list in parentheses shows explicitly that there are no arguments; otherwise no conclusions can be drawn. Operations may be omitted from high-level diagrams.

In Figure 3.4, the class *Person* has attributes *name* and *age* and operations *change-job* and *change-address. Name, age, change-job,* and *change-address* are features of *Person.*

| Person |
| --- |
| name<br>age |
| change-job<br>change-address |

| File |
| --- |
| file name<br>size in bytes<br>last update |
| print |

| Geometric<br>object |
| --- |
| color<br>position |
| move (delta: Vector)<br>select (p : Point): Boolean<br>rotate (angle) |

**Figure 3.4** Operations

*Feature* is a generic word for either an attribute or operation. Similarly, *File* has a *print* operation. *Geometric object* has *move*, *select*, and *rotate* operations. *Move* has argument *delta*, which is a *Vector*; *select* has one argument *p* which is of type *Point* and returns a *Boolean*; and *rotate* has argument *angle*.

During modeling, it is useful to distinguish operations that have side effects from those that merely compute a functional value without modifying any objects. The latter kind of operation is called a *query*. Queries with no arguments except the target object may be regarded as derived attributes. For example, the width of a box can be computed from the positions of its sides. A derived attribute is like an attribute in that it is a property of the object itself, and computing it does not change the state of the object. In many cases, an object has a set of attributes whose values are interrelated, of which only a fixed number of values can be chosen independently. An object model should generally distinguish independent *base attributes* from dependent *derived attributes*. The choice of base attributes is arbitrary but should be made to avoid overspecifying the state of the object. The remaining attributes may be omitted or may be shown as derived attributes as described in Section 4.7.4.

### 3.1.6 Summary of Notation for Object Classes

Figure 3.5 summarizes object modeling notation for classes. A class is represented by a box which may have as many as three regions. The regions contain, from top to bottom: class name, list of attributes, and list of operations. Each attribute name may be followed by optional details such as type and default value. Each operation name may be followed by optional details such as argument list and result type. Attributes and operations may or may not be shown; it depends on the level of detail desired.

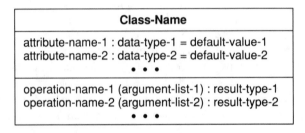

**Figure 3.5** Summary of object modeling notation for classes

## 3.2 LINKS AND ASSOCIATIONS

Links and associations are the means for establishing relationships among objects and classes.

### 3.2.1 General Concepts

A *link* is a physical or conceptual connection between object instances. For example, Joe Smith *Works-for* Simplex company. Mathematically, a link is defined as a tuple, that is, an ordered list of object instances. A link is an instance of an association.

An *association* describes a group of links with common structure and common semantics. For example, a person *Works-for* a company. All the links in an association connect objects from the same classes. Associations and links often appear as verbs in a problem statement. An association describes a set of potential links in the same way that a class describes a set of potential objects.

Associations are inherently bidirectional. The name of a binary association usually reads in a particular direction, but the binary association can be traversed in either direction. The direction implied by the name is the *forward* direction; the opposite direction is the *inverse* direction. For example, *Works-for* connects a person to a company. The inverse of *Works-for* could be called *Employs,* and connects a company to a person. In reality, both directions of traversal are equally meaningful, and refer to the same underlying association; it is only the names which establish a direction.

Associations are often implemented in programming languages as pointers from one object to another. A *pointer* is an attribute in one object that contains an explicit reference to another object. For example, a data structure for *Person* might contain an attribute *employer* that points to a *Company* object, and a *Company* object might contain an attribute *employees* that points to a set of *Employee* objects. Implementing associations as pointers is perfectly acceptable, but associations should not be modeled this way.

A link shows a relationship between two (or more) objects. Modeling a link as a pointer disguises the fact that the link is not part of either object by itself, but depends on both of them together. A company is not part of a person, and a person is not part of a company. Furthermore, using a pair of matched pointers, such as the pointer from *Person* to *Company* and the pointer from *Company* to a set of *Employee,* hides the fact that the forward and inverse pointers are dependent on each other. All connections among classes should therefore be modeled as associations, even in designs for programs. We must stress that associations are not just database constructs, although relational databases are built on the concept of associations.

Although associations are modeled as bidirectional they do not have to be implemented in both directions. Associations can easily be implemented as pointers if they are only traversed in a single direction. Chapter 10 discusses some trade-offs to consider when implementing associations.

Figure 3.6 shows a one-to-one association and corresponding links. Each association in the class diagram corresponds to a set of links in the instance diagram, just as each class corresponds to a set of objects. Each country has a capital city. *Has-capital* is the name of the

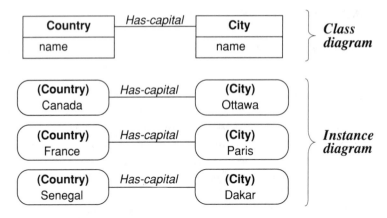

**Figure 3.6** One-to-one association and links

association. The OMT notation for an association is a line between classes. A link is drawn as a line between objects. Association names are italicized. An association name may be omitted if a pair of classes has a single association whose meaning is obvious. It is good to arrange the classes to read from left-to-right, if possible.

Figure 3.7 is a fragment of an object model for a program. A common task that arises in computer-aided design (CAD) applications is to find connectivity networks: Given a line, find all intersecting lines; given an intersection point, find all lines that pass through it; given an area on the screen, find all intersection points. (We use the word *line* here to mean a finite line segment.)

In the class diagram, each point denotes the intersection of two or more lines; each line has zero or more intersection points. The instance diagram shows one possible set of lines. Lines *L1*, *L2*, and *L3* intersect at point *P1*. Lines *L3* and *L4* intersect at point *P2*. Line *L5* has no intersection points and thus has no link. The solid balls and "2+" are multiplicity symbols. Multiplicity specifies how many instances of one class may relate to each instance of another class and is discussed in the next section.

Associations may be binary, ternary, or higher order. In practice, the vast majority are binary or qualified (a special form of ternary discussed later). We have encountered a few general ternary and few, if any, of order four or more. Higher order associations are more complicated to draw, implement, and think about than binary associations and should be avoided if possible.

Figure 3.8 shows a *ternary* association: Persons who are programmers use computer languages on projects. This ternary association is an atomic unit and cannot be subdivided into binary associations without losing information. A programmer may know a language and work on a project, but might not use the language on the project. The OMT symbol for general ternary and n-ary associations is a diamond with lines connecting to related classes. The name of the association is written next to the diamond. Note that we did not name the association or links in Figure 3.8. Association names are optional and a matter of modeling judgment. Associations are often left unnamed when they can be easily identified by their classes. (This convention does not work if there are multiple associations between the same classes.)

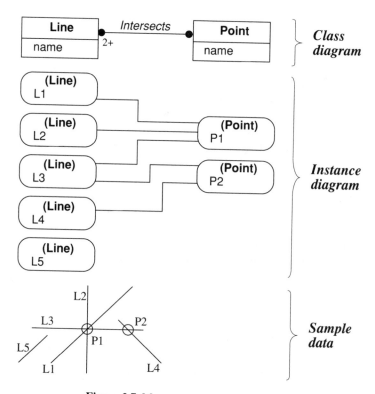

**Figure 3.7** Many-to-many association and links

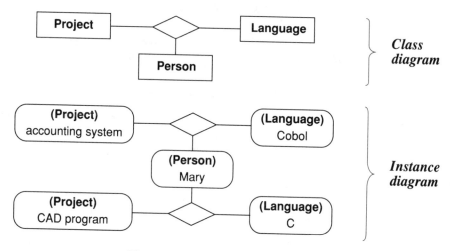

**Figure 3.8** Ternary association and links

### 3.2.2 Multiplicity

*Multiplicity* specifies how many instances of one class may relate to a single instance of an associated class. Multiplicity constrains the number of related objects. Multiplicity is often described as being "one" or "many," but more generally it is a (possibly infinite) subset of the non-negative integers. Generally the multiplicity value is a single interval, but it may be a set of disconnected intervals. For example, the number of doors on a sedan is 2 or 4. Object diagrams indicate multiplicity with special symbols at the ends of association lines. In the most general case, multiplicity can be specified with a number or set of intervals, such as "1" (exactly one), "1+" (one or more), "3-5" (three to five, inclusive), and "2,4,18" (two, four, or eighteen). There are special line terminators to indicate certain common multiplicity values. A solid ball is the OMT symbol for "many," meaning zero or more. A hollow ball indicates "optional," meaning zero or one. A line without multiplicity symbols indicates a one-to-one association. In the general case, the multiplicity is written next to the end of the line, for example, "1+" to indicate one or more.

Reviewing our past examples, Figure 3.6 illustrates one-to-one multiplicity. Each country has one capital city. A capital city administers one country. (In fact, some countries, such as Netherlands and Switzerland, have more than one capital city for different purposes. If this fact were important, the model could be modified by changing the multiplicity or by providing a separate association for each kind of capital city.)

The association in Figure 3.7 exhibits many-to-many multiplicity. A line may have zero or more intersection points. An intersection point may be associated with two or more lines. In this particular case, *L1*, *L2*, and *L4* have one intersection point; *L3* has two intersection points; *L5* has no intersection points. *P1* intersects with three lines; *P2* intersects with two lines.

Figure 3.9 illustrates zero-or-one, or optional, multiplicity. A workstation may have one of its windows designated as the console to receive general error messages. It is possible, however, that no console window exists. (The word "console" on the diagram is a role name, discussed in Section 3.3.3.)

**Figure 3.9** Zero-or-one multiplicity

Multiplicity depends on assumptions and how you define the boundaries of a problem. Vague requirements often make multiplicity uncertain. You should not worry excessively about multiplicity early in software development. First determine objects, classes, and associations, then decide on multiplicity.

Determining multiplicity often exposes hidden assumptions built into the model. For example, is the *Works-for* association between *Person* and *Company* one-to-many or many-to-many? It depends on the context. A tax collection application would permit a person to work for multiple companies. On the other hand, an auto workers' union maintaining member records may consider second jobs irrelevant. Explicitly representing a model with object diagrams helps elicit these hidden assumptions, making them visible and subject to scrutiny.

The most important multiplicity distinction is between "one" and "many." Underestimating multiplicity can restrict the flexibility of an application. For example, many phone number utility programs are unable to accommodate persons with multiple phone numbers. On the other hand, overestimating multiplicity imposes extra overhead and requires the application to supply additional information to distinguish among the members of a "many" set. In a true hierarchical organization, for example, it is better to represent "boss" with a multiplicity of "zero or one," rather than allow for nonexistent matrix management.

This chapter only considers multiplicity for binary associations. The solid and hollow ball notation is ambiguous for n-ary (n > 2) associations, for which multiplicity is a more complex topic. Section 4.6 extends our treatment of multiplicity to n-ary associations.

### 3.2.3 The Importance of Associations

The notion of an association is certainly not a new concept. Associations have been widely used throughout the database modeling community for years. (See Chapter 12 for details.) In contrast, few programming languages explicitly support associations. We nevertheless emphasize that associations are a useful modeling construct for programs as well as databases and real-world systems, regardless of how they are implemented. During conceptual modeling, you should not bury pointers or other object references inside objects as attributes. Instead you should model them as associations to indicate that the information they contain is not subordinate to a single class, but depends on two or more classes [Rumbaugh-87].[*]

Some object-oriented authors feel that every piece of information should be attached to a single class, and they argue that associations violate encapsulation of information into classes. We do not agree with this viewpoint. Some information inherently transcends a single class, and the failure to treat associations on an equal footing with classes can lead to programs containing hidden assumptions and dependencies.

Most object-oriented languages implement associations with object pointers. Pointers can be regarded as an implementation optimization introduced during the later stages of design. It is also possible to implement association objects directly, but the use of association objects during implementation is really a design decision (see Chapter 10).

## 3.3 ADVANCED LINK AND ASSOCIATION CONCEPTS

### 3.3.1 Link Attributes

An attribute is a property of the objects in a class. Similarly, a *link attribute* is a property of the links in an association. In Figure 3.10, *access permission* is an attribute of *Accessible by*. Each link attribute has a value for each link, as illustrated by the sample data at the bottom

---

[*] The term *association* as used in this book is synonymous with the term *relation* used in [Rumbaugh-87] and with the use of the term *relation* as used in discrete mathematics. We have used the term *association* to avoid confusion with the more restricted use of the term *relation* as used in relational databases, which usually permit relations between pure values only, not between objects with identity.

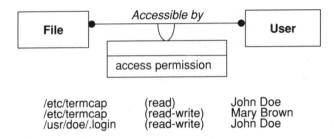

**Figure 3.10** Link attribute for a many-to-many association

of the figure. The OMT notation for a link attribute is a box attached to the association by a loop; one or more link attributes may appear in the second region of the box. This notation emphasizes the similarity between attributes for objects and attributes for links.

Many-to-many associations provide the most compelling rationale for link attributes. Such an attribute is unmistakably a property of the link and cannot be attached to either object. In Figure 3.10, *access permission* is a joint property of *File* and *User,* and cannot be attached to either *File* or *User* alone without losing information.

Figure 3.11 presents link attributes for two many-to-one associations. Each person working for a company receives a salary and has a job title. The boss evaluates the performance of each worker. Link attributes may also occur for one-to-one associations.

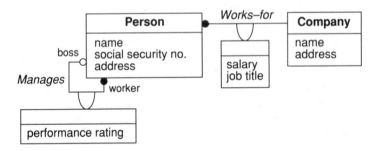

**Figure 3.11** Link attributes for one-to-many associations

Figure 3.12 shows link attributes for a ternary association. A pitcher may play for many teams in a given year. A pitcher may also play many years for the same team. Each team has many pitchers. For each combination of team and year, a pitcher has a won-loss record. Thus for instance, Harry Eisenstat pitched for the Cleveland Indians in 1939, winning 6 games and losing 7 games.

Figure 3.13 shows how it is possible to fold link attributes for one-to-one and one-to-many associations into the class opposite the "one" side. This is not possible for many-to-many associations. As a rule, link attributes should not be folded into a class because future flexibility is reduced if the multiplicity of the association should change. Either form in Figure 3.13 can express a one-to-many association. However, only the link attribute form remains correct if the multiplicity of *Works-for* is changed to many-to-many.

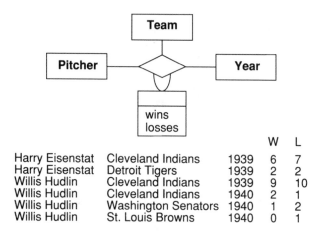

**Figure 3.12** Link attributes for a ternary association

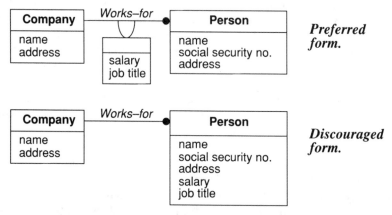

**Figure 3.13** Link attribute versus object attribute

## 3.3.2 Modeling an Association as a Class

Sometimes it is useful to model an association as a class. Each link becomes one instance of the class. The link attribute box introduced in the previous section is actually a special case of an association as a class, and may have a name and operations in addition to attributes. Figure 3.14 shows the authorization information for users on workstations. Users may be authorized on many workstations. Each authorization carries a priority and access privileges, shown as link attributes. A user has a home directory for each authorized workstation, but the same home directory can be shared among several workstations or among several users. The home directory is shown as a many-to-one association between the authorization class and the directory class. It is useful to model an association as a class when links can participate in associations with other objects or when links are subject to operations.

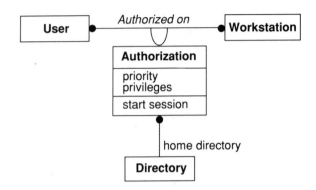

**Figure 3.14** Modeling an association as a class

### 3.3.3 Role Names

A *role* is one end of an association. A binary association has two roles, each of which may have a *role name*. A *role name* is a name that uniquely identifies one end of an association. Roles provide a way of viewing a binary association as a traversal from one object to a set of associated objects. Each role on a binary association identifies an object or set of objects associated with an object at the other end. From the point of view of the object, traversing the association is an operation that yields related objects. The role name is a derived attribute whose value is a set of related objects. Use of role names provides a way of traversing associations from an object at one end, without explicitly mentioning the association. Roles often appear as nouns in problem descriptions.

Figure 3.15 specifies how *Person* and *Company* participate in association *Works-for*. A person assumes the role of *employee* with respect to a company; a company assumes the role of *employer* with respect to a person. A role name is written next to the association line near the class that plays the role (that is, the role name appears on the destination end of the traversal). Use of role names is optional, but it is often easier and less confusing to assign role names instead of, or in addition to, association names.

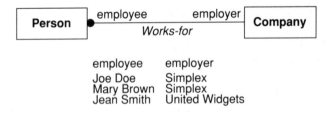

**Figure 3.15** Role names for an association

Role names are necessary for associations between two objects of the same class. For example, *boss* and *worker* distinguish the two employees participating in the *Manages* association in Figure 3.11. Role names are also useful to distinguish between two associations between the same pair of classes. When there is only a single association between a pair of distinct classes, the names of the classes often serve as good role names, in which case the role names may be omitted on the diagram.

Because role names serve to distinguish among the objects directly connected to a given object, all role names on the far end of associations attached to a class must be unique. Although the role name is written next to the destination object on an association, it is really a derived attribute of the source class and must be unique within it. For the same reason, no role name should be the same as an attribute name of the source class.

Figure 3.16 shows both uses of role names. A directory may contain many other directories and may optionally be contained in another directory. Each directory has exactly one user who is an owner, and many users who are authorized to use the directory.

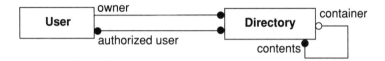

**Figure 3.16** Role names for a directory hierarchy

An n-ary association has a role for each end. The role names distinguish the ends of the association and are necessary if a class participates in an n-ary association more than once. Associations of degree 3 or more cannot simply be traversed from one end to another as binary associations can, so the role names do not represent derived attributes of the participating classes. For example, in Figure 3.12, both a team and a year are necessary to obtain a set of pitchers.

### 3.3.4 Ordering

Usually the objects on the "many" side of an association have no explicit order, and can be regarded as a set. Sometimes, however, the objects are explicitly ordered. For example, Figure 3.17 shows a workstation screen containing a number of overlapping windows. The windows are explicitly ordered, so only the topmost window is visible at any point on the screen. The ordering is an inherent part of the association. An ordered set of objects on the "many" end of an association is indicated by writing "{ordered}" next to the multiplicity dot for the role. This is a special kind of constraint. (See Section 4.7 for a discussion of constraints.)

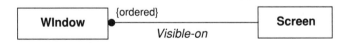

**Figure 3.17** Ordered sets in an association

### 3.3.5 Qualification

A *qualified association* relates two object classes and a *qualifier*. The qualifier is a special attribute that reduces the effective multiplicity of an association. One-to-many and many-to-many associations may be qualified. The qualifier distinguishes among the set of objects at the many end of an association. A qualified association can also be considered a form of ternary association.

For example, in Figure 3.18 a directory has many files. A file may only belong to a single directory.[*] Within the context of a directory, the file name specifies a unique file. *Directory* and *File* are object classes and *file name* is the qualifier. A directory plus a file name yields a file. A file corresponds to a directory and a file name. Qualification reduces the effective multiplicity of this association from one-to-many to one-to-one. A directory has many files, each with a unique name.

**Figure 3.18** A qualified association

Qualification improves semantic accuracy and increases the visibility of navigation paths. It is much more informative to be told that a directory and file name combine to identify a file, rather than be told that a directory has many files. The qualification syntax also indicates that each file name is unique within its directory. One way to find a file is to first find the directory and then traverse the file name link.

A qualifier is drawn as a small box on the end of the association line near the class it qualifies. *Directory* + *file name* yields a *File*, therefore *file name* is listed in a box contiguous to *Directory*.

Qualification often occurs in real problems, frequently because of the need to supply names. There normally is a context within which a name has meaning. For instance, a directory provides the context for a file name.

Figure 3.19 provides another example of qualification. A stock exchange lists many companies. However, a stock exchange lists only one company with a given ticker symbol. A company may be listed on many stock exchanges, possibly under different symbols. (This may actually not be true for stocks.) The unqualified notation cannot accommodate different ticker symbols for the same company on different exchanges.

Qualification usually reduces multiplicity from many to one, but not always. In Figure 3.20, a company has one president and one treasurer but many persons serving on the board of directors. Qualification partitions a set of related objects into disjoint subsets, but the subsets may contain more than one object.

### 3.3.6 Aggregation

*Aggregation* is the "part-whole" or "a-part-of" relationship in which objects representing the *components* of something are associated with an object representing the entire *assembly*. One

---

[*] This is only true for some operating systems. For example, a PC-DOS file does belong to a single directory. A UNIX file may belong to multiple directories. Once again, the precise nature of an object model depends upon the application.

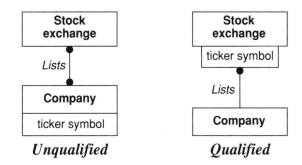

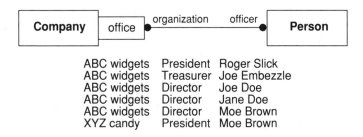

**Figure 3.19** Unqualified and qualified association

**Figure 3.20** Many-to-many qualification

common example is the bill-of-materials or parts explosion tree. For example, a name, argument list, and a compound statement are part of a C-language function definition, which in turn is part of an entire program. Aggregation is a tightly coupled form of association with some extra semantics. The most significant property of aggregation is *transitivity,* that is, if *A* is part of *B* and *B* is part of *C,* then *A* is part of *C.* Aggregation is also *antisymmetric,* that is, if *A* is part of *B,* then *B* is not part of *A.* Finally, some properties of the assembly *propagate* to the components as well, possibly with some local modifications. For example, the environment of a statement within a function definition is the same as the environment of the whole function, except for changes made within the function. The speed and location of a door handle is obtained from the door of which it is a part; the door in turn obtains its properties from the car of which it is a part. Unless there are common properties of components that can be attached to the assembly as a whole, there is little point in using aggregation. A parts tree is clearly an aggregation, but there are borderline cases where the use of aggregation is not clear-cut. When in doubt, use ordinary association. Section 4.1 explores the use of aggregation in more detail.

We define an aggregation relationship as relating an assembly class to *one* component class. An assembly with many kinds of components corresponds to many aggregation relationships. We define each individual pairing as an aggregation so that we can specify the multiplicity of each component within the assembly. This definition emphasizes that aggregation is a special form of association.

Aggregation is drawn like association, except a small diamond indicates the assembly end of the relationship. Figure 3.21 shows a portion of an object model for a word processing program. A document consists of many paragraphs, each of which consists of many sentences.

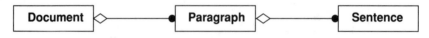

**Figure 3.21** Aggregation

The existence of a component object may depend on the existence of the aggregate object of which it is part. For example, a binding is a part of a book. A binding cannot exist apart from a book. In other cases, component objects have an independent existence, such as mechanical parts from a bin.

Figure 3.22 demonstrates that aggregation may have an arbitrary number of levels. A microcomputer is composed of one or more monitors, a system box, an optional mouse, and a keyboard. A system box, in turn, has a chassis, a CPU, many RAM chips, and an optional fan. When we have a collection of components that all belong to the same assembly, we can combine the lines into a single aggregation tree in the diagram. The aggregation tree is just a shorthand notation that is simpler than drawing many lines connecting components to an assembly. An object model should make it easy to visually identify levels in a part hierarchy.

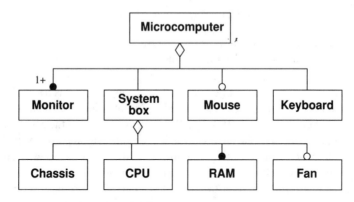

**Figure 3.22** Multilevel aggregation

## 3.4 GENERALIZATION AND INHERITANCE

### 3.4.1 General Concepts

Generalization and inheritance are powerful abstractions for sharing similarities among classes while preserving their differences. For example, we would like to be able to model the following situation: Each piece of equipment has a manufacturer, weight, and cost.

Pumps also have suction pressure and flow rate. Tanks also have volume and pressure. We would like to define equipment features just once and then add details for pump, tank, and other equipment types.

*Generalization* is the relationship between a class and one or more refined versions of it. The class being refined is called the *superclass* and each refined version is called a *subclass*. For example, *Equipment* is the superclass of *Pump* and *Tank*. Attributes and operations common to a group of subclasses are attached to the superclass and shared by each subclass. Each subclass is said to *inherit* the features of its superclass. For example, *Pump* inherits attributes *manufacturer, weight,* and *cost* from *Equipment*. Generalization is sometimes called the "is-a" relationship because each instance of a subclass is an instance of the superclass as well.

Generalization and inheritance are transitive across an arbitrary number of levels. The terms *ancestor* and *descendent* refer to generalization of classes across multiple levels. An instance of a subclass is simultaneously an instance of all its ancestor classes. The state of an instance includes a value for every attribute of every ancestor class. Any operation on any ancestor class can be applied to an instance. Each subclass not only inherits all the features of its ancestors but adds its own specific attributes and operations as well. For example, *Pump* adds attribute *flow rate*, which is not shared by other kinds of equipment.

The notation for generalization is a triangle connecting a superclass to its subclasses. The superclass is connected by a line to the apex of the triangle. The subclasses are connected by lines to a horizontal bar attached to the base of the triangle. For convenience, the triangle can be inverted, and subclasses can be connected to both the top and bottom of the bar, but if possible the superclass should be drawn on top and the subclasses on the bottom.

Figure 3.23 shows an equipment generalization. Each piece of equipment is a pump, heat exchanger, tank, or another type of equipment. There are several kinds of pumps: centrifugal, diaphragm, and plunger. There are several kinds of tanks: floating roof, pressurized, and spherical. *Pump type* and *tank type* both refine second level generalization classes down to a third level; the fact that the tank generalization symbol is drawn below the pump generalization symbol is not significant. Several object instances are displayed at the bottom of the figure. Each object inherits features from one class at each level of the generalization. Thus *P101* embodies the features of equipment, pump, and diaphragm pump. *E302* assumes the properties of equipment and heat exchanger.

The dangling subclass ellipsis (triple dot) in Figure 3.23 indicates that there are additional subclasses that are not shown on the diagram, perhaps because there is no room on the sheet and they are shown elsewhere, or maybe because enumeration of subclasses is still incomplete.

The words written next to the triangles in the diagram, such as *equipment type, pump type,* and *tank type,* are discriminators. A *discriminator* is an attribute of enumeration type that indicates which property of an object is being abstracted by a particular generalization relationship. Only one property should be discriminated at once. For example, class *Vehicle* can be discriminated on propulsion (wind, gas, coal, animal, gravity) and also on operating environment (land, air, water, outer space). The discriminator is simply a name for the basis of generalization. Discriminator values are inherently in one-to-one correspondence with the subclasses of a generalization. For example, the operating environment discriminator for

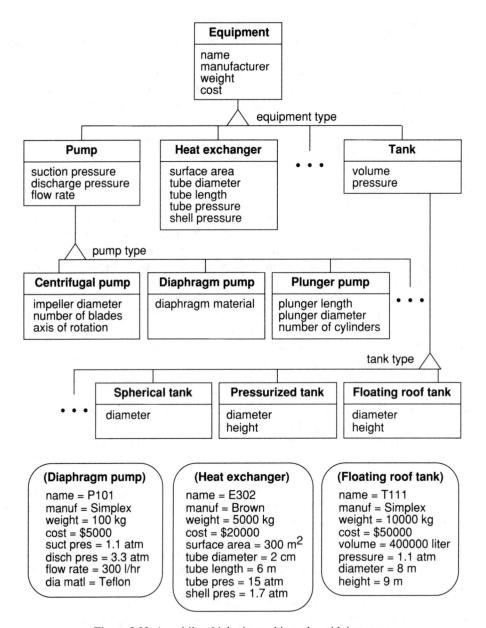

**Figure 3.23** A multilevel inheritance hierarchy with instances

*Boat* is *water*. The discriminator is an optional part of a generalization relationship; if a discriminator is included, it should be drawn next to the generalization triangle.

Figure 3.24 shows classes of graphic geometric figures. This example has more of a programming flavor and emphasizes inheritance of operations. *Move*, *select*, *rotate*, and *display*

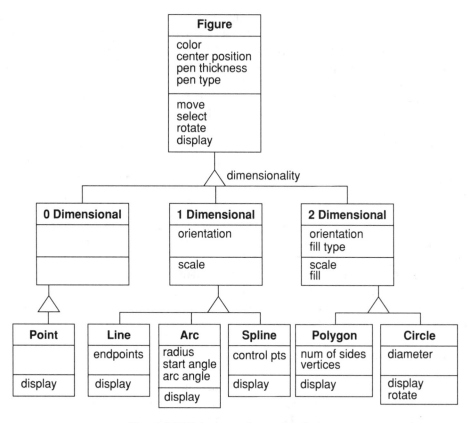

**Figure 3.24** Inheritance for graphic figures

are operations inherited by all subclasses. *Scale* applies to one- and two-dimensional figures. *Fill* applies only to two-dimensional figures.

Do not nest subclasses too deeply. Deeply nested subclasses can be difficult to understand, much like deeply nested blocks of code in a procedural language. Often with some careful thought and a little restructuring, you can reduce the depth of an overextended inheritance hierarchy. In practice, whether or not a subclass is "too deeply nested" depends upon judgment and the particular details of a problem. The following guidelines may help: An inheritance hierarchy that is two or three levels deep is certainly acceptable; ten levels deep is probably excessive; five or six levels may or may not be proper.

## 3.4.2 Use of Generalization

Generalization is a useful construct for both conceptual modeling and implementation. Generalization facilitates modeling by structuring classes and succinctly capturing what is similar and what is different about classes. Inheritance of operations is helpful during implementation as a vehicle for reusing code.

Object-oriented languages provide strong support for the notion of inheritance. (The concept of inheritance was actually invented far earlier, but object-oriented languages made it popular.) In contrast, current database systems provide little or no support for inheritance. Object-oriented database programming languages (Section 15.8.5) and extended relational database systems (Section 17.4) show promise of correcting this situation.

Inheritance has become synonymous with code reuse within the object-oriented programming community. After modeling a system, the developer looks at the resulting classes and tries to group similar classes together and reuse common code. Often code is available from past work (such as a class library) which the developer can reuse and modify, where necessary, to get the precise desired behavior. The most important use of inheritance, however, is the conceptual simplification that comes from reducing the number of independent features in a system.

The terms inheritance, generalization, and specialization all refer to aspects of the same idea and are often used interchangeably. We use *generalization* to refer to the relationship among classes, while *inheritance* refers to the mechanism of sharing attributes and operations using the generalization relationship. Generalization and specialization are two different viewpoints of the same relationship, viewed from the superclass or from the subclasses. The word *generalization* derives from the fact that the superclass generalizes the subclasses. *Specialization* refers to the fact that the subclasses refine or specialize the superclass. In practice, there is little danger of confusion.

### 3.4.3 Overriding Features

A subclass may *override* a superclass feature by defining a feature with the same name. The overriding feature (the subclass feature) refines and replaces the overridden feature (the superclass feature). There are several reasons why you may wish to override a feature: to specify behavior that depends on the subclass, to tighten the specification of a feature, or for better performance. For example, in Figure 3.24, *display* must be implemented separately for each kind of figure, although it is defined for any kind of figure. Operation *rotate* is overridden for performance in class *Circle* to be a null operation. Chapter 4 discusses overriding features in more detail.

You may override default values of attributes and methods of operations. You should never override the *signature,* or form, of a feature. An override should preserve attribute type, number, and type of arguments to an operation and operation return type. Tightening the type of an attribute or operation argument to be a subclass of the original type is a form of *restriction* (Section 4.3) and must be done with care. It is common to boost performance by overriding a general method with a special method that takes advantage of specific information but does not alter the operation semantics (such as *rotate-circle* in Figure 3.24).

A feature should never be overridden so that it is inconsistent with the signature or semantics of the original inherited feature. A subclass *is* a special case of its superclass and should be compatible with it in every respect. A common, but unfortunate, practice in object-oriented programming is to "borrow" a class that is similar to a desired class and then modify it by changing and ignoring some of its features, even though the new class is not really a special case of the original class. This practice can lead to conceptual confusion and hidden assumptions built into programs. (See Section 4.3 for further discussion of overrides.)

## 3.5 GROUPING CONSTRUCTS

### 3.5.1 Module

A *module* is a logical construct for grouping classes, associations, and generalizations. A module captures one perspective or view of a situation. For example, electrical, plumbing, and ventilation modules are different views of a building. The boundaries of a module are somewhat arbitrary and subject to judgment.

An object model consists of one or more modules. Modules enable you to partition an object model into manageable pieces. Modules provide an intermediate unit of packaging between an entire object model and the basic building blocks of class and association. Class names and association names must be unique within a module. As much as possible, you should use consistent class and association names across modules. The module name is usually listed at the top of each sheet. There is no other special notation for modules.

The same class may be referenced in different modules. In fact, referencing the same class in multiple modules is the mechanism for binding modules together. There should be fewer links between modules (external binding) than within modules (internal binding).

### 3.5.2 Sheet

A complex model will not fit on a single piece of paper. A *sheet* is the mechanism for breaking a large object model down into a series of pages. A sheet is a single printed page. Each module consists of one or more sheets. As a rule, we never put more than one module per sheet. A sheet is just a notational convenience, not a logical construct.

Each sheet has a title and a name or number. Each association and generalization appears on a single sheet. Classes may appear on multiple sheets. Multiple copies of the same class form the bridge for connecting sheets in an object model. Sheet numbers or sheet names inside circles contiguous to a class box indicate other sheets that refer to a class. Use of sheet cross-reference circles is optional.

## 3.6 A SAMPLE OBJECT MODEL

Figure 3.25 shows an object model of a workstation window management system, such as the X Window System or SunView. This model is greatly simplified—a real model of a windowing system would require a number of pages—but it illustrates many object modeling constructs and shows how they fit together into a large model.

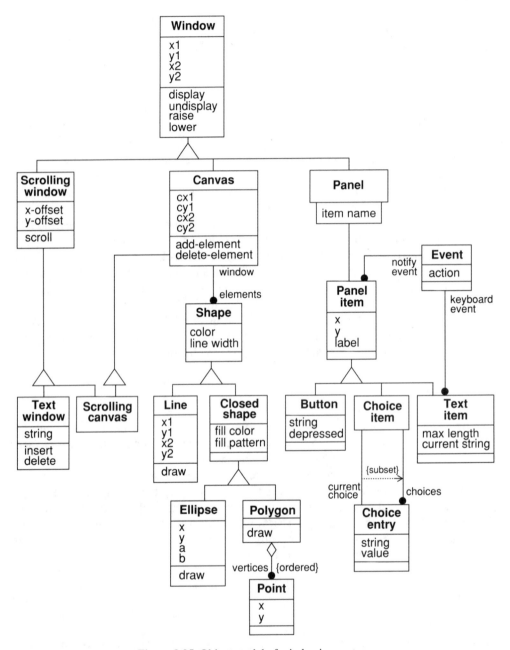

**Figure 3.25** Object model of windowing system

Class *Window* defines common parameters of all kinds of windows, including a rectangular boundary defined by the attributes *x1, y1, x2, y2*, and operations to display and undisplay a window and to raise it to the top (foreground) or lower it to the bottom (background) of the entire set of windows. *Panel, Canvas,* and *Text window* are varieties of windows. A canvas is a region for drawing graphics. It inherits the window boundary from *Window* and adds the dimensions of the underlying canvas region defined by attributes *cx1, cy1, cx2, cy2.* A canvas contains a set of elements, shown by the association to class *Shape.* All shapes have color and line width. Shapes can be lines, ellipses, or polygons, each with their own parameters. A polygon consists of an ordered list of vertices, shown as an aggregation of many points. Ellipses and polygons are both closed shapes, which have a fill color and a fill pattern. Lines are one-dimensional and cannot be filled. Canvas windows have operations to add elements and to delete elements.

*Text window* is a kind of a *Scrolling window,* which has a 2-dimensional scrolling offset within its window, as specified by *x-offset* and *y-offset,* as well as an operation *scroll* to change the scroll value. A text window contains a string, and has operations to insert and delete characters. *Scrolling canvas* is a special kind of canvas that supports scrolling; it is both a *Canvas* and a *Scrolling window.* This is an example of *multiple inheritance,* to be explained in Section 4.4.

A *Panel* contains a set of *Panel item* objects, each identified by a unique *item name* within a given panel, as shown by the qualified association. Each panel item belongs to a single panel. A panel item is a predefined icon with which a user can interact on the screen. Panel items come in three kinds: buttons, choice items, and text items. A button has a string which appears on the screen; a button can be pushed by the user and has an attribute *depressed.* A choice item allows the user to select one of a set of predefined *choices,* each of which is a *Choice entry* containing a string to be displayed and a value to be returned if the entry is selected. There are two associations between *Choice item* and *Choice entry;* a one-to-many association defines the set of allowable choices, while a one-to-one association identifies the current choice. The current choice must be one of the allowable choices, so one association is a subset of the other as shown by the arrow between them labeled "{subset}." This is an example of a constraint, to be explained in Section 4.7.

When a panel item is selected by the user, it generates an *Event,* which is a signal that something has happened together with an action to be performed. All kinds of panel items have *notify event* associations. Each panel item has a single event, but one event can be shared among many panel items. Text items have a second kind of event, which is generated when a keyboard character is typed while the text item is selected. Association *keyboard event* shows these events. Text items also inherit the *notify event* from superclass *Panel item;* the *notify event* is generated when the entire text item is selected with a mouse.

There are many deficiencies in this model. For example, perhaps we should define a type *Rectangle,* which can then be used for the window and canvas boundaries, rather than having two similar sets of four position attributes. Maybe a line should be a special case of a polyline (a connected series of line segments), in which case maybe both *Polyline* and *Polygon* should be subclasses of a new common superclass that defines an ordered list of points. Many attributes, operations, and classes are missing from a description of a realistic windowing system. Certainly the windows have associations among themselves, such as overlapping one another. Nevertheless, this simple model gives a flavor of the use of object modeling. We can criticize its details because it says something precise. It would serve as the basis for a fuller model.

## 3.7 PRACTICAL TIPS

We have gleaned the following tips for constructing object diagrams from our application work. Many of these tips have been mentioned throughout this chapter.

- Don't begin constructing an object model by merely jotting down classes, associations, and inheritance. First, you must understand the problem to be solved. The content of an object model is driven by relevance to the solution.

- Strive to keep your model simple. Avoid needless complications.

- Carefully choose names. Names are important and carry powerful connotations. Names should be descriptive, crisp, and unambiguous. Names should not be biased towards one aspect of an object. Choosing good names is one of the most difficult aspects of object modeling.

- Do not bury pointers or other object references inside objects as attributes. Instead model these as associations. This is clearer and captures the true intent rather than an implementation approach.

- Try to avoid general ternary and n-ary associations. Most of these can be decomposed into binary associations, with possible qualifiers and link attributes.

- Don't try to get multiplicity perfect too early in software development.

- Do not collapse link attributes into a class.

- Use qualified associations where possible.

- Try to avoid deeply nested generalizations.

- Challenge one-to-one associations. Often the object on either end is optional and zero-or-one multiplicity may be more appropriate. Other times many multiplicity is needed.

- Don't be surprised if your object model requires revision. Object models often require multiple iterations to clarify names, repair errors, add details, and correctly capture structural constraints (Section 4.7). Some of our most complex models, which are only a few pages long, have required half a dozen iterations.

- Try to get others to review your model. Object models can be a focal point for stimulating the involvement of others.

- Always document your object models. The diagram specifies the structure of a model but cannot describe the reasons behind it. The written explanation guides the reader through the model and explains subtle reasons why the model was structured a particular way. The written explanation clarifies the meaning of names in the model and should convey the reason for each class and relationship.

- Do not feel bound to exercise all object modeling constructs. The OMT notation is an idealization. Not all constructs are needed for every problem. Many constructs are optional and a matter of taste. Use only what you need for the problem at hand.

## 3.8  CHAPTER SUMMARY

Object models describe the static data structure of objects, classes, and their relationships to one another. The content of an object model is a matter of judgment and is driven by its relevance to an application. An object is a concept, abstraction, or thing with crisp boundaries and meaning for an application. All objects have identity and are distinguishable. An object class describes a group of objects with common attributes, operations, and semantics. An attribute is a property of the objects in a class; an operation is an action that may be applied to objects in a class.

Links and associations establish relationships among objects and classes. A link connects two or more objects. An association describes a group of links with common structure and common semantics. Multiplicity specifies how many instances of one class may relate to each instance of another class. An association is a logical construct, of which a pointer is an implementation alternative. There are other ways of implementing associations besides using pointers.

Additional constructs for modeling associations include: link attribute, role, qualifier, and aggregation. A link attribute is a property of the links in an association. Many-to-many associations demonstrate the most compelling rationale for link attributes. Such an attribute is unmistakably a property of the link and cannot be attached to either object. A role is a direction across an association. Roles are particularly useful in dealing with associations between objects of the same class. A qualifier reduces the effective multiplicity of an association by selecting among the set of objects at the many end. Names are often qualifiers. Aggregation is a tightly coupled form of association with special semantics, such as transitive closure and attribute value propagation. Aggregation is commonly encountered in bill-of-material or parts explosion problems.

Generalization and inheritance are fundamental concepts in object-oriented languages that are missing in conventional languages and databases. Generalization is a useful construct for both conceptual modeling and implementation. During conceptual modeling, generalization enables the developer to organize classes into a hierarchical structure based on their similarities and differences. During implementation, inheritance facilitates code reuse. The term *generalization* refers to the relationship among class; the term *inheritance* refers to the mechanism of obtaining attributes and operations using the generalization structure. Generalization provides the means for refining a superclass into one or more subclasses. The superclass contains features common to all classes; the subclasses contain features specific to each class. Inheritance may occur across an arbitrary number of levels where each level represents one aspect of an object. An object accumulates features from each level of a generalization hierarchy.

Module and sheet are grouping constructs. An object model consists of one or more modules. A module is a logical grouping construct which captures one perspective or view of a situation. Most references to classes lie within modules; a few span modules. Each module has one or more sheets. A sheet is merely a notational convenience for fitting object models onto fixed sized pieces of paper.

The various object modeling constructs work together to describe a complex system precisely, as shown by our example of a model for a windowing system. Once an object model is available, even a simplified one, the model can be compared against knowledge of the real world or the desired application, criticized, and improved.

| aggregation | generalization | method | override |
| association | identity | module | qualification |
| attribute | inheritance | multiplicity | role |
| class | instance | object | sheet |
| discriminator | link | operation | signature |
| feature | link attribute | ordering | specialization |

**Figure 3.26** Key concepts for Chapter 3

## BIBLIOGRAPHIC NOTES

The object modeling approach described in this book builds on the OMT notation originally proposed in [Loomis-87]. [Blaha-88] extends the OMT notation for the purpose of database design. This book redefines the term *OMT*; in this book OMT does not merely refer to a notation but refers to our entire methodology. Our *object model* is analogous to the *OMT notation* discussed in the papers. This book refines object modeling notation beyond that shown in the papers and sets forth a complete methodology for its use.

The object modeling notation is one of a score of approaches descended from the seminal entity-relationship (ER) model of [Chen-76]. All the descendents attempt to improve on the ER approach. Enhancements to the ER model have been pursued for several reasons. The ER technique has been successful for database modeling and as a result, there has been great demand for additional power. Also, ER modeling only addresses database design and not programming. There are too many extensions to ER for us to discuss them all here. (Chapter 12 discusses some extensions to ER.)

A noteworthy aspect of our approach to object modeling is the emphasis we place on associations. Just as inheritance is useful for conceptual modeling and implementation, so too associations are important for conceptual modeling and implementation. Most existing object-oriented programming languages ([Cox-86], [Goldberg-83], and [Meyer-88]) lack the notion of associations and require the use of pointers. Most database design techniques recognize the importance of associations. [Rumbaugh-87] is the original source of our association ideas. The use of the term *relation* in [Rumbaugh-87] is synonymous with our use of *association* in this book.

[Khoshafian-86] defines the concept of object identity and its importance to programming languages and database systems.

## REFERENCES

[Blaha-88] Michael Blaha, William Premerlani, James Rumbaugh. Relational database design using an object-oriented methodology. *Communications of the ACM 31*, 4 (April 1988) 414-427.

[Chen-76] P.P.S. Chen. The Entity-Relationship model—toward a unified view of data. *ACM Transactions on Database Systems 1*, 1 (March 1976).

[Cox-86] Brad J. Cox. *Object-Oriented Programming*. Reading, Mass.: Addison-Wesley, 1986.

[Goldberg-83] Adele Goldberg, David Robson. *Smalltalk-80: The Language and its Implementation.* Reading, Mass.: Addison-Wesley, 1983.

[Khoshafian-86] S.N. Khoshafian, G.P. Copeland. Object identity. *OOPLSA'86* as *ACM SIGPLAN 21,* 11 (Nov. 1986), 406-416.

[Loomis-87] Mary E.S. Loomis, Ashwin V. Shah, James E. Rumbaugh. An object modeling technique for conceptual design. *European Conference on Object-Oriented Programming,* Paris, France, June 15-17, 1987, published as *Lecture Notes in Computer Science, 276,* Springer-Verlag.

[Meyer-88] Bertrand Meyer. *Object-Oriented Software Construction.* Hertfordshire, England: Prentice Hall International, 1988.

[Rumbaugh-87] James E. Rumbaugh. Relations as semantic constructs in an object-oriented language. *OOPSLA'87* as *ACM SIGPLAN 22,* 12 (Dec.1987), 466-481.

## EXERCISES

**3.1**    (2) Prepare a class diagram from the instance diagram in Figure E3.1.

**Figure E3.1**  Instance diagram for a portion of Europe

**3.2**    (2) Prepare a class diagram from the instance diagram in Figure E3.2. Explain your multiplicity decisions. Each point has an x coordinate and a y coordinate. What is the smallest number of points required to construct a polygon? Does it make a difference whether or not a given point may be shared between several polygons? How can you express the fact that points are in a sequence?

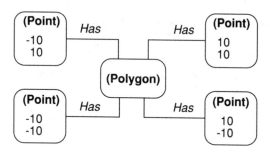

**Figure E3.2**  Instance diagram of a polygon that happens to be a square

**3.3**    (3) Consistent with the object diagram that you prepared in exercise 3.2, draw an instance diagram for two triangles with a common side under the following conditions:
a. A point belongs to exactly one polygon.
b. A point belongs to one or more polygons.

**3.4**    (3) Prepare a class diagram from the instance diagram in Figure E3.3. Explain your multiplicity decisions. How does your diagram express the fact that points are in a sequence?

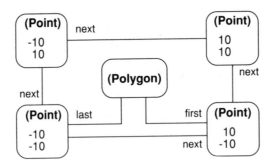

**Figure E3.3**  Another instance diagram of a polygon that happens to be a square

**3.5**    (5) Prepare a written description for the object diagrams in exercise 3.2 and exercise 3.4.

**3.6**    (5) Prepare a class diagram from the instance diagram in Figure E3.4.

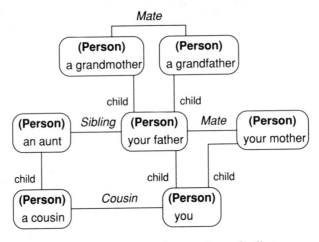

**Figure E3.4**  Instance diagram for part of your family tree

**3.7**    (3) Prepare a class diagram from the instance diagram of a geometrical document shown in Figure E3.5. This particular document has 4 pages. The first page has a red point and a yellow square displayed on it. The second page contains a line and an ellipse. An arc, a circle, and a rectangle appear on the last two pages. In preparing your diagram, use exactly one aggregation relationship and one or more generalization relationships.

**3.8**    (6) a. Prepare an instance diagram for the class diagram in Figure E3.6 for the expression $(X + Y/2) / (X/3 + Y)$. Parentheses are used in the expression for grouping, but are not needed in the diagram. The many multiplicity indicates that a term may be used in more than one expression.
b. Modify the class diagram so that terms are not shared and to handle unary minus.

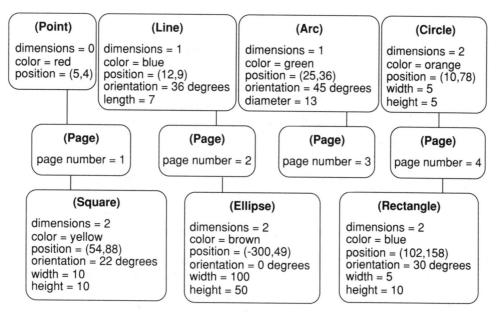

**Figure E3.5** Instance diagram for a geometrical document

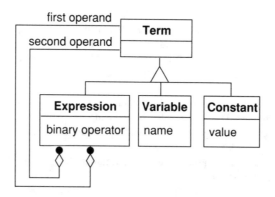

**Figure E3.6** Class diagram for simple arithmetic expressions

**3.9**   (3) Figure E3.7 is a partially completed object diagram of an air transportation system. Multiplicity balls have been left out. Add them to the diagram. Defend your decisions. Demonstrate how multiplicity decisions depend on your perception of the world.

**3.10**  (4) Revise Figure E3.7 to make seat location a qualifier.

**3.11**  (3) Add association names to the unlabeled associations in Figure E3.7.

**3.12**  (3) Add role names to the unlabeled associations in Figure E3.7.

**3.13**  (4) Prepare an instance diagram for an imaginary round trip you took last weekend to London. Include at least one instance of each object class. Fortunately, direct flights on a hypersonic

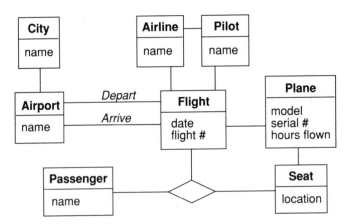

**Figure E3.7** Partially completed model of an air transportation system

plane were available. A friend of yours went with you but decided to stay a while and is still there. Captain Johnson was your pilot on both flights. You had a different seat each way, but you noticed it was on the same plane because of a distinctive dent in the tail section.

**3.14** (1) Add the following operations to the object diagram in Figure E3.7: heat, hire, fire, refuel, reserve, clean, de-ice, takeoff, land, repair, cancel, delay. It is permissible to add an operation to more than one object class.

**3.15** Prepare object diagrams showing at least 10 relationships among the following object classes. Include associations, aggregations, and generalizations. Use qualified associations and show multiplicity balls in your diagrams. You do not need to show attributes or operations. Use association names where needed. As you prepare the diagrams, you may add additional object classes.
   a. (4) school, playground, principal, school board, classroom, book, student, teacher, cafeteria, rest room, computer, desk, chair, ruler, door, swing
   b. (4) castle, moat, drawbridge, tower, ghost, stairs, dungeon, floor, corridor, room, window, stone, lord, lady, cook
   c. (7) expression, constant, variable, function, argument list, relational operator, term, factor, arithmetic operator, statement, program
   d. (6) file system, file, directory, file name, ASCII file, executable file, directory file, disk, drive, track, sector
   e. (4) automobile, engine, wheel, brake, brake light, door, battery, muffler, tail pipe
   f. (6) gas furnace, blower, blower motor, room thermostat, furnace thermostat, humidifier, humidity sensor, gas control, blower control, hot air vents
   g. (5) chess piece, rank, file, square, board, move, position, sequence of moves
   h. (5) sink, freezer, refrigerator, table, light, switch, window, smoke alarm, burglar alarm, cabinet, bread, cheese, ice, door, kitchen

**3.16** (5) Add at least 15 attributes and at least 5 operations to each of the object diagrams you prepared in the previous exercise.

**3.17** (5) Figure E3.8 is a portion of an object diagram for a computer program for playing several types of card games. Deck, hand, discard pile, and draw pile are collections of cards. The initial size of a hand depends on the type of game. Each card has a suit and rank. Add the following operations to the diagram: display, shuffle, deal, initialize, sort, insert, delete, top-of-pile, bottom-of-pile, draw, and discard. Some operations may appear in more than one object class. For each class in which an operation appears, describe the arguments to the operation and what the operation should do to an instance of that class.

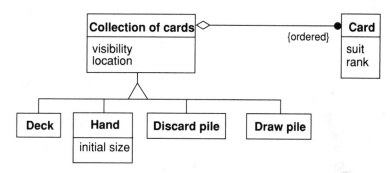

**Figure E3.8** Portion of an object diagram for a card playing system

**3.18** (5) Figure E3.9 is a portion of an object diagram for a computer system for laying out a newspaper. The system handles several pages which may contain, among other things, columns of text. The user may edit the width and length of a column of text, move it around on a page, or move it from one page to another. As shown, a column is displayed on exactly one page. It is desired to modify the system so that portions of the same column may appear on more than one page. If the user edits the text on one page, the changes should appear automatically on other pages. Modify the object diagram to handle this enhancement. You should change x location and y location into link attributes.

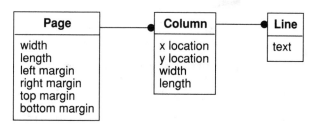

**Figure E3.9** Portion of an object diagram for a newspaper publishing system

**3.19** (4) Figure E3.10 is an object diagram that might be used in designing a system to simplify the scheduling and scoring of judged athletic competitions such as gymnastics, diving, and figure skating. There are several events and competitors. Each competitor may enter several events and each event has many competitors. Each event has several judges who subjectively rate the performance of competitors in that event. A judge rates every competitor for an event. In some cases, a judge may score more than one event. The focal points of the competition are trials. Each trial is an attempt by one competitor to turn in the best performance possible in one event. A trial is scored by the panel of judges for that event and a net score determined. Add role names and multiplicity balls to the associations.

**Figure E3.10** Portion of an object diagram for an athletic event scoring system

**3.20** (3) Add the following attributes to Figure E3.10: address, age, date, difficulty factor, name. In some cases, you may wish to use the same attribute in more than one class.

**3.21** (2) Add an association to Figure E3.10 to make it possible to directly determine what events a competitor intends to try without involving the class *Trial*.

**3.22** (6) Prepare an object diagram for the dining philosopher's problem. There are 5 philosophers and 5 forks around a circular table. Each philosopher has access to 2 forks on either side. Each fork is shared by 2 philosophers. Each fork may be either on the table or in use by one philosopher. A philosopher must have 2 forks to eat.

**3.23** (5) Prepare an object model to describe undirected graphs. An undirected graph consists of a set of vertices and a set of edges. Edges connect pairs of vertices. Your model should capture only the structure of graphs (i.e., connectivity), and need not be concerned with geometrical details such as location of vertices or lengths of edges. A typical graph is shown in Figure E3.11.

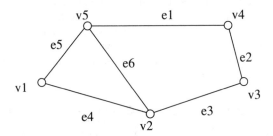

**Figure E3.11** Sample undirected graph

**3.24** (3) Prepare an instance diagram for Figure E3.11.

**3.25** (4) Extend the object diagram you prepared in exercise 3.23 to accommodate geometrical details, including locations of vertices and names of vertices and edges.

**3.26** (5) Prepare an object model to describe directed graphs. A directed graph is similar to an undirected graph, except the edges are oriented. A typical graph is shown in Figure E3.12. Use direction as a qualifier in your diagram so that it is possible to determine the vertex that is connected to the head or to the tail of each edge.

**3.27** (3) Prepare an instance diagram for Figure E3.12.

**3.28** (6) Several object classes shown in Figure E3.13 have attributes that are really pointers to other object classes and which could be replaced with associations. A person may have up to three companies as employers. Each person has an ID. A car is assigned an ID. Cars may be owned

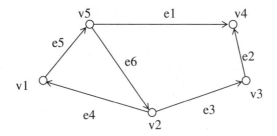

**Figure E3.12** Sample directed graph

by persons, companies, or banks. Car owner ID is the ID of the person, company, or bank who owns the car. A car loan may be involved in the purchase of a car.

Burying object references as pointers is the incorrect way to construct an object model. Prepare an object diagram in which the pointers are replaced with relationships. Try to get multiplicities right. You may need to add one or more object classes of your own. Eliminate all IDs. Some attributes may be converted to discriminators.

| **Person** | **Car** | **Car loan** | **Company** | **Bank** |
|---|---|---|---|---|
| name | owner ID | vehicle ID | name | name |
| age | vehicle ID | customer type | company ID | bank ID |
| employer 1 ID | owner type | customer ID | | |
| employer 2 ID | model | account number | | |
| employer 3 ID | year | bank ID | | |
| person ID | | interest rate | | |
| address | | current balance | | |

**Figure E3.13** Object classes with some attributes that are pointers.

**3.29** (3) A problem arises when several independent systems need to identify the same object. For example, the department of motor vehicles, an insurance company, a bank, and the police may wish to identify a given motor vehicle. Discuss the relative merits of using the following identification methods:
a. Identify by its owner
b. Identify by attributes such as manufacturer, model, and year
c. Use the vehicle identification number (VIN) assigned to the car by its manufacturer
d. Use IDs generated internally by each interested agency

**3.30** (7) Prepare an object model that might be used to troubleshoot a 4-cycle lawn mower engine. Use three sheets for the model, with one sheet for each of the following paragraphs:

Power is developed in such an engine by the combustion of a mixture of air and gasoline against a piston. The piston is attached to a crankshaft via a connecting rod, and moves up and down inside a cylinder as the shaft rotates. As the piston moves down, an intake valve opens, allowing the piston to draw a mixture of fuel and air into the cylinder. At the bottom of the stroke, the intake valve closes. The piston compresses and heats the mixture as it moves upward. Rings in grooves around the piston rub against the cylinder wall providing a seal necessary for compression and spreading lubricating oil. At the top of the stroke, an electrical spark from a spark plug detonates the mixture. The expanding gases develop power during the downward stroke. At the bottom, an exhaust valve is opened. On the next upward stroke, the exhaust gases are driven out.

Fuel is mixed with air in a carburetor. Dust and dirt in the air, which could cause excessive mechanical wear, are removed by an air filter. The optimum ratio of fuel to air is set by adjusting a tapered mixture screw. A throttle plate controls the amount of mixture pulled into the cylinder. The throttle plate, in turn, is controlled through springs by the operator throttle control and a governor, a mechanical device which stabilizes the engine speed under varying mechanical loads. Intake and exhaust valves are normally held closed by springs, and are opened at the right time by a cam shaft which is gear driven by the crankshaft.

The electrical energy for the spark is provided and timed by a magnet, coil, condenser, and a normally closed switch called the points. The coil has a low voltage primary circuit connected to the points and a high voltage secondary connected to the spark plug. The magnet is mounted on a flywheel and as it rotates past the coil, it induces a current in the shorted primary circuit. The points are driven open at the right instant by a cam on the crankshaft. With the aid of the condenser, they interrupt the current in the primary circuit, inducing a high voltage pulse in the secondary.

**3.31** (5) The tower of Hanoi is a problem frequently used to teach recursive programming techniques. The object is to move a stack of disks from one of three long pegs to another, using the third peg for maneuvering. Each disk is a different size. Disks may be moved from the top of a stack on a peg to the top of the stack on any other peg, one at a time, provided a disk is never placed on another disk that is smaller than itself. The details of the algorithm for listing the sequence of required moves will depend on the structure of the object diagram used. Prepare object diagrams for each of the following descriptions. Show object classes and associations. Do not show attributes or operations:

a. A tower consists of several (3) pegs. Each peg has several disks on it, in a certain order.

b. A tower consists of several (3) pegs. Disks on the pegs are organized into subsets called stacks. A stack is an ordered set of disks. Every disk is in exactly one stack. A peg may have several stacks on it, in order.

c. A tower consists of several (3) pegs. Disks on the pegs are organized into subsets called stacks, as in (b), with several stacks on a peg. However, the structure of a stack is recursive. A stack consists of one disk (the disk that is physically on the bottom of the stack) and zero or one stack, depending on the height of the stack.

d. Similar to (c), except only one stack is associated with a peg. Other stacks on the peg are associated in a linked list.

**3.32** (7) The recursive algorithm for producing the sequence of moves described in the previous exercise focuses on a stack of disks. To move a stack of height N, where N>1, first move the stack of height N-1 to the free peg using a recursive call. Then move the bottom disk to the desired peg. Finally, move the stack on the free peg to the desired peg. The recursion terminates, because moving a stack of height 1 is trivial. Which one of the several object diagrams that you prepared in the previous exercise is best suited for this algorithm? Discuss why. Also, add attributes and operations to the diagram. What are the arguments for each operation? Describe what each operation is supposed to do to each class for which it is defined.

# 4

# Advanced Object Modeling

Chapter 4 continues our discussion of object modeling concepts with treatment of advanced topics such as aggregation, inheritance, metadata, and constraints. This chapter provides subtleties for improved modeling that can be skipped upon a first reading of this book.

## 4.1 AGGREGATION

Aggregation is a strong form of association in which an aggregate object is *made of* components. Components are *part of* the aggregate. The aggregate is semantically an extended object that is treated as a unit in many operations, although physically it is made of several lesser objects. A single aggregate object may have several parts; each part-whole relationship is treated as a separate aggregation in order to emphasize the similarity to association. Parts may or may not exist apart from the aggregate or appear in multiple aggregates. Aggregation is inherently transitive; an aggregate has parts, which may in turn have parts. Many aggregate operations imply transitive closure* and operate on both direct and indirect parts. Recursive aggregation is common.

---

* Transitive closure is a term from graph theory. If $E$ denotes an edge and $N$ denotes a node and $S$ is the set of all pairs of nodes connected by an edge, then $S^+$ (the transitive closure of $S$) is the set of all pairs of nodes directly or indirectly connected by a sequence of edges. Thus $S^+$ includes all nodes which are directly connected, nodes connected by two edges, nodes connected by three edges, and so forth.

### 4.1.1 Aggregation Versus Association

Aggregation is a special form of association, not an independent concept. Aggregation adds semantic connotations in certain cases. If two objects are tightly bound by a part-whole relationship, it is an aggregation. If the two objects are usually considered as independent, even though they may often be linked, it is an association. Some tests include:

- Would you use the phrase *part of*?
- Are some operations on the whole automatically applied to its parts?
- Are some attribute values propagated from the whole to all or some parts?
- Is there an intrinsic asymmetry to the association, where one object class is subordinate to the other?

Aggregations include part explosions and expansions of an object into constituent parts. In Figure 4.1 a company is an aggregation of its divisions, which are in turn aggregations of their departments; a company is indirectly an aggregation of departments. A company is not an aggregation of its employees, since company and person are independent objects of equal stature.

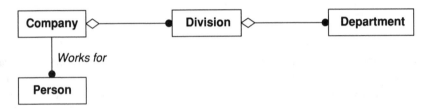

**Figure 4.1** Aggregation and association

The decision to use aggregation is a matter of judgment and is often arbitrary. Often it is not obvious if an association should be modeled as an aggregation. To a large extent this kind of uncertainty is typical of modeling; modeling requires seasoned judgment and there are few hard and fast rules. Our experience has been that if you exercise careful judgment and are consistent, the imprecise distinction between aggregation and ordinary association does not cause problems in practice.

### 4.1.2 Aggregation Versus Generalization

Aggregation is not the same thing as generalization. Aggregation relates instances. Two distinct objects are involved; one of them is a part of the other. Generalization relates classes and is a way of structuring the description of a single object. Both superclass and subclass refer to properties of a single object. With generalization, an object is simultaneously an instance of the superclass and an instance of the subclass. Confusion arises because both aggregation and generalization give rise to trees through transitive closure. An aggregation tree is composed of object instances that are all part of a composite object; a generalization tree is composed of classes that describe an object. Aggregation is often called "a-part-of" relationship; generalization is often called "a-kind-of" or "is-a" relationship.

Figure 4.2 illustrates aggregation and generalization for the case of a desk lamp. Parts explosions are the most compelling examples of aggregation. Base, cover, switch, and wiring are all part of a lamp. Lamps may be classified into several different subclasses: fluorescent and incandescent, for example. Each subclass may have its own distinct parts. For example, a fluorescent lamp has a ballast, twist mount, and starter; an incandescent lamp has a socket.

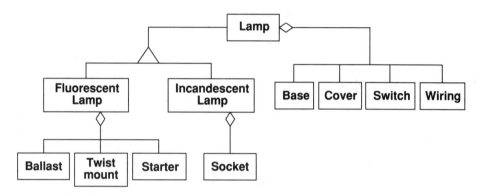

**Figure 4.2** Aggregation and generalization

Aggregation is sometimes called an "and-relationship" and generalization an "or-relationship." A lamp is made of a base and a cover and a switch and wiring and so on. A lamp is a fluorescent lamp or an incandescent lamp.

### 4.1.3 Recursive Aggregates

Aggregation can be fixed, variable, or recursive. A fixed aggregate has a fixed structure; the number and types of subparts are predefined. The lamp in Figure 4.2 has a fixed aggregate structure.

A variable aggregate has a finite number of levels, but the number of parts may vary. The company in Figure 4.1 is a variable aggregate with a two-level tree structure. There are many divisions per company and many departments per division.

A recursive aggregate contains, directly or indirectly, an instance of the same kind of aggregate; the number of potential levels is unlimited. Figure 4.3 shows the example of a computer program. A computer program is an aggregation of blocks, with optionally recursive compound statements; the recursion terminates with simple statements. Blocks can be nested to arbitrary depth.

Figure 4.3 illustrates the usual form of a recursive aggregate: a superclass and two subclasses, one of which is an intermediate node of the aggregate and one of which is a terminal node of the aggregate. The intermediate node is an assembly of instances of the abstract superclass.

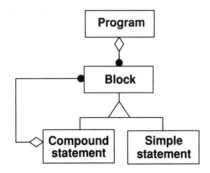

**Figure 4.3** Recursive aggregate

### 4.1.4 Propagation of Operations

*Propagation* (also called *triggering*) is the automatic application of an operation to a network of objects when the operation is applied to some starting object [Rumbaugh-88].[*] For example, moving an aggregate moves its parts; the move operation propagates to the parts. Propagation of operations to parts is often a good indicator of aggregation.

Figure 4.4 shows an example of propagation. A person owns multiple documents. Each document is composed of paragraphs that are, in turn, composed of characters. The copy operation propagates from documents to paragraphs to characters. Copying a paragraph copies all the characters in it. The operation does not propagate in the reverse direction; a paragraph can be copied without copying the whole document. Similarly, copying a document copies the owner link but does not spawn a copy of the person who is owner.

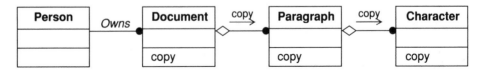

**Figure 4.4** Propagation of operations

Most other approaches present an all-or-nothing option: copy an entire network with deep copy, or copy the starting object and none of the related objects with shallow copy. The concept of propagation of operations provides a concise and powerful way for specifying an entire continuum of behavior. An operation can be thought of as starting at some initial object and flowing from object to object through links according to propagation rules. Propagation is possible for other operations including save/restore, destroy, print, lock, and display.

Propagation is indicated on object models with a special notation. The propagation behavior is bound to an association (or aggregation), direction, and operation. Propagation is

---

* The term *association* as used in this book is synonymous with the term *relation* used in [Rumbaugh-88].

indicated with a small arrow and operation name next to the affected association. The arrow indicates the direction of propagation.

## 4.2 ABSTRACT CLASSES

An *abstract class* is a class that has no direct instances but whose descendent classes have direct instances. A *concrete class* is a class that is instantiable; that is, it can have direct instances. A concrete class may have abstract subclasses (but they in turn must have concrete descendants). A concrete class may be a leaf class in the inheritance tree; only concrete classes may be leaf classes in the inheritance tree. Figure 4.5 summarizes the definition of abstract and concrete class. (The dotted line is the object modeling notation for instantiation and is discussed in Section 4.5.1.)

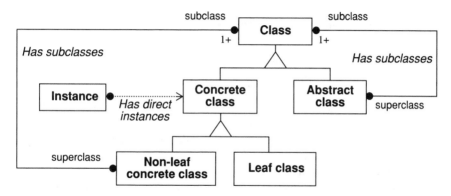

**Figure 4.5** Object model defining abstract and concrete class

All the occupations shown in Figure 4.6 are concrete classes. *Butcher, Baker,* and *Candlestick Maker* are concrete classes because they have direct instances. The ellipsis notation (...) indicates that additional subclasses exist but have been omitted from the diagram, perhaps for lack of space or lack of relevance to the present concern. *Worker* also is a concrete class because some occupations may not be further specified.

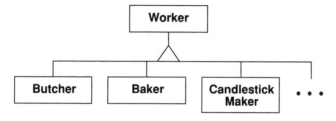

**Figure 4.6** Concrete classes

Class *Employee* in Figure 4.7 is an example of an abstract class. All employees must be either hourly, salaried, or exempt.

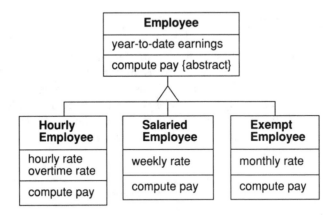

**Figure 4.7** Abstract class and abstract operation

Abstract classes organize features common to several classes. It is often useful to create an abstract superclass to encapsulate classes that participate in the same association or aggregation. Some abstract classes appear naturally in the application domain. Other abstract classes are artificially introduced as a mechanism for promoting code reuse.

Abstract classes are frequently used to define methods to be inherited by subclasses. On the other hand, an abstract class can define the protocol for an operation without supplying a corresponding method. We call this an abstract operation. (Recall that in Chapter 3 we defined an operation as the protocol for an action that may be applied to objects in a class. A method is the actual implementation of an operation.) An abstract operation defines the form of an operation for which each concrete subclass must provide its own implementation. A concrete class may not contain abstract operations because objects of the concrete class would have undefined operations.

Figure 4.7 shows an abstract operation. An abstract operation is designated by a comment in braces. *Compute-pay* is an abstract operation of class *Employee*; its form but not its implementation is defined. Each subclass must supply a method for this operation.

The *origin class* of a feature is the topmost defining class. The origin class defines the *protocol* of the feature, that is the type of an attribute or the number and type of arguments and result type for operations, as well as the semantic intent. Descendent classes can refine the protocol by further restricting the types or by overriding the initialization or method code. Descendent classes may not expand or change the protocol.

Note that the abstract nature of a class is always provisional, depending on the point of view. A concrete class can usually be refined into several subclasses, making it abstract. Conversely, an abstract class may become concrete in an application in which the difference among its subclasses is unimportant.

## 4.3 GENERALIZATION AS EXTENSION AND RESTRICTION

An instance of a class is an instance of all ancestors of the class. This is part of the definition of generalization. Therefore all ancestor class features must apply to the subclass instances. A descendent class cannot omit or suppress an ancestor attribute because then it would not truly be an ancestor instance. Similarly operations on an ancestor class must apply to all descendent classes. A subclass may reimplement an operation for reasons of efficiency but cannot change the external protocol.

A subclass may add new features. This is called *extension*. For example, Figure 4.7 extends class *Employee* with three subclasses that inherit all *Employee* features and add new features of their own.

A subclass may also constrain ancestor attributes. This is called *restriction* because it restricts the values that instances can assume. For example, a circle is an ellipse whose major and minor axes are equal. Arbitrary changes to the attribute values of a restricted subclass may cause it to violate the constraints, such that the result no longer belongs to the original subclass. This is not a problem from the perspective of the superclass because the result is still a valid superclass instance. For example, a circle that is scaled unequally in the x and y dimensions remains an ellipse but is no longer a circle. Class *Ellipse* is closed under the scaling operation, but *Circle* is not.

Inherited features can be renamed in a restriction. The inherited major and minor axes of a circle must be equal and could be renamed the *diameter*.

Class membership can be defined in two ways: implicitly by rule or explicitly by enumeration. A rule defines a condition for membership in a class; all objects whose values satisfy the rule belong to the class. This is the usual mathematical usage. Polygons, triangles, ellipses, circles, and other mathematical objects are defined by rule. This works well for immutable values but not so well for objects that can undergo changes yet remain the same object. Most object-oriented languages consider an object to be a discrete unit with explicit properties, one of which is the class of the object. An object has explicit class membership and the attributes it bears flows from its class. In contrast, for rule-based definition, class membership flows from attribute values.

In an explicit definition of class membership, operations that would invalidate class membership constraints must be disallowed on semantic grounds. Restriction implies that a subclass may not inherit all the operations of its ancestors. In an ideal world, such operations would be automatically detected by a support system, but for now they must be specified by the designer. Thus the *Circle* class must suppress the unequal scale operation. On the other hand, an object declared to be an ellipse is not restricted to remain a circle even if its major and minor axes happen to be temporarily equal.

Failing to note the difference between restriction and extension has caused confusion in the past. Some authors have been bothered by the fact that subclasses must suppress some operations. Chapter 10 of [Meyer-88] notes that subclasses can be viewed as both specializing and extending superclass features. These meanings are complementary. Some operations are meaningful only to a subset of instances; narrowing the set of instances broadens the number of applicable operations. Meyer also notes that the internal implementation of an operation can be overridden, provided the external protocol remains the same.

### 4.3.1 Overriding Operations

There is tension between use of inheritance for abstract data types and for sharing implementation. Most of this tension relates to overriding methods. The trouble arises when the overriding method substantially differs from the overridden method, rather than just refining it. Overriding is done for the following reasons:

*Overriding for extension.* The new operation is the same as the inherited operation, except it adds some behavior, usually affecting new attributes of the subclass. This concept is supported by Eiffel (redefine) and Smalltalk (SUPER). For example, *Window* may have a *draw* operation that draws the window boundary and contents. *Window* could have a subclass called *LabeledWindow* that also has a *draw* operation. The *draw-LabeledWindow* method could be implemented by invoking the method to draw a *Window* and then adding code to draw the label.

*Overriding for restriction.* The new operation restricts the protocol, such as tightening the types of arguments. This may be necessary to keep the inherited operation closed within the subclass. For example, the superclass *Set* may have the operation *add(object)*. The subclass *IntegerSet* would then have the more restrictive operation *add(integer)*.

*Overriding for optimization.* An implementation can take advantage of the constraints imposed by a restriction to improve the code for an operation, and this is a valid use of overriding. The new method must have the same external protocol and results as the old one, but its internal representation and algorithm may differ completely.

For example, superclass *IntegerSet* could have an operation to find the maximum integer. The method for finding the maximum of an *IntegerSet* may be implemented as a sequential search. The subclass *SortedIntegerSet* could provide a more efficient implementation of the *maximum* operation, since the contents of the set are already sorted.

*Overriding for convenience.* A common practice in developing new classes is to look for a class similar to what is desired. The new class is made a subclass of the existing class and overrides the methods that are inconvenient. This ad hoc use of inheritance is semantically wrong and leads to maintenance problems because there is no inherent relationship between the parent and child classes. A better approach is to generalize the common aspects of the original and new classes into a third class, from which the first two classes both inherit.

We propose the following semantic rules for inheritance. Adherence to these rules will make your software easier to understand, easier to extend, and less prone to errors of oversight.

- All query operations (operations that read, but do not change, attribute values) are inherited by all subclasses.

- All update operations (operations that change attribute values) are inherited across all extensions.

- Update operations that change constrained attributes or associations are blocked across a restriction. For example, the *scale-x* operation is permitted for class *Ellipse*, but must be blocked for subclass *Circle*.

- Operations may not be overridden to make them behave differently (in their externally-visible manifestations) from inherited operations. All methods that implement an operation must have the same protocol.

- Inherited operations can be refined by adding additional behavior.

The implementation and use of many existing object-oriented languages violates these principles.

## 4.4 MULTIPLE INHERITANCE

*Multiple inheritance* permits a class to have more than one superclass and to inherit features from all parents. This permits mixing of information from two or more sources. This is a more complicated form of generalization than single inheritance, which restricts the class hierarchy to a tree. The advantage of multiple inheritance is greater power in specifying classes and an increased opportunity for reuse. It brings object modeling closer to the way people think. The disadvantage is a loss of conceptual and implementation simplicity. In principle, all kinds of different mixing rules can be defined to resolve conflicts among features defined on different paths.

### 4.4.1 Definition

A class may inherit features from more than one superclass. A class with more than one superclass is called a *join class*. A feature from the same ancestor class found along more than one path is inherited only once; it is the same feature. Conflicts among parallel definitions create ambiguities that must be resolved in implementations. In practice, such conflicts should be avoided or explicitly resolved to avoid ambiguities or misunderstandings, even if a particular language provides a priority rule for resolving conflicts.

In Figure 4.8, *AmphibiousVehicle* is both *LandVehicle* and *WaterVehicle*. In Figure 4.9, *VestedHourlyEmployee* is both *VestedEmployee* and *HourlyEmployee*. *AmphibiousVehicle* and *VestedHourlyEmployee* are join classes.

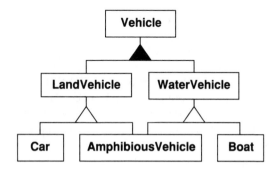

**Figure 4.8** Multiple inheritance from overlapping classes

Each generalization should cover a single property, for example where a vehicle travels. If a class can be refined on several distinct and independent dimensions, then use multiple generalizations. Recall that the content of an object model is driven by its relevance to an

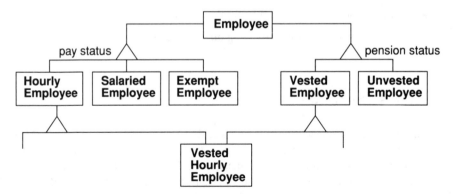

**Figure 4.9** Multiple inheritance from disjoint classes

application solution, so do not list all possible generalizations, just show the important ones. In Figure 4.9, class *Employee* independently specializes on pay status and pension status. This is shown with two separate generalizations.

The generalization subclasses may or may not be disjoint. For example, *LandVehicle* and *WaterVehicle* overlap because some vehicles travel on both land and water. *HourlyEmployee*, *SalariedEmployee*, and *ExemptEmployee* are disjoint; each employee must belong to exactly one of these. A hollow triangle indicates disjoint subclasses; a solid triangle indicates overlapping subclasses. A class can multiply inherit from distinct generalizations or from different classes within an overlapping generalization but never from two classes in the same disjoint generalization.

The term *multiple inheritance* is used somewhat imprecisely to mean either the conceptual relationship between classes or the language mechanism that implements that relationship by sharing of behavior and data. Whenever possible, we try to distinguish between *generalization* (the conceptual relationship) and *inheritance* (the language mechanism), but in the case of multiple inheritance the term is so widely used already that use of the term "multiple generalization" would be confusing.

### 4.4.2 Accidental Multiple Inheritance

An instance of a join class is inherently an instance of all the ancestors of the join class. For example, an instructor is inherently both faculty and student. But what about a Harvard Professor taking classes at MIT? There is no class to describe the combination (it would be artificial to make one). This is an example of "accidental" multiple inheritance, in which one instance happens to participate in two overlapping classes. This case is poorly handled by most object-oriented languages. As shown in Figure 4.10, the best approach using conventional languages is to treat *Person* as an object composed of multiple *UniversityMember* objects. This workaround replaces inheritance with delegation (discussed in the next section). This is not totally satisfactory because there is a loss of identity between the separate roles, but the alternatives involve radical changes to the OO framework [McAllester-86].

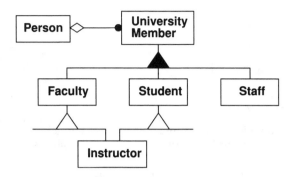

**Figure 4.10** Workaround for accidental multiple inheritance

### 4.4.3 Workarounds

Dealing with lack of multiple inheritance is really an implementation issue, but early restructuring of a model is often the easiest way to work around its absence. Some restructuring techniques are described below. Two of the following approaches make use of *delegation*, which is an implementation mechanism by which an object forwards an operation to another object for execution. See Section 10.6.3 for further discussion of delegation.

*Delegation using aggregation of roles.* A superclass with multiple independent generalizations can be recast as an aggregate in which each component replaces a generalization. This approach is similar to that for accidental multiple inheritance in the previous section. This approach replaces a single object having a unique ID by a group of related objects that compose an extended object. Inheritance of operations across the aggregation is not automatic. They must be caught by the join class and delegated to the appropriate component.

For example, in Figure 4.11 *EmployeePayroll* becomes a superclass of *HourlyEmployee*, *SalariedEmployee*, and *ExemptEmployee*. *EmployeePension* becomes a superclass of *VestedEmployee* and *UnvestedEmployee*. Then *Employee* can be modeled as an aggregation of *EmployeePayroll* and *EmployeePension*. An operation such as *compute-pay* sent to an *Employee* object would have to be redirected to the *EmployeePayroll* component by the *Employee* class.

In this approach, the various join classes need not actually be created as explicit classes. All combinations of subclasses from the different generalizations are possible.

*Inherit the most important class and delegate the rest.* Figure 4.12 makes a join class a subclass of its most important superclass. The join class is treated as an aggregation of the remaining superclasses and their operations are delegated as in the previous alternative. This approach preserves identity and inheritance across one generalization.

*Nested generalization.* Factor on one generalization first, then the other. This approach multiplies out all possible combinations. For example, in Figure 4.13 under each of *HourlyEmployee*, *SalariedEmployee*, and *ExemptEmployee*, add two subclasses for vested and unvested employees. This preserves inheritance but duplicates declarations and code and violates the spirit of object-oriented programming.

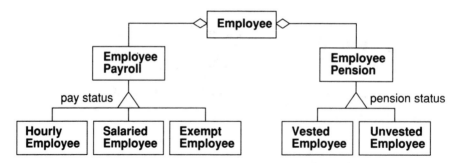

**Figure 4.11** Multiple inheritance using delegation

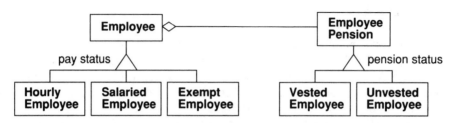

**Figure 4.12** Multiple inheritance using inheritance and delegation

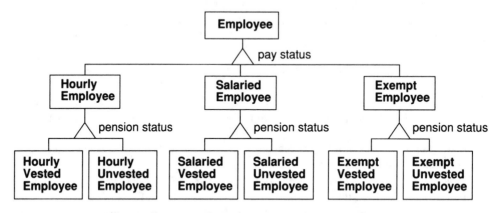

**Figure 4.13** Multiple inheritance using nested generalization

Any of these workarounds can be made to work, but all compromise logical structure and maintainability. Some issues to consider when selecting the best workaround are:

- If a subclass has several superclasses, all of equal importance, it may be best to use delegation (Figure 4.11) and preserve symmetry in the model.

- If one superclass clearly dominates and the others are less important, implementing multiple inheritance via single inheritance and delegation may be best (Figure 4.12).

- If the number of combinations is small, consider nested generalization (Figure 4.13). If the number of combinations is large, avoid it.

- If one superclass has significantly more features than the other superclasses or one superclass clearly is the performance bottleneck, preserve inheritance through this path (Figure 4.12 or Figure 4.13).

- If you choose to use nested generalization (Figure 4.13), factor on the most important criterion first, the next most important second, and so forth.

- Try to avoid nested generalization (Figure 4.13) if large quantities of code must be duplicated.

- Consider the importance of maintaining strict identity. Only nested generalization (Figure 4.13) preserves this.

## 4.5 METADATA

*Metadata* is data that describes other data. For example, the definition of a class is metadata. Models are inherently metadata, since they describe the things being modeled (rather than *being* the things). Many real-world applications have metadata, such as parts catalogs, blueprints, and dictionaries. Computer language implementations also use metadata heavily. Figure 4.5 is another example of metadata. In Section 4.2 while explaining the modeling concept of concrete and abstract classes we found it useful to use an object model to explain object modeling constructs. The case study in Chapter 18 presents an actual application that required a model of metadata (a metamodel).

Relational database management systems (see Chapter 17) also use metadata. A person can define database tables for storing information. Similarly, a relational DBMS has several metatables that store table definitions. Thus a data table may store the fact that the capital of Japan is Tokyo, the capital of Thailand is Bangkok, and the capital of India is New Delhi. A metatable would store the fact that a country has a capital city.

Metadata is frequently confusing because it blurs the normal separation between the model and the real world. With ordinary applications, the same terms can be used to refer to both the model and the real world; the context of usage distinguishes which is meant. With metadata, the context is not sufficient to distinguish the description from the thing being described, so a more precise distinction must be made.

### 4.5.1 Patterns and Metadata

A class describes a set of object instances of a given form. *Instantiation* relates a class to its instances. In a broader sense, any pattern describes examples of the pattern; the relationship between pattern and example can be regarded as an extension of instantiation.

Figure 4.14 shows an example of instantiation. *Joe Smith* and *Mary Wilson* are instances of class *Person*. The dotted arrows connect the instances to the class. Explicitly showing the instantiation relationship is useful when both instances and classes must be manipulated as objects, for example in interpreters, modeling tools, and language support mechanisms. Instantiation is also useful for documenting examples and test cases. For most problems, however, classes and their instances need not be shown together.

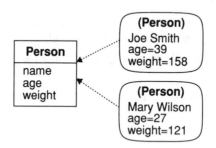

**Figure 4.14**  Notation for instantiation

Real-world things may be metadata. There are real-world things that describe other real-world things. A part description in a catalog describes manufactured parts. A blueprint describes a house. An engineering drawing describes a system.

For example, consider models of cars made by different manufacturers, such as a 1969 Ford Mustang or a 1975 Volkswagen Rabbit. Each *CarModel* in Figure 4.15 describes a particular kind of car; each *CarModel* has its own attributes and associations. Each *CarModel* object also describes a set of physical cars owned by persons. For example, John Doe may own a blue Ford with serial number *1FABP* and a red Volkswagen with serial number *7E81F*. Each car receives the common attributes from *CarModel* but also has its own list of particular attributes, such as serial number, color, and list of options. It would be possible to create a class to describe each kind of car, but the list of models keeps growing. It is better to consider the *CarModel* object as a pattern, a piece of metadata, that describes *Car* objects.

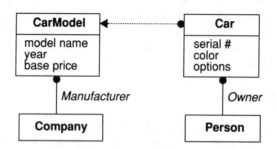

**Figure 4.15**  Patterns and individuals

### 4.5.2 Class Descriptors

Classes can also be considered as objects, but they are meta-objects and not real-world objects. Class descriptor objects have features, and they in turn have their own classes, which are called *metaclasses*. Treating everything as an object provides a more uniform implementation and greater functionality for solving complex problems.

A *class attribute* describes a value common to an entire class of objects, rather than data peculiar to each instance. Class attributes are useful for storing default information for creating new objects or summary information about instances of the class.

A *class operation* is an operation on the class itself. The most common kind of class operations are operations to create new class instances. Operations to create instances must be class operations because the instance being operated on does not initially exist. A query that provides summary information for instances in a class is also a class operation. Operations on class structure, such as scanning the list of attributes or methods, are class operations.

Figure 4.16 shows a class *Window* with class features indicated by leading dollar signs. *Window* has class attributes for the set of all windows, the set of visible windows, default window size, and maximum window size. *Window* contains class operations to create a new window object and to find the existing window with the highest priority.

| Window |
| --- |
| size: Rectangle<br>visibility: Boolean<br>$all-windows: Set[Window]<br>$visible-windows: Set[Window]<br>$default-size: Rectangle<br>$maximum-size: Rectangle |
| display<br>$new-Window<br>$get-highest-priority-Window |

**Figure 4.16** Class with class features

## 4.6 CANDIDATE KEYS

The ball notation discussed in Chapter 3 works fine when discussing multiplicity for binary associations and is the preferred notation for binary associations. However, multiplicity balls are ambiguous for n-ary (n>2) associations. The best approach for n-ary associations is to specify candidate keys.

A *candidate key* is a minimal set of attributes that uniquely identifies an object or link. By minimal, we mean that you cannot discard an attribute from the candidate key and still distinguish all objects and links. A class or association may have one or more candidate keys, each of which may have different combinations and numbers of attributes. The object ID is always a candidate key for a class. One or more combinations of related objects are candidate keys for associations.

Candidate key is a term commonly used within the database community. However candidate key is really not a database concept; candidate key is a logical concept. Each candidate key constrains the instances in a class or the multiplicity of an association. Most programming languages lack the notion of a candidate key. A candidate key is delimited in an object model with braces. (This is the object modeling notation for constraints, which are discussed in the next section.)

Figure 4.17 compares multiplicity and candidate keys for binary associations. Multiplicity and candidate keys have nearly the same expressive power for binary associations. (Multiplicity also includes the notion of existence dependency—whether an object must participate in an association.) A many-to-many association requires both related objects to uniquely identify each link. A one-to-many association has a single candidate key: the object on the many end. A one-to-one association has two candidate keys: either of the objects. If we specify the country, or specify the capital city, there is no ambiguity. Note that a candidate key may be specified even when one or both classes are optional. For example, a city may not be a capital at all, but a city is capital of at most one country.

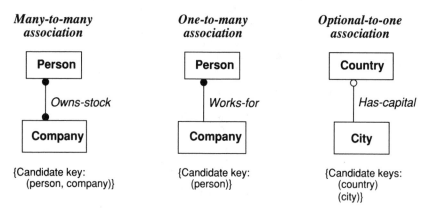

**Figure 4.17** Comparison of multiplicity with candidate keys for binary associations

Figure 4.18 shows a ternary association that has one candidate key consisting of all three objects. Persons who are programmers use computer languages on projects. Several links are presented at the bottom of the figure. No combination of just one or two objects will uniquely identify each link.

Figure 4.19 contains another ternary association. A student has one advisor at a university. A student may attend more than one university. A professor may be an advisor at more than one university. Here the instances suggest that (student, university) is the only candidate key. This candidate key involves only two of the three related objects.

We deduce the candidate key by considering all the possibilities. *Student* is not a candidate key; two links have the value *Mary*. *Professor* and *University* are not candidate keys. *Student+Professor*, *Professor+University* are not candidate keys; *Susan+Weaver*,

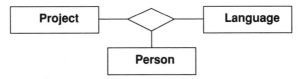

{Candidate key: (project, person, language)}

| Project | Person | Language |
|---------|--------|----------|
| CAD program | Mary | C |
| control software | Susan | Ada |
| C++ compiler | Mike | C |
| CAD program | Bob | assembler |
| CAD program | Mike | C |
| CAD program | Mike | assembler |

**Figure 4.18** Ternary association

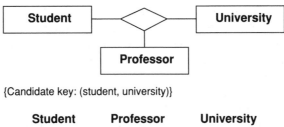

{Candidate key: (student, university)}

| Student | Professor | University |
|---------|-----------|------------|
| Mary | Prof Weaver | SUNY |
| Mary | Prof Rumrow | RPI |
| Susan | Prof Weaver | RPI |
| Susan | Prof Weaver | SUNY |
| Bob | Prof Shapiro | Oxford |

**Figure 4.19** Ternary association

*Weaver+SUNY* appear twice. *Student+University* may be a candidate key, since no links share the same values. Based on the problem statement, we decide that *Student+University* really is a candidate key and would distinguish other links beyond the five in Figure 4.19. *Student+Professor+University* is not a candidate key, because it is not a minimal set of attributes.

## 4.7 CONSTRAINTS

### 4.7.1 Definition

*Constraints* are functional relationships between entities of an object model. The term *entity* includes objects, classes, attributes, links, and associations. A constraint restricts the values that entities can assume. Examples include: No employee's salary can exceed the salary of the employee's boss (a constraint between two things at the same time). No window will have an aspect ratio (length/width) of less than 0.8 or greater than 1.5 (a constraint between properties of a single object). The priority of a job may not increase (constraint on the same object over time). Figure 4.20 lists these examples. Simple constraints may be placed in object models. Complex constraints should be specified in the functional model (see Chapter 6).

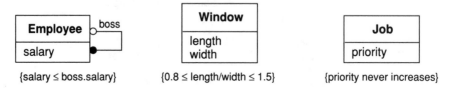

**Figure 4.20**  Constraints on objects

We favor expressing constraints in a declarative manner. Ordinarily, constraints must be converted to procedural form before they can be stated in a programming language. Ideally conversion should be automatic, but this may be difficult or impossible to achieve. Object models capture some constraints through their very structure. For example, single inheritance implies that subclasses are mutually exclusive.

Constraints provide one criterion for measuring the quality of an object model; a "good" object model captures many constraints through its structure. It often requires several iterations to get the structure of a model right from the perspective of constraints. In principle, we could embellish object modeling notation with all kinds of special constructs to capture more and more structural constraints. This is probably not a good idea. The object modeling notation advanced by this book represents a compromise between expressive power and simplicity. There will always be constraints that must be expressed in natural language.

Object modeling syntax for constraints is as follows: Constraints are delimited by braces and positioned near the constrained entity. A dotted line connects multiple constrained entities. An arrow may be used to connect a constrained entity to the entity it depends on. Instantiation is a kind of constraint and therefore uses the same notation.

### 4.7.2  Constraints on Links

Multiplicity constrains an association. It restricts the number of objects related to a given object. Object modeling notation has a special syntax for showing common multiplicity values ([0,1], exactly 1, and 0+). Other values of multiplicity can be shown by a numerical interval near an association role. For example, Figure 4.5 specifies "1+" for two association roles.

The notation "{ordered}" indicates that the elements of the "many" end of an association have an explicit order that must be preserved. Figure 4.21 shows an object model for the officers of a country. Each office (such as president, chief justice, king) for each country has a set of persons who have held the office, ordered chronologically.

**Figure 4.21** Constraints on association links

### 4.7.3 General Constraints

General constraints must be expressed with natural language or equations. You should draw a dotted line between classes involved in the constraint and specify the details with comments in braces. Sometimes it may be impractical to draw lines to all the classes, so make the best of it. Sometimes it is better to have an unattached constraint than to draw lines all over the place.

For example, one association may be a subset of another. In Figure 4.22 the chair of a committee must be a member of the committee; the *Chair-of* association is a subset of the *Member-of* association.

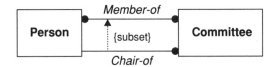

**Figure 4.22** Subset constraint between associations

### 4.7.4 Derived Objects, Links, and Attributes

A *derived object* is defined as a function of one or more objects, which in turn may be derived. The derived object is completely determined by the other objects. Ultimately, the derivation tree terminates with base objects. Thus a derived object is redundant but may be included in an object model to ease comprehension; it often represents a meaningful real-world concept. Similarly, there are also *derived links* and *derived attributes*.

The notation for a derived entity is a slash or diagonal line (on the corner of a class box, on an association line, or in front of an attribute). You should show the constraint that determines the derived value. Like most of the object modeling notation, the derived value notation is optional.

As shown in Figure 4.23, age provides a good example of a derived attribute. Age can be derived from birth date and the current date.

In Figure 4.24, a machine consists of several assemblies that in turn consist of parts. An assembly has a geometrical offset with respect to machine coordinates; each part has an offset with respect to assembly coordinates. We can define a coordinate system for each part that is derived from machine coordinates, assembly offset, and part offset. This coordinate system can be represented as a derived object class called *Offset* related to each part by a derived association called *NetOffset*.

{age = currentdate − birthdate}

**Figure 4.23**  Derived attribute

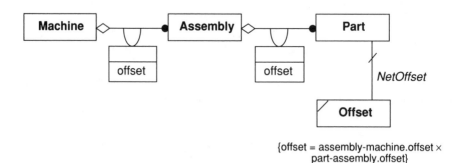

{offset = assembly-machine.offset ×
part-assembly.offset}

**Figure 4.24**  Derived object and association

Real world concepts are highly redundant, therefore we expect to see many derived entities in models; it is desirable to use concepts that appear in the application domain. Nevertheless it is important to distinguish independent and dependent entities in a model so that the true complexity can be seen. Derived entities are constrained by their base entities and the derivation rule.

### 4.7.5 Homomorphisms

A *homomorphism* maps between two associations as illustrated by Figure 4.25. For example, in a parts catalog for an automobile, a catalog item may contain other catalog items. Each catalog item is specified by a model number that corresponds to thousands or millions of individual manufactured items, each with its own serial number. The individual items are also composed of subitems. Each physical item's parts explosion tree has the same form as the catalog item's parts explosion tree. The *contains* aggregation on catalog items is a homomorphism of the *contains* aggregation on physical items. This form of homomorphism between two trees is common.

In general, a homomorphism involves four relationships among four classes as shown in Figure 4.26. The homomorphism maps links of one general association (*u*) into links of another general association (*t*) as a many-to-one mapping. Two instantiation relationships map elements of one class into another: *r* is a many-to-one mapping from class *B* to class *A* and *s* is a many-to-one mapping from class *D* to class *C*. In the common case where *t* is on a single class and *u* is on a single class, then $A=C$, $B=D$, and $r=s$, as in Figure 4.25.

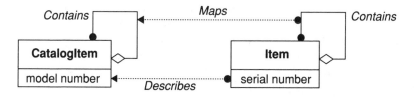

{item1 contains item2 ⇒ item1.model contains item2.model}

**Figure 4.25** Homomorphism for a parts catalog

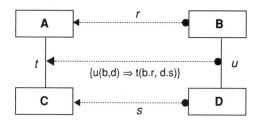

**Figure 4.26** General homomorphism

At first, the homomorphism may seem to be an esoteric concept. However, our experience has been that they really do appear in practice. Homomorphisms are most likely to occur for complex applications that deal with metadata. The homomorphism is essentially just an analogy—a special type of relationship between relationships. Proper use of homomorphisms constrain the structure of an object model and improve the correspondence between the model and the real world.

## 4.8 CHAPTER SUMMARY

This chapter covers several diverse topics that explain subtleties of object modeling. These concepts are not needed for simple models but may be important for complex applications. Remember, the content of any object model should be driven by its relevance to an application. Only use the advanced concepts in this chapter if they truly add to your application, either by improving clarity, tightening structural constraints, or permitting expression of a difficult concept.

Aggregation is a special form of transitive association where a group of component objects form a single semantic entity. Operations on an aggregate often propagate to the components. Recursive aggregates allow a component to also be an aggregate. Aggregation must not be confused with generalization, even though both constructs form trees; aggregation is a tree of instances, generalization is a tree of classes.

*Abstract* and *concrete* are useful terms for referring to classes in an inheritance hierarchy. Abstract classes help organize the class hierarchy and have no direct instances. Concrete classes may have direct instances. Abstract classes are frequently used to define methods in one place for use by several subclasses. Abstract classes can also be used to define the form or protocol of an operation, leaving the implementation to each subclass.

Inheritance has two different but complementary aspects. Extension means that a subclass may add new features. Restriction means that a subclass may constrain inherited features. For semantic reasons, a subclass should not suppress a superclass attribute or change the external protocol of a superclass operation. An instance of a subclass is simultaneously an instance of a superclass; thus it is not permissible for a subclass to violate superclass behavior. Unfortunately, it is common practice in existing object-oriented languages to abuse inheritance in this way. The price that is paid is more obscure code and awkward maintenance.

Multiple inheritance permits a subclass to inherit features from more than one superclass. A class with more than one superclass is called a join class. Each generalization should discriminate a single semantic quality. The subclasses of a given superclass should be arranged into more than one generalization if the superclass specializes on more than one discriminator. A join class may combine classes from different generalizations, or it may combine classes from an overlapping generalization, but it may not combine classes from the same disjoint generalization. Accidental inheritance is a property of instances and must be represented by delegation.

Metadata is data that describes other data. Object classes are metadata, since they describe objects. The instantiation relationship links class descriptor objects to class instances. Metadata is a useful concept for two reasons: It occurs in the real world and it is a powerful tool for implementing complex systems. Modeling metadata can be confusing because the distinction between descriptor and referent is blurred.

A candidate key is a minimal set of attributes that uniquely identifies an object or link. Candidate keys constrain the multiplicity of an association. Multiplicity balls serve as a shorthand notation; candidate keys express the fundamental abstraction. Multiplicity balls are fine for binary associations but are ambiguous for n-ary associations. The best approach for n-ary associations is to use candidate keys.

Explicit constraints among objects, links, and attributes are sometimes needed to express application semantics. The notation for a constraint is a comment in braces near the constrained entity; a dotted line can be added to bind constrained entities. Generalization and multiplicity are examples of constraints built into the fabric of object modeling. Homomorphisms are mappings between associations; a frequent usage is the mapping between a descriptor tree and a part tree. Derived entities may appear in a model for organizational or naming purposes, but do not add fundamental information.

| abstract class | constraint | instantiation | origin class |
|---|---|---|---|
| aggregation | derived entity | join class | override |
| candidate key | generalization | metaclass | propagation |
| class feature | homomorphism | metadata | protocol |
| concrete class | inheritance | multiple inheritance | |

**Figure 4.27** Key concepts for Chapter 4

## BIBLIOGRAPHIC NOTES

There have been a number of attempts to understand types, sometimes going considerably beyond the object-oriented paradigm. [Cardelli-85] describes a lattice of type definition models, of which object-oriented models are seen to be just one case (and not the most general). Extremely powerful type definition systems tend to be hard to understand and implement, so most language implementors have been more restrained.

[Teorey-89] presents an interesting approach to improving the understandability of large, complex models. The basic idea is that a model can be viewed at various levels of detail. High-level views hide low-level details within clusters. A *cluster* is a group of classes, associations, generalizations, and possibly other clusters which are abstracted into a single entity for presentation in a higher level view. Clusters can be recursively constructed until the proper level of abstraction is achieved. Teorey uses a heavy outline box to indicate clustering which is compatible with our OMT notation.

We choose not to present clustering as a section in this book because there are several unresolved issues. We are uncomfortable with Teorey's approach for handling associations between the external world and an entity within a cluster. In one sense, a cluster hides the fact that an entity is buried within, but this is contradicted by the visibility required to make the association. Also we regard the priority rules for forming clusters as vague and confusing. Nevertheless, we recommend the reading of Teorey's paper as it represents significant progress in an important area.

Many of the basic premises and details of object-oriented technology are controversial. The annual OOPSLA (Object-Oriented Programming Systems, Languages, and Applications) and ECOOP (European Conference on Object-Oriented Programming) conferences are the vehicles for new concepts, novel implementations, and philosophical arguments about the object-oriented field. Past theoretical controversies include the proper role of inheritance (single versus multiple, inheritance versus delegation, the need for metaclasses), more general forms of type systems, handling of metadata, treatment of constraints, and handling of aggregation.

## REFERENCES

[Atwood-85] Thomas M. Atwood. An object-oriented DBMS for design support applications. *IEEE COMPINT'85*. 299-307.

[Cardelli-85] Luca Cardelli, Peter Wegner. On understanding types, data abstraction, and polymorphism. *ACM Computing Surveys 17*, 4, 471-522.

[McAllester-86] David McAllester, Ramin Zabih. Boolean classes. *OOPSLA'87* as *SIGPLAN 22*, 12 (Dec. 1987), 417-424.

[Meyer-88] Bertrand Meyer. *Object-Oriented Software Construction*. Hertfordshire, England: Prentice Hall International, 1988.

[Rumbaugh-88] James E. Rumbaugh. Controlling propagation of operations using attributes on relations. *OOPSLA'88* as *ACM SIGPLAN 23*, 11 (Nov. 1988), 285-296.

[Teorey-89] Toby J. Teorey, Guangping Wei, Deborah L. Bolton, John A Koenig. ER model clustering as an aid for user communication and documentation in database design. *Communications of the ACM 32*, 8 (August 1989), 975-987.

## EXERCISES

**4.1**   (4) The object diagram in Figure E4.1 is a partial representation of the structure of an automobile. Improve it by changing some of the associations to aggregations.

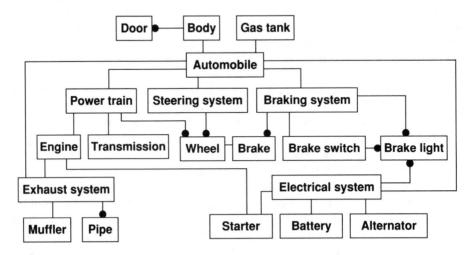

**Figure E4.1**   Portion of an object diagram of the assembly hierarchy of an automobile

**4.2**   (4) Figure E4.2 is a partially completed object diagram for an interactive diagram editor. A sheet is a collection of links and boxes. A link is a sequence of line segments that connect two boxes. Each line segment is specified by two points. A point may be shared by a vertical and a horizontal line segment in the same link. A selection is a collection of links and boxes that have been highlighted in anticipation of an editing operation. A buffer is a collection of links and boxes that have been cut or copied from the sheet. As it stands, the diagram does not express the constraint that a link or a box belongs to one buffer or one selection or one sheet. Revise the object diagram and use generalization to express the constraint by creating a superclass for the classes *Buffer*, *Selection*, and *Sheet*. Discuss the merits of the revision.

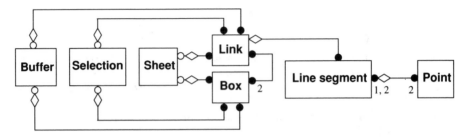

**Figure E4.2**   Portion of an object diagram for a simple diagram editor

**4.3**   (3) Categorize the following relationships into generalization, aggregation, or association. Beware, there may be ternary or n-ary associations in the list, so do not assume every relationship involving three or more object classes is a generalization. Defend your answers.

    a. A country has a capital city.

    b. A dining philosopher is using a fork.

    c. A file is an ordinary file or a directory file.

    d. Files contain records.

    e. A polygon is composed of an ordered set of points.

    f. A drawing object is text, a geometrical object, or a group.

    g. A person uses a computer language on a project.

    h. Modems and keyboards are input/output devices.

    i. Object classes may have several attributes.

    j. A person plays for a team in a certain year.

    k. A route connects two cities.

    l. A student takes a course from a professor.

**4.4**    (7) Prepare an object diagram for a graphical document editor that supports grouping, which is a concept used in a variety of graphical editors. Assume that a document is composed of several sheets. Each sheet contains drawing objects, including text, geometrical objects, and groups. A group is simply a set of drawing objects, possibly including other groups. A group must contain at least two drawing objects. A drawing object can be a direct member of at most one group. Geometrical objects include circles, ellipses, rectangles, lines, and squares.

**4.5**    (6) A directory file contains information about files in a directory, including both ordinary files as well as other directory files. Prepare an object diagram which models directory files and ordinary files. Since a directory plus a file name uniquely identifies a file, you will probably want to use file name as a qualifier.

**4.6**    (6) Prepare a verbal description of a situation that involves recursion, similar to the previous two exercises, and prepare the corresponding object diagram. Defend the need for recursion in your description.

**4.7**    (8) Descriptions of operations on some object classes in exercise 4.2 are given below. The notation is class::operation(arguments).Think about how operations on some classes trigger operations on other classes through associations. For each operation on each class, prepare a list of propagated operations. The list should contain class-operation pairs that are triggered through associations.

    buffer::paste(offset) - Copy and translate the contents of the buffer into the sheet. The x and y translation is specified by *offset*.

    selection::cut() - Transport the selected contents of the sheet from the sheet to the buffer. Links between a box that is selected and a box that is not selected are deleted. The previous contents of the buffer, if any, are deleted.

    selection::copy() - Make a copy of the selected contents of the sheet in the buffer. Links between a box that is selected and a box that is not selected are not copied. The previous contents of the buffer, if any, are deleted.

    selection::move(offset) - Translate the selected contents of the sheet by the specified offset. Links between a box that is selected and a box that is not selected are stretched.

    link::select() - Highlight the link and add it to the selected links if it has not already been selected.

    link::deselect() - Turn off highlighting of the link and remove it from the selected list if it has not already been deselected.

    link::toggle_selection() - Select the link if it is not selected, otherwise deselect it.

box::select() - Highlight the box and add it to the selected boxes if it has not already been selected.

box::deselect() - Turn off highlighting of the box and remove it from the selected list if it has not already been deselected.

box::toggle_selection() - Select the box if it is not selected, otherwise deselect it.

**4.8** (6) The following is a partial taxonomy of rotating electrical machines. Electrical machines may be categorized for analysis purposes into alternating current (ac) or direct current (dc). Some machines run on ac, some on dc, and some will run on either. An ac machine may be synchronous or induction. A few examples of electrical machines include large synchronous motors, small induction motors, universal motors, and permanent magnet motors. Most motors found in the home are usually induction machines or universal motors. Universal motors are typically used in where high speed is needed such as in blenders or vacuum cleaners. They will run on either ac or dc. Permanent magnet motors are frequently used in toys and will work only on dc. Prepare an object diagram showing how the categories and the machines just described relate to one another. Use multiple inheritance where it is appropriate to do so.

**4.9** (6) Revise the object diagram that you prepared for the previous exercise to eliminate all use of multiple inheritance. You may wish to use delegation and/or nested generalizations.

**4.10** (7) Prepare a metamodel that supports only the following subset of the OMT notation: object classes, attributes, and binary associations, including multiplicity and roles. Use only object classes, attributes, and binary associations to build your metamodel.

**4.11** (8) Prepare an instance diagram of the metamodel you prepared in the previous diagram. Treat the metamodel as an object diagram that can be represented by instances of the classes of the metamodel. As a minimum your instance diagram should include an instance for each class, attribute, and binary association in the metamodel.

**4.12** (10) (a) Prepare an object diagram for undirected graphs. Refer to exercise 3.23.
(b) Two undirected graphs G and H are isomorphic to each other if there exists a 1:1 correspondence between the edges of G and H such that the incidence relationships will be preserved. Extend your object diagram using a homomorphism to express the conditions under which two undirected graphs are isomorphic to each other.

**4.13** (5) Figure E4.3 is a portion of a metamodel which describes generalization. A generalization is associated with several generalization roles, which are the roles that object classes play in generalization relationships. Role type is either subclass or superclass. Does this model support multiple inheritance? Explain your answer.

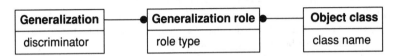

**Figure E4.3**  Metamodel of generalization relationships

**4.14** (7) Describe how to find which class is the superclass of a generalization using the metamodel in Figure E4.3. Revise the metamodel to simplify the query. Describe how to determine the superclass of a generalization using your revised metamodel. Make sure that your revised metamodel supports multiple inheritance.

**4.15** (7) How well does the metamodel in Figure E4.3 enforce the constraint that every generalization has exactly one superclass? Discuss how accurately it reflects the logical structure of generalization relationships as it stands. Revise it to improve the enforcement of the constraint.

**4.16** (9) Figure E4.3 is a metamodel which describes object models such as in Figure E4.4. Prepare an instance diagram using the object classes from the metamodel to describe the model in Figure E4.4. To simplify the problem of identifying instances in your diagram, the generalizations have been labeled. Use the same labels in your answer.

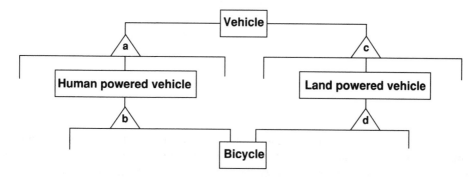

**Figure E4.4** Object diagram with multiple inheritance

**4.17** (7) Prepare a portion of an object diagram for a library book checkout system that shows the date a book is due and the late charges for an overdue book as derived objects.

**4.18** (10) Prepare a metamodel of Backus-Naur (BNF) representations of computer languages. The model could be used by a compiler-compiler (such as the UNIX program YACC) that accepts these representations in graphical form as input and which produces a compiler for the represented language. An example of a Backus-Naur form that the compiler-compiler will accept is shown in Figure E4.5. Nonterminals are shown in rectangles and terminals are shown in circles or rectangles with rounded corners. Circles are used for single characters. Rectangles with rounded edges are used for a sequence of several characters. Arrows indicate the direction of flow through the diagram. Where several directed paths diverge, it is permissible to take any one of them. The name of the nonterminal being described appears at the beginning of its representation.

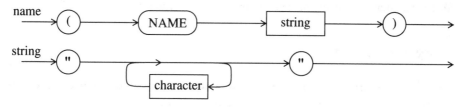

**Figure E4.5** Portion of a BNF diagram

# 5

# Dynamic Modeling

Temporal relationships are difficult to understand. A system can best be understood by first examining its static structure, that is, the structure of its objects and their relationships to each other at a single moment in time. Then we examine changes to the objects and their relationships over time. Those aspects of a system that are concerned with time and changes are the *dynamic model,* in contrast with the static, or object model. *Control* is that aspect of a system that describes the sequences of operations that occur in response to external stimuli, without consideration of what the operations do, what they operate on, or how they are implemented.

This chapter describes concepts dealing with flow of control, interactions, and sequencing of operations in a system of concurrently-active objects. The major dynamic modeling concepts are *events,* which represent external stimuli, and *states,* which represent values of objects. The *state diagram* is a standard computer science concept (a graphical representation of finite state machines) that has been handled in different ways in the literature, depending on its use. We emphasize the use of events and states to specify control, rather than as algebraic constructs. We show that states and events can be organized into generalization hierarchies to share structure and behavior.

In this chapter we mainly follow the notation of David Harel [Harel-87] for drawing structured state diagrams using nested contours to show structure.

## 5.1 EVENTS AND STATES

An object model describes the possible patterns of objects, attributes, and links that can exist in a system. The attribute values and links held by an object are called its *state*. Over time, the objects stimulate each other, resulting in a series of changes to their states. An individual stimulus from one object to another is an *event*. The response to an event depends on the state of the object receiving it, and can include a change of state or the sending of another event to the original sender or to a third object. The pattern of events, states, and state transitions for a given class can be abstracted and represented as a *state diagram*. A state diagram is a network of states and events, just as an object diagram is a network of classes and relationships. The *dynamic model* consists of multiple state diagrams, one state diagram for each class with important dynamic behavior, and shows the pattern of activity for an entire system. Each state machine executes concurrently and can change state independently. The state diagrams for the various classes combine into a single dynamic model via shared events.

## 5.1.1 Events

An *event* is something that happens at a point in time, such as *user depresses left button* or *Flight 123 departs from Chicago.* An event has no duration. Of course, nothing is really instantaneous; an event is simply an occurrence that is fast compared to the granularity of the time scale of a given abstraction.

One event may logically precede or follow another, or the two events may be unrelated. Flight 123 must depart Chicago before it can arrive in San Francisco; the two events are causally related. Flight 123 may depart before or after Flight 456 departs Rome; the two events are causally unrelated. Two events that are causally unrelated are said to be *concurrent;* they have no effect on each other. If the communications delay between two locations exceeds the difference in event times, then the events must be concurrent because they cannot influence each other. Even if the physical locations of two events are not distant, we consider the events concurrent if they do not affect each other. In modeling a system we do not try to establish an ordering between concurrent events because they can occur in any order. Any realistic model of a distributed system must include concurrent events and activities.

An event is a one-way transmission of information from one object to another. It is not like a subroutine call that returns a value. In the real world, all objects exist concurrently. An object sending an event to another object may expect a reply, but the reply is a separate event under the control of the second object, which may or may not choose to send it.

Every event is a unique occurrence, but we group them into *event classes* and give each event class a name to indicate common structure and behavior. This structure is hierarchical, just as object class structure is hierarchical. For example, *Flight 123 departs from Chicago* and *Flight 456 departs from Rome* are both instances of event class *airplane flight departs.* Some events are simple signals, but most event classes have attributes indicating the information they convey. For example, *airplane flight departs* has attributes *airline, flight number,* and *city.* The time at which an event occurs is an implicit attribute of all events.

An event conveys information from one object to another. Some classes of events may be simply signals that something has occurred, while other classes of events convey data values. The data values conveyed by an event are its *attributes,* like the data values held by objects. Attributes are shown in parentheses after the event class name. Figure 5.1 shows some examples of event classes with attributes. Showing attributes is optional.

The term *event* is often used ambiguously. Sometimes event refers to an event instance, at other times to an event class. In practice, this ambiguity is usually not a problem and the precise meaning is apparent from the context.

```
airplane flight departs (airline, flight number, city)
mouse button pushed (button, location)
input string entered (text)
phone receiver lifted
digit dialed (digit)
engine speed enters danger zone
```

**Figure 5.1** Event classes and attributes

Events include error conditions as well as normal occurrences. For example, *motor jammed, transaction aborted,* and *time-out* are typical error events. There is nothing different about an error event; only our interpretation makes it an "error."

### 5.1.2 Scenarios and Event Traces

A *scenario* is a sequence of events that occurs during one particular execution of a system. The scope of a scenario can vary; it may include all events in the system, or it may include only those events impinging on or generated by certain objects in the system. A scenario can be the historical record of executing a system or a thought experiment of executing a proposed system.

Figure 5.2 shows a scenario for using a telephone line. This scenario only contains events affecting the phone line.

```
caller lifts receiver
dial tone begins
caller dials digit (5)
dial tone ends
caller dials digit (5)
caller dials digit (5)
caller dials digit (1)
caller dials digit (2)
caller dials digit (3)
caller dials digit (4)
called phone beings ringing
ringing tone appears in calling phone
called party answers
called phone stops ringing
ringing tone disappears in calling phone
phones are connected
called party hangs up
phones are disconnected
caller hangs up
```

**Figure 5.2** Scenario for phone call

Each event transmits information from one object to another. For example, *dial tone begins* transmits a signal from the phone line to the caller. The next step after writing a scenario is to identify the sender and receiver objects of each event. The sequence of events and the objects exchanging events can both be shown in an augmented scenario called an *event trace* diagram. This diagram shows each object as a vertical line and each event as a horizontal arrow from the sender object to the receiver object. Time increases from top to bottom, but the spacing is irrelevant; it is only the sequences of events that are shown, not their exact timing. (Real-time systems impose time constraints on event sequences, but that is a separate matter requiring extra notation.) Figure 5.3 shows an event trace for a phone call. Note that concurrent events can be sent (*Phone line* sends events to *Caller* and *Callee* concurrently) and events between objects need not alternate (*Caller* dials several digits in succession).

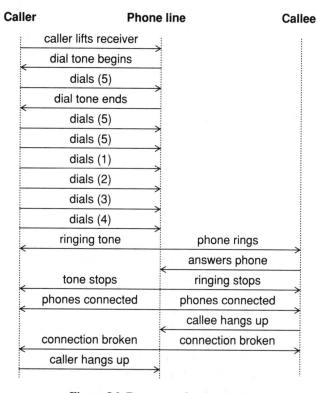

**Figure 5.3** Event trace for phone call

## 5.1.3 States

A *state* is an abstraction of the attribute values and links of an object. Sets of values are grouped together into a state according to properties that affect the gross behavior of the object. For example, the state of a bank is either solvent or insolvent, depending on whether its assets exceed its liabilities. A state specifies the response of the object to input events. The response to an event received by an object may vary quantitatively depending on the exact values of its attributes, but the response is qualitatively the same for all values within the same state, and may be qualitatively different for values in different states. The response of an object to an event may include an action or a change of state by the object. For example, if a digit is dialed in state *Dial tone,* the phone line drops the dial tone and enters state *Dialing*; if the receiver is replaced in state *Dial tone*, the phone line goes dead and enters state *Idle.*

A state corresponds to the interval between two events received by an object. Events represent points in time; states represent intervals of time. For example, after the receiver is lifted and before the first digit is dialed, the phone line is in state *Dial tone*. The state of an object depends on the past sequence of events it has received, but in most cases past events are eventually hidden by subsequent events. For example, events that happened before the phone is hung up have no effect on future behavior; the *Idle* state "forgets" events received prior to the *hang up* event.

A state has duration; it occupies an interval of time. A state is often associated with a continuous activity, such as the ringing of a telephone, or an activity that takes time to complete, such as flying from Chicago to San Francisco. Events and states are duals of one another; an event separates two states, and a state separates two events.

A state is often associated with the value of an object satisfying some condition. For example, *water is liquid* is equivalent to saying "the temperature of the water is greater than 0 C and less than 100 C." In the simplest case, each enumerated value of an attribute defines a separate state. For example, an automobile transmission might be in states *Reverse, Neutral, First, Second,* or *Third.*

In defining states, we ignore those attributes that do not affect the behavior of the object, and we lump together in a single state all combinations of attribute values and links that have the same response to events. Of course, every attribute has some effect on behavior or it would be meaningless, but often some attributes do not affect the pattern of control and can be thought of as simple parameter values within a given state. Recall that the purpose of modeling is to focus on those qualities of an entity that are relevant to the solution of an application problem and abstract away those that are irrelevant. The three different OMT models (object, dynamic, and functional) present different views of a system; the particular choice of attributes and values are not equally important in these three different views. For example, except for leading 0s and 1s, the exact digits dialed do not affect the control of the phone line, so we can summarize them all with state *Dialing* and track the phone number as a parameter. Sometimes, all possible values of an attribute are important but usually only when the number of possible values is small.

Both events and states depend on the level of abstraction used. For example, a travel agent planning an itinerary would treat each segment of a journey as a single event; a flight status board in an airport would distinguish departures and arrivals; an air traffic control system would break each flight into many geographical legs.

A state can be characterized in various ways. Figure 5.4 shows various characterizations of the state *Alarm ringing* on a watch. The state has a suggestive name and a natural-language description of its purpose. The event sequence that leads to the state consists of setting the alarm, doing anything that doesn't clear the alarm, and then having the target time occur. A declarative condition for the state is given in terms of parameters, such as *alarm* and *target time*; the alarm stops ringing after 20 seconds. Finally, a stimulus-response table shows the

---

**State:** *Alarm ringing*

**Description:** alarm on watch is ringing to indicate target time

Event sequence that produces the state:

    *set alarm* (target time)

    any sequence not including *clear alarm*

    current time = target time

Condition that characterizes the state:

    alarm = on, and target time ≤ current time ≤ target time + 20 seconds,
        and no button has not been pushed since target time

Events accepted in the state:

| event | action | next state |
|-------|--------|------------|
| current time = target time + 20 | reset alarm | *normal* |
| *button pushed* (any button) | reset alarm | *normal* |

---

**Figure 5.4** Various characterizations of a state

effect of events *current time* and *button pushed*, including the action that occurs and the next state. The different descriptions of a state may overlap.

Can links have state? In as much as they can be considered objects, links can have state. As a practical matter, it is generally sufficient to associate state only with objects. The state of an object can include the values of its links.

### 5.1.4 State Diagrams

A *state diagram* relates events and states. When an event is received, the next state depends on the current state as well as the event; a change of state caused by an event is called a *transition*. A state diagram is a graph whose nodes are states and whose directed arcs are transitions labeled by event names. A state is drawn as a rounded box containing an optional name. A transition is drawn as an arrow from the receiving state to the target state; the label on the arrow is the name of the event causing the transition. All the transitions leaving a state must correspond to different events.

The state diagram specifies the state sequence caused by an event sequence. If an object is in a state and an event labeling one of its transitions occurs, the object enters the state on the target end of the transition. The transition is said to *fire*. If more than one transition leaves a state, then the first event to occur causes the corresponding transition to fire. If an event occurs that has no transition leaving the current state, then the event is ignored. A sequence of events corresponds to a path through the graph.

Figure 5.5 shows a state diagram describing the behavior of a telephone line. The diagram is drawn for one phone line, not the caller or callee. The diagram contains sequences associated with normal calls as well as some abnormal sequences, such as timing out while

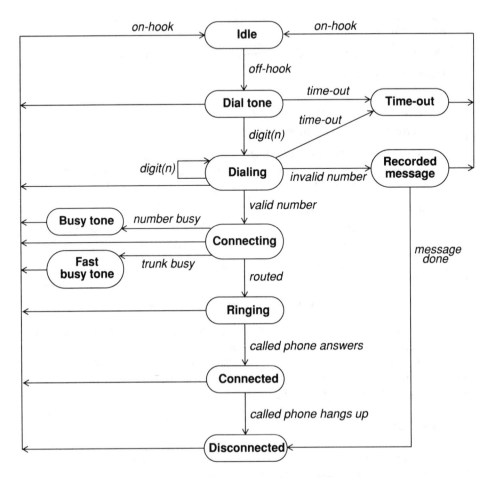

**Figure 5.5** State diagram for phone line

dialing or getting busy lines. The event *on-hook* causes a transition from any state to the *Idle* state; this is drawn as a bundle of transitions leading to *Idle*. Later we will show a more general notation that represents events applicable to groups of states with a single transition.

Note that the states do not totally define all values of the object. For example, state *Dialing* includes all sequences of incomplete phone numbers. It is not necessary to distinguish between different numbers as separate states since they all have the same behavior, but the actual number dialed must of course be saved as an attribute.

A state diagram describes the behavior of a single class of objects. Since all instances of a class have the same behavior (by definition), they all share the same state diagram, as they all share the same class features. But as each object has its own attribute values, so too each object has its own state, the result of the unique sequence of events that it has received. Each object is independent of other objects and proceeds at its own pace.

State diagrams can represent one-shot life cycles or continuous loops. The diagram for the phone line is a continuous loop. In describing ordinary usage of the phone, we do not know or care how the loop is started. (If we were describing installation of new lines, the initial state would be important.) One-shot diagrams represent objects with finite lives. A one-shot diagram has initial and final states. The initial state is entered on creation of an object; entering the final state implies destruction of the object. An initial state is shown by a solid circle. The circle can be labeled to indicate different initial conditions. A final state is shown by a bull's-eye. The bull's-eye can be labeled to distinguish final conditions. Figure 5.6 shows the life cycle of a chess game (with some simplifications). A one-shot diagram can be considered a state diagram "subroutine" that can be referenced from various places in a high-level diagram. Later we will show how creation and termination of an object fit into an overall system.

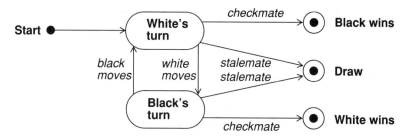

**Figure 5.6** One-shot state diagram for chess game

The *dynamic model* is a collection of state diagrams that interact with each other via shared events. An object model represents the static structure of a system, while a dynamic model represents the control structure of a system. A state diagram, like an object class, is a pattern; it describes an entire, possibly infinite, range of sequences. A scenario is to a dynamic model as an instance diagram is to an object model.

## 5.1.5 Conditions

A *condition* is a Boolean function of object values, such as "the temperature is below freezing." A condition is valid over an interval of time. For example, "the temperature was below freezing from November 15, 1921 until March 3, 1922." It is important to distinguish conditions from events, which have no time duration. A state can be defined in terms of a condition; conversely, being in a state is a condition.

Conditions can be used as *guards* on transitions. A guarded transition fires when its event occurs, but only if the guard condition is true. For example, "when you go out in the morning (*event*), if the temperature is below freezing (*condition*), then put on your gloves (*next state*)." A guard condition on a transition is shown as a Boolean expression in brackets following the event name.

Figure 5.7 shows a state diagram with guarded transitions for traffic lights at an intersection. One pair of electric eyes checks the north-south left turn lanes; another pair checks

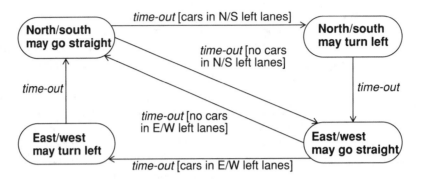

**Figure 5.7** State diagram with guarded transitions

the east-west turn lanes. If no car is in the north-south and/or east-west turn lanes then the traffic light control logic is smart enough to skip the left turn portion of the cycle.

## 5.2 OPERATIONS

The state diagrams presented so far describe the patterns of events and states for a single object class. In this section we show how events trigger operations.

### 5.2.1 Controlling Operations

State diagrams would be of little use if they just described patterns of events. A behavioral description of an object must specify what the object does in response to events. Operations attached to states or transitions are performed in response to the corresponding states or events.

An *activity* is an operation that takes time to complete. An activity is associated with a state. Activities include continuous operations, such as displaying a picture on a television screen, as well as sequential operations that terminate by themselves after an interval of time, such as closing a valve or performing a computation. A state may control a continuous activity, such as ringing a telephone bell, that persists until an event terminates it by causing a transition from the state. The notation "*do: A*" within a state box indicates that activity *A* starts on entry to the state and stops on exit. A state may also control a sequential activity, such as a robot moving a part, that progresses until it completes or until it is interrupted by an event that terminates it prematurely. The same notation "*do: A*" indicates that sequential activity *A* begins on entry to the state and stops when complete. If an event causes a transition from the state before the activity is complete, then the activity is terminated prematurely. For example, a robot might encounter resistance, causing it to cease moving. The two uses are not really different; a continuous activity may be viewed as a sequential activity that lasts indefinitely.

An *action* is an instantaneous operation. An action is associated with an event. An action represents an operation whose duration is insignificant compared to the resolution of the state diagram. For example, *disconnect phone line* might be an action in response to an *on-hook* event for the phone line in Figure 5.5. A real-world operation is not really instantaneous, of course, but modeling it as an action indicates that we do not care about its internal structure for control purposes. If we do care, then an operation should be modeled as an activity, with a starting event, ending event, and possibly some intermediate events.

Actions can also represent internal control operations, such as setting attributes or generating other events. Such actions have no real-world counterparts but instead are mechanisms for structuring control within an implementation. For example, an internal counter might be incremented every time a particular event occurs. In a computer, of course, even simple operations take some time, but they can be considered instantaneous with respect to the granularity of real events under consideration.

The notation for an action on a transition is a slash ('/') and the name (or description) of the action, following the name of the event that causes it. Figure 5.8 shows the state diagram for a pop-up menu on a workstation. When the right button is depressed, the menu is displayed; when the right button is released, the menu is erased. While the menu is visible, the highlighted menu item is updated whenever the cursor moves.

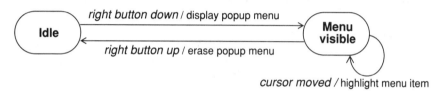

**Figure 5.8** Actions for pop-up menu

## 5.2.2 Summary of Notation for State Diagrams with Operations

Figure 5.9 summarizes the notation presented in Sections 5.1 and 5.2 for unstructured state diagrams. Section 5.3 discusses extensions for structured state diagrams.

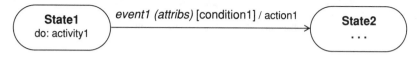

**Figure 5.9** Summary of notation for unstructured state diagrams

As shown in Figure 5.9, a state name is written in boldface within a rounded box. An event name is written on a transition arrow and may optionally be followed by one or more attributes within parentheses. A condition may be listed within square brackets after an event name. An activity is indicated within a state box by the keyword "*do:*" followed by the name or description of the activity. An action is indicated on a transition following the event name by a "/" character followed by the event name. All these constructs are optional in state diagrams.

Figure 5.10 shows the state diagram for the phone line, previously shown in Figure 5.5, but now with actions and activities.

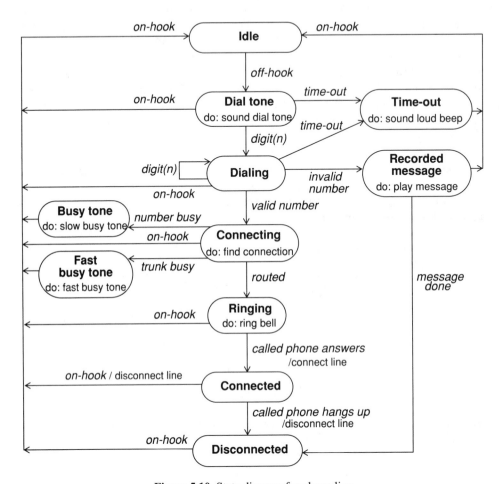

**Figure 5.10**  State diagram for phone line

## 5.3 NESTED STATE DIAGRAMS

State diagrams can be structured to permit concise descriptions of complex systems. The ways of structuring state machines are similar to the ways of structuring objects: generalization and aggregation. Generalization is equivalent to expanding nested activities. It allows an activity to be described at a high level, then expanded at a lower level by adding details, similar to a nested procedure call. In addition, generalization allows states and events to be arranged into generalization hierarchies with inheritance of common structure and behavior, similar to inheritance of attributes and operations in classes. Aggregation allows a state to be broken into orthogonal components, with limited interaction among them, similar to an object aggregation hierarchy. Aggregation is equivalent to concurrency of states. Concurrent states generally correspond to object aggregations, possibly an entire system, that have interacting parts.

### 5.3.1 Problems with Flat State Diagrams

State diagrams have often been criticized because they allegedly lack expressive power and are impractical for large problems. These problems are true of flat, unstructured state diagrams. Consider an object with $n$ independent Boolean attributes that affect control. Representing such an object with a single flat state diagram would require $2^n$ states. By partitioning the state into $n$ independent state machines, however, only $2n$ states are required. Or consider the state diagram shown in Figure 5.11, in which $n^2$ transitions are needed to connect every state to every other state. If this model can be reformulated using structure, the number of transitions could be reduced as low as $n$. All complex systems contain a large amount of redundancy that can be used to simplify state diagrams, provided appropriate structuring mechanisms are available.

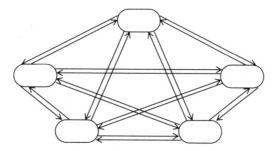

**Figure 5.11**  Combinatorial explosion of transitions in flat state diagram

### 5.3.2 Nesting State Diagrams

An activity in a state can be expanded as a lower-level state diagram, each state representing one step of the activity. Nested activities are one-shot state diagrams with input and output transitions, similar to subroutines. The set of nested state diagrams forms a lattice. (It is a tree if we expand out different copies of the same nested diagram.).

Figure 5.12 shows a top-level model for a vending machine. This diagram contains an activity *dispense item* and an event *select(item)* that are expanded in more detail in nested state diagrams. The diagram also shows a bit of alternate notation. The event *coins in(amount)* is written within the *Collecting money* state. This indicates a transition that remains within a single state. Also, the transition from the unnamed state containing "do: dispense item" to state *Idle* has no event label. The lack of event label indicates that the transition fires automatically when the activity in the state is complete.

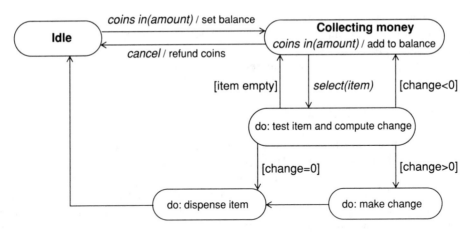

**Figure 5.12** Vending machine model

Figure 5.13 shows a subdiagram for the *dispense item* activity of Figure 5.12. This activity corresponds to a sequence of lower-level states and events that are invisible in the original high-level state diagram.

**Figure 5.13** *Dispense item* activity of vending machine

Events can also be expanded into subordinate state diagrams. Figure 5.14 shows the *select item* event from Figure 5.12, which actually involves several low-level events. The customer keys in an item number and can start over by hitting *clear*; the selection is confirmed by hitting *enter*. The label on the bull's-eye indicates the event generated on the higher-level state diagram.

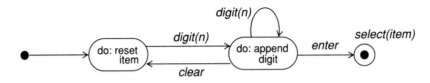

**Figure 5.14** *Select item* transition of vending machine

### 5.3.3 State Generalization

A nested state diagram is actually a form of generalization on states. Generalization is the "or-relationship." An object in a state in the high-level diagram must be in exactly one state in the nested diagram. It must be in the first state, *or* the second state, *or* in one of the other states. The states in the nested diagram are all refinements of the state in the high-level diagram. In the previous section, the states in the nested diagram are unaffected by transitions in the high-level diagram, but in general the states in a nested state diagram may interact with other states.

States may have substates that inherit the transitions of their superstates, just as classes have subclasses that inherit the attributes and operations of their superclasses. Any transition or action that applies to a state applies to all its substates, unless overridden by an equivalent transition on the substate. For example, the phone line model in Figure 5.5 could be simplified by replacing the transitions from each state to *Idle* on event *on-hook* with a single transition from a superstate *Active* to *Idle*. All the original states except *Idle* are substates of *Active*. The occurrence of event *on-hook* in any active substate causes a transition to state *Idle*.

Figure 5.15 shows a state diagram for an automatic transmission. The transmission can be in reverse, neutral, or forward; if it is in forward, it can be in first, second, or third gear. States *First, Second,* and *Third* are substates of state *Forward*. The generalization notation for states is different from that used for classes, to avoid a large number of lines that could be confused with transitions. A superstate is drawn as a large rounded box enclosing all of its substates. Substates in turn can enclose further substates. Because the rounded boxes representing the various states are nested, Harel calls them *contours*.

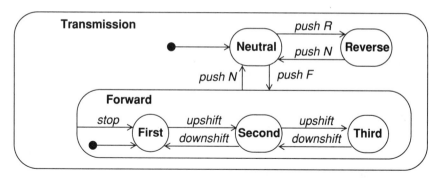

**Figure 5.15** State diagram of car transmission with generalization

The transitions of a superstate are inherited by each of its substates. Selecting "N" in any forward gear causes a transition to neutral. The transition from *Forward* to *Neutral* implies three inherited transitions, one from each forward gear to neutral. Selecting "F" in neutral causes a transition to forward. Within state *Forward*, substate *First* is the default initial state, shown by the unlabeled transition from the solid circle within the *Forward* contour. *Forward* is just an abstract state; control must be in a real state, such as *First*.

The transition on event *stop* from the *Forward* contour to state *First* represents a transition inherited by all three substates. In any forward gear, stopping the car causes a transition to *First*.

It is possible to represent more complicated situations, such as an explicit transition from a substate to a state outside the contour, or an explicit transition into the contour. In such cases, all the states must appear on one diagram using the contour notation. In simpler cases where there is no interaction except for initiation and termination, the nested states can simply be drawn as a separate diagram and referenced by name in a "do" statement, as in the vending machine example of Figure 5.12.

### 5.3.4 Event Generalization

Events can be organized into a generalization hierarchy with inheritance of event attributes. Figure 5.16 shows part of a tree of input events for a workstation. Events *mouse button down* and *keyboard character* are two kinds of user input. Both events inherit attribute *time* from event *event (*the root of the hierarchy) and attribute *device* from event *user input. Mouse button down* and *mouse button up* inherit *location* from *mouse button.* Keyboard characters can be divided into control characters and graphic characters. Ultimately every actual event can be viewed as a leaf on a generalization tree of events. Inherited event attributes are shown in the second part of each box. An input event triggers transitions on any ancestor event type. For example, typing an 'a' would trigger a transition on event *alphanumeric* as well as event *keyboard character.*

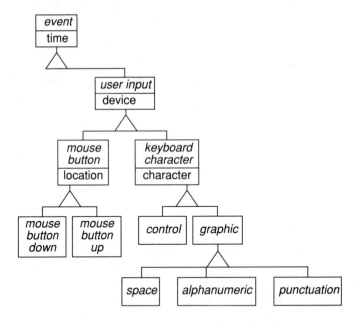

**Figure 5.16** Partial event hierarchy for keyboard events

Providing an event hierarchy permits different levels of abstraction to be used at different places in a model. For example, in some states all input characters might be handled the same and would lead to the same next state; in other states control characters would be treated differently from printing characters; still others might have different actions on individual characters.

## 5.4 CONCURRENCY

### 5.4.1 Aggregation Concurrency

A dynamic model describes a set of concurrent objects, each with its own state and state diagram. The objects in a system are inherently concurrent and can change state independently. The state of the entire system cannot be represented by a single state in a single object; it is the product of the states of all the objects in it. In many systems, the number of objects can change dynamically as well.

A state diagram for an assembly is a collection of state diagrams, one for each component. Aggregation implies concurrency. The aggregate state corresponds to the combined states of all the component diagrams. Aggregation is the "and-relationship." The aggregate state is one state from the first diagram, *and* a state from the second diagram, *and* a state from each other diagram. In the more interesting cases, the component states interact. Guarded transitions for one object can depend on another object being in a given state. This allows interaction between the state diagrams, while preserving modularity.

Figure 5.17 shows the state of a *Car* as an aggregation of component states: the *Ignition*, *Transmission*, *Accelerator*, and *Brake* (plus other unmentioned objects). Each component state also has substates. The state of the car includes one substate from each component. Each component undergoes transitions in parallel with all the others. The state diagrams of the components are almost, but not quite, independent: The car will not start unless transmission is in neutral. This is shown by the guard expression *Transmission in Neutral* on the transition from *Ignition-Off* to *Ignition-Starting*.

### 5.4.2 Concurrency within an Object

Concurrency within the state of a single object arises when the object can be partitioned into subsets of attributes or links, each of which has its own subdiagram. The state of the object comprises one state from each subdiagram. The subdiagrams need not be independent; the same event can cause transitions in more than one subdiagram. Concurrency within a single composite state of an object is shown by partitioning the composite state into subdiagrams with dotted lines. The name of the overall composite state can be written in a separate region of the box, separated by a solid line from the concurrent subdiagrams. Figure 5.18 shows the state diagram for the play of a bridge rubber. When a side wins a game, it becomes "vulnerable"; the first side to win two games wins the rubber. During the play of the rubber, the state of the rubber consists of one state from each subdiagram. When the *Playing rubber* composite state is entered, both subdiagrams are initially in their respective default states *Not vulnerable*. Each subdiagram can independently advance to state *Vulnerable* when its side wins a game. When one side wins a second game, a transition occurs to the corresponding *Wins rubber* state. This transition terminates both concurrent subdiagrams because they are part of the same composite state *Playing rubber* and are only active when the top-level state diagram is in that state.

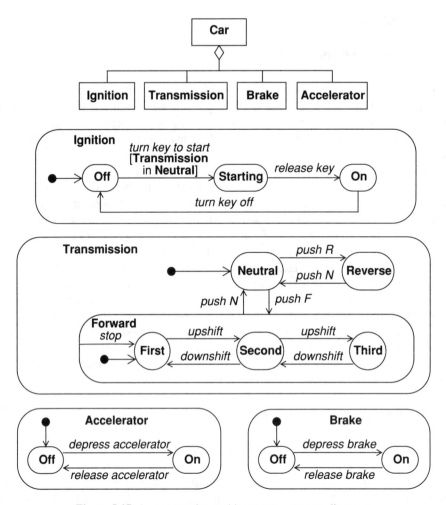

**Figure 5.17**  An aggregation and its concurrent state diagrams

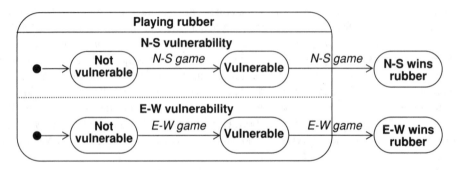

**Figure 5.18**  Bridge game with concurrent states

## 5.5 ADVANCED DYNAMIC MODELING CONCEPTS

In this section we present advanced dynamic modeling concepts as well as some refinements on the notation.

### 5.5.1 Entry and Exit Actions

As an alternative to showing actions on transitions, actions can be associated with entering or exiting a state. There is no difference in expressive power between the two notations, but frequently all transitions into a state perform the same action, in which case attaching the action to the state is more concise.

For example, Figure 5.19 shows the control of a garage door opener. The user generates *depress* events with a push-button to open and close the door. Each event reverses the direction of the door, but for safety the door must open fully before it can be closed. The control generates *motor up* and *motor down* actions for the motor. The motor generates *door open* and *door closed* events when the motion has been completed. Both transitions entering state *Opening* cause the door to open.

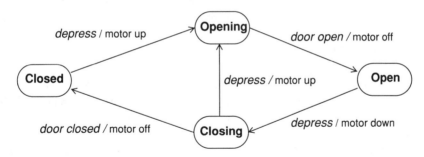

**Figure 5.19** Actions on transitions

Figure 5.20 shows the same model using actions on entry to states. An entry action is shown inside the state box following the keyword *entry* and a "/" character. Whenever the state is entered, by any incoming transition, the entry action is performed. An entry action is equivalent to attaching the action to every incoming transition. If an incoming transition already has an action, its action is performed first.

Exit actions are less common than entry actions, but they are occasionally useful. An exit action is shown inside the state box following the keyword *exit* and a "/" character. Whenever the state is exited, by any outgoing transition, the exit action is performed first.

If multiple operations are specified on a state, they are performed in the following order: actions on the incoming transition, entry actions, do activities, exit actions, actions on the outgoing transition. Do activities can be interrupted by events that cause transitions out of the state, but entry actions and exit actions are completed regardless, since they are considered to be instantaneous actions. If a do activity is interrupted, the exit action is nevertheless performed.

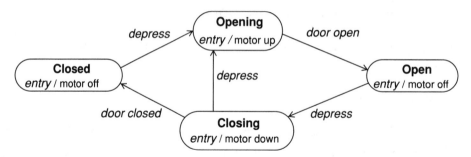

**Figure 5.20**  Actions on entry to states

Entry and exit actions are particularly useful in nested state diagrams because they permit a state (possibly an entire subdiagram) to be expressed in terms of matched entry-exit actions without regard for what happens before or after the state is active. It is possible to use actions attached to transitions as well as entry and exit actions in a diagram.

Transitioning into or out of a substate in a nested diagram can cause execution of several entry or exit actions, if the transition reaches across several levels of generalization. The entry actions are executed from the outside in and the exit actions from the inside out. This permits behavior similar to nested subroutine calls.

### 5.5.2  Internal Actions

An event can cause an action to be performed without causing a state change. The event name is written inside the state box, followed by a "/" and the name of the action. (Keywords *entry, exit,* and *do* are reserved words within the state box.) When such an event occurs, its action is executed but not the entry or exit actions for the state. There is therefore a difference between an internal action and a self-transition; the self-transition causes the exit and entry actions for the state to be executed. Figure 5.12 shows an internal action within the *Collecting money* state.

Figure 5.21 summarizes the additional notation for entry, exit, and internal actions.

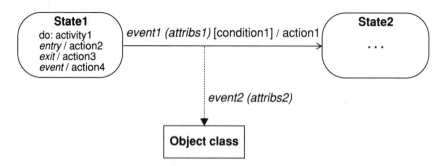

**Figure 5.21**  Summary of extended notation for state diagrams

### 5.5.3 Automatic Transition

Frequently the only purpose of a state is to perform a sequential activity. When the activity is completed, a transition to another state fires. An arrow without an event name indicates an automatic transition that fires when the activity associated with the source state is completed. If there is no activity, the unlabeled transition fires as soon as the state is entered (but the entry and exit actions are always performed). Such unlabeled transitions are sometimes called *lambda transitions,* after the Greek letter used to indicate them in some textbooks. Figure 5.12 shows four unlabeled transitions from the state containing activity "test item and compute change." Each transition has a guard condition. When the activity is complete, the transition with a valid guard condition fires.

If a state has one or more automatic transitions, but none of the guard conditions are satisfied, then the state remains active until one of the conditions is satisfied or until an event causes another transition to fire. The change in value of a condition is an implicit event (referred to in digital hardware as "edge triggering"). For example, "the temperature is below freezing" is a condition. "The temperature goes belong freezing" is the edge-triggered event associated with the condition.

### 5.5.4 Sending Events

An object can perform the action of sending an event to another object. A system of objects interacts by exchanging events.

The action *"send E(attributes)"* sends event E with the given attributes to the object or objects that receive it. For example, the phone line sends a *connect(phone-number)* event to the switcher when a complete phone number has been dialed. An event can be directed at a set of objects or a single object. Any and all objects with transitions on the event can accept it concurrently. The word "send" can be omitted if it is clear that E is the name of an event. In our diagrams, event names are shown in italics and action names in normal text, so there is no confusion.

Figure 5.21 shows another notation for sending an event from one object to another. The dotted line from a transition to an object indicates that an event is sent to the object when the transition fires. The arrow could be connected directly to a transition within the state diagram of the target object to indicate that the target transition depends on the event.

If a state can accept events from more than one object, the order in which concurrent events are received may affect the final state; this is called a *race condition.* For example, in Figure 5.20 the door may or may not remain open if the button is pressed at about the time the door becomes fully open. A race condition is not necessarily a design error, but concurrent systems frequently contain unwanted race conditions which must be avoided by careful design. A requirement of two events being received simultaneously is never a meaningful condition in the real world, as slight variations in transmission speed are inherent in any distributed system.

When an object interacts with an external object, such as a person or device, sending an event is often indistinguishable from an action. For example, in the event trace of Figure 5.3, actions *dial tone begins* and *ringing tone* are actually events between the phone line and the caller.

### 5.5.5 Synchronization of Concurrent Activities

Sometimes one object must perform two (or more) activities concurrently. The internal steps of the activities are not synchronized, but both activities must be completed before the object can progress to its next state. For example, consider a cash dispensing machine that dispenses cash and returns the user's card at the end of a transaction. The machine must not reset itself until the user takes both the cash and the card, but the user may take them in either order or even simultaneously. The order in which they are taken is irrelevant, only the fact that both of them have been taken. This is an example of *splitting control* into concurrent activities and later *merging control*.

Figure 5.22 shows a concurrent state diagram for the emitting activity. Concurrent activities within a single composite activity are shown by partitioning a state into regions with dotted lines, as explained previously. Each region is a subdiagram that represents a concurrent activity within the composite activity. The composite activity assumes exactly one state from each subdiagram.

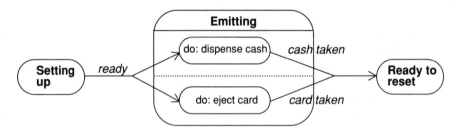

**Figure 5.22** Synchronization of control

Splitting of control into concurrent parts is shown by an arrow that forks. The forked arrow selects one state from each concurrent subdiagram. In the example, the transition on event *ready* splits into two concurrent parts, one to each concurrent subdiagram. When this transition fires, two concurrent substates become active and execute independently. Each concurrent substate could be a whole state diagram.

Any transition into a state with concurrent subdiagrams activates each of the subdiagrams. If any subdiagrams are omitted from the transition, they start in their default initial states. In this example, a forked arrow is not actually necessary. A transition could be drawn to the *Emitting* state, with a default initial state indicated in each subdiagram.

Merging of concurrent control is shown by an arrow with a forked tail. The target state becomes active when both events occur in any order. The events need not be simultaneous. Each subdiagram terminates as soon as its part of the transition fires, but all parts of the transition must fire before the entire transition fires and the composite state is terminated. If there are any subdiagrams in the composite state that are not part of the merge, then they are automatically terminated when the merge transition fires. The exit actions (if any) of all sub-diagrams are performed when the merge transition fires. In the example, the transitions *cash taken* and *card taken* are part of a single merge transition. When both parts of the merge transitions fire, state *Ready to reset* becomes active. Drawing a separate transition from each sub-state to the target state would have a different meaning; either transition would terminate the other subdiagram without waiting for the other transition.

In this example, the number of concurrently-active states varies during execution from one to two and back to one again.

## 5.6  A SAMPLE DYNAMIC MODEL

We present a sample dynamic model of a real device to show how the various modeling constructs fit together. This is a model of a Sears "Weekender" Programmable Thermostat. This model was constructed by reading the instruction manual and by experimenting with the actual device. This device controls a furnace and air conditioner according to time-dependent attributes which the owner enters using a pad of buttons.

While running, the thermostat operates the furnace or air conditioner to keep the current temperature equal to the target temperature. The target temperature is taken from a table of program values supplied by the user. The table specifies target temperature for 8 different time periods, 4 on weekdays and 4 on weekends, with start times specified by the user. The target temperature is reset from the table at the beginning of each program period. The user can override the target temperature for the remainder of the current period or indefinitely. The user programs the thermostat using a pad of 10 push buttons and 3 switches. The user sees parameters on an alphanumeric display. A switch illuminates a night light. The thermostat has a temperature sensor that reads the air temperature. The thermostat operates power relays for a furnace and an air conditioner, and an indicator lights up when the furnace or air conditioner is operating.

Each push button generates an event every time it is pushed. We assign one input event per button:

| | |
|---|---|
| TEMP UP | raises target temperature or program temperature |
| TEMP DOWN | lowers target temperature or program temperature |
| TIME FWD | advances clock time or program time |
| TIME BACK | retards clock time or program time |
| SET CLOCK | sets current time of day |
| SET DAY | sets current day of the week |
| RUN PRGM | leaves setup or program mode and runs the program |
| VIEW PRGM | enters program mode to examine and modify 8 program time and program temperature settings |
| HOLD TEMP | holds current target temperature in spite of the program |
| F-C BUTTON | alternates temperature display between Fahrenheit and Celsius |

Each switch supplies a parameter value chosen from two or three possibilities. We model each switch as an independent concurrent subdiagram with one state per switch setting. Although we assign event names to a change in state, it is the state of each switch that is of interest. The switches and their settings are:

Light switch      Lights the alphanumeric display. Values: light off, light on.

Season switch     Specifies which device the thermostat controls. Values: heat (furnace), cool (air conditioner), off (none).

Fan switch       Specifies when the ventilation fan operates. Values: fan on (fan runs continuously), fan auto (fan runs only when furnace or air conditioner is operating).

The thermostat controls the furnace, air conditioner, and fan power relays. We model this control by activities "run furnace," "run air conditioner," and "run fan."

The thermostat has a temperature sensor that it reads continuously, which we model by an external parameter *temp*. The thermostat also has an internal clock that it reads and displays continuously. We model the clock as another external parameter *time*, since we are not interested in building a state model of the clock. In building a dynamic model, it is important to only include states that affect the flow of control and to model other information as parameters or variables. We introduce an internal state variable *target temp*, which represents the current temperature that the thermostat is trying to maintain. This state variable is read by some actions and set by other actions; it permits communication among parts of the dynamic model.

Figure 5.23 shows the top-level state diagram of the programmable thermostat. It contains 7 concurrent subdiagrams. The user interface is too large to show and is expanded separately. The diagram includes trivial subdiagrams for the season switch and the fan switch. The other 4 subdiagrams show the output of the thermostat: the furnace, air conditioner, and fan relays, and the run indicator light. Each of these subdiagrams contains an *Off* and an *On* substate. The state of each subdiagram is totally determined by conditions on input parameters and the state of other subdiagrams, such as the season switch or the fan switch. The state of the 4 subdiagrams on the right is totally derived and contains no additional information.

Figure 5.24 shows the subdiagram for the user interface. The diagram contains 3 concurrent subdiagrams, one for the interactive display, one for the temperature mode, and one for the night light. The night light is controlled by a physical switch, so the default initial state is irrelevant; its value can be determined directly. The temperature display mode is controlled by a single push button that toggles the temperature units between Fahrenheit and Celsius. The default initial state is necessary; when the device is powered on, the initial temperature mode is Fahrenheit.

The subdiagram for the interactive display is more interesting. The device is either operating or being set up. Substate *Operate* contains two substates, *Run* and *Hold,* in addition to two concurrent substates, one which controls the target temperature display and one which controls the current time and temperature display. Every 2 seconds the display alternates between the current time and current temperature.

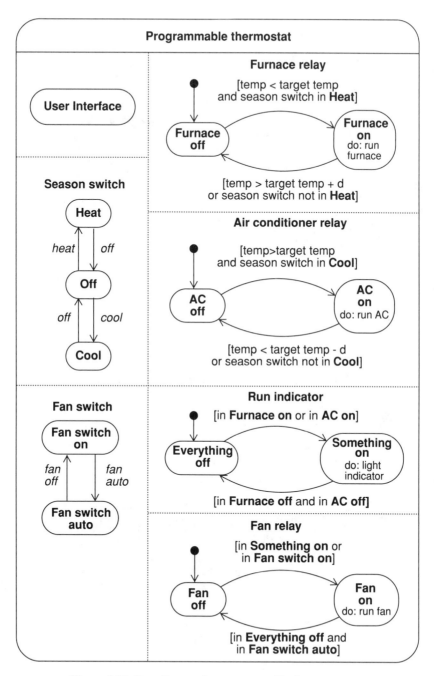

**Figure 5.23** State diagram for programmable thermostat

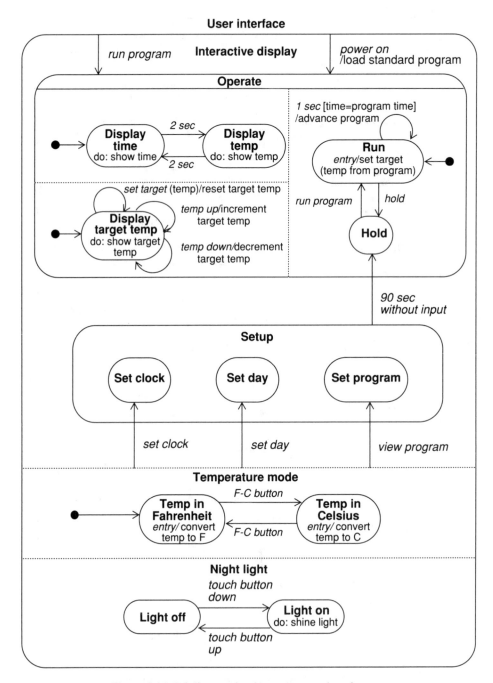

**Figure 5.24** Subdiagram for thermostat user interface

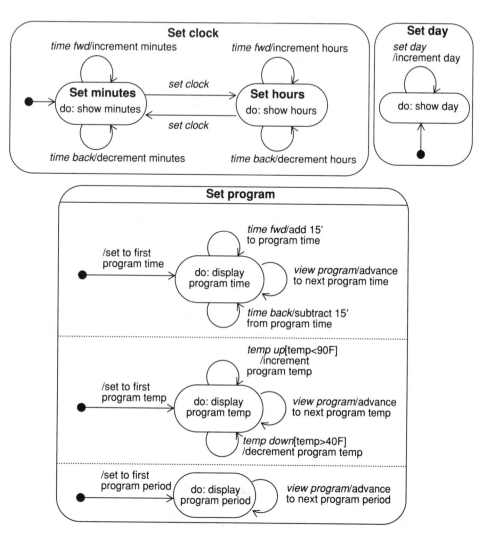

**Figure 5.25** Subdiagrams for thermostat user interface setup

The target temperature is displayed continuously and is modified by the *temp up* and *temp down* buttons, as well as the *set target* event that is generated only in the *Run* state. Note that the *target temp* parameter set by this subdiagram is the same parameter that controls the output relays.

While in the *Operate* state, the device is either in the *Run* or *Hold* substates. Every second in the *Run* state, the current time is compared to the stored program times in the program table; if they are equal, then the program advances to the next program period, and the *Run* state is reentered. The run state is also entered whenever the *run program* button is pressed in any state, as shown by the transition from the contour to the *Operate* state and the default initial transition to *Run*. Whenever the *Run* state is entered, the entry action on the state resets the target temperature from the program table. While the program is in the *Hold* state, the program temperature cannot be advanced automatically, but the temperature can still be modified directly by the *temp up* and *temp down* buttons. The default substate on *power on* is the *Run* substate. If the interface is in one of the setup states for 90 seconds without any input, the system enters the *Hold* state. This transition is shown as an arrow from the *Setup* contour directly to the *Hold* substate. Entering the *Hold* substate also forces entry to the default initial states of the other two concurrent subdiagrams of *Operate*. The *Setup* state was included in the model just to group the three setup substates for the 90-second time-out transition. Note a small anomaly of the device: The *hold* button has no effect within the *Setup* state, although the *Hold* state can be entered by waiting for 90 seconds.

The three setup subdiagrams are shown in Figure 5.25. Pressing *set clock* enters the *Set minutes* substate as initial default. Subsequent *set clock* presses toggle between the *Set hours* and the *Set minutes* substates. The *time fwd* and *time back* buttons modify the program time. Pressing *set day* enters the *Set day* substate and shows the day of the week. Subsequent presses increment the day directly. Pressing *view program* enters the *Set program* substate, which has three concurrent subdiagrams, one each controlling the display of the program time, program temperature, and program period. The *Set program* state always starts with the first program period, while subsequent *view program* events cycle through the 8 program periods. The *view program* event is shown on all three subdiagrams, each diagram advancing the setting that it controls. Note that the *time fwd* and *time back* events modify time in 15 minute increments, unlike the same events in the *set clock* state. Note also that the *temp up* and *temp down* transitions have guard conditions to keep the temperature in a fixed range.

None of the *Interactive display* substates has an explicit exit transition. Each substate is implicitly terminated by a transition into another substate from the main *Interactive display* contour.

## 5.7 RELATION OF OBJECT AND DYNAMIC MODELS

The dynamic model specifies allowable sequences of changes to objects from the object model. A state diagram describes all or part of the behavior of one object of a given class. States are equivalence classes of attribute and link values for the object. Events can be represented as operations on the object model.

Dynamic model structure is related to and constrained by object model structure. A substate refines the attribute and link values that the object can have. Each substate restricts the values that the object can have. But this refinement of object values is exactly generalization by restriction, as discussed in Section 4.3. A hierarchy of states of an object is equivalent to a restriction hierarchy of the object class. Object-oriented models and languages do not usually support restriction in the generalization hierarchy, so the dynamic model is the proper place to represent it. Both generalization of classes and generalization of states partition the set of possible object values. A single object can have different states over time—the object preserves its identity—but it cannot have different classes. Inherent differences among objects are therefore properly modeled as different classes, while temporary differences are properly modeled as different states of the same class.

A composite state is the aggregation of more than one concurrent substate. There are three sources of concurrency within the object model. The first is aggregation of objects: Each component of an aggregation has its own independent state, so the assembly can be considered to have a state that is the composite of the states of all its parts. The second source is aggregation within an object: The attributes and links of an object are its parts, and groups of them taken together define concurrent substates of the composite object state. The third source is concurrent behavior of an object, such as found in Figure 5.22. The three sources of concurrency are usually interchangeable. For example, an object could contain an attribute to indicate that it was performing a certain activity.

The dynamic model of a class is inherited by its subclasses. The subclasses inherit both the states of the ancestor and the transitions. The subclasses can have their own state diagrams. But how do the state diagrams of the superclass and the subclass interact? We have noted that states are equivalent to restriction on classes. If the superclass state diagrams and the subclass state diagrams deal with disjoint sets of attributes, there is no problem. The subclass has a composite state composed of concurrent state diagrams. If, however, the state diagram of the subclass involves some of the same attributes as the state diagram of the superclass, a potential conflict exists. The state diagram of the subclass must be a refinement of the state diagram of the superclass. Any state from the parent state diagram can be generalized or split into concurrent parts, but new states or transitions cannot be introduced into the parent diagram directly because the parent diagram must be a projection of the child diagram.Although refinement of inherited state diagrams is possible, usually the state diagram of a subclass should be an independent, orthogonal, concurrent addition to the state diagram inherited from a superclass, defined on a different set of attributes (usually the ones added in the subclass).

The event hierarchy is independent of the class hierarchy, in practice if not in theory. Events can be defined across different classes of objects. Events are more fundamental than states and more parallel to classes. States are defined by the interaction of objects and events. Transitions can often be implemented as operations on objects. The operation name corresponds to the event name. Events are more expressive than operations, however, because the effect of an event depends not only on the class of an object but also on its state.

## 5.8 PRACTICAL TIPS

The precise content of all OMT models depends on the needs of the application. This is true for the object, dynamic, and functional models. The examples in this chapter illustrate the various modeling constructs without showing the process for constructing a model in the first place. Parts 2 and 3 of this book show how to apply these principles; Part 4 presents several real applications.

The following practical tips have been mentioned throughout the chapter but are summarized here for convenience.

- Only construct state diagrams for object classes with meaningful dynamic behavior. Not all object classes require a state model.

- Check the various state diagrams for consistency on shared events so that the full dynamic model will be correct.

- Use scenarios to help you begin the process of constructing state diagrams. (Chapter 8 describes this process in detail.)

- Only consider *relevant* attributes when defining a state. All attributes shown in an object model need not be used in state diagrams.

- Consider the needs of the application when deciding on the granularity of events and states.

- Let the application distinguish between activities and actions. Activities occur over a period of time; actions are instantaneous compared to the time scale of an application.

- When a state has multiple incoming transitions and all transitions cause the same action to occur, put actions within state boxes preceded by an *entry* event instead of listing them on transition arcs. Do likewise for *exit* events.

- Use nested states when the same transaction applies to many states.

- Most concurrency arises from object aggregation and need not be expressed explicitly in the state diagram. Use composite states to show independent facets of the behavior of a single object.

- Try to make the state diagrams of subclasses independent of the state diagrams of their superclasses. The subclass state diagrams should concentrate on attributes unique to the subclasses.

- Beware of unwanted race conditions in state diagrams. Race conditions may occur when a state can accept events from more than one object.


## 5.9 CHAPTER SUMMARY

The dynamic model represents control information: the sequences of events, states, and operations that occur within a system of objects. Like the object model, the dynamic model is a pattern that specifies the allowable scenarios that may occur. The notation for the dynamic model represents a compromise between simplicity and expressiveness; there are some meaningful constraints that cannot be expressed by the notation we present. As with the object model, these constraints must be expressed in natural language.

An event is a signal that something has happened. A state represents the interval between events and specifies the context in which events are interpreted. A transition between states represents the response to an event, including the next state and possible actions and events sent to other objects. A condition is a Boolean function that controls whether a transition is allowed to occur. A state diagram is a graph of states and transitions labeled by events.

An action is an instantaneous operation in response to an event, often purely formal or internal. One kind of action is sending an event to another object. Actions can be attached to transitions or to entering or exiting a state. An activity is a sequence of actions that takes time to complete. An activity can be equated with a state or an entire state diagram. The result of an activity can be used as a decision to choose the next state.

States and events can both be expanded into nested state diagrams to show greater detail. Events and states can both be organized into inheritance hierarchies. Substates inherit the transitions of their superstates. Subevents trigger the same transitions as their superevents.

Objects are inherently concurrent. Each object is a collection that has its own state. State diagrams show concurrency as an aggregation of concurrent states, each operating independently. Concurrent objects interact by exchanging events and by testing conditions of other objects, including states. Transitions can split or merge flow of control.

Entry and exit actions permit actions to be associated with a state, to indicate all the transitions entering or exiting the state. They make self-contained state diagrams possible for use in multiple contexts. Internal actions represent transitions that do not leave the state. Automatic transitions fire when the their conditions are satisfied and any activity in the source state has terminated.

States are really restriction generalizations on a class and are complementary to ordinary extension generalizations. A subclass inherits the state diagrams of its ancestors, to be concurrent with any state diagram that it defines. It is also possible to refine an inherited state diagram by expanding states into substates or concurrent subdiagrams.

A realistic model of a programmable thermostat takes three pages and illustrates subtleties of behavior that are not apparent from the instruction manual or from everyday operation.

| action | contour | generalization | scenario |
|---|---|---|---|
| activity | control | guard | state |
| aggregation | dynamic model | nested diagram | state diagram |
| concurrency | event | operation | transition |
| condition | event trace | race condition | |

**Figure 5.26** Key concepts for Chapter 5

## BIBLIOGRAPHIC NOTES

A comparison of several techniques for specifying dynamic behavior of systems is given in [Davis-88].

Much of this chapter follows the work of David Harel, who has formalized his concepts in a notation called statecharts [Harel-87]. Harel's treatment is the most successful attempt to date to structure finite state machines and avoid the combinatorial explosion that has plagued them. Harel's statecharts are part of a larger development methodology that has been implemented as a commercial product called STATEMATE [Harel-88a]. Harel describes a contour-based notation for state diagrams, as well as object diagrams as special cases of a general diagram notation that he calls *higraphs* [Harel-88b].

We have used treelike notation for object diagrams and contour notation for state diagrams, although the notations are logically equivalent. As Harel indicates, the contour notation could also be used for object diagrams. Nested contours are good for conveying the intuitive feel that the general case includes all its specialized varieties. Contours have the disadvantage of being awkward to draw if nesting exceeds two or three levels. It is particularly inconvenient to develop top-down diagrams because the initial outer contours are usually too small and have to be redrawn. On the other hand, trees extend cleanly to any depth, and nodes at all levels can be drawn at the same resolution. We have chosen to use contours for states, which do not have a lot of text contents, but to use trees of object class boxes in a flat space to describe classes, which do have a lot of contents. In an earlier work, we had developed a treelike notation for states called *state trees* [Rumbaugh-88], but Harel's notation seems superior in most cases.

Finite state machines are a basic computer science concept that are described in any standard text on automata theory, such as [Hopcroft-79]. They are often described as recognizers or generators of formal languages. Basic finite state machines are limited in expressive power. They have been extended with local variables and recursion as Augmented Transition Networks [Woods-70] and Recursive Transition Networks. These extensions expand the range of formal languages they can express but do little to address the combinatorial explosion that makes them unwieldy for practical control problems.

[Shlaer-90] attaches a finite state machine to each object class. Actions attached to state entry are expressed in natural language. An object interacts with another object by sending an event to it as part of an action. There is no multilevel structure on the state machines and the interactions between objects tend to get buried in the code for actions.

Traditional finite automata have been approached from a synchronous viewpoint. Petri nets [Reisig-85] are a formalization of concurrency and synchronization of systems with distributed activity without resort to any notion of global time. Although they succeed well as an abstract conceptual model, they are too low level and inexpressive to be useful for specifying large systems.

Finite state machines have been used widely for specifying control of computer architectures and programs. Typically the problem is divided into data flow and control parts, the control part being specified by a finite state machine. Much of the thrust of previous work is to transform the finite state machines to minimize the size of the hardware. Details can be found in a standard text on switching theory or logic design, such as [Comer-84] or [Miller-79].

The need to specify interactive user interfaces has created several techniques for specifying control. This work is directed toward finding notations that clearly express powerful kinds of interactions while also being easily implementable. See [Green-86] for a comparison of some of these techniques.

## REFERENCES

[Comer-84] David J. Comer. *Digital Logic and State Machine Design*. New York: Holt, Rinehart, 1984.

[Davis-88] Alan M. Davis. A comparison of techniques for the specification of external system behavior. *Communications of ACM 31, 9* (September 1988), 1098-1115.

[Green-86] Mark Green. A survey of three dialogue models. *ACM Transactions on Graphics 5, 3* (July 1986), 244-275.

[Harel-87] David Harel. Statecharts: a visual formalism for complex systems. *Science of Computer Programming 8* (1987), 231-274.

[Harel-88a] D. Harel, H. Lachover, A. Naamad, A. Pnueli, M. Politi, R. Sherman, A. Shtul-Trauring. STATEMATE: A working environment for the development of complex reactive systems. *Proceedings of 10th IEEE International Conference on Software Engineering*, Singapore, April 1988.

[Harel-88b] David Harel. On visual formalisms. *Communications of ACM 31, 5* (May 1988), 514-530.

[Hopcroft-79] J.E. Hopcroft, J.D. Ullman. *Introduction to Automata Theory, Languages, and Computation*. Reading, Mass.: Addison-Wesley, 1979.

[Miller-79] Raymond A. Miller. *Switching Theory*. Huntington, New York: Robert E. Krieger, 1979.

[Reisig-85]. W. Reisig. *Petri Nets: An Introduction*. Berlin: Springer-Verlag, 1985.

[Rumbaugh-88] James Rumbaugh. State trees as structured finite state machines for user interfaces. *ACM SIGGRAPH Symposium on User Interface Software*, Banff, Alberta, October 17-19, 1988.

[Shlaer-90] Sally Shlaer, Stephen J. Mellor. *Object Life Cycles: Modeling the World in States*. Englewood Cliffs, New Jersey: Yourdon Press, 1990.

[Woods-70] W.A. Woods. Transition network grammars for natural language analysis. *Communications of ACM 13, 10* (Oct. 1970), 591-606.

## EXERCISES

**5.1**   (3) Write scenarios for the following activities:

  a. Moving a bag of corn, a goose, and a fox across a river in a boat. Only one thing may be carried in the boat at a time. If the goose is left alone with the corn, the corn will be eaten. If the goose is left alone with the fox, the goose will be eaten. Prepare two scenarios, one in which something gets eaten and one in which everything is safely transported across the river.

  b. Getting ready to take a trip in your car. Assume an automatic transmission. Don't forget your seat belt and emergency brake.

  c. An elevator ride to the top floor.

  d. Operation of a car cruise control. Include an encounter with slow moving traffic that requires you to disengage and then resume control.

**5.2**   (4) Some combined bath–showers have two faucets and a lever for controlling the flow of the water. The lever controls whether the water flows from the shower head or directly into the tub. When the water is first turned on, it flows directly into the tub. When the lever is pulled, a valve closes and latches, diverting the flow of water to the shower head. To switch from shower to bath with the water running, one must push the lever. Shutting off the water releases the lever so that the next time the water is turned on, it flows directly into the tub. Write a scenario for a shower that is interrupted by a telephone call.

**5.3**    (3) The direction control for some of the first toy electric trains was accomplished by interrupting the power to the train. Prepare state diagrams for the headlight and wheels of the train, corresponding to the following scenario:

       Power is off, train is not moving.
       Power is turned on, train moves forward and train headlight shines.
       Power is turned off, train stops and headlight goes out.
       Power is turned on, headlight shines and train does not move.
       Power is turned off, headlight goes out.
       Power is turned on, train runs backward with its headlight shining.
       Power is turned off, train stops and headlight goes out.
       Power is turned on, headlight shines and train does not move.
       Power is turned off, headlight goes out.
       Power is turned on, train runs forward with its headlight shining.

**5.4**    (4) An extension ladder has a rope, pulley, and latch for raising, lowering, and locking the extension. When the latch is locked, the extension is mechanically supported and you may safely climb the ladder. To release the latch, you raise the extension slightly with the rope. You may then freely raise or lower the extension. The latch produces a clacking sound as it passes over rungs of the ladder. The latch may be reengaged while raising the extension by reversing direction just as the latch is passing a rung. Prepare a state diagram of an extension ladder.

**5.5**    (4) A simple digital watch has a display and two buttons to set it, the A button and the B button. The watch has two modes of operation, display time and set time. In the display time mode, hours and minutes are displayed, separated by a flashing colon. The set time mode has two submodes, set hours and set minutes. The A button is used to select modes. Each time it is pressed, the mode advances in the sequence: display, set hours, set minutes, display, etc. Within the submodes, the B button is used to advance the hours or minutes once each time it is pressed. Buttons must be released before they can generate another event. Prepare a state diagram of the watch.

**5.6**    (5) Revise the dynamic model from the previous exercise to provide for more rapid setting of the time by pressing and holding the B button. If the B button is pressed and held for more than 5 seconds in set time mode, the hours or minutes (depending on the submode) increment once every 1/2 second.

**5.7**    (6) Figure E5.1 is a partially completed, simplified, state diagram for the control of a telephone answering machine. Calls are automatically answered as follows: An incoming call is detected on the first ring and the machine answers the call with a prerecorded announcement. When the announcement is complete, the caller's message is recorded. When the caller hangs up, the machine hangs up and shuts off. Place the following in the diagram: call detected, answer call, play announcement, record message, caller hangs up, announcement complete.

**Figure E5.1** Partially completed state diagram for an answering machine

**5.8**    (7) The telephone answering machine in the previous exercise is activated on the first ring. Revise the state diagram to have the machine answer after five rings. If the telephone is answered before five rings, the machine should do nothing. Be careful to distinguish between five calls in which the telephone is answered on the first ring and one call that rings five times.

**5.9** (3) In a personal computer, a disk controller is typically used to transfer a stream of bytes from a floppy disk drive to a memory buffer with the help of a host such as the central processing unit (CPU) or a direct memory access (DMA) controller. A partially completed, simplified, state diagram for the control of the data transfer is shown in Figure E5.2. The controller signals the host each time a new byte is available. The data must then be read and stored before another byte is ready. When the disk controller senses the data has been read, it indicates that data is not available, in preparation for the next byte. If any byte is not read before the next one comes along, the disk controller asserts a data lost error signal until the disk controller is reset. Add the following to the diagram: reset, indicate data not available, indicate data available, data read by host, new data ready, indicate data lost.

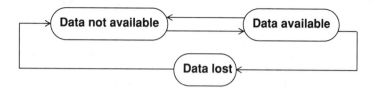

**Figure E5.2** Partially completed state diagram of a data transfer protocol

**5.10** (6) Figure E5.3 is a partially completed state diagram for one kind of motor control that is commonly used in household appliances. A separate appliance control determines when the motor should be on and continuously asserts "on" as an input to the motor control when the motor should be running.

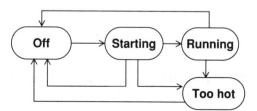

**Figure E5.3** Partially completed state diagram for a motor control

When "on" is asserted, the motor control should start and run the motor. Starting is accomplished by applying power to both the "start" and the "run" windings of the motor. A sensor, called a "starting relay," determines when the motor has started, at which point the "start" winding is turned off, leaving only the "run" winding powered. Both windings are shut off when "on" is not asserted.

Appliance motors could be damaged by overheating if they are overloaded or fail to start. To protect against thermal damage, the motor control often includes an over-temperature sensor. If the motor becomes too hot, the motor control removes power from both windings and ignores any "on" assertion from the appliance control until a reset button on the motor control is pressed and the motor has cooled off.

Add the following to the diagram. Activities: apply power to run winding, apply power to start winding. Conditions: motor is overheated, on is asserted, motor is running. Events: reset.

**5.11** (8) Convert the state diagram that you prepared in the previous exercise into a nested state diagram to take advantage of the commonality between the starting and running state. There is a transition from either the starting or the running state to the off state when "on" is not wanted.

**5.12** (8) There was a single, continuously active input to the control in exercise 5.10. In another common motor control, the user is provided two push buttons, one for "start" and one for "stop." To start the motor, the user depresses the "start" button. The motor continues to run after the "start" button is released. To stop the motor, the "stop" button is pressed. The "stop" button takes precedence over the "start" button so that the motor does not run while both buttons are depressed. If both buttons are depressed and released, whether or not the motor starts depends on the order in which the buttons are released. If the "stop" button is released first, the motor starts. Otherwise the motor does not start. Modify the state diagram that you prepared in exercise 5.10 to accommodate "start" and "stop" buttons.

**5.13** (8) Figure E5.4 is a partially completed, simplified, state diagram for the receiver in a universal asynchronous receiver transmitter (UART). A UART is used to transmit digital information one character at a time over a serial communications link. To simplify the exercise, we have ignored several features of actual UARTs, such as detection of parity, framing, and overrun errors.

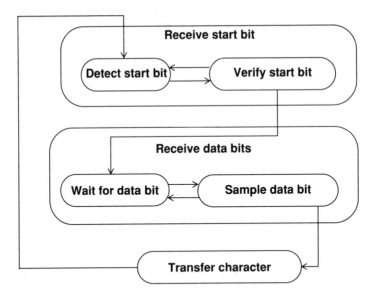

**Figure E5.4** Partially completed state diagram for an asynchronous receiver

Characters are transmitted as a sequence of bits at a fixed and predefined rate. A character consists of a start bit, several data bits, and a stop bit. The number of data bits in a character varies between 5 and 8 and can be set by the user. Within a character, bits are assigned precise time slots. A transmitter sends a 1 or a 0 bit by setting the polarity of its output throughout the time slot for that bit. The receiver decides whether a bit is a 1 or a 0 by sampling it at the center of its time slot. The transmitter sends a start bit at the beginning of each character to resynchronize the receiver. The edge of the start bit triggers the receiver, which then verifies the start bit at the center of the time slot. If it is not the correct polarity at that time, the assumption is that a short pulse of noise falsely triggered the receiver, and it goes back to waiting for a valid start bit. A 0 stop bit is used at the end of a character to separate characters, otherwise a 1 bit at the end of a character could interfere with the detection of the next start bit.

Once a valid start bit is found, the receiver proceeds to assemble bits into a character by sampling them in the centers of their time slots. When all of the bits have been assembled into a character, the receiver transfers it to an interface.

Complete the state diagram in Figure E5.4 with events, actions, activities, etc. The *Transfer character* state is used to move a character from the shift register to a holding register.

**5.14**  (9) Prepare concurrent state diagrams to control the buffered copying of an ASCII file to a personal computer from a remote computer through a UART (see exercise 5.13 for a description of a UART). You may assume that a program has already initiated the transfer from the remote computer and is waiting for data. The program must process interrupts from the UART and from a disk controller. The UART and the disk controller operate independently.

There will be an interrupt from the UART each time it receives a byte. To process the interrupt, the program must check for UART errors and add the byte into a buffer. If there is a UART error, the program must close the file, terminate the transfer and display an error message.

The disk controller generates an interrupt when it is ready for more data. Whenever the disk driver is ready and there is data in the buffer, write a byte to the file.

A special control character is used to signify the end of transmission. When the UART receives this character the program should close the file, terminate the transfer, and display a message that the transfer is complete.

Because the remote computer may send data faster than the disk can handle, the program will need to control the buffer. Whenever the buffer becomes nearly full, the program must send a request to the remote computer to suspend transmission. When the buffer becomes nearly empty, send a request to resume transmission.

**5.15**  (5) Three phase induction motors will spin either clockwise or counterclockwise, depending on the connection to the power lines. In applications requiring motor operation in both directions, two separate contactors (power relays) might be used to make the connections, one for each direction. Also, in some applications of large motors, the motor starts through a transformer that reduces the impact on the power supply. The transformer is bypassed by a third contactor after the motor has been given enough time to come up to speed. There are three momentary control inputs: requests for forward, reverse, or off. When the motor is off, forward or reverse requests cause the motor to start up and run in the requested direction. A reverse request is ignored if the motor is starting or running in the forward direction. and vice versa. An off request at any time shuts the motor off.

Figure E5.5 is a state diagram for one possible motor control. Convert it from a single state diagram into two concurrent state diagrams, one to control the direction of the motor and one for starting control.

**5.16**  (3) The control in the previous exercise does not provide for thermal protection.
  a. Modify the state diagram in Figure E5.5 to shut the motor off if an overheating condition is detected at any time.

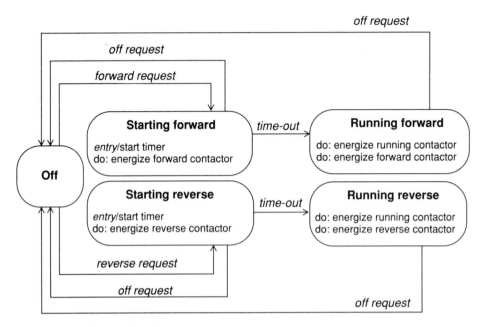

**Figure E5.5**  State diagram for a reduced-voltage-start, reversing,
three phase induction motor control

b. Modify the concurrent state diagrams that you produced in exercise 5.15 to shut the motor off if an overheating condition is detected at any time.

**5.17**  (2) Place the following event classes into a generalization hierarchy with inheritance of event attributes: pick operation, character input, line pick, circle pick, box pick, text pick, event.

**5.18**  (6) Prepare a state diagram for selecting and dragging items with the diagram editor described in exercises 4.2 and 4.7.

A cursor on the diagram tracks a two-button mouse. If the left button is pressed with the cursor on an item (a box or a link), the item is selected, otherwise previously selected items are deselected. Moving the mouse with the left button held down drags any selected items.

**5.19**  (9) A gas-fired, forced hot air, home heating system maintains room temperature and humidity in the winter using distributed controls. The comfort of separate rooms may be controlled somewhat independently. Heat is requested from the furnace for each room based on its measured temperature and the desired temperature for that room. When one or more rooms require heat, the furnace is turned on. When the temperature in the furnace is high enough, a blower on the furnace is turned on to send hot air through heating ducts. If the temperature in the furnace exceeds a safety limit, the furnace is shut off and the blower continues to run. Flappers in the ducts are controlled by the system to deliver heat only to those rooms which need it. When the room(s) no longer requires heat, the furnace is shut off, but the blower continues to deliver hot air until the furnace has cooled off.

Humidity is also maintained based on a strategy involving desired humidity, measured humidity, and outside temperature. The desired humidity is set by the user for the entire home. Humidity of the cool air returning to the blower is measured. When the system determines that the humidity is too low, a humidifier in the furnace is turned on, whenever the blower is on, to inject moisture into the air leaving the blower.

Partition the control of this system into concurrent state machines. Describe the functioning of each state machine without actually going into the details of states, actions, or activities.

**5.20** (7) While exploring an old castle, you and a friend discovered a bookcase that you suspected to be the entrance to a secret passageway. While you examined the bookcase, your friend removed a candle from its holder, only to discover that the candle holder was the entrance control. The bookcase rotated a half turn, pushing you along, separating you from your friend. Your friend put the candle back. This time the bookcase rotated a full turn, still leaving you behind it. Your friend took the candle out. The bookcase started to rotate a full turn again, but this time you stopped it just shy of a full turn by blocking it with your body. Your friend handed you the candle and together you managed to force the bookcase back a half turn, but this left your friend behind it and you in front of it. You put the candle back. As the bookcase began to rotate, you took out the candle, and the bookcase stopped after a quarter turn. You and your friend then entered to explore further.

Develop a state diagram for the control of the bookcase that is consistent with the previous scenario. What should you have done at first to gain entry with the least fuss?

**5.21** (10) Figure E5.6 is a portion of the state diagram for the control of a video cassette recorder (VCR). The VCR has several buttons, including *select*, *on/off*, and *set* for setting the clock and automatic start–stop timers, *auto* for enabling automatic recording, *vcr* for bypassing the VCR, and *timed* for recording for a while. Many of the events in Figure E5.6 correspond to pressing the button with the same name. Several buttons have a toggling behavior. For example, pressing *vcr* toggles between VCR and TV mode. Several buttons used for manual control of the VCR are not accounted for in Figure E5.6 such as *play*, *record*, *fast forward*, *rewind*, *pause*, and *eject*. These buttons are enabled only in the *Manual* state. Do the following:

a. Prepare lists of events, actions, and activities.
b. Prepare a user's manual explaining how to operate the VCR.
c. By adding states, extend the state diagram to accommodate another start–stop timer for a second channel.
d. There is a great deal of commonality in your answer to the previous part. For example, setting the hour may be done in several contexts with similar results. Discuss how duplication of effort could be reduced.

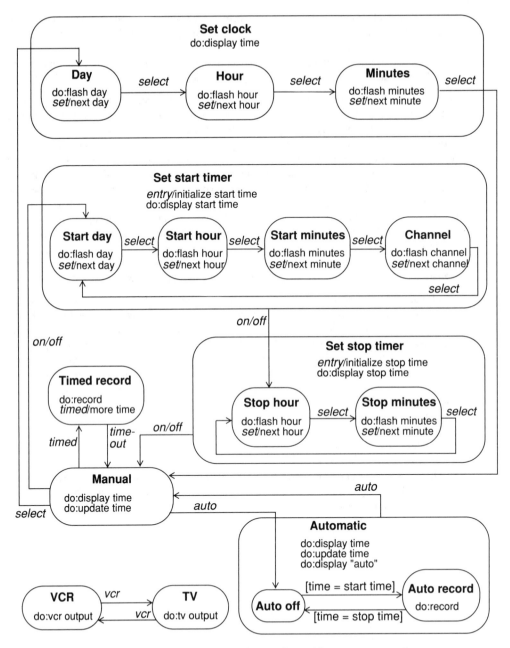

**Figure E5.6** Portion of a state diagram for a video cassette recorder

# 6

---

# Functional Modeling

The functional model describes computations within a system. The functional model is the third leg of the modeling tripod, in addition to the object model and the dynamic model. The functional model specifies what happens, the dynamic model specifies when it happens, and the object model specifies what it happens to.

The functional model shows how output values in a computation are derived from input values, without regard for the order in which the values are computed. The functional model consists of multiple data flow diagrams which show the flow of values from external inputs, through operations and internal data stores, to external outputs. The functional model also includes constraints among values within an object model. Data flow diagrams do not show control or object structure information; these belong to the dynamic and object models. We mainly follow the traditional exposition of data flow diagrams.

## 6.1 FUNCTIONAL MODELS

The functional model specifies the results of a computation without specifying how or when they are computed. The functional model specifies the meaning of the operations in the object model and the actions in the dynamic model, as well as any constraints in the object model. Noninteractive programs, such as compilers, have a trivial dynamic model; their purpose is to compute a function. The functional model is the main model for such programs, although the object model is important for any problem with nontrivial data structures. Many interactive programs also have a significant functional model. By contrast, databases often have a trivial functional model, since their purpose is to store and organize data, not to transform it.

A spreadsheet is a kind of functional model. In most cases, the values in the spreadsheet are trivial and cannot be structured further. The only interesting object structure is the cells in the spreadsheet itself. The purpose of the spreadsheet is to specify values in terms of other values.

A compiler is almost a pure computation. The input is the text of a program in a particular language; the output is an object file that implements the program in another language, often the machine language of a particular computer. The mechanics of compilation are irrelevant to the application.

The tax code is a large functional description. It specifies formulas for computing taxes based on income, expenses, donations, marital status, and so on. The tax code also defines objects (income, deductions) and contains dynamic information (when taxes are due, when estimated taxes are due, when income forms must be sent to employees). A set of tax forms and instructions is an algorithm implementing the functional model. Tax forms specify how to compute taxes based on a set of input values, such as income, expenses, deductions, and withholding. Note that tax forms only provide an algorithm for computing taxes; they do not define the actual tax due function. By contrast, the tax code usually defines the tax due function without specifying the algorithm for computing it. A taxpayer need not fill in the form in the exact sequence given in the instructions to get the correct answer.

## 6.2 DATA FLOW DIAGRAMS

The functional model consists of multiple data flow diagrams which specify the meaning of operations and constraints. A data flow diagram (DFD) shows the functional relationships of the values computed by a system, including input values, output values, and internal data stores. A data flow diagram is a graph showing the flow of data values from their sources in objects through *processes* that transform them to their destinations in other objects. A data flow diagram does not show control information, such as the time at which processes are executed or decisions among alternate data paths; this information belongs to the dynamic model. (Some authors do include control information in DFDs, primarily to show everything on one diagram, but we have broken out the control information into a separate diagram, the state diagram.) A data flow diagram does not show the organization of values into objects; this information belongs to the object model.

A data flow diagram contains *processes* that transform data, *data flows* that move data, *actor* objects that produce and consume data, and *data store* objects that store data passively. Figure 6.1 shows a data flow diagram for the display of an icon on a windowing system. The icon name and location are inputs to the diagram from an unspecified source. The icon is expanded to vectors in the application coordinate system using existing icon definitions. The vectors are clipped to the size of the window, then offset by the location of the window on the screen, to obtain vectors in the screen coordinate system. Finally the vectors are converted to pixel operations that are sent to the screen buffer for display. The data flow diagram shows the sequence of transformations performed, as well as the external values and objects that affect the computation.

### 6.2.1 Processes

A *process* transforms data values. The lowest-level processes are pure functions without side effects. Typical functions include the sum of two numbers, the finance charge on a set of

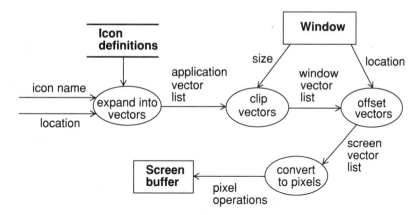

**Figure 6.1** Data flow diagram for windowed graphics display

credit card transactions, and the spline through a list of points. An entire data flow graph is a high-level process. A process may have side effects if it contains nonfunctional components, such as data stores or external objects. The functional model does not uniquely specify the results of a process with side effects. The functional model only indicates the possible functional paths; it does not show which path will actually occur. The results of such a process depend on the behavior of the system, as specified by the dynamic model. Examples of nonfunctional processes include reading and writing files, a voice recognition algorithm that learns from experience, and the display of images within a workstation windowing system.

A process is drawn as an ellipse containing a description of the transformation, usually its name. Each process has a fixed number of input and output data arrows, each of which carries a value of a given type. The inputs and outputs can be labeled to show their role in the computation, but often the type of value on the data flow is sufficient. Figure 6.2 shows two processes. Note that a process can have more than one output. The *display icon* process represents the entire data flow diagram of Figure 6.1 at a higher level of abstraction.

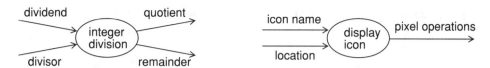

**Figure 6.2** Processes

The diagram only shows the pattern of inputs and outputs. The computation of output values from input values must also be specified. A high-level process can be expanded into an entire data flow diagram, much as a subroutine can be expanded into lower-level subroutines. Eventually the recursion must stop, and the atomic processes must be described directly, in natural language, mathematical equations, or by some other means. For example, "integer division" could be defined mathematically and "display icon" would be defined in terms of Figure 6.1. Frequently the atomic processes are trivial and simply access a value from an object, for example.

Processes are implemented as methods (or method fragments) of operations on object classes. The target object is usually one of the input flows, especially if the same class of object is also an output flow. In some cases, however, the target object is implicit. For example, in Figure 6.2, the target of *display icon* is the window that receives the pixel operations.

### 6.2.2 Data Flows

A *data flow* connects the output of an object or process to the input of another object or process. It represents an intermediate data value within a computation. The value is not changed by the data flow.

A data flow is drawn as an arrow between the producer and the consumer of the data value. The arrow is labeled with a description of the data, usually its name or type. The same value can be sent to several places; this is indicated by a fork with several arrows emerging from it. The output arrows are unlabeled because they represent the same value as the input. Figure 6.3 shows some data flows.

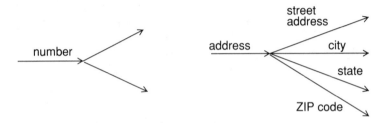

**Figure 6.3** Data flows to copy a value and split an aggregate value

Sometimes an aggregate data value is split into its components, each of which goes to a different process. This is shown by a fork in the path in which each outgoing arrow is labeled with the name of its component. The combination of several components into an aggregate value is just the opposite.

Each data flow represents a value at some point in the computation. The data flows internal to the diagram represent intermediate values within a computation and do not necessarily have any significance in the real world.

Flows on the boundary of a data flow diagram are its inputs and outputs. These flows may be unconnected (if the diagram is a fragment of a complete system), or they may be connected to objects. The inputs of Figure 6.1 are *icon name* and *location*; their sources must be specified in the larger context in which the diagram is used. The outputs of Figure 6.1 are *pixel operations*, which are sent to the screen buffer object. The same inputs and outputs appear in the bottom part of Figure 6.2, in which the entire data flow diagram of Figure 6.1 has been abstracted into a process.

### 6.2.3 Actors

An *actor* is an active object that drives the data flow graph by producing or consuming values. Actors are attached to the inputs and outputs of a data flow graph. In a sense, the actors lie on the boundary of the data flow graph but terminate the flow of data as sources and sinks of data, and so are sometimes called *terminators*. Examples of actors include the user of a program, a thermostat, and a motor under computer control. The actions of the actors are outside the scope of the data flow diagram but should be part of the dynamic model.

An actor is drawn as a rectangle to show that it is an object. Arrows between the actor and the diagram are inputs and outputs of the diagram. The screen buffer in Figure 6.1 is an actor that consumes pixel operations.

## 6.2.4 Data Stores

A *data store* is a passive object within a data flow diagram that stores data for later access. Unlike an actor, a data store does not generate any operations on its own but merely responds to requests to store and access data. A data store allows values to be accessed in a different order than they are generated. Aggregate data stores, such as lists and tables, provide access of data by insertion order or index keys. Sample data stores include a database of airline seat reservations, a bank account, and a list of temperature readings over the past day.

A data store is drawn as a pair of parallel lines containing the name of the store. Input arrows indicate information or operations that modify the stored data; this includes adding elements, modifying values, or deleting elements. Output arrows indicate information retrieved from the store. This includes retrieving the entire value or some component of it. The actual structure of the object must be described in the object model, together with a description of the update and access operations permitted.

Figure 6.4a shows a data store for temperature readings. Every hour a new temperature reading enters the store. At the end of the day, the maximum and minimum reading are retrieved from the store. In addition to introducing delays in the use of data, data stores permit many pieces of data to be accumulated and then used at once.

Figure 6.4b shows a data store for a bank account. The double-headed arrow indicates that *balance* is both an input and an output of the subtraction operation. This could be drawn with two separate arrows, but accessing and updating a value in a data store is a common operation.

Figure 6.4c shows a price list for items. Input to the store consists of pairs of item name and cost values. Later an item is given, and the corresponding cost is found. The unlabeled arrow from the data store to the process indicates that the entire price list is an input to the selection operation. Note that the item name is not an input to the data store during the selection operation because it does not modify the store but merely supplies input to the selection process.

Figure 6.4d shows the periodic table being accessed to find the atomic weight of an element. Obviously the properties of chemical elements are constant and not a variable of the program. It is convenient to represent the operation as a simple access of a *constant data store* object. Such a data store has no inputs.

Both actors and data stores are objects. We distinguish them because their behavior and usage is generally different, although in an object-oriented language they might both be implemented as objects. On the other hand, a data store might be implemented as a file and an actor as an external device. Some data flows are also objects, although in many cases they

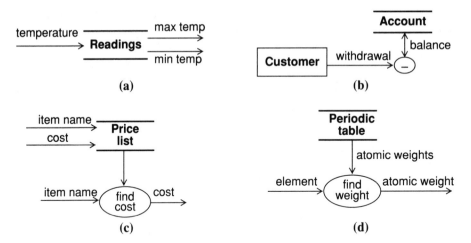

**Figure 6.4** Data stores

are pure values, such as integers, which lack individual identity. (In an object-oriented language, however, objects and pure values are often implemented the same.)

There is a difference between viewing an object as a single value and as a data store containing many values. In Figure 6.5, the customer name selects an account from the bank. The result of this operation is the account object itself, which is then used as a data store in the update operation. A data flow that generates an object used as the target of another operation is indicated by a hollow triangle at the end of the data flow. In contrast, the update operation modifies the balance in the account object, as indicated by the small arrowhead. The hollow triangle indicates a data flow value that subsequently is treated as an object, usually a data store. (This is a new construct that we have introduced. Traditional data flow notation does not adequately represent the dynamic creation or selection of an object for later use in the diagram as an aggregate.)

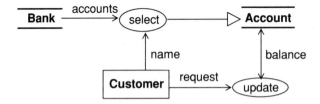

**Figure 6.5** Selection with an object as result

Figure 6.6 shows the creation of a new account in a bank. The result of the *create account* process is a new account, which is stored in the bank. The customer's name and deposit are stored in the account. The account number from the new account is given to the customer. In this example, the account object is viewed both as a data value (stored in the bank) and as a data store (used to store and retrieve values).

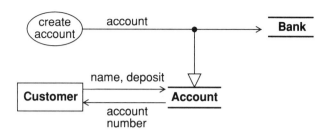

**Figure 6.6** Creation of a new object

## 6.2.5 Nested Data Flow Diagrams

A data flow diagram is particularly useful for showing the high-level functionality of a system and its breakdown into smaller functional units. A process can be expanded into another data flow diagram. Each input and output of the process is an input or output of the new diagram. The new diagram may have data stores that are not shown in the higher-level diagram. The *display icon* process of Figure 6.2 corresponds to the data flow diagram of Figure 6.1. Diagrams can be nested to an arbitrary depth, and the entire set of nested diagrams forms a tree. Nesting of a data flow diagram permits each level to be coherent and understandable yet the overall functionality can be arbitrarily complex. A diagram that references itself represents a recursive computation. (The nesting of diagrams has also been called *leveling,* since the diagrams are organized into different levels.)

Eventually the nesting of diagrams terminates with simple functions. These functions must be specified as operations, to be explained in Section 6.3.

## 6.2.6 Control Flows

A data flow diagram shows all possible computation paths for values; it does not show which paths are executed and in what order. Decisions and sequencing are control issues that are part of the dynamic model. A decision affects whether one or more functions are even performed, rather than supplying a value to the functions. Even though the functions do not have input values from these decision functions, it is sometimes useful to include them in the functional model so that they are not forgotten and so their data dependencies can be shown. This is done by including *control flows* in the data flow diagram.

A control flow is a Boolean value that affects whether a process is evaluated. The control flow is not an input value to the process itself. A control flow is shown by a dotted line from a process producing a Boolean value to the process being controlled.

Figure 6.7 shows a data flow diagram for a withdrawal from a bank account. The customer supplies a password and an amount. The withdrawal occurs only if the password is successfully verified. The update process could be expanded with a similar control flow to guard against overdrafts.

Control flows can occasionally be useful, but they duplicate information in the dynamic model and should be used sparingly.

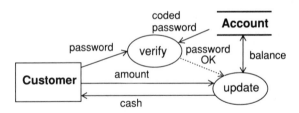

**Figure 6.7** Control flow

## 6.3 SPECIFYING OPERATIONS

Processes in data flow diagrams must eventually be implemented as operations on objects. Each bottom-level, atomic process is an operation. Higher-level processes may also be considered operations, although an implementation may be organized differently from the data flow diagram it represents because of optimization. Each operation may be specified in various ways, including the following:

- mathematical functions, such as trigonometric functions;

- table of input and output values (enumeration) for small finite sets;

- equations specifying output in terms of input;

- pre- and post-conditions (axiomatic definition);

- decision tables;

- pseudocode;

- natural language.

Specification of an operation includes a signature and a transformation. The signature defines the interface to the operation: the arguments it requires (number, order, and types) and the values it returns (number, order, and types). The operation is usually listed in the object model to show the pattern of inheritance; the signature of all methods implementing an operation must match. The transformation defines the effect of an operation: the output values as functions of the input values and the side effects of the operation on its operand objects.

The external specification of an operation only describes changes visible outside the operation. During the implementation of an operation, internal values may be created for convenience or optimization. Some values may even be part of the internal state of an object. For example, a sorted list of values can be implemented using various data structures, such as a linear list or a balanced tree, whose internal organization can be freely changed provided it does not change the external ordering of the list. Such internal details are private to an operation (and possibly to an object class) and do not appear in its external specification. The purpose of the specification is to indicate what an operation must do logically, not how it must be implemented. Therefore the state of the object itself must be divided into externally visible information and private internal information. Changes to the internal state of an object that are not externally visible do not change the value of the object.

*Access operations* are operations that read or write attributes or links of an object. It is unnecessary to list or specify access operations during analysis, since they are trivial. During design, it is necessary to note which access operations will be public and which will be private to the object class. (See Section 1.2.2 for an explanation of analysis and design.) The reason for restricting access is not for reasons of logical correctness but rather to encapsulate classes for protection against bugs and to permit modifications to the implementation in the future. Access operations are derived directly from the attributes and associations of a class in the object model.

Nontrivial operations can be divided into three categories: queries, actions, and activities. A *query* is an operation that has no side effects on the externally visible state of any object; it is a pure function. A query with no parameters (except for the target object) is a *derived attribute*; it has the form (although not necessarily the implementation) of an attribute. For example, if a point is specified in Cartesian coordinates, then the radius and angle are derived attributes. In the object model, query operations can be grouped with attributes, but their derived status should be indicated because they do not contribute additional information to the state of the object. In many cases, the choice of certain attributes as base attributes and others as derived attributes is arbitrary. For example, a point may be expressed in both Cartesian and polar coordinates; neither is more correct. Because query operations have no external effects, they are less important in analyzing and designing a system than base attributes and actions. They can often be specified with equations written in terms of other attributes and do not require a control component. Query operations are derived from paths in the object model or by repackaging data from the object model.

An *action* is a transformation that has side effects on the target object or other objects in the system reachable from the target object. An action has no duration in time; it is logically instantaneous (although any actual implementation will take some time, of course). Because the state of an object is defined by its attributes and links, all actions must be definable in terms of updates to base attributes and links. An action can be defined in terms of the state of the system before and after the action; a control component is unnecessary. For example, the action of scaling a window on a workstation involves scaling the window boundary and all of the contents of the window by a fixed factor. The order in which the scaling is performed is irrelevant to the specification of the action; only the final result matters. Actions are usually derived from processes in the functional model.

Actions can be described in various ways, including mathematical equations, decision trees, decision tables, enumeration of all possible inputs, predicate calculus, and natural language. It is important that a specification be clear and unambiguous, not that it be formal. Figure 6.8 shows the specification for a telephone switcher connecting a call. There are several elements of a specification: the function name, the inputs and outputs, the transformations to values, and the constraints that must be observed. Note that no algorithm for determining connections is given. The specification is informal and still ambiguous. For example, the topology of the network must be specified in more detail. Nevertheless, this will do for an initial top-level specification.

One way of specifying an action is to give an algorithm (English, pseudocode, or actual code) for computing it. Frequently a simple but inefficient algorithm for a function is easy to define. This does not imply that the program must use the same algorithm, only that the results be identical, although proving that two algorithms yield the same result can be diffi-

---

**Function**: connect call

**Inputs**: phone line, number dialed, current settings of switches

**Outputs**: new settings of switches, connection status

**Transformation**: Connect the calling phone to the dialed phone by closing connections in the switcher, observing the following constraints:

**Constraints**: Only two lines are a time may be connected on any one circuit.

Previous connections must not be disturbed.

If the called line is already in use, then no switches are closed, and the status is reported as busy.

If a connection is impossible because too many switches are in use, then no switches are closed, and the status is reported as switcher busy.

---

**Figure 6.8** Action for telephone switcher connection

cult. Some functions can be specified in ways that do not provide a basis for an algorithm, even an inefficient one. For example, the inverse of a matrix A is defined as "that matrix B such that A times B yields the identity matrix." Matrix multiplication is easily defined, but deriving an algorithm to compute the inverse requires a considerable amount of linear algebra. Supplying an algorithm is part of design.

An *activity* is an operation to or by an object that has duration in time, as opposed to queries and actions, which are considered as instantaneous (logically, if not actually). An activity inherently has side effects because of its extension in time. Activities only make sense for actors, objects that generate operations on their own, because passive objects are mere data repositories. An operating system demon, such as an output spooler, is considered an actor because it has an active role in controlling the flow of information. The details of an activity are specified by the dynamic model as well as the functional model and cannot be considered just as a transformation. In most cases, an activity corresponds to a state diagram in the dynamic model.

## 6.4 CONSTRAINTS

A *constraint* shows the relationship between two objects at the same time (such as frequency and wavelength) or between different values of the same object at different times (such as the number of outstanding shares of the mutual fund). A constraint may be expressed as a total function (one value is completely specified by another) or a partial function (one value is restricted, but not completed specified, by another). For example, a coordinate transformation might specify that the scale factor for the x-coordinate and the y-coordinate will be equal; this constraint totally defines one value in terms of the other. The Second Law of Thermodynamics expresses a partial constraint; it states that the entropy (disorder) of the Universe can never decrease.

Constraints can appear in each of the kinds of model. Object constraints specify that some objects depend entirely or partially on other objects. Dynamic constraints specify relationships among the states or events of different objects. Functional constraints specify restrictions on operations, such as the scaling transformation described above.

A constraint between values of an object over time is often called an *invariant*. Conservation laws in physics are invariants: The total energy, or charge, or angular momentum of a system remains constant. Invariants are useful in specifying the behavior of operations.

## 6.5 A SAMPLE FUNCTIONAL MODEL

In this section, we describe the functional model for a flight simulator. The simulator is responsible for handling pilot input controls, computing the motion of the airplane, computing and displaying the outside view from the cockpit window, and displaying the cockpit gauges. The simulator is intended to be an accurate but simplified model of flying an airplane, ignoring some of the smaller effects and making some simplifying assumptions. For example, we omit the rudder, under the assumption that it is held so as to keep the plane pointing in the direction of motion. Figure 6.9 shows the top-level data flow diagram for the flight simulator. There are two input actors: the *Pilot*, who operates the airplane controls, and the *Weather*, which varies according to some specified pattern. There is one output actor: the *Screen*, which displays the pilot's view. There are two read-only data stores: the *Terrain database*, which specifies the geometry of the surrounding terrain as a set of colored polygonal surfaces, and the *Cockpit database*, which specifies the shape and location of the cockpit viewport and the locations of the various gauges. There are three internal data stores: *Spatial parameters*, which holds the 3-D position, velocity, orientation, and rotation of the plane; *Fuel*, which holds the amount of fuel remaining; and *Weight*, which holds the total weight of the plane (consumption of fuel causes the weight to decrease). The initialization of the internal data stores is necessary but is not shown on the data flow diagram.

The processes in the diagram can be divided into three kinds: handling controls, motion computation, and display generation. The control handling processes are *adjust controls*, which transforms the position of the pilot's controls (such as joysticks) into positions of the airplane control surfaces and engine speed; *consume fuel*, which computes fuel consumption as a function of engine speed; and *compute weight*, which computes the weight of the airplane as the sum of the base weight and the weight of the remaining fuel. Process *adjust controls* is expanded on Figure 6.10, where it can be seen as comprising three distinct controls: the elevator, the ailerons, and the throttle. There is no need to expand these processes further, as they can be described by input-output functions (we do not attempt to specify them here).

The motion computation processes are *compute forces*, which computes the various forces and torques on the plane and sums them to determine the net acceleration and the rotational torques, and *integrate motion*, which integrates the differential equations of motion. Process *compute forces* incorporates both geometrical and aeronautical computations. It is expanded on Figure 6.11. Net force is computed as the vector sum of drag, lift, thrust, and

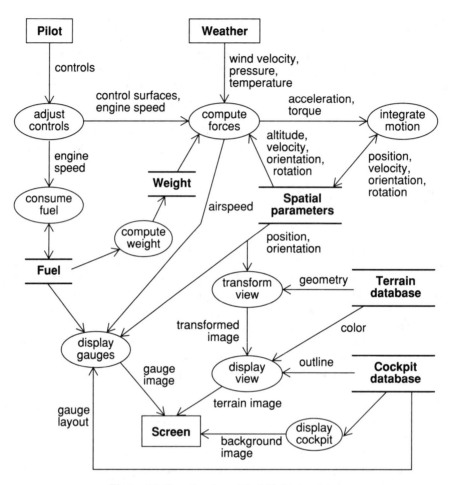

**Figure 6.9** Functional model of flight simulator

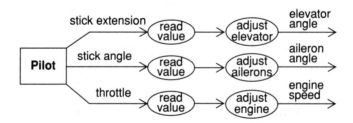

**Figure 6.10** Expansion of *adjust controls* process

weight. These forces in turn depend on intermediate parameters, such as airspeed, angle of attack, and air density. The aerodynamic calculations must be made relative to the air mass, so the wind velocity is subtracted from the plane's velocity to give the airspeed relative to

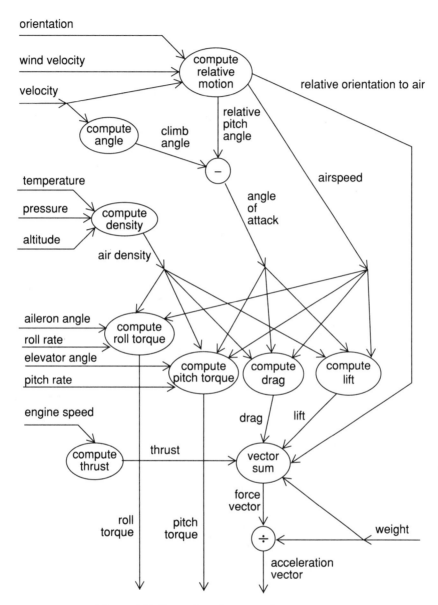

**Figure 6.11** Expansion of *compute forces* processes

the air mass; the orientation of the plane must be transformed also. Air density is also computed and used in subsequent processes. The intermediate parameters are computed in terms of data store parameters, such as airplane velocity, orientation, rotation rates roll rate and pitch rate, and altitude, obtained from *Spatial parameters*; wind velocity, temperature, and pressure, obtained from *Weather*; weight, obtained from *Weight*; and in terms of output data flows from other processes, such as elevator angle, aileron angle, and engine speed, obtained

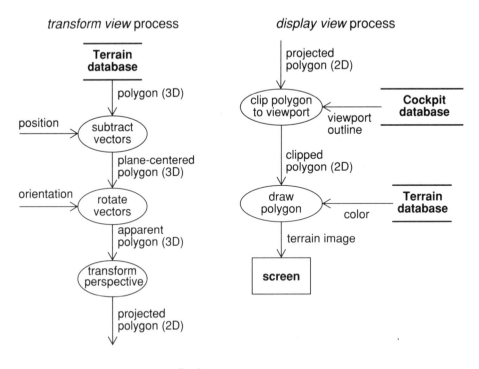

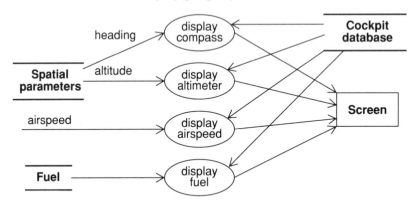

**Figure 6.12** Expansion of display processes

from process *adjust controls*. The internal processes, such as *compute drag, compute lift,* and *compute density*, would be specified by aeronautical formulas and look-up tables for the specific airplane. For example, *compute lift* is specified by the equation $L = C(\alpha)S\rho V^2/2$, where L is lift, $\alpha$ is the angle of attack, S is the wing area, $\rho$ is the air density, V is the airspeed, and C is the coefficient of lift as a function of angle of attack, specified by a table for the particular kind of wing. Process *integrate motion* is the solution to the differential equations of motion. It is easy to specify, but its implementation involves careful numerical analysis considerations.

The display processes are *transform view, display view, display gauges,* and *display cockpit.* These processes convert the airplane parameters and terrain into a simulated view on the screen. They are expanded on Figure 6.12. Process *transform view* transforms the coordinates of a set of polygons in the *Terrain database* into the pilot's coordinate system, by first offsetting them by the plane's position, rotating the polygons by the plane's orientation, and then transforming the polygons' perspective onto the viewing plane to produce a 2-D image in the pilot's eye view. The position and orientation of the plane are input parameters. Process *display view* clips the image of the transformed polygons to remain within the output of the cockpit viewport, whose shape is specified in a *Cockpit database.* The clipped 2-D polygons are drawn on the screen using the colors specified in the *Terrain database.* Process *display gauges* displays various airplane parameters as gauges, using locations specified in the cockpit database. Process *display cockpit* displays a fixed image of the stationary parts of the cockpit and needed not be expanded.

Note that the functional model does not specify when, why, and how often values are computed. In a simulation such as this one, the motion integration might be performed more often than view computation because integration is subject to cumulative errors if too large an interval is used. Other computations can be omitted by sorting data cleverly. A smart view-mapping algorithm would quickly eliminate most of the terrain polygons using crude direction or distance checks so that only a few polygons would require costly full transformations and visibility checks. The set of active polygons would have to be updated occasionally as the plane moves, but hopefully not too often. Such considerations are part of the implementation algorithm but do not show up in the data flow diagram, which shows the underlying flow of data and computations but not the control decisions added by an implementation.

## 6.6 RELATION OF FUNCTIONAL TO OBJECT AND DYNAMIC MODELS

The functional model shows what "has to be done" by a system. The leaf processes are the operations on objects. The object model shows the "doers"—the objects. Each process is implemented by a method on some object. The dynamic model shows the sequences in which the operations are performed. Each sequence is implemented as a sequence, loop, or alternation of statements within some method. The three models come together in the implementation of methods. The functional model is a guide to the methods.

The processes in the functional model correspond to operations in the object model. Often there is a direct correspondence at each level of nesting. A top-level process corresponds to an operation on a complex object, and lower-level processes correspond to operations on more basic objects that are part of the complex object or that implement it. Sometimes one process corresponds to several operations, and sometimes one operation corresponds to several processes.

Processes in the functional model show objects that are related by function. Often one of the inputs to a process can be identified as the target object, with the rest being parameters to the operation. The target object is a *client* of the other objects (called *suppliers)* because it uses them in performing the operation. The target knows about the clients, but the clients do not necessarily know about the target. The target object class is dependent on the argument classes for its operations. The client-supplier relationship establishes implementation dependencies among classes; the clients are implemented in terms of, and are therefore dependent on, the supplier classes.

A process is usually implemented as a method. If the same class of object is an input and an output, then the object is usually the target, and the other inputs are arguments. If the output of the process is a data store, the data store is the target. If an input of the process is a data store, the data store is the target. Frequently a process with an input from or output to a data store corresponds to two methods, one of them being an implicit selection or update of the data store. If an input or output is an actor, then it is the target. If an input is an object and an output is a part of the object or a neighbor of the object in the object model, then the object is the target. If an output object is created out of input parts, then the process represents a class method. If none of these rules apply, then the target is often implicit and is not one of the inputs or outputs. Often the target of a process is the target of the entire subdiagram. For example, in Figure 6.9, the target of *compute forces* is actually the airplane itself. Data stores *weight* and *spatial parameters* are simply components of the airplane accessed during the process.

Actors are explicit objects in the object model. Data flows to or from actors represent operations on or by the objects. The data flow values are the arguments or results of the operations. Because actors are "self-motivated" objects, the functional model is not sufficient to indicate when they act. The dynamic model for an actor object specifies when it acts.

Data stores are also objects in the object model, or at least fragments of objects, such as attributes. Each flow into a data store is an update operation. Each flow out of a data store is a query operation, with no side effects on the data store object. Data stores are passive objects that respond to queries and updates, so the dynamic model of the data store is irrelevant to its behavior. The dynamic model of the actors in a diagram is necessary to determine the order of operations.

Data flows are values in the object model. Many data flows are simply pure values, such as numbers, strings, or lists of pure values. Pure values can be modeled as classes and implemented as objects in most languages, but they do not have identity. A pure value is not a container whose value can change but just the value itself. A pure value therefore has no state and no dynamic model. Operations on pure values yield other pure values and have no side effects. Arithmetic operations are examples of such operations.

Other data flows represent normal objects. The selection data flow notation of Figure 6.5 explicitly produces a data store object to be operated on by other flows. Some input data flows to processes represent objects that are the targets of the processes. For example, the polygons in the top half of Figure 6.12 are the targets of several operations. In the object model, class *polygon* would have operations *subtract position, rotate, transform perspective,* and *clip to viewport.* In still other cases, a data flow represents an object that remains encapsulated; it is created by one process and passed through to another without change. Such data flows represent arguments to operations, rather than targets. For example, in Figure 6.6, the input *account* to *bank* is an object that is stored within *bank* without being operated on; the same object is treated as a target object with respect to deposits from the customer.

Relative to the functional model: The object model shows the structure of the actors, data stores, and flows in the functional model. The dynamic model shows the sequence in which processes are performed.

Relative to the object model: The functional model shows the operations on the classes and the arguments of each operation. It therefore shows the supplier-client relationship among classes. The dynamic model shows the states of each object and the operations that are performed as it receives events and changes state.

Relative to the dynamic model: The functional model shows the definitions of the leaf actions and activities that are undefined with the dynamic model. The object model shows what changes state and undergoes operations.

## 6.7 CHAPTER SUMMARY

The functional model shows a computation and the functional derivation of the data values in it without indicating how, when, or why the values are computed. The dynamic model controls which operations are performed and the order in which they are applied. The object model defines the structure of values that the operations operate on. For batch-like computations, such as compilers or numerical computations, the functional model is the primary model, but in large systems all three models are important.

Data flow diagrams show the relationship between values in a computation. A data flow diagram is a graph of processes, data flows, data stores, and actors. Processes transform data values. Low-level processes are simple operations on single objects, but higher-level processes can contain internal data stores subject to side effects. A data flow diagram is a process. Data flows relate values on processes, data stores, and actors. Actors are independent objects that produce and consume values. Data stores are passive objects that break the flow of control by introducing delays between the creation and the use of data. As a rule, control information should be shown in the dynamic model and not the functional model, although control flows in data flow diagrams are occasionally useful.

Data flow diagrams can be nested hierarchically, but ultimately the leaf processes must be specified directly as operations. Operations can be specified by a variety of means, including mathematical equations, tables, and constraints between the inputs and outputs. An operation can be specified by pseudocode, but a specification does not imply a particular implementation; it may be implemented by a different algorithm that yields equivalent results. Operations have signatures that specify their external interface and transformations that specify their effects. Queries are operations without side effects; they can be implemented as pure functions. Actions are operations with side effects but without duration; they can be implemented as procedures. Activities are operations with side effects and duration; they must be implemented as tasks. Operations can be attached to classes within the object model and implemented as methods.

Constraints specify additional relationships that must be maintained between values in the object model. Invariants specify that some functions of values remain constant over time.

The object model, dynamic model, and functional model all involve the same concepts, namely data, sequencing, and operations, but each model focuses on a particular aspect and leaves the other aspects uninterpreted. All three models are necessary for a full understanding of a problem, although the balance of importance among the models varies according to the kind of application. The three models come together in the implementation of methods, which involve data (target object, arguments, and variables), control (sequencing constructs), and operations (calls, expressions, and data access). Data flow diagrams are particularly useful for showing the high-level functionality of a system and for showing complex transformations with multiple inputs, outputs, and intermediate values.

| | | |
|---|---|---|
| action | data flow diagram | nested data flow diagram |
| activity | data store | operation |
| actor | derived attribute | process |
| client | function | query |
| constraint | functional model | signature |
| control flow | invariant | terminator |
| data flow | leveling | |

**Figure 6.13** Key concepts for Chapter 6

## BIBLIOGRAPHIC NOTES

Data flow diagrams are the primary modeling construct in a number of traditional software development methodologies. Many readers will be familiar with these concepts from previous work. [Yourdon-89] presents the classic exposition of the leading traditional methodology, including an explanation of data flow diagrams. [DeMarco-79] and [Gane-78] are earlier pioneering books in the area. [Ward-86] adds control concepts to the standard data flow diagram notation. Engineers commonly use several equivalent data flow notations, such as signal processing diagrams. PERT charts are another familiar example, albeit with some additional semantics.

## REFERENCES

[DeMarco-79] Tom DeMarco. *Structured Analysis and Systems Specification.* Englewood Cliffs, New Jersey: Prentice Hall, 1979.

[Gane-78] Chris Gane and Trish Sarson. *Structured Systems Analysis: Tools and Techniques.* Englewood Cliffs, New Jersey: Prentice Hall, 1978.

[Ward-86] Paul Ward and Steve Mellor. *Structured Development of Real-Time Systems.* Englewood Cliffs, New Jersey: Yourdon Press, 1986.

[Yourdon-89] Edward Yourdon. *Modern Structured Analysis.* Englewood Cliffs, New Jersey: Yourdon Press, 1989.

## EXERCISES

**6.1**   (2) Describe the meaning of the data flow diagram in Figure E6.1.

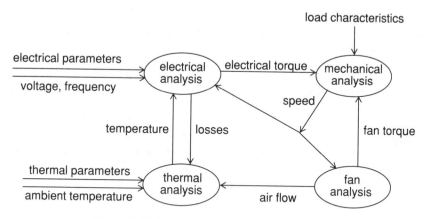

**Figure E6.1**  Data flow diagram of motor analysis

**6.2**   (6) Figure E6.1 cannot be considered a description of how to actually compute the performance of a motor because it contains circular dependencies. For example, electrical analysis uses speed as an input and computes electrical torque. Mechanical analysis uses electrical torque as an input in computing speed. Suppose you were given four subroutines that performed the computations involved in each of the four processes. Each subroutine computes the outputs of the associated process from the inputs. Discuss how to compute the temperature of a motor in view of the circular dependencies.

**6.3**   (6) Prepare a data flow diagram for computing the net score for a trial in judged athletic competitions that describes the following method. Each attempt of a competitor in an event is observed by several judges. Each judge rates the attempt and holds up a score. A reader assigned to the group of judges announces the scores one at a time to a panel of scorekeepers. Three scorekeepers write the scores down, cross off the highest and the lowest scores, and total up the rest. They check each other's total to detect errors in recording and/or arithmetic. In some cases, they may ask the reader to repeat the scores. When they are satisfied, they hand their figures to three other scorekeepers who multiply the total score by a difficulty factor for the event and take the average to determine a net score. The net scores are compared to detect and correct scoring errors.

**6.4**   (3) Prepare a data flow diagram for computing the volume and surface area of a cylinder. Inputs are the height and radius of the cylinder. Outputs are volume and surface area. Discuss several ways of implementing the data flow diagram.

**6.5**   (6) Prepare a data flow diagram for computing the mean of a sequence of input values. A separate control input is provided to reset the computation. Each time a new value is input, the mean of all values input since the last reset command should be output. Since you have no way of knowing how many values will be processed between resets, the amount of data storage that you use should not depend on the number of input values. Detail your diagram down to the level of multiplications, divisions, and additions.

**6.6**   (3) Using the quadratic formula as a starting point, prepare a data flow diagram for computing the roots of the quadratic equation $ax^2 + bx + c = 0$. Real numbers, a, b and c are inputs. Outputs are values of x = R1 and x = R2, which satisfy the equation. Remember, R1 and R2 may be real or complex, depending on the values of a, b, and c. The quadratic formula for R1 and R2 is $(-b \pm SQRT(b^2 - 4ac))/(2a)$.

**6.7**   (6) Some types of computer architectures perform arithmetic quickly but are slow at performing control branching. On these machines, computation time may be reduced in some cases by avoiding the use of conditions, which may be eliminated by converting them into calculations. For example, suppose that it is desired to compute the function y = Y(x) without using a condition, where Y(x) is defined conditionally as Y(x) = F(x) when x is positive and Y(x) = G(x) otherwise, with both F(x) and G(x) given. The two statements may be combined into a single calculation, $Y(x) = SIGN(x) \times F(x) + (1 - SIGN(x)) \times G(x)$, where $SIGN(x) = 1$ if $x > 0$, else $SIGN(x) = 0$. ($SIGN(x)$ could be itself computed or provided by the hardware.)

   a.  Using if statements, express an algorithm for computing the following real periodic function $T(x)$ for all real values of $x$: For a portion of the domain of $T(x)$, $-3 < x \le 3$, $T(x)$ can be described as 3+x for $-3 < x \le -2$, as $-x-1$ for $-2 < x \le -1$, as 1+x for $-1 < x \le 0$, as 1–x for $0 < x \le 1$, as x–1 for $1 < x \le 2$ and as 3–x for $2 < x \le 3$.

   b.  Sketch the function $T(x)$ for $-5 < x < 5$.

   c.  Using the $SIGN(x)$ function, prepare a data flow diagram for $T(x)$ that uses only functions and arithmetic.

**6.8**   (8) Figure E6.2 is an object diagram for a simple diagram editor. Prepare a data flow diagram showing how cutting and pasting works. Refer to exercise 4.7 for a synopsis of some operations.

**6.9**   (7) A data flow diagram expresses functional dependencies. The outputs of each process are functionally dependent on the inputs to the process. For example, in Figure E6.1, losses depend on electrical parameters, voltage, frequency, temperature, and speed. Air flow depends only on speed.

   a.  Prepare an object diagram (metamodel) that could be used to represent functional dependencies.

   b.  A graph of processes and data flows represents a partial ordering of the processes. Describe an operation whose inputs are processes and data flows and whose output is an ordered list of processes. Each process in the list does not require the outputs of any process later on in the list.

   c.  Place the following processes in a partial order, and also prepare a data flow diagram. If an input to a process is not listed as the output of another process, you may assume it comes from an actor or from a data store.
   Process: p1; Inputs: in1, in2; Outputs: d1, d2;
   Process: p2; Inputs: d1, d3, d4; Outputs: d7;
   Process: p3; Inputs: in3, in4; Outputs: d4, d5;
   Process: p4; Inputs: d2, d5; Outputs: d6;
   Process: p5; Inputs: d6, d7; Outputs: out;
   Process: p6; Inputs: in5, in6; Outputs: d3;

**6.10**  (3) There is a clear distinction between the definition and the implementation of a function. The definition describes the behavior of the function while the implementation actually computes the function. The definition of a function may be used to test the accuracy of the implementation.

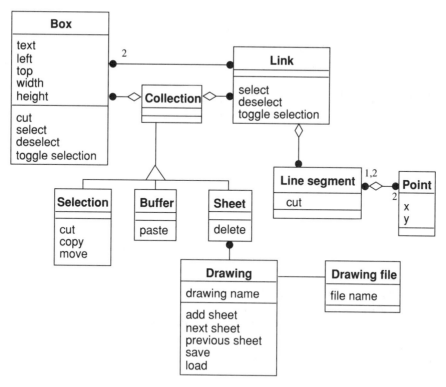

**Figure E6.2**   Object diagram used by an interactive editor of simple diagrams

Prepare definitions of each of the following functions using mathematics, diagrams, or pre- and post-conditions.
a.  absolute value
b.  trigonometric sine
c.  natural logarithm
d.  square root

**6.11**   (4) Write pseudocode to implement each of the functions in the previous exercise. You may wish to refer to a book on numerical analysis. Describe the accuracy of your implementations.

# PART 2: DESIGN METHODOLOGY

# 7

# Methodology Preview

Part 1 of this book presents OMT *concepts*, specifically the concepts and notation for the object, dynamic, and functional models. We now shift our focus in Part 2 and discuss the *process* for devising the three OMT models. Part 1 discusses *what constitutes* a model; Part 2 explains *how to* formulate a model. Our treatment in Part 2 of this book is language-independent and applies equally well to object-oriented languages, traditional procedural languages, and databases. Part 3 shows how this generic design maps to specific implementation targets.

## 7.1 OMT AS A SOFTWARE ENGINEERING METHODOLOGY

A *software engineering methodology* is a process for the organized production of software, using a collection of predefined techniques and notational conventions. A methodology is usually presented as a series of steps, with techniques and notation associated with each step. The concepts and notations that support the OMT methodology have been presented in Part 1 of this book. The steps of software production are usually organized into a life cycle consisting of several phases of development. The complete software life cycle spans from initial formulation of the problem, through analysis, design, implementation, and testing of the software, followed by an operational phase during which maintenance and enhancement are performed.

The OMT methodology supports the entire software life cycle. This book covers life cycle phases from problem formulation through requirements analysis, design, and implementation. This book does not cover testing and maintenance. Both testing and maintenance are simplified by an object-oriented approach, but the traditional methods used in these phases are not significantly altered. However, an object-oriented approach produces a clean, well-understood design that is easier to test, maintain, and extend than non-object-oriented designs because the object classes provide a natural unit of modularity.

Some software developers prefer a rapid prototyping approach, whereby a small portion of the software is initially developed and evaluated through use. The software is gradually made robust through incremental improvements to the specification, design, and implementation. In contrast, with the life cycle approach, software is fully specified, fully designed, then fully implemented.

Other authors have made various arguments for and against the merits of rapid prototyping. These arguments do not concern us here, since the OMT methodology applies equally well in either case. The notion of objects provides a solid basis for specifying, designing, and implementing software in one pass, or gradually building software through multiple passes. Object-oriented software development is anchored to real-world objects; software objects can easily assume additional behavior associated with their real-world counterparts. In contrast, rapid prototyping is more difficult with function-based software development, since a functional breakdown suitable for a prototype may not be suitable for a full implementation.

## 7.2 THE OMT METHODOLOGY

The OMT methodology consists of several phases:

*Analysis* (Chapter 8) is concerned with understanding and modeling the application and the domain within which it operates. The initial input to the analysis phase is a problem statement which describes the problem to be solved and provides a conceptual overview of the proposed system. Subsequent dialogue with the customer and real-world background knowledge are additional inputs to analysis. The output from analysis is a formal model that captures the three essential aspects of the system: the objects and their relationships, the dynamic flow of control, and the functional transformation of data subject to constraints.

The overall architecture of the system is determined during *System Design* (Chapter 9). Using the object model as a guide, the system is organized into subsystems. Concurrency is organized by grouping objects into concurrent tasks. Overall decisions are made about interprocess communication, data storage, and implementation of the dynamic model. Priorities are established for making design trade-offs.

During the *Object Design* phase (Chapter 10), the analysis models are elaborated, refined, and then optimized to produce a practical design. During object design there is a shift in emphasis from application concepts towards computer concepts. First the basic algorithms are chosen to implement each major function of the system. Based on these algorithms, the structure of the object model is then optimized for efficient implementation. The design must also account for concurrency and dynamic control flow as determined during system design. The implementation of each association and attribute is determined. Finally, the subsystems are packaged into modules.

Chapter 11 summarizes the OMT methodology presented in Chapters 8, 9, and 10. Chapter 12 compares the OMT methodology with other software engineering methodologies.

## 7.3 IMPACT OF AN OBJECT-ORIENTED APPROACH

The OMT methodology is an object-oriented software construction approach which differs from traditional software development approaches. These differences affect the process of software development, and ultimately the software product, itself.

*Shifting of development effort into analysis.* An object-oriented approach moves much of the software development effort up to the analysis phase of the life cycle. It is sometimes disconcerting to spend more time during analysis and design, but this extra effort is more than compensated by faster and simpler implementation. Because the resulting design is cleaner and more adaptable, future changes are much easier.

*Emphasis on data structure before function.* An object-oriented approach focuses attention on data structure instead of the functions to be performed. This change of emphasis gives the development process a more stable base and allows the use of a single unifying software concept throughout the process: the concept of an object. All other concepts, such as functions, relationships, and events, are organized around objects so that information recorded during analysis is not lost or transformed when design and implementation take place.

The data structures of an application and the relationships between them are much less vulnerable to changing requirements than the operations performed on the data. Organizing a system around objects rather than around functions gives the development process a stability that is lacking in function-oriented approaches. Encapsulated objects, with public interfaces that hide their private internal implementation, are further protected from the effects of change.

*Seamless development process.* Because an object-oriented approach defines a set of problem-oriented objects early in the project and continues to use and extend these objects throughout the development cycle, the separation of life cycle phases is much less distinct. In the Object Modeling Technique, the object model developed during analysis is used for design and implementation, and work is channeled into refining the model at progressively more detailed levels rather than converting from one representation into another. The process is seamless because there are no discontinuities in which a notation at one phase is replaced by a different notation at another phase.

*Iterative rather than sequential.* Although the description of the Object Modeling Technique is of necessity linear, the actual development process is iterative. The seamlessness of object-oriented development makes it easier to repeat the development steps at progressively finer levels of detail. Each iteration adds or clarifies features rather than modifies work that has already been done, so there is less chance of introducing inconsistencies and errors.

## 7.4 CHAPTER SUMMARY

A software engineering methodology consists of a process for organized development based on a set of coordinated techniques. The OMT methodology is based on the development of a three-part model of the system, which is then refined and optimized to constitute a design. The object model captures the objects in the system and their relationships. The dynamic model describes the reaction of objects in the system to events, and the interactions between objects. The functional model specifies the transformations of object values and constraints on these transformations. The Object Modeling Technique produces systems that are more stable with respect to changes in requirements than traditional function-oriented approaches.

| | |
|---|---|
| analysis | object design |
| impact of OO methodology | OMT methodology |
| life cycle | system design |

**Figure 7.1** Key concepts for Chapter 7

## EXERCISES

**7.1**   (2) "It seems there is never enough time to do a job right the first time, but there is always time to do it over." Discuss how the methodology presented in this chapter overcomes this tendency of human behavior. What kinds of errors do you make if you rush into the implementation phase of a software project? Compare the relative effort required to prevent errors with that needed to detect and correct them.

**7.2**   (5) This book explains how to use object–oriented techniques to implement programs and data-bases. Discuss how object–oriented techniques could be applied in other arenas, such as language design, knowledge representation, and hardware design, for example.

# 8

# Analysis

*Analysis,* the first step of the OMT methodology, is concerned with devising a precise, concise, understandable, and correct model of the real-world. Before building anything complex, such as a house, a computer program, or a hardware-software system, the builder must understand the requirements and the real-world environment in which it will exist.

The purpose of object-oriented analysis is to model the real-world system so that it can be understood. To do this, you must examine requirements, analyze their implications, and restate them rigorously. You must abstract important real-world features first and defer small details until later. The successful analysis model states what must be done, without restricting how it is done, and avoids implementation decisions. The result of analysis should be understanding the problem as a preparation for design.

In this chapter you will learn how to take the concepts discussed in Part 1 of this book and apply them to construct a formal and rigorous model of the real-world problem. This real-world model consists of the object, dynamic, and functional models. The analysis model serves several purposes: It clarifies the requirements, it provides a basis for agreement between the software requestor and the software developer, and it becomes the framework for later design and implementation.

## 8.1 OVERVIEW OF ANALYSIS

As shown in Figure 8.1, analysis begins with a problem statement generated by clients and possibly the developers. The statement may be incomplete or informal; analysis makes it more precise and exposes ambiguities and inconsistencies. The problem statement should not be taken as immutable but should serve as a basis for refining the real requirements.

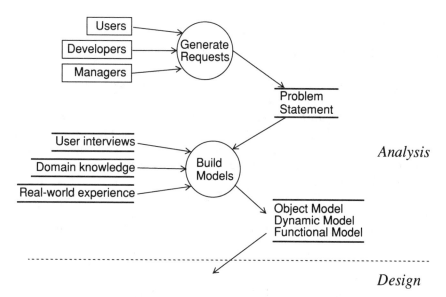

**Figure 8.1** Overview of analysis process

Next, the real-world system described by the problem statement must be understood, and its essential features abstracted into a model. Statements in natural language are often ambiguous, incomplete, and inconsistent. The analysis model is a precise, concise representation of the problem that permits answering questions and building a solution. Subsequent design steps refer to the analysis model, rather than the original vague problem statement. Perhaps even more important, the process of constructing a rigorous model of the problem domain forces the developer to confront misunderstandings early in the development process while they are still easy to correct.

The analysis model addresses the three aspects of objects: static structure (object model), sequencing of interactions (dynamic model), and data transformations (functional model). All three submodels are not equally important in every problem. Almost all problems have useful object models derived from real-world entities. Problems concerning interactions and timing, such as user interfaces and process control, have important dynamic models. Problems containing significant computation, such as compilers and engineering calculations, have important functional models. All three submodels contribute operations which are summarized on the object model.

Analysis cannot always be carried out in a rigid sequence. Large models are built up iteratively. First a subset of the model is constructed, then extended, until the complete problem is understood.

Analysis is not a mechanical process. Most problem statements lack essential information, which must be obtained from the requestor or from the analyst's knowledge of the real-world problem domain. The analyst must communicate with the requestor to clarify ambiguities and misconceptions. The analysis models facilitate precise communication.

## 8.2 PROBLEM STATEMENT

The first step in developing anything is to state the requirements. This applies just as much to leading-edge research as to simple programs and to personal programs, as well as to large team efforts. Being vague about your objective only postpones decisions to a later stage where changes are much more costly.

As summarized in Figure 8.2, the problem statement should state what is to be done and not how it is to be done. It should be a statement of needs, not a proposal for a solution. A user manual for the desired system is a good problem statement. The requestor should indicate which features are mandatory and which are optional, to avoid overly constraining design decisions. The requestor should avoid describing system internals, as this restricts implementation flexibility. Performance specifications and protocols for interaction with external systems are legitimate requirements. Software engineering standards, such as modular construction, design for testability, and provision for future extensions, are also proper.

| Requirements Statement | Design & Implementation |
|---|---|
| • Problem scope | • General approach |
| • What is needed | • Algorithms |
| • Application context | • Data structures |
| • Assumptions | • Architecture |
| • Performance needs | • Optimizations |

**Figure 8.2**  Overview of analysis process

Many problem statements, from individuals, companies, and government agencies, mix true requirements with design decisions. There may sometimes be a compelling reason to require a particular computer or language; there is rarely justification to specify the use of a particular algorithm. The analyst must separate the true requirements from design and implementation decisions disguised as requirements. The analyst should challenge such pseudorequirements, as they restrict flexibility. There may be political or organizational reasons for the pseudorequirements, but at least the analyst should recognize that these externally imposed design decisions are not essential features of the problem domain.

A problem statement may have more or less detail. A requirement for a conventional product, such as a payroll program or a billing system, may have considerable detail. A requirement for a research effort in a new area may lack many details, but presumably the research has some objective, which should be clearly stated.

Most problem statements are ambiguous, incomplete, or even inconsistent. Some requirements are just plain wrong. Some requirements, although precisely stated, have unpleasant consequences on the system behavior or impose unreasonable implementation costs. Some requirements seem reasonable at first but do not work out as well as the requestor thought. The problem statement is just a starting point for understanding the problem, not an immutable document. The purpose of the subsequent analysis is to fully understand the problem and its implications. There is no reason to expect that a problem statement prepared without a full analysis will be correct.

The analyst must work with the requestor to refine the requirements so they represent the requestor's true intent. This involves challenging the requirements and probing for missing information. The psychological, organizational, and political considerations of doing this are beyond the scope of this book, except for the following piece of advice: If you do exactly what the customer asked for, but the result does not meet the customer's real needs, you will probably be blamed anyway.

## 8.3 AUTOMATED TELLER MACHINE EXAMPLE

The following problem statement for an automated teller machine (ATM) network shown in Figure 8.3 serves as an example throughout the chapter:

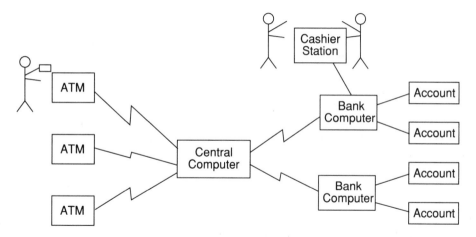

**Figure 8.3** ATM network

Design the software to support a computerized banking network including both human cashiers and automatic teller machines (ATMs) to be shared by a consortium of banks. Each bank provides its own computer to maintain its own accounts and process transactions against them. Cashier stations are owned by individual banks and communicate directly with their own bank's computers. Human cashiers enter account and transaction data. Automatic teller machines communicate with a central computer which clears transactions with the appropriate banks. An automatic teller machine accepts a cash card, interacts with the user, communicates with the central system to carry out the transaction, dispenses cash, and prints receipts. The system requires appropriate recordkeeping and security provisions. The system must handle concurrent accesses to the same account correctly. The banks will provide their own software for their own computers; you are to design the software for the ATMs and the network. The cost of the shared system will be apportioned to the banks according to the number of customers with cash cards.

## 8.4  OBJECT MODELING

The first step in analyzing the requirements is to construct an object model. The object model shows the static data structure of the real-world system and organizes it into workable pieces. The object model describes real-world object classes and their relationships to each other. Most crucial is the top level organization of the system into classes connected by associations; lower-level partitions within classes (generalizations) are less critical. The object model precedes the dynamic model and functional model because static structure is usually better defined, less dependent on application details, more stable as the solution evolves, and easier for humans to understand.

Information for the object model comes from the problem statement, expert knowledge of the application domain, and general knowledge of the real world. If the designer is not a domain expert, the information must be obtained from the application expert and checked against the model repeatedly. Object model diagrams promote communication between computer professionals and application-domain experts.

Identify classes and associations first, as they affect the overall structure and approach to the problem. Next add attributes to further describe the basic network of classes and associations. Then combine and organize classes using inheritance. Attempts to specify inheritance directly without first describing low-level classes and their attributes often distort the class structure to match preconceived notions. Add operations to classes later as a by-product of constructing the dynamic and functional models. Operations modify objects and therefore cannot be fully specified until the dynamics and functionality are understood.

It is best to get ideas down on paper before trying to organize them too much, even though they may be redundant and inconsistent, so as not to lose important details. An initial analysis model is likely to contain flaws that must be corrected by later iterations. The entire model need not be constructed uniformly. Some aspects of the problem can be analyzed in depth through several iterations while other aspects are still sketchy. Analysis and design are rarely completely linear.

The following steps are performed in constructing an object model:

- Identify objects and classes [8.4.1-8.4.2]

- Prepare a data dictionary [8.4.3]

- Identify associations (including aggregations) between objects [8.4.4-8.4.5]

- Identify attributes of objects and links [8.4.6-8.4.7]

- Organize and simplify object classes using inheritance [8.4.8]

- Verify that access paths exist for likely queries [8.4.9]

- Iterate and refine the model [8.4.10]

- Group classes into modules [8.4.11]

### 8.4.1 Identifying Object Classes

The first step in constructing an object model is to identify relevant object classes from the application domain. Objects include physical entities, such as houses, employees, and machines, as well as concepts, such as trajectories, seating assignments, and payment schedules. All classes must make sense in the application domain; avoid computer implementation constructs, such as linked lists and subroutines. Not all classes are explicit in the problem statement; some are implicit in the application domain or general knowledge.

As shown in Figure 8.4, begin by listing candidate object classes found in the written description of the problem. Don't be too selective; write down every class that comes to mind. Classes often correspond to nouns. For example, in the statement "a reservation system to sell tickets to performances at various theaters" tentative classes would be *Reservation, System, Ticket, Performance,* and *Theater.*

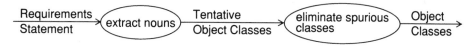

**Figure 8.4** Identifying object classes

Don't worry much about inheritance or high-level classes; first get specific classes right so that you don't subconsciously suppress detail in an attempt to fit a preconceived structure. For example, if you are building a cataloging and checkout system for a library, identify different kinds of materials, such as books, magazines, newspapers, records, videos, and so on. You can organize them into broad categories later, by looking for similarities and differences among basic classes.

*ATM example.* Examination of the nouns in the ATM problem statement of Figure 8.3 yields the tentative object classes listed in Figure 8.5. Additional classes that do not appear directly in the statement, but can be identified from our knowledge of the problem domain, are listed in Figure 8.6.

### 8.4.2 Keeping the Right Classes

Now discard unnecessary and incorrect classes according to the following criteria. Figure 8.7 shows the classes eliminated from the ATM example.

- *Redundant classes.* If two classes express the same information, the most descriptive name should be kept. For example, although customer might describe a person taking an airline flight, passenger is more descriptive. On the other hand, if the problem concerns contracts for a charter airline, customer is also an appropriate word, since a contract might involve several passengers.

  In the ATM example, *Customer* and *User* are redundant; *Customer* is retained because it is more descriptive.

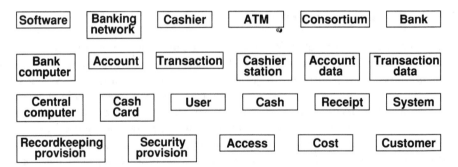

**Figure 8.5** ATM classes extracted from problem statement nouns

**Figure 8.6** ATM classes identified from knowledge of problem domain

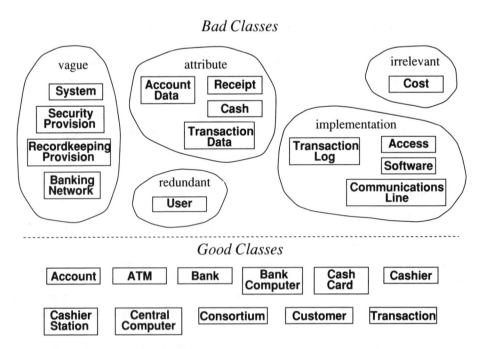

**Figure 8.7** Eliminating unnecessary classes from ATM problem

- *Irrelevant classes.* If a class has little or nothing to do with the problem, it should be eliminated. This involves judgment, because in another context the class could be important. For example, in a theater ticket reservation system, the occupations of the ticket holders are irrelevant, but the occupations of the theater personnel may be relevant.

  In the ATM example, apportioning *Cost* is outside the scope of the ATM transaction software.

- *Vague classes.* A class should be specific. Some tentative classes may have ill-defined boundaries or be too broad in scope. For example, *Recordkeeping provision* is vague. In the ATM problem, this is part of *Transaction.* In other applications, this might be included in other classes, such as *Stock sales, Telephone calls,* or *Machine failures.*

- *Attributes.* Names that primarily describe individual objects should be restated as attributes. For example, name, age, weight, and address are usually attributes. If the independent existence of a property is important, then make it a class and not an attribute. For example, an employee's room would be a class in an application to reassign rooms after a reorganization.

  The ATM example contains several names that are best modeled as attributes. *Account data* is underspecified but in any case probably describes an account. An ATM dispenses cash and receipts, but beyond that cash and receipts do not affect the problem, so they should be treated as ATM attributes.

- *Operations.* If a name describes an operation that is applied to objects and not manipulated in its own right, then it is not a class. For example, a telephone call is a sequence of actions involving a caller and the telephone network. If we are simply building telephones, then *Call* is part of the dynamic model and not an object class.

  An operation that has features of its own should be modeled as a class, however. For example, in a billing system for telephone calls a *Call* would be an important class with attributes such as date, time, and destination.

- *Roles.* The name of a class should reflect its intrinsic nature and not a role that it plays in an association. For example, *Owner* would be a poor name for a class in a car manufacturer's database. What if a list of drivers is added later? What about persons who lease cars? The proper class is *Person* (or possibly *Customer*), which assumes various different roles, such as *owner, driver,* and *lessee.*

  One physical entity sometimes corresponds to several classes. For example, *Person* and *Employee* may be distinct classes in some circumstances and redundant in others. From the viewpoint of a company database of employees, the two may be identical. In a government tax database, a person may hold more than one job, so it is important to distinguish *Person* from *Employee;* each person can correspond to zero or more instances of employee information.

- *Implementation constructs.* Constructs extraneous to the real world should be eliminated from the analysis model. They may be needed later during design, but not now. For example, CPU, subroutine, process, algorithm, and interrupt are implementation constructs for most applications, although they are a legitimate classes for an operating system. Data structures, such as linked lists, trees, arrays, and tables, are almost always implementation constructs.

Some tentative ATM classes are really implementation constructs. *Transaction log* is simply the set of transactions; its exact representation is a design issue. Communication links can be shown as associations; *Communications line* is simply the physical implementation of such a link.

### 8.4.3 Preparing a Data Dictionary

Isolated words have too many interpretations, so prepare a data dictionary for all modeling entities. Write a paragraph precisely describing each object class. Describe the scope of the class within the current problem, including any assumptions or restrictions on its membership or use. The data dictionary also describes associations, attributes, and operations. Figure 8.8 shows a data dictionary for the classes in the ATM problem.

### 8.4.4 Identifying Associations

Next, identify associations between classes. Any dependency between two or more classes is an association. A reference from one class to another is an association. As we discussed in Chapter 3, attributes should not refer to classes; use an association instead. For example, class *Person* should not have an attribute *employer*; relate class *Person* and class *Company* by association *Works-for.* Associations show dependencies between classes at the same level of abstraction as the classes themselves, while object-valued attributes hide dependencies and obscure their two-way nature. Associations can be implemented in various ways, but such implementation decisions should be kept out of the analysis model to preserve design freedom.

Associations often correspond to stative verbs or verb phrases. These include physical location (*next to, part of, contained in*), directed actions (*drives*), communication (*talks to*), ownership (*has, part of*), or satisfaction of some condition (*works for, married to, manages*). Extract all the candidates from the problem statement and get them down on paper first; don't try to refine things too early.

Don't spend much time trying to distinguish between association and aggregation. Aggregation is just an association with extra connotations. Use whichever seems most natural at the time and move on.

Figure 8.9 shows associations for the ATM example. The majority are taken directly from verb phrases in the problem statement. For some associations the verb phrase is implicit in the statement. Finally, some associations depend on real-world knowledge or assumptions. These must be verified with the requestor, as they are not in the problem statement.

Account—a single account in a bank against which transactions can be applied. Accounts may be of various types, at least checking or savings. A customer can hold more than one account.

ATM—a station that allows customers to enter their own transactions using cash cards as identification. The ATM interacts with the customer to gather transaction information, sends the transaction information to the central computer for validation and processing, and dispenses cash to the user. We assume that an ATM need not operate independently of the network.

Bank—a financial institution that holds accounts for customers and that issues cash cards authorizing access to accounts over the ATM network.

Bank computer—the computer owned by a bank that interfaces with the ATM network and the bank's own cashier stations. A bank may actually have its own internal network of computers to process accounts, but we are only concerned with the one that talks to the network.

Cash card—a card assigned to a bank customer that authorizes access of accounts using an ATM machine. Each card contains a bank code and a card number, most likely coded in accordance with national standards on credit cards and cash cards. The bank code uniquely identifies the bank within the consortium. The card number determines the accounts that the card can access. A card does not necessarily access all of a customer's accounts. Each cash card is owned by a single customer, but multiple copies of it may exist, so the possibility of simultaneous use of the same card from different machines must be considered.

Cashier—an employee of a bank who is authorized to enter transactions into cashier stations and accept and dispense cash and checks to customers. Transactions, cash, and checks handled by each cashier must be logged and properly accounted for.

Cashier station—a station on which cashiers enter transactions for customers. Cashiers dispense and accept cash and checks; the station prints receipts. The cashier station communicates with the bank computer to validate and process the transactions.

Central computer—a computer operated by the consortium which dispatches transactions between the ATMs and the bank computers. The central computer validates bank codes but does not process transactions directly.

Consortium—an organization of banks that commissions and operates the ATM network. The network only handles transactions for banks in the consortium.

Customer—the holder of one or more accounts in a bank. A customer can consist of one or more persons or corporations; the correspondence is not relevant to this problem. The same person holding an account at a different bank is considered a different customer.

Transaction—a single integral request for operations on the accounts of a single customer. We only specified that ATMs must dispense cash, but we should not preclude the possibility of printing checks or accepting cash or checks. We may also want to provide the flexibility to operate on accounts of different customers, although it is not required yet. The different operations must balance properly.

**Figure 8.8** Data dictionary for ATM classes

*Verb phrases:*
Banking network includes cashiers and ATMs
Consortium shares ATMs
Bank provides bank computer
Bank computer maintains accounts
Bank computer processes transaction against account
Bank owns cashier station
Cashier station communicates with bank computer
Cashier enters transaction for account
ATMs communicate with central computer about transaction
Central computer clears transaction with bank
ATM accepts cash card
ATM interacts with user
ATM dispenses cash
ATM prints receipts
System handles concurrent access
Banks provide software
Cost apportioned to banks

*Implicit verb phrases:*
Consortium consists of banks
Bank holds account
Consortium owns central computer
System provides recordkeeping
System provides security
Customers have cash cards

*Knowledge of problem domain:*
Cash card accesses accounts
Bank employs cashiers

**Figure 8.9** Associations from ATM problem statement

### 8.4.5 Keeping the Right Associations

Now discard unnecessary and incorrect associations, using the following criteria:

- *Associations between eliminated classes.* If one of the classes in the association has been eliminated, then the association must be eliminated or restated in terms of other classes. In the ATM example, we can eliminate *Banking network includes cashier stations and ATMs, Cost apportioned to banks, ATM prints receipts, ATM dispenses cash, System provides recordkeeping, System provides security*, and *Banks provide software.*

- *Irrelevant or implementation associations.* Eliminate any associations that are outside the problem domain or deal with implementation constructs. For example, *System handles concurrent access* is an implementation concept. Real-world objects are inherently concurrent; it is the implementation of the access algorithm that is required to be concurrent.

- *Actions.* An association should describe a structural property of the application domain, not a transient event. For example, *ATM accepts cash card* describes part of the interaction cycle between an ATM and a customer, not a permanent relationship between ATMs and cash cards. We can also eliminate *ATM interacts with user.*

Sometimes, a requirement expressed as an action implies an underlying structural relationship and should be rephrased accordingly. For example, *Central computer clears transaction with bank* describes an action that implies the structural relationship *Central computer communicates with bank.*

- *Ternary associations.* Most associations between three or more classes can be decomposed into binary associations or phrased as qualified associations. For example, *Cashier enters transaction for account* can be broken into *Cashier enters transaction* and *Transaction concerns account. Bank computer processes transaction against account* can be broken similarly. *ATMs communicate with central computer about transaction* is really the binary associations *ATMs communicate with central computer* and *Transaction entered on ATM.*

  If a term in a ternary association is purely descriptive and has no features of its own, then the term is a link attribute on a binary association. Association *Company pays salary to person* can be rephrased as binary association *Company employs person* with a *salary* value for each *Company-Person* link.

  Occasionally a general ternary association is required. *Professor teaches course in room* cannot be decomposed without losing information. We have not encountered associations with four or more classes in our work.

- *Derived associations.* Omit associations that can be defined in terms of other associations because they are redundant. For example, *Grandparent of* can be defined in terms of a pair of *Parent of* associations. Also omit associations defined by conditions on object attributes. For example, *younger than* expresses a condition on the birth dates of two persons, not additional information.

  As much as possible, classes, attributes, and associations in the object model should represent independent information. Multiple paths between classes often indicate derived associations which are compositions of primitive associations. *Consortium shares ATMs* is a composition of the associations *Consortium owns central computer* and *Central computer communicates with ATMs.*

  Be careful because not all associations that form multiple paths between classes indicate redundancy. Sometimes the existence of an association can be derived from two or more primitive associations and the multiplicity can not. Keep the extra association if the additional multiplicity constraint is important. For example, in Figure 8.10 a company employs many persons and owns many computers. Each employee is assigned zero or more computers for the employee's personal use; some computers are for public use and are not assigned to anyone. The multiplicity of the *Assigned-to* association cannot be deduced from the *Employs* and *Owns* associations.

  Although derived associations do not add information, they are useful in the real world and in design. For example, kinship relationships such as *Uncle, Mother-in-law,* and *Cousin* have names because they describe familiar relations considered important within our society. You may show derived associations in object diagrams, but they should be drawn using dotted lines to indicate their dependent status and to distinguish them from fundamental associations.

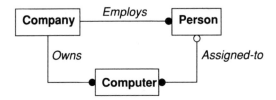

**Figure 8.10** Nonredundant associations

Further specify the semantics of associations as follows:

- *Misnamed associations*. Don't say how or why a situation came about, say what it is. Names are important to understanding and should be chosen with great care. *Bank computer maintains accounts* is a statement of action; rephrase as *Bank holds account*.

- *Role names*. Add role names where appropriate. The role name describes the role that a class in the association plays from the point of view of the other class. For example, in the *Works-for* association *Company* has the role *employer* and *Person* has the role *employee*. If there is only one association between a pair of classes, and the name of a class adequately describes its role, you may omit role names. For example, the roles in the association *Central computer communicates with ATM* are clear from the class names. An association between two instances of the same class (a reflexive association) requires role names to distinguish the instances. For example, the association *Person manages person* would have the roles *boss* and *worker*.

- *Qualified associations*. Usually a name identifies an object within some context; most names are not globally unique. The context combines with the name to uniquely identify the object. For example, the name of a company must be unique within the chartering state but may be duplicated in other states (there once was a Standard Oil Company in Ohio, Indiana, California, and New Jersey). The name of a company qualifies the association *State charters company*; *State* and *company name* uniquely identify *Company*.

    A qualifier distinguishes objects on the "many" side of an association. For example, the qualifier *bank code* distinguishes the different banks in a consortium. Each cash card needs a bank code so that transactions can be directed to the appropriate bank.

- *Multiplicity*. Specify multiplicity, but don't put too much effort into getting it right, as multiplicity often changes during analysis. Challenge multiplicity values of "one." For example, the association *one Manager manages many employees* precludes matrix management or an employee with divided responsibilities. For multiplicity values of "many," consider whether a qualifier is needed; also ask if the objects need to be ordered in some way.

- *Missing associations*. Add any missing associations that are discovered. For example, we overlooked *Transaction entered on cashier station*, *Customers have accounts*, and *Transaction authorized by cash card*. If cashiers are restricted to specific stations, then the association *Cashier authorized on cashier station* would be needed.

*ATM example.* Figure 8.11 shows an object diagram with the remaining associations. Note that *Transaction* as been split into *Remote transaction* and *Cashier transaction* to accommodate different associations. The diagram shows multiplicity values. Some analysis decisions could have been made differently. Don't worry; there are many possible correct models of a problem. We have shown the analysis process in small steps; with practice, you can elide several steps together in your mind.

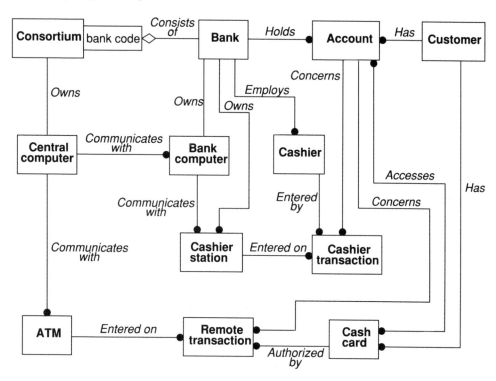

**Figure 8.11** Initial object diagram for ATM system

### 8.4.6 Identifying Attributes

Next identify object attributes. Attributes are properties of individual objects, such as name, weight, velocity, or color. Attributes should not be objects; use an association to show any relationship between two objects.

Attributes usually correspond to nouns followed by possessive phrases, such as "the color of the car" or "the position of the cursor." Adjectives often represent specific enumerated attribute values, such as *red, on,* or *expired.* Unlike classes and associations, attributes are less likely to be fully described in the problem statement. You must draw on your knowledge of the application domain and the real world to find them. Fortunately attributes seldom affect the basic structure of the problem.

Do not carry discovery of attributes to excess. Only consider attributes that directly relate to a particular application. Get the most important attributes first; fine details can be added later. During analysis, avoid attributes which are solely for implementation. Be sure to give each attribute a meaningful name.

Derived attributes should be omitted or clearly labeled. For example, *age* is derived from *birth date* and *current time* (which is a property of the environment). Derived attributes, like derived objects and associations, can be useful in abstracting meaningful properties of an application, but they should be clearly distinguished from base attributes, which define the state of the object. Derived attributes should not be expressed as operations, such as *get-age*, although they may eventually be implemented as such.

Link attributes should also be identified. A link attribute is a property of the link between two objects, rather than being a property of an individual object. For example, the many-to-many association between *Stockholder* and *Company* has a link attribute of *number of shares*. Link attributes are sometimes mistaken for object attributes.

### 8.4.7 Keeping the Right Attributes

Eliminate unnecessary and incorrect attributes with the following criteria:

- *Objects.* If the independent existence of an entity is important, rather than just its value, then it is an object. For example, *Boss* is an object and *salary* is an attribute. The distinction often depends on the application. For example, in a mailing list *city* might be considered as an attribute, while in a census *City* would be an object. An entity that has features of its own within the given application is an object.

- *Qualifiers.* If the value of an attribute depends on a particular context, then consider restating the attribute as a qualifier. For example, *employee number* is not a unique property of a person with two jobs; it qualifies the association *Company employs person.*

- *Names.* Names are often better modeled as qualifiers rather than object attributes. Test: Does the name select among objects in a set? Can an object in the set have more than one name? If so, the name qualifies an association. If a name appears to be unique, you may have missed the object class that is being qualified. For example, *department name* may be unique within a company, but eventually the program may need to deal with more than one company.

  A name is an object attribute when it does not depend on context, especially when it need not be unique. Names of persons, unlike names of companies, may be duplicated and are therefore object attributes.

- *Identifiers.* Object-oriented languages incorporate the notion of an object identifier for unambiguously referencing an object. Do not list these object identifiers in object models, as object identifiers are implicit in object models. Only list attributes which exist in the application domain. For example, *account code* is a bonafide attribute; *Banks* assign *account codes.* In contrast, *transaction ID* should not be listed as an attribute, although it may be convenient to generate one during implementation.

- *Link attributes.* If a property depends on the presence of a link, then the property is an attribute of the link and not of a related object. Link attributes are usually obvious on many-to-many associations; they cannot be attached to either class because of their multiplicity. Link attributes are more subtle on many-to-one associations because they could be attached to the "many" object without losing information. Link attributes are also subtle on one-to-one associations.

- *Internal values.* If an attribute describes the internal state of an object that is invisible outside the object, then eliminate it from the analysis.

- *Fine detail.* Omit minor attributes which are unlikely to affect most operations.

- *Discordant attributes.* An attribute that seems completely different from and unrelated to all other attributes may indicate a class that should be split into two distinct classes. A class should be simple and coherent. Unfocused classes frequently result from premature consideration of implementation decisions during analysis.

We apply these criteria to the ATM problem to obtain attributes for each class (Figure 8.12). Some tentative attributes are actually qualifiers on associations. Some observations are:

- *Bank code* and *card code* are present on the card. Their format is an implementation detail, but we must add a new association *Bank issues cash card*. *Card code* is a qualifier on this association; *bank code* is the qualifier of *Bank* with respect to *Consortium*.

- The computers do not have state relevant to this problem. Whether the machine is up or down is a transient attribute that is part of implementation.

- Avoid the temptation to omit *Consortium*, even though it is currently unique. It provides the context for the *bank code* qualifier and may be useful for future expansion.

Keep in mind that the ATM problem is an example and not a full application. Real applications, when fleshed out, tend to have many more attributes per class than shown in Figure 8.12.

## 8.4.8 Refining with Inheritance

The next step is to organize classes by using inheritance to share common structure. Inheritance can be added in two directions: by generalizing common aspects of existing classes into a superclass (bottom up) or by refining existing classes into specialized subclasses (top down).

You can discover inheritance from the bottom up by searching for classes with similar attributes, associations, or operations. For each generalization, define a superclass to share common features. For example, *Remote transaction* and *Cashier transaction* are similar, except in their initiation, and can be generalized by *Transaction*. On the other hand, *Central computer* and *Bank computer* have little in common for purposes of the ATM example. Some attributes or even classes may have to be redefined slightly to fit in properly. This is acceptable, but don't push too hard if it doesn't fit; you may have the wrong generalization. Some generalizations will suggest themselves based on existing taxonomy in the real world; use existing concepts whenever possible. Symmetry will suggest classes that are missing from certain generalizations.

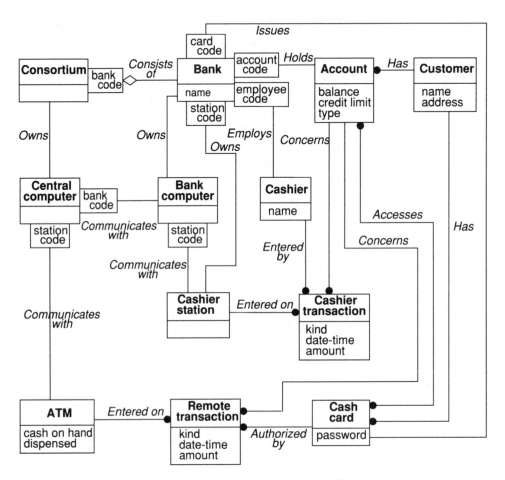

**Figure 8.12**  ATM object model with attributes

Top-down specializations are often apparent from the application domain. Look for noun phrases composed of various adjectives on the class name: *fluorescent* lamp, *incandescent* lamp; *fixed* menu, *pop-up* menu, *sliding* menu. Avoid excessive refinement. If proposed specializations are incompatible with an existing class, the existing class may be improperly formulated. Enumerated subcases in the application domain are the most frequent source of specializations. Often, it is sufficient to note that a set of enumerated subcases exists, without actually listing them. For example, an ATM account could be refined into *Checking account* and *Savings account*. While undoubtedly useful in some banking applications, this distinction does not affect behavior within the ATM application; *account type* can be made a simple attribute of *Account*.

Multiple inheritance may be used to increase sharing, but only if necessary, because it increases both conceptual and implementation complexity. In using multiple inheritance, it is often possible to designate a primary superclass which supplies most of the inherited structure and behavior. Secondary superclasses add orthogonal details.

When the same association name appears more than once with substantially the same meaning, try to generalize the associated classes. For example, *Transaction* is entered on both *Cashier station* and *ATM; Entry station* generalizes *Cashier station* and *ATM*. Sometimes the classes have nothing in common but the association, but more often you will uncover an underlying generality that you have overlooked.

Attributes and associations must be assigned to specific classes in the class hierarchy. Each one should be assigned to the most general class for which it is appropriate. Some adjustment may be needed to get everything right. Symmetry may suggest additional attributes to distinguish among subclasses more clearly.

Figure 8.13 shows the ATM object model after adding inheritance.

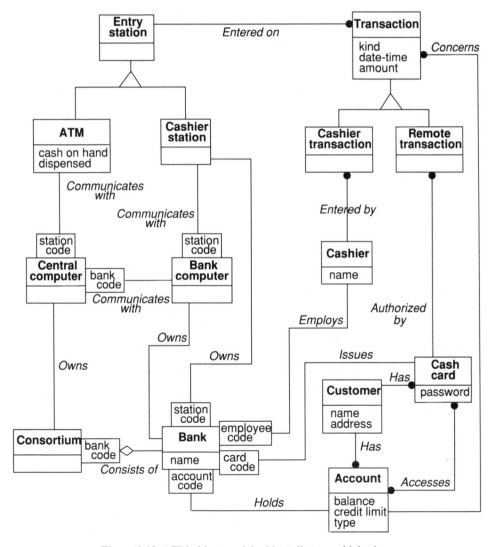

**Figure 8.13** ATM object model with attributes and inheritance

## 8.4.9 Testing Access Paths

Trace access paths through the object model diagram to see if they yield sensible results. Where a unique value is expected, is there a path yielding a unique result? For multiplicity "many" is there a way to pick out unique values when needed? Think of questions you might like to ask. Are there useful questions which cannot be answered? They indicate missing information. If something that seems simple in the real world appears complex in the model, you may have missed something (but make sure that the complexity is not inherent in the real world).

*ATM example.* A cash card itself does not uniquely identify an account, so the user must choose an account somehow. If the user supplies an account type (savings or checking), each card can access at most one savings and one checking account. This is probably reasonable, and many cash cards actually work this way, but it limits the system. The alternative is to require customers to remember account numbers. If a cash card accesses a single account, then transfers between accounts are impossible.

We have assumed that the ATM network serves a single consortium of banks. Real cash machines today often serve overlapping networks of banks and accept credit cards as well as cash cards. The model would have to be extended to handle that situation. We will assume that the customer is satisfied with this limitation on the system.

## 8.4.10 Iterating Object Modeling

An object model is rarely correct after a single pass. The entire software development process is one of continual iteration; different parts of a model are often at different stages of completion. If a deficiency is found, go back to an earlier stage if necessary to correct it. Some refinements can only come after the dynamic and functional models are completed.

Signs of missing objects include:

- asymmetries in associations and generalizations: Add new classes by analogy.

- disparate attributes and operations on a class: Split a class so that each part is coherent.

- difficulty in generalizing cleanly: One class may be playing two roles. Split it up and one part may then fit in cleanly.

- an operation with no good target class: Add the missing target class.

- duplicate associations with the same name and purpose: Generalize to create the missing superclass that unites them.

- a role substantially shapes the semantics of a class: Maybe it should be a separate class. This often means converting an association into a class. For example, a person can be employed by several companies with different conditions of employment at each; *Employee* is then a class denoting a person working for a particular company, in addition to class *Person* and *Company*.

Signs of unnecessary classes include:

- lack of attributes, operations, and associations on a class: Why is it needed?

Signs of missing associations include:

- missing access paths for operations: Add new associations so that queries can be answered.

Signs of unnecessary associations include:

- redundant information in the associations: Remove associations that do not add new information or mark them as derived.

- lack of operations that traverse an association: If no operations use a path, maybe the information is not needed. This test must wait until operations are specified. [See Section 8.7]

Signs of incorrect placement of associations:

- role names that are too broad or too narrow for their classes: Move the association up or down in the class hierarchy.

Signs of incorrect placement of attributes:

- need to access an object by one of its attribute values: Consider a qualified association.

In practice, model building is not as rigidly ordered as we have shown. You can combine several steps once you are experienced. For example, you can identify classes, reject the incorrect ones without writing them down, and add them to the object diagram together with their associations. You can take some parts of the model through several steps and develop them in some detail, while other parts are still sketchy. The order of steps can be interchanged when appropriate. If you are just learning object modeling, however, we recommend that you follow the steps in full detail the first few times.

*ATM example.* Cash card really has a split personality—it is both an authorization unit within the bank allowing access to the customer's accounts and also a piece of plastic data that the ATM reads to obtain coded IDs. In this case, the codes are actually part of the real world, not just computer artifacts; the codes, not the cash card, are communicated to the central computer. We should split cash card into two objects: *Card authorization*, an access right to one or more customer accounts; and *Cash card*, a piece of plastic that contains a bank code and a cash card number meaningful to the bank. Each card authorization may have several cash cards, each containing a serial number for security reasons. The card code, present on the physical card, identifies the card authorization within the bank. Each card authorization identifies one or more accounts, for example, one checking account and one savings account.

Transaction is not general enough to permit transfers between accounts because it concerns only a single account. In general, a *Transaction* consists of one or more *updates* on individual accounts. An *update* is a single action (withdrawal, deposit, or query) on a single account. All updates in a single transaction must be processed together as an atomic unit; if any one fails, then they all are canceled.

The distinction between *Bank* and *Bank computer* and between *Consortium* and *Central computer* doesn't seem to affect the analysis. The fact that communications are processed by computers is actually an implementation concept. Merge *Bank computer* into *Bank* and *Central computer* into *Consortium*.

*Customer* doesn't seem to enter into the analysis so far. However, when we consider operations to open new accounts, it may be an important concept, so leave it alone for now.

Figure 8.14 shows a revised object model diagram that is simpler and cleaner.

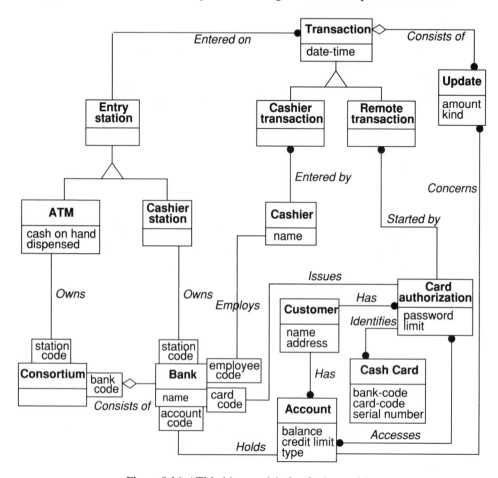

**Figure 8.14**  ATM object model after further revision

### 8.4.11  Grouping Classes into Modules

The last step of object modeling is to group classes into sheets and modules. Diagrams may be divided into sheets of uniform size for convenience in drawing, printing, and viewing. Tightly-coupled classes should be grouped together, but since a sheet holds a fixed amount of information the breakdown is occasionally arbitrary. A module is a set of classes (one or more sheets) that captures some logical subset of the entire model. For example, a model of a computer operating system might contain modules for process control, device control, file maintenance, and memory management. Modules may vary in size.

Each association should generally be shown on a single sheet, but some classes must be shown more than once to connect different sheets. Look for cut points among the classes: a class that is the sole connection between two otherwise disconnected parts of the object network. Such a class forms the bridge between two sheets or modules. For example, in a file management system, a file is the cut point between the directory structure and the file contents. If a single cut point cannot be found, try to minimize the number of bridge classes. Try to choose modules to reduce the number of crossovers in the object diagram. With a little care, most object diagrams can be drawn as planar graphs, without crossing lines.

A "star" pattern is frequently useful for organizing modules: a single core module contains the top-level structure of high-level classes. Other modules expand each high-level class into a generalization hierarchy and add associations to additional low-level classes.

Reuse a module from a previous design if possible, but avoid forcing a fit. Reuse is easiest when part of the problem domain matches a previous problem. If the new problem is similar to a previous problem but different, the original design may have to be extended to encompass both problems. Use your judgment about whether this is better than building a new design.

*ATM example.* The model we have presented is small and would not require breakdown into modules, but it could serve as a core for a more detailed model. The modules might be:

- tellers—cashier, entry station, cashier station, ATM
- accounts—account, cash card, card authorization, customer, transaction, update, cashier transaction, remote transaction
- banks—consortium, bank

Each module could add details: The account module could contain varieties of transactions, information about customers, interest payments and fees; the banks module could contain information about branches, addresses, and cost allocations.

## 8.5 DYNAMIC MODELING

The dynamic model shows the time-dependent behavior of the system and the objects in it. Begin dynamic analysis by looking for events—externally-visible stimuli and responses. Then summarize permissible event sequences for each object with a state diagram. Algorithm execution is not relevant during analysis if there are no externally-visible manifestations; algorithms are part of implementation.

The dynamic model is insignificant for a purely static data repository, such as a database. The dynamic model is important for interactive systems. For most problems, logical correctness depends on the sequences of interactions, not the exact times of interactions. Real-time systems, however, do have specific timing requirements on interactions that must be considered during analysis. We do not address real-time analysis in this book.

First prepare scenarios of typical dialogs. Even though these scenarios may not cover every contingency, they at least ensure that common interactions are not overlooked. Extract events from the scenarios. It is usually best to identify events first and then assign each event to its target object. Organize the sequences of events and states into a state diagram. Finally compare state diagrams for different objects to make sure the events exchanged by them match. The resulting set of state diagrams constitute the dynamic model.

In summary, the following steps are performed in constructing a dynamic model:

- Prepare scenarios of typical interaction sequences [8.5.1]
- Identify events between objects [8.5.3]
- Prepare an event trace for each scenario [8.5.3]
- Build a state diagram [8.5.4]
- Match events between objects to verify consistency [8.5.5]

### 8.5.1 Preparing a Scenario

Prepare one or more typical dialogs between user and system to get a feel for expected system behavior. These scenarios show the major interactions, external display formats, and information exchanges. Approach the dynamic model by scenarios, rather than trying to write down the general model directly, to ensure that important steps are not overlooked and that the overall flow of the interaction is smooth and correct.

Sometimes the problem statement describes the full interaction sequence, but most of the time you will have to invent (or at least flesh out) the interaction format. For example, the ATM problem statement indicates the need to obtain transaction data from the user but is vague about exactly what parameters are needed and what order to ask for them. The problem statement may specify needed information but leaves open the manner in which it is obtained. In many applications, gathering input is a major task or sometimes the only major task. The dynamic model is crucial in such applications.

First prepare scenarios for "normal" cases, interactions without any unusual inputs or error conditions. Then consider "special" cases, such as omitted input sequences, maximum and minimum values, and repeated values. Then consider user error cases, including invalid values and failures to respond. For many interactive applications, error handling is the most difficult part of the implementation. If possible, allow the user to abort an operation or roll back to a well-defined starting point at each step. Finally consider various other kinds of interactions that can be overlaid on basic interactions, such as help requests and status queries.

A *scenario* is a sequence of events. An event occurs whenever information is exchanged between an object in the system and an outside agent, such as a user, a sensor, or another task. The information values exchanged are parameters of the event. For example, the event *password entered* has the password value as a parameter. Events with no parameters are meaningful and even common. The information in such an event is the fact that it has occurred—a pure signal. Anytime information is input to the system or output from the system, an event occurs.

For each event, identify the actor (system, user, or other external agent) that caused the event and the parameters of the event. The screen layout or output format generally doesn't affect the logic of the interaction or the values exchanged. Don't worry about output formats for the initial dynamic model; describe output formats during refinement of the model.

*ATM example.* Figure 8.15 shows a normal ATM scenario. Figure 8.16 shows a scenario with exceptions.

---

The ATM asks the user to insert a card; the user inserts a cash card.
The ATM accepts the card and reads its serial number.
The ATM requests the password; the user enters "1234."
The ATM verifies the serial number and password with the consortium; the
    consortium checks it with bank "39" and notifies the ATM of acceptance.
The ATM asks the user to select the kind of transaction (withdrawal, deposit,
    transfer, query); the user selects withdrawal.
The ATM asks for the amount of cash; the user enters $100.
The ATM verifies that the amount is within predefined policy limits and asks the
    consortium to process the transaction; the consortium passes the request to
    the bank, which eventually confirms success and returns the new account
    balance.
The ATM dispenses cash and asks the user to take it; the user takes the cash.
The ATM asks whether the user wants to continue; the user indicates no.
The ATM prints a receipt, ejects the card, and asks the user to take them; the
    user takes the receipt and the card.
The ATM asks a user to insert a card.

**Figure 8.15** Normal ATM scenario

---

The ATM asks the user to insert a card; the user inserts a cash card.
The ATM swallows the card and reads its serial number.
The ATM requests the password; the user enters "9999."
The ATM verifies the serial number and password with the consortium, which
    rejects it after consulting the appropriate bank.
The ATM indicates a bad password and asks the user to renter it; the user enters
    "1234" which the ATM successfully verifies with the consortium.
The ATM asks the user to select the kind of transaction; the user selects
    withdrawal.
The ATM asks for the amount of cash; the user has a change of mind and hits
    "cancel."
The ATM ejects the card and asks the user to take it; the user takes it.
The ATM asks a user to insert a card.

**Figure 8.16** ATM scenario with exceptions

Many other variations can be described: The user fails to insert the card in time, the ATM can't read the card, the card has expired, the transaction is inappropriate to the account, the amount is invalid, the machine is out of cash or paper, the remote communication lines are down, or the transaction is rejected because of suspicious patterns of usage on the card.

Additional scenarios should be written for administrative parts of the ATM system, such as authorizing new cards, opening accounts, adding banks to the consortium, and obtaining transaction logs. We will not explore these aspects.

### 8.5.2 Interface Formats

Most interactions can be separated into two parts: application logic and the user interface. The analysis should concentrate first on the information flow and control, rather than the presentation format. The same program logic can accept input from command lines, files, mouse buttons, touch panels, physical push buttons, or remote links, if the surface details are carefully isolated. The dynamic model captures the control logic of the application.

It is hard to evaluate a user interface without actually testing it. Often the interface can be mocked up so that users can try it. Application logic can often be simulated with dummy procedures. Decoupling application logic from the user interface allows the "look and feel" of the user interface to be evaluated while the application is under development.

Figure 8.17 shows a possible ATM layout. Its exact details are not important at this point, even less the wording of the messages. The important thing is the information exchanged, in whatever form. For example, don't worry about the sequence of keystrokes needed to enter a password; treat "enter password" as an atomic event. Nevertheless, it is good to draw at least one possible illustration of each interaction format, to help make sure nothing important is forgotten.

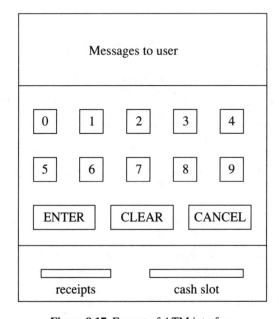

**Figure 8.17** Format of ATM interface

### 8.5.3 Identifying Events

Examine the scenarios to identify all external events. Events include all signals, inputs, decisions, interrupts, transitions, and actions to or from users or external devices. Internal computation steps are not events, except for decision points that interact with the external world. Use scenarios to find normal events, but don't forget error conditions and unusual events.

An action by an object that transmits information is an event. For example, *enter password* is an event sent from external agent *User* to application object *ATM*. Most object-to-object interactions and operations correspond to events. For example, *insert card* is an event sent from *User* to *ATM*. Some information flows are implicit. For example, *dispense cash* is an event from *ATM* to *User*.

Group together under a single name events that have the same effect on flow of control, even if their parameter values differ. For example, *enter password* should be an event class, since the password value does not affect the flow of control. Similarly *dispense cash* is also an event class, since the amount of cash dispensed does not affect the flow of control. Events that affect the flow of control should be distinguished. *Account OK, bad account,* and *bad password* are all different events; don't group them under *card status*.

You must decide when differences in quantitative values are important enough to distinguish. For example, different digits from a keyboard would usually be considered the same event, since the high-level control does not depend on numerical values. Pushing the "enter" key, however, would probably be considered a distinct event, since the application would respond differently. The distinction depends on the application. You may have to construct the state diagram before you can classify all events; some distinctions between events may have no effect on behavior and can be ignored.

Allocate each type of event to the object classes that send it and receive it. The event is an output event for the sender and an input event for the receiver. Sometimes an object sends an event to itself, in which case the event is both an output and an input for the same class.

Show each scenario as an *event trace*—an ordered list of events between different objects assigned to columns in a table. Figure 8.18 shows an event trace for an ATM scenario. If more than one object of the same class participates in the scenario, assign a separate column to each object. By scanning a particular column in the trace, you can see the events that directly affect a particular object. Only these events can appear in the state diagram for the object.

Show the events between a group of classes (such as a module) on an *event flow diagram*, as in Figure 8.19. This diagram summarizes events between classes, without regard for sequence. Include events from all scenarios, including error events. The event flow diagram is a dynamic counterpart to an object diagram. Paths in the object diagram show possible information flows; paths in the event flow diagram show possible control flows.

### 8.5.4 Building a State Diagram

Prepare a state diagram for each object class with nontrivial dynamic behavior, showing the events the object receives and sends. Every scenario or event trace corresponds to a path through the state diagram. Each branch in control flow is represented by a state with more than one exit transition.

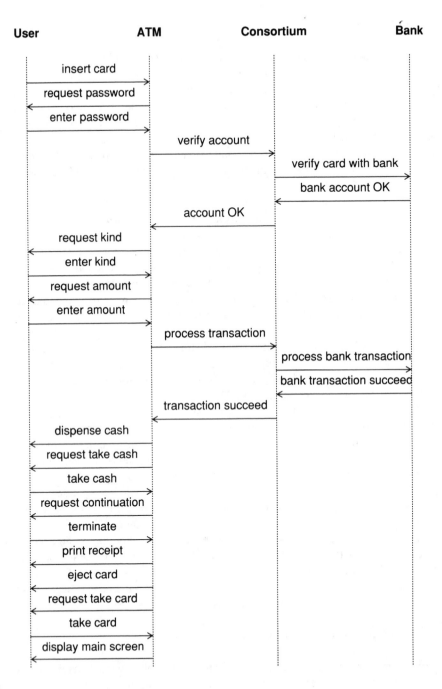

**Figure 8.18** Event trace for ATM scenario

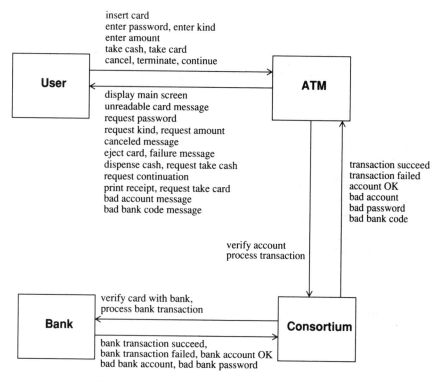

insert card
enter password, enter kind
enter amount
take cash, take card
cancel, terminate, continue

display main screen
unreadable card message
request password
request kind, request amount
canceled message
eject card, failure message
dispense cash, request take cash
request continuation
print receipt, request take card
bad account message
bad bank code message

transaction succeed
transaction failed
account OK
bad account
bad password
bad bank code

verify account
process transaction

verify card with bank,
process bank transaction

bank transaction succeed,
bank transaction failed, bank account OK
bad bank account, bad bank password

**Figure 8.19** Event flow diagram for ATM example

Start with the event trace diagrams that affect the class being modeled. Pick a trace showing a typical interaction and only consider the events affecting a single object. Arrange the events into a path whose arcs are labeled by the input and output events found along one column in the trace. The interval between any two events is a state. Give each state a name, if a name is meaningful, but don't bother if it is not. The initial diagram will be a sequence of events and states. If the scenario can be repeated indefinitely, close the path in the state diagram.

Now find loops within the diagram. If a sequence of events can be repeated indefinitely, then they form a loop. Replace finite sequences of events with loops when possible. In a loop, the first state and the last state are identical. If the object "remembers" that it has traversed a loop, then the two states are not really identical, and a simple loop is incorrect. At least one state in a loop must have multiple transactions leaving it or the loop will never terminate.

Now merge other scenarios into the state diagram. Find the point in each scenario where it diverges from previous scenarios. This point corresponds to an existing state in the diagram. Attach the new event sequence to the existing state as an alternative path. While examining states and scenarios, you may think of other possible events that can occur at each state; add them to the state diagram as well.

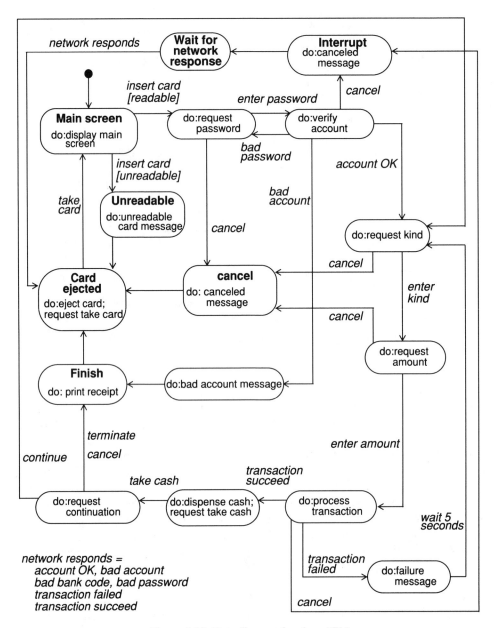

**Figure 8.20** State diagram for class *ATM*

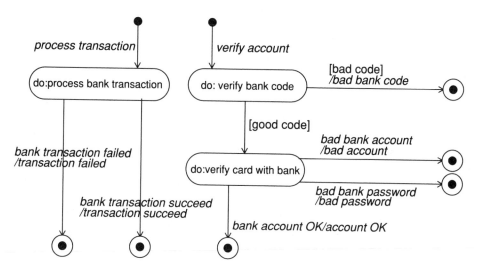

**Figure 8.21** State diagram for class *Consortium*

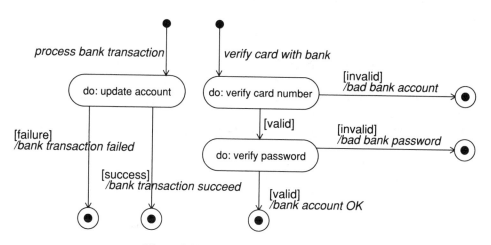

**Figure 8.22** State diagram for class *Bank*

The hardest thing is deciding at which state an alternate path rejoins the existing diagram. Two paths join at a state if the object "forgets" which one was taken. In many cases, it is obvious from your knowledge of the application that two states are identical. For example, inserting two nickels into a vending machine is equivalent to inserting one dime.

Beware of two paths that appear identical but which can be distinguished under some circumstances. For example, some systems repeat the input sequence if the user makes an error entering information but give up after a certain number of failures. The repeat sequence is almost the same except that it remembers the past failures. The difference can be glossed over by adding a parameter, such as *number of failures,* to remember information. At least one transition must depend on the value of the parameter. The judicious use of parameters and conditional transitions can simplify state diagrams considerably but at the cost of mixing together state information and data. State diagrams with too much data dependency can be confusing and counterintuitive. Another alternative is to partition a state diagram into two concurrent subdiagrams, using one subdiagram for the main line and the other for the distinguishing information. For example, a subdiagram to allow for one user failure might have states *No error* and *One error.*

After normal events have been considered, add boundary cases and special cases, as discussed in Section 8.5.1. Consider events that occur at awkward times, for example, a request to cancel a transaction after it has been submitted for processing. In cases when the user (or other external agent) may fail to respond promptly and some resource must be reclaimed, a *time-out* event can be generated after a given interval. Handling user errors cleanly often requires more thought and code than the normal case. Error handling often complicates an otherwise clean and compact program structure, but it must be done.

You are finished with the state diagram of a class when the diagram covers all scenarios, and the diagram handles all events that can affect an object of the class in each of its states. You can use the state diagram to suggest new scenarios by considering how some event not already handled should affect the state of the object. Posing "What if" questions is a good way to test completeness and error-handling capabilities of a class (and should be repeated at the module and system levels as well).

If there are complex interactions with independent inputs, you can organize the dynamic model using a nested state diagram, as described in Chapter 5. Otherwise a flat state diagram is usually adequate.

Repeat the above process of building state diagrams for each class of objects. Concentrate on classes with important interactions.

Not all classes need a state diagram. Many objects respond to input events independently of their past history, or capture all important history as parameters that do not affect control. Such objects may receive and send events. List the input events for each object and the output events sent in response to each input event, but there will be no further state structure.

Eventually you may be able to write down state diagrams directly without preparing event traces. A few scenarios are usually helpful, in any case.

*ATM example.* Objects *ATM, Cashier station, Consortium,* and *Bank* are actors that exchange events. Objects *Cash card, Transaction,* and *Account* are passive objects that are acted on and do not exchange events. The customer and cashier are actors, but their interactions with the entry stations are already shown; the customer and cashier objects are external to the system and need not be implemented within it anyway. Figure 8.20 shows the state machine for the ATM. Figure 8.21 shows the state diagram for the consortium. Many copies of the diagram may be active concurrently; each diagram corresponds to one transaction. Figure 8.22 shows the state machine for the bank. Again, each diagram corresponds to one transaction. These state diagrams are all simplistic, especially with regard to their error handling. For example, Figure 8.20 makes no provision for failure of the network communication link. In such a case, an ATM would be expected to eject the customer's card; we do not show this behavior. The state machine for *Cashier station* has been omitted to save space; it is similar to *ATM*.

### 8.5.5 Matching Events Between Objects

Check for completeness and consistency at the system level when the state diagrams for each class are complete. Every event should have a sender and a receiver, occasionally the same object. States without predecessors or successors are suspicious; make sure they represent starting or termination points of the interaction sequence. Follow the effects of an input event from object to object through the system to make sure that they match the scenarios. Objects are inherently concurrent; beware of synchronization errors where an input occurs at an awkward time. Make sure that corresponding events on different state diagrams are consistent. The set of state diagrams for object classes with important dynamic behavior constitute the dynamic model for an application.

*ATM example.* An account can potentially be accessed concurrently by more than one machine. Access to an account needs to be controlled to ensure that only one update at a time is applied.

Examination of the state diagrams shows that *bad bank code* is sent by consortium but not received by ATM. It needs to be added, followed by action *print bad bank code* and a transition to *card ejected*.

## 8.6 FUNCTIONAL MODELING

The functional model shows how values are computed, without regard for sequencing, decisions, or object structure. The functional model shows which values depend on which other values and the functions that relate them. Data flow diagrams are useful for showing functional dependencies. Functions are expressed in various ways, including natural language, mathematical equations, and pseudocode.

The processes on a data flow diagram correspond to activities or actions in the state diagrams of the classes. The flows on a data flow diagram correspond to objects or attribute values in an object diagram. It is best to construct the functional model after the object and dynamic models.

The following steps are performed in constructing a functional model:

- Identify input and output values [8.6.1]
- Build data flow diagrams showing functional dependencies [8.6.2]
- Describe functions [8.6.3]
- Identify constraints [8.6.4]
- Specify optimization criteria [8.6.5]

### 8.6.1 Identifying Input and Output Values

Begin by listing input and output values. Input and output values are parameters of events between the system and the outside world. Examine the problem statement to find any input or output values that you missed.

Figure 8.23 shows input and output values for the ATM application. Since all interactions between the system and the outside world pass through the ATM (or the cashier station, which is not elaborated here), all input and output values are parameters of ATM events. Input events that only affect the flow of control, such as *cancel, terminate,* or *continue,* do not supply input values. Acknowledgment events, such as *take cash* or *take card* similarly, do not supply data.

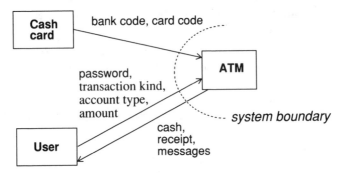

**Figure 8.23** Input and output values for ATM system

### 8.6.2 Building Data Flow Diagrams

Now construct a data flow diagram showing how each output value is computed from input values. A data flow diagram is usually constructed in layers. The top layer may consist of a single process, or perhaps one process each to gather inputs, compute values, and generate outputs. Figure 8.24 shows the top-level data flow diagram for the ATM example; input and output values are supplied and consumed by external objects, such as *User* and *Cash card.*

Within each data flow diagram layer, work backward from each output value to determine the function that computes it. If the inputs to the operation are all inputs of the entire diagram, you are done. Otherwise some of the operation inputs are intermediate values that

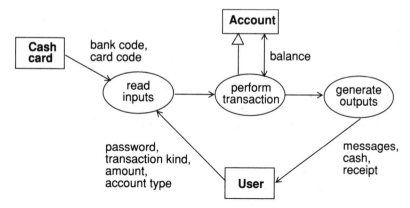

**Figure 8.24** Top level data flow diagram for ATM

must be traced backward in turn. You can also trace forward from inputs to outputs, but it is usually harder to identify all the uses of an input than to identify all the sources of an output.

Expand each nontrivial process in the top-level diagram into a lower-level data flow diagram. If second-level processes still contain nontrivial processes, they can be expanded recursively. Figure 8.25 expands the *perform transaction* process from Figure 8.24. Much of the *perform transaction* process selects the appropriate account, based on bank code, card code, and account type. The actual update process applies the transaction kind and amount to the selected account.

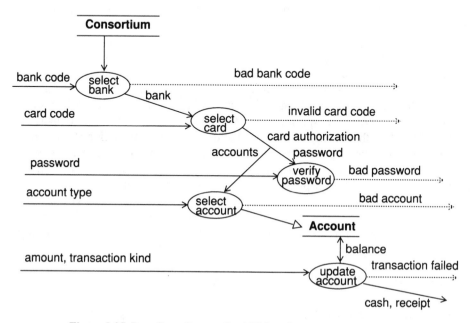

**Figure 8.25** Data flow diagram for ATM *perform transaction* process

Most systems contain internal storage objects that retain values between iterations. The ATM computation reads and writes values from the *Account* object. An internal store can be distinguished from a data flow or a process because it receives values that do not result in immediate outputs but instead are used at some distant time in the future.

Data flow diagrams specify only dependencies among operations. They do not show decisions or sequencing of operations; in fact, some operations can be optional or mutually exclusive. For example, the password must be verified before the account is updated; if it fails, then the account is not updated. Such sequencing decisions are part of the dynamic model, not the functional model.

Some data values affect decisions in the dynamic model. Decisions do not directly affect output values in the data flow model, as the data flow model shows all possible computation paths. However, it can be useful to capture decision functions in the data flow model, since they may be complicated functions of input values. Decision functions can be shown on the data flow diagram, but their outputs are control signals, indicated by dotted output arrows. These functions are "data sinks" within the data flow diagram; their outputs affect the flow of control in the dynamic model and not output values directly. For example, *verify password* is a decision function. We have shown the error signal that it may produce but left implicit the control arrow to the *update account* process. If you wish, you can draw a control arrow to a process controlled by a decision.

### 8.6.3  Describing Functions

When the data flow diagram has been refined enough, write a description of each function. The description can be in natural language, mathematical equations, pseudocode, decision tables, or some other appropriate form. Focus on what the function does, not how to implement it. The description can be declarative or procedural. A declarative description specifies the relationships between input and output values and the relationships among the output values. For example, the description of a "sort and remove duplicate values" function might be "every value in the input list appears exactly once in the output list, the output list contains only values from the input list, and the values in the output list are in strictly increasing order." A procedural description specifies a function by giving an algorithm to compute it. The purpose of the algorithm is only to specify what the function does; during implementation, any other algorithm that computes the same values can be substituted. Declarative descriptions are preferable to procedural descriptions, because they do not imply an implementation, but if the procedural description is much easier to write it should be used.

Most of the functions in the ATM example are trivial. Figure 8.26 shows the description of the *update account* function. The primary purpose is to specify what is to happen in all cases; for example, if the request exceeds the account balance, will a partial withdrawal be permitted?

### 8.6.4  Identifying Constraints Between Objects

Identify constraints between objects. Constraints are functional dependencies between objects that are not related by an input-output dependency. Constraints can be on two objects

```
update account (account, amount, transaction-kind) -> cash, receipt, message
    If the amount on a withdrawal exceeds the current account balance,
        reject the transaction and dispense no cash
    If the amount on a withdrawal does not exceed the current account balance,
        debit the account and dispense the amount requested
    If the transaction is a deposit
        credit the account and dispense no cash
    If the transaction is a status request
        dispense no cash
    In any case,
        the receipt shows ATM number, date, time, account number,
        transaction-kind, amount transacted (if any), and new balance
```

**Figure 8.26** Function description for *update account* function

at the same time, between instances of the same object at different times (an *invariant)*, or between instances of different objects at different times (although the latter are usually input-output functions). Preconditions on functions are constraints that the input values must satisfy, and postconditions are constraints that the output values are guaranteed to hold. State the times or conditions under which the constraints hold.

A constraint in the ATM problem is "no account balance may ever be negative." If we add accounts with overdraft privileges, the constraint becomes "no negative account balance may exceed the credit limit for the account." These constraints do not specify what to do if an excessive withdrawal is attempted; the analyst must incorporate the constraint into the dynamic and functional models to complete the specification.

### 8.6.5 Specifying Optimization Criteria

Specify values to be maximized, minimized, or otherwise optimized. If there are several optimization criteria that conflict, indicate how the trade-off is to be decided. Don't worry about making this too precise; you usually won't be able to, and the criteria are likely to change before the project is done anyway.

Optimization criteria for the ATM example might include: Minimize the number of physical messages sent between different sites. Minimize the time an account is locked for concurrency reasons. It is extremely urgent to minimize the time an entire bank is locked for concurrency reasons, if such locking is needed.

### 8.7 ADDING OPERATIONS

Our style of object-oriented analysis places much less emphasis on defining operations than more traditional programming-based object-oriented methodologies. The list of potentially-useful operations is open-ended and it is difficult to know when to stop adding them. Operations in object-oriented programming languages can correspond to queries about attributes or associations in the object model (such as *account.balance* or *cash-card.bank*), to events in the dynamic model (such as *cancel* sent from *user* to *ATM*), and to functions in the functional model (such as *update account*). We find it more useful to distinguish these various kinds of operations during analysis. In some object-oriented languages, such as Smalltalk, all these operations would be implemented the same, but other languages, such as DSM [Shah-89] provide separate mechanisms for each of them.

Key operations should now be summarized in the object model. They are discovered during the following analysis steps.

### 8.7.1 Operations from the Object Model

Operations from object structure include reading and writing attribute values and association links. These operations need not be shown explicitly on the object model, but are implied by the presence of an attribute. During analysis it is assumed that all attributes are accessible. A "dot" notation is convenient to indicate an attribute access, such as "ATM.cash-on-hand". Navigating a path from one object to another through the object model can be expressed as a series of "pseudo-attribute" accesses on association roles, such as "account.bank" or "remote-transaction.card-authorization.customer". Accessing a qualified link can be shown using an "index" notation, such as "consortium.bank[bank-code].account[account-code]". This notation can be used in pseudocode to define functions and actions.

### 8.7.2 Operations from Events

Each event sent to an object corresponds to an operation on the object. Depending on system architecture, events can be implemented directly by including an event handler as part of the system substrate, or they can be converted into explicit methods. During analysis, events are best represented as labels on state transitions and should not be explicitly listed in the object model.

### 8.7.3 Operations from State Actions and Activities

Actions and activities in the state diagram may be functions. These functions having interesting computational structure should be defined as operations on the object model. For example, in the ATM example *Consortium* has the activity *verify bank code* and *Bank* has the activity *verify password*.

### 8.7.4 Operations from Functions

Each function in the data flow diagram corresponds to an operation on an object (or possibly several objects). These functions frequently have interesting computational structure and should be summarized on the object model. Organize the functions into operations on objects. Omit access functions that traverse the object model.

If the same series of equations or pseudocode fragments describes more than one function, then a new operation can be introduced to simplify the functional model.

If we consider Figure 8.25, the *select* operations are all really path traversals in the object model. The only interesting operations are *verify-password* and *update-account*. We can define *verify-password* as an operation on class *Card-authorization* and *update-account* as an operation on class *Account*. In expanding the definition of *update-account*, it may be convenient to define simpler operations for each kind of transaction:

```
account :: withdraw (kind, amount)→status
account :: deposit (kind, amount)→status
```

### 8.7.5  Shopping List Operations

Sometimes the real-world behavior of classes suggests operations. Meyer [Meyer-88] calls this a "shopping list" because the operations are not dependent on a particular application nor subject to a particular order of execution but are meaningful in their own right. Shopping list operations permit considering future possible needs while the organization of classes is still fluid. They provide an opportunity to broaden the base of an object definition beyond the narrow needs of the immediate problem. They are meaningless for a purely function-oriented problem decomposition but make sense because we have insisted that objects have a real-world meaning that transcends their use in a single problem. Omit operations that correspond to path traversals.

Some operations not already required by the ATM problem include:

```
account :: close
account :: authorize-cash-card (cash-card-authorization)
bank :: create-savings-account(customer)→account
bank :: create-checking-account(customer)→account
bank :: create-cash-card(customer)→cash card-authorization
cash-card-authorization :: remove-account (account)
cash-card-authorization :: close
```

### 8.7.6  Simplifying Operations

Examine the object model for similar operations and variations in form on a single operation. Try to broaden the definition of an operation to encompass such variations and special cases. Use inheritance where possible to reduce the number of distinct operations. Introduce new superclasses as needed to simplify the operations, provided that the new superclasses are not forced and unnatural. Locate each operation at the correct level within the class hierarchy. A result of this refinement is often fewer, more powerful operations that are nevertheless simpler to specify than the original operations, because they are more uniform and general.

The ATM example is not complex enough to require simplification.

## 8.8  ITERATING THE ANALYSIS

Most analysis models require more than one pass to complete. Most problem statements contain circularities and most applications cannot be approached in a completely linear way, because different parts of the problem interact. To understand a problem with all its implications, you must attack the analysis iteratively, preparing a first approximation to the model and then iterating the analysis as your understanding increases. There is no firm line between analysis and design, so don't overdo it. Verify the final analysis with the requestor and application domain experts.

## 8.8.1 Refining the Analysis Model

The overall analysis model may show inconsistencies and imbalances within and across models. Iterate the different stages to produce a cleaner, more coherent design. Attempt to refine object definitions to increase sharing and improve structure. Add details that you glossed over during the first pass.

Some constructs will feel awkward and won't seem to fit in right. Reexamine them carefully; you may have the wrong concepts. Sometimes major restructuring in the model is needed as your understanding increases. It is easier to do now than it will ever be, so don't avoid changes that seem right just because you already have a model in place. When there are many constructs that appear similar but don't fit together right, you have probably missed or miscast a more general concept. Watch out for generalizations factored on the wrong attributes.

A common omission is a physical object that has two logically-distinct aspects. These should be modeled with a distinct object for each aspect. An indication of this is an object that doesn't fit in cleanly because of its need to fill two roles.

Other indications to watch for include exceptions, many special cases, lack of expected symmetry, and an object with two or more sets of unrelated attributes or operations. Consider restructuring your model to better capture constraints within its structure.

Remove objects or associations that seemed useful at first but now appear extraneous. Often two distinct objects in the analysis can be combined because the distinction between them doesn't affect the rest of the model in any meaningful way.

A good model feels right and does not appear to have extraneous detail. Don't worry if it doesn't seem perfect; even a good model will often have a few small areas where the design is adequate but never feels quite right.

## 8.8.2 Restating the Requirements

When the analysis is complete, the model serves as the basis for the requirements and defines the scope of future discourse. Most of the real requirements will be part of the model. Some requirements specify performance constraints; these should be stated clearly together with optimization criteria. Other requirements specify the method of solution; these should be separated and challenged, if possible.

The final model should be verified with the requestor. During analysis some requirements may appear to be incorrect or impractical; corrections to the requirements should be confirmed. The analysis model should also be verified by application domain experts to make sure that it correctly models the real world. We have found analysis models to be an effective means of communication with application experts who are not computer experts.

The final verified analysis model serves as the basis for system architecture, design, and implementation. The original problem statement should be revised to incorporate corrections and understanding discovered during analysis.

### 8.8.3 Analysis and Design

The goal of the analysis is to fully specify the problem and application domain without introducing a bias to any particular implementation, but it is impossible in practice to avoid all taints of implementation. There is no absolute line between the various design phases, nor is there any such thing as a perfect analysis. Don't treat the rules we have given too rigidly. The purpose of the rules is to preserve flexibility and permit changes later, but remember that the goal of modeling is to accomplish the total job, and flexibility is just a means to an end.

## 8.9 CHAPTER SUMMARY

The purpose of analysis is to state and understand the problem and the application domain so that a correct design can be constructed. A good analysis captures the essential features of the problem without introducing implementation artifacts that prematurely restrict design decisions.

First write an initial problem statement, in consultation with requestors, users, and domain experts. The requirements should describe what needs to be done, not how it will be implemented. The problem statement may be incomplete, ambiguous, and erroneous—it is just a starting point.

The object model shows the static structure of the real world. First identify object classes. Then identify associations between objects, including aggregations. Object attributes and links should be identified, although minor ones can be deferred. Inheritance should be used to organize and simplify the class structure. Organize tightly-coupled classes and associations into modules. Information in object models should be supplemented with brief textual descriptions, including the purpose and scope of each entity.

The dynamic model shows the behavior of the system, especially sequencing of interactions. First prepare scenarios of typical and exceptional sessions. Then identify external events between the system and the outside world. Build a state diagram for each active object showing the patterns of events it receives and sends, together with actions that it performs. Match events between state diagrams to verify consistency; the resulting set of state diagrams constitute the dynamic model.

The functional model shows the functional derivation of values, without regard for when they are computed. First identify input and output values of the system as parameters of external events. Then construct data flow diagrams to show the computation of each output value from other values and ultimately input values. Data flow diagrams interact with internal objects that serve as data stores between iterations. Finally specify constraints and optimization criteria.

Operations are derived from several sources in this methodology and we do not find it useful to group them together during analysis. Only operations from the functional model (and possibly shopping list operations) need be shown on the object diagram.

Methodologies are never as linear as they appear in books. This one is no exception. Any complex analysis is constructed by iteration on multiple levels. All parts of the model need not be developed at the same pace. The result of analysis replaces the original problem statement and serves as the basis for design.

| | |
|---|---|
| analysis | identifying attributes |
| analysis model | identifying classes |
| building the dynamic model | identifying events |
| building the functional model | identifying operations |
| building the object model | problem statement |
| data dictionary | scenario |
| identifying associations | testing the model |

**Figure 8.27** Key concepts for Chapter 8

## BIBLIOGRAPHIC NOTES

Shlaer and Mellor [Shlaer-88] present a similar approach to analyzing a problem in terms of real-world objects, attributes, and relationships, and constructing state machines for each object. Their approach is oriented more to relational database representations than ours. Our methodology stresses the freedom of an analysis model from implementation constructs, such as relational tables and identifiers. Shlaer and Mellor construct state models for passive objects, such as accounts, while we would restrict state models to active objects. Nevertheless the reader can easily make the correspondence between the notations and approaches.

Meyer [Meyer-88] provides many useful insights into principles underlying a good design. He advocates the use of data-directed bottom-up design, discovery of "shopping list operations," and the lack of any "main program" in a system. We would not reject his goals, although we have found that operations can be derived from the dynamic and functional models as part of design. He makes effective use of assertions, pre- and post-conditions for specifying operations.

Booch presents perhaps the best short explanation of object-oriented design in his brief paper [Booch-86]. He discusses how to find objects and operations by looking at nouns and verbs in the problem statement.

A more thorough comparison with other methodologies and notations is given in Chapter 12.

## REFERENCES

[Booch-86] Grady Booch. Object-oriented development. *IEEE Transactions on Software Engineering SE-12*, 2 (February 1986), 211-221.

[Meyer-88] Bertrand Meyer. *Object-Oriented Software Construction*. Hertfordshire, England: Prentice Hall International, 1988.

[Shah-89] Ashwin Shah, James Rumbaugh, Jung Hamel, Renee Borsari. DSM: an object-relationship modeling language. *OOPSLA '89* as *ACM SIGPLAN 24*, 11 (Nov. 1989), 191-210.

[Shlaer-88] Sally Shlaer, Stephen J. Mellor. *Object-Oriented Systems Analysis*. Englewood Cliffs, New Jersey: Yourdon Press, 1988.

## EXERCISES

**8.1**   (3) For each of the following systems, identify the relative importance of the three aspects of modeling: 1) object modeling, 2) dynamic modeling, 3) functional modeling. Explain your answers. For example, for a compiler, the answer might be 3, 1, and 2. Functional modeling is most important for a compiler because it is dominated by data transformation concerns.

    a.  bridge player
    b.  change-making machine
    c.  car cruise control
    d.  electronic typewriter
    e.  spelling checker
    f.  telephone answering machine

**8.2**   (4) Prepare functional specifications, similar to the problem statement given for the ATM system in Section 8.3, for each of the systems in exercise 8.1. You may limit the scope of the system, but be precise and avoid making implementation decisions. Use 150-300 words per specification.

**8.3**   (3) Rephrase the following requirements to make them more precise. Remove any design decisions posing as requirements:

    a.  A system to transfer data from one computer to another over a telecommunication line. The system should transmit data reliably over noisy channels. Data must not be lost if the receiving end cannot keep up or if the line drops out. Data should be transmitted in packets, using a master–slave protocol in which the receiving end acknowledges or negatively acknowledges all exchanges.

    b.  A system for automating the production of complex machined parts is needed. The parts will be designed using a three–dimensional drafting editor that is part of the system. The system will produce tapes that can be used by numerical control (N/C) machines to actually produce the parts.

    c.  A desktop publishing system is needed, based on a what-you-see-is-what-you-get philosophy. The system will support text and graphics. Graphics includes lines, squares, boxes, polygons, circles, and ellipses. Internally, a circle is represented as a special case of an ellipse and a square as a special case of a box. The system should support interactive, graphical editing of documents.

    d.  A system for generating nonsense is desired. The input is a sample document. The output is random text that mimics the input text by imitating the frequencies of combinations of letters of the input. The user specifies the order of the imitation and the length of the desired output. For order N, every output sequence of N characters is found in the input and at approximately the same frequency. As the order increases, the style of the output more closely matches the input. The system should generate its output with the following method: Select a position at random in the document being imitated. Scan forward in the input text until a sequence of characters is found that exactly matches the last N-1 characters of the output. If you reach the end of the input, continue scanning from the beginning. When a match is found, copy the letter that follows the matched sequence from the input to the output. Repeat until the desired amount of text is generated.

    e.  A system for distributing electronic mail over a network is needed. Each user of the system should be able to send mail from any computer account and receive mail on one designated account. There should be provisions for answering or forwarding mail, as well as saving messages in files or printing them. Also, users should be able to send messages to several other users at once through distribution lists. Each computer on the net should hold any messages destined for computers which are down.

**8.4**    (7) Create an object diagram for each system from exercise 8.3.

Exercises 8.5–8.15 are related. Exercise 8.5 should be done first. The following are tentative functional specifications for a simple diagram editor that could be used as the core of a variety of applications:

The editor will be used interactively to create and modify drawings. A drawing contains several sheets. Drawings are saved to and loaded from named ASCII files. Sheets contain boxes and links. Each box may optionally contain a single line of text. Text is allowed only in boxes. The editor must automatically adjust the size of a box to fit any enclosed text. The font size of the text is not adjustable. Any pair of boxes on the same sheet may be linked by a series of alternating horizontal and vertical lines. A simple, one sheet drawing is shown in Figure E8.1.

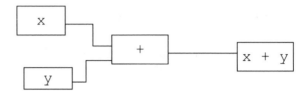

**Figure E8.1**  Sample drawing

The editor will be menu driven, with pop-up menus. A three button mouse will be used for menu, object, and link selections. The following are some operations the editor should provide: create sheet, delete sheet, next sheet, previous sheet, create box, link boxes, enter text, group selection, cut, move or copy selections, paste, edit text, save drawing, and load drawing. Copy, cut, and paste will work through a buffer. Copy will create a copy of selections from a sheet to the buffer. Cut will remove selections to the buffer. Paste will copy the contents of the buffer to the sheet. Each copy and cut operation overwrites the previous contents of the buffer. Pan and zoom will not be allowed; drawings will have fixed size. When boxes are moved, enclosed text should move with them and links should be stretched.

**8.5**    (3) The following is a list of candidate object classes. Prepare a list of classes that should be eliminated for any of the reasons given in this chapter. Give a reason for each elimination. If there is more than one reason, give the main one:

character, line, x coordinate, y coordinate, link, position, length, width, collection, selection, menu, mouse, button, computer, drawing, drawing file, sheet, pop-up, point, menu item, selected object, selected line, selected box, selected text, file name, box, buffer, line segment coordinate, connection, text, name, origin, scale factor, corner point, end point, graphics object.

**8.6**    (3) Prepare a data dictionary for the previous exercise.

**8.7**    (3) The following is a list of candidate associations and generalizations for the diagram editor described in exercise 8.5. Prepare a list of associations and generalizations that should be eliminated or renamed for any of the reasons given in this chapter. Give a reason for each elimination or renaming. If there is more than one reason, give the main one.

a box has text, a box has a position, a link logically associates two boxes, a box is moved, a link has points, a link is defined by a sequence of points, a selection or a buffer or a sheet is a collection, a character string has a location, a box has a character string, a character string has characters, a line has length, a collection is composed of links and boxes, a link is deleted, a line is moved, a line is a graphical object, a point is a graphical object, a line has two points, a point has an x coordinate, a point has a y coordinate

**8.8**   (8) Figure E8.2 is a partially completed object diagram for the diagram editor described in exercise 8.5. How could it be used for each of the following queries?

a.   What are all selected boxes and links?

b.   Given a box, determine all other boxes that are directly linked to it.

c.   Given a box, find all other boxes that are directly or indirectly linked to it.

d.   Given a box and a link, determine if the link involves the box.

e.   Given a box and a link, find the other box logically connected to the given box through the other end of the link.

f.   Given two boxes, determine all links between them.

g.   Given a selection, determine which links are "bridging" links. If a selection does not include all boxes on a sheet, "bridging" links may result. A "bridging" link is a link that connects a box that has been selected to a box that has not. A link that connects two boxes that are selected or two boxes that are not selected is not a "bridging" link. "Bridging" links require special handling during a *cut* or a *move* operation on a selection.

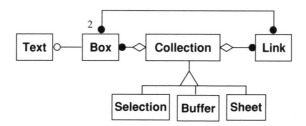

**Figure E8.2**  Partially completed object diagram for a diagram editor

**8.9**   (6) Figure E8.3 is a variation of the object diagram for the previous exercise in which the class *Connection* is used to explicitly represent the connection of a link to a box. Explain how to carry out those queries from the previous exercise that become simpler with this representation. Do any of them become more difficult? If so, which ones? Discuss the merits of this variation.

**8.10**   (4) Prepare a scenario for the preparation of the drawing in Figure E8.1. Include at least one of each of the editor operations listed in exercise 8.5. Do not worry about error conditions.

**8.11**   (3) Prepare 3 error scenarios, starting from the previous exercise.

**8.12**   (4) Prepare event traces for the scenarios you prepared in the previous two exercises.

**8.13**   (4) Prepare an event flow diagram for the diagram editor.

**8.14**   (6) What object classes require state diagrams? (You may want to consider adding the classes *Editor* and/or *Mouse* if your object diagram does not already have them.) Prepare state diagrams for the classes that need them. Check corresponding events for consistency.

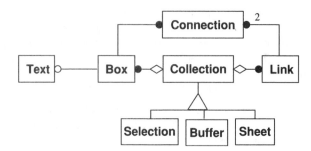

**Figure E8.3** Partially completed object diagram for a diagram editor

**8.15** (5) Prepare a functional model for the diagram editor.

Exercises 8.16–8.27 are related. Exercise 8.16 should be done first. These exercises are concerned with a computerized scoring system you have volunteered to create for the benefit of a local children's synchronized swimming league. Teams get together for competitions called meets during which the children perform in two types of events: figures and routines. Figure events, which are performed individually, are particular water ballet maneuvers such as swimming on your back with one leg raised straight up. Routines, which are performed by the entire team, are water ballets. Both figures and routines are scored, but your system is concerned only with figures.

Children must provide their names, ages, addresses, and team names to register prior to the meet. To simplify scoring, each contestant is assigned a number.

During a meet, figure events are held simultaneously at several stations that are set up around a swimming pool, usually one at each corner. There are volunteer judges and scorekeepers. Scorekeepers tend to become burned out, so there is a fair amount of turnover in their ranks. Several judges and scorekeepers are assigned to each station during a meet. Over the course of a season each judge and scorekeeper may serve several stations. For scoring uniformity, each figure is held at exactly one station with the same judges. A station may process several figure events in the course of a meet.

Contestants are split up into groups, with each group starting at a different station. When a child is finished at one station, he or she proceeds to another station for another event. When everyone has been processed at a station for a given event, the station switches to the next event assigned to it.

Each competitor gets one try at each event, called a trial. Just before a trial, the child's number is announced to the child and to the scorekeepers. Sometimes the children get out of order or the scorekeepers get confused and the station stops while things get straightened out. Each judge indicates a raw score for each observed trial by holding up numbered cards. The raw scores are read to the scorekeepers, who record them and compute a net score for the trial. The highest and lowest raw scores are discarded and the average of the remaining is multiplied by a difficulty factor for the figure.

Individual and team prizes are awarded at the conclusion of a meet based on top individual and team scores. There are several age categories, with separate prizes for each category. Individual prizes are based on figures only. Team prizes are based on figures and routines.

Your system will be used to store all information needed for scheduling, registration, and scoring. At the beginning of a season, all swimmers will be entered into the system and a season schedule will be prepared, including deciding which figures will be judged at which meets. Prior to a meet, the system will be used to process registrations. During a meet, it will record scores and determine winners.

**8.16** (3) The following is a list of candidate object classes for the scoring system. Prepare a list of classes that should be eliminated for any of the reasons given in this chapter. Give a reason for each elimination. If there is more than one reason, give the main one:

address, age, age category, average score, back, card, child, child's name, competitor, compute average, conclusion, contestant, corner, date, difficulty factor, event, figure, file of team member data, group, individual, individual prize, judge, league, leg, list of scheduled meets, meet, net score, number, person, pool, prize, register, registrant, raw score, routine, score, scorekeeper, season, station, team, team prize, team name, trial, try, water ballet.

**8.17** (3) Prepare a data dictionary for the previous exercise.

**8.18** (4)The following is a list of candidate associations and generalizations for the scoring system. Prepare a list of associations and generalizations that should be eliminated or renamed for any of the reasons given in this chapter. Give a reason for each elimination or renaming. If there is more than one reason, give the main one:

a season consists of several meets, a competitor registers, a competitor is assigned a number, a number is announced, competitors are split into groups, a meet consists of several events, several stations are set up at a meet, several events are processed at a station, several judges are assigned to a station, routines and figures are events, raw scores are read, highest score is discarded, lowest score is discarded, figures are processed, a league consists of several teams, a team consists of several competitors, a trial of a figure is made by a competitor, a trial receives several scores from the judges, prizes are based on scores.

**8.19** (8) Figure E8.4 is a partially completed object diagram for the scoring system. Explain how it could be used for each of the following queries. You may need to revise the diagram to process some of the queries:
a. Find all the members of a given team.
b. Find which figures were held more than once in a given season.
c. Find the net score of a competitor for a given figure at a given meet.
d. Find the team average over all figures in a given season.
e. Find the average score of a competitor over all figures in a given meet.
f. Find the team average in a given figure at a given meet.
g. Find the set of all individuals who competed in any events in a given season.
h. Find the set of all individuals who competed in all of the events held in a given season.
i. Find all the judges who judged a given event in a given season.
j. Find the judge who awarded the lowest score during a given event.
k. Find the judge who awarded the lowest score for a given figure.
l. Modify the diagram so that the competitors registered for an event can be determined.

**8.20** (3) Prepare a scenario for setting up the scoring system at the beginning of a season. Data on teams, competitors, and judges will be entered. A schedule of meets for the season will be prepared and events for each meet will be selected. Enter difficulty factors for events. Include at least 2 teams, 6 competitors, 3 judges, 3 meets, and 12 events. Do not worry about error conditions.

**8.21** (3) Prepare 3 error scenarios, starting from exercise 8.20.

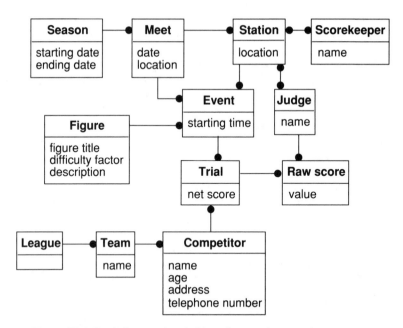

**Figure E8.4** Partially completed object diagram for a scoring system

**8.22** (3) Prepare a scenario for printing and processing preregistration forms for the scoring system. Include entering changes in address in two of the returned forms and two children unable to attend. Assign a number to each contestant.

**8.23** (5) Prepare scenarios for scoring on the day of a meet. To simplify matters, limit the scenario to 2 teams, 4 competitors, 2 stations, 6 judges, and 4 events. Include both scoring during events and determination of winners at the end.

**8.24** (6) What object classes require state diagrams? You may want to consider adding classes. Prepare state diagrams for the classes that need them. Check corresponding events for consistency.

**8.25** (5) Prepare a functional model for the scoring system.

**8.26** (3) Prepare a shopping list of operations for the scoring system and place them in an object diagram.

**8.27** (5) For each operation listed in the previous exercise, summarize what the operation should do.

Exercises 8.28–8.33 illustrate additional fine points of performing object-oriented analysis.

**8.28** (6) Revise the diagrams in Figure E8.5, Figure E8.6, Figure E8.7, and Figure E8.8 to eliminate ternary associations. In some cases you will have to promote the association to a class.
    Figure E8.5 is a relationship between *Doctor, Patient,* and *Date-time* which might be encountered in a system used by a clinic with several doctors on the staff. Candidate keys for the relationship include *Date-time + Patient* or *Date-time + Doctor.*

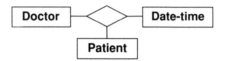

**Figure E8.5** Ternary association for doctor, patient, and date-time

**Figure E8.6** Ternary association for student, professor, and university

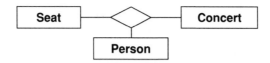

**Figure E8.7** Ternary association for seat, person, and concert

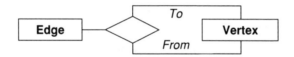

**Figure E8.8** Ternary association for directed graphs

Figure E8.6 is a relationship between *Student*, *Professor*, and *University* which might be used to express the contacts between students and professors who teach at or attend several universities.

There is one link in the relationship for a student that takes one or more classes from a professor at a university. The candidate key is *Student + Professor + University*.

Figure E8.7 shows the relationship expressing the seating arrangement at a concert. *Concert + Seat* is a candidate key.

Figure E8.8 expresses the connectivity of a directed graph. Each edge of a directed graph is connected in a specific order to exactly 2 vertices. More than one edge can be connected between a given pair of vertices. The only candidate key of the relationship is *Edge*.

In each case, try to come as close as possible to the original intent and discuss what is lost.

**8.29** (4) Figure E8.9 is an object diagram for exercise 8.3a. *Sender* and *Receiver* are the only classes with important dynamic behavior. Construct an event trace for the following scenario: Sender tries to establish a connection to the receiver by sending a start of transaction packet. The receiver successfully reads the packet and replies with an acknowledgment. The sender then transmits a start of file packet, which is acknowledged. Then, the file data is transmitted in three acknowledged packets, followed by end of file, and end of transaction, which are also acknowledged.

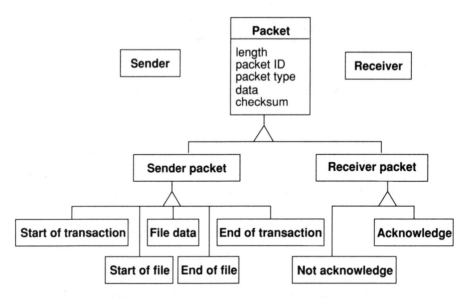

**Figure E8.9** An object diagram for a file transfer system

**8.30** (3) Prepare additional event traces for the previous example to include errors caused by noise corruption of each type of sender packet. Revise your previous answer.

**8.31** (5) Prepare a state–event diagram for a file transfer system from the event traces prepared in exercises 8.29 and 8.30.

**8.32** (3) Prepare a state diagram for the class *Cashier station* for the ATM problem described in this chapter.

**8.33** (6) In an airline reservation system, there could be a ternary relationship between flight, seat, and passenger. What are the candidate keys of the relationship under the following conditions?
  a. A given seat on a given flight is assigned to zero or one passenger. A passenger may travel on many flights but must have exactly one seat on a traveled flight and must be sitting in it during the flight.
  b. A given seat on a given flight is assigned to zero or one passenger, as in the previous. A passenger may travel on many flights and may have several seats on a traveled flight, as long as the extra seats are paid for. (Some passengers may be willing to pay for the extra elbow room, or may have some delicate electronic equipment that they want to strap into a seat.)

**8.34** (4) Use generalization to improve the object diagram for a file system shown in Figure E8.10.

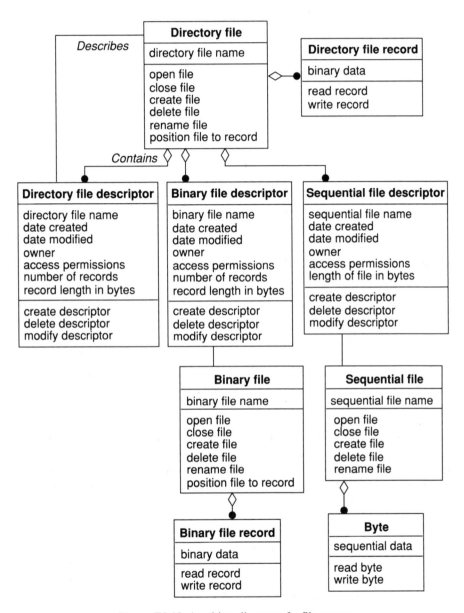

**Figure E8.10** An object diagram of a file system

# 9

---

# System Design

After you have analyzed a problem, you must decide how to approach the design. *System design* is the high-level strategy for solving the problem and building a solution. System design includes decisions about the organization of the system into subsystems, the allocation of subsystems to hardware and software components, and major conceptual and policy decisions that form the framework for detailed design.

The overall organization of a system is called the *system architecture*. There are a number of common architectural styles, each of which is suitable for certain kinds of applications. One way to characterize an application is by the relative importance of its object, dynamic, and functional models. Different architectures place differing emphasis on the three models.

In this chapter you will learn about the many aspects of an application problem that you should consider when formulating a system design. We also present several common architectural styles that you can use as a starting point for your designs. This list of architectural styles is not meant to be complete; new architectures can always be invented or adapted as needed. The treatment of system design in this chapter is intended for small to medium software development efforts; large complex systems, involving more than about ten developers, are limited by human communication issues and require a much greater emphasis on design logistics. Most of the suggestions in this chapter are suitable for non-object-oriented as well as object-oriented systems.

## 9.1 OVERVIEW OF SYSTEM DESIGN

During analysis, the focus is on *what* needs to be done, independent of *how* it is done. During design, decisions are made about how the problem will be solved, first at a high level, then at increasingly detailed levels.

*System design* is the first design stage in which the basic approach to solving the problem is selected. During system design, the overall structure and style are decided. The *system architecture* is the overall organization of the system into components called *subsystems*.

The architecture provides the context in which more detailed decisions are made in later design stages. By making high-level decisions that apply to the entire system, the system designer partitions the problem into subsystems so that further work can be done by several designers working independently on different subsystems.

The system designer must make the following decisions:

- Organize the system into subsystems [9.2]
- Identify concurrency inherent in the problem [9.3]
- Allocate subsystems to processors and tasks [9.4]
- Choose an approach for management of data stores [9.5]
- Handle access to global resources [9.6]
- Choose the implementation of control in software [9.7]
- Handle boundary conditions [9.8]
- Set trade-off priorities [9.9]

Often the overall architecture of a system can be chosen based on its similarity to previous systems. Certain kinds of system architecture are useful for solving several broad classes of problems. Section 9.10 surveys several common architectures and describes the kinds of problems for which they are useful. Not all problems can be solved by one of these architectures but many can. Many other architectures can be constructed by combining these forms.

## 9.2 BREAKING A SYSTEM INTO SUBSYSTEMS

For all but the smallest applications, the first step in system design is to divide the system into a small number of components. Each major component of a system is called a *subsystem*. Each subsystem encompasses aspects of the system that share some common property—similar functionality, the same physical location, or execution on the same kind of hardware. For example, a spaceship computer might include subsystems for life support, navigation, engine control, and running scientific experiments.

A subsystem is not an object nor a function but a package of classes, associations, operations, events, and constraints that are interrelated and that have a reasonably well-defined and (hopefully) small interface with other subsystems. A subsystem is usually identified by the *services* it provides. A *service* is a group of related functions that share some common purpose, such as I/O processing, drawing pictures, or performing arithmetic. A subsystem defines a coherent way of looking at one aspect of the problem. For example, the file system within an operating system is a subsystem; it comprises a set of related abstractions that are largely, but not entirely, independent of abstractions in other subsystems, such as the memory management subsystem or the process control subsystem.

Each subsystem has a well-defined interface to the rest of the system. The interface specifies the form of all interactions and the information flow across subsystem boundaries but does not specify how the subsystem is implemented internally. Each subsystem can then be designed independently without affecting the others.

Subsystems should be defined so that most interactions are within subsystems, rather than across subsystem boundaries, in order to reduce the dependencies among the subsystems. A system should be divided into a small number of subsystems; 20 is probably too many. Each subsystem may in turn be decomposed into smaller subsystems of its own. The lowest level subsystems are called *modules*, as discussed in Chapter 3.

The relationship between two subsystems can be *client-supplier* or *peer-to-peer*. In a client-supplier relationship, the client calls on the supplier, which performs some service and replies with a result. The client must know the interface of the supplier, but the supplier does not have to know the interfaces of its clients because all the interactions are initiated by clients using the supplier's interface. In a peer-to-peer relationship, each of the subsystems may call on the others. A communication from one subsystem to another is not necessarily followed by an immediate response. Peer-to-peer interactions are more complicated because the subsystems must know each other's interfaces. Communications cycles can exist that are hard to understand and liable to subtle design errors. Look for supplier-client decompositions whenever possible because a one-way interaction is much easier to build, understand, and change than a two-way interaction.

The decomposition of systems into subsystems may be organized as a sequence of horizontal *layers* or vertical *partitions*.

## 9.2.1 Layers

A layered system is an ordered set of virtual worlds, each built in terms of the ones below it and providing the basis of implementation for the ones above it. The objects in each layer can be independent, although there is often some correspondence between objects in different layers. Knowledge is one-way only: A subsystem knows about the layers below it, but has no knowledge of the layers above it. A supplier-client relationship exists between lower layers (providers of services) and upper layers (users of services).

In an interactive graphics system, for example, windows are made from screen operations, which are implemented using pixel operations, which execute as device I/O operations. Each layer may have its own set of classes and operations. Each layer is implemented in terms of the classes and operations of lower layers.

Layered architectures come in two forms: closed and open. In a *closed architecture*, each layer is built only in terms of the immediate lower layer. This reduces the dependencies between layers and allows changes to be made most easily because a layer's interface only affects the next layer. In an *open architecture*, a layer can use features of any lower layer to any depth. This reduces the need to redefine operations at each level, which can result in a more efficient and compact code. However, an open architecture does not observe the principle of information hiding. Changes to a subsystem can affect any higher subsystem, so an open architecture is less robust than a closed architecture. Both kinds of architectures are useful; the designer must weigh the relative value of efficiency and modularity.

Usually only the top and bottom layers are specified by the problem statement: The top is the desired system, the bottom is the available resources (hardware, operating system, existing libraries). If the disparity between the two is too great (as it often is), then the system designer must introduce intermediate layers to reduce the conceptual gap between adjoining layers.

A system constructed in layers can be ported to other hardware/software platforms by rewriting one layer. It is a good practice to introduce at least one layer of abstraction between the application and any services provided by the operating system or hardware. Define a layer of interface classes providing logical services and map them onto the concrete services that are system-dependent.

### 9.2.2 Partitions

Partitions vertically divide a system into several independent or weakly-coupled subsystems, each providing one kind of service. For example, a computer operating system includes a file system, process control, virtual memory management, and device control. The subsystems may have some knowledge of each other, but this knowledge is not deep, so major design dependencies are not created.

A system can be successively decomposed into subsystems using both layers and partitions in various possible combinations: Layers can be partitioned and partitions can be layered. Figure 9.1 shows a block diagram of a typical application, which involves simulation of the application and interactive graphics. Most large systems require a mixture of layers and partitions.

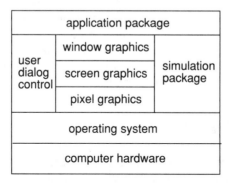

**Figure 9.1** Block diagram of a typical application

### 9.2.3 System Topology

When the top-level subsystems are identified, the designer should show the information flow among subsystems with a data flow diagram (see the examples of architectural styles in Section 9.10). Sometimes, all subsystems interact with all other subsystems, but often the flow is simpler. For example, many computations have the form of a pipeline; a compiler is an example. Other systems are arranged as a star, in which a master subsystem controls all interactions with other subsystems. Use simple topologies when they are suitable for a problem to reduce the number of interactions among subsystems.

## 9.3 IDENTIFYING CONCURRENCY

In the analysis model, as in the real world and in hardware, all objects are concurrent. In an implementation, however, not all software objects are concurrent because one processor may support many objects. In practice, many objects can be implemented on a single processor if the objects cannot be active together. One important goal of system design is to identify which objects must be active concurrently and which objects have activity that is mutually exclusive. The latter objects can be folded together in a single thread of control, or task.

### 9.3.1 Identifying Inherent Concurrency

The dynamic model is the guide to identifying concurrency. Two objects are inherently concurrent if they can receive events at the same time without interacting. If the events are unsynchronized, the objects cannot be folded onto a single thread of control. For example, the engine and the wing controls on an airplane must operate concurrently (if not completely independently). Independent subsystems are desirable because they can be assigned to different hardware units without any communication cost.

Two subsystems that are inherently concurrent need not necessarily be implemented as separate hardware units. The purpose of hardware interrupts, operating systems, and tasking mechanisms is to simulate logical concurrency in a uniprocessor. Physically-concurrent input must of course be processed by separate sensors, but if there are no timing constraints on response then a multitasking operating system can handle the computation.

Often the problem statement specifies that objects must be implemented as distinct hardware units. For example, if the ATM statement from Chapter 8 contained the requirement that each machine should continue to operate locally in the event of a central system failure (perhaps with reduced limits on transactions), then we would have no choice but to include a CPU in each ATM machine with a full control program.

### 9.3.2 Defining Concurrent Tasks

Although all objects are conceptually concurrent, in practice many objects in a system are interdependent. By examining the state diagrams of individual objects and the exchange of events among them, many objects can often be folded together onto a single thread of control. A *thread of control* is a path through a set of state diagrams on which only a single object at a time is active. A thread remains within a state diagram until an object sends an event to another object and waits for another event. The thread passes to the receiver of the event until it eventually returns to the original object. The thread splits if the object sends an event and continues executing.

On each thread of control, only a single object at a time is active. Threads of control are implemented as *tasks* in computer systems. For example, while the bank is verifying an account or processing a bank transaction, the ATM machine is idle. If the ATM is controlled directly by a central computer, then the ATM object can be folded together with the bank transaction object as a single task.

## 9.4 ALLOCATING SUBSYSTEMS TO PROCESSORS AND TASKS

Each concurrent subsystem must be allocated to a hardware unit, either a general purpose processor or a specialized functional unit. The system designer must:

- Estimate performance needs and the resources needed to satisfy them.

- Choose hardware or software implementation for subsystems.

- Allocate software subsystems to processors to satisfy performance needs and minimize interprocessor communication.

- Determine the connectivity of the physical units that implement the subsystems.

### 9.4.1 Estimating Hardware Resource Requirements

The decision to use multiple processors or hardware functional units is based on a need for higher performance than a single CPU can provide. The number of processors required depends on the volume of computations and the speed of the machine. For example, a military radar system generates too much data in too short a time to handle in a single CPU, even a very large one. The data must be digested by many parallel machines before the final analysis about a threat can be performed.

The system designer must estimate the required CPU processing power by computing the steady state load as the product of the number of transactions per second and the time required to process a transaction. The estimate will usually be imprecise. Often some experimentation is useful. The estimate should then be increased to allow for transient effects, due to both random variations in load as well as synchronized bursts of activity. The amount of excess capacity needed depends on the acceptable rate of failure due to insufficient resources.

### 9.4.2 Hardware-Software Trade-offs

Hardware can be regarded as a rigid but highly optimized form of software. The object-oriented view is a good way of thinking about hardware. Each device is an object that operates concurrently with other objects (other devices or software). The system designer must decide which subsystems will be implemented in hardware and which in software. Subsystems are implemented in hardware for two main reasons:

- Existing hardware provides exactly the functionality required. Today it is easier to buy a floating point chip than to implement floating point in software. Sensors and actuators must be hardware, of course.

- Higher performance is required than a general purpose CPU can provide, and more efficient hardware is available. For example, chips that perform the Fast Fourier Transform (FFT) are widely used in signal processing applications.

Much of the difficulty of designing a system comes from meeting externally-imposed hardware and software constraints. Object-oriented design provides no magic solution, but the external packages can be modeled nicely as objects. You must consider compatibility, cost, and performance issues. You should also think about flexibility for future changes, both design changes and future product enhancements. Providing flexibility costs something; the architect must decide how much it is worth.

### 9.4.3  Allocating Tasks to Processors

The tasks for the various software subsystems must be allocated to processors. Tasks are assigned to processors because:

- Certain tasks are required at specific physical locations, to control hardware or to permit independent or concurrent operation. For example, an engineering workstation needs its own operating system to permit operation when the interprocessor network is down.

- The response time or information flow rate exceeds the available communication bandwidth between a task and a piece of hardware. For example, high performance graphics devices require tightly-coupled controllers because of their high internal data generation rates.

- Computation rates are too great for a single processor, so tasks must be spread among several processors. Those subsystems that interact the most should be assigned to the same processor to minimize communication costs. Independent subsystems should be assigned to separate processors.

### 9.4.4  Determining Physical Connectivity

After determining the kinds and relative numbers of physical units, the system designer must choose the arrangement and form of the connections among the physical units. The following decisions must be made:

- Choose the topology of connecting the physical units. Associations in the object model often correspond to physical connections. Client-supplier relationships in the functional model also correspond to physical connections. Some connections may be indirect, of course, but the designer must attempt to minimize the connection cost of important relationships.

- Choose the topology of repeated units. If several copies of a particular kind of unit or group of units are included for performance reasons, their topology must be specified. The object model and functional model are not useful guides because the use of multiple units is primarily a design optimization not required by analysis. The topology of repeated units usually has a regular pattern, such as a linear sequence, a matrix, a tree, or a star. The designer must consider the expected arrival patterns of data and the proposed parallel algorithm for processing it.

- Choose the form of the connection channels and the communication protocols. The system design phase may be too soon to specify the exact interfaces among units, but the general interaction mechanisms and protocols must usually be chosen. For example, interactions may be asynchronous, synchronous, or blocking. The bandwidth and latency of the communication channels must be estimated and the correct kind of connection channels chosen.

Even when the connections are logical and not physical, the connections must be considered. For example, the units may be tasks within a single operating system connected by interprocess communication calls. On most operating systems, such IPC calls are much slower than subroutine calls within the same program and may be impractical for certain time-critical connections. In that case, the tightly-linked tasks must be combined into a single task and the connections made by simple subroutine calls.

## 9.5 MANAGEMENT OF DATA STORES

The internal and external data stores in a system provide clean separation points between subsystems with well-defined interfaces. In general each data store may combine data structures, files, and databases implemented in memory or on secondary storage devices. For example, a personal computer application may use memory data structures, a RAM disk, and a hard disk. An accounting system may use a database and files to connect subsystems. Different kinds of data stores provide various trade-offs between cost, access time, capacity, and reliability.

Files are a cheap, simple, and permanent form of data store. However, file operations are low level and applications must include additional code to provide a suitable level of abstraction. File implementations vary for different computer systems, so portable applications must carefully isolate file system dependencies. Implementations for sequential files are mostly standard, but commands and storage formats for random access files and indexed files vary widely.

Databases, managed by database management systems (DBMS), are another kind of data store. Various types of DBMS are available from vendors: hierarchical, network, relational, object-oriented, and logic. DBMS attempt to cache frequently accessed data in memory in order to achieve the best combination of cost and performance from memory and disk storage. Databases are powerful and make applications easier to port to different hardware and operating system platforms, since the vendor ports the DBMS code. One disadvantage is that DBMS have a complex interface. Many database languages integrate awkwardly with programming languages.

The following guidelines characterize the kind of data that belongs in a formal database:

- Data that requires access at fine levels of detail by multiple users
- Data that can be efficiently managed with DBMS commands
- Data that must port across many hardware and operating system platforms
- Data that must be accessible by more than one application program

The following guidelines characterize the kind of data that belongs in a file and not in a relational database:

- Data that is voluminous in quantity but difficult to structure within the confines of DBMS (such as a graphics bit map)
- Data that is voluminous in quantity and of low information density (such as archival files, debugging dumps, or historical records)
- "Raw" data that is summarized in the database
- Volatile data that is kept a short time and then discarded

### 9.5.1 Advantages of Using a Database

There are many advantages to using a DBMS instead of simple files:

- *Many infrastructure features*, such as crash recovery, sharing between multiple users, sharing between multiple applications, data distribution, integrity, extensibility, and transaction support have already been programmed by the DBMS vendor.
- *Common interface for all applications*. Each application accesses the subset of the information it needs and ignores the rest.
- *A standard access language*. The SQL language is supported by most commercial relational database management systems.

### 9.5.2 Disadvantages of Using a Database

DBMS also have disadvantages that complicate and sometimes prevent their use on real problems. DBMS provide a general purpose engine for flexible management of data. But at times, DBMS functionality is not powerful enough or the performance overhead from providing general services too high. Some limitations of current DBMS, particularly relational DBMS, are:

- *Performance overhead*. Few relational DBMS can exceed 50 simple transactions per second on a computer such as a VAX 11/785. A simple transaction updates one row of a relational DBMS table. For demanding applications, system designers must work with the DBMS vendor to wring out extra performance or develop a custom solution.
- *Insufficient functionality for advanced applications*. Relational DBMS were developed for business applications that have large quantities of data with simple structure. Relational DBMS are difficult to use for applications that require richer data types or nonstandard operations.
- *Awkward interface with programming languages*. Relational DBMS support set-oriented operations that are expressed through a nonprocedural language. Most programming languages are procedural in nature and can only access relational DBMS tables a row at a time. [Premerlani-90] discusses a solution to integrating object-oriented languages with relational DBMS.

Some of these disadvantages may disappear as efficient object-oriented DBMS are implemented.

## 9.6 HANDLING GLOBAL RESOURCES

The system designer must identify global resources and determine mechanisms for controlling access to them. Global resources include: physical units, such as processors, tape drives, and communication satellites; space, such as disk space, a workstation screen, and the buttons on a mouse; logical names, such as object IDs, filenames, and class names; and access to shared data, such as databases.

If the resource is a physical object, then it can control itself by establishing a protocol for obtaining access within a concurrent system. If the resource is a logical entity, such as an object ID or a database, then there is danger of conflicting access in a shared environment. Independent tasks could simultaneously use the same object ID, for example. Each global resource must be owned by a "guardian object" that controls access to it. One guardian object can control several resources. All access to the resource must pass through the guardian object. For example, most database managers are free-standing tasks that other tasks can call to obtain data from the database. Allocating each shared global resource to a single object is a recognition that the resource has identity.

A logical resource can also be partitioned logically, such that subsets are assigned to different guardian objects for independent control. For example, one strategy for object ID generation in a parallel distributed environment is to preallocate a range of possible IDs to each processor in a network; each processor allocates the IDs within its preallocated range without the need for global synchronization.

In a time-critical application, the cost of passing all access to a resource through a guardian object is sometimes too high, and clients must access the resource directly. In this case, locks can be placed on subsets of the resource. A *lock* is a logical object associated with some defined subset of a resource that gives the lock holder the right to access the resource directly. A guardian object must still exist to allocate the locks, but after one interaction with the guardian to obtain a lock the user of the resource can access the resource directly. This approach is more dangerous because each resource user must be trusted to behave itself in its access to the resource. The use of direct access to shared resources should be discouraged in an object-oriented design unless absolutely necessary.

## 9.7 CHOOSING SOFTWARE CONTROL IMPLEMENTATION

During analysis, all interactions are shown as events between objects. Hardware control closely matches the analysis model, but the system designer must choose among several ways to implement control in software. Although there is no logical necessity that all subsystems use the same implementation, usually the designer chooses a single control style for the whole system. There are two kinds of control flows in a software system: external control and internal control.

External control is the flow of externally-visible events among the objects in the system. There are three kinds of control for external events: procedure-driven sequential, event-driven sequential, and concurrent. The control style adopted depends on the resources available (language, operating system) and on the pattern of interactions in the application. External control is discussed in this section.

Internal control is the flow of control within a process. It exists only in the implementation and therefore is not inherently concurrent or sequential. The designer may choose to decompose a process into several tasks for logical clarity or for performance (if multiple processors are available). Unlike external events, internal transfers of control, such as procedure calls or inter-task calls, are under the direction of the program and can be structured for convenience. Three kinds of control flow are common: procedure calls, quasi-concurrent inter-task calls, and concurrent inter-task calls. Quasi-concurrent inter-task calls, such as coroutines or lightweight processes, are programming conveniences in which multiple address spaces or call stacks exist but in which only a single thread of control can be active at once.

### 9.7.1 Procedure-driven Systems

In a procedure-driven sequential system, control resides within the program code. Procedures issue requests for external input and then wait for it; when input arrives, control resumes within the procedure that made the call. The location of the program counter and the stack of procedure calls and local variables define the system state.

The major advantage of procedure-driven control is that it is easy to implement with conventional languages; the disadvantage is that it requires the concurrency inherent in objects to be mapped into a sequential flow of control. The designer must convert events into operations between objects. A typical operation corresponds to a pair of events: an output event that performs output and requests input and an input event that delivers the new values. Asynchronous input cannot be easily accommodated with this paradigm because the program must explicitly request input. The procedure-driven paradigm is suitable only if the state model shows a regular alternation of input and output events. Flexible user interfaces and control systems are hard to build using this style.

Note that all major object-oriented languages, such as Smalltalk, C++, and CLOS, are procedural languages. Do not be fooled by the Smalltalk phrase *message passing*. A message *is* a procedure call with a built-in case statement that depends on the class of the target object. A major drawback of conventional object-oriented languages is that they fail to support the concurrency inherent in objects. Some concurrent object-oriented languages have been designed, but they are not yet widely used.

### 9.7.2 Event-driven Systems

In an event-driven sequential system, control resides within a dispatcher or monitor provided by the language, subsystem, or operating system. Application procedures are attached to events and are called by the dispatcher when the corresponding events occur ("callback"). Procedure calls to the dispatcher send output or enable input but do not wait for it in-line. All procedures return control to the dispatcher, rather than retaining control until input arrives. Events are handled directly by the dispatcher. Program state cannot be preserved using the program counter and stack because procedures return control to the dispatcher. Procedures must use global variables to maintain state or the dispatcher must maintain local state for them. Event-driven control is more difficult to implement with standard languages than procedure-driven control but is often worth the extra effort.

Event-driven systems permit more flexible patterns of control than procedure-driven systems. Event-driven systems simulate cooperating processes within a single multi-threaded task; an errant procedure can block the entire application, so care must be taken. Event-driven user interface subsystems are particularly useful; some commercial examples include SunView and X-Windows.

Use an event-driven system for external control in preference to a procedure-driven system whenever possible because the mapping from events to program constructs is much simpler and more powerful. Event-driven systems are also more modular and can handle error conditions better than procedure-driven systems.

### 9.7.3 Concurrent Systems

In a concurrent system, control resides concurrently in several independent objects, each a separate task. Events are implemented directly as one-way messages (*not* Smalltalk "messages") between objects. A task can wait for input, but other tasks continue execution. The operating system usually supplies a queuing mechanism for events so that events are not lost if a task is executing when they arrive. The operating system resolves scheduling conflicts among tasks. Examples of concurrent systems include tasks on an operating system and Ada tasks. If there are multiple CPUs, then different tasks can actually execute concurrently.

Ada supports concurrent tasks within the language. Programs in other languages, such as Fortran, C, or C++, can of course be run as tasks within a standard operating system, but inter-task communication usually requires costly operating system calls that are not portable to other operating systems. None of the current major object-oriented languages directly support tasking. Research is currently underway to develop concurrent object-oriented languages, some of which are in limited use.

### 9.7.4 Internal Control

During the design process, operations on objects are expanded into lower-level operations on the same or other objects. Internal interactions between objects can be viewed similarly to external interactions among objects, as events passed between objects, and the same implementation mechanisms can be used. There is an important difference: External interactions inherently involve waiting for events because different objects are independent and cannot force other objects to respond; internal operations are generated by objects as part of the implementation algorithm, so their response patterns are predictable. Most internal operations can therefore be thought of as procedure calls, in which the caller issues a request and waits for the response. There are algorithms in which concurrency can be used profitably, if parallel processing is available, but many computations are well represented sequentially and can easily be folded onto a single thread of control.

### 9.7.5 Other Paradigms

We assume that the reader is primarily interested in procedural programming, but other paradigms are possible, such as rule-based systems, logic programming systems, and other forms of nonprocedural programs. These constitute another control style in which explicit control is replaced by declarative specification with implicit evaluation rules, possibly nondeterministic or highly convoluted. Such languages are currently used in limited areas, such as artificial intelligence and knowledge-based programming, but we expect their use to grow in the future. Because these languages are totally different from procedural languages (including object-oriented languages), the remainder of this book has little to say about their use.

## 9.8 HANDLING BOUNDARY CONDITIONS

Although most of the design effort in many systems is concerned with the steady-state behavior, the system designer must consider boundary conditions as well: initialization, termination, and failure. The following kinds of issues must be addressed:

*Initialization.* The system must be brought from a quiescent initial state to a sustainable steady state condition. Things to be initialized include constant data, parameters, global variables, tasks, guardian objects, and possibly the class hierarchy itself. During initialization only a subset of the functionality of the system is usually available. Initializing a system containing concurrent tasks is most difficult because independent objects must not get either too far ahead or too far behind other independent objects during initialization.

*Termination.* Termination is usually simpler than initialization because many internal objects can simply be abandoned. The task must release any external resources that it had reserved. In a concurrent system, one task must notify other tasks of its termination.

*Failure.* Failure is the unplanned termination of a system. Failure can arise from user errors, from the exhaustion of system resources, or from an external breakdown. The good system designer plans for orderly failure. Failure can also arise from bugs in the system and is often detected as an "impossible" inconsistency. In a perfect design, such errors would never happen, but the good designer plans for a graceful exit on fatal bugs by leaving the remaining environment as clean as possible and recording or printing as much information about the failure as possible before terminating.

## 9.9 SETTING TRADE-OFF PRIORITIES

The system designer must set priorities that will be used to guide trade-offs during the rest of design. The designer is often required to choose among desirable but incompatible goals. For example, a system can often be made faster by using extra memory. Design trade-offs must be made regarding not only the software itself but also regarding the process of developing it. Sometimes it is necessary to sacrifice complete functionality to get a piece of software into use (or into the marketplace) earlier. Sometimes the problem statement specifies which goals are of highest priority, but often the burden falls on the designer to reconcile the incompatible desires of the client and decide how the trade-offs should be made.

The system designer must determine the relative importance of the various criteria as a guide to making trade-off decisions during design. All the trade-offs are not *made* during system design, but the priorities for making them are established. For example, the first video games ran on processors with limited memory. Conserving memory was the highest priority, followed by fast execution. Designers had to use every programming trick in the book, at the expense of maintainability, portability, and understandability. As another example, there are several mathematical subroutine packages available on a wide range of machines. Well-conditioned numerical behavior is crucial to such packages, as well as portability and understandability. These cannot be sacrificed for fast development. In another case, a user interface is hard to evaluate without actually using it. The designer often uses *rapid prototyping,* which is a "quick and dirty" implementation of part of the system to be evaluated, while ignoring or simulating the rest of the system. Rapid prototyping minimizes initial design time by sacrificing completeness of functionality, efficiency, and robustness. Once the prototype is evaluated, the interface can be reimplemented using different design trade-offs, and the remainder of the system can be implemented.

The entire character of a system is affected by the trade-off decisions made by the designer. The success or failure of the final product may depend on whether its goals are well-chosen. Even worse, if no system-wide priorities are established, then the various parts of the system may optimize opposing goals ("suboptimization"), resulting in a system that wastes resources. Even on small projects, programmers often forget the real goals and become obsessed with "efficiency" when it really is not important.

Setting trade-off priorities is at best vague. You cannot expect numerical accuracy ("speed 53%, memory 31%, portability 15%, cost 1%"). Priorities are rarely absolute; for example, trading memory for speed does not mean that any increase in speed, no matter how small, is worth any increase in memory, no matter how large. We cannot even give a full list of design criteria that might be subject to trade-offs. Instead, the priorities are a statement of design philosophy by the system designer to guide the design process. Judgment and interpretation are required when trade-offs are actually made during the rest of the design.

## 9.10 COMMON ARCHITECTURAL FRAMEWORKS

There are several prototypical architectural frameworks that are common in existing systems. Each of these is well-suited to a certain kind of system. If you have an application with similar characteristics, you can save effort by using the corresponding architecture, or at least using it as a starting point for your design. The kinds of systems include:

- Batch transformation—a data transformation executed once on an entire input set.

- Continuous transformation—a data transformation performed continuously as inputs change.

- Interactive interface—a system dominated by external interactions.

- Dynamic simulation—a system that simulates evolving real-world objects.

- Real-time system—a system dominated by strict timing constraints.

- Transaction manager—a system concerned with storing and updating data, often including concurrent access from different physical locations.

This is not meant to be a complete list of known systems and architectures but a list of common forms. Some problems require a new kind of architecture, but most can use an existing framework or at least a variation on it. Many problems combine aspects of these architectures.

### 9.10.1 Batch Transformation

A *batch transformation* is a sequential input-to-output transformation, in which inputs are supplied at the start, and the goal is to compute an answer; there is no ongoing interaction with the outside world. Examples include standard computational problems: compiler, payroll program, VLSI automatic layout, stress analysis of a bridge, and many others.

The state model is trivial or nonexistent for batch transformation problems. The object model may be simple or complex. The most important aspect of a batch transformation is the functional model which specifies how input values are transformed into output values. This is probably the area best addressed by current methodologies emphasizing data flow diagrams and functional decomposition. However, the use of object models for data structures improves on previous methods of representing data for problems that have complex, often polymorphic data. A compiler is an example of a batch transformation with complex data structures. Figure 9.2 shows the data flow diagram for a compiler.

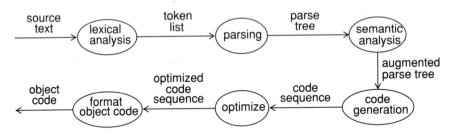

**Figure 9.2** Data flow diagram of compiler

The steps in designing a batch transformation are:

- Break the overall transformation into stages, each stage performing one part of the transformation. The system diagram is a data flow diagram. This can usually be taken straight from the functional model, although additional detail may be added during system design.

- Define intermediate object classes for the data flows between each pair of successive stages. Each stage knows only about the objects on either side of it, its own inputs and outputs. Each set of classes forms a coherent object model in the design, loosely coupled to the object models from neighboring stages.

- Expand each stage in turn until the operations are straightforward to implement.
- Restructure the final pipeline for optimization.

### 9.10.2 Continuous Transformation

A *continuous transformation* is a system in which the outputs actively depend on changing inputs and must be periodically updated. Unlike a batch transformation, in which the outputs are computed only once, the outputs in an active pipeline must be updated frequently (in theory continuously, although in practice they are computed discretely at a fine time scale). Because of severe time constraints, the entire set of outputs cannot usually be recomputed each time an input changes (otherwise the application would be a batch transformation). Instead, the new output values must be computed incrementally. Typical applications include signal processing, windowing systems, incremental compilers, and process monitoring systems.

The functional model together with the object model defines the values being computed. The dynamic model is less important because most of the structure of the application is due to the steady flow of data and not due to discrete interactions.

Because a complete recomputation is impossible for every input value change, an architecture for a continuous transformation must facilitate incremental computation. The transformation can be implemented as a pipeline of functions. The effect of each incremental change in an input value must be propagated through the pipeline. To make incremental computation possible, intermediate objects may be defined to hold intermediate values. Redundant values may be introduced for performance reasons.

Synchronization of values within the pipeline may be important for high-performance systems, such as signal processing applications. In such cases, operations are performed at well-defined times and the flow path of operations must be carefully balanced so that values arrive at the right place at the right time without bottlenecks.

The steps in designing a pipeline for a continuous transformation are:

- Draw a data flow diagram for the system. The input and output actors correspond to data structures whose values change continuously. Data stores within the pipeline show parameters that affect the input-to-output mapping. Figure 9.3 shows a graphics application in three stages: First geometric figures in user-defined coordinates are mapped into window coordinates; then the figures are clipped to fit the window bounds; finally each figure is offset by the position of its window to yield a position on the screen.

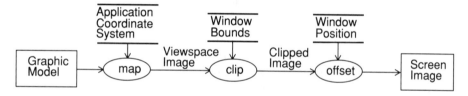

**Figure 9.3** Data flow diagram for a graphics application

- Define intermediate objects between each pair of successive stages, as in the batch transformation. For example, each geometric figure from the graphic model has a mapped version of itself at each stage in the computation.

- Differentiate each operation to obtain incremental changes to each stage. That is, propagate the incremental effects of each change to an input object through the pipeline as a series of incremental updates. For example, a change in the position of a geometric figure requires its old image to be erased, its new position computed, and its new image displayed; the images of other figures are unchanged and need not be recomputed.

- Add additional intermediate objects for optimization.

### 9.10.3 Interactive Interface

An *interactive interface* is a system that is dominated by interactions between the system and external agents, such as humans, devices, or other programs. The external agents are independent of the system, so their inputs cannot be controlled, although the system may solicit responses from them. An interactive interface usually includes only part of an entire application, one that can often be handled independently from the computational part of the application. The major concerns of an interactive interface are the communications protocol between the system and the external agents, the syntax of possible interactions, the presentation of output (the appearance on the screen, for instance), the flow of control within the system, the ease of understanding and user interface, performance, and error handling. Examples of interactive systems include a forms-based query interface, a workstation windowing system, the command language for an operating system, and the control panel for a simulation.

Interactive interfaces are dominated by the dynamic model. Objects in the object model represent interaction elements, such as input and output tokens and presentation formats. The functional model describes which application functions are executed in response to input event sequences, but the internal structure of the functions is usually unimportant to the behavior of the interface. An interactive system is concerned with external appearances, not deep semantic structure.

The steps in designing an interactive interface are:

- Isolate the objects that form the interface from the objects that define the semantics of the application.

- Use predefined objects to interact with external agents, if possible. For example, workstation windowing systems such as X-Windows, NeWS, and MacAPP have extensive collections of predefined windows, menus, buttons, forms, and other kinds of objects ready to be adapted to applications.

- Use the dynamic model as the structure of the program. Interactive interfaces are best implemented using concurrent control (multi-tasking) or event-driven control (interrupts or call-backs). Procedure-driven control (writing output and then waiting for input in-line) is awkward for anything but rigid control sequences.

- Isolate physical events from logical events. Often a logical event corresponds to multiple physical events. For example, a graphical interface can take input from a form, from a pop-up menu, from a function button on the keyboard, by typing a command sequence, or from an indirect command file.

- Fully specify the application functions that are invoked by the interface. Make sure that the information to implement them is present.

### 9.10.4 Dynamic Simulation

A *dynamic simulation* models or tracks objects in the real world. Examples include molecular motion modeling, spacecraft trajectory computation, economic models, and video games. Traditional methodologies built on data flow diagrams are poor at representing these problems because simulations involve many distinct objects that constantly update themselves, rather than a single large transformation. Simulations are perhaps the simplest system to design using an object-oriented approach. The objects and operations come directly from the application. Control can be implemented in two ways: an explicit controller external to the application objects can simulate a state machine, or objects can exchange messages among themselves, similar to the real-world situation.

Unlike an interactive system, the internal objects in a dynamic simulation do correspond to real-world objects, so the object model is usually important and often complex. Like an interactive system, the dynamic model is an important part of simulation systems. Simulators often have a complex functional model as well.

The steps in designing a dynamic simulation are:

- Identify actors, active real-world objects, from the object model. The actors have attributes that are periodically updated.

- Identify discrete events. Discrete events correspond to discrete interactions with the object, such as turning power on or applying the brakes. Discrete events can be implemented as operations on the object.

- Identify continuous dependencies. Real-world attributes may be dependent on other real-world attributes or vary continuously with time, altitude, velocity, or steering wheel position. These attributes must be updated at periodic intervals using numerical approximation techniques to minimize quantization error.

- Generally a simulation is driven by a timing loop at a fine time scale. Discrete events between objects can often be exchanged as part of the timing loop.

The hardest problem with simulations is usually providing adequate performance. In an ideal world, an arbitrary number of parallel processors would execute the simulation in an exact analogy to the real-world situation. In practice, the system designer must estimate the computational cost of each update cycle and provide adequate resources. Continuous processes must be approximated as discrete steps.

### 9.10.5  Real-time System

A *real-time system* is an interactive system for which time constraints on actions are particularly tight or in which the slightest timing failure cannot be tolerated. For critical actions, the system must be guaranteed to respond within an absolute interval of time. Typical applications include process control, data acquisition, communications devices, device control, and overload relays. To guarantee response time, the worst case scenario has to be determined and provided for. This can simplify analysis because it is usually easier to determine the worst case behavior than the average case behavior.

Real-time design is complex and involves issues such as interrupt handling, prioritization of tasks, and coordinating multiple CPUs. Unfortunately, real-time systems are frequently designed to operate close to their resource limits so that severe, nonlogical restructuring of the design is often needed to achieve the necessary performance. Such contortions come at the cost of portability and maintainability. Real-time design is a specialized topic that we do not cover in detail in this book.

### 9.10.6  Transaction Manager

A *transaction manager* is a database system whose main function is to store and access information. The information comes from the application domain. Most transaction managers must deal with multiple users and concurrency. A transaction must be handled as a single atomic entity without interference from other transactions. Examples of transaction managers include airline reservation systems, inventory control systems, and database management systems.

The object model is the most important. The functional model in a transaction management system is less important because operations tend to be predefined and to focus on updating and querying information. The dynamic model shows concurrent access of distributed information. Distribution is an inherent part of the real-world problem and must be modeled as part of the analysis. The dynamic model is also important for estimating transaction throughput.

Frequently you can use an existing database management system. In such cases, the main problem is to construct the object model and choose the granularity of transactions that must be considered atomic by the system.

The steps in designing a transaction management system are:

- Map the object model directly into a database. See Chapter 17 for advice on using a relational database.

- Determine the units of concurrency, that is, the resources that inherently or by specification cannot be shared. Introduce new classes as needed.

- Determine the unit of transaction, that is, the set of resources that must be accessed together during a transaction. Typically a transaction succeeds or fails in its entirety.

- Design concurrency control for transactions. Most database management systems incorporate this. The system may need to retry failed transactions several times before giving up.

## 9.11 ARCHITECTURE OF THE ATM SYSTEM

The ATM system introduced in Chapter 8 is a hybrid of an interactive interface and a transaction management system. The entry stations are interactive interfaces—their purpose is to interact with a human to gather information needed to formulate a transaction. Specifying the entry stations consists of constructing an object model and a dynamic model; the functional model is trivial. The consortium and banks are primarily a distributed transaction management system. Their purpose is to maintain a database of information and to allow it to be updated over a distributed network under controlled conditions. Specifying the transaction management part of the system consists primarily of constructing an object model.

Figure 9.4 shows the architecture of the ATM system. There are three major subsystems: the ATM stations, the consortium computer, and the bank computers. The topology is a simple star; the consortium computer communicates with all the ATM stations and with all the bank computers. Each connection is a dedicated phone line. The station code and the bank code are used to distinguish the phone lines to the consortium computer.

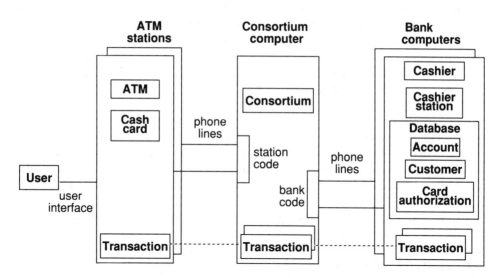

**Figure 9.4** Architecture of ATM system

The only permanent data stores are in the bank computers. Because the data must be kept consistent but may be accessed by several concurrent transactions, the data is kept in a database. Each transaction is processed as a single batch operation; an account is locked by a transaction until the transaction is complete.

Concurrency arises because there are many ATM stations, each of which can be active at once. There can be only one transaction per ATM station, but each transaction requires the assistance of the consortium computer and a bank computer. A transaction cuts across physical units; each transaction is shown in the diagram as three connected pieces. During design, each piece will become a separate implementation class. Although there is only one transaction per ATM station, there may be many concurrent transactions per consortium computer or bank computer. This does not pose any special problem because access to any one account is synchronized through the database.

The ATM station is little more than a state diagram. The consortium computer and bank computers will be event driven. Each of them queues input events but processes them one at a time in the order received.

The consortium computer must be large enough to handle the expected maximum number of simultaneous transactions. It may be acceptable to occasionally block a transaction, provided the user receives an appropriate message. The bank computers must also be large enough to handle the expected worst-case load, and they must have enough disk storage to record all transactions.

The system must contain operations to allow ATM stations and bank computers to be added and deleted. Each physical unit must protect itself against the failure or disconnection of the rest of the network. A database will provide protection against loss of data. However, special attention must be paid to failure during a transaction so that neither the user nor the bank lose money. A complicated acknowledgment protocol before committing the transaction may be required. The ATM station should display an appropriate message if the connection is down. Other kinds of failure must be handled as well, such as exhaustion of cash or paper for receipts.

On a financial system such as this, fail-safe transactions are the highest priority. If there is any doubt about the integrity of a transaction, then it must be aborted with an appropriate message to the user.

There is little need for a lower layer of system implementation. The ATM station is just a state machine; its functional model is trivial. The consortium computer simply forwards a message from an ATM station to a bank computer and from a bank computer to an ATM station. It has minimal functionality. The bank computer is the only unit with any non-trivial procedures, but even those are mostly just database updates. The only complexity might come from failure handling.

All in all, the ATM system is a simple architecture, but many applications are similar.

## 9.12 CHAPTER SUMMARY

After analyzing an application and before beginning the detailed design, the system designer must decide on the basic approach to the solution. The form of the high-level structure of the system, including its breakdown into subsystems, its inherent concurrency, allocation of subsystems to hardware and software, data management, coordination of global resources, software control implementation, boundary conditions, and trade-off priorities, is called the system architecture.

A system can be divided into horizontal layers and vertical partitions. Each layer defines a different abstract world that may differ completely from other layers. Each layer is a client of services of the layer or layers below it and a supplier of services for the layer or layers above it. Systems can also be divided into partitions, each performing a general kind of service. Simple system topologies, such as pipelines or stars, reduce system complexity. Most systems are a mixture of layers and partitions.

Inherently concurrent objects execute in parallel and cannot be combined on a single thread of control. These objects must be assigned to separate hardware devices or to separate tasks in a processor. Other objects can be folded together on a single thread of control and implemented as a single task.

Enough processors and special-purpose hardware units must be provided to achieve the needed performance. Objects must be assigned to hardware such that the use of hardware is balanced and meets concurrency constraints. The system designer must estimate computational throughput and allow for queuing effects in configuring the hardware. Some compute-intensive computations can be performed by special-purpose hardware. One goal in partitioning a hardware network is to minimize communications traffic between physically-distinct modules.

Data stores may be used to cleanly separate subsystems within an architecture and to give application data some degree of permanence. In general data stores may be implemented with memory data structures, files, and/or databases. Files are simple, cheap, and permanent but may provide too low a level of abstraction for an application and necessitate much additional programming. Databases provide a higher level of abstraction than files, but they too involve compromises in terms of overhead costs and complexity.

The system designer must identify global resources and determine mechanisms for controlling access to them. Some common mechanisms are: establishing a "guardian" object that serializes all access, partitioning global resources into disjoint subsets which are managed at a lower level, and locking.

Hardware control is inherently concurrent, but software control can be procedure-driven, event-driven, and concurrent. Control for a procedure-driven system resides within the program code; the location of the program counter and the stack of procedure calls and local variables define the system state. In an event-driven system control resides within a dispatcher or monitor; application procedures are attached to events and are called by the dispatcher when the corresponding events occur. In a concurrent system, control resides concurrently in multiple independent objects. Event-driven and concurrent implementations are much more flexible than procedure-driven control.

Most of system design is concerned with steady-state behavior but boundary conditions must be considered as well: initialization, termination, and failure.

An essential aspect of system architecture is making trade-offs between time and space, hardware and software, simplicity and generality, and efficiency and maintainability. These trade-offs depend on the goals of the application. The system designer must state the priorities so that trade-off decisions during subsequent design will be consistent.

Several kinds of systems are frequently encountered for which standard architectural frameworks exist. These include two kinds of functional transformations: batch computation and continuous transformation; three kinds of time-dependent systems: interactive interface, dynamic simulation, and real-time; and a database system: transaction manager. Most application systems are usually a hybrid of several forms, possibly one for each major subsystem. Other kinds of architecture are possible.

| | | |
|---|---|---|
| architecture | inherent concurrency | subsystem |
| client-supplier | layer | system design |
| concurrency | partition | system topology |
| data management | peer-to-peer | thread of control |
| event-driven system | real-time system | trade-off priorities |
| hardware requirements | service | |

**Figure 9.5** Key concepts for Chapter 9

## BIBLIOGRAPHIC NOTES

Software systems design is addressed by several books on design methodology, such as [Ward-85], [Page-Jones-88], and [Yourdon-89]. Recent years have seen greater emphasis on system design and issues of distributed and concurrent systems. The introduction of tasking constructs in Ada has spurred a new emphasis on modularity and concurrency in programming; [Buhr-84] addresses these issues and introduces notation for them.

The design of large real-time hardware-software systems, such as military weapons systems, air traffic control systems, and spacecraft launch and support systems, is another matter entirely. Although the techniques in this book should be applicable to any kind of system, very large systems are dominated by logistical concerns. Analysis in such systems can involve extensive experiments to establish the requirements themselves and to determine what is realizable by current technology. There are few if any books proposing methodologies for such systems, and we do not profess to be experts.

For a description of an active transformation pipeline for a graphics processor, see Chapter 10 of [Foley-82].

## REFERENCES

[Buhr-84] R.J.A. Buhr. *System Design with Ada*. Englewood Cliffs, New Jersey: Prentice Hall, 1984.

[Foley-82] James D. Foley, Andries Van Dam. *Fundamentals of Interactive Computer Graphics*. Reading, Mass.: Addison-Wesley, 1982.

[Page-Jones-88] Meilir Page-Jones. *The Practical Guide to Structured Systems Design*. Englewood Cliffs, New Jersey: Prentice Hall, 1988.

[Premerlani-90] William J. Premerlani, Michael R. Blaha, James E. Rumbaugh, Thomas A. Varwig. Building an object-oriented DBMS on top of a relational database. Expected to be published in CACM, September 1990.

[Ward-85] Paul Ward, Steve Mellor. *Structured Development for Real-Time Systems, Volume 3*. Englewood Cliffs, New Jersey: Yourdon Press, 1986.

[Yourdon-89] Edward Yourdon, Larry Constantine. *Structured Design: Fundamentals of a Discipline of Computer Program and Systems Design*. Englewood Cliffs, New Jersey: Prentice Hall, 1989.

## EXERCISES

**9.1** (4) For each of the following systems, list the applicable style(s) of system architecture: batch transformation, continuous transformation, interactive interface, dynamic simulation, real time system, and transaction manager. Explain your selection(s). For systems which fit more than one style, group features of the system by style.

a. *An electronic chess companion.* The system consists of a chess board with a built-in computer, lights, and membrane switches. The human player registers moves by pressing chess pieces on the board, activating membrane switches mounted under each square. The computer indicates moves through lights also mounted under each square. The human moves the chess pieces for the computer. The computer should make only legal moves, should reject attempted illegal human moves, and should try to win.

b. *An airplane flight simulator for a video game system.* The video game system has already been implemented and consists of a computer with joystick and push–button inputs and an output interface for a color television. Your job is to develop the software for the computer to display the view from the cockpit of an airplane. The joystick and push button are used to control the airplane. The display should be based on a terrain description stored in memory. When your program is complete, it will be sold on cartridges that plug into the video game system.

c. *A floppy disk controller chip.* The chip is going to use a microprogram for internal control. You are concerned with the microprogram. The chip bridges the gap between a computer and a floppy disk drive. Your portion of the control will be responsible for positioning the read/write head and reading the data. Information on the diskette is organized into tracks and sectors. Tracks are equally spaced circles of data on the diskette. Data within a track is organized into sectors. Your architecture will need to support the following operations: Find track 0, find a given track, read a track, read a sector, write a track, and write a sector.

d. *A sonar system.* You are concerned with the portion of the system that detects undersea objects and computes how far away they are (range). This is done by transmitting an acoustic pulse and analyzing any resulting echo. A technique called correlation is used to perform the analysis, in which a time delayed copy of the transmitted pulse is multiplied by the returned echo and integrated for many values of time delay. If the result is large for a particular value of time delay, it is an indication that there is an object with a range that corresponds to that delay.

**9.2** (3) Discuss how you would implement control for the applications described in the previous exercise.

**9.3** (7) As the system architect for a new signal processing product, you must decide how to store data in real time. The product uses analog to digital convertors to sample an analog input signal at the rate of 16000 bytes/second (128000 bits/second) for 10 seconds. Unfortunately, the needed calculations are too time consuming to do as the samples are received, so you are going to have to store the samples temporarily. The decision has already been made to limit the amount of memory used for buffers to 64000 bytes. The system has a floppy disk drive that uses diskettes organized into 77 tracks for a total of 243000 bytes of storage per diskette. It takes 10 milliseconds to move the disk drive read/write head from one track to another and 83 milliseconds, on average, to find the beginning of a track once the head is positioned. The disk drive will be positioned at the correct track prior to the start of data acquisition.

Two solutions to the problem are being considered: (1) Simply write the data samples on the diskette as they become available. Why doesn't this work? (2) Use memory as a buffer. Data samples are placed in memory as they are acquired and written to the floppy disk as fast as possible on sequential tracks. Will this method work? Describe the method in more detail. How much memory is needed for the buffer? How many tracks will be used on the diskette? Prepare a few scenarios. Describe how the control might work.

**9.4**    (6) A system is desired for automating the drilling of holes in rectangular metal plates. The size and location of holes is described interactively using a graphical editor on a personal computer. When the user is satisfied with a particular drawing, a peripheral device on the personal computer punches a numerical control (N/C) tape. The tape can then be used on a variety of commercially available N/C drilling machines which have moving drill heads and which can change drill sizes. You are concerned only with the editing of the drawings and the punching of the N/C tapes. The tapes contain sequences of instructions to move the drill head, change drills, and drill. Since it takes some time to move the drill between holes, and even longer to change drills, the system should determine a reasonably efficient drilling sequence. It is not necessary to achieve the absolute minimum time, but the system should not be grossly inefficient either. The drill head is controlled independently in the x and y directions, so the time it takes to move between holes is proportional to the larger of the required displacements in the x and the y direction. Prepare a system architecture. How would you characterize the style of the system?

**9.5**    (5) A system for interactive symbolic manipulation of polynomials is desired. The basic idea is to allow a mathematician to be more accurate and productive in developing formulas. The user enters mathematical expressions and commands a line at a time. Expressions are ratios of polynomials, which are constructed from constants and variables. Intermediate expressions may be assigned to variables for later recall. Operations include addition, subtraction, multiplication, division, and differentiation with respect to a variable. Develop an architecture for the system. How would you characterize the style of the system? How would you save work in progress to resume at a future time?

**9.6**    (4) The following modules have been suggested for the system described in the previous exercise. Organize them into partitions and layers.
a.  line syntax—scan a line of user input for tokens
b.  line semantics—determine meaning of line input
c.  command processing—execute user input, error checking
d.  construct expression—build an internal representation of an input expression
e.  apply operation—carry out an operation on one or more expressions
f.  save work—save the current context
g.  load work—read in previously saved context
h.  substitute—substitute one expression for a variable in another expression
i.  rationalize—convert an expression to canonical form
j.  evaluate—replace a variable in an expression with a constant and simplify the expression

**9.7**    (6) A system for editing, saving, and printing object diagrams and generating relational database schema is desired. Only a limited subset of the object modeling notation is to be supported: object classes with attributes and binary associations with multiplicity. Editing functions such as create object class, create association, cut, copy, and paste are required. Diagrams span several sheets. The editor must understand the semantics of object diagrams. For example, when an object class rectangle is moved, the lines representing any attached associations are stretched. If an object class is deleted, attached associations are also deleted. When the user is satisfied with the diagram, the system will generate the corresponding relational database schema. Discuss the relative advantages of a single program which performs all functions versus two programs, one which edits object diagrams and the other which generates database schema from object diagrams.

**9.8**   (6) In the previous exercise, there are both physical and logical aspects of object diagrams to be considered. Physical aspects include location and sizes of lines, boxes, circles, and text. Logical aspects include connectivity, classes, attributes, and associations. Discuss basing your architecture on the following strategies. Consider issues involved in editing and saving object diagrams as well as generating database schema:
   a. Model only the geometrical aspects of object diagrams. Treat logical aspects as derived attributes.
   b. Model both the geometrical and logical aspects of object diagrams.

**9.9**   (5) Another approach to the system described in exercise 9.7 is to use a commercially available desktop publishing system for object diagram preparation instead of implementing your own object diagram editor. The desktop editor can dump its output in an ASCII markup language. The vendor supplies the grammar for the markup language. Compare the two approaches. One approach is to build your own editor that understands the semantics of object diagrams. The other is to use a commercially available desktop publishing system to edit object diagrams. What happens if new versions of the desktop publishing system become available? Can you assume that the user prepares a diagram using a notation that your database generator will understand? Is it worth the effort to implement functions such as cut, copy, and paste that commercial systems already do so well? Who is going to help the user if they run into problems? How is your system going to be supported and maintained? How soon can you get the system completed?

**9.10**  (6) One architectural decision that could be made for the system described in the previous exercise is to perform a batch transformation, with the desktop publishing system file as input and relational database schema as output. The following are proposed intermediate objects, not necessarily in the right order. Each is a model or file that is a distinct transform of the original object diagram. Prepare a block diagram showing all steps in the transformation from input to output. Describe what must be done in each step of the transformation:
   a. database model—collection of tables
   b. connection model—a collection of interconnected blocks containing text
   c. document model— collection of lines, ellipses, and text
   d. object model—collection of object classes and relationships
   e. output file—list of database commands to create tables
   f. input file—lists of graphic primitives on pages

**9.11**  (6) A common issue in many systems is how to store data so it is preserved in the event of power loss or hardware failure. The ideal solution should be reliable, low cost, small, fast, maintenance free, simple to incorporate into a system. Also, it should be immune to heat, dirt, and humidity. Compromises in the available technology often influence the functional requirements. Compare each of the following solutions in terms of the ideal.
   a. Do not worry about it at all. Reset all data every time the system is turned on.
   b. Never turn the power off if it can be helped. Use a special power supply, including backup generators, if necessary.

    c. Keep critical information on a magnetic disk drive. Periodically make full and/or incremental copies on magnetic tape.

    d. Use a battery to maintain power to the system memory when the rest of the system is off. It might even be possible to continue to provide limited functionality.

    e. Use a special memory component, such as a magnetic bubble memory or an electronically erasable programmable read only memory.

    f. Critical parameters are entered by the user through switches. Several types of switches are commercially available for this use, including several toggle switches in a package that connects the same way as an integrated circuit.

**9.12** (7) For each of the following systems, select one or more of the strategies for data storage from the previous exercise. In each case explain your reasoning and give an estimate (order of magnitude) of how much memory, in bytes, is required:

    a. *Four function pocket calculator.* Main source of power is sunlight. Performs basic arithmetic.

    b. *Electronic typewriter.* Main source of power is either rechargeable batteries or alternating current. Operates in two modes. In one mode, documents are typed a line at a time. Editing may be performed on a line before it is typed. A liquid crystal display will display up to 16 characters for editing purposes. In the other mode, an entire document can be entered and edited before printing. It is desired to save the working document for up to a year with the main power off.

    c. *System clock for a personal computer.* Main power is direct current supplied by the personal computer when it is on. Provides time and date information to the computer. Must maintain the correct date and time for at least 5 years with the main power off.

    d. *Airline reservation system.* Main power is alternating current. Used to reserve seats on airline flights. The system must be kept running at all times, at all costs. If, for some reason, the system must be shut off, no data should be lost.

    e. *Digital control and thermal protection unit for a motor.* The device provides thermal protection for motors over a wide range of horsepower ratings by calculating motor temperature based on measured current and a simulation of motor heat dissipation. If the calculated motor temperature exceeds safe limits, the motor is shut off and not allowed to be restarted until it cools down. The main source of power is alternating current, which may be interrupted. The system must provide protection as soon as it is turned on. Parameters needed for thermal simulation are initially set at the factory, but provision must be made to change them, if necessary, after the system is installed. Because the motor temperature is not measured directly, it is necessary to continue to simulate the motor temperature for at least an hour after loss of main power, in case power is restored before the motor cools.

**9.13** (9) Designing file formats is a common activity that may be carried out during system design. A BNF diagram is a convenient way to express file formats. Figure E9.1 is a portion of a BNF diagram of a language for describing object classes and binary associations. Nonterminal symbols are shown in rectangles and terminal symbols are shown in circles or rectangles with rounded corners. With the exception of *character*, all nonterminals are defined in the diagram. A diagram consists of classes and associations. A class has a unique name and many attributes. An association has an optional name and two roles, one for each end of the association. A role contains the name one of the object classes being associated and multiplicity information. Textual information is described by quoted strings. A character is any ASCII character except quote.

    a. Use the language in Figure E9.1 to describe the object diagram in Figure E9.2.

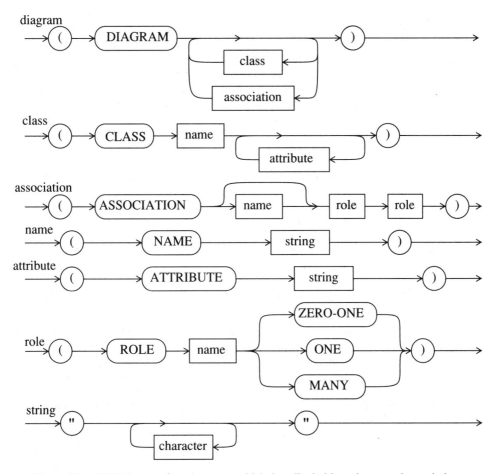

**Figure E9.1** BNF diagram for a language which described object classes and associations

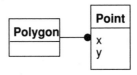

**Figure E9.2** Object diagram of polygons

b. Discuss similarities and differences between data in storage and data in motion. For example, the description you prepared in the previous part could be used to store an object diagram in a file or to transmit a diagram from one location to another.

c. The language in this problem is used to describe the structure of object diagrams. Invent a language to describe two dimensional polygons. Use BNF to describe your language. Describe a square and a triangle in your language.

**9.14** (6) A common problem encountered in digital systems is data corruption due to noise or hardware failure. One solution is to use a cyclic redundancy code (CRC). When data is stored or transmitted, a code is computed from the data and appended to it. When data is retrieved or received, the code is recomputed and compared with the value that was appended to the data. A match is necessary but not sufficient to indicate that the data is correct. The probability that errors will be detected depends on the sophistication of the function used to compute the CRC. Some functions can be used for error correction as well as detection. Parity is an example of a simple function that detects single bit errors.

The function to compute a CRC can be implemented in hardware or software. The choice for a given problem is a compromise involving speed, cost, flexibility, and complexity. The hardware solution is fast, but may add unnecessary complexity and cost to the system hardware. The software solution is cheaper and more flexible, but may not be fast enough and may make the system software more complex.

For each of the following subsystems, decide whether or not a CRC is needed. If so, decide whether to implement the CRC in hardware or software. Defend your choices.
a.  floppy disk controller
b.  system to transmit data files from one computer to another over telephone lines
c.  memory board on a computer board in the space shuttle
d.  magnetic tape drive
e.  validation of an account number (a CRC can be used to distinguish between valid accounts and those generated at random)

**9.15** (Project) Advances in technology have made it possible to put banking functions in a credit card. (See "The very smart card: a plastic pocket bank," IEEE Spectrum, October 1988.) It is often the case that new systems are constrained by considerations of compatibility with old methods. What changes would you make in the architecture of the very smart card if it did not have to be compatible with existing credit cards? For example, what would happen if the card was not going to be used to make imprints and did not have to be read magnetically. How would the architecture change if size constraints were relaxed? Do you think the bending requirement would be necessary if the smart card were not preceded by credit cards? Explain your answers.

# 10

---

# Object Design

The analysis phase determines what the implementation must do, and the system design phase determines the plan of attack. The object design phase determines the full definitions of the classes and associations used in the implementation, as well as the interfaces and algorithms of the methods used to implement operations. The object design phase adds internal objects for implementation and optimizes data structures and algorithms. Object design is analogous to the preliminary design phase of the traditional software development life cycle.

This chapter shows how to take the analysis model and flesh it out to provide a basis for implementation. In the OMT methodology, there is no need to transform from one model to another, as the object-oriented paradigm spans analysis, design, and implementation. The object-oriented paradigm applies equally well in describing the real-world specification and computer-based implementation.

## 10.1 OVERVIEW OF OBJECT DESIGN

During object design the designer carries out the strategy chosen during system design and fleshes out the details. There is a shift in emphasis from application domain concepts toward computer concepts. The objects discovered during analysis serve as the skeleton of the design, but the object designer must choose among different ways to implement them with an eye toward minimizing execution time, memory, and other measures of cost. In particular, the operations identified during analysis must be expressed as algorithms, with complex operations decomposed into simpler internal operations. The classes, attributes, and associations from analysis must be implemented as specific data structures. New object classes must be introduced to store intermediate results during program execution and to avoid the need for recomputation. Optimization of the design should not be carried to excess, as ease of implementation, maintainability, and extensibility are also important concerns.

### 10.1.1  Working from Analysis and Architecture

The object model describes the classes of objects in the system, including their attributes and the operations that they support. The information in the analysis object model must be present in the design in some form. Usually the simplest and best approach is to carry the classes from analysis directly into design. Object design then becomes a process of adding detail and making implementation decisions. Occasionally, an analysis object does not appear explicitly in the design but is distributed among other objects for computational efficiency. More often, new redundant classes are added for efficiency.

The functional model describes the operations that the system must implement. During design we must decide how each operation should be implemented, choosing an algorithm for the operation and breaking complex operations into simpler operations. This decomposition is an iterative process that must be repeated at successively lower levels of abstraction. The algorithms and decomposition must be chosen to optimize important implementation measures, such as ease of implementation, understandability, and performance.

The dynamic model describes how the system responds to external events. The control structure for a program is primarily derived from the dynamic model. The flow of control within a program must be realized either explicitly (by an internal scheduler that recognizes events and maps them into operation calls) or implicitly (by choosing algorithms that perform the operations in the order specified by the dynamic model).

In choosing an architecture, we have already taken some steps toward making the decisions necessary to implement the system. We have chosen the overall flow of control and data through the system and have partitioned the system into manageable subsystems. If multiple processors are involved, we have decided how objects will be allocated to processors. The choice of architecture will also influence the decision of how to map events into operations.

Object-oriented design is primarily a process of refinement or adding detail. This chapter shows how to evolve an analysis model into a design by organizing and augmenting the analysis model.

### 10.1.2  Steps of Object Design

During object design, the designer must perform the following steps:

- Combine the three models to obtain operations on classes [10.2]
- Design algorithms to implement operations [10.3]
- Optimize access paths to data [10.4]
- Implement control for external interactions [10.5]
- Adjust class structure to increase inheritance [10.6]
- Design associations [10.7]
- Determine object representation [10.8]
- Package classes and associations into modules [10.9]

Object-oriented design is an iterative process. When you think that the object design is complete at one level of abstraction, add more detail and flesh out the design further at a finer level of detail. You may find that new operations and attributes must be added to classes in the object model, and possibly new classes will be identified. It may even be necessary to revise the relationships between objects (including changes to the inheritance hierarchy). You should not be surprised if you find yourself iterating several times.

### 10.1.3 Object Modeling Tool Example

Many of the examples in this chapter come from the design of the Object Modeling Tool (OMTool), a program written by one of the authors. OMTool is a graphic editor for constructing object diagrams. With OMTool a person can easily create, load, edit, save, and print object diagrams. A major design goal for OMTool has been to provide simple and natural user interaction.

Before the advent of OMTool, we constructed object diagrams with a general purpose graphic editor. It is tedious to construct object diagrams by drawing lines, boxes, text, and so forth. OMTool permits the user to build object diagrams directly from OMT modeling symbols. For instance, as the user moves a class box, relationship lines stay connected and move with it. OMTool prevents illogical constructs, such as dangling relationship lines. With OMTool, it is easy to quickly sketch out and then clean up an object diagram. We have also developed several backend programs that take acquired OMTool data and generate programming code stubs and relational database schema.

One major architectural decision that we made for OMTool was to store both a logical and graphical model. The graphical model stores the picture that is drawn on the screen: the choice of symbols, position of symbols, length of lines, and so forth. The logical model stores the underlying meaning of the picture, that is, classes, attributes, operations, and their relationships. The graphical model is useful for interacting with the user of OMTool and preparing printouts. The logical model is useful for semantic checking and interacting with the backend programs which need to know what the diagram means but do not care about the precise manner in which it is drawn. The examples in this chapter are taken from both the OMTool graphical and logical models.

## 10.2 COMBINING THE THREE MODELS

After analysis we have the object, dynamic, and functional models, but the object model is the main framework around which the design is constructed. The object model from analysis may not show operations. The designer must convert the actions and activities of the dynamic model and the processes of the functional model into operations attached to classes in the object model. In making this conversion, we begin the process of mapping the logical structure of the analysis model into a physical organization of a program.

Each state diagram describes the life history of an object. A transition is a change of state of the object and maps into an operation on the object. We can associate an operation with each event received by an object. In the state diagram, the action performed by a transition depends on both the event and the state of the object. Therefore the algorithm implementing an operation depends on the state of the object. If the same event can be received by more than one state of an object, then the code implementing the algorithm must contain a case statement dependent on the state. (If the language permits an object to change its class at run time, then the states of the object can be implemented as subclasses of the original class, and the method resolution mechanism eliminates the need for a case statement. State can be considered an example of generalization by restriction, as explained in Section 4.3, but most object-oriented languages do not support dynamic changing of an object's class.) However, in many cases, an event can only be received in a single state, or all transitions on the event result in the same action, so no case statement is necessary.

An event sent by an object may represent an operation on another object. Events often occur in pairs, with the first event triggering an action and the second event returning the result or indicating the completion of that action. In this case, the event pair can be mapped into an operation performing the action and returning control provided that the events are on a single thread of control passing from object to object.

An action or activity initiated by a transition in a state diagram may expand into an entire data flow diagram in the functional model. The network of processes within the data flow diagram represents the body of an operation. The flows in the diagram are intermediate values in the operation. The designer must convert the graph structure of the diagram into a linear sequence of steps in an algorithm. The processes in the data flow diagram constitute suboperations. Some of them, but not necessarily all, may be operations on the original target object or on other objects. Determine the target object of a suboperation as follows:

- If a process extracts a value from an input flow, then the input flow is the target.

- If a process has an input flow and an output flow of the same type, and the output value is substantially an updated version of the input flow, then the input/output flow is the target.

- If a process constructs an output value from several input flows, then the operation is a class operation (constructor) on the output class.

- If a process has an input from or an output to a data store or an actor, then the data store or actor is a target of the process. (In some cases, such a process must be broken into two operations, one for the actor or data store and one for a flow value.)

The original target class is a client of any classes that supply internal operations to one of its operations. The client-supplier relationship defines the structure of the operation calling graph (sometimes called the program structure chart).

## 10.3 DESIGNING ALGORITHMS

Each operation specified in the functional model must be formulated as an *algorithm*. The analysis specification tells *what* the operation does from the view point of its clients, but the algorithm shows *how* it is done. An algorithm may be subdivided into calls on simpler operations, and so on recursively, until the lowest-level operations are simple enough to implement directly without further refinement.

The algorithm designer must:

- Choose algorithms that minimize the cost of implementing operations
- Select data structures appropriate to the algorithms
- Define new internal classes and operations as necessary
- Assign responsibility for operations to appropriate classes

### 10.3.1 Choosing Algorithms

Many operations are simple enough that the specification in the functional model already constitutes a satisfactory algorithm because the description of what is done also shows how it is done. Many operations simply traverse paths in the object-link network to retrieve or change attributes or links. For example, Figure 10.1 shows a *Class box* object containing an *Operation list*, which in turn contains a set of *Operation entry* objects. There is no need to write an algorithm to find the class box containing a given operation entry because the value is found by a simple traversal of unique links. Nontrivial algorithms are primarily needed for two reasons: to implement functions for which no procedural specification is given and to optimize functions for which a simple but inefficient algorithm serves as definition.

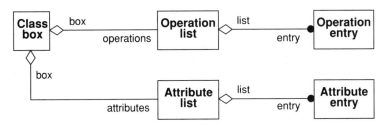

**Figure 10.1** Fragment of OMTool model

Some functions are specified as declarative constraints, without any procedural definition. For example, "the circle passing through three noncolinear points" is a nonprocedural specification of a circle. In such cases, you must use your knowledge of the situation (and appropriate reference books) to invent an algorithm. The essence of most geometry problems, such as the example given, is the discovery of appropriate algorithms and the proof that they are correct.

Most functions have simple mathematical or procedural definitions. Often the simple definition is also the best algorithm for computing the function or else is so close to any other algorithm that any loss in efficiency is worth the gain in clarity. For example, a class box from Figure 10.1 is drawn by first drawing its outline and then iteratively drawing its parts, the operation list and the attribute list.

In other cases, the simple definition of an operation would be hopelessly inefficient and must be implemented with a more efficient algorithm. For example, searching for a value in a set of size *n* by scanning the set requires an average of *n*/2 operations, whereas a binary search takes *log n* operations and a hash search takes less than 2 operations on average, regardless of the size of the set.

The level of abstraction of the algorithms should not go below the level of granularity of the objects in your object model. For example, in sketching the recursive draw algorithm for the class box in Figure 10.1, it is inappropriate to worry about the low-level graphics calls that will draw the box icon. It is not necessary to write algorithms for trivial operations that are internal to one object, such as setting or accessing the value of an attribute.

Considerations in choosing among alternative algorithms include:

- *Computational complexity.* How does processor time increase as a function of the size of the data structures? Don't worry about small factors in efficiency—avoid "bit pushing." For example, an extra level of indirection is insignificant if it improves clarity. It is essential, however, to think about the complexity of the algorithm, that is, how the execution time (or memory) grows with the number of input values—constant time, linear, quadratic, or exponential—as well as the cost of processing each input value. For example, the infamous "bubble sort" algorithm requires time proportional to $n^2$, where *n* is the size of the list, while most alternative sort algorithms require time proportional to *n log n*.

- *Ease of implementation and understandability.* It is worth giving up some performance on noncritical operations if they can be implemented quickly with a simple algorithm. For example, a pick operation on an OMTool diagram is implemented as a recursive search of top-level diagram elements, such as class boxes and associations, working down toward primitive elements, such as individual attribute entries. This is not the most efficient algorithm theoretically, but it is simple to implement and extensible. Here, speed is not a problem because the operation is only performed when the user pushes a button, and the number of elements on the page is limited.

- *Flexibility.* Most programs will be extended sooner or later. A highly optimized algorithm often sacrifices readability and ease of change. One possibility is to provide two implementations of critical operations—a simple but inefficient algorithm that can be implemented quickly and used to validate the system, and a complicated but efficient algorithm, whose correct implementation can be checked against the simple one. For example, a more complicated algorithm for picking objects in a diagram could be implemented by spatially sorting all the objects in a large, flat data structure. This algorithm would be faster for large diagrams, but it imposes constraints on the form of the objects and requires that the algorithm know details for all objects. In any case, the original simple algorithm could be used as a correctness check.

- *Fine tuning the object model.* If the object model were structured differently, would there be other alternatives? For example, Figure 10.2 shows two designs of the mapping between diagram elements and windows in OMTool. In the original upper design, each diagram element contains a list of windows in which it is visible. This is inefficient because operations on a set of elements must be computed separately for each window. In the lower design, each element belongs to one sheet, which may appear in any number

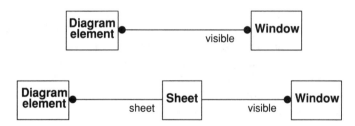

**Figure 10.2** Alternative structure

of windows. The image on the sheet can be computed once, and then copied to each window as a bitmap operation. The reduction in repeated operations is worth the extra level of indirection.

### 10.3.2 Choosing Data Structures

Choosing algorithms involves choosing the data structures they work on. During analysis, we concentrated only on the logical structure of the information in the system, but during object design we must choose the form of the data structures that will permit efficient algorithms. The data structures do not add information to the analysis model, but they organize it in a form convenient for the algorithms that use it. Many implementation data structures are instances of *container classes*. Such data structures include arrays, lists, queues, stacks, sets, bags, dictionaries, associations, trees, and many variations on these, such as priority queues and binary trees. Most object-oriented languages provide an assortment of generic data structures as part of their predefined class libraries.

For example, the diagram elements in a picture must be drawn on the screen in some specific order because the ones drawn last may overlap the ones drawn first. To permit consistent ordering, they are organized into an ordered list.

### 10.3.3 Defining Internal Classes and Operations

During the expansion of algorithms, new classes of objects may be needed to hold intermediate results. New, low-level operations may be invented during the decomposition of high-level operations.

A complex operation can be defined in terms of lower-level operations on simpler objects. These low-level operations must be defined during object design because most of them are not visible externally. Some of the required lower-level operations may be found among the "shopping-list" operations that were identified during analysis as being potentially useful. But there will usually be a need to add new internal operations as we expand high-level functions. For example, the OMTool erase operation on a diagram element is conceptually simple, but its implementation on a pixel-based screen is more complicated. To erase an object, it must be drawn in the background color, then objects uncovered by the erasure or damaged by the draw must be repaired by being redrawn. The repair operation is purely an internal operation needed because we are working on a pixel-based screen.

When you reach this point during the design phase, you may have to add new classes that were not mentioned directly in the client's description of the problem. These low-level classes are the implementation elements out of which the application classes are built. For example, an OMTool class box image is made of rectangles, lines, and text strings in various fonts. In OMTool, the low-level graphics elements come from the graphics toolkit module, which supplies its services to the rest of the system. Typically low-level implementation classes are placed in a distinct module.

### 10.3.4 Assigning Responsibility for Operations

Many operations have obvious target objects, but some operations can be performed at several places in an algorithm, by one of several objects, as long as they eventually get done. Such operations are often part of a complex high-level operation with many consequences. Assigning responsibility for such operations can be frustrating, and they are easy to overlook in laying out object classes because they are not an inherent part of any one class.

For example, OMTool has a *drag* operation applicable to diagram elements. Dragging a box moves the box and all the lines attached to it, provided nothing pushes up against an obstacle. The drag operation propagates from object to object along connections between objects. Some drags can fail because of obstacles, and backtracking may be required. Eventually the picture must be redrawn on the screen. When should each object image be redrawn on the screen? After it is dragged by another object? After it drags other objects? After all objects have been dragged? Is each object responsible for redrawing itself, or is the entire picture responsible for redrawing itself? Such questions are hard to answer because the breakdown on a complex externally meaningful operation into internal operations is arbitrary.

When a class is meaningful in the real world, then the operations on it are usually clear. During implementation, however, internal classes are introduced that do not correspond to real-world objects but merely some aspect of them. Since the internal classes are invented for implementation, they are somewhat arbitrary, and their boundaries are more a matter of convenience than of logical necessity.

How do you decide what class owns an operation? When only one object is involved in the operation, the decision is easy: Ask (or tell) that object to perform the operation. The decision is more difficult when more than one object is involved in an operation. You must decide which object plays the lead role in the operation. Ask yourself the following questions:

- Is one object acted on while the other object performs the action? In general, it is best to associate the operation with the *target* of the operation, rather than the *initiator*.

- Is one object modified by the operation, while other objects are only queried for the information they contain? The object that is changed is the target of the operation.

- Looking at the classes and associations that are involved in the operation, which class is the most centrally-located in this subnetwork of the object-model? If the classes and associations form a star about a single central class, it is the target of the operation.

- If the objects were not software, but were the real-world objects being represented internally, what real object would you push, move, activate, or otherwise manipulate to initiate the operation?

Assigning an operation to a class within a generalization hierarchy can sometimes be difficult because the definitions of the subclasses within the hierarchy are often fluid and can be adjusted during design as convenient. It is common to move an operation up and down in the hierarchy during design, as its scope is adjusted.

## 10.4 DESIGN OPTIMIZATION

The basic design model uses the analysis model as the framework for implementation. The analysis model captures the logical information about the system, while the design model must add details to support efficient information access. The inefficient but semantically-correct analysis model can be optimized to make the implementation more efficient, but an optimized system is more obscure and less likely to be reusable in another context. The designer must strike an appropriate balance between efficiency and clarity.

During design optimization, the designer must:

- Add redundant associations to minimize access cost and maximize convenience
- Rearrange the computation for greater efficiency
- Save derived attributes to avoid recomputation of complicated expressions

### 10.4.1 Adding Redundant Associations for Efficient Access

During analysis, it is undesirable to have redundancy in the association network because redundant associations do not add any information. During design, however, we evaluate the structure of the object model for an implementation. Is there a specific arrangement of the network that would optimize critical aspects of the completed system? Should the network be restructured by adding new associations? Can existing associations be omitted? The associations that were useful during analysis may not form the most efficient network when the access patterns and relative frequencies of different kinds of access are considered.

To demonstrate the analysis of access paths, consider the design of a company's employee skills database. A portion of the object model from the analysis phase is shown in Figure 10.3. The operation *Company::find-skill* returns a set of persons in the company with a given skill. For example, we might ask for all employees who speak Japanese.

**Figure 10.3** Chain of associations

For this example, suppose that the company has 1000 employees each of whom has 10 skills on average. A simple nested loop would traverse *Employs* 1000 times and *Has-skill* 10,000 times. If only 5 employees actually speak Japanese, then the test-to-hit ratio is 2000.

Several improvements are possible. First, *Has-skill* need not be implemented as an unordered list but instead as a hashed set. Hashing can be performed in constant time, so the cost of testing whether a person speaks Japanese is constant, provided *Speaks Japanese* is represented by a unique skill object. This rearrangement reduces the number of tests from 10,000 to 1,000, one per employee.

In cases where the number of hits from a query is low because only a fraction of objects satisfy the test, we can build an *index* to improve access to objects that must be frequently retrieved. For example, we can add a qualified association *Speaks language* from *Company* to *Employee,* where the qualifier is the language spoken (Figure 10.4). This permits us to immediately access all employees who speak a particular language with no wasted accesses. There is a cost of the index: It requires additional memory, and it must be updated whenever the base associations are updated. The designer must decide when it is worthwhile to build indexes. Note that if most queries return all or most of the objects in the search path, then an index really does not save much because the test-to-hit ratio is near 1.

**Figure 10.4** Index for personal skills database

*Speaks language* is a derived association, defined in terms of underlying base associations. The derived association does not add any information to the network but permits the model information to be accessed in a more efficient manner.

Analyze the use of paths in the association network as follows:

• Examine each operation and see what associations it must traverse to obtain its information. Note which associations are traversed in both directions (usually not by a single operation) and which are traversed in a single direction only; the latter can be implemented efficiently with one-way pointers.

For each operation, note the following items:

• How often is the operation called? How costly is it to perform?

• What is the "fan-out" along a path through the network? Estimate the average count of each "many" association encountered along the path. Multiply the individual fan-outs to obtain the fan-out of the entire path, which represents the number of accesses on the last class in the path. Note that "one" links do not increase the fan-out, although they increase the cost of each operation slightly; don't worry about such small effects.

• What is the fraction of "hits" on the final class, that is, objects that meet selection criteria (if any) and are operated on? If most objects are rejected during the traversal for some reason, then a simple nested loop may be inefficient at finding target objects.

Provide indexes for frequent, costly operations with a low hit ratio because such operations are inefficient to implement using nested loops to traverse a path in the network.

### 10.4.2 Rearranging Execution Order for Efficiency

After adjusting the structure of the object model to optimize frequent traversals, the next thing to optimize is the algorithm itself. Actually, data structures and algorithms are directly related to each other, but we find that usually the data structure should be considered first.

One key to algorithm optimization is to eliminate dead paths as early as possible. For example, suppose we want to find all employees who speak both Japanese and French. Suppose 5 employees speak Japanese and 100 speak French; it is better to test and find the Japanese speakers first, then test if they speak French. In general, it pays to narrow the search as soon as possible. Sometimes the execution order of a loop must be inverted from the original specification in the functional model.

### 10.4.3 Saving Derived Attributes to Avoid Recomputation

Data that is redundant because it can be derived from other data can be "cached" or stored in its computed form to avoid the overhead of recomputing it. New objects or classes may be defined to retain this information. The class that contains the cached data must be updated if any of the objects that it depends on are changed.

Figure 10.5 shows a use of a derived object and derived attribute in OMTool. Each class box contains an ordered list of attributes and operations, each represented as a text string (left of diagram). Given the location of the class box itself, the location of each attribute can be computed by adding up the size of all the elements in front of it. Since the location of each element is needed frequently, the location of each attribute string is computed and stored. The region containing the entire attribute list is also computed and saved so that input points need not be tested against attribute text elements in other boxes (right of diagram). If a new attribute string is added to the list, then the locations of the ones after it in the list are simply offset by the size of the new element.

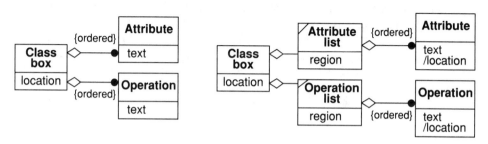

**Figure 10.5** Derived attribute to avoid recomputation

The use of an association as a cache is shown in Figure 10.6. A sheet contains a priority list of partially overlapping elements. If an element is moved or deleted, the elements under it must be redrawn. Overlapping elements can be found by scanning all elements in front of the deleted element in the priority list for the sheet and comparing them to the deleted element. If the number of elements is large, this algorithm grows linearly in the number of elements. The *Overlaps* association stores those elements that overlap an object and precede it in the list. This association must be updated when a new element is added, but testing for overlap using the association is more efficient.

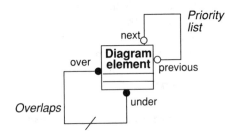

**Figure 10.6** Association as a cache

Derived attributes must be updated when base values change. There are three ways to recognize when an update is needed: by explicit code, by periodic recomputation, or by using active values.

*Explicit update.* Each derived attribute is defined in terms of one or more fundamental base objects. The designer determines which derived attributes are affected by each change to a fundamental attribute and inserts code into the update operation on the base object to explicitly update the derived attributes that depend on it.

*Periodic recomputation.* Base values are often updated in bunches. Sometimes it is possible to simply recompute all the derived attributes periodically without recomputing derived attributes after each base value is changed. Recomputation of all derived attributes can be more efficient than incremental update because some derived attributes may depend on several base attributes and might be updated more than once by an incremental approach. Also periodic recomputation is simpler than explicit update and less prone to bugs. On the other hand, if the data set changes incrementally a few objects at a time, periodic recomputation is not practical because too many derived attributes must be recomputed when only a few are affected.

*Active values.* An *active value* is a value that has dependent values. Each dependent value *registers* itself with the active value, which contains a set of dependent values and update operations. An operation to update the base value triggers updates of all the dependent values, but the calling code need not explicitly invoke the updates. Separating the calling code from the dependent object updates provides the same kind of modularity advantage as separating the call of an operation from the methods that it might invoke. Some programming languages implement active values.

## 10.5 IMPLEMENTATION OF CONTROL

The designer must refine the strategy for implementing the state-event models present in the dynamic model. As part of system design, you will have chosen a basic strategy for realizing the dynamic model (Section 9.7). Now during object design you must flesh out this strategy.

There are three basic approaches to implementing the dynamic model:

- Using the location within the program to hold state (procedure-driven system)

- Direct implementation of a state machine mechanism (event-driven system)

- Using concurrent tasks

### 10.5.1 State as Location within a Program

This is the traditional approach to representing control within a program. The location of control within a program implicitly defines the program state. Any finite state machine can be implemented as a program (easily using gotos, somewhat harder using nested program structures). Each state transition corresponds to an input statement. After input is read, the program branches depending on the input event received. Each input statement needs to handle any input value that could be received at that point. In highly nested procedural code, low-level procedures must accept inputs that they may know nothing about and pass them up through many levels of procedure calls until some procedure is prepared to handle them. The lack of modularity is the biggest drawback of this approach.

One technique of converting a state diagram to code is as follows:

1.  Identify the main control path. Beginning with the initial state, identify a path through the diagram that corresponds to the normally expected sequence of events. Write the names of states along this path as a linear sequence. This becomes a sequence of statements in the program.

2.  Identify alternate paths that branch off the main path and rejoin it later. These become conditional statements in the program.

3.  Identify backward paths that branch off the main loop and rejoin it earlier. These become loops in the program. If there are multiple backward paths that do not cross, they become nested loops in the program. Backward paths that cross do not nest and can be implemented with gotos if all else fails, but these are rare.

4.  The states and transitions that remain correspond to exception conditions. They can be handled by several techniques including error subroutines, exception handling supported by the language, or setting and testing of status flags. Exception handling is a legitimate use for gotos in a programming language because their use frequently simplifies breaking out of a nested structure, but do not use them unless necessary.

Let's see how the above approach could be applied to the state model for the ATM class introduced in Chapter 8. Figure 10.7 shows the state model and the pseudocode derived from it. First, we identify the main path of control, which corresponds to the reading of a card, querying the user for transaction information, processing the transaction, printing a receipt, and ejecting the card. Alternative flows of control occur if the customer wants to process more than one transaction or if the password is bad and the customer is asked to try again.

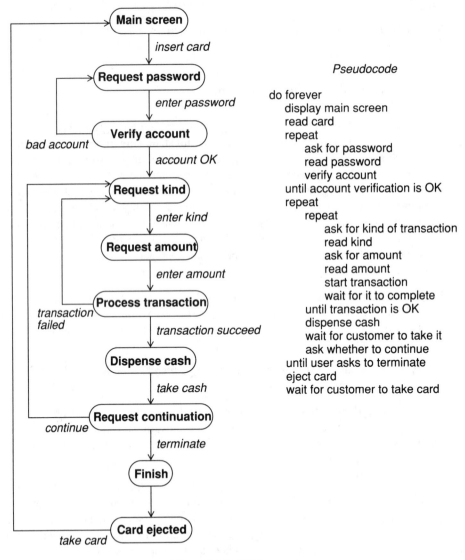

**Figure 10.7** ATM control

Putting these all together, the right portion of Figure 10.7 shows the pseudocode for the ATM control loop. The *cancel* events could be added to the flow of control and implemented as *goto* exception handling code.

Input events within a single-threaded program are coded as blocking I/O reads, that is, I/O statements that wait for input (usually immediately following a write). In a multitasking language, such as Ada, input events can also be coded as wait statements for an inter-task call. The operating system is responsible for catching interrupts and queuing them up for ordinary programs.

## 10.5.2 State Machine Engine

The most direct approach to implementing control is to have some way of explicitly representing and executing state machines. For example, a general "state machine engine" class could provide the capability to execute a state machine represented by a table of transitions and actions provided by the application. Each object instance would contain its own independent state variables but would call on the state engine to determine the next state and action. (The state machines are objects but not application objects. They are part of the language substrate to support the semantics of application objects.)

This approach allows you to quickly progress from the analysis model to a skeleton prototype of the system by defining classes from the object model, state machines from the dynamic model, and creating "stubs" of the action routines. A stub is the minimal definition of a function or subroutine without any internal code (code to return a precalculated or contrived value may be included). Thus if each stub prints out its name, this technique allows you to execute the skeleton application to verify that the basic flow of control is correct.

A parser, such as Unix *yacc* or *lex,* produces an explicit state machine to implement a user interface. Some application packages, especially in the user interface area, permit state machines to be supplied as tables to be interpreted by the package.

Creation of a state machine mechanism is not particularly difficult using an object-oriented language and should be considered as a practical alternative if you do not have a state machine package already available.

## 10.5.3 Control as Concurrent Tasks

An object can be implemented as a task in the programming language or operating system. This is the most general approach, as it preserves the inherent concurrency of real objects. Events are implemented as inter-task calls using the facilities of the language or operating system. As in the previous implementation, the task uses its location within the program to keep track of its state.

Some languages, such as Concurrent Pascal or Concurrent C++, support concurrency, but acceptance of such languages in production environments is still limited. Ada supports concurrency, provided an object is equated with an Ada task, although the run-time cost is high. The major object-oriented languages do not yet support concurrency.

## 10.6  ADJUSTMENT OF INHERITANCE

As object design progresses, the definitions of classes and operations can often be adjusted to increase the amount of inheritance. The designer should:

- Rearrange and adjust classes and operations to increase inheritance
- Abstract common behavior out of groups of classes
- Use delegation to share behavior when inheritance is semantically invalid

### 10.6.1  Rearranging Classes and Operations

Sometimes the same operation is defined across several classes and can easily be inherited from a common ancestor, but more often operations in different classes are similar but not identical. By slightly modifying the definitions of the operations or the classes, the operations can often be made to match so that they can be covered by a single inherited operation.

Before inheritance can be used, each operation must have the same interface and the same semantics. All operations must have the same signature, that is, the same number and types of arguments and results. If the signatures match, then the operations must be examined to see if they have the same semantics. The following kinds of adjustments can be used to increase the chance of inheritance:

- Some operations may have fewer arguments than others. The missing arguments can be added but ignored. For example, a draw operation on a monochromatic display does not need a color parameter, but the parameter can be accepted and ignored for consistency with color displays.

- Some operations may have fewer arguments because they are special cases of more general arguments. Implement the special operations by calling the general operation with appropriate parameter values. For example, appending an element to a list is a special case of inserting an element into list; the insert point simply follows the last element.

- Similar attributes in different classes may have different names. Give the attributes the same name and move them to a common ancestor class. Then operations that access the attributes will match better. Also watch for similar operations with different names. A consistent naming strategy is important to avoid hiding similarities.

- An operation may be defined on several different classes in a group but be undefined on the other classes. Define it on the common ancestor class and declare it as a no-op on the classes that don't care about it. For example, in OMTool the *begin-edit* operation places some figures, such as class boxes, in a special draw mode to permit rapid resizing while the text in them is being edited. Other figures have no special draw mode, so the *begin-edit* operation on these classes has no effect.

### 10.6.2  Abstracting Out Common Behavior

Opportunities to use inheritance are not always recognized during the analysis phase of development, so it is worthwhile to reexamine the object model looking for commonality between classes. In addition, new classes and operations are often added during design. If a set of operations and/or attributes seems to be repeated in two classes, it is possible that the two classes are really specialized variations of the same thing when viewed at a higher level of abstraction.

When common behavior has been recognized, a common superclass can be created that implements the shared features, leaving only the specialized features in the subclasses. This transformation of the object model is called *abstracting out* a common superclass or common behavior. Usually the resulting superclass is abstract, meaning that there are no direct instances of it, but the behavior it defines belongs to all instances of its subclasses. For example, a *draw* operation of a geometric figure on a display screen requires setup and rendering of the geometry. The rendering varies among different figures, such as circles, lines, and splines, but the setup, such as setting the color, line thickness, and other parameters, can be inherited by all figure classes from abstract class *Figure*.

Sometimes it is worthwhile to abstract out a superclass even when there is only one subclass in your project that inherits from it. Although this does not result in any sharing of behavior in the immediate project, the abstract superclass thus created may be reusable in future projects. It may even be a worthwhile addition to your class library. When a project is completed, the potentially reusable classes should be collected, documented, and generalized so that they may be used in future projects.

Abstract superclasses have benefits other than sharing and reuse. The splitting of a class into two classes that separate the specific aspects from the more general aspects is a form of *modularity*. Each class is a separately maintained component with a well documented interface.

The creation of abstract superclasses also improves the *extensibility* of a software product. Imagine that you are developing a temperature-sensing module for a larger computerized control system. There is a specific type of sensor (Model J55) that you must use, with a particular way of reading the temperature, and a formula for converting the raw numeric reading into degrees Celsius. You could implement all this behavior in a single class, with one instance for every sensor in the system. But realizing that the J55 sensor is not the only type available, you create an abstract *Sensor* superclass that defines the general behavior common to all sensors. A particular subclass called *Sensor-J55* implements reading and conversion that is particular to this model.

Now, when your control system converts to use a new model of sensor, all you have to do is implement a new subclass for that model with only the specialized behavior that is different. The common behavior has already been implemented. Perhaps best of all, you will not have to change a single line of code in the large control system that uses these sensors because the interface is the same, as defined by the *sensor* superclass.

There is a subtle but important way that abstract superclasses improve the *configuration management* aspect of software maintenance and distribution. Suppose that your control system software must be distributed to many plants throughout the country, each of which has a different system configuration involving (among other things) a different mix of temperature sensors. Some plants still use the old J55 model, while others have converted to the newer K99 model, and some plants may have a mixture of both types. Generating customized versions of your software to match each different configuration could be tedious.

Instead, you distribute one version of software that contains a subclass for each known model of sensor. When the software starts up, it reads a configuration file provided by the customer that tells it which model of sensor is used in which location and creates an instance of the particular subclass that handles that type of sensor. All the rest of the code treats the sensors as if they were all the same as defined by the *Sensor* superclass. It is even possible to change from one type of sensor to another *on-the-fly* (while the system is running) if the software is told to create a new object to manage the new type of sensor.

### 10.6.3 Use Delegation to Share Implementation

Inheritance is a mechanism for implementing generalization, in which the behavior of a superclass is shared by all its subclasses. Sharing of behavior is justifiable only when a true generalization relationship occurs, that is, only when it can be said that the subclass *is* a form of the superclass. Operations of the subclass that override the corresponding operation of the superclass have a responsibility to provide the same services provided by the superclass, and possibly more. When class B *inherits the specification* of class A, we can assume that every instance of class B *is* an instance of class A because it behaves the same.

Sometimes programmers use inheritance as an implementation technique with no intention of guaranteeing the same behavior. It often happens that an existing class already implements some of the behavior that we want to provide in a newly-defined class, although in other respects the two classes are different. The designer is then tempted to inherit from the existing class to achieve part of the implementation of the new class. This can lead to problems if other operations that are inherited provide unwanted behavior. We discourage this *inheritance of implementation* because it can lead to incorrect behavior.

As an example of implementation inheritance, suppose that you are about to implement a *Stack* class, and you already have a *List* class available. You may be tempted to make *Stack* inherit from *List*. Pushing an element onto the stack can be achieved by adding an element to the end of the list and popping an element from a stack corresponds to removing an element from the end of the list. But we are also inheriting unwanted list operations that add or remove elements from arbitrary positions in the list. If these are ever used (by mistake or as a "short-cut") then the *Stack* class will not behave as expected.

Often when you are tempted to use inheritance as an implementation technique, you could achieve the same goal in a safer way by making one class an attribute or associate of the other class. In this way, one object can selectively invoke the desired functions of another class, using *delegation* rather than inheritance. Delegation consists of catching an operation on one object and sending it to another object that is part of or related to the first object. Only meaningful operations are delegated to the second object, so there is no danger of inheriting meaningless operations by accident.

A safer implementation of *Stack* would delegate to the *List* class as shown in Figure 10.8. Every instance of *Stack* contains a private instance of *List*. (The actual implementation of this aggregation is optimized as discussed in Section 10.7, possibly using an embedded object or a pointer attribute.) The *Stack::push* operation delegates to the list by calling its *last* and *add* operations to add an element at the end of the list, and the *pop* operation has a similar implementation using the *last* and *remove* operations. The ability to corrupt the stack by adding or removing arbitrary elements is hidden from the client of the *Stack* class.

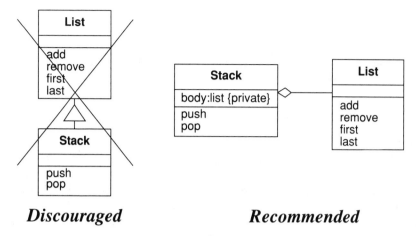

**Discouraged**                          **Recommended**

**Figure 10.8** Alternative implementations of a Stack
using inheritance (left) and delegation (right)

In general, it is best not to use inheritance for strictly implementation reasons. Reserve the use of inheritance for cases where you can say that an instance of one class also *is* an instance of some other class.

Some languages, such as Eiffel and C++, permit a subclass to inherit the form of a superclass but to selectively inherit operations from ancestors and selectively export operations to clients. This is tantamount to the use of delegation, because the subclass *is not* a form of the superclass in all respects and is not confused with it.

## 10.7 DESIGN OF ASSOCIATIONS

Associations are the "glue" of our object model, providing access paths between objects. Associations are conceptual entities useful for modeling and analysis. During the object design phase we must formulate a strategy for implementing the associations in the object model. We can either choose a global strategy for implementing all associations uniformly, or we can select a particular technique for each association, taking into account the way it will be used in the application. To make intelligent decisions about associations, we first need to analyze the way they are used.

### 10.7.1 Analyzing Association Traversal

We have assumed until now that associations are inherently bidirectional, which is certainly true in an abstract sense. But if some associations in your application are only traversed in one direction, their implementation can be simplified. Be aware, however, that the requirements on your application may change, and you may add a new operation later that needs to traverse the association in the reverse direction.

For prototype work, we always use bidirectional associations so that we can add new behavior and expand or modify the application rapidly. For production work we optimize some associations. Whichever implementation strategy you choose, you should hide the implementation using access operations to traverse and update the association. This will allow you to change your decision with minimal effort.

### 10.7.2 One-way Associations

If an association is only traversed in one direction, it may be implemented as a *pointer*—an attribute which contains an object reference. If the multiplicity is "one," as shown in Figure 10.9, then it is a simple pointer; if the multiplicity is "many," then it is a set of pointers. If the "many" end is ordered, then a list can be used instead of a set. A qualified association with multiplicity "one" can be implemented as a dictionary object. (A dictionary is a set of value pairs that maps selector values into target values. Dictionaries are implemented efficiently in most object-oriented languages using hashing.) Qualified associations with multiplicity "many" are rare, but they can be implemented as a dictionary of sets of objects.

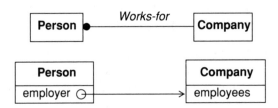

**Figure 10.9** Implementation of one-way association using pointers

### 10.7.3 Two-way Associations

Many associations are traversed in both directions, although not usually with equal frequency. There are three approaches to their implementation:

- Implement as an attribute in one direction only and perform a search when a backward traversal is required. This approach is useful only if there is a great disparity in traversal frequency in the two directions and minimizing both the storage cost and the update cost are important. The rare backward traversal will be expensive.

- Implement as attributes in both directions, using the techniques outlined in the previous section and shown in Figure 10.10. This approach permits fast access, but if either attribute is updated then the other attribute must also be updated to keep the link consistent. This approach is useful if accesses outnumber updates.

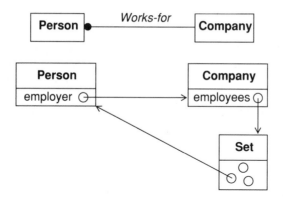

Figure 10.10 Implementation of two-way association using pointers

- Implement as a distinct association object, independent of either class, as shown in Figure 10.11 [Rumbaugh-87]. An association object is a set of pairs of associated objects (triples for qualified associations) stored in a single variable-size object. For efficiency, an association object can be implemented using two dictionary objects, one for the forward direction and one for the backward direction. Access is slightly slower than with attribute pointers, but if hashing is used then access is still constant time. This approach is useful for extending predefined classes from a library which cannot be modified, because the association object can be added without adding any attributes to the original classes. Distinct association objects are also useful for sparse associations, in which most objects of the classes do not participate because space is used only for actual links.

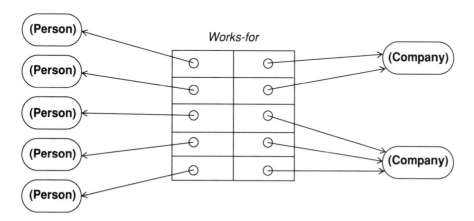

Figure 10.11 Implementation of association as an object

### 10.7.4 Link Attributes

If an association has link attributes, then its implementation depends on the multiplicity. If the association is one-to-one, the link attributes can be stored as attributes of either object. If the association is many-to-one, the link attributes can be stored as attributes of the "many" object, since each "many" object appears only once in the association. If the association is many-to-many, the link attributes cannot be associated with either object; the best approach is usually to implement the association as a distinct class, in which each instance represents one link and its attributes.

## 10.8  OBJECT REPRESENTATION

Implementing objects is mostly straightforward, but the designer must choose when to use primitive types in representing objects and when to combine groups of related objects.

Classes can be defined in terms of other classes, but eventually everything must be implemented in terms of built-in primitive data types, such as integers, strings, and enumerated types. For example, consider the implementation of a social security number within an employee object as shown in Figure 10.12. The social security number attribute can be implemented as an integer or a string, or as an association to a social security number object, which itself can contain either an integer or a string. Defining a new class is more flexible but often introduces unnecessary indirection.

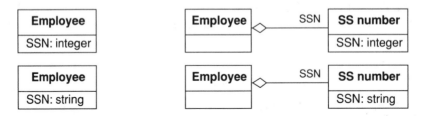

**Figure 10.12** Alternative representations for an attribute

In a similar vein, the designer must often choose whether to combine groups of related objects. Figure 10.13 shows two common implementations of 2-dimensional lines, one as a separate class and one embedded as attributes within the *Point* class. Neither representation is inherently superior because both are mathematically correct.

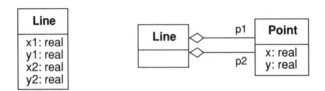

**Figure 10.13** Embedded and explicit objects

## 10.9 PHYSICAL PACKAGING

Programs are made of discrete physical units that can be edited, compiled, imported, or otherwise manipulated. In some languages, such as C and Fortran, the units are source files. In Ada, the *package* is an explicit language construct for modularity. Object-oriented languages have various degrees of packaging. In any large project, careful partitioning of an implementation into packages (of whatever form) is important to permit different persons to cooperatively work on a program. Packaging involves the following issues:

- Hiding internal information from outside view

- Coherence of entities

- Constructing physical modules

### 10.9.1 Information Hiding

One design goal is to treat classes as "black boxes," whose external interface is public but whose internal details are hidden from view. Hiding internal information permits implementation of a class to be changed without requiring any clients of the class to modify code. Furthermore, additions and changes to the class are surrounded by "fire walls" that limit the effects of any changes so that changes can be understood clearly. There is a trade-off between information hiding and the optimization activities as discussed in Section 10.4. From the packaging viewpoint, we seek to minimize dependencies, while optimization takes advantage of details and may lead to redundant components and associations. The designer must balance these conflicting demands.

During analysis, we were not concerned with information hiding. During design, however, the public interface of each class must be carefully defined. The designer must decide what attributes should be accessible from outside the class. These decisions should be recorded in the object model by adding the annotation *{private}* after attributes that are to be hidden, or by separating the list of attributes into two parts.

Taken to an extreme, a method on a class could traverse all the associations of the object model to locate and access another object in the system. This unconstrained visibility is appropriate during analysis, but methods that know too much about the entire model are fragile because any change in representation invalidates them. During design we try to limit the scope of any one method. We need to define the bounds of visibility that each method requires. Specifying what other classes a method can see defines the dependencies between classes.

Each operation should have a limited knowledge of the entire model, including the structure of classes, associations, and operations. The fewer things that an operation knows about, the less likely it will be affected by any changes. Conversely, the fewer operations know about details of a class, the easier the class can be changed if needed. The following design principles help to limit the scope of knowledge of any operation:

- Allocate to each class the responsibility of performing operations and providing information that pertains to it.

- Call an operation to access attributes belonging to an object of another class.

- Avoid traversing associations that are not connected to the current class.

- Define interfaces at as high a level of abstraction as possible.

- Hide external objects at the system boundary by defining abstract interface classes, that is, classes that mediate between the system and the raw external objects.

- Avoid applying a method to the result of another method, unless the result class is already a supplier of methods to the caller. Instead consider writing a method to combine the two operations.

### 10.9.2  Coherence of Entities

One important design principle is *coherence* of entities. An entity, such as a class, an operation, or a module, is coherent if it is organized on a consistent plan and all its parts fit together toward a common goal. An entity should have a single major theme; it should not be a collection of unrelated parts.

A method should do one thing well. A single method should not contain both *policy* and *implementation*. *Policy* is the making of context-dependent decisions. *Implementation* is the execution of fully-specified algorithms. Policy involves making decisions, gathering global information, interacting with the outside world, and interpreting special cases. A policy method contains I/O statements, conditionals, and accesses data stores. A policy method does not contain complicated algorithms but instead calls various implementation methods. An implementation method does exactly one operation, without making any decisions, assumptions, defaults, or deviations. All its information is supplied as arguments, so the argument list may be long.

Separating policy and implementation greatly increases the possibility of reusability. The implementation methods do not contain any context dependencies, so they are likely to be reusable. The policy methods must usually be rewritten in a new application, but they are often simple and consist mostly of high-level decisions and calls on low-level methods.

For example, consider an operation to credit interest on a checking account. Interest is compounded daily based on the daily balance, but all interest for a month is lost if the account is closed. The interest crediting should be separated into two parts: an implementation method that computes the interest due between a pair of days, without regard to any forfeitures or other provisions; and a policy method that decides whether and for what interval the implementation method is called. This separation permits either the policy or the implementation to be modified independently and greatly increases the chance of reusing the implementation method, which is likely to be the more complicated. Policy methods are less likely to be reusable, but they are not usually as complicated because they do not contain computational algorithms.

A class should not serve too many purposes at once. If it is too complicated, it can be broken up using either generalization or aggregation. Smaller pieces are more likely to be reusable than large complicated pieces. Exact numbers are somewhat risky, but as a rule of thumb consider breaking up a class if it contains more than about 10 attributes, 10 associations, or 20 operations. Always break a class if the attributes, associations, or operations sharply divide into two or more different groups that seem unrelated.

### 10.9.3 Constructing Modules

During the analysis and system design phases we partitioned the object model into modules (and because of limitations on screen or paper size the modules may have been further partitioned into sheets). This initial organization may not be suitable or optimal for the final packaging of the system implementation. The new classes that we have added during design either add to an existing module or layer or can be organized into a separate module or layer that did not exist in the analysis.

Modules should be defined so that their interfaces are minimal and well-defined. The interface between two modules consists of the associations that relate classes in one module with classes in the other and operations which access classes across module boundaries (these operations define the client-supplier relationship of classes, taken from the functional model).

The connectivity of the object model can be used as a guide for partitioning modules. A rough rule of thumb is that classes that are closely connected by associations should be in the same module, while classes that are not connected, or are loosely connected may be in separate modules. The binding strength of client-supplier relationships, due to the functional model, is weaker than the strength of associations, which are an inherent part of a set of objects.

Of course there are other aspects to be considered. Modules should have some functional cohesiveness or unity of purpose. The classes in a module should represent similar kinds of things in the application or should be components of the same composite object.

The number of different operations that traverse a given association is a good measure of its coupling strength. This number expresses the number of different ways that the association is used, not the frequency of traversal. Try to encapsulate strong coupling within a single module.

## 10.10  DOCUMENTING DESIGN DECISIONS

The design decisions discussed in this chapter must be documented when they are made, or you will become confused. This is especially true if you are working with other developers. It is impossible to remember design details for any nontrivial software system, and documentation is often the best way of transmitting the design to others and recording it for reference during maintenance.

The Design Document should be an extension of the Requirements Analysis Document. Thus the Design Document will include a revised and much more detailed description of the

Object Model, in both graphical form (object model diagrams) and textual form (class descriptions). Additional notation is appropriate for showing implementation decisions, such as arrows showing the traversal direction of associations and pointers from attributes to other objects.

The Functional Model will also be extended during the design phase, and it must be kept current. Again, this is a seamless process because design uses the same notation as analysis but with more detail and specifics. It is particularly important to specify all operation interfaces by giving their arguments, results, input-output mappings, and side effects.

If the Dynamic Model is implemented using an explicit state control or concurrent tasks, then the analysis model or its extension is adequate. If the dynamic model is implemented by location within program code, then structured pseudocode for algorithms is needed.

Despite the seamless conversion from analysis to design, it is probably a good idea to keep the Design Document distinct from the Analysis Document. Because of the shift in viewpoint from an external user's view to an internal implementor's view, the design document includes many optimizations and implementation artifacts. It is important to retain a clear, user-oriented description of the system for use in validation of the completed software and for reference during the maintenance phase. Traceability from an element in the original analysis to the corresponding element in the design document should be straightforward since the design document is an evolution of the analysis model and retains the same names.

## 10.11 CHAPTER SUMMARY

Object design follows analysis and system design. Object design does not begin from scratch but rather elaborates on the previous analysis and system design. The object design phase adds implementation details, such as restructuring classes for efficiency, internal data structures and algorithms to implement operations, implementation of control, implementation of associations, and packaging into physical modules. Object design extends the analysis model with specific implementation decisions and additional internal classes, attributes, associations, and operations.

The designer must transfer operations from the functional and dynamic models onto the object model for implementation. A process from the functional model becomes an operation on an object. An event form the dynamic model may also become an operation on an object, depending on the implementation of control.

Each operation from the analysis model must be assigned an algorithm that implements it clearly and efficiently, according to the optimization goals selected during system design. The design must consider computational complexity but should sacrifice small amounts of performance for greater clarity of the code. Internal classes and operations may be added to implement algorithms efficiently.

The initial design derived from analysis must be extended and restructured for purposes of optimization. The original information is not discarded, but new redundant information is added to optimize access paths and preserve intermediate results that would otherwise have to be recomputed. Algorithms can be rearranged to reduce the number of operations to be executed.

State-event interactions can be implemented using one of three different styles of control: use of the location within a program to preserve the control state, explicit state machine representation, or concurrent tasks.

During object design, the definitions of internal classes and operations can be adjusted to increase the amount of inheritance. These adjustments include modifying the argument list of a method, moving attributes and operations from a class into a superclass, defining an abstract superclass to cover the shared behavior of several classes, and splitting an operation into an inherited part and a specific part. Delegation should be used rather than inheritance when a class is similar to another class but not truly a subclass.

Associations subsume many implementation techniques under a single uniform notation during analysis, but they can be implemented as pointers within objects or distinct objects depending on their access patterns. An association traversed in a single direction can be implemented as an attribute pointing to another object or a set of objects, depending on the multiplicity of the association. A bidirectional association can be implemented as a pair of pointers, but operations that update the association must always modify both directions of access. Associations can also be implemented as association objects.

The exact representation of objects must be chosen. At some point, user-defined objects must be implemented in terms of primitive objects or data types supplied by the programming language. Some classes can be combined.

Programs must be packaged into physical modules for editors and compilers as well as for the convenience of programming teams. Information hiding is a primary goal of packaging to ensure that future changes affect few modules. Modules should be coherent and organized about a common theme.

Design decisions should be documented by extending the analysis model, by adding detail to the object, dynamic, and functional models. Implementation constructs are appropriate, such as pointers (in the object model), structured pseudocode (in the dynamic model), and functional expressions (in the function model).

| | |
|---|---|
| abstracting out a superclass | implementation of control flow |
| algorithm | optimization of design |
| analyzing association traversal | physical packaging |
| combining the three models | policy versus implementation |
| container class | redundancy to improve speed |
| delegation | visibility of associations |
| deriving operations | visibility of attributes |
| implementation of associations | visibility of operations |

**Figure 10.14** Key concepts for Chapter 10

## BIBLIOGRAPHIC NOTES

Algorithms and data structures are part of the basic computer science curriculum. Knuth's classic series covers basic concepts as well as many advanced practical algorithms and data structures. There are several good books which cover algorithms from the viewpoint of computational complexity, such as [Aho-75] and [Sedgewick-83]. There are many bewildering variations on common algorithms for searching and sorting, however, and their performance on different problems can be difficult to analyze; see [Gonnet-84] for empirical measurements of algorithm performance.

Adding indexes and rearranging access order to improve performance is a mature technique in data base optimization. See [Ullman-88] or [Loomis-87] for examples.

Much of software engineering practice has been concerned with rules for packaging programs into modules with appropriate visibility rules. [Yourdon-89] gives the standard approach. [Buhr-84] is heavily focused on packaging of Ada programs, but the notation should be extendible to object-oriented applications.

[Lieberherr-88] is an early attempt to provide visibility guidelines that preserve maximum modularity within an object-oriented context. [Meyer-88] suggests style rules for using classes and operations.

## REFERENCES

[Aho-75] Alfred Aho, John Hopcroft, Jeffrey Ullman. *The Design and Analysis of Computer Algorithms*. Reading, Mass.: Addison-Wesley, 1975.

[Buhr-84] R.J.A. Buhr. *System Design with Ada*. Englewood Cliffs, New Jersey: Prentice Hall, 1984.

[Gonnet-84] G.H. Gonnet. *Handbook of Algorithms and Data Structures*. Reading, Mass.: Addison-Wesley, 1984.

[Knuth-75] Donald Knuth. *The Art of Computer Programming, Volumes 1-3*. Reading, Mass.: Addison-Wesley, 1975.

[Lieberherr-88] K. Lieberherr, I. Holland, A. Riel. Object-Oriented programming: an objective sense of style. *OOPSLA'88* as *ACM SIGPLAN 23*, 11 (Nov. 1988), 323-334.

[Loomis-87] Mary Loomis. *The Database Book*. New York: Macmillan, 1987.

[Meyer-88] Bertrand Meyer. *Object-Oriented Software Construction*. Hertfordshire, England: Prentice Hall International, 1988.

[Rumbaugh-87] James E. Rumbaugh. Relations as semantic constructs in an object-oriented language. *OOPSLA'87* as *ACM SIGPLAN 22*, 12 (Oct. 1987), 466-481

[Sedgewick-83] Robert Sedgewick. *Algorithms*. Reading, Mass.: Addison-Wesley, 1983.

[Ullman-88] Jeffrey Ullman. *Principles of Database and Knowledge-Base Systems, Volumes 1, 2*. Rockville, Maryland: Computer Science Press, 1988.

[Yourdon-89] Edward Yourdon, Larry Constantine. *Structured Design: Fundamentals of a Discipline for Computer Program and Systems Design*. Englewood Cliffs, New Jersey: Prentice Hall, 1989.

## EXERCISES

**10.1** (3) Write algorithms to draw the following figures on a graphics terminal. The figures are not filled. Assume pixel based graphics. State any assumptions that you make.
   a. circle
   b. ellipse
   c. square
   d. rectangle

**10.2** (2) Discuss whether or not the algorithm that you wrote in the previous exercise to draw an ellipse is suitable for drawing circles and whether or not the rectangle algorithm is suitable for squares.

**10.3** (3) By careful ordering of multiplications and additions, the total number of arithmetic steps needed to evaluate a polynomial can be minimized. For example, one way to evaluate the polynomial $a_4x^4 + a_3x^3 + a_2x^2 + a_1x + a_0$ is to compute each term separately, adding each term to the total as it is computed, which requires 10 multiplications and 4 additions. Another way is to rearrange the order of the arithmetic to $x \cdot (x \cdot (x \cdot (x \cdot a_4 + a_3) + a_2) + a_1) + a_0$, which requires only 4 multiplications and 4 additions. How many multiplications and additions are required by each method for an $n$th order polynomial? Discuss the relative merits of each approach.

**10.4** (5) Many conventional data structures can be replaced with associations. Draw sample object diagrams in which each of the following conventional data structures is replaced by one or more associations. Keep your answers simple.
   a. array
   b. list
   c. stack
   d. queue
   e. binary tree

**10.5** (4) Improve the object diagram in Figure E10.1 by generalizing the classes *Ellipse* and *Rectangle* to the class *Graphics primitive*, transforming the object diagram so that there is only a single one-to-one association to the object class *Boundary*. In effect, you will be changing the 0,1 multiplicity to exactly-one multiplicity. As it stands, the class *Boundary* is shared between *Ellipse* and *Rectangle*. A *Boundary* is the smallest rectangular region that will contain the associated *Ellipse* or *Rectangle*.

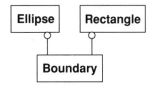

**Figure E10.1** Portion of an object diagram with a shared class

**10.6** (5) Which class(es) in the object diagram that you produced for the previous exercise would be the most suitable owner of a delete operation? Explain your answer.

**10.7** (3) Assign a data type to each attribute in Figure E10.2.

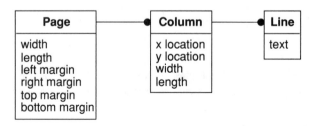

**Figure E10.2** Portion of an object diagram of a newspaper

**10.8** (3) Express an operation that moves a *Column* of a newspaper in terms of an operation on a *Line* of text, in Figure E10.2.

**10.9** (4) Modify the object diagram in Figure E10.2 so that margins are described in a separate class and so that default margins may be specified for the entire newspaper. Also, the default margins may be overridden on specific pages.

**10.10** (4) Characterize each association in Figure E10.2 in terms of traversal directionality and ordering. State any assumptions that you make. Describe how you would implement each association.

**10.11** (3) Modify Figure E10.2 to make it possible to be able to determine what *Page* a *Line* is on without first determining what *Column* it is in.

**10.12** (4) Assign a data type to each attribute in Figure E10.3. V*isibility* controls whether the fronts or the backs of cards are displayed. *Location* is the place where the collection is to be displayed. List enumeration values.

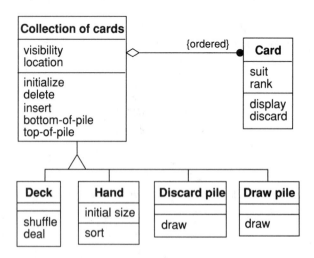

**Figure E10.3** Portion of an object diagram of a card playing program

**10.13** (7) Write pseudocode for each operation in Figure E10.3. *Initialize* causes a deck to start with 52 cards and anything else to become empty. *Delete* and *insert* take a card as a single argument and delete or insert the card into a collection, forcing the collection to redisplay itself afterwards. *Delete* is allowed only on the top card of a deck, a draw pile, or a discard pile. *Top-of-pile and bottom-of-pile* are queries. *Shuffle* mixes a deck. *Deal* selects cards from the top of the deck one at a time, deleting them from the deck and inserting them into hands which are created and returned as an array of hands. *Sort* is used to sort a hand by suit and rank. *Display* displays a card. *Discard* deletes a card from the collection that contains it and places it on top of the draw pile, which is passed as an argument. *Draw* deletes the top card from a draw or discard pile and inserts the card into a hand, which is passed as an argument.

**10.14** (3) Characterize the association in Figure E10.3 in terms of traversal directionality and ordering. State any assumptions that you make. Describe how you would implement the association.

**10.15** (5) Assign a data type to each attribute in Figure E10.4. Refer to exercise 8.16 for a description of the application.

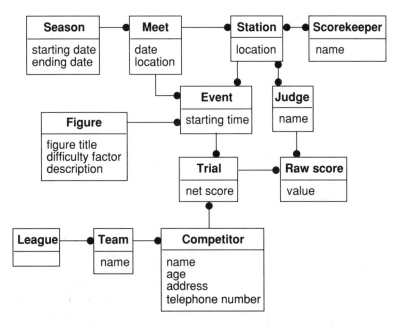

**Figure E10.4** Portion of an object diagram of a scoring system

**10.16** (7) Characterize each of the associations in Figure E10.4 in terms of traversal directionality and ordering. State any assumptions that you make.

**10.17** (5) Write pseudocode for computing the net score for a trial in Figure E10.4. Refer to exercise 6.3 for a description of how a trial is scored.

**10.18** Prepare pseudocode for the following operations to classes in Figure E10.4.
   a. (4) register a competitor for an event
   b. (3) register a competitor for all events at a meet

c.  (4) select and schedule events for a meet

d.  (4) schedule meets in a season

e.  (4) assign events, judges, and scorekeepers to stations

**10.19**  (9) Figure E10.5 is a portion of an object diagram meta model which might be used in a compiler of an object-oriented language. Write pseudocode for an algorithm for the operation *trace_inheritance_path* that traces an inheritance hierarchy as follows: input to the operation is a pair of classes. The operation returns an ordered list of classes on the path from the more general class to the more specific class. Tracing is only through generalizations; aggregations and associations are ignored. If tracing fails, an empty list is returned. You may assume that multiple inheritance is not allowed.

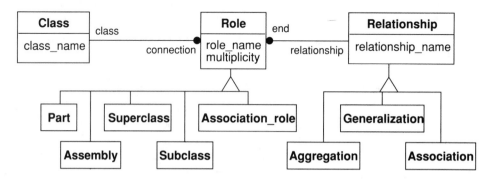

**Figure E10.5**  Portion of an object diagram meta model

**10.20**  (8) Refine Figure E10.5 by eliminating the associations to the classes *Role* and *Relationship*, replacing them with associations to the subclasses of *Role* and *Relationship*. This is an example of a transformation on an object diagram. Write pseudocode for the *trace_inheritance_path* algorithm for the diagram that you produce.

**10.21**  (7) Referring to Figure E10.5, prepare an algorithm for an operation that will generate a name for an association that does not already have one. This operation would be useful in a program that generates database schema from an object diagram, to assure that all associations in an object diagram have names, whether or not they were named by the user. Input to the operation is an instance of *Association*. The operation must return a globally unique *relationship_name*. If the association already has a name, the operation should return it. Otherwise the operation should generate a name using a strategy that you must devise. The precise strategy is not critical, but the generated names must be unique, and anyone reading the names should be able to determine which association the name refers to. Assume all associations are binary. You may assume that a similar operation on the class *Role* already has been designed that will return a *role_name* unique within the context of a relationship. If the name that would be formed collides with an existing name, modify the name in some way to make it unique. If you feel you need to modify the diagram or use additional data structures, go ahead, but be sure to describe them.

**10.22**  (7) Improve the object diagram in Figure E10.6 by transforming it, adding the class *Political party*). Associate *Voter* with a party. Discuss why the transformation is an improvement.

**10.23**  (7) Sometimes an airline will substitute a smaller aircraft for a larger one for a flight with few passengers. Write an algorithm for reassigning seats so that passengers with low row numbers do not have to be reassigned. Assume both aircraft have the same number of seats per row.

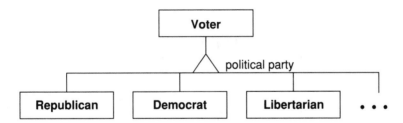

**Figure E10.6** Object diagram representing voter membership in a political party

**10.24** (8) The need for implementation efficiency may force you to create classes that are not in the original problem statement. For example, a two dimensional CAD system may use specialized data structures to determine which points fall within a rectangular window specified by the user. One technique is to maintain a collection of points sorted on x and then y. Points that fall within a rectangular window can usually be found without having to check all points. Prepare an object diagram that describes collections of points sorted on x and y. Write pseudocode for the operations *delete, add*, and *search*. The input to *search* is a description of a rectangular region and a collection of points. The output of *search* is a set of points from the input collection which fall within the region. Inputs to both *delete* and *add* are a point and a collection of points. The input point is added or deleted from the collection.

**10.25** (8) Determine how the time required by the search operation in the previous exercise depends on the number of points in a collection. Explicitly state any assumptions you make.

**10.26** (3) In selecting an algorithm, it may be important to evaluate its resource requirements. How does the time required to execute the following algorithms depend on the following parameters?

a. The algorithm in exercise 10.19 on the depth of the inheritance hierarchy.

b. The algorithm in exercise 10.23 on the number of passengers.

**10.27** (5) Figure E10.7 is a state diagram for a garage door opener. Implement it by using state as location within a program. You may use pseudocode or any structured programming language.

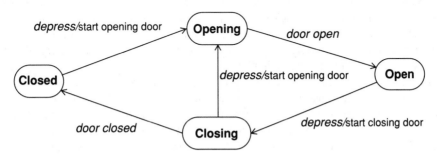

**Figure E10.7** State diagram for a garage door opener

**10.28** (Project) As a class project, design a state machine engine. The design should include descriptions of data structures and algorithms needed to make the engine run.

# 11

## Methodology Summary

This chapter summarizes the methodology of the Object Modeling Technique. The techniques discussed in previous chapters are listed below as numbered steps. While this implies that the order is important, we find that:

- Experienced developers are able to combine several steps or perform certain steps in parallel for portions of a project.

- Iteration of the steps is necessary at successively lower levels of abstraction, adding more detail to the model.

- After the overall analysis has been completed at a high level of abstraction, subsystems within a large project can be designed independently and concurrently at lower levels of abstraction.

The distinction between analysis and design may at times seem arbitrary and confusing. The following simple rules should guide your decisions concerning the proper scope of analysis and design.

The *analysis* model should include information that is meaningful from a real-world perspective and should present the external view of the system. The analysis model should be understandable to the client for a system and should provide a useful basis for eliciting the true requirements for a system. The true requirements are those that are really needed, internally consistent, and feasible to achieve.

In contrast, the *design* model is driven by relevance to the computer implementation. Thus the design model must be reasonably efficient and practical to encode. In practice, many portions of the analysis model can often be readily implemented without change; thus there may be considerable overlap between the analysis and design models. The design model must address low level details that are elided in the analysis model. The analysis and design models combine to provide valuable documentation for a system from two different, but complementary, perspectives.

## 11.1 ANALYSIS

The goal of analysis is to develop a model of what the system will do. The model is expressed in terms of objects and relationships, dynamic control flow, and functional transformations. The process of capturing requirements and consulting with the requestor should continue throughout analysis.

1. Write or obtain an initial description of the problem (Problem Statement).

2. Build an Object Model:

   • Identify object classes.

   • Begin a data dictionary containing descriptions of classes, attributes, and associations.

   • Add associations between classes.

   • Add attributes for objects and links.

   • Organize and simplify object classes using inheritance.

   • Test access paths using scenarios and iterate the above steps as necessary.

   • Group classes into modules, based on close coupling and related function.

   $\Rightarrow$ **Object Model** = object model diagram + data dictionary.

3. Develop a Dynamic Model:

   • Prepare scenarios of typical interaction sequences.

   • Identify events between objects and prepare an event trace for each scenario.

   • Prepare an event flow diagram for the system.

   • Develop a state diagram for each class that has important dynamic behavior.

   • Check for consistency and completeness of events shared among the state diagrams.

   $\Rightarrow$ **Dynamic Model** = state diagrams + global event flow diagram.

4. Construct a Functional Model:

   • Identify input and output values.

   • Use data flow diagrams as needed to show functional dependencies.

   • Describe what each function does.

   • Identify constraints.

   • Specify optimization criteria.

   $\Rightarrow$ **Functional Model** = data flow diagrams + constraints.

5.  Verify, iterate, and refine the three models:

- Add key operations that were discovered during preparation of the functional model to the object model. Do not show all operations during analysis as this would clutter the object model; just show the most important operations.

- Verify that the classes, associations, attributes, and operations are consistent and complete at the chosen level of abstraction. Compare the three models with the problem statement and relevant domain knowledge, and test the models using scenarios.

- Develop more detailed scenarios (including error conditions) as variations on the basic scenarios. Use these "what-if" scenarios to further verify the three models.

- Iterate the above steps as needed to complete the analysis.

⇒  **Analysis Document** = Problem Statement + Object Model + Dynamic Model + Functional Model.

## 11.2 SYSTEM DESIGN

During system design, the high-level structure of the system is chosen. Chapter 9 presents several canonical architectures that may serve as a suitable starting point. The object-oriented paradigm introduces no special insights into system design, but we include system design for complete coverage of the software development process.

1.  Organize the system into subsystems.

2.  Identify concurrency inherent in the problem.

3.  Allocate subsystems to processors and tasks.

4.  Choose the basic strategy for implementing data stores in terms of data structures, files, and databases.

5.  Identify global resources and determine mechanisms for controlling access to them.

6.  Choose an approach to implementing software control:

- Use the location within the program to hold state, or

- Directly implement a state machine, or

- Use concurrent tasks.

7.  Consider boundary conditions.

8.  Establish trade-off priorities.

⇒  **System Design Document** = structure of basic architecture for the system as well as high level strategy decisions.

## 11.3 OBJECT DESIGN

During object design we elaborate the analysis model and provide a detailed basis for implementation. We make the decisions that are necessary to realize a system without descending into the particular details of an individual language or database system. Object design starts a shift away from the real-world orientation of the analysis model towards the computer orientation required for a practical implementation.

1. Obtain operations for the object model from the other models:

- Find an operation for each process in the functional model.

- Define an operation for each event in the dynamic model, depending on the implementation of control.

2. Design algorithms to implement operations:

- Choose algorithms that minimize the cost of implementing operations.

- Select data structures appropriate to the algorithms.

- Define new internal classes and operations as necessary.

- Assign responsibility for operations that are not clearly associated with a single class.

3. Optimize access paths to data:

- Add redundant associations to minimize access cost and maximize convenience.

- Rearrange the computation for greater efficiency.

- Save derived values to avoid recomputation of complicated expressions.

4. Implement software control by fleshing out the approach chosen during system design.

5. Adjust class structure to increase inheritance:

- Rearrange and adjust classes and operations to increase inheritance.

- Abstract common behavior out of groups of classes.

- Use delegation to share behavior where inheritance is semantically invalid.

6. Design implementation of associations:

- Analyze the traversal of associations.

- Implement each association as a distinct object or by adding object-valued attributes to one or both classes in the association.

7. Determine the exact representation of object attributes.

8. Package classes and associations into modules.

⇒ **Design Document** = Detailed Object Model + Detailed Dynamic Model + Detailed Functional Model.

## 11.4  CHAPTER SUMMARY

The OMT Methodology is based on the use of an object-oriented notation to describe classes and relationships throughout the life-cycle. The Object Model is augmented with a Dynamic Model and a Functional Model to describe all aspects of a system. The analysis phase consists of developing a model of what the system is supposed to do, regardless of how it is implemented. The design phase consists of optimizing, refining, and extending the Object Model, Dynamic Model, and Functional Model until they are detailed enough for implementation. As we shall see in Part 3, implementation of the design is a straightforward matter of translating the design into code, since most difficult decisions are made during design.

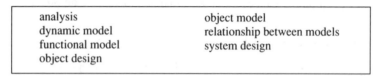

| analysis | object model |
| dynamic model | relationship between models |
| functional model | system design |
| object design | |

**Figure 11.1**  Key concepts for Chapter 11

## EXERCISES

Use the Object Modeling Technique to develop the following systems. Prepare scenarios, diagrams, models, specifications, and documents as appropriate. For each diagram and model that you prepare, show both your first version and your last refinement. State any assumptions you make concerning functional requirements. Also, summarize the order in which you followed the steps of the methodology.

**11.1**   (Project) A simple flight simulator. Using a bit mapped display, present a perspective view from the cockpit of a small airplane, periodically updated to reflect the motion of the plane. The world in which flights take place includes mountains, rivers, lakes, roads, bridges, a radio tower and, of course, a runway. Control inputs are from two joysticks. The left joystick operates the rudder and engine. The right one controls ailerons and elevator. Make the simulator as realistic as possible without being too complex.

**11.2**   (Project) A system for automatically executing the actions needed to build a software system from its components, similar to the UNIX Make facility. The system reads a file which describes what must be done in the form of dependency rules. Each rule has one or more targets, one or more sources, and an optional action. Targets and sources are names of files. If any of the sources of a rule are newer than any of its targets, the action of the rule is executed by the system to rebuild the targets from the sources.

**11.3**   (Project) A computer tic-tac-toe player. Inputs and outputs are provided through a dedicated hardware interface. The user indicates moves by pressing membrane switches, one for each of the nine squares. X's and O's are displayed by a liquid crystal display. The user may select a level of skill and who is to go first.

**11.4** (Project) A system for compressing data, using the method described by Edward R. Fiala and Daniel H. Greene, "Data Compression with Finite Windows," on pages 490-505 of the *Communications of the ACM*, Volume 32, Number 4, April 1989.

**11.5** (Project) A program to provide a computer opponent for the game Othello. Rules of the game are simple. Players take turns placing their markers on squares in an 8-by-8 board. One player has black markers, the other white. When one player places a marker so that one or more of the opponent's markers are surrounded in a straight line vertically, horizontally, or diagonally, the surrounded markers change color. A player who cannot place a marker must pass. The object of the game is to occupy as many squares as possible with your markers. The skill of the computer will be set at the start of the game by entering a skill level. The game starts with two black markers and two white markers arranged as shown in Figure E11.1. The board and markers should be displayed using bit mapped graphics. Human moves will be entered by a light pen.

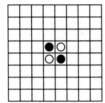

**Figure E11.1** Starting position for Othello

# 12

# Comparison of Methodologies

This chapter summarizes other software engineering approaches and compares them to the Object Modeling Technique (OMT). Specifically, we survey Structured Analysis/Structured Design (SA/SD), Jackson Structured Design (JSD), various information modeling notations, and other object-oriented work. We identify the strengths and weaknesses of each approach.

Our purpose is to clearly identify the major differences and similarities between the OMT and other approaches. The reader will gain deeper insight into the OMT by comparing it with other methodologies that may already be familiar. Our coverage of these other methodologies is brief; interested readers are referred to the references for additional information. This chapter can be skipped by readers unfamiliar with or uninterested in other methodologies.

## 12.1 STRUCTURED ANALYSIS/STRUCTURED DESIGN (SA/SD)

Currently, the most widely-used software engineering methodologies are those based on data flow diagrams. Several variations of the data flow approach are used in practice. We discuss Structured Analysis/Structured Design (SA/SD) as a representative of the data flow approach. Yourdon, Constantine, DeMarco, Page-Jones, and others have written about SA/SD. Ward and Mellor have added real-time extensions to SA/SD. SA/SD is pervasive, applicable to many problems, and well-documented.

The OMT and SA/SD methodologies both incorporate similar modeling components. Both methodologies support three orthogonal views of a system—the object, dynamic, and functional models. The OMT and SA/SD methodologies differ in the relative emphasis that they place on the various modeling components. OMT designs are dominated by the object model. The real-world paradigm of objects and relationships provides the context for understanding dynamic and functional behavior. In contrast, SA/SD stresses functional decomposition. A system is viewed primarily as providing one or more functions to the end user.

### 12.1.1 Summary of SA/SD Approach

SA/SD includes a variety of notations for formally specifying software. During the analysis phase, data flow diagrams, process specifications, a data dictionary, state transition diagrams, and entity-relationship diagrams are used to logically describe a system. In the design phase, details are added to the analysis models and the data flow diagrams are converted into *structure chart* descriptions of programming language code.

*Data flow diagrams* model the transformations of data as it flows through a system and are the focus of SA/SD. A data flow diagram consists of processes, data flows, actors, and data stores. Chapter 6 discusses data flow diagrams in detail. Starting from the top level data flow diagram, SA/SD recursively divides complex processes into subdiagrams, until many small processes are left that are easy to implement. When the resulting processes are simple enough, the decomposition stops, and a *process specification* is written for each lowest-level process. Process specifications may be expressed with decision tables, pseudocode, or other techniques.

The *data dictionary* contains details missing from data flow diagrams. The data dictionary defines data flows and data stores and the meaning of various names. Chapter 8 presents a sample data dictionary.

*State transition diagrams* model time dependent behavior and are similar to the dynamic model presented in Chapter 5 of this book. Most state transition diagrams describe control processes or timing of function execution and data access triggered by events.

*Entity-relationship (ER) diagrams* highlight relationships between data stores that otherwise would only be seen in the process specifications. Each ER data element corresponds to one data flow diagram data store. The object modeling notation described in this book (primarily Chapter 3) is an enhanced form of ER diagram. (Section 12.3 discusses ER diagrams.)

The above tools are used during the process of *structured analysis. Structured design* follows structured analysis and addresses low-level details. For example, during structured design, data flow diagram processes are grouped into tasks and allocated to operating system processes and CPUs. Data flow diagram processes are converted into programming language functions, and a *structure chart* is created showing the procedure call tree.

### 12.1.2 Comparison with OMT

SA/SD and OMT modeling have much in common. Both methodologies use similar modeling constructs and support the three orthogonal views of a system. The difference between SA/SD and OMT is primarily a matter of style and emphasis. In the SA/SD approach, the functional model dominates, the dynamic model is next most important, and the object model least important. In contrast, OMT modeling regards the object model as most important, then the dynamic model, and finally the functional model.

SA/SD organizes a system around procedures. In contrast, an object-oriented design technique (such as OMT) organizes a system around real-world objects, or conceptual objects that exist in the user's view of the world. Most changes in requirements are changes in function rather than in the objects, so change can be disastrous to procedure-based design. By contrast, changes in function are readily accommodated in an object-oriented design by adding or changing operations, leaving the basic object structure unchanged. SA/SD is useful for problems where functions are more important and complex than data. SA/SD assumes that this often occurs.

An SA/SD design has a clearly-defined system boundary, across which the software procedures must communicate with the real world. The structure of a SA/SD design is derived in part from the system boundary, so it can be difficult to extend a SA/SD design to a new boundary. It is much easier to extend an object-oriented design; one merely adds objects and relationships near the boundary to represent objects that existed previously only in the outside world. An object-oriented design is more resilient to change and more extensible.

The direct analogy between objects in an object-oriented design and the objects in the problem domain results in systems that are easier to understand. This makes the design more intuitive and simplifies traceability between requirements and software code. It also makes a design more coherent to persons who are not part of the original design team.

In SA/SD the decomposition of a process into subprocesses is somewhat arbitrary. Different people will produce different decompositions. In object-oriented design the decomposition is based on objects in the problem domain, so developers of different programs in the same domain tend to discover similar objects. This increases reusability of components from one project to the next.

An object-oriented approach better integrates databases with programming code. One uniform paradigm, the object, can model both database and programming structure. Research on object-oriented databases may further improve this situation. In contrast, a procedural design approach is inherently awkward at dealing with databases. It is difficult to merge programming code organized about functions with a database organized about data.

There are many reasons why data flow approaches are in such wide use. Programmers have tended to think in terms of functions, so data flow based methodologies have been easier to learn. Another reason is historical; SA/SD was one of the first well-thought-out, formal approaches to software and system development. We believe that the benefits of an object-oriented approach and the maturation of object-oriented technology will gradually promote its wide use for analysis, design, and implementation.

## 12.2 JACKSON STRUCTURED DEVELOPMENT (JSD)

Jackson Structured Development (JSD) is another mature methodology, which has a different style than SA/SD or OMT. The JSD methodology was developed by Michael Jackson and is especially popular in Europe. JSD does not distinguish between analysis and design and instead lumps both phases together as specification. JSD divides system development into two stages: specification, then implementation. JSD first determines the "what" and then the "how." JSD is intended especially for applications in which timing is important.

JSD uses graphical models, as do SA/SD, OMT, and other techniques, but we will not show any JSD diagrams in this chapter. Sample diagrams are not required to communicate the flavor of JSD. In our opinion, JSD is less graphically oriented than SA/SD and OMT.

### 12.2.1 Summary of JSD Approach

A JSD model begins with consideration of the real world. The purpose of a system is to provide functionality, but Jackson feels that one must first consider how this functionality fits in with the real world. A JSD model describes the real world in terms of entities, actions, and ordering of actions. Entities usually appear as nouns in requirements statements and actions appear as verbs. JSD software development consists of six sequential steps: entity action step, entity structure step, initial model step, function step, system timing step, and implementation step.

During the *entity action step* the software developer lists entities and actions for part of the real world. The purpose of the overall system guides the choice of entities and actions. The input to the entity action step is the requirements statement; the output is a list of entities and actions.

[Jackson-83] presents several examples, one of which is the design of an elevator control system. We will refer to Jackson's elevator example in our discussion. The elevator control system controls two elevators which service six floors. Each elevator has six inside buttons—one for each floor. Each floor has up and down buttons in the waiting area. Jackson identifies two entities for the elevator control example: button and elevator. He identifies three actions: Press a button, elevator arrives at floor $n$, and elevator leaves floor $n$.

Actions occur in the real world and are not an artifact of the system. Actions take place at a point in time, are atomic, and not decomposable. The *entity structure step* partially orders the actions of each entity by time. The elevator control system illustrates the importance of ordering actions. It is permissible for an elevator to arrive at floor 3, leave floor 3, arrive at floor 2, leave floor 2, and so on. It does not make sense for two arrive actions to occur in succession; arrive and leave operations must alternate.

The *initial model step* states how the real world connects to the abstract model. JSD supports state-vector and data stream connection.

The elevator control system illustrates state-vector connection. What happens if someone presses the up-button five times rapidly in succession? The elevator user does not want the control system to remember each button press and send an elevator five times to service the request. Instead pressing the up-button sets an "up-flag" to true. Pressing the up-button extra times has no further effect. The JSD model of the computer system is unaware of the number of presses and only communicates with the real world via the "up-flag." Jackson calls this "up-flag" a state-vector connection.

A computer print buffer illustrates data stream connection. The computer user does not want to lose information if the computer can transmit faster than the printer can print. A print buffer partially decouples the computer from the printer; CPU processing and printing can overlap. A real printer buffer is of finite size; when the buffer is full, the computer must wait before sending further data. JSD data stream connections are buffers of infinite size. The initial model step of a JSD design, does not address physical buffer limitations.

The *function step* uses pseudocode to state outputs of actions. At the end of this step the developer has a complete specification of the required system. In the elevator example, turning the display panel lights on and off as an elevator arrives at each floor is a function that must be specified.

The *system timing step* considers how much the model is permitted to lag the real world. For the most part, the result of the timing step is a set of informal notes on performance constraints. For example, an elevator control system must detect when up and down buttons are pressed. How long must the user keep the button contact closed upon a press? It is annoying to press an elevator button and not have the system respond. A low threshold means that the control system is more likely to detect a service request. However if a button press is detected via a polling scheme, a low value demands more computer resources. The designer explicitly makes performance trade-offs during the system timing step.

The *implementation step* focuses on the problems of process scheduling and allocates processors to processes. The number of processes may be different from the number of processors. Jackson's elevator control model has 50 processes. The developer must decide whether to match each process to one of 50 CPUs or how to get several processes to share the same CPU. After the six JSD steps comes writing of code and database design.

### 12.2.2 Comparison with OMT

Some authors refer to JSD as being "object-oriented." We disagree. JSD does begin with consideration of the real world and in this sense is object-oriented. However, Jackson identifies few entities (objects) and shows little of their structure. Each of the three examples presented in [Jackson-83] have only two or three entities. We believe that an object-oriented model should have a rich mixture of data structure and relationships.

We find the JSD approach complex and difficult to fully comprehend. We think that JSD is more obscure than data-flow and object-oriented approaches. One reason for JSD's complexity is its heavy reliance on pseudocode; graphic models are easier to understand. JSD is also complex because it was specifically designed to handle difficult real-time problems. For these problems, JSD may produce a superior design and be worth the effort. However, JSD's complexity is unnecessary and a bit overwhelming for the more common, simpler problems.

Jackson places more emphasis on actions and less on attributes than we do. Some JSD actions look similar to OMT associations. For example, *a clerk allocates product to an order.* We call *allocates* an association; Jackson calls it an action. Jackson finds attributes confusing and prefers to avoid them. Actions have such a prominent role in JSD modeling that they preempt attributes, in much the same way that attributes diminish the importance of operations in OMT object models.

JSD is a useful methodology for the following types of applications:

- Concurrent software where processes must synchronize with each other.

- Real time software. JSD modeling is extremely detailed and focuses on time.

- Microcode. JSD is thorough, makes no assumptions about the availability of an operating system, and considers concurrent processing and timing.

- Programming parallel computers. The JSD paradigm of many processes may be helpful here.

JSD is ill-suited for some other applications:

- High level analysis. JSD does not foster broad understanding of a problem. JSD is ineffective at abstraction and simplification. JSD meticulously handles details but does not help a developer grasp the essence of a problem.

- Databases. Database design is a more complex topic than Jackson implies. JSD modeling is biased towards actions and away from entities and attributes. As a natural consequence, it is a poor technique for database design.

- Conventional software running under an operating system. JSD's abstraction of hundreds or thousands of processes is confusing and unnecessary.

## 12.3 INFORMATION MODELING NOTATIONS

OMT object modeling combines object-oriented concepts (class and inheritance) with information modeling concepts (entities and associations). Information modeling originated within the database community and is concerned with modeling the structure of data so that it can be properly managed with a database.

The Entity-Relationship (ER) approach [Chen-76] is the most common approach to information modeling. ER is a graphical technique that is popular because the notation is easy to understand, yet powerful enough to model real problems. ER diagrams are readily translated into a database implementation.

There really is no "standard ER"; all practical implementations, and there are many of them, extend ER in various ways. For instance, [Teorey-86] discusses the LRDM approach. LRDM is a useful extension to ER and supports basic concepts such as inheritance, association, and entities that are described by attributes. [Shlaer-88a] describes another enhancement to ER.

OMT object modeling is also an enhanced form of ER. We add several new concepts, such as qualification, and a methodology for programming and database design. Figure 12.1 and Figure 12.2 compare the readability and expressability of ER and OMT notations for the same problem. Our presentation of ER syntax was taken from [Ullman-88] and [Chen-76].

In these figures, a person has a name, address, and social security number. A person may charge time to projects and earn a salary. A company has a name, address, phone number, and primary product. A company hires and fires persons. *Person* and *Company* have a many-to-many relationship. Job title depends on both person and company.

There are two types of persons: workers and managers. Each worker works on many projects; each manager is responsible for many projects. A project is staffed by many workers and exactly one manager. Each project has a name, budget, and internal priority for securing resources.

A company is composed of multiple departments; each department within a company is uniquely identified by its name. A department usually, but not always, has a manager. Most managers manage a department; a few managers are not assigned to any department. Each department manufactures many products; while each product is made by exactly one department. A product has a name, cost, and weight.

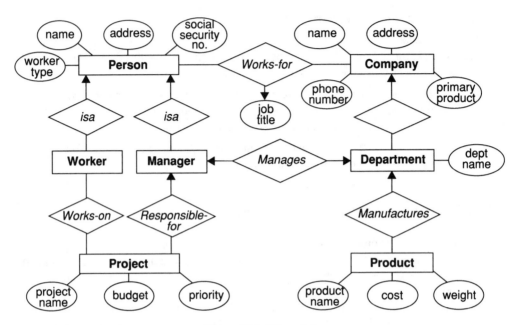

**Figure 12.1** ER model

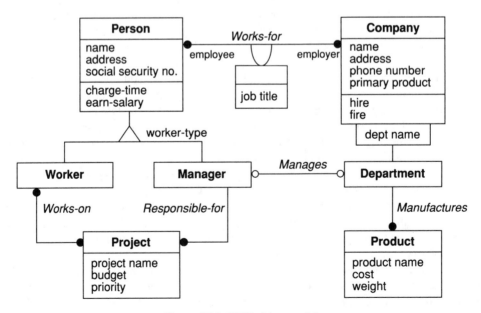

**Figure 12.2** OMT object model

## 12.4  OBJECT-ORIENTED WORK

Now we compare the OMT with other object-oriented approaches. Our comparison is necessarily limited because little has been published on object-oriented methodologies for software engineering. Our approach is compatible with the few publications we have encountered to date. To a large extent, our work synthesizes several different camps of thought: databases, object-oriented concepts, and software engineering. We consider our work to be a consolidation of past efforts with some incremental improvements.

[Booch-86] describes the rudiments of object-oriented software development. He explains that object-oriented development is fundamentally different from traditional functional approaches to design, such as those based on data flow. Object-oriented software decomposition more closely models a person's perception of reality, while functional decomposition is only achieved through a transformation of the problem space. Thus it is not surprising that software developed with an object-oriented approach is more understandable, extensible, and maintainable.

[Booch-91] extends previous Ada-oriented work to the entire object-oriented design area. His excellent discussion of inheritance and classification are particularly worth reading. Booch's methodology includes a variety of models that address the object, dynamic, and functional aspects of a software system. We would say that his book places less emphasis on analysis and more emphasis on design than we do. A major distinction between Booch's approach and the OMT approach is the emphasis we place on associations. Booch mentions associations in referring to our past work but has not truly incorporated them into his methodology. The similarities between the approaches are more striking than the differences, and both approaches complement one another.

[Meyer-88] is really not a methodology (and does not claim to be) but has many tips on good design. Meyer's book is heavily oriented towards using language as a vehicle for expressing a design; we use graphics. Meyer does not deal with conceptual modeling or analysis.

[Shlaer-88b] describes a complete methodology for object-oriented analysis which is similar to ours. Shlaer and Mellor's methodology, like our OMT methodology, breaks analysis down into three phases: static modeling of objects, dynamic modeling of states and events, and functional modeling. All in all, we think that their methodology is quite good. A flaw with Shlaer and Mellor's treatment is their excessive preoccupation with relational database tables and database keys.

Shlaer and Mellor only claim their methodology as an approach to analysis, and caution that the final design might be different. We have tried to show how the object-oriented paradigm can permeate the entire software development process—from analysis to design to implementation.

Coad and Yourdon [Coad-90] present an approach to object-oriented analysis that is similar to the original OMT approach taken by us [Loomis-87] and by Shlaer and Mellor. They touch briefly on design.

Jacobsen [Jacobsen-87] claims to have a full object-oriented development methodology, but only limited details of his methodology have been published; the rest is available through a commercial course. He analyzes a system in terms of entities (an object model) and *use cases* (prototypical scenarios covering dynamic behavior). For implementation, functionality is grouped into *services,* groups of related functional requirements. Design consists of constructing a system architecture in terms of modular *blocks.*

All of the object-oriented methodologies, including ours, have much in common, and should be contrasted more with non-object-oriented methodologies than with each other.

## 12.5 CHAPTER SUMMARY

Several popular software engineering approaches are based on the notion of data flow. The Structured Analysis/Structured Design (SA/SD) methodology is representative of the data flow approach. SA/SD begins with a single process or function that represents the overall purpose of the desired software. SA/SD recursively divides complex processes, until one is left with many small functions that are easy to implement.

SA/SD and OMT modeling have much in common. Both methodologies support the three orthogonal views of a system—the object, dynamic, and functional models. The difference is that SA/SD emphasizes the functional model while OMT emphasizes the object model. We believe that for most problems an object-oriented approach is superior to a data flow approach. An object-oriented design is more extensible, provides better traceability, and better integrates database and programming code.

Michael Jackson advocates a different approach to system development, called JSD. A JSD model begins with consideration of the real world. One culls out the most important entities and actions in the real world, from the perspective of the application. The remaining JSD steps develop detailed pseudocode that precisely specify desired software behavior and their correspondence to real-world actions.

We regard JSD as a valuable approach, as are SA/SD and OMT. Each methodology has its niche where it clearly excels. JSD is an excellent methodology for real-time and microcode applications. We consider JSD a poor approach for high-level analysis and database design.

We have compared OMT object modeling to the entity-relationship (ER) information modeling notation. In essence, OMT object modeling is an enhanced form of ER. OMT object modeling improves on ER in the areas of expressiveness and readability.

The OMT methodology builds on earlier object-oriented work and benefits from insights that have come with experience.

```
entity-relationship (ER) diagram
information modeling notations
Jackson Structured Development (JSD)
Object Modeling Technique (OMT)
other approaches to object-oriented development
Structured Analysis/Structured Design (SA/SD)
```

**Figure 12.3** Key concepts for Chapter 12

## REFERENCES

[Booch-86] Grady Booch. Object-oriented development. *IEEE Transactions on Software Engineering 12*, 2 (Feb.1986), 211-221.

[Booch-91] Grady Booch. *Object-Oriented Design*. Redwood City, Calif.: Benjamin/Cummings, 1991.

[Cameron-89] John Cameron. *JSP & JSD: The Jackson Approach to Software Development*. Washington, DC: IEEE Computer Society Press, 1989.

[Chen-76] P.P.S. Chen. The entity-relationship model—toward a unified view of data. *ACM Transactions on Database System 1*, 1 (March 1976).

[Coad-90] Peter Coad, Edward Yourdon. *Object-Oriented Analysis*. Englewood Cliffs, New Jersey: Yourdon Press, 1990.

[Jackson-83] Michael A. Jackson. *System Development*. Englewood Cliffs, New Jersey: Prentice Hall International, 1983.

[Jacobsen-87] Ivar Jacobsen. Object oriented development in an industrial environment. *OOPSLA'87* as *ACM SIGPLAN 22*, 12 (December 1987), 183-191.

[Loomis-87] Mary E.S. Loomis, Ashwin V. Shah, James E. Rumbaugh. An object modeling technique for conceptual design. *European Conference on Object-Oriented Programming*, Paris, France, June 15-17, 1987, published as *Lecture Notes in Computer Science, 276*, Springer-Verlag.

[Meyer-88] Bertrand Meyer. *Object-Oriented Software Construction*. Hertfordshire, England: Prentice Hall International, 1988.

[Shlaer-88a] Sally Shlaer and Stephen J. Mellor. *Object-Oriented Systems Analysis: Modeling the World in Data*. Englewood Cliffs, New Jersey: Yourdon Press, 1988.

[Shlaer-88b] Sally Shlaer, Stephen J. Mellor, Deborah Ohlsen, and Wayne Hywari. The object-oriented method for analysis. *Proceedings of the Tenth Structured Development Forum*, 1988.

[Teorey-86] Toby J. Teorey, Dongqing Yang, James P. Fry. A logical design methodology for relational databases using the extended entity-relationship model. *Computing Surveys 18*, 2 (June 1986), 197-222.

[Ullman-88] Jeffrey Ullman. *Principles of Database and Knowledge-Base Systems, Volumes 1 and 2*. Rockville, Maryland: Computer Science Press, 1988.

[Yourdon-79] Edward Yourdon, Larry L. Constantine. *Structured Design*. Englewood Cliffs, New Jersey: Yourdon Press, 1979.

[Yourdon-89] Edward Yourdon. *Modern Structured Analysis*. Englewood Cliffs, New Jersey: Yourdon Press, 1989.

## EXERCISES

**12.1**  (6) You are designing a portable tester for integrated circuits. The tester will have several different types of sockets. An integrated circuit will be tested by placing it in the socket that matches its pin configuration and identifying the type of circuit. The tester will then run through a series of tests, applying power and signals to the appropriate pins and measuring the response of the circuit. A portion of the object diagram for the tester is shown in Figure E12.1. There is a doubly qualified association between test case and socket. Each test case applies several named signals to pins of a socket. The same signal may be applied to more than one pin. Each pin may receive signals from several test cases. Prepare a corresponding ER diagram; preserve as much semantic content as you can.

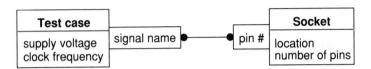

**Figure E12.1** Portion of an object diagram for an integrated circuit tester

**12.2** (3) Figure E12.2 is an object diagram for a portion of a simplified simulator for training glider pilots. The simulator is for one glider with wings and rudder only. Effects of the wind and forces generated by the body of the glider are neglected. Details of the user interface to the simulator are outside the scope of this exercise. A glider has several associated lifting surfaces, in this case two wings and a rudder. The wings provide lift and the rudder is used to steer. Methods would be provided to perform simulation. For instance, the force on each surface would be calculated from its attribute values, and the orientation, velocity, and rotational rate of the glider. The force on the rudder would also depend on its deflection. The translational acceleration would be computed by retrieving the results of force calculations and masses of associated surfaces. The accelerations would be numerically integrated to update position, orientation, velocity, and rotational rate.

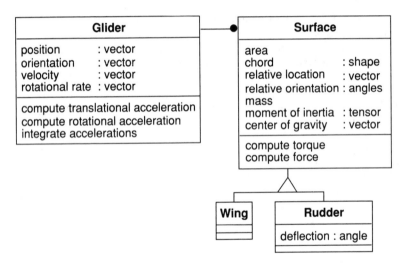

**Figure E12.2** Object diagram of a portion of a glider simulator

Figure E12.3 is the corresponding data flow diagram for the glider. Position, orientation, velocity, and rotation vectors are data stores which serve as state variables for the simulator.

a. Modify both diagrams to add an elevator to the tail of the glider to provide additional control and to add another small wing on the nose of the glider to provide additional lift and stability.

b. How would each diagram be modified to simulate the behavior of the glider after any combination of surfaces falls off, including elevator, rudder, left main wing, right main wing, left nose wing, and right nose wing. (There are 63 combinations.)

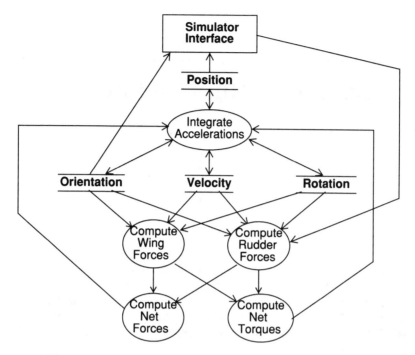

**Figure E12.3** Data flow diagram for a portion of a glider simulator

**12.3** (Project) Consult a few of the references at the end of the chapter and compare and contrast the way inheritance, methods, and ternary relationships are handled by Shlaer and Mellor, Booch, Teorey, and OMT.

# 13

From Design to Implementation

Part 1 of this book presents object modeling concepts; Parts 2 and 3 deal with the development process for applying these concepts. Part 2 presents the front end of the development process, the portion that is generic in nature and spans implementation targets. Part 3 covers the tail end of software development and discusses the specific details for implementing a system using object-oriented languages, non-object-oriented languages, and database management systems.

Writing code is an extension of the design process. Writing code should be straightforward, almost mechanical, because all the difficult decisions should already have been made during design. The code should be a simple translation of the design decisions into the peculiarities of a particular language. Decisions do have to be made while writing code, but each one should affect only a small part of the program so they can be changed easily. Nevertheless, the program code is the ultimate embodiment of the solution to the problem, so the way in which it is written is important for maintainability and extensibility.

## 13.1 IMPLEMENTATION USING A PROGRAMMING LANGUAGE

Most executable languages are capable of expressing the three aspects of software specification: data structure, dynamic flow of control, and functional transformation.

Data structure is expressed in a declarative (nonprocedural) subset of a language. The statements that are used to declare data structures are sometimes mixed in with the procedural statements but are not executable. In some languages, such as Ada, a sharp distinction is made between external specification, which is purely declarative, and internal specification, which is often combined with procedural statements.

Flow of control may be expressed either procedurally (conditionals, loops, and calls) or nonprocedurally (rules, constraints, tables, and state machines). Traditional languages are purely procedural, although the programmer can implement nonprocedural constructs as data. Nonprocedural languages, such as rule-based systems, constraint maintenance systems, and logic programming languages, support entirely different ways of organizing programs. Their relationship to object-oriented concepts is still under exploration, and we do not cover them in this book.

Support for concurrent threads of control is lacking in most major languages (except for Ada). Multitasking and interprocess communication are provided by modern operating systems but must be accessed from programs using awkward subroutine calls. Concurrency can also be simulated within programs using coroutines, control modules, or event handlers.

Functional transformations are expressed in terms of the primitive operators of the language, as well as calls to subprograms. Most procedural languages are similar in the kinds of functionality they support and do not differ greatly from Fortran. Lisp permits constructions of functions at run time, which permits interesting (and confusing) operations.

Implementation of an object-oriented design is easiest using an object-oriented language, but even object-oriented languages vary in their degree of support for object-oriented concepts. Each language represents a compromise among conceptual power, efficiency, and compatibility with previous work. Chapter 15 describes various characteristics and limitations of object-oriented languages and how to work around them.

Even when a non-object-oriented language must be used, an object-oriented design is beneficial. Object-oriented concepts can be mapped into non-object-oriented language constructs. There is really not a problem of power—after all, programming languages are eventually converted to machine language anyway—as much as an issue of expressiveness. Use of a non-object-oriented language requires greater care and discipline to preserve the object-oriented structure of the program, and the programmer cannot obtain help from the language in finding violations. Chapter 16 describes implementation of object-oriented designs using C, Ada, and Fortran.

Any language, object-oriented or non-object-oriented, is a tool that can be used well or poorly. Object-oriented programming can greatly improve the expressiveness of programs, but it can also increase the opportunity for obfuscation by careless programmers. As with any craft, good programming requires discipline and adherence to principles of good style. Chapter 14 describes style guidelines that promote the effective use of object-oriented techniques.

## 13.2 IMPLEMENTATION USING A DATABASE SYSTEM

When the main concern is access to persistent data, rather than the operations on the data, a database is often the appropriate form of implementation. The main focus of a database is the structure and constraints on the data. Database commands typically operate on sets of data from the database, incorporating a high degree of parallelism, while most conventional languages are highly serial. Database operations are much less procedural than conventional programming language statements, although they are more procedural than a rule-based system. Databases provide concurrent operations on data by different users as part of their fundamental structure.

We discuss implementation of database applications using existing relational database management systems (RDBMS) in Chapter 17. Most RDBMS provide separate languages for data declarations and operations, analogous to the distinction in programming languages.

The data definition language is used to declare the structure of the data. A query language may be provided which allows the expression of functional transformations (record locking and update) and flow of control. The query language may be limited to simple record access based on fields that act as keys, or it might offer more of the features of a general purpose programming language.

Some recent object-oriented database systems attempt to integrate an object-oriented language with a database in a single seamless package. Operations may be defined for each class of object, but the programmer need not explicitly read and write information to persistent storage. Although object-oriented database systems promise better performance and easier use in the long run, they are not yet as mature as conventional relational database systems and may also pose problems integrating with existing conventional applications. Integrated object-oriented languages and databases are discussed as part of Chapter 15.

## 13.3 IMPLEMENTATION OUTSIDE A COMPUTER

The specification and design techniques described in this book are useful for implementation targets besides programming languages and databases. Often the design of a computer application involves an implementation that will consist of a mixture of software and some other structure. Typical domains include design of hardware, design of a knowledge base, and modeling business enterprises. Object modeling techniques can be useful in capturing structural, dynamic, and functional relationships in such domains in a way that can be communicated to domain experts. It is beyond the scope of this book to explore implementation in these other domains.

## 13.4 OVERVIEW OF PART 3

Part 3 of the book discusses implementation of object-oriented designs in various target languages:

- Chapter 14 contains style guidelines for writing programs in object-oriented and non-object-oriented languages in a proper object-oriented spirit, maximizing the possibility of readability, reusability, and extensibility.

- Chapter 15 describes implementation using object-oriented languages having varying degrees of support for object-oriented concepts. It includes a survey of several commercially available languages. It also discusses integrated object-oriented languages and databases.

- Chapter 16 shows how to implement object-oriented designs in a non-object-oriented language and addresses the limitations of such an implementation. Various object-oriented concepts are mapped into C, Ada, and Fortran code.

- Chapter 17 describes implementation of object-oriented designs using existing relational database management systems, including alternate ways of mapping various object-oriented constructs and ways to optimize performance.

# 14

---

# Programming Style

As any chess player, cook, or skier can attest, there is a great difference between knowing something and doing it well. Writing object-oriented programs is no different. It is not enough to know the basic constructs and to be able to assemble them together into programs. The experienced programmer follows principles to make readable programs that live beyond the immediate need. These principles include general design principles, programming idioms ("how to do common tasks with the tools at hand"), rules-of-thumb, tricks of the trade, and cautionary advice. Good style is important in all programming, but it is even more important in object-oriented design and programming because much of the benefit of the object-oriented approach is predicated on producing reusable, extensible, understandable programs.

## 14.1 OBJECT-ORIENTED STYLE

Good programs do more than simply satisfy their functional requirements. Programs that follow proper design guidelines are more likely to be correct, reusable, extensible, and quickly debugged. Most style guidelines that are intended for conventional programs also apply to object-oriented programs. In addition, facilities such as inheritance are peculiar to object-oriented languages and require new guidelines. We present object-oriented style guidelines under the following categories, although many guidelines contribute to more than one category:

- Reusability
- Extensibility
- Robustness
- Programming-in-the-large

## 14.2 REUSABILITY

Reusable software reduces design, coding, and testing cost by amortizing effort over several designs. Reducing the amount of code also simplifies understanding, which increases the likelihood that the code is correct. Reuse is possible in conventional languages, but object-oriented languages greatly enhance the possibility of code reuse.

### 14.2.1 Kinds of Reusability

There are two kinds of reuse: sharing of newly-written code within a project and reuse of previously-written code on new projects. Similar guidelines apply to both kinds of reuse. Sharing of code within a project is a matter of discovering redundant code sequences in the design and using programming language facilities, such as procedures or methods, to share their implementation. This kind of code sharing almost always pays off immediately by producing smaller programs, faster debugging, and faster iteration of the design.

Planning for future reuse takes more foresight and represents an investment. It is unlikely that a class in isolation will be used for multiple projects. Programmers are more likely to reuse carefully thought out subsystems, such as abstract data types, graphics packages, and numerical analysis libraries.

### 14.2.2 Style Rules for Reusability

*Keep methods coherent.* A method is coherent if it performs a single function or a group of closely related functions. If it does two or more unrelated things, break it apart into smaller methods.

*Keep methods small.* If a method is large, break it into smaller methods. A method that exceeds one or two pages is probably too large. By breaking a method into smaller parts, you may be able to reuse some parts even when the entire method is not reusable.

*Keep methods consistent.* Similar methods should use the same names, conditions, argument order, data types, return value, and error conditions. Maintain parallel structure when possible. The Unix operating system offers many examples of inconsistent functions. For example, in the C library, there are two inconsistent functions to output strings, *puts* and *fputs*. The *puts* function writes a string to the standard output, followed by a newline character; *fputs* writes a string to a specified file, without a newline character. Avoid this kind of inconsistency.

*Separate policy and implementation.* Policy methods make decisions, shuffle arguments, and gather global context. Policy methods switch control among implementation methods. Policy methods should check for status and errors; they should not directly perform calculations or implement complex algorithms. Policy methods are often highly application-dependent, but they are simple to write and easy to understand. Policy methods are the "mortar."

Implementation methods perform specific detailed operations, without deciding whether or why to do them. If implementation methods can encounter errors, they should only return status, not take action. Implementation methods perform specific computations on fully-specified arguments and often contain complicated algorithms. Implementation methods do not access global context, make decisions, contain defaults, or switch flow of control. Because implementation methods are self-contained algorithms, they are likely to be meaningful and reusable in other contexts. Implementation methods are the "bricks."

Do not combine policy and implementation in a single method. Isolate the core of the algorithm into a distinct, fully-specified implementation method. This requires abstracting out the particular parameters of the policy method as arguments in a call to the implementation method.

For example, a method to scale a window by a factor of 2 is a policy method. It should set the target scale factor for the window and call on an implementation method that scales the window by an arbitrary scale factor. Later if you decide to change the default scale factor to another value, such as 1.5, you just have to modify the parameter in the policy method, without changing the implementation method which actually does the work.

*Provide uniform coverage.* If input conditions can occur in various combinations, write methods for all combinations, not just the ones that you currently need. For example, if you write a method to get the last element of a list, also write one to get the first element.

*Broaden the method as much as possible.* Try to generalize argument types, preconditions and constraints, assumptions about how the method works, and the context in which the method operates. Take meaningful actions on empty values, extreme values, and out-of-bounds values. Often a method can be made more general with a slight increase in code.

*Avoid global information.* Minimize external references. Referring to a global object imposes required context on the use of a method. Often the information can be passed in as an argument. Otherwise store global information as part of the target object so that other methods can access it uniformly.

*Avoid modes.* Functions that drastically change behavior depending on current context are hard to reuse. Try to replace them with modeless functions. For example, a text processing application requires insert and replace operations. One approach is to set a mode to *insert* or *replace,* then use a *write* operation to insert or replace text depending on the current mode. A modeless approach uses two operations, *insert* and *replace,* that do the same operations without a mode setting. The danger of modes is that an object left in a mode in one part of an application can affect an operation applied later in the application.

### 14.2.3 Using Inheritance

The preceding guidelines improve the chance of inheriting shared code. Sometimes, however, methods on different classes are similar but not similar enough to represent with a single inherited method. There are several techniques of breaking up methods to inherit some code.

*Subroutines.* The simplest approach is to factor out the *common* code into a single method that is called by each method. The common method can be assigned to an ancestor class. This is effectively a subroutine call and is shown in Figure 14.1.

*Factoring.* In some cases the best way to increase code reuse between similar classes is to factor out the differences between the methods of different classes, leaving the remainder of

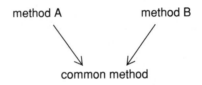

**Figure 14.1** Code reuse via subroutines

the code as a shared method. This approach is effective when the differences between methods are small and the similarities are great. As shown in Figure 14.2, the common portion of two methods is made into a new method. The new method calls an operation that is implemented by a different method containing the code differences in each subclass. Sometimes an abstract class must be added to hold the top-level method. This approach makes it easier to add new subclasses because only the difference code need be written.

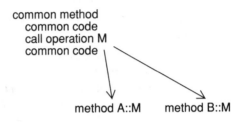

**Figure 14.2** Code reuse via factoring

A package for plotting numerical data provides a good illustration of factoring. *DataGraph* is an abstract class that organizes common data and operations for its subclasses. One of *DataGraph*'s methods is *draw,* consisting of the following steps:

1) Draw border
2) Scale data
3) Draw axes
4) Plot data
5) Draw title
6) Draw legend

Subclasses of *DataGraph*, such as *LineGraph, BarGraph,* and *ScatterGraph,* draw borders, titles, and legends the same way but differ in the way they scale data, draw axes, and plot data. Each subclass inherits the methods *drawBorder, drawTitle,* and *drawLegend* from abstract class *DataGraph,* but each subclass defines its own methods for *scaleData, drawAxes,* and *plotData.* The method *draw* need only be defined once, on class *DataGraph,* and inherited by each subclass. Each time the draw method is invoked, it applies *drawBorder, drawTitle,* and *drawLegend* inherited from the superclass and *scaleData, drawAxis,* and *plotData* supplied by the subclass for the object. To add a new subclass, only the three specialized methods need be written.

*Delegation.* Sometimes it appears that use of inheritance would increase code reuse within a program, when a true superclass/subclass relationship does not exist. Do not give in to the temptation to use this *implementation inheritance*; use delegation instead. Inheritance should only be used when the generalization relationship is semantically valid. Inheritance means that each instance of a subclass truly is an instance of the superclass; thus all operations and attributes of the superclass must uniformly apply to the subclass. Improper use of inheritance leads to programs that are hard to maintain and extend. Object-oriented languages are permissive in their use of inheritance and will not enforce the good programming practice that we recommend.

Delegation provides a proper mechanism to achieve the desired code reuse. The operation is caught in the desired class and forwarded to another class for actual execution. Since each operation must be explicitly forwarded, unexpected side effects are less likely to occur. The names of operations in the catching class may differ from those in the class supplying the operations. Each class should choose names which are most appropriate for its purposes.

*Encapsulate external code.* Often you will want to reuse code that may have been developed for an application with different interfacing conventions. Rather than inserting a direct call to the external code, it is safer to encapsulate its behavior within an operation or a class. This way the external routine or package can be changed or replaced, and you will only have to change your code in one place.

For example, you may have a numerical analysis application but, knowing that reliable matrix inversion software already exists, you do not want to reimplement the algorithm in your object-oriented language. A matrix class might be written to encapsulate the functionality provided by the external subroutine package. The matrix class would have, for example, an inverse operation that takes the tolerance-for-singularity as an argument and returns a new matrix that is the inverse of the operation's target.

## 14.3 EXTENSIBILITY

Most software is extended in ways that its original developers may not expect. The guidelines for reusability enhance extensibility as well. In addition, the following object-oriented principles enhance extensibility.

*Encapsulate classes.* A class is encapsulated if its internal structure is hidden from other classes. Only methods on the class should access its implementation. Many compilers are smart enough to optimize operations into direct access to the implementation, but the programmer should not. Respect the information in other classes by never reaching inside the class for data.

*Hide data structures.* Do not export data structures from a method. Internal data structures are specific to a method's algorithm. If you export them, you limit flexibility to change the algorithm later.

*Avoid traversing multiple links or methods.* A method should have limited knowledge of an object model. A method must be able to traverse links to obtain its neighbors and must be able to call operations on them, but it should not traverse a second link from the neighbor to a third class because the second link is not directly visible to it. Instead, call an operation on the neighbor object to traverse the operation; if the association network changes, the operation method can be rewritten without changing the call. Similarly, avoid applying a second operation to the result of an operation call unless the class of the result is already known as an attribute, argument, or neighbor, or the result class is from a lower-level library. Instead, write a new operation on the original target class to perform the combined operation itself. The principles in this paragraph were proposed in [Lieberherr-89] as the "Law of Demeter."

*Avoid case statements on object type.* Use methods instead. Case statements can be used to test internal attributes of an object but should not be used to select behavior based on object type. Dispatching operations based on object type is the whole point of methods, so don't circumvent them.

*Distinguish public and private operations.* Public operations are visible outside a class and have published interfaces. Once a public operation is used by other classes, it is costly to change its interface, so public operations should be carefully defined. Private operations are internal to a class and are used to help implement the public operations. Private operations can be deleted or their interfaces can be changed to modify the implementation of the class with impact limited to other methods on the class.

Why classify operations as public and private?

- There is no need to bother the user of a class with internal details. Private methods just confuse the external user of the class.

- Since private methods depend on internal implementation decisions, the method designer may change the number and types of arguments if the implementation changes.

- Private methods may rely on preconditions or state information created by other methods in the class. Applied out of context, a private operation may calculate incorrect results or cause the object to fail.

- Private methods add modularity. Internal details of the method only affect methods on the class, not other methods.

Similarly, attributes and associations should be classified as public or private. In addition, public attributes and associations may be classified as read-only or writable outside the owner class.

## 14.4 ROBUSTNESS

You should strive for efficiency in writing methods but not at the expense of robustness. A method is robust if it does not fail even if it receives improper parameters. Robustness against internal bugs may be traded off against efficiency. Robustness against user errors should never be sacrificed.

*Protect against errors.* Software should protect itself against incorrect user input. Incorrect user input should never cause a crash. Any method that accepts user input must validate input that could cause trouble.

The method designer must consider two kinds of error conditions. Application (user) errors are identified during analysis and report on conditions that exist in the problem domain. For example, an automatic teller machine application should report or process errors about the ATM card scanner and communications lines. The response to these errors is part of the analysis. On the other hand, low-level system errors concern programming aspects of a method. These low-level errors include operating system errors, such as memory allocation errors or file input/output errors, and hardware faults. Your program should check for these errors and at least try to die gracefully if nothing else is possible.

Try to guard against programming bugs as well as possible, and give good diagnostic information even if fatal bugs occur. During development, it is often worthwhile to insert internal assertions into the code to uncover bugs, even though the checks will be removed for efficiency in the production version. A strongly-typed object-oriented language provides greater protection against type mismatches, but assertions can be manually inserted in any language.

*Optimize after the program runs.* Don't optimize a program until you get it working. Often programmers spend too much effort trying to improve portions of code that are infrequently executed. Measure the performance within the program before optimizing it; you may be surprised to find that most parts consume little of the total time. Study your application to learn what measures are important, such as worst case times and operation frequencies. If an operation may be implemented in more than one way, assess the trade-offs of the alternatives as they relate to memory, speed, and simplicity of implementation. In general, avoid optimizing more of the program than you have to, as optimization compromises extensibility, reusability, and understandability. If methods are properly encapsulated, they can be replaced with optimized versions without affecting the rest of the program.

*Validate arguments.* External operations, those available to users of the class, must rigorously check their arguments to prevent failure. But internal methods may assume their arguments are valid for efficiency reasons. Public methods must take more care to check the validity of arguments because external users are more likely to violate restrictions on arguments. Internal, or private, methods can often assume preconditions since the implementor has tighter control and can rely on the public methods that call them for error checking.

Don't include arguments that cannot be validated. For example, the infamous *scanf* function in Unix reads a line of input into an internal buffer without checking the size of the buffer. This loophole has been exploited to write virus programs that force a buffer overflow in system software that did not validate its arguments. Don't write or use operations whose arguments can't be validated.

*Avoid predefined limits.* When possible use dynamic memory allocation to create data structures that do not have predefined limits. During design, it is difficult to predict the maximum capacity expected of data structures in an application, so don't set any limits. The day of fixed limits on symbol table entries, user names, file names, compiler entries, and other things should be long over. Most object-oriented languages have excellent dynamic memory allocation facilities.

*Instrument the program for debugging and performance monitoring.* Just as a hardware circuit designer instruments an IC board with test points, you should instrument your code for debugging, statistics, and performance. The level of debugging that you must build into your code depends on the programming environment presented by the language. In Smalltalk, for example, a class browser allows a developer to explore the class hierarchy, displaying attributes and the code for methods. An inspector lets the user interrupt execution and print the internal state of an instance. If your implementation language does not have similar capabilities, then you can provide print methods for each class. These methods can be accessed from your system debugger. Also, you can add debug statements to the methods. These debug statements are conditionally executed depending on an instance variable that contains the debug level. You can print a message on entry or exit and selectively print input or output values.

Adding code to gather statistics will help you understand the behavior of your classes. Some operating systems, such as Unix and VMS, offer tools to create execution profiles of an application. Typically, these tools report the number of times each method was called and the amount of processor time spent in each method. If your system does not have comparable tools, you can instrument your code for gathering statistics much like for debugging.

## 14.5 PROGRAMMING-IN-THE-LARGE

Programming-in-the-large refers to writing large, complex programs with teams of programmers. Human communication becomes paramount on such projects and requires proper software engineering practices. The following guidelines should be observed:

*Do not prematurely begin programming.* It is important to first complete the generic thought process before confronting the quirks of an implementation target. All software development methodologies emphasize the importance of first designing, then coding.

*Keep methods understandable.* A method is understandable if someone other than the creator of the method can understand the code (as well as the creator after a time lapse). Keeping methods small and coherent helps to accomplish this.

*Make methods readable.* Meaningful variable names increase readability. Typing a few extra characters is cheaper than the misunderstanding that can come later when another programmer tries to decipher your variable names. Check the readability of your methods by running them through a spelling checker. Avoid abbreviations that may confuse other programmers. Use temporary variables instead of deeply nested expressions. Do not use the same temporary variable for two different purposes within a method, even if their usage does not overlap; stack space is cheap anyway.

*Use exactly the same names as in the object model.* The choice of names used within a program should exactly match those found in the object model. A program may need to introduce additional names for implementation reasons, and this is fine, but the uniformity of names where they carry forward should be preserved. This practice improves traceability, documentation, and understandability for the software as a whole.

*Choose names carefully.* Make sure your names accurately describe the operations, classes, and attributes they label. Follow a uniform pattern in making up names. For example, you might use the pattern *"verb_object"* in making up operation names, such as *add_element* or *draw_highlight*. Be sure to define the verbs being used frequently (for example, you may want to distinguish between *copy* and *deepcopy* or between *new* and *create*). Many object-oriented languages automatically build method names from the class name and operation.

Do not use the same operation name for semantically different operations. All classes that use the same name should have the same origin class and the same signature (number and types of arguments).

| Good | Bad |
|------|-----|
| Circle::Area | Matrix::Invert (performs matrix inversion) |
| Rectangle::Area | Figure::Invert (turns figure upside down) |

*Use programming guidelines.* Project teams should use programming guidelines available in their organizations. If guidelines do not exist, the software team should create guidelines that address issues such as the form of variable names, indentation style for control structures, method documentation headers, and in-line documentation.

*Package into modules.* Group classes with similar functions into a module.

| Module | Classes |
|--------|---------|
| plotting | line plot, bar chart, pie chart |
| geometry | polygon, circle |
| windows | menus, buttons, toggles, panels |
| animation | scenes, cues, key frames |

*Document classes and methods.* The documentation of a method describes its purpose, function, context, inputs, and outputs as well as any assumptions and preconditions about the state of the object. You should describe the algorithm, including why it was chosen. Internal comments within the method should describe major steps.

*Publish the specification.* The specification is a contract between the producer and the consumer of the class. Once a specification is written, the producer cannot break the contract, for doing so would affect the consumer. The specification only contains declarations. The user of a method should be able to use the method just by looking at the specification. Some languages, such as Ada and C++, support separation of specification and implementation. On-line descriptions of the class and its features help promote the correct use of the class. Each operation should also be documented by itself (apart from its method on each class), giving its origin, generic meaning, telling what each subclass must do to implement the operation, and what related methods are needed by the subclass. A partial sample specification follows.

Class Description
Class Name: Circle
Version:   1.0
Description: Ellipse whose major and minor axes are equal
Super Classes: Ellipse
Features:
    Public Attributes:
        center: Point — location of its center
        radius: Real — its radius
    Public Methods:
        draw (Window) — draws a circle in the window
        intersectLine (Line): Set of Points — finds the intersection of a line and a
            circle, returns set of 0-2 points
        area (): Real — calculates area of circle
        perimeter (): Real — calculates circumference of circle
    Private Methods: none
Method Description
Method Circle::intersectLine (line: Line) : Set of Points
    Description: Given a circle and a line, finds the intersection, returns a set of
        0-2 intersection points. If the line is tangent to the circle, the set contains
        a single point.
    Inputs:
        self:Circle — circle to be intersected with line
        line:Line — line to be intersected with circle
    Returns:
        A set of intersection points. Set may contain 0, 1, or 2 points
    Side Effects: none
    Errors: If the figures do not intersect, returns an empty set.
        If the line is tangent to the circle, returns the tangent point.
        If the circle's radius is 0, returns a single point if the point is on the line.
Operation Description
Operation intersectLine (line: Line) : Set of Points
    Origin Class: GeometricFigure
    Description: Returns a set of intersection points between the geometric object
        and the line. The set may contain 0, 1, or more points. Each tangent
        point only appears once. If the line is colinear with a line segment in the
        figure, only the two end points of the segment are included.
    Status: Abstract operation in the origin class, must be overridden.
    Inputs:
        self: GeometricFigure — figure to be intersected with line
        line:Line — line to be intersected with circle
    Returns:
        A set of intersection points. Set may contain 0 or more points.
    Side Effects: none

Errors: If the figures do not intersect, returns an empty set.
If the line is colinear with a line segment in the figure, the set includes only the end points of the segment.
If the figure is an area, then its boundary is used.

## 14.6 CHAPTER SUMMARY

Good style is important to maximize the benefits of object-oriented design and programming; most benefits come from greatly reduced maintenance and enhancement costs and in reuse of the new code on future projects. Object-oriented programming style guidelines include conventional programming style guidelines as well as principles uniquely applicable to object-oriented concepts such as inheritance.

A major goal of object-oriented design is maximizing reusability of classes and methods. Reuse within a program or project is a matter of looking for similarities and consolidating them using inheritance. Planning for reuse by future projects takes more foresight because designing reusable software takes more time and effort up front. Reusability is enhanced by keeping methods small, coherent, and local. Separation of policy and implementation is important. One way to use inheritance is by factoring a generic method into suboperations, some of which are inherited from the origin class and some of which are overridden by each subclass. Delegation should be used when methods must be shared but classes are not in a true generalization relationship.

Most software is eventually extended. Extensibility is enhanced by encapsulation of classes and methods, minimizing dependencies between classes and methods, using methods to access attributes of other classes, and distinguishing public from private operations on a class.

Robustness should not be sacrificed for efficiency. Because objects contain references to their own classes, they are less vulnerable to mismatched typing than conventional programming variables and can be checked dynamically to see that they match the assumptions within a method. Programs should always protect against user and system errors. Testing assertions to catch programming bugs takes time but can be used during debugging and removed during production.

Writing large programs with teams of programmers requires more discipline, better documentation, and better communication than one-person or small projects. Writing readable, well-documented methods is essential.

| | |
|---|---|
| delegation | public versus private |
| encapsulation | reusability |
| extensibility | robustness |
| factoring | specification of public interface |
| programming-in-the-large | |

**Figure 14.3** Key concepts for Chapter 14

## BIBLIOGRAPHIC NOTES

In object-oriented programming, application concepts must be rendered into programming language constructs without obscuring either application meaning or program structure, so good programming style is important. Most conventional programming principles are also valid for object-oriented programming. [Kernighan-78] is a classic style guide for programming, a bit low-level perhaps for current languages, but useful nevertheless. [Dijkstra-76] stresses elegance in the design of demonstrably-correct programs.

## REFERENCES

[Dijkstra-76] Edsger W. Dijkstra. *A Discipline of Programming*. Englewood Cliffs, New Jersey: Prentice Hall, 1976.

[Kernighan-78] Brian W. Kernighan, P.J. Plauger. *The Elements of Programming Style*. New York: McGraw-Hill, 1978.

[Lieberherr-89] Karl J. Lieberherr, Arthur J. Riel. Contributions to teaching object-oriented design and programming. *OOPSLA'89* as *ACM SIGPLAN 24*, 11 (Nov. 1989) 11-22.

## EXERCISES

**14.1**  (4) A technique that can occasionally be used to reuse code is to use a method itself as an argument for another method. For example, one operation that can be performed on a binary tree is ordered printing. The subroutine *Print(node)* could print the values in a tree rooted at *node* by a recursive call to *Print(node.left_subtree)*, if there is a left subtree, followed by printing *node.-value*, followed by a recursive call for the right subtree. This approach could be generalized to apply other operations. List at least three operations that could be performed on the nodes of a binary tree. Prepare pseudocode for a subroutine *Ordered_visit(node, method)* that applies *method* to the nodes of the tree rooted at *node*, in order.

**14.2**  (3) Combining similar operations into a single operation can improve code reuse. Revise, extend, or generalize the following two operations into a single operation. Also list the attributes needed to track both types of accounts.

    a. *Cash_check(normal_account, check)* If the amount of the *check* is less than the balance in *normal_account*, cash the check and debit the account. Otherwise, bounce the check.

    b. *Cash_check(reserve_account, check)* If the amount of the *check* is less than the balance in *reserve_account*, cash the check and debit the account. Otherwise, examine the reserve balance. If the check can be covered by transferring funds from the reserve without going over the reserve limit, cash the check and update the balances. Otherwise, bounce the check.

**14.3**  (4) Figure E14.1 is a function coded in C to create a new sheet for a computer-aided design application. A sheet is a named, displayable, two-dimensional region containing text and graphics. Several sheets may be required to completely represent a system being designed. The function given in the figure creates a new vertical or horizontal sheet and constructs a name from a root and a suffix. The C functions it calls are *strlen* to compute the length of a string, *strcpy* to copy a string, *strcat* to concatenate two strings, and *malloc* to allocate memory. The data types *Sheet_type* and *Sheet* are defined outside of the function in the same module. The functions *strlen*, *strcpy*, and *strcat* will cause a crash if they are called with 0 for any argument. As it stands, the subroutine is exposed to several types of errors. The arguments *root_name* and *suffix* could be zero and *sheet_type* could be an illegal enumerated value. The call to *malloc* could fail to allocate memory.

a. Prepare a list of all the ways the function could fail. For each way, describe the consequences.

b. Revise the function so that it does not crash as a result of any of the errors you listed in part *a* and so that it prints out a descriptive error message for each kind of error as an aid in debugging programs in which it is called.

```
Sheet create_sheet (sheet_type, root_name, suffix)
Sheet_type sheet_type;
char *root_name, *suffix;
{ char *malloc(), *strcpy(), *strcat(), *sheet_name;
  int strlen(), root_length, suffix_length;
  Sheet sheet, vert_sheet_new(), horiz_sheet_new();
  root_length = strlen(root_name);
  suffix_length = strlen(suffix);
  sheet_name = malloc(root_length + suffix_length + 1);
  sheet_name = strcpy(sheet_name, root_name);
  sheet_name = strcat(sheet_name, suffix);
  switch(sheet_type)
  { case VERTICAL:
      sheet = vert_sheet_new();
      break;
    case HORIZONTAL:
      sheet = horiz_sheet_new();
      break;
  }
  sheet->name = sheet_name;
  return sheet;
}
```

**Figure E14.1** Function to create a new named sheet

**14.4** (3) Rewrite the C function in Figure E14.2 by using better names. The corresponding object diagram is in Figure E14.3. The function determines the value of a term by recursively expanding expressions. The function *compute* applies a binary operation to two values and *var_get* returns the value of a variable. Rename these functions as well.

```
Value ptree_get(top_nde)
Term top_nde;
{ Value val, val1, val2, compute(), var_get();
  switch(top_nde->node_type)
  { case CNSTNT:
      val = top_nde->value;
      return val;
      break;
    case VAR:
      val = var_get(top_nde->name);
      return val;
      break;
    case EXP:
      val1 = ptree_get(top_nde->left_nde);
      val2 = ptree_get(top_nde->right_nde);
      val = compute(val1, val2, top_nde->binary_operator);
      return val;
      break;
  }
}
```

**Figure E14.2** Function to evaluate a *Term*

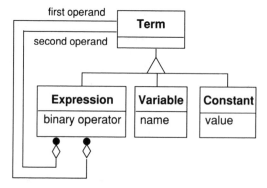

**Figure E14.3** Object diagram of a *Term*

**14.5** (7) Add methods to the object diagram in Figure E14.4 to satisfy the following queries. You may wish to review exercise 8.19. Write pseudocode for each method that you add and indicate whether the method is public or private. Separate policy from implementation. Avoid traversing multiple links.

a. Find all the members of a given team.

b. Find which figures were held more than once in a given season.

c. Find the net score of a competitor for a given figure at a given meet.
d. Find the team average score over all figures in a given season.
e. Find the average score of a competitor over all figures in a given meet.
f. Find the team average score in a given figure at a given meet.
g. Find the set of all individuals who competed in any events in a given season.
h. Find the set of all individuals who competed in all of the events held in a given season.
i. Find all the judges who judged a given event in a given season.
j. Find the judge who awarded the lowest score during a given event.
k. Find the judge who awarded the lowest score for a given figure.

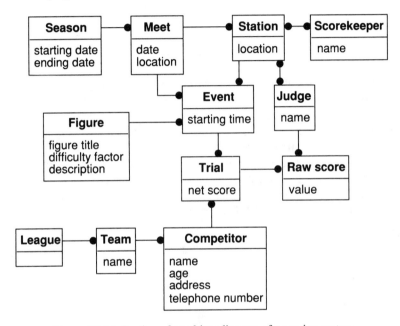

**Figure E14.4** Portion of an object diagram of a scoring system

# 15

---

# Object-Oriented Languages

Not surprisingly, the most natural implementation target for an object-oriented design is an object-oriented language. This chapter discusses how to take a generic design and make the final implementation decisions that are required to realize the design in a specific object-oriented language. The goal of the techniques in this chapter is to produce code for a program. The chapter also surveys, compares, and contrasts various object-oriented languages in order to show how the choice of a language influences these implementation decisions.

This chapter is one of three chapters included in Part 3 of the book covering implementation in a particular kind of target language, and is in parallel to Chapter 16 (Non-Object-Oriented Languages) and Chapter 17 (Relational Databases).

After reading this chapter, you will understand how to map an object-oriented design into an object-oriented language, and you will understand some factors to consider in choosing an object-oriented language.

## 15.1 TRANSLATING A DESIGN INTO AN IMPLEMENTATION

It is relatively easy to implement an object-oriented design with an object-oriented language since language constructs are similar to design constructs. A precise definition of an OO language is not crucial for selecting one. In general, an OO language supports *objects* (combining data and operations), *polymorphism* at run-time, and *inheritance*. A more formal discussion of the essential concepts of OO languages and the diverse ways in which these concepts are supported is found in [Stefik-86] and [Wegner-87].

We use C++, Eiffel, and Smalltalk to explain how to implement an OMT design with OO languages. We discuss implementation of the basic object-oriented concepts common to all object-oriented languages, describing the various ways in which different languages support the concepts. Section 15.7 discusses more advanced features of object-oriented languages, including some features that are not well supported by current languages. Section 15.8 discusses distinctive aspects of several commercially available OO languages: Smalltalk, C++, Eiffel, CLOS, and object-oriented database languages.

All three OMT models contribute to code development. The object model contains most of the declarative structure: the specification of classes, attributes, inheritance hierarchy, and associations. The dynamic model specifies the high-level control strategy for the system: procedure-driven, event-driven, or multi-tasking. The functional model captures functionality of objects that must be incorporated into methods.

The following considerations apply to implementing an object-oriented design in an object-oriented language:

- Class definitions [15.2]
- Creating objects [15.3]
- Calling operations [15.4]
- Using inheritance [15.5]
- Implementing associations [15.6]

### 15.1.1 Graphics Editor Example

Figure 15.1 shows a part of an object model for a graphics editor, which will be used as an example throughout the chapter. The editor permits recursive groups of shapes to be constructed from boxes and circles. A window contains a set of shapes. Groups can be built from shapes or smaller groups. Items (shapes or groups) that are not part of a group are root items in the window and are available for manipulation. A root item can be selected by picking one of its embedded shapes with a locator cursor controlled by a mouse. A shape is picked if the cursor point lies within it. Selected items can be grouped, ungrouped, cut from the window, or moved by an offset. Commands are also provided to clear the selections or create new shapes. Shapes are erased by writing over them in the background color.

The diagram shows the attributes and operations of each class. Abstract operations are indicated by the word *abstract* in the origin class

## 15.2 CLASS DEFINITIONS

The first step in implementing an object-oriented design is to declare object classes. Each attribute and operation in an object diagram must be declared as part of its corresponding class. It is good practice to carry forward the names from the design diagram. If you have not already assigned data types to attributes, you must now do so. Declare attributes and operations as either public or private, if the language supports the distinction. Public features can be accessed by any method, while private features are only accessible by methods of the same class.

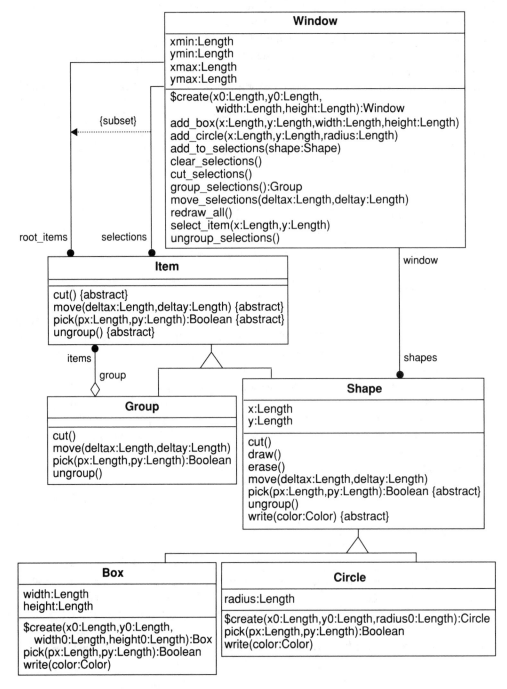

**Figure 15.1** Simple graphics editor

### 15.2.1 Class Definitions in C++

In C++, the declaration for the class *Window* is:

```
class Window
{
public:
    // constructor method must have same name as the class
    Window (Length x0,Length y0,Length width, Length height);
    // destructor method must have same name as the class
    ~Window ();
    // instance methods
    void add_box (Length x, Length y,
                    Length width, Length height);
    void add_circle (Length x, Length y, Length radius);
    void clear_selections();
    void cut_selections();
    Group * group_selections();
    void move_selections (Length deltax, Length deltay);
    void redraw_all();
    void select_item (Length x, Length y);
    void ungroup_selections();
private:
    Length xmin;
    Length ymin;
    Length xmax;
    Length ymax;
    void add_to_selections(Shape* shape);
};
```

In C++, both attributes and methods are declared together as *members* of a class. A method may not have the same name as an attribute. The object creation routine, called a *constructor,* must have the same name as the class (Section 15.3.1).

In C++, you must declare members as either public or private (the default is private). Public members can be accessed by any function; private members can only be accessed by methods on the same class (not necessarily the same object, however). All attributes in this example are private because arbitrary changes to a window are not permitted. In general, it is good practice to keep attributes private and provide access to them only through methods, to prevent client code from being dependent on the exact implementation of a class. All operations are public, except *add_to_selections,* which is used internally by the *Window* class. We have omitted the associations from this declaration. Later, we explain how to represent associations in an object-oriented language.

*Length* is a user-defined type (not a class) that hides the actual implementation of the length (so that it could be either integer or real, for example). It could be declared as a *typedef* in C++:

```
typedef float Length;
```

or

```
typedef int Length;
```

### 15.2.2 Class Definitions in Eiffel

In Eiffel, the class declaration for the class *Window* is:

```
class WINDOW
export
    add_box, add_circle, clear_selections, cut_selections,
    group_selections, move_selections,
    redraw_all, select_item, ungroup_selections
feature
    xmin, ymin, xmax, ymax: REAL;
    Create (x0, y0, width, height: REAL) is body end;
    add_box (x, y, width, height: REAL) is body end;
    add_circle (x, y, radius: REAL) is body end;
    add_to_selections (ashape: SHAPE) is body end;
    clear_selections is body end;
    cut_selections is body end;
    group_selections: Group is body end;
    move_selections (deltax, deltay: REAL) is body end;
    redraw_all is body end;
    select_item (x, y: REAL) is body end;
    ungroup_selections is body end
end -- class WINDOW
```

In Eiffel, features (attributes and operations) are private unless they are explicitly made public with the *export* keyword. Create is automatically public. *REAL* is a simple, or predefined, type. Although Eiffel is not case-sensitive, by convention simple types and class names are capitalized.

### 15.2.3 Class Definitions in Smalltalk

Smalltalk programs are normally entered using the Smalltalk browser. The printed code we show here would normally be added interactively. All Smalltalk classes are ultimately descended from class *object*.

```
class name            Window
superclass            Object
instance variables    xmin ymin xmax ymax
class methods
    instantiating
    createAt: aPoint ofWidth: width ofHeight: height
instance methods
    adding shapes
    addBoxAt: aPoint ofWidth: width ofHeight: height
    addCircleAt: aPoint ofRadius: radius

    refreshing window
    redrawAll
```

```
manipulating selections
clearSelections
cutSelections
groupSelections
moveSelectionsBy: deltaPoint
selectItemAt: aPoint
ungroupSelections

private
addToSelections: aShape
```

To make attributes (*instance variables* in Smalltalk) private, we omit methods to query and set the attributes. The groupings in italics are called *categories*, used to organize methods of a class. They have no other semantic meaning. By convention, methods that are for internal use only are put in the category *private*, but Smalltalk does not enforce the privacy. The programmer must be careful to honor the convention.

We have replaced separate $x$ and $y$ coordinates by class *Point* in several places. Smalltalk has a convenient method '@' to create a point from a pair of numbers. For example:

```
aPoint ← 3 @ 4
```

## 15.3 CREATING OBJECTS

Object-oriented languages create new objects in one of two ways. Some languages, such as Smalltalk and DSM, have classes that are full objects in their own right. In these languages, an operation applied to a class object (called a *class operation*) creates a new object of the class. Other languages, such as C++ and Eiffel, do not have class objects. These languages have special operations that create new objects.

When a new object is created, the language must allocate storage for its attribute values and must assign it a unique object ID, either the address of the storage block or an index in a table. Object-oriented languages free the programmer of the necessity to explicitly allocate memory for objects.

Different languages use one of two styles of destroying objects that are no longer needed. In some languages, objects are destroyed by an explicit operation (such as *destroy*). The programmer must take care that no references to a destroyed object remain, or memory access errors may result. Explicit memory management is error-prone, so some languages, such as Smalltalk, include automatic garbage collectors that destroy objects that are inaccessible, without requiring (or permitting) any explicit deallocation.

### 15.3.1 Creating Objects in C++

C++ does not have class objects or class operations to create instances of a class. Instead it has a special *constructor* operation to initialize new instances. The name of the method for the class constructor has the same name as the class, such as:

```
Window::Window (Length x0,Length y0,
                Length width, Length height)
{
    xmin = x0; ymin = y0;
    xmax = x0 + width; ymax = y0 + height;
}
```

In C++, multiple constructors for a single class can be defined, distinguished by the number and types of their arguments (this is an example of *overloading*). For example, we might have constructors with the following arguments:

```
Window (); // default position and size
Window (Length x0, Length y0); // default size
Window (Length x0, Length y0, Length width, Length height);
```

A constructor is executed whenever a new object instance is allocated. At the time of allocation, the programmer can specify the arguments for the constructor; the constructor with matching argument types is executed. If no arguments are specified, then the default constructor with no arguments is executed.

C++ provides three kinds of memory allocation for objects: preallocated by the compiler in fixed global memory (*static*), allocated on the stack (*automatic*), and allocated from a heap (*dynamic*).

Static storage is obtained by declaring a variable outside of any function or by using the keyword *static* on an attribute. A static attribute is a class attribute common to all instances of the class. Static storage is preallocated by the compiler and does not change during execution. A constructor can be specified, which is executed during program initialization. The following statement declares a static global variable to hold an initialized W*indow* object:

```
Window main_window = Window (0.0,0.0,8.5,11.0);
```

Local variables within functions normally use automatic storage. When a function is entered, enough space on the hardware stack is reserved to hold all the local variables of the function. The storage is deallocated when the function exits, so references to automatic variables must not be stored in other objects whose lifetimes might exceed the automatic variables. The declaration of local variables has the same form as the declaration of global variables shown above, except they are declared within a function body.

Each class can have one *destructor*. A destructor performs any necessary cleanup before an object is destroyed. Destructors do not take any arguments. Destructor methods have the name of the class prefixed by a tilde, '~':

```
Window :: ~Window ()
{
    // erase the window and repaint the underlying region
}
```

When a function exits, the *destructor* for each automatic variable is called. After the destructors have been run, the storage for automatic variables is implicitly deallocated when the function return instruction adjusts the stack to its pre-call value.

Dynamic storage is allocated from a heap on an explicit request from the programmer. The *new* operator allocates storage for a new object and returns a pointer to it, which can be stored in a pointer variable. The *new* operator can include arguments for the constructor:

```
Window * window = new Window (0.0,0.0,8.5,11.0);
```

A dynamic object may outlive the function in which it is created. Dynamic objects can only be deallocated by applying the *delete* operator to the object pointer. The programmer must make sure that no references to the object remain. The *delete* operator first invokes the destructor for the class and then deallocates the storage for the object:

```
delete window;
```

Standard implementations of C++ do not have a garbage collector and heap-based objects must be explicitly deallocated by the *delete* operator, so there is danger of dangling object references to incorrectly deleted objects, as well as the loss of memory to inaccessible objects which have not been deleted. A dangling reference is a reference by one object to another object that no longer exists.

Note that constructors and destructors simply initialize and clean up objects. Memory allocation and deallocation are invoked explicitly by the *new* and *delete* operators or implicitly by declaration of local variables.

C++ permits considerable flexibility in memory allocation. The programmer can override the built-in memory allocator for a given class and supply a new one. Because operators such as assignment and type conversion can also be overridden on a class-by-class basis, it is possible to completely control allocation and creation of objects, although most programmers will not need to use such techniques.

## 15.3.2 Creating Objects in Eiffel

Eiffel separates the declaration of a variable (called an *entity* in Eiffel) from the creation of an object. A declaration of an entity makes a name that can hold a reference to an object of a given type, but the reference is initially void, that is, it does not refer to any object:

```
w: WINDOW
```

This declaration makes a variable that can hold a reference to a window, but does not store an actual object in the variable. It is similar to a C++ declaration for a pointer or reference variable.

All Eiffel objects are dynamic; there is no equivalent of the C++ static or automatic objects. To create an object of the given type and store its reference in the entity, the *Create* operation is applied to the entity:

```
w.Create (0.0, 0.0, 8.5, 11.0);
```

There is a default *Create* operation for each class that allocates a new instance of a class and initializes its attributes to zero values. The programmer can override the default *Create* operation to perform additional actions or accept arguments:

```
class WINDOW
...
feature
   Create (x0, y0, width, height: REAL) is
      do
         xmin := x0; ymin := y0;
         xmax := x0 + width; ymax := y0 + height
      end; -- Create
   ...
end -- class WINDOW
```

A second special operation, *Clone*, copies an existing object and creates a new object whose attributes are identical.

There is no way to explicitly destroy an Eiffel object (such as the C++ *delete* operator). The *Forget* operation removes the object reference from an entity, but it does not destroy the object itself. The Eiffel garbage collector is responsible for destroying objects that are no longer accessible because they cannot be reached from the root object or from any program variables. This simplifies the programmer's job considerably and prevents many insidious bugs, but imposes a run-time cost on the system.

Eiffel's garbage collector runs as a coroutine that checks for unused objects when memory usage reaches predefined thresholds. The garbage collector can be explicitly turned on and off.

### 15.3.3 Creating Objects in Smalltalk

All Smalltalk objects are dynamic and are allocated from a heap. Deallocation is performed by a built-in garbage collector. All variables are untyped and can hold objects of any class. New objects are created using the same *message passing* (operation calling) mechanism used for operations on objects. Smalltalk does not require any special creation operations, as do C++ and Eiffel.

To allocate a new object in Smalltalk, a message is sent to a *class object*, that is, an object that describes the class itself. Instance creation is a *class operation*, that is, it is an operation on a class, rather than an operation on an instance object. By convention, the *new* operation creates a new instance of a class:

```
w ← Window new
```

Unlike in C++ and Eiffel, there are no restrictions on the names of instance creation operations. Because a creation operation is explicitly applied to a class object, it cannot be confused with an instance operation. The developer can write custom instance creation methods that accept arguments:

```
w ← Window createAt: 0 @ 0 ofWidth: 8.5 ofHeight: 11.0
```

The method would be defined as follows:

```
class name Window
class methods
```

```
createAt: aPoint ofWidth: width ofHeight: height
   | w |
   w ← self new.
   w initialize: aPoint width: width height: height.
   ↑w
```
**instance methods**
```
   initialize: aPoint width: width height: height
      xmin ← aPoint x.
      ymin ← aPoint y.
      xmax ← xmin + width.
      ymax ← ymin + height
```
The class method cannot directly access the attributes of the new instance, so an instance method *initialize:width:height:* must be written to initialize the attributes.

Objects cannot be explicitly deallocated. Storage is reclaimed by an automatic built-in garbage collector.

## 15.4 CALLING OPERATIONS

In most OO languages, each operation has at least one implicit argument, the target object, indicated with a special syntax. Operations may or may not have additional arguments. Some languages permit a choice between passing arguments as read-only values or as references to values that can be updated by a procedure.

### 15.4.1 Calling Operations in C++

A C++ operation is declared as a member of a class along with attributes. An operation is invoked using a similar notation to attribute access: the member selection operator "->" is applied to an object pointer:
```
Shape* shape;
shape->move (dx, dy);
```
Additional arguments may be objects, built-in types such as *int*, *float*, and *char*, and user-defined types, such as *typedef* types.

An attribute name or operation name used as an identifier within a C++ method implicitly refers to the target object of the method. In the following example, *x* and *y* are attributes of the target object of class *Shape*:
```
void Shape::move (Length deltax, Length deltay)
{
    x = x + deltax;
    y = y + deltay;
}
```
The implicit argument *this* contains a reference to the target object (usually to pass it as an argument to another operation). The previous code could be written as:

```
    void Shape::move (Length deltax, Length deltay)
    {
        this->x = this->x + deltax;
        this->y = this->y + deltay;
    }
```

Reference to an attribute of an object that is not the target requires a qualified reference:

```
    window->xmin = x1;
```

Unless the qualified object is of the same class as the method, such direct attribute access should be avoided because it violates encapsulation of classes. Use an access method on the class instead, which permits the internal representation of the class to be changed.

Unlike Smalltalk and Eiffel, C++ makes a distinction between the object record and a reference to an object. Use of the object record directly permits the attributes of the object to be updated, but does not permit references to the object to be inserted into associations. Most of the time it is best to consider the object reference as "the object." To use object records directly, omit the C++ indirection operator (* or &):

```
    Box box(10.0,13.4,5.12,3.14);
    box.move (dx, dy);
```

### 15.4.2 Calling Operations in Eiffel

Methods in Eiffel are called *routines*. Arguments to routines can be simple types (*REAL*, *IN-TEGER*, *BOOLEAN*, and *CHARACTER*) or user-defined classes. Although all objects are kept as pointers, Eiffel does not permit a routine to modify a formal parameter through assignment or by applying an operation (such as *Create*, *Clone*, or *Forget*) that can modify the reference. However, other operations can be applied to an object that is a formal parameter, and these operations may result in changes to the state of the object.

The Eiffel syntax for calling an operation is similar to C++. Note that the Eiffel attribute selection operator '.' is equivalent to the C++ operator '->':

```
    local
        aShape: SHAPE;
        dx, dy: REAL
    do

        ...
        aShape.move (dx, dy);
    end
```

Eiffel permits implicit access to the features of the target object by writing the name of the feature. Identifiers $x$ and $y$ are attributes of the target *SHAPE*:

```
    move (deltax, deltay: REAL) is
        -- move a shape by delta
    do
        x := x + deltax;
        y := y + deltay
    end
```

Eiffel supplies a predefined identifier, *Current*, that names the target object of an operation. This identifier is equivalent to *this* in C++ and *self* in Smalltalk. The code above is equivalent to:

```
move (deltax, deltay: REAL) is
   -- move a shape by delta
do
    Current.x := Current.x + deltax;
    Current.y := Current.y + deltay
end
```

Reference to a feature of an object that is not the target requires a qualified reference:

```
window.xmin := x1;
```

## 15.4.3 Calling Operations in Smalltalk

All arguments and variables in Smalltalk are objects. All operations are methods associated with objects. The programmer *sends messages* (applies operations) to objects. A *message* is the name of an operation with a list of argument values. Smalltalk binds the message to a method at run-time by examining the class of the object and searching the methods on the class and its ancestors. Formal parameters to methods cannot be changed by assignment within a method. The Smalltalk syntax for message passing does not use punctuation marks but does use keywords to separate the arguments:

```
aShape moveDelta: aPoint
```

This method would be implemented as follows:

```
class name Shape
instance variables
   x  y
instance methods
   moveDelta: aPoint
       x ← x + aPoint x
       y ← y + aPoint y
```

Within a method, attributes of the target object (*instance variables* in Smalltalk) may be accessed directly by writing the name of the attribute, as in C++ and Eiffel.

Smalltalk provides a pseudovariable, *self*, that refers to the receiver of the message. There is no Smalltalk equivalent of the C++ and Eiffel operations to access an attribute from an object. Only the attributes of the target object can be accessed directly. Attributes of other objects must be accessed by (user-provided) access operations:

```
aPoint ← aWindow getLocation
```

All attributes are therefore private to the class. Unfortunately, there is no way to restrict access to operations of a class; all operations are public.

## 15.5  USING INHERITANCE

Object-oriented languages vary in the mechanisms provided to implement inheritance. [Kim-88a, Chapter 3] discusses three independent dimensions for classifying inheritance mechanisms: static or dynamic, implicit or explicit, and per object or per group. Many of the popular languages are static (inheritance is bound at compile time), implicit (behavior of an object depends on its class, which cannot be changed), and per group (inheritance character-istics are specified for a class, not for specific objects). In most languages, the declaration of each class includes a list of superclasses from which it inherits attributes and methods.

### 15.5.1  Using Inheritance in C++

The superclass or superclasses of a class are specified as part of the class declaration. A sub-class is called a *derived* class. The C++ code that follows declares *Shape* to be a subclass of *Item*. *Box* and *Circle* are subclasses of *Shape*.

```
class Item
{
public:
    virtual void cut() = 0;
    virtual void move (Length deltax, Length deltay) = 0;
    virtual Boolean pick (Length px, Length py) = 0;
    virtual void ungroup() = 0;
};
class Shape: public Item
{
protected:
    Length x;
    Length y;
public:
    void cut();
    void draw() {write (COLOR_FOREGROUND);}
    void erase () {write (COLOR_BACKGROUND);}
    void move (Length deltax, Length deltay);
    virtual Boolean pick (Length px, Length py) = 0;
    void ungroup() {}
    virtual void write (Color color) = 0;
};
class Box: public Shape
{
protected:
    Length width;
    Length height;
public:
    Box (Length x0, Length y0, Length width0, Length height0);
    Boolean pick (Length px, Length py);
    void write (Color color);
};
```

```
class Circle: public Shape
{
protected:
    Length radius;
public:
    Circle (Length x0, Length y0, Length radius0);
    Boolean pick (Length px, Length py);
    void write (Color color);
};
```

The attributes declared in a superclass are inherited by its subclasses and need not be repeated. They can be accessed from any subclass unless they are declared *private*. Only methods of a class can access its private attributes. Attributes declared *protected* are accessible to subclasses but not to client classes.

```
Boolean Box::pick (Length px, Length py)
{
    return x<=px && px<=x+width && y<=py && py<=y+height;
}
```

Methods declared in a superclass are also inherited. If a method can be overridden by a subclass, then it must be declared *virtual* in its first appearance in a superclass. For example, method *write* in class *Shape* can be overridden in classes *Box* and *Circle* and is therefore virtual. Methods *draw* and *erase* on class *Shape* are not overridden by the subclasses so they need not be declared virtual (they are implemented by calling virtual function *write* with a color of black or white). Method *Shape::write* is declared virtual and "initialized" to 0; this identifies it as a *pure virtual function*, that is, an abstract operation. Any class with a pure virtual function is an abstract class and cannot be instantiated directly. The compiler verifies that any concrete subclass defines or inherits implementations for all pure virtual functions.

Methods that override inherited methods must be redeclared in the subclass, but those that are inherited (and not overridden) need not be repeated. Likewise, inherited attributes need not be repeated. Virtual operations are called using the same syntax as nonvirtual operations:

```
Shape * shape;
Length x,y;
Boolean status;
status = shape->pick (x,y);
```

The knowledge of a class's ancestry can be declared *public* or *private*. If a superclass derivation is *private*, then clients of the class cannot call inherited operations directly nor access attributes of the ancestors. Masking inherited operations permits the safe use of inheritance for implementation purposes where a true generalization relationship does not exist, although we would discourage this kind of usage.

C++ supports multiple inheritance, by specifying a list of superclasses in the derivation statement. The use of conflicting attribute or operation names from different superclasses is not allowed. C++ supports several complicated variations on multiple inheritance, including a chain of constructors that are automatically invoked when a new instance is created.

### 15.5.2 Using Inheritance in Eiffel

In Eiffel, inheritance is indicated with the *inherit* clause as shown in the following example:

```
class ITEM
export
    cut, move, pick, ungroup
feature
    cut is deferred end;
    move (deltax, deltay: REAL) is deferred end;
    pick (x,y: REAL):BOOLEAN is deferred end;
    ungroup is deferred end
end

class SHAPE
export cut, draw, erase, move, ungroup, write
inherit ITEM
feature
    x,y: REAL;
    cut is body end;
    draw is body end;
    erase is body end;
    move (deltax, deltay: REAL) is body end;
    ungroup is body end;
    write (acolor: COLOR) is deferred end
end

class BOX
export pick, write
inherit SHAPE redefine pick, write
feature
    width, height: REAL;
    Create (x0, y0, width0, height0: REAL) is body end;
    pick (x,y: REAL): BOOLEAN is body end;
    write (acolor: COLOR) is body end
end

class CIRCLE
export pick, write
inherit SHAPE redefine pick, write
feature
    radius: REAL;
    Create (x0, y0, radius0: REAL) is body end;
    pick (x,y: REAL): BOOLEAN is body end;
    write (acolor: COLOR) is body end
end
```

Abstract operations are indicated with the *deferred* declaration. These operations must be implemented by all subclasses. Features in the subclass that override features in the superclass must be indicated with the *redefine* clause (not shown in this example). Features that are inherited and not overridden, such as operation *move* within class *CIRCLE*, need not be listed in either the *export* clause nor the *redefine* clause.

External visibility of features is specified by the *export* list, which replaces the *public* and *private* declarations of C++. All the features of a superclass are available to its descendents (there is no distinction corresponding to C++ *private* and *protected*). Features can be selectively exported to a specified class (and all its descendents), similar to the C++ *friend* declaration. Eiffel features can be renamed in a subclass.

Eiffel supports multiple inheritance. Renaming of inherited features can help to reduce name conflicts from different superclasses.

### 15.5.3 Using Inheritance in Smalltalk

In Smalltalk, inheritance is indicated by supplying the name of the superclass for an object. As in C++ and Eiffel, only those features that are unique to a subclass are specified. Any methods to be overridden are defined in the subclass.

```
class name          Item
superclass          Object

class name          Shape
superclass          Item
instance variables
   x
   y
instance methods
   cut
   draw
   erase
   move: aPoint
   ungroup

class name          Box
superclass          Shape
instance variables
   width
   height

instance methods
   pick: aPoint
   write: aColor
class methods
   createAt: aPoint width: widthSize length: lengthSize

class name          Circle
superclass          Shape
instance variables
   radius
instance methods
   pick: aPoint
   write: aColor
class methods
   createAt: aPoint radius: radiusSize
```

All the attributes of a superclass are available to all of its descendents. There is no need to indicate that a method can be overridden; all methods can be overridden. In C++ and Eiffel, an operation must be defined in its *origin* class, that is, the least common ancestor of all the classes that implement methods on the operation. In Smalltalk, by contrast, there is no need to declare abstract methods, but the programmer must ensure that an undefined operation is not applied to an object. A normal convention and good practice is to define abstract methods as "*self subclassResponsibility*" in case a method on a subclass is forgotten. The method *subclassResponsibility* then prints an error message if an undefined abstract operation is invoked. Errors in Smalltalk programs are more likely to show up at run time, because of its weak typing. There is no way to block the use of an operation by any class, so complete encapsulation is not possible in Smalltalk.

The standard implementations of Smalltalk do not support multiple inheritance, although some experimental implementations have supported it.

## 15.6 IMPLEMENTING ASSOCIATIONS

Chapter 10 discussed how to implement associations and aggregations. There are two general approaches: buried pointers and distinct association objects.

If your language does not explicitly support association objects (and most currently do not), then buried pointers are easiest to implement. Buried pointers may be added during design or deferred until now. In either case, the attributes needed to implement the buried pointers must be added to the class definitions. A binary association is usually implemented as an attribute in each associated object, containing a pointer to the related object or to a set of related objects. In many cases, however, the association is only traversed in one direction, so a pointer need only be added to one of the classes. Pointers in the "one" direction are simple to implement; they simply contain object references. Pointers in the "many" direction require a set of objects, or an array if the association is ordered, implemented most easily with a collection class object from a class library.

An association can also be implemented as a distinct container object. An explicit association object is conceptually a set of tuples, each tuple containing one value from each associated class. A binary association object can be implemented as two *Dictionary* objects, each dictionary mapping in one direction across the association.

There is an important consequence of buried pointers that is overlooked by many users and designers of object-oriented languages. Associations cannot be simulated by attributes on classes without violating encapsulation of classes because the paired attributes composing an association are not independent. Updating one pointer in the implementation of an association implies that the other pointer must be updated as well to keep the implementation consistent. The individual attributes should not be made freely available externally because they must not be updated separately. On the other hand, an externally-available method to update the attributes cannot be attached to either class of the association without access to the internal implementation of the other class because the attributes are mutually constrained. C++ allows limited relaxation of encapsulation using the *friend* construct, and

Eiffel provides export of features to selected classes, but there is no clean way to encapsulate associations as attributes in Smalltalk or most other languages.

Associations are intrinsically important since they arise when capturing and describing requirements. (See Section 3.2.3.) The real-world need for associations does not go away merely because most existing OO languages are not rich enough to directly capture them. The best solution to this problem would be for language designers to provide support for association objects as a basic concept, as is done in the DSM language [Shah-89].

### 15.6.1 Implementing Associations in C++

The many-to-one association between *Item* and *Group* could be implemented in C++ using pointers:

```
class Item
{
    // other declarations as before
private:
    Group * group;
    friend Group::add_item (Item *);
    friend Group::remove_item (Item *);
public:
    Group * get_group () {return group;}
};
class Group: public Item
{
    // other declarations as before
private:
    ItemSet * items;
public:
    void add_item (Item *);
    void remove_item (Item *);
    ItemSet * get_items () {return items;}
};
```

Whenever a new link is added to the association, both pointers must be updated. When a link is removed, both pointers must also be updated. The code might look as follows:

```
void Group::add_item (Item *item)
{
    item->group = this;
    items->add (item);
}
void Group::remove_item (Item *item)
{
    item->group = 0;
    items->remove (item);
}
```

The *Group* methods can update the *group* attribute in an *Item* object because they are declared as *friend*s of class *Item*. The *friend* construct provides a clean mechanism for allowing access to internal details without totally destroying encapsulation.

In this example we have omitted code to check whether an item is already in a group. Before putting an item in a group, we should first check to see if it is already in an group, and remove it if necessary. This check is not absolutely necessary if we can guarantee that we will never put an item in a group without first removing it from a previous group, but an explicit check adds protection against bugs.

Class *ItemSet* is a collection class that holds sets of items. It has the following protocol:

```
class ItemSet
{
public:
    ItemSet (); // create an empty set
    ~ItemSet (); // destroy a set
    void add (Item *); // add an item to the set
    void remove (Item *); // delete an item from the set
    Boolean includes (Item *); // test for an item in the set
    int size (); // report the number of items in the set
};
```

Collection classes that are more general (but weakly-typed) are found in available class libraries, such as the NIH class library [Gorlen-90] produced at the USA National Institutes of Health. This library also includes *iterator* objects to scan collections in *for*-loops without knowing the internal structure of the collection. There are operations to create an iterator, to advance it while testing for the end of the collection, and to get the current object from the collection:

```
Boolean Group::pick (Length x, Length y)
{
    ItemIterator it(items);
    while (it++)
        if (it()->pick (x,y)) return TRUE;
    return FALSE;
}
```

Variable-length array classes can be used to implement ordered associations. Some applications may require other data structures, such as circular lists or trees. (We have omitted the details of adapting a generic class, such as *Set*, to hold a specific kind of object, such as *Item*. This will eventually be done using parameterized types in C++. Until those are part of the standard C++ language, class libraries implement various tricks to permit storing specific classes in generic containers.)

Distinct association objects are not difficult to implement if the class library does not already contain them. *Association* can be implemented as a new container class and placed in the class library. The simplest approach is to implement an association object as two dictionary objects. (A dictionary is a look-up table that maps one value into another. It is provided by most class libraries.) One dictionary maps the association in the forward direction and the other in the reverse direction. Both dictionaries must be updated when the association is updated, but traversal of an association is efficient.

Each association in the object model is implemented by an association object. The links in the association are the elements of the association object. Using association objects preserves encapsulation of the constraint between the classes implicit in an association. For example, the previous routine could be written as:

```
Association* item_group_asn = new Association (many_to_one);

void Group::add_item (Item *item)
{
    item_group_asn->add (item, this);
}

void Group::remove_item (Item *item)
{
    item_group_asn->remove (item, this);
}

Group * Item::get_group ()
{
    return (Group*) item_group_asn->index_forward (this);
}

ItemSet * Group::get_items ()
{
    return (ItemSet*)item_group_asn->index_reverse (this);
}
```

We have glossed over the details of storing specific object classes in generic container objects, which can be done either by casting the contents (as we have shown) or by using parameterized classes (when they are added to C++).

If an association is implemented as a separate object, then no attributes need be added to either class in the association. If the association is sparse (that is, a small fraction of objects participate in it), then a separate association object uses less storage than a pointer in each object. Access of values is somewhat slower than with pointers in objects, but if associations are implemented with dictionaries that contain hash tables, the access time should be a small constant, independent of the number of links in the association.

### 15.6.2 Implementing Associations in Eiffel

The options for implementing associations in Eiffel are basically the same as in C++. Eiffel supports parameterized (*generic* in Eiffel) container objects, which are parameterized according to the type of objects they hold. The Eiffel *LINKED_LIST*, supplied in the basic class library, may be used to implement the many-to-one association between *ITEM* and *GROUP*:

```
class ITEM
export
   get_group
     -- selective export to class GROUP
   set_group {GROUP}, forget_group {GROUP}
feature
   mygroup: GROUP;
   get_group: GROUP is
       do
          Result := mygroup
       end;
   set_group(g:GROUP) is
       do
          mygroup := g
       end;
   forget_group is
       do
          forget(mygroup)
       end;
end -- ITEM
class GROUP
export add_item, remove_item, get_items
inherit
   ITEM
feature
   items:LINKED_LIST[ITEM]; -- parameterized type
   Create is
       do
          items.Create
       end;
   add_item(value:ITEM) is
       do
          items.finish;
          items.insert_right(value);
          value.set_group(Current)
       end;
   remove_item(value:ITEM) is
       do
          items.search (value, 1);
          items.delete;
          value.forget_group
       end;
   get_items(number:INTEGER):ITEM is
       do
          Result := items
       end;
end -- GROUP
```

Eiffel permits selective export of any feature. Here, we have exported *ITEM*'s *set_group* and *forget_group* features to the *GROUP* class. This maintains encapsulation by limiting write access to participants in the *ITEM/GROUP* association.

The Eiffel *forget* operator is for storage deallocation. It frees the object denoted by the object-id it operates on, and also sets the object-id to *void*.

### 15.6.3 Implementing Associations in Smalltalk

Smalltalk's rich class library helps developers to implement a variety of associations. For the many-to-one association (in Figure 15.1) between a Group and the Items it contains, we use a *Set*, found in the Smalltalk class library:

```
class name        Item
super class       Object
instance variables
   group
instance methods
   other instance methods as before
   getGroup
      ↑group
   private methods
   putGroup: aGroup
      group ← aGroup


class name        Group
super class       Item
instance variables
   items
class methods
   new
      ↑((super new) putItems: (Set new))
instance methods
   other instance methods as before
   addItem: anItem
      items add: anItem.
      anItem putGroup: self
   removeItem: anItem
      items remove: anItem.
      anItem putGroup: nil
   getItems
      ↑items copy
   private methods
   putItems: aSet
      items ← aSet
```

Since Smalltalk does no type checking, there are no restrictions on the class of items that can be added to a *Group*. Any object that responds to the *putGroup:* message is allowed. Note that proper encapsulation of the association is impossible in Smalltalk. The method *put-Group:* on class *Item* is marked as "private," but it is up to the programmer to respect the privacy of the method, because all methods are actually public.

## 15.7 OBJECT-ORIENTED LANGUAGE FEATURES

Object-oriented languages vary in their support of advanced object-oriented concepts. There is no single language that matches all styles and meets all needs. In this section we discuss various features of object-oriented languages that vary among languages. Select a language appropriate to your requirements. For example, if your design requires multiple inheritance, you should consider languages that support it well. Interpreted languages are useful for rapid prototyping but may not be adequate if you have stringent timing constraints. There is no point in building your own class library if the language provides one with suitable classes for your design. If you want extra compile-time error-checking, use a strongly-typed language. If memory usage is convoluted in your application, consider languages which provide automatic garbage collection. If you require persistent data accessible by multiple users, you may want to consider an OO database. Unless a language is exceptionally clumsy to use, syntax should only be a minor consideration.

This chapter refers to a variety of OO languages. C++, Eiffel, Objective-C, Smalltalk-80 and CLOS are commercially available languages. Trellis-Owl and DSM are research languages. GemStone and ORION are database languages. Figure 15.2 at the end of the chapter summarizes the features supported by certain commercially-available languages.

### 15.7.1 Multiple Inheritance

Some languages, such as C++ (Version 2), CLOS, Eiffel, and DSM, support multiple inheritance. Many others do not. If the language you select supports multiple inheritance, there is a direct translation from your design to implementation. Otherwise, you must use some of the workarounds suggested in Chapter 4.

Multiple inheritance introduces the possibility of conflict among attribute and operation names. A class could have more than one ancestor with the same attribute. There are several approaches that languages take to solving the problem. For example, the Eiffel compiler rejects programs with such clashes. CLOS, on the other hand, has a protocol for resolving them. In any case, we strongly recommend that you avoid such conflicts. Relying on the compiler to resolve conflicts is a matter of poor style because it damages extensibility and can lead to confusion.

### 15.7.2 Class Library

Most OO languages include a library of useful generic classes, which may be used as is or customized to meet a specific need through the creation of subclasses. The availability of a class library means that many components need not be reimplemented by the programmer.

The most useful kinds of classes implement general purpose data structures, such as sets, dynamic arrays, lists, queues, stacks, dictionaries, trees, and so forth. These classes, often referred to as *container classes*, serve as a framework for organizing collections of other objects. Classes implementing various kinds of associations should also be available in the class library.

More complete class libraries might include device-independent abstractions of interface classes (such as streams, input devices, display devices, file systems) or concurrent processes. A separate library of user interface classes for use with one or more windowing systems is useful, as is a graphics library. Support for string manipulation is needed by most programs.

### 15.7.3 Efficiency

Object-oriented languages have an undeserved reputation for inefficiency because some early languages (Smalltalk and Lisp-based languages) were interpreted rather than compiled. The availability of compiled languages and more efficient interpreters has given developers more latitude in choosing an appropriate language. Use of an OO language with a mature class library often results in code that runs *faster* than that written with a non-OO language. This is because the overhead of an OO language is often more than compensated by better implementations of data structures and algorithms available in a mature class library. For example, many programmers would not bother to implement hash tables or balanced trees for small programs, but such data structures are available in a good class library.

One aspect of object-oriented languages that seems inefficient is the use of *method resolution* at run-time (also known as dynamic binding) to implement polymorphic operations. Method resolution is the process of matching an operation on an object to a specific method. This would seem to require a search up the inheritance tree at run time to find the class that implements the operation for a given object. Most languages, however, optimize the look-up mechanism to make it more efficient. As long as the class structure remains unchanged during program execution, the correct method for every operation can be stored locally in the subclass. With this technique, known as *method caching*, dynamic binding can be reduced to a single hash table look-up and performed in constant time regardless of the depth of the inheritance tree or the number of methods in the class. Clever compiler tricks can reduce even the size of the constant cost.

In a strongly-typed language, such as C++, the cost of run-time method resolution can be reduced to a single structure reference, almost insignificant compared to the cost of calling a procedure. Each class has a structure containing methods accessible by objects of the class. A pointer to each method is stored at a known location with the structure. A pointer to the method structure for the class is stored in each object. Run-time method resolution is performed by retrieving the method structure and indexing it by the known offset of the method. This technique cannot be used if new methods can be created at run time (because the structure cannot be precomputed) or if the name of a method can be constructed at run time (because the offset cannot be precomputed).

A language system can further optimize method resolution to use dynamic look-up only where it is needed. A large percentage of the method calls in a typical application can be statically bound by the compiler if it is provided with enough information. There are two ways the compiler can acquire this information. One way is for the programmer to declare which operations may be overridden, thus limiting dynamic binding to only those functions. The virtual functions of C++ and the generic functions of CLOS reflect this approach. The other approach is to provide a final optimization pass that analyzes the application as a whole, decides what methods are not overridden, and then recompiles the application, taking advantage of this information. This approach is adopted by the Eiffel language system. Note that the declaration of types for variables allows the compiler to be much more precise in its determination of which method calls can be optimized.

### 15.7.4  Strong Typing Versus Weak Typing

Object-oriented languages vary greatly in their approach to typing. The term *typing* refers to whether each variable and attribute value is merely known to be an object (*weak typing*) or may be declared more precisely as belonging to a particular class or one of its descendents (*strong typing*). The sample design in Figure 15.1 assumes strong typing. For example, the attribute *radius* is declared to be of type *Length*. Smalltalk is a weakly typed language—all variables in Smalltalk are objects of unspecified class. Eiffel, DSM, Objective-C, and C++ are strongly typed languages. CLOS and Objective-C support strong typing but do not require its use—a variable that references an object may optionally by declared, and the compiler will check usage of that variable. Hybrid languages, such as DSM, C++, and Objective-C, even permit an attribute to assume a value which is not an object but rather is an underlying C language type. Permitting nonobject values increases efficiency of common operations, such as arithmetic, at some cost in uniformity of reference.

Strong typing in a language serves two purposes. Strong typing provides active support to the programmer in detecting mismatched method arguments and assignment statements. Strong typing also increases opportunities for optimization. The compiler can detect when a general purpose operation can be replaced by a specific function call (see Section 15.7.3). No power is lost by the use of strong typing; the programmer can always declare everything to be of class *Object* to get the same effect as weak typing.

Although weak typing is flexible and powerful, it permits dangerous coding practices. Modern programming language theory has been evolving in the direction of strong type checking. Much of the advances in programming language theory have derived from restricting the programmer's ability to perform dangerous operations. Most new languages support strong typing. The premise behind strong typing is that it is easier to detect and correct software bugs at compile-time rather than at run-time. Strong typing improves the reliability of delivered software.

### 15.7.5  Memory Management

The freedom with which objects can be created and accessed causes a problem when memory space must be reclaimed. Most OO languages allocate memory from a heap rather than using fixed blocks of global memory or a stack. A dynamic memory allocation system can run out of memory unless objects that are no longer needed are deallocated. The principal problem lies in determining when an object is not needed or can no longer be accessed. The severity of the problem depends on the type of application and the memory architecture. Many programs that have access to a large amount of virtual memory can simply ignore the problem. On the other hand, a highly interactive application expected to run indefinitely must consider memory management no matter how large the available memory space.

There are two approaches to memory management: either it is done automatically by the run-time system of the language or it is done explicitly by deallocation statements written by the programmer. The preferred approach, automatic memory management, relieves the programmer of the responsibility of deciding when to deallocate memory and avoids the risk of dangling object references that explicit deallocation is vulnerable to. However, users are understandably dissatisfied with some garbage collection schemes that result in long pauses at unpredictable points during execution. Incremental garbage collection schemes avoid long delays but impose a higher average cost. Improved garbage collection algorithms offer some hope in this area.

CLOS and Smalltalk offer fully automatic garbage collection. C++ requires the programmer to deallocate unneeded objects, but the C++ language allows the programmer to define destructor functions, which are called automatically when a variable goes out of scope. This gives the programmer a convenient way of organizing and invoking explicit storage deallocation but is not a garbage collector. Dynamically-allocated objects must be explicitly deallocated by the *delete* operator. Explicit deallocation runs the dual risk of deallocating objects that are still referenced (leading to program crashes) and failing to deallocate objects that are inaccessible (leading to memory waste), but it does not impose any additional time or memory costs on the program.

### 15.7.6 Encapsulation

*Encapsulation* (also *information hiding*) consists of separating the *protocol,* the external aspects of an object that are accessible to other objects, from the internal implementation details of the object, which are hidden from other objects. Encapsulation prevents a program from becoming so interlaced that a small change has massive ripple effects. You can change the implementation of a class without affecting its clients. You may want to change the implementation of an object in order to improve performance, fix a bug, consolidate code, or port it to a different system. Encapsulation is not unique to object-oriented languages, but the ability to combine data structure and behavior in a single entity makes encapsulation cleaner and more powerful than in conventional languages that separate data structure and behavior. Languages differ greatly in the degree to which the class boundary is enforced.

One way that encapsulation can be violated occurs when code associated with one class directly accesses the attributes of another class. Direct access makes assumptions about the storage format and location of the data. These implementation details should be hidden within a class. For example, an attribute value may actually be computed from other information. The proper way to access an attribute of another object is to "ask for it" by invoking an operation of the object, rather than simply "taking it." Many languages (such as Smalltalk) forbid direct access to the attributes of another object or (as in C++ and Trellis-Owl) permit attributes to be declared either public or private. Eiffel provides perhaps the finest control of encapsulation through its *export* statement, which lists attributes that may be read and operations that may be executed. The C++ *friend* declaration allows limited loosening of encapsulation for access by specified classes or functions.

Encapsulation can be violated through careless use of inheritance. A subclass inherits the attributes of its superclass, but if the methods of the subclass directly access superclass attributes, the encapsulation of the superclass is defeated. CLOS, Owl, Eiffel, and C++ permit a class to restrict its visibility from its subclasses. There are arguments in favor of allowing a class to access its superclasses, but the cost is tight binding between the classes.

Often it is useful to write some "private" operations that are for internal use only by other methods of the same class. It is desirable to restrict the visibility of these operations so that other classes cannot use them. It is often necessary to allow subclasses to access these internal operations, so a simple distinction between public and private is not possible. Some languages permit a third level of access to subclasses (such as the C++ *protected* declaration).

A more complete discussion of encapsulation is found in [Micallef-88].

### 15.7.7 Packaging

The class is not an adequate structuring construct for large systems. Most OO languages lack partitioning mechanisms for controlling visibility between classes. We have suggested the use of modules containing classes as a structuring mechanism during analysis.

A related problem is that object-oriented languages typically require that the names of classes must be unique. Often this is not the case when two or more applications that were developed independently are combined. For example, two designers working independently might define different versions of a class called *Symbol* with different operations and semantics. The problem is similar to name clashes in block-structured languages.

In the Ada language and in CLOS, the *package* construct provides the means to structure a system into separate components with their own name-spaces. In Ada, names declared in the specification of a package are not visible outside the package unless explicitly requested, allowing control of both the name-space and inter-package dependencies. Entities that are known by one name outside the package can be renamed within. Packages may be nested, allowing an entire subsystem to be encapsulated within a well-defined interface.

Object-oriented languages would benefit by the addition of packaging capability. In particular, the ability to nest the packaging components of a system allows better control of visibility.

### 15.7.8 Development Environment

The tools that are available for browsing and editing source code, compilation, debugging, system integration, and testing have a big effect on your productivity. Support tools are especially important in object-oriented languages because of the difficulty of managing inherited and dynamically-bound features in a large system.

A *browser* allows you to explore the source code in a structured way, asking what classes are present and what operations are defined for each class. The Smalltalk-80 browser, described in [Goldberg-84], is the most prominent example.

The *compiler* or *interpreter* is the most important implementation tool. Whether the language is interpreted, compiled, or translated affects the speed with which you can make small changes and test their effect. An interpreter allows more flexible debugging. Interpreted systems such as Smalltalk and Lisp allow an executing program to be stopped, edited to correct a bug, and resumed. Objective-C offers an optional interpreter in addition to the compiler.

Some compilers translate an object-oriented language to an intermediate language (such as C) which is then compiled. The C++ language was first implemented by translation into C, but true compilers are now available. Translation may pose problems for *symbolic debuggers* because they do not understand the original object-oriented code. In evaluating the debugger, find out whether it shows you the original object-oriented source code or the intermediate code (which may be hard to read). The debugger should be able to inspect attribute values and evaluate object-oriented expressions.

Tools for *system-building* and *change control* are essential for large projects but are also valuable for individual programmers. Consider whether the proposed language provides them or integrates smoothly with existing tools. System rebuilding can consume much time if a simple change in one module requires that client modules must be recompiled as well. Try to determine what kinds of change trigger recompilation of clients. Experience has shown that the use of conventional building tools, such as UNIX *make*, are too crude for many purposes. Finer-grained development environments are needed but are only recently available.

### 15.7.9 Metadata

METADATA (discussed in Chapter 4) is data about data. METADATA that is present at run-time allows an application to reason about, and possibly even change, its own structure and capabilities, including the operations an object supports, the attributes it possesses, or the types of attributes. There are also more conventional uses of metadata, such as writing a generic procedure that prints or saves any object using the attribute names and types.

Languages containing explicit class descriptor objects (such as Smalltalk and DSM) contain run-time metadata about classes. A class object acts as a template for the creation of new instances. The class may also contain descriptions of the attributes and operations, such as name, type, or arguments. For example, a *Complex number* class might define *real part* and *imaginary part* attributes each of which is represented as a 32-bit floating point number.

Of course, the designer of the system knows the metadata, so in principle this data could be embedded in the code. But if the design changes (say, by adding a new attribute to a class) then all the code that depends on embedded data will become invalid. The use of metadata at run-time rather than at compile-time allows the construction of extensible systems with generic procedures and abstract classes that are reusable in unforeseen applications. META-DATA also can be used to support data persistence or by programming support tools such as debuggers, browsers, and inspectors.

### 15.7.10  Parameterized Classes

Parameterized classes, or generics [Meyer-86], allow a parameterized template to be written that can then be applied in several cases that differ only in the types of the parameters. For example, a generic *List* class can be instantiated as a *list of points* or a *list of integers*. The generic *add-element* method on the list implicitly depends on the type of element. Local variables within the method have generic type that depends on the instance. Parameterized classes are present in the Ada language and in Eiffel. Parameterized templates have been proposed for C++ [Stroustrup-88].

### 15.7.11  Assertions and Constraints

Assertions and constraints improve the odds that the behavior of a class matches the expectations of its clients. We can do this informally by writing a natural language description of the desired behavior, but how can we be sure that the description will be understood in the same way (or even read) by another programmer who wants to use the class?

Usually there are a few critical assumptions about the behavior of a class, operation, or method that can be expressed mathematically. These assumptions take the form of *assertions* that must be true at particular points during execution (such as preconditions and postconditions), and *constraints* that must be maintained, or *invariants* that must always be true.

Chapter 8 showed how to use assertions and constraints as part of the functional model. Assertions should also be written into the software in a form that can be optionally compiled and automatically checked at run-time. While this technique can be used in many languages (such as the *assert* macro available in many C implementations), it is particularly well-supported in the Eiffel language [Meyer-88].

Constraints can be more than simply conditions to be tested. They can be viewed as a way of expressing declaratively what might otherwise have to be written as procedural code. A language system could understand constraints that are declared and insure that they remain true by taking action at run-time to maintain the constraints. The Prolog logic programming language has such capabilities. It would not be surprising to see such constraint maintenance systems become widely available under object-oriented languages.

### 15.7.12  Data Persistence

All computer programs operate on data. If you require data that persists beyond the lifetime of a single program execution, then you will need to use a permanent data store. There are various reasons for wanting persistent data:

- Persistent data may provide the easiest mechanism for passing data from one program to another.

- Persistent data allows the same program to resume processing at a later date.

- Data stores are often useful for historical or archival purposes.

There are several approaches to providing persistent data services: files, special purpose hardware devices, databases, and intrinsic language support. Some new object-oriented databases are especially convenient in their data storage services. To a large extent, such an advanced object-oriented database looks like an object-oriented language, except that the orthogonal property of persistence may be specified for data structures. The advantages and disadvantages of object-oriented databases, relative to conventional databases, are discussed in Section 15.8.5.

## 15.8 SURVEY OF OBJECT-ORIENTED LANGUAGES

Having considered various language characteristics, we now examine how they have been combined in several commercially available object-oriented languages: Smalltalk, C++, Eiffel, CLOS, and database programming languages.

### 15.8.1 Smalltalk

Smalltalk was the first popular object-oriented language, developed at Xerox PARC, and its success engendered many other object-oriented languages. Smalltalk is not only a language but also a development environment incorporating some functions of an operating system. For single-user development, it offers arguably the best features of both language and environment. Smalltalk falls short in areas where it was not intended to be used—in multiple person projects and in its weak or unspecified ability to interface with external software or hardware devices. Smalltalk elegantly articulates the goals of extensibility and reusability.

All aspects of the Smalltalk language system are available through an on-line interpreter and class browser. The language syntax is simple. Variables and attributes are untyped. Everything is an object, including classes. Classes can be added, extended, tested, and debugged interactively. A garbage collector frees the programmer of the burden of memory management.

What does Smalltalk provide the implementor? Perhaps the most important contribution is the highly interactive development environment, which avoids the edit-compile-link cycle delays of the traditional compiler-based language. The Smalltalk environment permits rapid development of programs. Another strength is the class library, which was designed to be extended and adapted by adding subclasses to meet the needs of the application. Because Smalltalk is an untyped language, library components can be combined to rapidly prototype an application.

The Model/View/Controller (MVC) architecture for user interface design is another important contribution of Smalltalk. A user interface is divided into an underlying application-defined model, any number of different views of the model, and controllers that synchronize changes to the model and the views. MVC makes it possible to concentrate on the essentials of an application (the Model) and add the user-interface (the Views and Controllers) independently. The class library provides standard versions of each of these components, which can be subclassed and extended incrementally. There can be many different view/controller pairs for each model, and the views and controllers can be modified extensively with little or no change in the model. However, the MVC is a complex system that is not easy to learn.

Smalltalk is a pure object-oriented system with extensive metadata available and modifiable at run-time. Implementation of the language as an interpreter, tightly integrated with other parts of the its self-contained environment, gives ideal support for rapid incremental development and debugging.

### 15.8.2 C++

C++ is a hybrid language, in which some entities are objects and some are not. C++ is an extension of the C language, implemented not only to add object-oriented capabilities but also to redress some of the weaknesses of the C language. Many added features are orthogonal to object-oriented programming, such as inline expansion of subroutines, overloading of functions, and function prototypes. Because of its origin as an extension of C, its backing by major computer vendors, the perception of it as a nonproprietary language, and the availability of free compilers, C++ seems likely to become the dominant object-oriented language for general use.

C++ is a strongly-typed language developed by Bjarne Stroustrup at AT&T Bell Laboratories. It was originally implemented as a preprocessor that translates C++ into standard C. As a preprocessor, C++ introduced problems for symbolic debuggers, but direct compilers are now available, and symbolic debuggers that support objects with inheritance and dynamic binding are now available. Commercial vendors offer C++ implementations for a variety of operating systems. A C++ compiler with debugger and library are available for no charge from the Free Software Foundation (with restrictions on commercial use).

Unlike several other OO languages, C++ does not contain a standard class library as part of its environment, although the standard AT&T release includes libraries for I/O, coroutine tasking, and complex arithmetic. Class libraries have been implemented by various developers, including a class library developed by the USA National Institutes of Health (NIH), which is achieving wide usage [Gorlen-90]. Class libraries for object-oriented windowing systems include Interviews [Vlissides-88] and ET++ [Weinand-88]. Unfortunately, because C++ provides no guidelines for library organization, different libraries may be incompatible. The emergence of a consensus in favor of a standard foundation class library would be an important asset to C++.

C++ contains facilities for inheritance and run-time method resolution, but a C++ data structure is not automatically object-oriented. Method resolution and the ability to override an operation in a subclass are only available if the operation is declared *virtual* in the superclass. Thus, the need to override a method must be anticipated and written into the origin class definition. Unfortunately, the writer of a class may not expect the need to define specialized subclasses or may not know what operations will have to be redefined by a subclass. This means that the superclass often must be modified when a subclass is defined and places a serious restriction on the ability to reuse library classes by creating subclasses, especially if source code for the library is not available. (Of course, you could declare *all* operations as *virtual*, at a slight cost in memory and function-calling overhead.)

The implementation of run-time method resolution is efficient. For each class, a predefined *struct* is initialized with pointers to each method available to the class. Each object contains a pointer to the method structure for its class. At run-time, a virtual operation is resolved by retrieving the method structure from the object and selecting a member to find the method address. C++ does not support run-time class descriptor objects other than the method pointer structure. C++ 2.0 supports multiple inheritance.

C++ contains good facilities for specifying access to attributes and operations of a class. Access may be permitted by methods of any class (*public*), restricted to methods of subclasses of the class (*protected*), or restricted to direct methods of the class (*private*). In addition, "spot" access can be given to a particular class or function using the *friend* declaration.

As with C, the declaration syntax of C++ is awkward and its grammar is difficult to parse. C++ supports overloaded operators: several methods that share the same name but whose arguments vary in number or type. C++ supports several memory allocation strategies for objects—statically allocated by the compiler, stack-based, and allocated at run-time from a heap. The programmer must avoid mixing objects of different memory types or dangling references may cause run-time failures. Each class can have several *constructor* and *conversion* functions, which initialize new objects and convert between types for assignment and argument passing; these are semantically sound but perhaps somewhat confusing for normal use.

In summary, C++ is a complex, malleable language characterized by a concern for the early detection of errors, various implementation choices, and run-time efficiency at the expense of some design flexibility and simplicity.

### 15.8.3 Eiffel

Eiffel is a strongly typed object-oriented language written by Bertrand Meyer. Programs consist of collections of class declarations that include methods. Multiple inheritance, parameterized classes (*generics*), memory management, and assertions are supported. A modest class library is provided, including lists, trees, stacks, queues, files, strings, hash tables, and binary trees. For portability, the Eiffel compiler translates source programs into C. Eiffel has good software engineering facilities for encapsulation, access control, renaming, and scope. Eiffel is arguably the best commercial OO language in terms of its technical capabilities.

The focal point of Eiffel is the class declaration, which lists attributes and operations. Eiffel provides uniform access to both attributes and operations by abstracting them into a single concept called a feature. An Eiffel class declaration may include a list of exported features, a list of ancestor classes, and a list of feature declarations. Eiffel does not treat either classes or associations as first class objects.

Eiffel supports memory management through a coroutine which detects objects that are no longer referenced and releases the memory allocated to them. The Eiffel run-time system executes the coroutine whenever the available memory space is low. Several mechanisms are provided to control memory management. Automatic execution of the coroutine may be suppressed through a compiler switch or turned on or off at run-time. For operating systems that do not support virtual memory, there is a compiler switch to arrange for Eiffel's run-time system to provide automatic paging.

A contractual model of programming is supported by preconditions, postconditions, invariants, and exceptions. A *precondition* is a condition that the caller of an operation agrees to satisfy. A *postcondition* is one the operation itself agrees to achieve. An *invariant* is a condition that a class must satisfy at all stable times. Conditions and invariants are a part of the class declaration and must also be obeyed by all descendent classes. If they are violated at run-time, an exception occurs, which either causes the faulty operation to fail or executes an exception handler for the class if the programmer provides one. Compiler switches provide several levels of error checking. Once an application is debugged you can turn off assertion checking.

## 15.8.4 CLOS

The Common Lisp Object System (CLOS) is an object-oriented extension of Common Lisp which will soon become an official part of the Lisp language. It resulted from the work of a Lisp standardization group working on the X3J13 ANSII standard. This group studied the many existing object-oriented extensions of Lisp (such as Flavors and CommonLoops), but rather than selecting one of them as a standard, the group decided to formulate a new language based on language features that had proven successful. Because CLOS can be implemented in Common Lisp, it permits experimentation on new concepts to continue, while providing a common standard.

Although it was originally implemented in a hybrid fashion, CLOS is so well integrated with the traditional features of Common Lisp that it has most of the advantages of a "pure" object-oriented language. This is because every data object, including the atoms and lists of Lisp, is a member of a class. Methods for Lisp primitives belong to an inheritance structure. As a result, there is no practical distinction between Lisp primitives and objects.

The programming environment of Common Lisp and CLOS is an interpreter which also allows code to be compiled into a form that is more efficiently executed. Debugging facilities under Common Lisp depend on the specific implementation but are generally excellent. Commercial offerings of Common Lisp with CLOS should be expected to provide completely object-oriented debugger support.

CLOS currently does not have a standard class library. Organizations that use CLOS are currently collecting their own reusable classes, and there is some sharing of classes between organizations. Commercial vendors will undoubtedly provide extension classes such as window packages. One point in favor of CLOS is that the Common Lisp types already present form a common root for whatever new classes are added, so separately developed class libraries are more likely to be consistent.

CLOS provides powerful and flexible inheritance capabilities. Multiple inheritance is supported, and CLOS has rules for resolving the ambiguity resulting from inherited features with the same name.

Polymorphic operations requiring dynamic method resolution can be implemented as generic methods. All arguments to a generic method are explicit; there is no special variable like *self* in Smalltalk. Unlike most object-oriented languages, CLOS uses multiple arguments to resolve methods, allowing the direct implementation of operations that exhibit "multiple polymorphism" in which the specific method for an operation depends on more than one of its arguments (for example, binary arithmetic operations).

CLOS provides a rich collection of metadata that can be accessed and updated at runtime. New classes can be defined, and methods can be added to classes dynamically. These features are a standard part of the language, documented as the "meta-object protocol." Unlike most languages, Lisp-based languages permit new procedures to be constructed at run time out of source statements of other procedures.

Like Common Lisp, CLOS is a weakly-typed language. Native types are provided, and classes behave like types, but there is no requirement to declare the type of a variable, and there is no checking to insure that the use of an object is consistent with its declaration. While achieving maximal design flexibility, weak typing can affect performance and ease of debugging. The optional declarations could be used by the compiler to optimize access, but this optimization depends on the specific implementation.

The concept of encapsulation is not enforced by the CLOS language system. Programmers are encouraged to define and document the public interface of each class and to use only the advertised features of other classes, but there is nothing to prevent the code of one class from directly accessing the implementation details of another class. This lack of enforcement is consistent with Lisp's general policy of providing maximum flexibility and room for experimentation.

### 15.8.5 OO Database Programming Languages

An OO-DBMS unites two technologies: data base management and object-oriented programming. Object-oriented programming languages (OOPL) are expressive but lack data persistence (data that outlasts the execution of a single job). Conventional DBMSs have data persistence but lack expressibility. OO-DBMSs try to provide both data persistence and expressibility. An OO-DBMS must handle large programs that operate on large data stores.

For conventional applications that combine programs with DBMS access, the developer uses a procedural technique, such as hierarchical functional decomposition or data flow diagrams, to design the overall application. A technique such as Entity-Relationship (see Chapter 12) may then be used to design the database. The database design may be converted to SQL code which is embedded in a language such as C, Pascal, or Cobol.

To say the least, the above scenario is unattractive. The fundamental problem is twofold. First, different paradigms are used to design various parts of the system. Second, the implementation vehicles mismatch. This book targets the design problem by uniformly applying object-oriented models to systems, programming code, and databases. OO-DBMS research is striving to remedy the implementation side by providing one software system that has the richness of programming languages and the practical features of DBMSs.

In general there are two types of database queries: set-oriented and navigational. Relational DBMSs are intended to perform parallel operations on large sets of data. In contrast, OO programming languages are efficient at quickly navigating from one object to another by traversing pointers. A relational DBMS performs navigation by using joins, which are several orders of magnitude slower than pointer traversal. An OO-DBMS must efficiently perform both types of queries. One important feature of an OO-DBMS is the implicit assumption that the system is oriented towards operations on individual objects and the programmer can expect these to perform well. This is notable mainly because the relational model typically performs badly for single-object operations and navigation between objects [Cattell-86, Maier-86].

The first generation of OO-DBMSs were early products and did not provide the robustness and "industrial strength" users have come to expect of conventional DBMSs. The performance of these systems was disappointing for large applications. GemStone, which is marketed by Servio Logic, is a commercially marketed OO-DBMS. The GemStone language is similar to Smalltalk. The GemStone database has procedural interfaces to C and Pascal. GemStone uses an optimistic concurrency scheme and server-client model and supports single inheritance [Maier-86]. Another early OO-DBMS is ONTOS, marked by Ontologic Corporation. ONTOS has an object-oriented structure accessible by SQL queries and C++ program statements.

ORION is an OO database language prototype by MCC which is written in common LISP. ORION's syntax is similar to Flavors and LOOPS. ORION supports multiple inheritance, versioning, and concurrency with an IBM-like locking protocol. ORION supports set-oriented queries with a relational DBMS flavor. ORION permits some dynamic changes to the database schema. [Kim-88]

Second generation OO-DBMSs are under development by start-up companies whose principals have previous experience developing both object-oriented languages and commercial-quality relational database management systems. There is reasonable hope that one or more of these companies will succeed in producing a second-generation OO-DBMS that can compete effectively with commercial relational DBMSs.

### 15.8.6 Comparison of Object-Oriented Languages

Figure 15.2 summarizes the discussion of object-oriented languages contained in this section and in the previous section. As with any comparison table of this type, there will always be inaccuracies due to changes in the languages and differences between implementations. Nevertheless, we include this table because we think the benefits of comparing languages at a glance outweighs the shortcomings.

### 15.9 CHAPTER SUMMARY

This chapter shows how an object-oriented language can be used to implement a design developed using the OMT methodology. Practical advice has been given concerning the implementation of various design constructs and the selection of a language.

In the first part of the chapter we concentrated on language features that are common to most object-oriented languages, using C++, Eiffel, and Smalltalk as examples. Classes in the object model are implemented by declaring classes with the attributes and associations required. Implementation of inheritance is also accomplished by a simple declaration in OO

| | C++ 2.0 | Smalltalk 80 | CLOS | Eiffel | Objective C |
|---|---|---|---|---|---|
| Integration of classes with primitive types | hybrid | pure | integrated | integrated | hybrid |
| Strong type checking | Y | N | N | Y | Y |
| Ability to restrict access to attributes: | | | | | |
|    Control of access from clients | Y | Y | N | Y | Y |
|    Control of access from subclasses | Y | N | N | Y | N |
| Standard class library | N | Y | N | Y | Y |
| Parameterized classes | F | — | — | Y | N |
| Multiple inheritance | Y | N | Y | Y | N |
| Scoping of class names (packages) | N | N | Y | N | N |
| Messaging model: | | | | | |
|    Single target object | Y | Y | N | Y | Y |
|    Dynamic binding on multiple args | N | N | Y | N | N |
| Method combination features: | | | | | |
|    SUPER concept | N | Y | Y | Y | Y |
|    Before & after methods | N | N | Y | N | N |
| Assertions and constraints | N | N | N | Y | N |
| Metadata at run-time | N | Y | Y | N | Y |
| Garbage collection | N | Y | Y | Y | N |
| Efficiency: | | | | | |
|    Static binding when possible | Y | N | N | Y | Y |

Key to table entries:
   Y   = Yes, the feature is present.
   N   = No, the feature is not present in common current implementations.
   F   = Planned in a future release
   —   = Not Applicable: Parameterized classes are not needed in languages with weak typing.

**Figure 15.2** Comparison of commercially available object-oriented languages

languages. Associations are implemented either by using object references (pointers) or by defining a new collection class (*Association*) to serve as a template for creating specific associations in the design.

When writing methods to implement operations, object-oriented programming differs in a few respects from conventional languages. In most current OO languages, the target object is passed to the method as an implicit argument, available within the method under a special identifier (*self*, *this*, or *Current*). Other arguments should be passed as references to objects. Objects can be explicitly allocated or destroyed using special operations provided by the language.

The second part of the chapter discusses some important features which are not common to all OO languages. These features include multiple inheritance, a class library, efficiency of implementation, strong typing, automatic memory management, enforcement of encapsulation, packaging constructs, development environment, metadata accessible at run-time, parameterized classes, assertions and constraints, and persistent objects.

The final part of the chapter is a brief survey of OO languages, including OO database systems. Smalltalk is an interpreted language with weak type checking and garbage collection that is noted for its development environment and extensive class library. Such a language is ideal for rapid development of prototypes but does not support large team efforts well. The C++ language is a hybrid language based heavily on C but with improved type checking and extensions to support OO programming. Efficiency is obtained at the cost of some design flexibility. Eiffel is a strongly-typed language that provides many advanced features such as multiple inheritance, generic classes, automatic memory management, and assertion checking. CLOS is an integrated OO extension to Common Lisp. It provides powerful inheritance capabilities, rich metadata accessible at runtime, and an unusual but very flexible means of defining polymorphic operations. In the rapidly evolving area of OO database systems, the first generation products have been successful in providing basic OO structure accessible from both a query language and a program interface but do not quite meet industrial performance and robustness requirements. Research OO-DBMS have provided more sophisticated features, and a second generation of commercial systems is on the way.

| | |
|---|---|
| assertion | object-oriented database |
| class library | object-oriented language |
| container class | packages (name-space control) |
| encapsulation | parameterized class |
| implementation of associations | persistence of data |
| memory management | programming environment |
| meta-information | self-reference |
| method resolution | strong typing |

**Figure 15.3** Key concepts for Chapter 15

## BIBLIOGRAPHIC NOTES

A survey of various approaches to object-oriented language characteristics may be found in [Stefik-86]. A good comparison of specific languages is found in [Micallef-88]. The [Wegner-87] paper constructs a general design space of language characteristics within which existing languages may be classified and new research directions sought.

Descriptions of specific languages may be found in [Stroustrup-84] for C++, [Keene-89] for CLOS, [Cox-86] for Objective-C, [Meyer-88] for Eiffel, [Goldberg-83] for Smalltalk-80, [Schaffert-86] for Trellis-Owl, and [Shah-89] for DSM.

Despite his focus on Eiffel, [Meyer-88] provides a good general coverage of issues in strongly typed object-oriented languages. The same can be said of [Cox-86] for general coverage of languages with weakly typed object systems. Good descriptions of the general purpose objects in a class library as an important supplement to the language itself may be found in [Goldberg-83] and [Gorlen-90].

Specific treatment of unresolved issues in object-oriented languages may be found in the following sources: [Snyder-86] draws attention to the way that some views of inheritance violate encapsulation, [Stein-87] compares delegation and inheritance as means of sharing behavior, and [Meyer-86] contrasts genericity and inheritance.

## REFERENCES

[Cattell-86] R.G.G. Cattell, T.R. Rogers. Combining object-oriented and relational models of data. *1986 International Workshop on Object-Oriented Database Systems*, Pacific Grove, Calif., Sept. 1986.

[Cox-86] Brad Cox. *Object-Oriented Programming: An Evolutionary Approach*. Reading, Mass.: Addison-Wesley, 1986.

[Goldberg-83] Adele Goldberg, David Robson. *Smalltalk-80: The Language and its Implementation*. Reading, Mass: Addison-Wesley, 1983.

[Goldberg-84] Adele Goldberg. *Smalltalk-80: The Interactive Programming Environment*. Reading, Mass.: Addison-Wesley, 1984.

[Gorlen-90] Keith Gorlen, Sanfor Orlow, Perry Plexico. *Data Abstraction and Object-Oriented Programming in C++*. Chichester, England: John Wiley & Sons Ltd., 1990.

[Keene-89] Sonya Keene. *Object-Oriented Programming in Common Lisp: A Programmer's Guide to CLOS*. Reading, Mass.: Addison-Wesley, 1989.

[Kim-88a] Won Kim, Frederick H. Lochovsky. *Object-Oriented Concepts, Databases, and Applications*. New York: ACM Press, 1988.

[Kim-88b] Won Kim, Nat Ballou, Hong-Tai Chou, Jorge F. Garza, Jay Banerjee. Integrating an object-oriented programming system with a database system. *OOPSLA'88* as *ACM SIGPLAN 23*, 11 (Nov. 1988), 142-152.

[Lippman-89] Stanley B. Lippman. *A C++ Primer*. Reading, Mass.: Addison-Wesley, 1989.

[Liskov-87] Barbara Liskov, Alan Snyder, Russell Atkinson, Craig Schaffert. Abstraction mechanisms in CLU. *Communications of the ACM 20*, 8 (August 1977), 564-576.

[Maier-86] David Maier, Jacob Stein, Allen Otis, Alan Purdy. Development of an object-oriented DBMS. *OOPSLA'86* as *ACM SIGPLAN 21*, 11 (Nov. 1986), 472-482.

[Meyer-86] Bertrand Meyer. Genericity versus inheritance. *OOPSLA'86* as *ACM SIGPLAN 21*, 11 (Nov. 1986), 391-405.

[Meyer-88] Bertrand Meyer. *Object-Oriented Software Construction*. Hertfordshire, England: Prentice Hall International, 1988.

[Micallef-88] Josephine Micallef. Encapsulation, Reusability and extensibility in object-oriented languages. *Journal of Object-Oriented Programming 1*, 1 (April/May 1988), 12-38.

[Schaffert-86] Craig Schaffert, Topher Cooper, Bruce Bullis, Mike Kilian, Carrie Wilpolt. An introduction to Trellis-Owl.*OOPSLA'86* as *ACM SIGPLAN 21*, 11 (Nov. 1986), 9-16.

[Shah-89] Ashwin Shah, James Rumbaugh, Jung Hamel, Renee Borsari. DSM: an object-relationship modeling language. *OOPSLA'89* as *ACM SIGPLAN 24*, 11 (Nov. 1989), 191-202.

[Snyder-86] Alan Snyder. Encapsulation and inheritance in object-oriented programming languages. *OOPSLA'86* as *ACM SIGPLAN 21*, 11 (Nov. 1986), 38-45.

[Stefik-86] Mark Stefik, Daniel G. Bobrow. Object-oriented programming: themes and variations. *The AI Magazine 6*, 4 (1986), 40-62.

[Stein-87] Lynn Andrea Stein. Delegation is inheritance. *OOPSLA'87* as *ACM SIGPLAN 22,* 12 (Dec. 1987), 138-147.

[Stroustrup-84] Bjarne Stroustrup. *The C++ Programming Language.* Reading, Mass.: Addison-Wesley, 1986.

[Stroustrup-88] Bjarne Stroustrup. Parameterized types for C++. USENIX *C++ Conference.* Denver, Colo., October 17-21, 1988.

[Vlissides-88] John M. Vlissides, Mark A. Linton. Applying object-oriented design to structured graphics. *Proceedings of the 1988 USENIX C++ Conference,* Oct. 1988, 81-94.

[Weinand-88] André Weinand, Erich Gamma, Rudolf Marty. ET++—an object-oriented application framework in C++. *OOPSLA'88* as *ACM SIGPLAN 23,* 11 (Nov. 1988), 46-57.

[Wegner-87] Peter Wegner. Dimensions of object-based language design. *OOPSLA'87* as *ACM SIGPLAN 22,* 12 (Dec. 1987), 168-182.

## EXERCISES

**15.1**   (4) Write class declarations for the object diagram in Figure E15.1 in any language that does not directly support multiple inheritance. The application is a simulator that computes the performance of electrical machines.

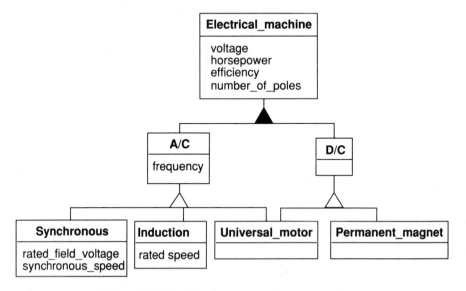

**Figure E15.1** Partial taxonomy for electrical machines

**15.2** (6) Write code, including class declarations and methods, to implement the following using pointers in any object-oriented language:

    a. One-to-one association which is traversed in both directions.

    b. One-to-many association which is traversed in the direction from one to many. The association is considered unordered.

    c. One-to-many association which is traversed in the direction from one to many. The association is considered ordered.

    d. Many-to-many association which is traversed in both directions. The association is considered ordered in one direction, and unordered in the other direction.

**15.3** (4) Describe some situations in which strong typing would help you. Describe some circumstances in which strong typing would cause problems.

**15.4** (8) Many object-oriented languages have libraries which support the creation and manipulation of container classes such as *Symbol, Set, Array, Dictionary,* and *Association.*

    A *Symbol* is a string object that enables you to determine if two strings match by simply checking for equality of the object IDs. The first time a symbol with a given string value is created, a new object ID is allocated. All subsequent attempts to create a symbol with the same string value will return the previously assigned ID.

    A *Set* is an unordered collection of unique values. Duplicate values are automatically discarded from a set. Values can be added, deleted, and tested.

    An *Array* is an ordered, dynamic, collection of values, indexed by nonnegative integer selector values. The number of elements is variable. Elements can be added or deleted at the end, beginning, or at any point in the middle. An insertion or deletion in the middle causes the positions of subsequent elements to change.

    A *Dictionary* is a many-to-one mapping function whose domain and range are objects, including possibly other container objects.

    An *Association* is a two-way mapping that can be composed from two dictionaries.

    Write pseudocode to construct the following from container classes. List any operations that you assume are defined on the container classes, and explain what they do.

    a. A *Sorted_dictionary*. Each entry in the dictionary maps a name to an object. Entries are sorted by name. Needed operations include *insert(name, object)*, which adds an entry to the dictionary; *delete(name)*, which deletes an entry; *find(name)*, which returns the *object* associated with *name*; *find_first()*, which returns the first object in the dictionary; *find_last()*, which returns the last; *find_previous(object)*, which returns the object just previous to *object*; and *find_next_object(object)*, which returns the object which follows *object.* Also needed is an initialization operation which creates a new, empty dictionary. The operation *insert(name, object)* replaces an entry in the dictionary if *name* is already in the dictionary.

    b. A *Polygon.* A *Polygon* is a two dimensional object whose x-y coordinates are stored as instances of the class *Point.* Needed operations on the class *Polygon* include *delete()*, which deletes a polygon, and *get_points()*, which returns an array of points which belong to a polygon. Needed operations on the class *Point* include *delete()*, which removes it from its polygon; *append(polygon)*, which adds it to a polygon; and *get_polygon()*, which returns the polygon to which it belongs. Also needed is an initialization operation to create a new polygon from an ordered list of points. Assume that a *Point* belongs to one *Polygon* rather than being shared. If two polygons share a common coordinate, two *Point*s are made with the same coordinates.

c. An *Index*. An *Index* is similar to a *Dictionary,* except the mapping is to a set instead of individual objects. An index might be used, for example, to determine all automobiles that were manufactured in a given year. Needed operations include *add(object_selector, object_target)*, which adds a target object to the set associated with the selector; *delete(object_selector, object_target)*, which deletes a target from the set associated with the selector; and *find(object_selector)*, which returns a set of objects which are indexed by *object_selector*. Unlike the *insert* operation in part (a), the *add* operation does not replace existing data but adds to it.

**15.5** (5) Describe how you would use tools included in software development environments such as browsers, compilers, interpreters, symbolic debuggers, system builders and change control systems to help solve the following problems:

a. You are using an unfamiliar subroutine in a subsystem library. There is not much documentation, so you would like to quickly find out how it works by experimenting with it.

b. Your program seems to have a bug in it which makes no sense to you as you glare at your source code for one of the program modules. Now you are not sure that the program that you just run was built from the source code that you are looking at. It is possible that you forgot to recompile this module before you ran the linker.

c. The program you are developing quits with a memory fault error. The line at which it fails is different each time you run the program, depending on the data. The problem is repeatable with the same data.

d. You are the leader of a team working on a large software project. You want to make sure that only one person works on a file at a time. The latest version of all modules must be accessible to the group as a whole, but individual users might want private copies for debugging purposes.

e. There are too many steps involved in building the application for you to execute all of them each time you make a change. Furthermore, you have trouble simply remembering all these steps, let alone trying to figure out which ones need to be redone as the result of your latest revision.

f. You have written your own preprocessor. The debugger you are using displays the output of the preprocessor, and you have trouble tracing errors back to the original source code.

**15.6** (7) Describe strategies for dealing with the following memory management problems, assuming that automatic garbage collection is not feasible. Your answer should be in the form of guidelines that a programmer could use during coding.

a. *A system for text manipulation.* A common operation is the creation of one large text segment in contiguous memory from an array of several smaller segments. The system is expected to handle a lot of text, and you cannot afford to waste memory. You cannot set an upper bound on either the text length or the array size. The following operations are convenient building blocks which you must provide if they are not available as library routines: Determine the size of a text segment, allocate a segment of memory of a given size, deallocate a previously allocated memory segment, copy text from one memory segment to another, and combine two text segments placing the result in a previously allocated segment of memory. Write pseudocode for a method that combines text, recovering memory space that is no longer used.

b. *A multi pass compiler.* Objects are created dynamically. Each pass examines the objects created on the previous pass and produces objects to be used on the next pass. The computer system on which the compiler will run has a practically unlimited virtual address space and an operating system with a good swapping algorithm. The routines in the run-time library for allocating and deallocating memory dynamically are inefficient. Discuss the relative merits of two alternatives: (1) Forget about garbage collection all together and let the operating system allocate a large amount of virtual memory. (2) Carefully deallocate memory when objects are no longer referenced.

c. *Banking software or an air traffic control system that runs for a long time.* You have the same computer system and run-time library as described in exercise 15.6(b). Discuss the relative merits of the two approaches.

d. *A subroutine which may create and return an object that uses a large block of memory.* The only operations allowed on the object class are implemented by other subroutines which you are going to write. You do not wish to leave garbage lying around. Discuss the relative merits of the following two approaches: (1) Each time the subroutine is called it destroys the object created the last time it was called, if any. (2) Each time the subroutine is called, it may create a new object. It is up to the calling routine to destroy the object when it is no longer needed by calling a routine that you will write. Consider both situations when the routine that calls your routine is recursive and when it is not.

**15.7** (4) Express the following as a constraint that is to be enforced in an application which handles points and polygons: Points are associated with polygons. Every point belongs to exactly one polygon. You do not want a polygon to be linked to a point that has been deleted.

**15.8** (7) Describe the attributes and methods of the generic class *Binary_tree* that will support the construction of unbalanced binary trees from any class whose instances can be ordered. A *compare* method must be provided for each class that is included. *Compare* compares two instances of a class, returning *less than*, *equal to*, or *greater than*, depending on the order. Operations on the class *Binary_tree* include *insert(object)* which inserts an object into a tree, *delete(object)* which deletes an object from a tree, *print()* which prints all objects in the tree in order, and *test(-object)* which determines if a given object is in a tree. Assume that a *print* method is available for all classes from which trees are constructed. Descriptions of attributes should include data types and whether the attribute is private or public. Descriptions of methods should include data types of arguments and returned values as well as assertions and constraints.

**15.9** (7) Write code in any object-oriented language to implement the generic class *Binary_tree* described in exercise 15.8. Test it on the following two classes: *Person* and *Page*. *Person* is ordered by *name* and *Page* is order by *page number*. You will need to write a *compare* method and a *print* method for each class. Make up a few attributes for each class.

**15.10** (3) Write code in any object-oriented language to shuffle a deck of cards and to deal 4 hands of 13 cards from the deck. Be sure to create new instances of the classes *Card, Deck* and *Hand* from Figure E15.2. The relationship between *Collection_of_cards* and *Card* preserves the order in which cards are placed into collection which is not necessarily according to *suit* and *rank*.

**15.11** (3) Using any object-oriented language, implement the aggregation between *Card* and *Collection_of_cards* in Figure E15.2 so that the order in which *Card*s are added to a *Collection_of_cards* is preserved and so that the aggregation can be traversed in both directions.

**15.12** (4) Write code in any object-oriented language to implement the *sort* operation on the class *Hand* shown in Figure E15.2. Sort the cards in each suit according to rank in descending order: ace, king, queen, jack, ten down to deuce. Suits should be arranged in a hand in the order: spades, hearts, clubs, and diamonds. There are no arguments to the operation.

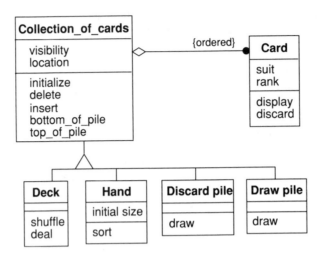

**Figure E15.2** Object diagram for a card-playing program

**15.13** (4) Implement the *insert* operation in Figure E15.2 with any object-oriented language. There is one argument, *card*, to the operation which inserts the card into the *Collection_of_cards*. A card is inserted at the top of a *Deck, Hand, Discard pile*, or *Draw_pile*.

You may wish to refer to exercise 8.5 for background for exercises 15.14-15.16.

**15.14** (4) Using an object-oriented language, implement all associations involving the classes *Box, Link, Line_segment,* or *Point* in Figure E15.3. Note that the editor allows links only between pairs of boxes.

**15.15** (5) Implement the *cut* operation on the class *Box* in Figure E15.3 using any object-oriented language. Propagate the operation from boxes to attached link objects. Update any associations that are involved. Be sure to recover any memory that is released by the operation. You may assume another routine will update the display.

**15.16** (5) Implement a routine using any object-oriented language that will create a logical link between two boxes. (See Figure E15.3.) Inputs to the routine are two boxes and a list of points. The routine should update associations and create object instances as needed. You may assume another routine will update the display.

**15.17** (8) Using any object oriented language, implement the following queries on Figure E15.3:
   a. Given a box, determine all other boxes that are directly linked to it.
   b. Given a box, find all other boxes that are directly or indirectly linked to it.
   c. Given a box and a link, determine if the link involves the box.
   d. Given a box and a link, find the other box logically connected to the given box through the other end of the link.
   e. Given two boxes, determine all links between them.
   f. Given a selection and a sheet, determine which links connect a selected box to a deselected box.

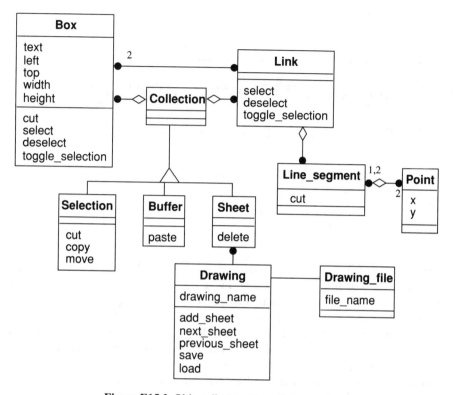

**Figure E15.3** Object diagram for a diagram editor

g. Given two boxes and a link, produce an ordered set of points. The first point is where the link connects to the first box, the last point is where the link connects to the second box and intermediate points trace the link.

**15.18** (Project) Write a program for simulating evolution, as described in the Computer Recreations column in the May 1989 issue of *Scientific American*, using any object oriented language.

# 16

---

# Non-Object-Oriented Languages

The analysis and design techniques introduced in this book can be implemented using non-object-oriented languages as well as object-oriented languages. In this chapter, we discuss techniques for mapping concepts into non-object-oriented languages. We present a general discussion of the issues and possible solutions and then show how to apply them to C, Ada, and Fortran in particular. Where appropriate, the chapter describes the shortcomings of each language that restrict the application of some principles. Many other languages, such as Pascal, face essentially the same problems as C and Ada.

Adhering to the object-oriented paradigm requires discipline and a non-object-oriented language offers no indications when you start to go astray. Nevertheless, if you must use a non-object-oriented language, you will benefit from object-oriented analysis and design, even if you lack some capabilities in the implementation language.

After reading this chapter, you will understand how to map an object-oriented design into a non-object-oriented programming language.

## 16.1 MAPPING OBJECT-ORIENTED CONCEPTS

Implementing an object-oriented design in a non-object-oriented language requires basically the same steps as implementing a design in an object-oriented language [Section 15.1]. The programmer using a non-object-oriented language must map object-oriented concepts into the target language, whereas the compiler for an object-oriented language performs such a mapping automatically. The steps required to implement a design are:

- Translate classes into data structures [16.2]
- Pass arguments to methods [16.3]
- Allocate storage for objects [16.4]
- Implement inheritance in data structures [16.5]

- Implement method resolution [16.6]

- Implement associations [16.7]

- Deal with concurrency [16.8]

- Encapsulate internal details of classes [16.9]

### 16.1.1 Graphics Editor Example

See Section 15.1.1 and Figure 15.1 for a description of a portion of an object model for a graphics editor, which will be used as an example throughout the chapter. This is the same example that was used to explain object-oriented language code in Chapter 15.

### 16.1.2 Implementation in C

The language C, with its loose type checking, provides the flexibility that allows several important object-oriented concepts to be implemented. The C pointer mechanism and run-time memory allocation also assist the implementation. It is fairly simple to implement classes, instances, single inheritance, and run-time method resolution in C with little loss of efficiency. (In fact, this is exactly the approach taken by several object-oriented languages which generate C code as output: Objective C, Eiffel, DSM, and C++.)

### 16.1.3 Implementation in Ada

Ada supports data abstraction and discrete objects but does not support inheritance. Therefore it cannot be considered object-oriented. The main obstacles to a straightforward mapping come from Ada's rigid typing system and lack of procedure pointers. From a practical point of view, though, an object-oriented design constructed using the OMT methodology can be implemented in Ada, although somewhat less easily than in C. Ada offers excellent encapsulation facilities that make possible development of large systems.

### 16.1.4 Implementation in Fortran

The lack of modern data structuring constructs and dynamic memory allocation makes Fortran difficult, if not impossible, to use for applications requiring complex nonnumeric data structures. On the other hand, Fortran is still widely used for numeric applications, and its provision for complex numbers and multidimensional arrays are unmatched in most "modern" programming languages. Object-oriented analysis and design can be used profitably, but you eventually have to translate data structures into arrays, the only data structuring mechanism in Fortran. The Fortran programmer must manually translate many constructs that would be supported directly by C or Ada.

If your application requires many numerical computations, including matrices and complex numbers, then Fortran does have advantages over most other languages. However, you may consider coding the numerical computations in Fortran and coding the other parts—set up, symbolic manipulation, data network traversal, user interaction—in another language.

The Fortran programs can be considered computational utilities and the non-Fortran programs can manage the overall system.

### 16.1.5 Other Languages

Pascal is much like Ada in its limitations. It has strong type-checking that is rigid, and it lacks function pointer variables.

Lisp, on the other hand, is such a malleable language that almost anything is possible. The implementation suggestions for C could easily be implemented in Lisp. On the other hand, many Lisp programmers will have access to an object-oriented Lisp, such as CLOS or Flavors, so there is less need to provide LISP workarounds.

## 16.2 TRANSLATING CLASSES INTO DATA STRUCTURES

Normally you will implement each class as a single contiguous block of attributes—a record structure. Each attribute in a class becomes an element in the record. Each attribute has a declared type, which can be a primitive type, such as *integer, real,* or *character,* or can be a structured value, such as an embedded record structure or a fixed-length array.

An object has state and identity and is subject to side effects. A variable that identifies an object must therefore be implemented as a sharable reference and not simply by copying the values of an object's attributes. A reference can be implemented as a memory address or an array index but in any case must permit the sharing (aliasing) of a single object in memory from multiple possible references.

### 16.2.1 Translating Classes into C Struct Declarations

Each class in the design becomes a C *struct.* Each attribute defined in the class becomes a field of the C *struct.* The structure for the *Window* class is declared as:

```
struct Window
{
    Length xmin;
    Length ymin;
    Length xmax;
    Length ymax;
};
```

*Length* is a C type (not a class) defined with a C *typedef* statement to provide greater modularity in the definition of values:

```
typedef float Length;
```

In C, an object reference can be represented by a pointer to its object record:

```
struct Window * window;
Length x1 = window->xmin;
```

An object can be allocated statically, automatically (on the stack), or dynamically (on the heap) because C can compose a pointer to any object, including one embedded within another structure.

### 16.2.2 Translating Classes into Ada Record Definitions

The Ada code for a class is similar to the C code. Ada uses a *record* type:

```
type Length is new FLOAT;
type WindowRecord is record
    xmin: Length;
    ymin: Length;
    xmax: Length;
    ymax: Length;
end record;
```

In Ada, an object reference, or pointer, can be represented by an *access type*:

```
type Window is access WindowRecord;
```

We use Ada access types to represent object references when the number of objects of a given class is unbounded. In this case, the object records are allocated at run time using the Ada *new* allocator, as shown below:

```
aWindow: Window := new WindowRecord;
```

Access types are needed for dynamic allocation and for associations between objects. The use of access types and dynamic allocation can be omitted when an object value is embedded within another object and does not have a distinct identity. In any case, the components within the record represent object attributes, and are accessed as follows:

```
x1: Length := aWindow.xmin;
```

### 16.2.3 Translating Classes into Fortran Arrays

Fortran has no user-defined data structure except the array, so the programmer must simulate records. A class is represented as an implicit group of arrays, one for each attribute in the class. The arrays all have the same dimension, which must be large enough to accommodate all the objects of the class that will exist at any time, since Fortran does not support dynamic memory allocation. The index into the arrays represents an object ID *within the given class*. Object IDs for different classes overlap, so you must know the class of a variable in the program (or determine it as explained later under inheritance). The arrays for a single class can be organized into a common block. For example, the storage for windows in the previous example would look like:

```
COMMON /WINDOW/ XMIN, YMIN, XMAX, YMAX, NWINDOW
REAL XMIN(1000), YMIN(1000), XMAX(1000), YMAX(1000)
INTEGER NWINDOW
```

The programmer must maintain a counter of the number of objects of a given class that have been allocated (NWINDOW) so that new object IDs can be assigned.

Fortran has no way to define new types, so you cannot define *Length* symbolically, but must expand it in terms of primitive data types (such as *REAL, COMPLEX, INTEGER, LOGICAL*, and *CHARACTER*).

Standard Fortran restricts the length of identifiers but many Fortran compilers allow identifier names of 32 or more characters. In our examples, we assume that long names including underscores are allowed. If your compiler requires short names, you must map meaningful names to abbreviations yourself at a considerable cost in readability.

In Fortran, an object can be represented by its index into the attribute arrays for its class. Attributes are accessed by indexing the corresponding array. The program must know the class of the object:

```
INTEGER AWINDOW
REAL X1
X1 = XMIN(AWINDOW)
```

## 16.3 PASSING ARGUMENTS TO METHODS

Every method has at least one argument, the implicit *self* argument. In a non-object-oriented language, the argument must be made explicit, of course. Methods may also have additional objects as arguments. Some of the arguments may be simple data values and not objects. In passing an object as an argument to a method, a reference to the object must be passed if the value of the object can be updated within the method. If the method is a query that simply extracts information from an object without modifying it, then a call-by-value mechanism can be used if the language permits. Passing all arguments as references is more uniform, however.

We advise a consistent naming convention for method function names. One that we have found useful in C is to concatenate the class name, two underscores, and the operation name. (The two underscores separate the class name from the operation name, each of which may contain single underscores.) Standard Fortran is overly restrictive on names, but many compilers permit long names and the use of underscores. Ada names may not contain double underscores and they are case-insensitive, but names can be as long as desired. Ada variable and argument names must differ from type names.

### 16.3.1 Passing Arguments in C

In C, an object should always be passed by pointer. Although C permits structures to be passed by value, passing a pointer to an object structure is usually more efficient and provides a uniform access mechanism for both query and update operations.

```
Window__add_to_selections (self, shape)
    struct Window * self;
    struct Shape * shape;
```

### 16.3.2 Passing Arguments in Ada

In Ada, an object can be passed as an access type:

```
type Window is access WindowRecord;
procedure Window_add_to_selections (self: Window;
                    aShape: Shape);
```

The object access parameter, *self,* is (by default) an *in* parameter because its value will not be changed in the method. If the value of a variable will be updated within the method, it must be passed as an *in out* parameter. Note, however, that the access type (or pointer) referencing an object will not be modified within the method, even though the record-object that it points to may be. An access type permits modification of the attributes of the referenced object.

Access to the same object concurrently from different tasks is likely to cause inconsistencies. If concurrent access to an object is possible, objects should be encapsulated entirely within a task and accessed only from within that task. This will serialize concurrent access, guaranteeing that each operation is completed before the next one is begun. In Section 9.3 we discussed how to identify inherently concurrent tasks in a system.

### 16.3.3 Passing Arguments in Fortran

In Fortran, an object can be passed as an index into the arrays for its class:

```
SUBROUTINE WINDOW__ADD_TO_SELECTIONS (SELF, SHAPE)
INTEGER SELF, SHAPE
```

An object whose contents will be queried but not updated can be passed as a list of attribute values if desired, although the index is usually shorter and therefore more convenient:

```
FUNCTION CIRCLE__PICK (X0, Y0, RADIUS, X, Y)
LOGICAL CIRCLE__PICK
REAL X0, Y0, RADIUS, X, Y
```

## 16.4 ALLOCATING OBJECTS

Objects can be allocated statically (at compile time), dynamically (from a heap), or on a stack. Statically allocated objects are implemented as global variables allocated by the compiler. Their lifetime is the duration of the program. They can be useful for system-level objects or constants, but it is poor object-oriented practice to use too many global variables because they defeat modularity.

Most temporary and intermediate objects will be implemented as stack-based variables (such as C *automatic* variables or Pascal *local* variables). The advantage of stack-based variables is that they are automatically allocated and deallocated. The programmer must ensure that no references to a stack-based object remain after the declaring block has been exited. Stack-based variables are not suitable for general objects whose lifetime outlasts the procedure that created them. Using such techniques can lead to subtle bugs which are hard to find.

Dynamically allocated objects are needed when the number of them is not known at compile time. A general object can be implemented as a data structure allocated on request at run time from a heap (a block of global storage managed by the storage allocator). Storage for dynamically allocated objects is requested explicitly by a special operator: *malloc* in C, *new* in Pascal or Ada, *make* in CommonLisp. Once allocated, dynamic objects persist until they are explicitly deallocated, so pointers to them can be stored in other objects. Knowing when to deallocate an object is not always simple, but this problem is shared with many object-oriented languages as well. Some languages, such as Lisp, provide garbage collection, which removes the burden of deallocation from the programmer and avoids the danger of dangling pointers.

### 16.4.1  Allocating Objects in C

Global objects can be declared as top-level *struct* variables. They can be initialized at compile time:

```
struct Window outer_window = {0.0, 0.0, 8.5, 11.0};
```

When calling a method, the address of the variable (&outer_window) must be passed.

Most objects should be allocated dynamically using *malloc* or *calloc*:

```
struct Window * create_window (xmin, ymin, width, height)
    Length xmin, ymin, width, height;
{
    struct Window * window;
    window= (struct Window *)malloc (sizeof (struct Window));
    window->xmin = xmin;
    window->ymin = ymin;
    window->xmax = xmin + width;
    window->ymax = ymin + height;
    return window;
}
```

When an object is no longer needed, it must be deallocated using the C *free* function. Make sure that there are no pointers to it before deallocating it. Also be sure to free any component objects that are pointed to by its instance variables.

Temporary and intermediate objects can be allocated as ordinary C *automatic* variables within a function body or block. When calling a method, the address of the variable must be passed. Stack-based variables cannot be used when their lifetime outlasts the function that created them.

### 16.4.2  Allocating Objects in Ada

Global objects can be allocated as constant access types and optionally initialized:

```
main_window: constant Window :=
                new WindowRecord'( 0.0, 0.0, 8.5, 11.0 );
```

Most objects will be allocated dynamically using *new*. Higher-level functions can be written that allocate a new object and initialize some of its attributes:

```
function create_window (xmin, ymin, width, height: Length)
    return Window is
begin
    return new WindowRecord'(xmin, ymin,
                xmin+width, ymin+height);
end;
```

An Ada compiler may provide garbage collection to recover allocated storage that can no longer be referenced. In most cases, however, you must explicitly deallocate access types, just as with C, using the generic function *UNCHECKED_DEALLOCATION*.

### 16.4.3 Allocating Objects in Fortran

As a programmer you must explicitly allocate new objects from predefined arrays. Programming a dynamic application would be much harder in Fortran than in C or Ada because you must implement the allocation mechanism yourself (by simulating a heap):

```
FUNCTION CREATE_WINDOW (X1, Y1, WIDTH, HEIGHT)
COMMON /WINDOW/ XMIN, YMIN, XMAX, YMAX, NWINDOW
REAL XMIN(1000), YMIN(1000), XMAX(1000), YMAX(1000)
INTEGER NWINDOW
INTEGER CREATE_WINDOW
REAL X1, Y1, X2, Y2
NWINDOW = NWINDOW + 1
XMIN(NWINDOW) = X1
YMIN(NWINDOW) = Y1
XMAX(NWINDOW) = X1 + WIDTH
YMAX(NWINDOW) = Y1 + HEIGHT
CREATE_WINDOW = NWINDOW
RETURN
END
```

### 16.5 IMPLEMENTING INHERITANCE

There are several ways to implement data structures for inheritance in a non-object-oriented language:

- *Avoid it.* Many applications do not require inheritance. Many other applications have only a few classes requiring inheritance. Those classes not needing inheritance can be implemented as simple records. [Booch-86] describes how to do object-oriented designs in this manner for Ada.

- *Flatten the class hierarchy.* Use inheritance during design but expand each concrete class as an independent data structure during implementation. Each inherited operation must be reimplemented as a separate method on each concrete class. Flattening the hierarchy introduces duplication, but the use of language constructs such as Ada generics or C macros can help. One useful technique is to group some inherited attributes into a record type and embed the record in each concrete class to reduce the number of duplicated lines in each declaration.

- *Break out separate objects.* Instead of inheriting common attributes from a superclass, a group of attributes can be pulled out of all the subclasses and implemented as a separate object with a reference to it stored within each subclass. Grouping attributes under a separate type permits a single method to be written to manipulate them. The subclasses must delegate operations to the referenced object.

These approaches avoid the implementation of inheritance. When inheritance is actually needed, the best implementation depends on the language and the application, as explained below.

### 16.5.1 Implementing Inheritance in C

To handle single inheritance, embed the declaration for the superclass as the first part of each subclass declaration. The first field of each *struct* is a pointer to a class descriptor object shared by all direct instances of a class. The class descriptor object is a *struct* containing the class attributes, including the name of the class (optional) and the methods for the class. Its format will be discussed later.

The class *Shape* is an abstract class, with concrete subclasses *Box* and *Circle*. The C declarations for classes *Shape, Box,* and *Circle* are as follows:

```
struct Shape
{
    struct ShapeClass * class;
    Length x;
    Length y;
};
struct Box
{
    struct BoxClass * class;
    Length x;
    Length y;
    Length width;
    Length height;
};
struct Circle
{
    struct CircleClass * class;
    Length x;
    Length y;
    Length radius;
};
```

A pointer to a *Box* or *Circle* structure can be passed to a C function expecting a pointer to a *Shape* structure because the first part of the *Box* or *Circle* structure is identical to the *Shape* structure. (To be strictly correct, you should *cast* such an argument to be a pointer to *Shape*, but most compilers won't notice the difference anyway.) Because the prefix of the structure is the same as the superclass structure, the superclass method simply ignores the extra fields on the end. For example, a pointer to *Box* is interpreted as a pointer to *Shape* in the following call:

```
struct Box * box;
struct Window * window;
Window__add_to_selections (window, box)
```

The first field of each structure is a pointer to the class descriptor for the actual class of each object instance. This field is needed only if run-time method resolution is to be done. Its form and use are described in Section 16.6.1.

Multiple inheritance cannot be implemented using this approach because a subclass with two superclasses cannot align its attributes with both of them. The best approach is to eliminate multiple inheritance using the workarounds discussed in Chapter 4.

### 16.5.2 Implementing Inheritance in Ada

Ada's *variant records* can be used to implement inheritance (single inheritance only). A variant record is a record structure with several alternatives. Each record contains a *discriminant*, which is a component to distinguish the alternate forms of the record. Declare a variant record for the root of each class hierarchy, with one variant for each subclass. The attributes in the superclass are common to all the variants. Multiple levels of variant nesting correspond to multiple levels of subclasses. A single method can operate on all variants of a single root class because they are all the same Ada type.

The root classes must be chosen carefully because it is usually inefficient to make everything a variant of class *object*. This approach works well when the hierarchy is shallow. The advantage of variant records is that no trickery is needed to use them, and all access is syntactically and semantically correct:

```
type ItemClass is (GroupClass, BoxClass, CircleClass);
subtype ShapeClass is ItemClass range BoxClass..CircleClass;
type ItemRecord (class: ItemClass) is record
    case class is
        when GroupClass => null;
        when ShapeClass =>
            x: Length;
            y: Length;
            case class is
                when BoxClass =>
                    width: Length;
                    height: Length;
                when CircleClass =>
                    radius: Length;
                when others => null;
            end case;
    end case;
end record;
type Item is access ItemRecord;
subtype Group is Item;
subtype Shape is Item;
subtype Box is Item;
subtype Circle is Item;
```

The record type above represents the inheritance tree from Figure 15.1 consisting of the classes *Item*, *Shape*, *Box*, and *Circle*. When an object is allocated from this record type, it is *constrained* to be a specific variant, representing exactly one of the four classes. The dynamic allocator of a good Ada compiler will allocate only the space required by the attributes of that class of object. The following code creates an object of the *Group* class:

```
item_group: Group := new ItemRecord (GroupClass);
```

### 16.5.3 Implementing Inheritance in Fortran

Fortran has no user-defined records, therefore variant records are not possible. One approach is to implement a given class hierarchy as a *universal record*. A universal record contains an attribute for every attribute found in any descendent class. Those attributes that do not apply in a particular case are simply ignored. This approach wastes storage but may be considered if the variant part of the record is small.

```
COMMON /SHAPE/X,Y,WIDTH,HEIGHT,RADIUS,NSHAPE
REAL X(1000),Y(1000),WIDTH(1000),HEIGHT(1000)
REAL RADIUS(1000)
INTEGER NSHAPE
```

A less wasteful approach, the Fortran equivalent of the variant record, is to separate a class into subclasses, each implemented as a separate class with its own arrays and object indexes. The original class is represented by a pair of integer arrays: One array stores a code for the subclass and the other stores the index of the object within its corresponding subclass array. The programmer must first assign an integer code to each class in the system. In this example we define class *Item* as either a *Shape* (1000 maximum) or a *Group* (100 maximum). Common block *CLASSES* defines the integer code for each class.

```
COMMON /ITEM/ ITEM_CLASS, ITEM_ID, NITEM
INTEGER ITEM_CLASS(1100), ITEM_ID(1100)
INTEGER NITEM/0/
COMMON /CLASSES/ GROUP, BOX, CIRCLE
INTEGER GROUP/1/, BOX/2/, CIRCLE/3/
```

When a new object is created, an index value must be allocated from the superclass as well as the subclass. For example, the following code creates a new circle:

```
FUNCTION CREATE_CIRCLE (X0, Y0, RADIUS0)
common blocks for ITEM, SHAPE, and CLASSES go here
INTEGER CREATE_CIRCLE
NSHAPE = NSHAPE + 1
X(NSHAPE) = X0
Y(NSHAPE) = Y0
RADIUS(NSHAPE) = RADIUS0
NITEM = NITEM + 1
ITEM_CLASS(NITEM) = CIRCLE
ITEM_ID(NITEM) = NSHAPE
CREATE_CIRCLE = NITEM
END
```

This same technique of representing an object in a generic situation by a pair of values, one indicating the class and the other indicating a class-specific ID, can be used by Ada, Pascal, and other languages.

## 16.6 IMPLEMENTING METHOD RESOLUTION

In an object-oriented language, a single operation may be implemented by many methods (polymorphism), depending on the run-time class of the object. Run-time method resolution is one of the main features of an object-oriented language that is lacking in a non-object-oriented language. Method resolution can be handled in several ways:

• *Avoid it.* If each operation is defined only once in the class hierarchy and not overridden, then there is no polymorphism and no need for run-time method resolution. Methods can still be inherited; all subclasses share the methods of a superclass, but they cannot override them. This advice is not as outrageous as it may seem. Casual overriding of operations to change their behavior is semantically questionable because a subclass should not modify the meaning of an inherited operation (Section 4.3.1).

• *Resolve methods at compile time.* If the class of each object is known at compile time, then the correct method can be determined and called directly, avoiding the need for run-time method resolution. It is sufficient to know that the object class is a descendent of the lowest class that overrides the method. In many applications, the classes of most objects are known at compile time. Of course, if the class hierarchy is changed or a new method is defined, then the programmer must manually reevaluate the method resolution and substitute a new function call.

• *Resolve methods at run time.* If you have a collection of objects of mixed classes to which you need to apply an abstract operation, then dynamic method resolution is required. You must test the class of the object to determine the correct method. An object-oriented language automatically makes this test. The C language supports an elegant and efficient technique of performing methods resolution using a predefined structure containing method pointers. Other languages, such as Ada and Fortran, do not support method pointers, so you must use *case* statements within a single dispatch method.

### 16.6.1 Method Resolution in C

Any methods that you can resolve at compile time can be implemented as straight C function calls. Many operations are implemented only once as methods and never overridden, so they do not need run-time method resolution. For example, all methods of *Window* are unique. The most general approach, however, is to define a class descriptor object for each class containing a pointer to the method function for each operation visible from the class, including inherited operations. Each class descriptor is a C *struct* containing all the operations defined in the class or inherited from a superclass. Each class descriptor contains inherited operations from its superclass as its first part, just as the *struct* for an object instance contains inherited attributes. The following code shows the declaration for the class descriptors for

*Item*, *Shape*, *Box*, and *Circle*. We append the word *Class* to the class name in declaring the *struct* for the class descriptor.

```
struct ItemClass
{
    char * class_name;
    void (* cut)  ();
    void (* move) ();
    Boolean (* pick) ();
    void (* ungroup) ();
};

struct ShapeClass
{
    char * class_name;
    void (* cut)  ();
    void (* move) ();
    Boolean (* pick) ();
    void (* ungroup) ();
    void (* write) ();
};

struct BoxClass
{
    char * class_name;
    void (* cut)  ();
    void (* move) ();
    Boolean (* pick) ();
    void (* ungroup) ();
    void (* write) ();
};

struct CircleClass
{
    char * class_name;
    void (* cut)  ();
    void (* move) ();
    Boolean (* pick) ();
    void (* ungroup) ();
    void (* write) ();
};
```

The class descriptor *struct* defines the names of the operations visible to a class, but you still have to define and initialize a class descriptor object for each class. Each descriptor object is a global variable, the single instance of its class descriptor *struct*. (We use the same name for the class descriptor object as the C *struct* because they belong to separate C name spaces and cannot be confused.) You must initialize each field of the class descriptor object with the name of the C method function defined or inherited by the class. You can determine the correct method by examining the object model. For example, class *Box* inherits operation *move* from class *Shape* but overrides operations *pick* and *write* with its own methods:

```
struct BoxClass BoxClass =
{
    "Box",
    Shape__cut,
    Shape__move,
    Box__pick,
    Shape__ungroup,
    Box__write
};
struct CircleClass CircleClass =
{
    "Circle",
    Shape__cut,
    Shape__move,
    Circle__pick,
    Shape__ungroup,
    Circle__write
};
```

If a class has class attributes, they can also be stored in the class descriptor as additional fields. For example, we store the name of each class in the class descriptor object for use during debugging, printing, or other uses.

Note that class descriptor objects are needed only for concrete classes and are unnecessary for abstract classes, such as *Shape*. The only use of the class descriptor objects is to store the methods and class variables available to objects. When a new object instance is created, the address of its class descriptor object is stored as the *class* field in the object record. The information about the class of an object, including its name, class attributes, and methods, can be obtained at run time from the objects's *class* field.

We omitted operations *draw* and *erase* from the class descriptor. These operations are implemented as methods only in the *Shape* class; they call the *write* operation with either the foreground or background color. Because they are not overridden, they can be implemented as direct function calls. Of course, we can include them in the class descriptor for uniformity and future extensions.

The *class* field of each object must be initialized with a pointer to the class descriptor:

```
struct Circle * create_circle (x0, y0, radius0)
    Length x0, y0, radius0;
{
    struct Circle * new_circle;
    new_circle =
            (struct Circle *) malloc (sizeof (struct Circle));
    new_circle->class = &CircleClass;
    new_circle->x = x0;
    new_circle->y = y0;
    new_circle->radius = radius0;
    return new_circle;
}
```

If an operation must be resolved at run time, the class descriptor object is used to determine the correct C function. The class descriptor object is obtained from the object and indexed by the name of the operation. For example, to call the *pick* operation on an unknown *Shape* requires the following code:

```
struct Shape *shape;
Length x, y;
Boolean status;
status = (*shape->class->pick) (shape, x, y);
```

Note that the target object must be included twice, once to find the method and once as the first argument of the method. Dynamic method resolution requires two more memory accesses and one more add than a direct function call. Compared to the overhead of calling an average function, the added cost is really insignificant.

### 16.6.2 Method Resolution in Ada

Ada permits overloading subprogram names based on the types of the subprogram arguments, but overloading must be resolved at compile time, and cannot be used for cases requiring run-time type discrimination. Ada has no procedure pointers, so a method table cannot be constructed. The best approach for dynamic method resolution in Ada is to define a "dispatch method" for each operation, a single procedure shared by all classes that is called whenever run-time method resolution on the operation is required. The dispatch method contains a *case* statement that tests the actual class of the object (represented by the discriminant of the variant record) and calls the corresponding implementation method directly. If you add a new subclass requiring a new method, you have to add it to the case statement in the dispatch method, but none of the client code that uses the operation need be modified. By using dynamic method resolution only when required, the number of dispatch methods can be reduced to a minimum.

The following code shows the implementation of the *move* operation by two specific methods followed by the more general dispatch method. We assume that the subclasses have been implemented as a variant record and declared as Ada subtypes:

```
procedure Shape_move (self: Shape; dx, dy: Length) is
begin
    self.x := self.x + dx;
    self.y := self.y + dy;
end;
procedure Group_move (self: Group; dx, dy: Length) is
    the_list: ItemList;
begin
    the_list := self.items;
    for i in 1..the_list.count loop
        move (the_list.values(i), dx, dy);
    end loop;
end;
```

```
procedure move (self: Item; dx, dy : Length) is
begin
    case self.class is
        when ShapeClass => Shape_move (self, dx, dy);
        when GroupClass => Group_move (self, dx, dy);
        when others => null;
    end case;
end;
```

The component named *items* in the *ItemRecord* implements the association between a group and its items, as described later in Section 16.7. The *ItemList* type is a dynamic array of items.

### 16.6.3 Method Resolution in Fortran

Methods for objects whose class is known at compile time can be resolved to direct procedure calls. The remaining objects must have class numbers stored in them (see the common block *CLASSES* in Section 16.5.3). A dispatch procedure can be written for each operation, with the class number and object index of each object as parameters. The dispatch procedure contains a computed goto or a conditional on each possible class value to call the correct method:

```
    FUNCTION PICK (CLASS, ID, PX, PY)
    LOGICAL PICK
    LOGICAL GROUP_PICK, BOX_PICK, CIRCLE_PICK
    INTEGER CLASS, ID
    GOTO (100, 200, 300) CLASS
    PICK = .FALSE.
    RETURN
100 PICK = GROUP_PICK (ID, PX, PY)
    RETURN
200 PICK = BOX_PICK (ID, PX, PY)
    RETURN
300 PICK = CIRCLE_PICK (ID, PX, PY)
    RETURN
    END
```

### 16.7 IMPLEMENTING ASSOCIATIONS

Implementing associations in a non-object-oriented language presents the same two possibilities as in an object-oriented language: mapping them into pointers or implementing them directly as association container objects. We have discussed these choices as part of object design in Section 10.7. To summarize their implementation:

• *Mapping associations to pointers*. The traditional approach to implementing binary associations is to map each role of an association into an object pointer stored as a field of the source object record. Each object contains a pointer to an associated object (if the multiplicity is "one" or "zero-one") or a pointer to a set of associated objects (if the multiplicity is greater than one). A set may be implemented using any appropriate available data structure—often a linked-list or array, but a hash table or binary tree may be used when the greater execution efficiency warrants the extra programming effort.

The association may be implemented in one direction or in both directions. If it is traversed in only a single direction, it may be implemented as a pointer from one object to another. If it is traversed in both directions, it must be implemented using pointers in both associated objects; the two pointers must be kept mutually consistent. It is best not to directly update the pointers within general application code but to write a utility procedure to add or delete links by updating both cross-linked pointers. You need not be so careful when accessing values from the association—the pointers can be accessed directly from either object—although there are maintenance advantages to hiding the implementation within an access procedure.

• *Implementing association objects.* An association can be implemented directly as a data structure. If an association relates more than two classes then it cannot be mapped into pointers, and a separate object must be used in any case. In its basic form (and its mathematical definition), an association is simply a set of records, each containing one object ID for each associated class. The simplest approach is to implement an association as an array or list of records or record pointers. To traverse a binary link, the list is searched to find a link in which one field is equal to the source object, and the value of the other field is returned as the target object.

The access of values from an unordered list is inefficient because the list must be linearly searched. A more efficient implementation is to sort the list on one or more key fields or to hash the elements on one or more key fields. Such a data structured is said to be *indexed* on the key fields. If the association is to be traversed or accessed from more than one direction, then multiple indexes must be built and maintained. Whenever an element is added, modified, or deleted, all the indexes must be updated accordingly. Depending on the relative numbers of updates and accesses in each direction of traversal, it is more efficient to either index the association on a single key (and search it linearly when an access occurs on a different key) or to index the association on multiple keys (and update several indexes when a link changes).

### 16.7.1 Implementing Associations in C

A binary association is usually implemented as a field in each associated object, containing a pointer to the related object or to an array of related objects. For example, the many-to-one association between *Item* and *Group* would be implemented as:

```
struct Item
{
    struct ItemClass * class;
    struct Group * group;
};
```

```
struct Group
{
    struct GroupClass * class;
    int item_count;
    struct Item ** items;
};
```

Other data structures, such as a linked list or a hash table, can also be used to store sets of objects. In this example, a group is created from a set of selected items. The memory for the *items* pointer can be allocated all at once, since the number of items in a group does not change. If it were possible to add a single new item to a group, then both pointers must be updated:

```
Group__add_item (self, item)
    struct Group * self;
    struct Item * item;
{
    item->group = self;
    self->items = (struct Item **) realloc (self->items,
            ++self->item_count * sizeof (struct Item *));
    self->items [self->item_count-1] = item;
}
```

You can build more sophisticated data structures to avoid calling *realloc* more than necessary. It is useful to have available a library of generic container objects, such as variable-length arrays, lists, and hash tables.

### 16.7.2 Implementing Associations in Ada

A binary association is normally implemented in Ada as mutual pointers between two objects. A pointer is implemented as an Ada *access* type. For example, the many-to-one association between *Item* and *Group* would be implemented by adding *group* and *items* to the fields of the *Item* type:

```
type ItemListRecord (capacity: Positive);
type ItemList is access ItemListRecord;

type ItemRecord (class: ItemClass) is record
    theGroup: Group := null;
    case class is
        when GroupClass =>
            items: ItemList := null;
        when ShapeClass =>
            -- [Code deleted: See Section 16.5.2]
    end case;
end record;

type ItemVector is array (Positive range <>) of Item;
```

```
type ItemListRecord (capacity: Positive) is record
    count: Natural := 0;
    values: ItemVector (1..capacity);
end record;
```

The type *ItemListRecord* is can be allocated with any initial size. The collection of items in a group can be expanded without bound if the ItemList is reallocated at a larger size when its capacity is outgrown.

The collection of related objects could instead can be stored as a linked list in which each item in the set contains a link to the next item in the set. In a linked list every object that may appear in a set must have an additional field to store the link to the next object in the set. The related object contains an access pointer to the first object in the list.

### 16.7.3 Implementing Associations in Fortran

The same approaches are possible in Fortran as in other languages. Represent an association by mutual pointers. An additional integer array is added to each class to hold the ID of an associated object. In the case of multiplicity "many," a set of related values is needed. Because Fortran does not have dynamic memory allocation, a linked list is usually the easiest way to represent a set of objects. To the common block *GROUP*, we add array *ITEMS* containing the index of the first item in the list of items related to the group object. To the common block *ITEM*, we add array *NEXT_IN_GROUP* to link together the items in one list of related items and also array *GROUP* containing the index of the related group. Null relationships are indicated by an index of zero.

```
COMMON /ITEM/ITEM_CLASS,ITEM_ID,NEXT_IN_GROUP,GROUP, NITEM
INTEGER ITEM_CLASS(1100),ITEM_ID(1100),NEXT_IN_GROUP(1100)
INTEGER GROUP(1100)
INTEGER NITEM/0/
COMMON /GROUP/ITEMS,NGROUP
INTEGER ITEMS(100),NGROUP
```

### 16.8 DEALING WITH CONCURRENCY

Most languages do not explicitly support concurrency. Even in the languages that support concurrency, such as Ada, the cost of a task is usually large compared to a statement or a procedure call, so it cannot be used freely. Although many algorithms could be implemented in parallel if suitable machines and languages were available, algorithms can generally be implemented sequentially with no loss of power and with less danger of programming errors. Concurrency is usually needed only when the external interactions force it, that is, when more than one external event can occur, and the behavior of the program depends on their timing.

Multiple tasks are required to implement true concurrency. Note that interrupts are logically equivalent to multiple tasks because the flow of control in the interrupt is independent of the flow of control in the main program. If an object is treated as a passive piece of data accessible to two or more tasks concurrently, then inconsistencies can occur because each task will have an incorrect picture of the state of the object. If, however, each object is "owned" by one task, then there is little danger of conflict in the use of data because an object cannot develop two concurrent threads of control. The use of shared data should therefore be avoided, and communication between separate tasks should occur through messages exchanged by tasks.

In a language lacking concurrent constructs, such as C or Pascal, there is no danger of violating these rules because the only way to create concurrency is to ask the operating system to create a parallel task. If the operating system supports interrupt routines, usually implemented by calling a procedure in the address space of the main program, then the interrupt procedure should not modify any objects accessible to the main program but should merely store its data in a reserved location, set a software flag, and allow the main program to come to a clean synchronization point for further processing.

In a language with tasking, such as Ada, there is danger of interference among concurrent tasks. The danger can be reduced by assigning each global variable to a single task and by allocating any dynamically created objects to a single task at a time. Communications among tasks should use the defined synchronization operations, such as the Ada entry call and *accept* statements.

There exist techniques, such as the use of semaphores, for sharing direct access to data among more than one task. These techniques are equivalent to simulating a task without actually creating one. They are less straightforward than the use of actual tasks and should be avoided in most cases.

## 16.9 ENCAPSULATION

Encapsulation of data representation and method implementation is one of the major themes of object-oriented programming. Object-oriented languages provide constructs to encapsulate implementation. Some of this encapsulation is lost when the programmer must manually translate object-oriented concepts into a non-object-oriented language, but you can still take advantage of the encapsulation facilities provided by the language.

### 16.9.1 Encapsulation in C

C has a reputation for encouraging loose programming style harmful to encapsulation. Nevertheless, you can take the following steps to improve encapsulation:

- Avoid the use of global variables.

- Package the methods for each class into a separate file. Only include the declarations for classes whose internal structure you need, such as ancestor classes of the current class. Do not access the fields of objects of different classes; call an access method instead.

- Treat objects of other classes as type "`void *`"; while technically illegal, most compilers treat all pointers the same (but watch out for word length or alignment problems on some machines).

### 16.9.2 Encapsulation in Ada

Ada provides strong enforcement of encapsulation by distinguishing between the external view of a package (the package specification) and the internal view of its implementation (the package body). The package specification and body may be compiled separately.

Private types provide further support for encapsulation. A type that is declared in the package specification is visible outside the package and is therefore said to be "exported" by the package. Ada provides mechanisms for declaring a *private* type whose implementation is hidden. External clients of a private type must access objects of that type only through operations defined by the package. The implementation of the type and its operations can be changed without impacting the clients.

A common style of Ada programming is to implement a class as a package that exports a private type. This kind of package is sometimes called a *type-manager* because it encapsulates the implementation of a type and operations that can be performed on it. Instances of the class can have attributes if the type is a record type. Operations on the class are implemented as subprograms that are visible in the package specification. Class variables can be implemented as variables declared in the context of the package specification or its body. Sometimes several classes are put in the same package to allow mutual visibility. The following code gives an example of this style of implementation, representing the *Item* class and its subclasses, *Shape*, *Box*, and *Circle* as private types exported by an Ada package.

```
package Item_pkg is
    type Length is new Float;
    type Item is private;
    subtype Shape is Item;
    subtype Box is Item;
    subtype Circle is Item;
    subtype Group is Item;

    function create_box (x, y, height, width: Length)
               return Box;
    function create_circle (x, y, radius: Length)
               return Circle;
    function create_group return Group;
    procedure add_item (self: Group; new_item: Item);
    procedure move (self: Item; dx, dy : Length);
    procedure draw (self: Item);
        -- [ Additional subprograms deleted ]
private
    type ItemClass is (GroupClass, BoxClass, CircleClass);
    subtype ShapeClass is ItemClass
               range BoxClass..CircleClass;
    type ItemRecord (class: ItemClass);
    type Item is access ItemRecord;
end Item_pkg;
```

The package specification above reveals only the external interface of the *Item* class and its subclasses. The declarations within the private section of the specification are hidden from external clients but are needed by the compiler in compiling external accesses. The implementation of these classes is hidden in the package body, which can be compiled separately:

```
package body Item_pkg is
    type ItemListRecord (capacity: Positive);
    type ItemList is access ItemListRecord;

    type ItemRecord (class: ItemClass) is record
        -- [ Code deleted: See Section 16.5.2 ]
    end record;
    type ItemVector is array (Positive range <>) of Item;
    type ItemListRecord (capacity: Positive) is record
        count: Natural := 0;
        values: ItemVector (1..capacity);
    end record;
        -- [ Subprogram bodies have been deleted ]
end Item_pkg;
```

Using the variant record implementation of inheritance requires that all subclasses of a given class be together in the same package because all subclasses are subtypes of the parent class. In Ada, strong type distinctions are not made between subtypes of a common base type. For purposes of type checking and overload resolution by the compiler they are viewed as the same base type.

### 16.9.3 Encapsulation in Fortran

The common blocks containing the storage of attributes for a class should be known only by methods on the class involved. Other classes should access an object only by its index value. All access to attributes of the class should be through an access procedure defined by the class. Because of the lack of pointers in Fortran, encapsulation is adequate. If a separate data manager is written in another language, encapsulation is even better because all objects in Fortran would be treated as encapsulated objects represented as coded integers.

### 16.10 WHAT YOU LOSE

Use of an object-oriented or non-object-oriented language is not a matter of functionality. By using the mappings described above, you can translate any object-oriented construct into a non-object-oriented language. Computational power is never an issue because any universal language can compute anything computable.

The real issue with languages is not power but expressiveness, convenience, protection from errors, and maintainability. An object-oriented language makes writing, maintaining, and extending programs easier and safer because it performs tasks that the non-object-oriented language programmer must perform manually. These include:

• *Expressiveness:* The non-object-oriented programmer must map object-oriented operations, such as method calling or subclass declaration, into explicit operations which are often ugly.

• *Convenience:* The programmer must manually traverse the class hierarchy when calling methods or passing arguments. If the class hierarchy changes, then the programmer must manually reevaluate the traversals.

• *Error protection:* The programmer must ensure that all methods are included in a dispatch method or dispatch structure. The programmer must initialize a new object with its class. The programmer must avoid accessing internal attributes of other classes.

• *Maintainability:* If changes are made to the object declarations, the programmer must determine their effects on the code and modify the code accordingly. An object-oriented language provides and enforces modularity of classes that prevents changes from propagating through the entire program. The non-object-oriented programmer requires discipline to achieve similar modularity without the help of the language.

Nevertheless, if you must use a non-object-oriented language, we feel that an object-oriented design will simplify your task and provide greater flexibility and extensibility if you are willing to program in a disciplined manner.

## 16.11 CHAPTER SUMMARY

Object-oriented designs can be implemented in conventional programming languages but require programming discipline. Classes can be implemented as records in any modern language. In Fortran, classes should usually be implemented as implicit collections of arrays. Method arguments should be address pointers or array indexes to permit shared access to an object by different access paths (aliasing). Objects should be allocated from a heap, if possible. In Fortran the programmer must preallocate storage for the maximum number of objects expected. Inheritance can be simulated easily in C by duplicating the structure of a superclass in a subclass and simply passing a subclass object to a superclass method. Inheritance can be implemented with greater difficulty using variant records in strongly-typed languages such as Ada and Pascal. Run-time method resolution is clean and efficient in C, using function pointers stored in a class descriptor object for each class. In Ada or Fortran, case statements within a single dispatch method must be used for run-time method resolution. In most applications, many operations can be resolved at compile time, and run-time method resolution can be reserved for special cases. Associations are usually implemented as pointers from one object to another. Sets of related objects can be implemented as arrays, linked lists, or other data structures. An association can also be implemented as a distinct object containing a set of paired values. Concurrency is handled by operating system calls in most languages except Ada, which contains explicit support for concurrent tasks. If concurrency exists, every object should be "owned" by a single task to prevent run-time conflicts. Ada contains excellent encapsulation facilities; other languages contain some facilities for encapsulation, but they rely upon the discipline of the programmer.

There is no support in non-object-oriented languages to generate object-oriented data structures and enforce proper use of the constructs. In particular, changes to code may force the programmer to manually retranslate the object-oriented constructs. Before deciding to accept these sacrifices, a design team should investigate using an object-oriented language such as C++ or Eiffel. A transition from C to C++ is not difficult for a programming team, yet offers object-oriented programming support. Nevertheless, if you must use a non-object-oriented language, use of object-oriented design will make your job easier. Any mappings that you must make are conceptual mappings that you must make in any case to use the language, and object-oriented notation makes them explicit.

| | |
|---|---|
| implementation of concurrency | implementation of classes |
| encapsulation | implementation of inheritance |
| implementation of associations | implementation of method resolution |

**Figure 16.1** Key concepts for Chapter 16

## BIBLIOGRAPHIC NOTES

Two workstation software libraries use C language object-based approaches to provide tools for creating window-based applications. SunView [Sun-86] uses attribute keywords and variable length argument lists to set and access the properties of windows, frames, panels, buttons, and sliders. The X Window toolkit intrinsics library [McCormack-88] allows software developers to use *widgets* that define the appearance and behavior of buttons, sliders, and menus. Attributes are called *resources*. An inheritance mechanism provides for the addition of new widgets by software developers.

Jacky [Jacky-86] describes a medical radiation therapy planning system implemented in Pascal. Objects are represented as Pascal *records*, using the fields in the record as attributes. A message passing mechanism in Pascal provides run-time procedure binding.

The Ada language is covered in [Barnes-89], which can serve either as a reference or as a tutorial manual for serious readers. For a concise description of graphical object-oriented design for Ada, see [Booch-86]. A good discussion of object-oriented programming in Ada is found in [Seidewitz-87], which includes treatment of the usefulness and limitations of generics. A taxonomy of general purpose data structures can be found in [Booch-87], showing Ada implementations that use generics. Before applying the Ada techniques, the reader is advised to obtain [AdaLRM], the official language reference manual.

## REFERENCES

[AdaLRM] ANSI/MIL-STD-1815A. *Military Standard--Ada Programming Language*, Ada Joint Program Office, U.S. Department of Defense.

[Barnes-89] John G. P. Barnes. *Programming in Ada, 3rd edition.* Reading, Mass.: Addison-Wesley, 1989.

[Booch-86] Grady Booch. Object-oriented development. *IEEE Transactions on Software Engineering*, March, 1986.

[Booch-87] Grady Booch. *Software Components with Ada.* Redwood City, Calif.: Benjamin/Cummings, 1987.

[Jacky-86] Jonathan Jacky, Ira Kalet. An object-oriented approach to a large scale scientific application. *OOPSLA'86* as *ACM SIGPLAN 21,* 11 (Nov. 1986) 368-376.

[McCormack-88] Joel McCormack, Paul Asente, Ralph R. Swick. *X Toolkit Intrinsics - C Language Interface.* MIT Project Athena, 1988.

[Seidewitz-87] Ed Seidewitz. Object-oriented programming in Smalltalk and Ada. *OOPSLA'87* as *ACM SIGPLAN 22,* 12 (Dec. 1987) 202-213.

[Sun-86] *SunView Programmer's Guide*, Sun Microsystems, Mt. View, Calif., 1986.

## EXERCISES

Any code requested in the following exercises should be written in a non-object-oriented language. Many of the exercises are taken from the previous chapter, so refer to the figures there.

**16.1**   (5) Implement the following library objects:
  a. A *Dictionary*, which is a one-way many-to-one mapping function whose domain and range are objects.
  b. A *Set*, which is an unordered collection of unique values. Duplicate values are automatically discarded from a set. Values can be added, deleted, and tested.
  c. A *VariableArray*, which is an ordered, dynamic, collection of values, indexed by nonnegative integer selector values. The number of elements is variable. Elements can be added or deleted at the end, beginning, or at any point in the middle

**16.2**   (6) Write code to implement the following:
  a. One-to-one association which is traversed in both directions.
  b. One-to-many association which is traversed in the direction from one to many. The association is considered unordered.
  c. One-to-many association which is traversed in the direction from one to many. The association is considered ordered.
  d. Many-to-many association which is traversed in both directions. The association is considered ordered in one direction and unordered in the other direction.

**16.3**   (6) Write library functions *allocate(size)*, which allocates and returns a block of memory, and *deallocate(block)*, which recovers an unused block of memory. These functions are useful in implementing object-oriented designs in a non-object-oriented language.

**16.4**   (4) Write code for the ordered aggregation between *Collection of cards* and *Card* in Figure E15.2. Operations include insertion, deletion, and traversing in both directions.

**16.5** (4) Implement all associations involving the classes *Box, Link, Line segment,* or *Point* in Figure E15.3 using any technique discussed in this chapter.

**16.6** (7) Write code for the *cut* operation on the class *Box* in Figure E15.3. Propagate the operation from boxes to attached link objects. Update any associations that are involved. Be sure to recover any memory that is released by the operation. You may assume another routine will update the display.

**16.7** (7) Prepare a routine that will create a logical link between two boxes. (See Figure E15.3.) Inputs to the routine are two boxes and a list of points that define the line segments of the link. The routine should update associations and create object instances as needed. You may assume another routine will update the display.

**16.8** (8) Implement the following queries on Figure E15.3:
   a. Given a box, determine all other boxes that are directly linked to it.
   b. Given a box, find all other boxes that are directly or indirectly linked to it.
   c. Given a box and a link, determine if the link involves the box.
   d. Given a box and a link, find the other box logically connected to the given box through the other end of the link.
   e. Given two boxes, determine all links between them.
   f. Given a selection and a sheet, determine which links connect a selected box to a deselected box.
   g. Given two boxes and a link, produce an ordered set of points. The first point is where the link connects to the first box, the last point is where the link connects to the second box, and intermediate points trace the link.

**16.9** (7) Implement the classes in Figure E15.1. Note the multiple inheritance.

**16.10** (8) Discuss how to implement the following classes described in exercise 15.4, using a non-object-oriented language:
   a. *Sorted_dictionary*
   b. *Polygon*
   c. *Index*

**16.11** (8) Write code in any non-object-oriented language to implement the generic class *Binary_tree* described in exercise 15.8. Make up at least three classes to test it. You will need to write a *compare* method and a *print* method for each class.

**16.12** (Project) Write a program for simulating evolution, as described in the Computer Recreations column in the May 1989 issue of *Scientific American*.

# 17

# Relational Databases

The object-oriented paradigm is versatile. It not only provides a sound basis for designing systems and programming code but can also be used to design databases. The use of an object-oriented design transcends the choice of database. You can design hierarchical, network, relational, and object-oriented databases. Object-oriented designs are efficient, coherent, and less prone to the update problems that plague many other database design techniques. As a side benefit, the use of a uniform design technique improves integration of database and programming language code.

You design a database by first performing the analysis steps described in Chapter 8 and constructing an object model. The remaining methodology chapters (9 and 10) primarily concern design of programming code and apply to database design to a lesser extent. This chapter resumes where Chapter 8 ends and considers implementation issues. How can we map an object model to database structures and tune the result for fast performance? This chapter also includes a brief introduction to databases for new readers.

Chapters 15 and 18 complement this chapter. Chapter 15 includes a section on object-oriented DBMS that have developed from object-oriented programming languages. Chapter 18 discusses automation of the object-model-to-database mapping process.

The coverage of this chapter is biased towards relational DBMS for the following reasons. Relational DBMS are gaining popularity at the expense of hierarchical and network DBMS. Relational DBMS are increasing their advantage in functionality and flexibility and are catching up in performance. Object-oriented DBMS look promising but have not yet reached the commercial mainstream. Logic DBMS also seem promising but are even further away from mass market acceptance.

## 17.1 GENERAL DBMS CONCEPTS

A *Data Base Management System (DBMS)* is a computer program for managing a permanent, self-descriptive repository of data. This repository of data is called a *database* and is stored in one or more files. There are many reasons why developers use a DBMS:

- *Crash recovery.* The database is protected from hardware crashes, disk media failures, and some user errors.

- *Sharing between users.* Multiple users can access the database at the same time.

- *Sharing between applications.* Multiple application programs (presumably related) can read and write data to the same database. A database is a neutral medium that facilitates communication between free-standing programs.

- *Security.* Data can be protected against unauthorized read and write access.

- *Integrity.* You can specify rules that data must satisfy. A DBMS can control the quality of its data over and above facilities that may be provided by application programs.

- *Extensibility.* Data may be added to the database without disrupting existing programs. Data can be reorganized for faster performance.

- *Data distribution.* The database may be partitioned across various sites, organizations, and hardware platforms.

The life cycle for most database applications includes the following steps.

1. Design the application.

2. Devise a specific architecture for coupling the application to a database.

3. Select a specific DBMS to serve as a platform.

4. Design the database. Write DBMS code to set up the proper database structures.

5. Write programming language code to compensate for DBMS shortcomings, provide a user interface, validate data, and perform computations. Many DBMS provide productivity tools to simplify routine applications.

6. Populate the database with information.

7. Run the application. Query and update the database as needed.

Of course, reality is more complex than this list implies, and there is feedback between steps. Often the DBMS platform is chosen first.

The most important and difficult task for many database applications is the database design. The design of the accompanying programming code is usually much easier. You should design a database for many of the same reasons that you should design any computer program: careful design of software before coding improves the quality and reduces the cost. A database design is often referred to as a *data model* or *schema*.

In general there are two approaches to database design. The first approach is attribute driven: Compile a list of attributes relevant to the application and synthesize groups of attributes that preserve functional dependencies. The other approach is entity driven: Discover entities that are meaningful to the application and describe them. In a typical design, there are ten times fewer entities than attributes, so entity design is much more tractable. Object modeling is a form of entity design.

The *three schema architecture*, summarized in Figure 17.1, is the standard architecture for a family of related database applications. This architecture was originally proposed by the ANSI/SPARC committee on DBMS. The basic idea is that a database design should comprise three layers: the external, conceptual, and internal schemas. Each external schema is a database design from the perspective of a single application. The external schema is a view or abstraction of the global, overall conceptual schema. The external schema isolates applications from most changes in the conceptual schema. To a large extent, future evolution in the conceptual schema can be resolved within the external-conceptual schema interface. The conceptual schema is a database design from the perspective of an enterprise. The conceptual schema integrates related applications and hides the peculiarities of the underlying DBMS. The internal schema deals with the limitations and features of a specific DBMS. The internal schema level consists of actual DBMS code required to implement the conceptual schema.

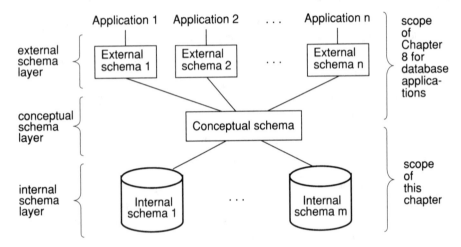

**Figure 17.1** ANSI/SPARC three schema architecture

Object modeling (discussed in Chapter 8) is useful for designing both the external and conceptual schema. You should construct one object model for each external schema and another object model for the conceptual schema. This chapter explains how to translate object models into DBMS code.

## 17.2 RELATIONAL DBMS CONCEPTS

The *relational data model* was invented by E.F. Codd and is based on one simple concept — the table. A *relational DBMS* (RDBMS) is a computer program for managing these tables. A RDBMS, as defined by Codd, has three major parts:

- Data that is presented as tables
- Operators for manipulating tables
- Integrity rules on tables

We will consider each of these parts in turn. Readers familiar with RDBMS may skip this section.

## 17.2.1 RDBMS Logical Data Structure

A relational database logically appears as simply a collection of tables. Tables have a specific number of columns and an arbitrary number of rows. The columns of tables are called *attributes* and directly correspond to attributes in object models. The rows are called *tuples* and correspond to object instances and links. A *simple value* is stored at each table row and column intersection.

Relational database theory dictates that each attribute must be assigned a domain. A *domain* is a set of legal values. Domains carry more information than just a data format and permit greater semantic checking. For instance, domains can be used to prevent operations on incompatible attributes, such as adding a cost to a weight. The concept of domain is similar to strong typing in a programming language. Unfortunately, most RDBMS do not support domains and only support simple data formats like number, date, and character string.

Each value in a table must belong to the domain of its attribute or be null. *Null* means that an attribute value is unknown or not applicable for a given row. There are complex theoretical issues concerning null values that often cause problems for real applications.

RDBMS use various devices for speeding access to tables, as literal tables are much too slow for practical needs. These tuning devices are transparent and not visible in the commands for reading and writing to tables. The RDBMS decides when tuning information is helpful in processing a query, and if so, automatically uses it. The RDBMS automatically updates tuning information whenever the corresponding tables are updated. Indexing, hashing, and sorting are common tuning techniques.

## 17.2.2 RDBMS Operators

SQL has become the most popular language for RDBMS, as well as an ANSI and ISO standard. Unfortunately, SQL is far from an ideal language and has many technical flaws. For example, SQL violates modern principles of language theory. The scope of the SQL standard is small and incomplete; it does not address important issues such as performance tuning and programming productivity tools. (See [Date-87] for a detailed critique of the SQL language.) Nevertheless, we will use SQL in this book, since it is a standard.

SQL provides operators for manipulating tables. The SQL *select* statement queries tables. The syntax of the *select* command looks something like:

```
SELECT attribute-list
FROM table-1, table-2, ...
WHERE predicate-is-true
```

Logically table-1, table-2, and any others are combined into one temporary table. The attribute list specifies which columns should be retained in the temporary table. The predicate expression specifies which rows should be retained. The contents of the temporary table are returned as the answer to the query. Additional SQL commands create tables, insert rows into tables, delete rows from tables, and perform other functions.

Interactive SQL commands are set-oriented; they operate on entire tables rather than individual rows or values. SQL provides a similar language for use with application programs through an awkward, row-at-a-time interface. RDBMS can deal with entire tables, but most programming languages cannot.

### 17.2.3 RDBMS Integrity

An important aspect of RDBMS, one that is often overlooked, is support for integrity. Most RDBMS lack proper support for integrity. The two aspects of integrity in Codd's model are entity integrity and referential integrity. Entity integrity dictates that each table have exactly one primary key. A *primary key* is a combination of one or more attributes whose value unambiguously locates each row in a table. (The primary key is always a candidate key. Candidate key was defined in Chapter 4.) In Figure 17.2, *person-ID* is the primary key of the *Person* table; *company-ID* is the primary key of the *Company* table.

|          | person-ID | person-name | address       | company-ID |
|----------|-----------|-------------|---------------|------------|
| Person table | 1         | Jim Smith   | 314 Olive St. | 1001       |
|          | 5         | Moe Brown   | 722 Short St. | 1002       |
|          | 999       | Jim Smith   | 1561 Main Dr. | 1001       |
|          | 14        | Jane Brown  | 722 Short St. | null       |

|          | company-ID | company-name   | address          |
|----------|------------|----------------|------------------|
| Company table | 1001       | Ajax Widgets   | 33 Industrial Dr. |
|          | 1002       | AAA liquors    | 724 Short St.    |
|          | 1003       | Win-more Sports | 1877 Broadway    |

person-ID is the primary key of Person table.
company-ID is the primary key of Company table.
company-ID is a foreign key in Person table.

**Figure 17.2**  Primary key and foreign key

Referential integrity requires that the RDBMS keep each foreign key consistent with its corresponding primary key. A *foreign key* is a primary key of one table that is embedded in another (or the same) table. In Figure 17.2 *company-ID* is a foreign key in the *Person* table. It would not be permissible to change Moe Brown's *company-ID* to 1004 since 1004 is not defined in the *Company* table. If the row for Ajax Widgets was deleted in the *Company* table, then both Jim Smith rows in the *Person* table must have their *company-ID* set to null. The link between foreign key and primary key forms a frequent navigation path between tables.

The SQL standard and commercial RDBMS implementations are slowly moving towards support for referential integrity. Referential integrity is useful when mapping object models to tables. Figure 17.2 happens to be a one-to-many association that has been converted to table form (see Section 17.3.4).

## 17.2.4 Normal Forms

*Normal forms* are rules developed to avoid logical inconsistencies from table update operations. Each normal form prohibits a form of redundancy in table organization that could yield meaningless results if one table were updated independently of other tables. There are multiple levels of normal form. Each higher level of normal form adds a constraint to the normal form below it. As the database designer satisfies higher normal form, tables tend to become fragmented; normal forms improve database consistency at the cost of added navigation and slower query execution. You should not inadvertently violate normal forms but may occasionally do so for a good reason, such as performance.

A table is in *first normal form* when each attribute value does not contain a repeating group. Figure 17.3a has a row with two entries under *equipment name* and thus violates first normal form. Restating the dual entries as two rows in Figure 17.3b satisfies first normal form.

A table is in *second normal form* when it satisfies first normal form and each row has a primary key. Each nonprimary key field must fully depend on the primary key. Figure 17.3b violates second normal form because *equipment manufacturer* and *manufacturer address* depend on the full primary key while *plant manager* only depends on part of the primary key. Figure 17.3c splits off the partial dependency into another table and satisfies second normal form.

A table is in *third normal form* when it satisfies second normal form and each nonprimary key attribute directly depends on the primary key. Figure 17.3c violates third normal because there is a transitive dependency; *manufacturer address* depends on *equipment manufacturer* which in turn depends on the primary key. Third normal form requires direct dependence on the primary key. Once again, splitting into two tables resolves the violation. Figure 17.3d satisfies third normal form.

There are higher normal forms that are usually not needed. [Kent-83] contains a more thorough explanation of normal forms. The motivation for observing normal form becomes much more compelling when there are thousands or millions of rows, instead of the few shown in Figure 17.3. The next section discusses how object models tend to preserve normal form.

## 17.2.5 Views

A *view* is a virtual table that is dynamically computed as needed. A view does not physically exist but is derived from one or more underlying tables. In theory, views are the means for deriving external schema from conceptual schema for the ANSI three schema architecture. In practice, views are less useful. Commercial RDBMS usually support reading through views but seldom support writing through views. There are subtle semantic issues associated with writing through views that most RDBMS avoid [Keller-86].

**(a)** *Violates 1st normal form.*

| plant name | equipment name | plant manager | equipment manufacturer | manufacturer address |
|---|---|---|---|---|
| ethylene styrene styrene | final cooler, feed heater feed pump feed heater | Jim Smith Bill Gunn Bill Gunn | ABC exchanger XYZ pumps ABC exchanger | 1247 Locust 432 Broadway 1247 Locust |

**(b)** *Satisfies 1st normal form. Violates 2nd normal form.*

| plant name | equipment name | plant manager | equipment manufacturer | manufacturer address |
|---|---|---|---|---|
| ethylene | final cooler | Jim Smith | ABC exchanger | 1247 Locust |
| ethylene | feed heater | Jim Smith | ABC exchanger | 1247 Locust |
| styrene | feed pump | Bill Gunn | XYZ pumps | 432 Broadway |
| styrene | feed heater | Bill Gunn | ABC exchanger | 1247 Locust |

Primary key: (plant-name, equipment-name)

**(c)** *Satisfies 2nd normal form. Violates 3rd normal form.*

| plant name | plant manager |
|---|---|
| ethylene | Jim Smith |
| styrene | Bill Gunn |

Primary key:
(plant-name)

| plant name | equipment name | equipment manufacturer | manufacturer address |
|---|---|---|---|
| ethylene | final cooler | ABC exchanger | 1247 Locust |
| ethylene | feed heater | ABC exchanger | 1247 Locust |
| styrene | feed pump | XYZ pumps | 432 Broadway |
| styrene | feed heater | ABC exchanger | 1247 Locust |

Primary key: (plant-name, equipment-name)

**(d)** *Satisfies 3rd normal form.*

| plant name | plant manager |
|---|---|
| ethylene | Jim Smith |
| styrene | Bill Gunn |

Primary key: (plant-name)

| plant name | equipment name | equipment manufacturer |
|---|---|---|
| ethylene | final cooler | ABC exchanger |
| ethylene | feed heater | ABC exchanger |
| styrene | feed pump | XYZ pumps |
| styrene | feed heater | ABC exchanger |

Primary key: (plant-name, equipment-name)

| equipment manufacturer | manufacturer address |
|---|---|
| ABC exchanger | 1247 Locust |
| XYZ pumps | 432 Broadway |

Primary key: (equipment-manufacturer)

**Figure 17.3** Normal forms

## 17.3 RELATIONAL DATABASE DESIGN

So far this chapter has reviewed DBMS in general and RDBMS. We now shift our focus towards database design. As stated earlier, we only consider relational database design, primarily because RDBMS technology is mature and dominates the marketplace.

### 17.3.1 Extended Three Schema Architecture for Object Models

Figure 17.4 shows how object modeling relates to the three schema architecture. First, you should formulate object models for the external and conceptual schema. Then, you should translate each object model to ideal tables, that is, the table model. Views and/or interface programs connect external tables to conceptual tables. Conceptual tables convert to internal schema. We will now study each part of the extended three schema architecture in detail.

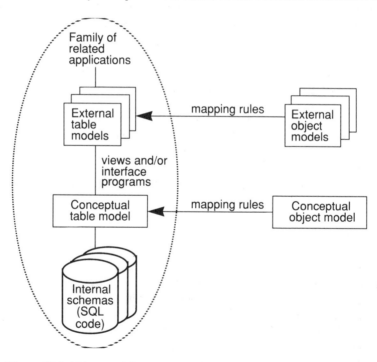

**Figure 17.4** Object modeling and the three schema architecture for RDBMS

The object models focus on logical data structure. Each object model consists of many classes, associations, generalizations, and attributes. Object modeling promotes deep, abstract thinking about a problem unencumbered by implementation details. Object models are effective for communicating with application experts and reaching a consensus about the important aspects of a problem. Object models help developers achieve a coherent, understandable, efficient, and correct database design.

374 Chapter 17 / RELATIONAL DATABASES

Each table model consists of many ideal tables. These ideal tables are generic and DBMS-independent. Ideal tables abstract common characteristics of RDBMS implementations. The table model decouples DBMS idiosyncrasies from object model to table model mapping rules. This improves documentation and eases porting.

In order to translate from an object model to ideal tables, you must choose among several mapping alternatives. For example, there are two ways to map an association to tables and four ways to map a generalization (discussed later in this chapter). You must also supply details that are missing from the object model, such as the primary key and candidate keys for each table and whether each attribute can be null. Attributes in candidate keys usually should not be null; the data modeler may choose to require values for additional attributes. You must assign a domain to each attribute and list groups of attributes subject to frequent access.

The internal schema of the three schema architecture consists of SQL commands that create the tables, attributes, and performance-tuning structures. Indexes are the most popular performance-tuning device so we will use them in our examples. This level exploits the features and compensates for the shortcomings and quirks of DBMS products.

Generation of SQL commands requires that you assign tables to DBMS files and honor DBMS restrictions on length and legal characters for names. You must define domains if the RDBMS has the ability or convert domains into data types.

The remainder of this chapter focuses on converting object models to table models. We will study various cases and formulate mapping rules. The mapping rules apply equally well to external and conceptual object models. We deemphasize conversion from the external table model to conceptual table model to internal schema (left hand side of Figure 17.4) because object modeling introduces nothing new here. The conversion between the various tabular representations is the same for tables derived from objects as it is for those derived from more conventional approaches.

## 17.3.2 The Use of Object IDs

Most of our examples will use IDs for primary keys to simplify exposition. Each class-derived table has an ID for the primary key; one or more object IDs form the primary key for association-derived tables. This strategy is compatible with the object-oriented language notion that objects have identity apart from their properties. Object-oriented languages implement identity with pointers or look-up tables into pointers; an ID is the equivalent database construct. Figure 17.2 uses IDs; Figure 17.3 does not.

There are benefits to using IDs. IDs are immutable and completely independent of changes in data value and physical location. The stability of IDs is particularly important for associations since they refer to objects. Contrast this with referring to objects by name. Then changing a name requires update of many associations. IDs provide a uniform mechanism for referencing objects.

On the other hand, IDs have disadvantages. Generating IDs is a nuisance, for which RDBMS provide no inherent support. For example, it is awkward to track previously allocated IDs and reclaim deleted IDs for reuse. Object-oriented languages usually avoid ID reuse by giving IDs many bits. Databases cannot be so cavalier, since they are specifically intended to be long lived.

IDs undermine the original intent of RDBMSs. RDBMS theory emphasizes that data is located and manipulated based on attribute values. In one sense, it certainly is permissible to define IDs as attributes and adopt a protocol for handling them. But on the other hand, an ID really is not a value and is an implementation artifact that RDBMSs are trying to eliminate.

So when should you use IDs? Do not use IDs for applications where users directly access the database. People think in terms of descriptive properties such as names and not in terms of artificial numbers. The advantages of IDs may prevail when database access is restricted via programs. Restricted access often occurs because application software is needed to compensate for DBMS deficiencies, enforce integrity, and provide a user interface. We will discuss object-to-table mapping rules that apply, regardless of whether IDs are used.

### 17.3.3 Mapping Object Classes to Tables

Each class maps to one or more tables. (Also a table may correspond to more than one class. See Section 17.3.4.) The objects in a class may be partitioned horizontally and/or vertically. For instance, if a class has many instances of which a few are often referenced, horizontal partitioning may improve efficiency by placing the frequently accessed objects in one table and the remaining objects in another table. Of course, an application will not benefit from horizontal partitioning unless it knows which table to search. Similarly, if a class has attributes with different access patterns, it may help to partition the objects vertically. Figure 17.5 shows horizontal and vertical partitioning.

Horizontal partition

| person-ID | person-name | address |
| --- | --- | --- |
| 1 | Mike Rumrow | 14 Center St. |
| 5 | Moe Brown | 722 Short St. |

| person-ID | person-name | address |
| --- | --- | --- |
| 999 | Jim Smith | 1561 Main Dr. |

Vertical partition

| person-ID | person-name |
| --- | --- |
| 1 | Mike Rumrow |
| 5 | Moe Brown |
| 999 | Jim Smith |

| person-ID | address |
| --- | --- |
| 1 | 14 Center St. |
| 5 | 722 Short St. |
| 999 | 1561 Main Dr. |

**Figure 17.5** Horizontal and vertical partitioning of tables

In Figure 17.6 an object class converts to one table. Class *Person* has attributes *person name* and *address*. The table model lists these attributes and adds the implicit object ID. As part of formulating the table model, we add details. We specify that *person ID* cannot be null since it is a candidate key. We decide that *person name* should not be null; a name must be entered for every person. (*Person name* is not a candidate key because two persons may have the same name.) Attribute *address* may be null. We assign a domain to each attribute, specify the primary key for each table, and note frequently accessed groups of attributes.

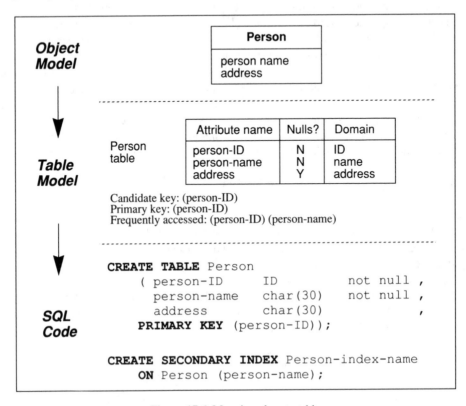

**Figure 17.6** Mapping class to table

The SQL code creates the *Person* table. (The SQL standard currently supports referential integrity. However many commercial products do not yet fully support this aspect of the standard.) The index on *person-name* ensures quick retrieval for this attribute since it is frequently accessed. The SQL level also maps domains to data types.

### 17.3.4 Mapping Binary Associations to Tables

In general, an association may, or may not, map to a table. It depends on the type and multiplicity of the association and the database designer's preferences in terms of extensibility, number of tables, and performance trade-offs.

Figure 17.7 shows that a many-to-many association always maps to a distinct table. This schema satisfies third normal form. The primary keys for both related classes and any link attributes become attributes of the association table. Attributes *company ID* and *person ID* combine to form the only candidate key for the *Owns-stock* table. In general, an association may be traversed starting from either class so both *company ID* and *person ID* could be frequently accessed. The foreign key clauses of the SQL code indicate that each *Owns-stock* tuple must reference a *Company* and *Person* that have been defined in their respective tables.

An association table always sets the foreign keys from the related objects to not null; by definition, a link between two objects requires that both objects be known. If a given pair of objects does not have a link, we omit an entry in the association table.

Many RDBMS do not semantically support primary keys; the workaround is to define unique indexes. (A RDBMS that explicitly supports primary keys may also generate a unique index as a side effect.) We use the primary key clause in our examples because it is part of standard SQL and we expect it to eventually become widely adopted. The primary key may subsume a secondary index. For example, if the *Owns-stock* primary key in Figure 17.7 is implemented as a unique index on *company-ID*, *person-ID*, the secondary index on *company-ID* would be superfluous.

Figures 17.8, 17.9, and 17.10 show two options for mapping a one-to-many association to tables. You may create a distinct table for the association or bury a foreign key in the table for the many class. We do not show SQL code for this example and some others because SQL code is voluminous, and the table model already makes the desired point. The advantages of merging an association into a class are:

- Fewer tables

- Faster performance due to fewer tables to navigate

The disadvantages of merging an association into a class are:

- *Less design rigor.* Associations are between independent objects of equal syntactic weight. In general, it seems inappropriate to contaminate objects with knowledge of other objects. This point is related to the argument in favor of encapsulation for object-oriented languages.

- *Reduced extensibility.* It is difficult to get multiplicity right on the first few design passes. One-to-one and one-to-many associations may be externalized. Many-to-many associations must be externalized.

- *More complexity.* An asymmetrical representation of the association complicates search and update.

The final decision on whether to collapse an association into a related class depends on the application.

You may also collapse a one-to-one association into an object table or merge even further and store both objects and the association all in one table.[*] Chapter 3 used *a country has a capital city* to illustrate a one-to-one association. *Country, Capital city*, and the association could all be stored in one table. Merging into a single table improves performance and reduces database storage at the cost of less extensibility and possible violation of third normal form.

---

[*] Be careful with collapsing cyclical associations. For example, if classes *A*, *B*, and *C* are related by one-to-one associations *A::B*, *B::C*, and *C::A*, it may not be correct to fold all three classes and three associations into one table. For example, the instances *a1::b1*, *b1::c1*, and *c1::a2* require that the cycle be implemented with at least two tables.

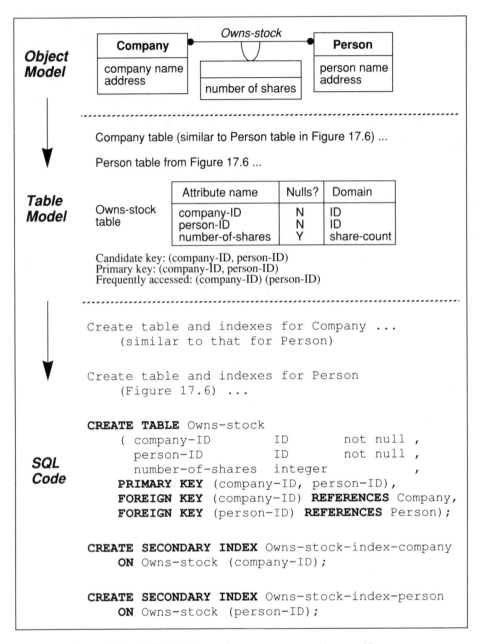

**Figure 17.7** Mapping many-to-many association to tables

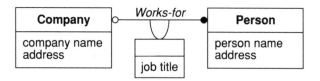

**Figure 17.8** Object model for one-to-many association

---

Company table (similar to Person table in Figure 17.6) ...

Person table from Figure 17.6 ...

| Works-for table | Attribute name | Nulls? | Domain |
|---|---|---|---|
| | company-ID | N | ID |
| | person-ID | N | ID |
| | job-title | Y | title |

Candidate key: (person-ID)
Primary key: (person-ID)
Frequently accessed: (company-ID) (person-ID)

**Figure 17.9** Table model for one-to-many association—distinct association table

---

Company table (similar to Person table in Figure 17.6) ...

| Person table | Attribute name | Nulls? | Domain |
|---|---|---|---|
| | person-ID | N | ID |
| | person-name | N | name |
| | address | Y | address |
| | company-ID | Y | ID |
| | job-title | Y | title |

Candidate key: (person-ID)
Primary key: (person-ID)
Frequently accessed:   (person-ID) (person-name) (company-ID)

**Figure 17.10** Table model for one-to-many association—buried foreign key

Note that for a one-to-many association you may also collapse both classes and the association all into one table. However, usually this is undesirable and may violate second normal form.

The hollow ball multiplicity symbol in Figure 17.8 indicates that a person need not be employed. In Figure 17.11, all persons within the scope of the model must be employed. This figure illustrates the issue of existence dependency that we mentioned in Section 4.6. Here, *Person* objects know about *Company* objects since each *Person* object requires a *Company* object. There is less benefit to having a distinct association table. The only change in the table model for the buried foreign key case is that *company ID* cannot be null.

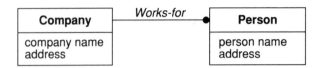

**Figure 17.11** Object model for association with existence dependency

### 17.3.5 Mapping Ternary Associations to Tables

Figure 17.12 shows an RDBMS implementation for a ternary association. Note that we show a table for each class participating in the ternary association even for a class that may be trivial like *Year*. Here, if the *Year* table merely pairs *year-ID* with *year*, we could perform a minor optimization: Discard the *Year* table and replace *year-ID* by *year* in the ternary table.

Figure 17.12 does not exhibit existence dependency. This certainly seems to make sense for the pitching example. A pitcher, team, and year have independent existence apart from whether a pitcher happens to pitch for a team in a given year. For a ternary association where a dependency between an object class and the ternary association is important, it is probably best to promote the ternary association to an object class (see Section 3.3.2) and handle the dependency as in Figure 17.11. The promotion of the ternary association to a class gives each ternary instance an ID that can then be referenced by the dependent object.

Note that the *Person* table refers to *person-ID* while the ternary table refers to *pitcher-ID*. The ternary table reflects that a person assumes the role of pitcher. *Pitcher-ID* is a more meaningful attribute name for the ternary table than *person-ID*. The object model shows that these two names refer to the same entity and would be expected to share a common navigational path. The role name of a class should be used for attributes buried in association tables. Figure 17.12 shows how to handle roles with SQL code. (We could have used roles in some of our earlier examples. For instance, in Figure 17.7 person assumes the role of shareholder. In Figure 17.8 and Figure 17.11 a company is the employer and a person is the employee.)

Figures 17.13 and 17.14 discuss one more association construct—qualification. A company has many persons serving as officers. Most offices within a company are held by one person, such as President and Treasurer. A few offices, such as member of the board of directors, may be served by many persons. A person may have many company-office combinations. For instance, a person may be an officer of more than one company or hold multiple offices for the same company.

The *Company* and *Person* tables are similar to earlier examples. The association table is more interesting. The association table has three attributes: the primary key for *Company*, the primary key for *Person*, and the qualifier *office*. None of these attributes can be null since they are all an essential part of the qualified association. All three attributes must appear in the primary key and candidate key since the association is many-to-many after qualification.

We have not explicitly discussed aggregations in any of our database examples. The design of aggregation tables follows the same mapping rules as for associations.

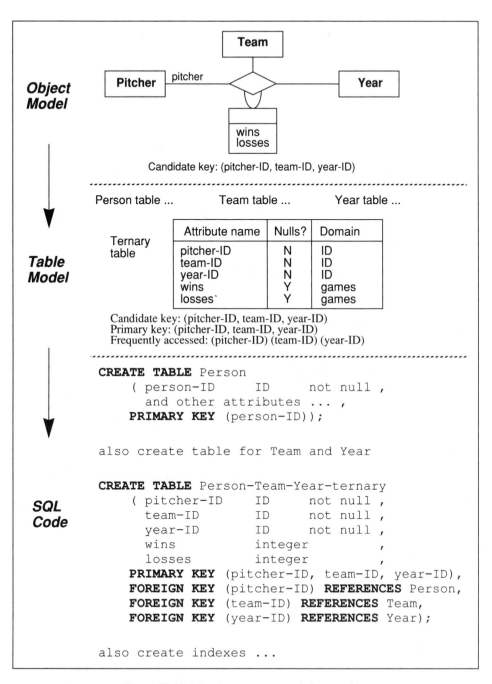

**Figure 17.12** Mapping ternary association to tables

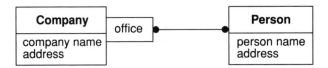

**Figure 17.13** Object model for a qualified association

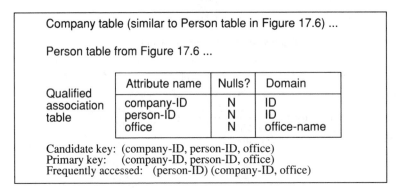

**Figure 17.14** Table model for a qualified association

## 17.3.6 Mapping Generalizations to Tables

There are four approaches to mapping generalizations to tables. We will use Figure 17.15 as our basis for exploring these strategies. We begin by discussing single inheritance.

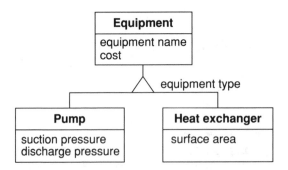

**Figure 17.15** Object model for generalization

Figure 17.16 shows the normal approach. The superclass and the subclasses each map to a table. The identity of an object across a generalization is preserved through the use of a shared ID. Thus *product pump* may have one row in the *Equipment* table with ID 101 and

| | Attribute name | Nulls? | Domain |
|---|---|---|---|
| Equipment table | equipment-ID | N | ID |
| | equipment-name | N | name |
| | cost | Y | money |
| | equipment-type | N | equip-type |

Candidate keys: (equipment-ID) (equipment-name)
Primary key: (equipment-ID)
Frequently accessed: (equipment-ID) (equipment-name)

| | Attribute name | Nulls? | Domain |
|---|---|---|---|
| Pump table | equipment-ID | N | ID |
| | suction-pressure | Y | pressure |
| | discharge-pressure | Y | pressure |

Candidate key: (equipment-ID)
Primary key: (equipment-ID)
Frequently accessed: (equipment-ID)

| | Attribute name | Nulls? | Domain |
|---|---|---|---|
| Heat exchanger table | equipment-ID | N | ID |
| | surface-area | Y | area |

Candidate key: (equipment-ID)
Primary key: (equipment-ID)
Frequently accessed: (equipment-ID)

**Figure 17.16** Table model for generalization—superclass and subclass tables

another row in the *Pump* table also with ID 101. This approach is logically clean and extensible. However, it involves many tables, and superclass to subclass navigation may be slow. You could navigate the tables as follows:

1. The user supplies an equipment name.

2. Find the *Equipment* row that corresponds to equipment name.

3. Retrieve the *equipment ID* and *equipment type* for this row.

4. Go to the subclass table indicated by *equipment type*, and find the subclass row with the same ID as the *Equipment* row.

For example, the user may specify equipment name "product pump." The application looks in the equipment table and finds that product pump has ID 101 and equipment type pump. The application then searches the *Pump* table and retrieves additional data for ID 101.

Figure 17.17 shows SQL code for Figure 17.16. Note that SQL cannot enforce the partitioning indicated by the generalization discriminator. You could store *product pump* in both the *Pump* and *Heat exchanger* tables, and SQL would permit it. The basic problem is the SQL has little support for integrity constraints. You would need to write special application code to enforce the generalization partition and use SQL permissions to block interactive access or access through other programs.

```
CREATE TABLE Equipment
    ( equipment-ID          ID          not null ,
      equipment-name        char(30)    not null ,
      cost                  money                ,
      equipment-type        char(10)    not null ,
    PRIMARY KEY (equipment-ID));


CREATE SECONDARY INDEX  Equipment-index-name
    ON Equipment (equipment-name);


CREATE TABLE Pump
    ( equipment-ID          ID          not null ,
      suction-pressure      real                 ,
      discharge-pressure    real                 ,
    PRIMARY KEY (equipment-ID),
    FOREIGN KEY (equipment-ID) REFERENCES Equipment);


Create table for Heat exchanger ...
    (similar to that for Pump)
```

**Figure 17.17**  SQL code for generalization—superclass and subclass tables

Figure 17.18 and Figure 17.19 are alternate mapping approaches. They are motivated by the desire to eliminate superclass-to-subclass navigation and thus speed performance. However, the improved performance incurs a price.

Figure 17.18 illustrates the "many subclass approach." This approach eliminates the superclass table and replicates all the superclass attributes in each subclass table. You might use this approach if a subclass has many attributes, the superclass has few attributes, and the application knows what subclass to search. Figure 17.18 observes third normal form but is less satisfying than the standard approach. You cannot enforce uniqueness of equipment names across subclass tables since RDBMS do not provide indexes that span tables.

The "one superclass table approach" shown in Figure 17.19 brings all subclass attributes up to the superclass level. Each record in the superclass table uses attributes pertinent to one subclass; the other attribute values are null. The table in this figure violates third normal form; *equipment-ID* or *equipment-name* is the primary key, but attribute values also depend on *equipment type*. This may be a useful approach if there are only two or three subclasses with few attributes.

The best way to handle generalization relationships that exhibit multiple inheritance from disjoint classes (see Section 4.4) is to use the standard approach shown in Figure

17.16—one table per superclass, one table per subclass. The best way to handle multiple inheritance from overlapping classes is to use one table for the superclass, one table for each subclass, and one table for the generalization relationship (the fourth approach for mapping generalizations to tables). Multiple inheritance infrequently occurs, so usually it is not worth the effort to try to optimize the mapping.

| | Attribute name | Nulls? | Domain |
|---|---|---|---|
| Pump table | equipment-ID | N | ID |
| | equipment-name | N | name |
| | cost | Y | money |
| | suction-pressure | Y | pressure |
| | discharge-pressure | Y | pressure |

Candidate keys: (equipment-ID) (equipment-name)
Primary key: (equipment-ID)
Frequently accessed: (equipment-ID) (equipment-name)

| | Attribute name | Nulls? | Domain |
|---|---|---|---|
| Heat exchanger table | equipment-ID | N | ID |
| | equipment-name | N | name |
| | cost | Y | money |
| | surface-area | Y | area |

Candidate keys: (equipment-ID) (equipment-name)
Primary key: (equipment-ID)
Frequently accessed: (equipment-ID) (equipment-name)

**Figure 17.18** Table model for generalization—many subclass tables

| | Attribute name | Nulls? | Domain |
|---|---|---|---|
| Equipment table | equipment-ID | N | ID |
| | equipment-name | N | name |
| | cost | Y | money |
| | equipment-type | N | equip-type |
| | suction-pressure | Y | pressure |
| | discharge-pressure | Y | pressure |
| | surface area | Y | area |

Candidate keys: (equipment-ID) (equipment-name)
Primary key: (equipment-ID)
Frequently accessed: (equipment-ID) (equipment-name)

**Figure 17.19** Table model for generalization — one superclass table

### 17.3.7 Summary of Object Model to Table Mapping Rules

Mapping object classes to tables

- Each class maps to one or more tables. (Similarly, a table may correspond to more than one class if they are connected with a one-to-one or one-to-many association.) [Figure 17.6]

Mapping associations to tables

- Each many-to-many association maps to a distinct table. [Figure 17.7]

- Each one-to-many association maps to a distinct table or may be buried as a foreign key in the table for the many class. [Figures 17.8 through 17.11]

- Each one-to-one association maps to a distinct table or may be buried as a foreign key in the table for either class.

- For one-to-many and one-to-one associations, if there are no cycles, you have the additional option of storing the association and both related objects all in one table. Be aware this may introduce redundancy and violate normal forms.

- Role names are incorporated as part of the foreign key attribute name. [Figure 17.12]

- N-ary (n>2) associations map to a distinct table. Sometimes, it helps to promote an n-ary association to a class. [Figure 17.12]

- A qualified association maps to a distinct table with at least three attributes — the primary key of each related class and the qualifier. [Figure 17.13, Figure 17.14]

- Aggregation follows the same rules as association.

Mapping single inheritance generalizations to tables

- The superclass and each subclass map to a table. [Figure 17.16, Figure 17.17]

- No superclass table, superclass attributes are replicated for each subclass. [Figure 17.18]

- No subclass tables, bring all subclass attributes up to the superclass level. [Figure 17.19]

*Mapping disjoint multiple inheritance to tables*

- The superclass and each subclass map to a table. [Figure 17.16, Figure 17.17]

*Mapping overlapping multiple inheritance to tables*

- The superclass and each subclass map to a table; the generalization relationship also maps to a table.

### 17.3.8 Another Approach for Mapping Object Models to Tables

Our approach to mapping object structures to tables has been to carry forward as much object model semantics as possible to RDBMS tables. Then we can avail ourselves of inherent RDBMS query, update, and integrity facilities. This is the approach that we describe in this chapter.

Another approach to mapping object models is to store <entity-name, key, attribute-name, value> tuples. Then, one table can store all classes, associations, and generalizations for an entire object model. For example, the object "John Smith" would be stored as <person, 123, person-name, "John Smith">, <person, 123, address, "456 Ocean Drive">, and <person, 123, salary, $25000>. Many knowledgebase-to-DBMS translators use this approach.

In general, putting all entities in one table is not a good approach to relational database design. The one table approach subverts an important benefit of databases: a database is more than just a repository of data, and is supposed to be self-descriptive. A database not only stores data but also stores the structure of its data (metadata). In a sense, the one table approach removes metadata from the database and puts it into the application code that must decipher the one large table.

## 17.4 ADVANCED RELATIONAL DBMS

Research is currently underway on DBMS more powerful than the conventional SQL RDBMS described in this chapter. Section 15.8.5 discussed one vein of research: object-oriented programming languages with persistent data. This section describes another approach: advanced RDBMS.

An explicit goal of advanced RDBMS is to make as few changes as possible to the relational model. The primary thrust is to extend the relational model with new data types, operators, and access methods. For example, a mathematical application may require complex numbers as a data type. A decision table application may require new operations that check a decision table for completeness and consolidate rows for cases where a decision criterion is irrelevant. Special access methods like a grid search would help spatial applications.

The rationale is that advanced applications demand a wide range of capabilities. No single DBMS can implement the features needed to satisfy all applications. Thus an advanced RDBMS must provide a support system that enables application developers to add custom features. The architecture is open as contrasted with the closed architecture of conventional RDBMS.

Some advantages of the advanced RDBMS approach are:

- *Definitely adds to existing RDBMS functionality.* It preserves the traditional strengths of RDBMS: many simultaneous users, large quantities of data, reliability, distributed data management, and programming support tools.

- *Integrates well with existing relational databases.* It provides for smooth flow of data between engineering and business applications.

- *Data sharing.* The database is truly a central repository and not wedded to any particular programming language or application.

Some potential disadvantages are:

- *Performance.* Is even an augmented RDBMS capable of efficient operations on individual objects?

- *Functionality*. Does the RDBMS paradigm interfere with the ability to deliver needed capabilities? If so, will these limitations cause a problem for real applications?

- *Security*. An open architecture may make it more difficult to protect data against unauthorized reading and writing.

POSTGRES is one example of the advanced RDBMS approach. POSTGRES is a prototype at UC Berkeley and the successor to the INGRES RDBMS. POSTGRES adopts the "one database approach"—one database that can be extended to serve a variety of applications. Supported data types include variable length data, QUEL (a query language similar to SQL) queries, and procedures. POSTGRES provides facilities for active databases, such as triggers and inferencing with forward and backward chaining [Stonebraker-86].

EXODUS is a prototype at the University of Wisconsin. EXODUS adopts the "database generator approach"—a host of custom DBMS each serving an application niche. EXODUS provides kernel facilities for use by all applications and a set of tools to aid the database implementor in generating the custom portion of each DBMS [Carey-86].

## 17.5 CHAPTER SUMMARY

A Data Base Management System (DBMS) is a computer program that is designed to provide general purpose functionality for storing, retrieving, and controlling access to permanent data. A DBMS protects data against accidental loss and makes it available for sharing. An entire branch of computer science is devoted to studying DBMS issues and answering questions such as:

- What paradigm is most conducive to representing database structure?

- What kind of language provides the most natural interaction?

- How can a database capture more of the true meaning of its data?

- How should a database be organized for maximum performance and flexibility?

Several DBMS paradigms are available: hierarchical, network, relational, and object-oriented. Hierarchical and network DBMS bring the conceptual DBMS close to the underlying physical data structures. Thus they are efficient but difficult to use and fading in the marketplace. Relational DBMS dominate today's marketplace. Relational DBMS present the database at a higher level of abstraction than hierarchies and networks and are easier to use. Relational DBMS implementations are improving in performance as they mature and use smarter optimization techniques. Object-oriented DBMS and/or advanced relational DBMS may be the wave of the future. Much research is underway that is motivated by the lessons learned from current relational DBMS. Many theoretical, performance, and practical issues must be resolved before we learn the fate of these new approaches.

Object-oriented concepts provide an excellent basis for modeling hierarchical, network, relational, and object-oriented DBMS. Object models permit developers to think about a problem at a high, abstract level and yet rest assured that the resulting design can be easily and practically implemented. The following simple rules enable designers to convert an object model to relational DBMS tables.

- An object class maps to a table.

- An association maps to a table.

- A generalization maps to a superclass table plus a series of subclass tables.

We presented various alternatives that deviate from the basic conversion formula. These alternatives trade-off performance, integrity, and extensibility.

| | |
|---|---|
| aggregation (in RDBMS schema) | object (in RDBMS schema) |
| association (in RDBMS schema) | primary key |
| class (in RDBMS schema) | qualified association (in RDBMS schema |
| foreign key | schema |
| generalization (in RDBMS schema) | table |
| integrity of data | ternary association (in RDBMS schema) |
| normal forms | three schema architecture |

**Figure 17.20** Key concepts for Chapter 17

## BIBLIOGRAPHIC NOTES

Many good books explain DBMS and relational DBMS principles. C.J. Date has written numerous books [Date-81] [Date-83] [Date-86] [Date-87]. Date is a polished writer and has deep insights into relational DBMS technology derived from his past work for IBM. [Loomis-87a] is another good DBMS reference.

Our approach to database design is not all that much different from other authors. After all, there is only so much a person can say about mapping to simple tables. Chapter 12 of this book reviews other approaches to database design. Part of [Loomis-87a] discusses database design but this has been superseded by her more recent work [Loomis-87b]. Our work improves on other approaches with: a better modeling notation, an intermediate table model, more attention paid to integrity, and more thorough mapping rules.

Our treatment of relational database design is detailed but is not complete. We make no provision for handling versions and alternatives; we have not decided how to model them. We do not address database security (SQL GRANT command) and how to analyze dynamic interaction with a database (transaction modeling). We have been automating the conversion of object models to relational DBMS schema, but this work is not described here. (A user interactively draws object models on the CRT screen, annotates them with database implementation decisions, and then asks the system to automatically generate a relational DBMS schema definition. Chapter 18 describes some of our early work in this area.) [Oertly-89] discusses evolutionary database design—how to accommodate changes in the structure of a database that is already populated with data. Oertly's treatment is compatible with our work.

## REFERENCES

[Blaha-88] Michael Blaha, William Premerlani, James Rumbaugh. Relational database design using an object-oriented methodology. *Communications of the ACM 31*, 4 (April 1988), 414-427.

[Carey-86] M. Carey, D. DeWitt, D. Frank, G. Graefe, M. Muralikrishna, J. Richardson, E. Shekita. The architecture of the EXODUS extensible DBMS. *International Workshop on Object-Oriented Database Systems*, Pacific Grove, Calif., September 1986.

[Date-81] Chris J. Date. *An Introduction to Database Systems, Third Edition*. Reading, Mass.: Addison-Wesley, 1981.

[Date-83] Chris J. Date. *An Introduction to Database Systems, Volume II*. Reading, Mass.: Addison-Wesley, 1983.

[Date-86] Chris J. Date. *Relational Database: Selected Writings*. Reading, Mass.: Addison-Wesley, 1986.

[Date-87] Chris J. Date. *A Guide to the SQL Standard*. Reading, Mass.: Addison-Wesley, 1987.

[Keller-86] Arthur M. Keller. The role of semantics in translating view updates. *IEEE Computer 19*, 1 (January 1986), 63-73.

[Kent-83] William Kent. A simple guide to five normal forms in relational database theory. *Communications of the ACM 26*, 2 (February 1983), 120-125.

[Loomis-87a] Mary E.S. Loomis. *The Database Book*. New York: Macmillan, 1987.

[Loomis-87b] Mary E.S. Loomis, Ashwin V. Shah, James E. Rumbaugh. An object modeling technique for conceptual design. *European Conference on Object-Oriented Programming*, Paris, France, June 15-17, 1987, published as *Lecture Notes in Computer Science, 276*, Springer-Verlag.

[Oertly-89] Fredy Oertly, Gerald Schiller. Evolutionary database design. *Fifth International Conference on Data Engineering*, Los Angeles, 1989.

[Stonebraker-86] Michael Stonebraker and Lawrence A. Rowe. The design of POSTGRES. *ACM SIGMOD'86*, Washington, D.C., May 28-30, 1986.

## EXERCISES

**17.1** (6) Four different object diagrams for directed graphs are shown in Figure E17.1 through Figure E17.4. A directed graph is constructed from named edges and vertices. Each directed edge in a graph is an arrow that starts at one vertex and ends at another vertex. Any number of edges may be connected to the same vertex. More than one edge may connect a given pair of vertices, and an edge may connect a vertex to itself.

Figure E17.1 depicts a graph as a many-to-many association between vertices. Directionality is indicated by the role names *from* and *to*. Edges are treated as link attributes. Figure E17.2 depicts a graph as a many-to-many association between edges. Vertices are link attributes. The qualifier, *end*, is an enumerated type with possible values of *to* and *from* indicating which ends of the edges are connected. Figure E17.3 treats both vertices and edges as objects. A graph is described by connections between vertices and edges. Two named associations, *To* and *From*, are used to store connections, one for each end of an edge. Figure E17.4 depicts connections with a qualified association. Each end of an edge connects to exactly one vertex. Once again, *end* is an enumerated type.

Which diagram most accurately models a graph? Discuss in detail the relative merits of each diagram. Consider what happens if more than one edge connects a given pair of vertices. What if an edge connects a vertex with itself? What happens if only one edge is connected to a vertex?

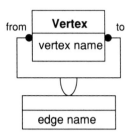

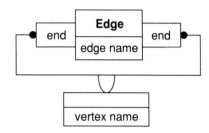

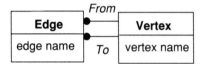

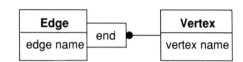

**Figure E17.1** Object diagram of directed graphs with edge name as a link attribute

**Figure E17.2** Object diagram of directed graphs with vertex name as a link attribute

**Figure E17.3** Object diagram of directed graphs with associations for each end of an edge

**Figure E17.4** Object diagram of directed graphs with an association for connections

**17.2** (5) Convert each diagram from the previous exercise into ideal tables (the table model described in the chapter).

**17.3** (4) Convert the ideal tables for the object diagrams in Figure E17.3 and Figure E17.4 into SQL commands to create empty database tables and indexes. Use your judgement to supply information that is missing from the object diagrams and needed for the conversion process.

**17.4** (4) Populate the database tables created by the SQL commands of exercise 17.3 for the directed graph in Figure E17.5.

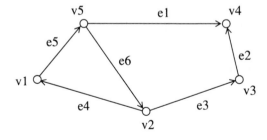

**Figure E17.5** Sample directed graph

**17.5** (6) For the object diagram in Figure E17.4, prepare queries for the following. You may express queries in SQL or in your own language. In some cases, you may need to embed a query within a procedure.

    a. Given the name of an edge, determine the two vertices that it connects.

    b. Given the name of a vertex, determine all edges connected to or from it.

    c. Given the names of a pair of vertices, determine the name of the edges, if any, that directly connects the pair in either direction.

    d. Given the name of a vertex, determine the names of all vertices that can be visited directly or indirectly from the given vertex by traversing one or more edges (transitive closure). Each edge must be traversed from its "from" end to its "to" end.

**17.6** (6) Convert Figure E17.6 into ideal tables. This is an object diagram of expressions formed from constants, variables, and arithmetic operators. Unary minus is not allowed. An expression is a binary tree of terms.

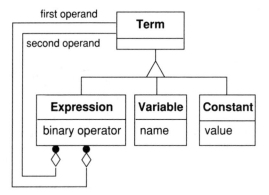

**Figure E17.6** Object diagram for expressions

**17.7** (4) Convert the ideal tables to RDBMS SQL commands for the previous exercise.

**17.8** (5) Indicate the contents of the database tables created by the SQL commands of the previous exercise for the expression $(X + Y/2) / (X/3 - Y)$. Consider the parentheses in establishing the precedence of operators; otherwise, ignore them in populating the database tables.

**17.9** (7) Convert the object diagram of a desktop publishing system in Figure E17.7 to ideal tables. A document consists of numbered pages. Each page contains many drawing objects, including ellipses, rectangles, polylines, and textlines. Ellipses and rectangles are embedded within a bounding box. A polyline is a sequence of line segments defined by vertex points. Textlines originate at a point and have a font. A group of objects is itself an object. Treat all associations and aggregations as unordered. For this exercise do not consider the ordering of pages in a document or the ordering of points in a polygon.

**17.10** (6) Revise your ideal tables from the previous exercise to treat the association between *Polyline* and *Point* and the aggregation between *Document* and *Page* as ordered. That is, given a polyline, it must be possible to query the database to retrieve the points in the correct order, and given a document it must be possible to scan its pages in order.

**17.11** (5) Modify the ideal tables produced in exercise 17.9 to reflect the revision to the object diagram shown in Figure E17.8. Discuss the relative merits of making the revision.

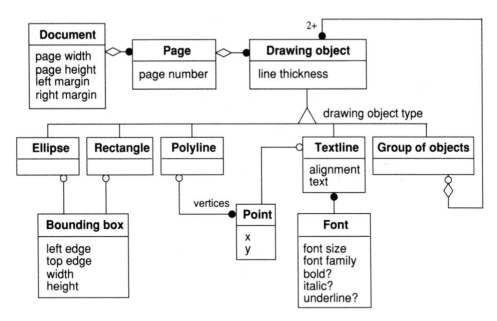

**Figure E17.7** Object diagram of a desktop publishing system

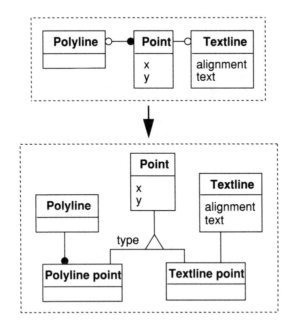

**Figure E17.8** Generalization of point to eliminate zero-or-one multiplicity

**17.12** (5) Convert the ideal tables for exercise 17.9 to RDBMS SQL commands. Develop an indexing strategy.

**17.13** (5) Explore some design trade-offs for exercises 17.9-17.12. For instance, consider the three different approaches to mapping the generalization. Look at each one-to-many association, and decide whether it should be a distinct table or merged with an object. Consider collapsing one-to-one associations. Defend your decisions and discuss ramifications.

**17.14** (4) Convert the RDBMS SQL commands in Figure E17.9 into an object diagram. The tables are used to store the straight line distances between pairs of cities.

```
CREATE TABLE City
     ( city-ID    ID        not null ,
       city-name  char(30) not null ,
     PRIMARY KEY (city-ID));


CREATE SECONDARY INDEX City-index-name
     ON City (city-name);


CREATE TABLE Route
     ( route-ID   ID          not null ,
       distance   real                 ,
     PRIMARY KEY (route-ID));


CREATE TABLE Distance-between-cities
     ( city-ID    ID          not null ,
       route-ID   ID          not null ,
     PRIMARY KEY (city-ID , route-ID),
     FOREIGN KEY (city-ID) REFERENCES City,
     FOREIGN KEY (route-ID) REFERENCES Route);
```

**Figure E17.9** SQL commands for creating tables to store distances between cities

**17.15** (4) Using the tables in exercise 17.14, formulate a query using pseudocode or SQL that will determine the distance between two cities given the names of the two cities.

**17.16** (4) Convert the RDBMS SQL commands in Figure E17.10 into an object diagram. The tables are used to store the straight line distances between pairs of cities.

**17.17** (4) Using the tables in exercise 17.16, formulate a query using pseudocode or SQL that will determine the distance between two cities given the names of the two cities. Assume that the distance between a given pair of cities is stored exactly once in the *Distance-between-cities* table. (The application must enforce a constraint such as *city1-ID* < *city2-ID* so that the distance is only entered once.)

**17.18** (5) Discuss the relative merits of the two approaches in the previous four exercises for storing distance information.

```
CREATE TABLE City
    ( city-ID      ID          not null ,
      city-name  char(30) not null ,
    PRIMARY KEY (city-ID));


CREATE SECONDARY INDEX City-index-name
    ON City (city-name);


CREATE TABLE Distance-between-cities
    ( city1-ID     ID          not null ,
      city2-ID     ID          not null ,
      distance     real        not null ,
    PRIMARY KEY (city1-ID , city2-ID),
    FOREIGN KEY (city1-ID) REFERENCES City,
    FOREIGN KEY (city2-ID) REFERENCES City);
```

**Figure E17.10** SQL commands for creating tables to store distances between cities

**17.19** (5) Discuss the similarities and differences between the database tables used to store edge and vertex information in exercises 17.1- 17.5 and the tables used to store distance information between cities in exercises 17.14 -17.18. How does fact that there is exactly one straight line distance between a pair of cities simplify the problem? Is the problem of storing distances between cities more nearly like a directed graph or an undirected graph? Why?

**17.20** (5) Convert the object diagrams in Figure E17.11, Figure E17.12, and Figure E17.13 into ideal tables and then into SQL commands. How does the presence of the zero-one multiplicity influence the conversion?

Figure E17.13 is a portion of an object model for a CAD system. A piece of equipment may be indicated on the screen with a special icon; minor equipment is not shown on the screen. Some icons are graphic-only and do not correspond to any piece of equipment.

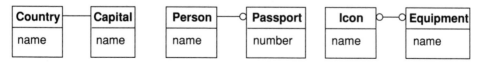

**Figure E17.11** Object diagram of capitals of countries

**Figure E17.12** Object diagram of passport ownership

**Figure E17.13** Object diagram for CAD system

**17.21** (5) Develop an object diagram for storing the status of forks and philosophers for the dining philosopher's problem. (See exercise 3.22.) Convert your diagram to RDBMS SQL commands. Show possible contents of the database tables for the situation in which each philosopher has exactly one fork.

**17.22** (8) Convert the diagram in Figure E17.14 into RDBMS SQL commands.

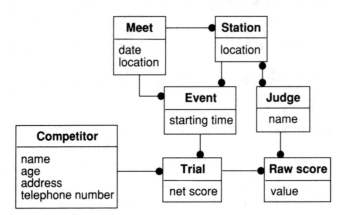

**Figure E17.14** Partial object diagram for a scoring system

**17.23** (5) What new features should be added to SQL to provide better support for OO concepts?

# 18

---

# Object Diagram Compiler

Compilers provide a natural application for the OMT methodology. Most compilers are batch programs that consist of one or more passes. Each pass works towards the goal of transforming the input to the output. For example, a C compiler may accept an input file of ASCII characters. Successive passes may parse into tokens, abstract the intended semantics, generate code, and then optimize code. Users expect that a compiler will carefully check its input during processing; the more errors the compiler can detect, the fewer errors will be encountered during program execution.

This chapter describes the development of a compiler for object diagrams for bill-of-material applications. The compiler is a batch program that accepts an object diagram as input and produces relational DBMS schema as output. The compiler input is limited to object diagrams of bill-of-material problems because of the special error checking built into the compiler. The compiler has served two purposes: It solved the immediate problems of the target applications and it was an important milestone in our continuing work on automating the OMT methodology.

The *Object Diagram Compiler* illustrates several concepts mentioned earlier in the book. The compiler architecture consists of four passes that step through a series of internal models. There are many relationships and functional dependencies within a model but few between models. As Chapter 9 notes, this kind of multipass architecture is common for compilers. The design of the compiler also touches upon some database issues discussed in Chapter 17 and metadata concepts described in Chapter 4.

## 18.1 BACKGROUND

General Electric has several internal applications that configure product assemblies. The business practice for these applications is that the customer specifies product function; the manufacturer must devise a corresponding product. For example, a customer might order a lawn mower that is lightweight, inexpensive, and energy efficient. The manufacturer may fill the order with a mower that has a 1 horsepower gasoline-powered engine, 45 cm diameter aluminum deck, and nonmulching blade. (GE does not manufacture lawn mowers; we use the lawn mower example for convenience.)

The list of parts chosen by a manufacturer to build a product is called a bill-of-material (BOM). A BOM is a tree of the direct and indirect parts that compose an assembly. The literature often refers to BOM as parts explosion problems. BOM are often printed out as indented parts lists, where the indentation corresponds to the depth in the hierarchy. Figure 18.1 shows a sample BOM for a lawn mower. The first value listed after each part type is the part number. Thus lawn mower *LM16G* has engine *E1*, deck *D16*, and so forth. Part properties follow the part number.

```
lawn mower: LM16G
        engine: E1, 1HP, gas powered
                piston: P1, 5 cm length, .5 cm diameter
                carburetor: CARB9
                wires: WI5, quantity 4, oil resistant

                ...

        deck: D16, 45 cm diameter, aluminum
        blade: B16, 40 cm long, non-mulching
        wheels: WH3, solid rubber, 8 cm diameter

        ...
```

**Figure 18.1** A portion of a bill-of-material (BOM)

In the past, most product assemblies have been manually designed by human experts. [Blaha-90] describes a new, automated approach to generating BOMs. The new approach uses a relational database to reverse engineer past product designs and extracts the implicit design rules for mapping specifications to choices of parts. The details of the new approach are beyond the scope of this book.

This chapter describes a portion of the new BOM configuration system: a subsystem called the *Object Diagram Compiler*. First, we draw an object diagram of a BOM parts explosion with an ordinary graphics editor by carefully placing many lines, triangles, boxes, text strings, and other primitives. The *Object Diagram Compiler* then processes the object diagram and ultimately generates DBMS commands that create tables and indexes. Whenever we change the object diagram, we rerun the compiler and generate new DBMS commands. Thus the object diagram is a living document. The *Object Diagram Compiler* simplifies documentation and DBMS schema generation by using the same source document for both. Our success with the *Object Diagram Compiler* has motivated further work towards developing more comprehensive tools for automating the OMT methodology.

## 18.2 PROBLEM STATEMENT

As shown in Figure 18.2, the objective of the *Object Diagram Compiler* is to translate BOM object diagrams into database commands and check for input errors.

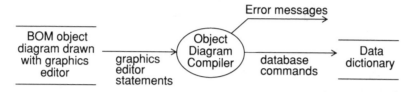

**Figure 18.2** Functional model of *Object Diagram Compiler*

### 18.2.1 Compiler Input

The compiler must read an ASCII description of a BOM object diagram produced by a general purpose graphics editor. We used FrameMaker,[*] but others such as MacDraw and Interleaf are also suitable. The graphics editor must be geometric-shape-based and not pixel-based. The compiler input is analogous to the source code of a conventional programming language compiler.

Figure 18.3 is a sample BOM object diagram. A lawn mower has a blade and engine. Each blade and engine may be associated with several lawn mowers. (Figure 18.3 refers to catalog descriptions of parts and not the physical parts. See Section 4.5, *Metadata*, for details.) *Lawn mower*, *Blade*, and *Engine* are described by attributes. Figure 18.4 shows some of the corresponding Framemaker language for the image of the *Blade* class.

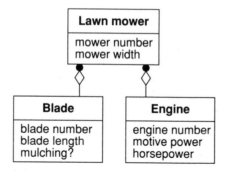

**Figure 18.3** Sample BOM object diagram

The *Object Diagram Compiler* must support basic object modeling constructs: classes, attributes, binary associations, binary aggregations, and generalizations. The compiler does not need to support object modeling constructs that are not needed for our BOM applications, such as qualified associations, n-ary relationships, and operations.

---

\* FrameMaker is a desktop publishing system that integrates word processing, graphics, page layout, and other features. We only used the graphic editing capabilities in the *Object Diagram Compiler*.

```
<Rectangle
      <BRect  3.06" 5.65" 1.06" 0.28">
> # end of Rectangle
<TextLine
      <TLOrigin  3.58" 5.83">   <TLAlignment Center >
      <Font    <FBold Yes >    > # end of Font
      <String 'Blade'>
> # end of TextLine
<Rectangle
      <BRect  3.06" 5.93" 1.06" 0.49">
> # end of Rectangle
<TextLine
      <TLOrigin  3.14" 6.08">   <TLAlignment Left >
      <Font    <FPlain Yes >   > # end of Font
      <String 'blade number'>
> # end of TextLine
<TextLine
      <TLOrigin  3.14" 6.22">   <TLAlignment Left >   <String 'blade length'>
> # end of TextLine
<TextLine
      <TLOrigin  3.14" 6.36">   <TLAlignment Left >   <String 'mulching?'>
> # end of TextLine
```

**Figure 18.4** Sample input for *Object Diagram Compiler*

## 18.2.2 Compiler Output

The compiler must produce a series of database commands. This output is executed as a script file to load a data dictionary. We used the Oracle DBMS, but any relational DBMS that supports the SQL language is suitable. The compiler must generate association names and determine how to implement relationships. Figure 18.5 shows some output that corresponds to Figure 18.3. The compiler output is analogous to the object code of a conventional programming language compiler.

The *Object Diagram Compiler* stores its output in a data dictionary custom designed for BOM applications. (Several downstream programs complete the process of creating the tables and indexes that store individual BOMs.) We used this custom dictionary rather than the DBMS dictionary because we required BOM specific extensions. Section 18.3.6 describes our data dictionary.

## 18.2.3 Miscellaneous Requirements

The *Object Diagram Compiler* was subject to further requirements on development time and performance. The compiler had to be developed quickly—in four months or less. It was part of the larger BOM generation project, and we did not want to divert our attention. Our requirements on execution time were more lax. An execution time of two hours or less is ad-

REMARK  Load object class ID, object class name, table name
Insert into meta_object_table Values ( 1000 , 'Lawn mower' , 'Lawn_mower' );
Insert into meta_object_table Values ( 1001 , 'Blade' , 'Blade' );
Insert into meta_object_table Values ( 1002 , 'Engine' , 'Engine' );

REMARK  Load relationship ID, relationship name, type
Insert into meta_relationship Values ( 2000 , 'Lawn_mower#Engine' , 'aggregation' );
Insert into meta_relationship Values ( 2001 , 'Lawn_mower#Blade' , 'aggregation' );

REMARK  Load relationship ID, assembly class ID, part class ID, part min and max multiplicity
Insert into meta_aggregation Values ( 2000, 1000, 1002, 1, 1 );
Insert into meta_aggregation Values ( 2001, 1000, 1001, 1, 1 );

.....

**Figure 18.5** Sample output from *Object Diagram Compiler*

equate because the compiler is a batch program that is only run at system set-up time. The compiler is not used for the day-to-day generation of BOMs. (As it turned out, because of skillful software engineering, performance was much better than required!)

The compiler must detect input errors but need not correct the errors. For instance, class names must be unique, have less than 31 characters, and begin with an alphabetic character. The compiler must not abort when it encounters user errors. The compiler must accept bad input and keep running so that the user can detect multiple errors from a single run.

The compiler must tolerate imperfect connections. Since object diagrams are prepared with a general purpose graphics editor, it is difficult to align and precisely connect everything. The compiler must accept input that looks correct when printed on paper. Also the compiler must detect mistakes that are not visible, such as superimposed drawing components.

The compiler must isolate dependencies on graphic editors and relational DBMS within one or two modules. Then the compiler can be ported without major rewriting.

## 18.3 ANALYSIS

Analysis is the first step towards solving the problem statement. It quickly became apparent that the difference in level of abstraction between input and output was too great to span in a single step. We decided that it would be best to use several passes. This conclusion is not surprising, since many compilers require multiple passes.

The disadvantage of a multipass approach is that the developer must prepare multiple object models and design multiple compilation phases. The advantage of multiple passes is that complexity is addressed in a divide and conquer fashion. The resulting code is easier to port since graphic editor and DBMS dependencies are isolated in small portions of code.

Figure 18.6 elaborates the functional model of the *Object Diagram Compiler* shown in Figure 18.2. Each ellipse represents a compiler pass. The three data stores at the bottom of the figure denote intermediate object models. The remainder of this section describes the compiler passes and intermediate object models. There is no significant dynamic model for the compiler, since it is a batch transformation.

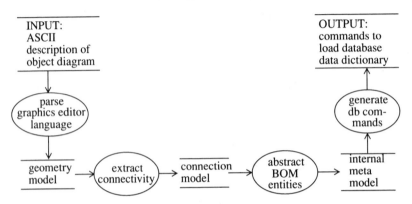

**Figure 18.6** Functional model of *Object Diagram Compiler*

## 18.3.1 Parse Graphics Editor Language

The first pass reads in the raw diagram Framemaker file generated by the graphics editor (a sample is shown in Figure 18.4) and builds the geometry model. The first pass corresponds to lexical analysis in a conventional programming language compiler. This pass required little analysis effort beyond figuring out a correct BNF syntax for the graphics editor language. Our development of a BNF grammar for the graphics editor was aided by vendor documentation.

## 18.3.2 Geometry Object Model

Figure 18.7 summarizes the geometry model. We have omitted some classes, associations, and attributes in order to conserve space and simplify explanation. The geometry model represents a diagram as a series of graphic primitives and is a convenient form for further processing. The geometry model regards an object diagram as simply a picture. The graphical objects (ellipses, rectangles, polylines, polygons, and textlines) coexist but have no interrelationships. We derived the geometry model directly from the BNF grammar of the graphics editor language.

The graphics editor that we used organizes components by page. A *Textline* is a single line of text that may be placed anywhere on a page. A *Textline* has a font and alignment and originates at a point. Each *Font* describes text size and special features such as italics, bold, and underlining. The geometry model includes *page number* for use in error messages.

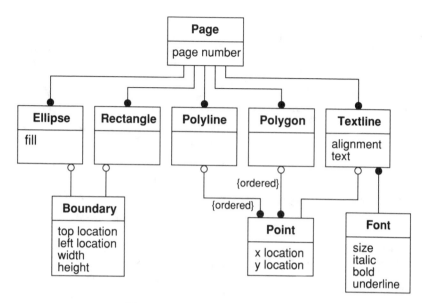

**Figure 18.7** Geometry object model

*Ellipse*, *Rectangle*, *Polyline*, and *Polygon* capture graphical information in the object diagram. Ellipses have a location and a bounding rectangle. An ellipse may have a hollow fill or solid fill. Rectangles have a location, width, and height. Polylines and polygons are composed of straight line segments that connect a sequence of points. A polyline is an arbitrary sequence of lines; a polygon is a closed geometric figure.

The geometric model for our lawn mower example (Figure 18.3) contains the following objects:

- 6 rectangles,
- 11 textlines (3 bold font, 8 normal font),
- 2 polygons (diamonds),
- 2 ellipses (which happen to be circles) with solid fill, and
- 2 polylines (vertical lines between *Lawn-mower* and *Blade*, *Lawn-mower* and *Engine*).

### 18.3.3 Extract Connectivity

The second pass consolidates raw geometry, classifies sizes and shapes, and detects intersections and attachments of geometrical primitives. We call the output from the second pass the connection model.

Figure 18.8 presents part of the data flow diagram for this pass. *Ellipses*, *Rectangles*, *Polylines*, *Polygons*, and *Textlines* from the geometry model are input data stores in the functional model. Every class and association in the connection model is the output of one or

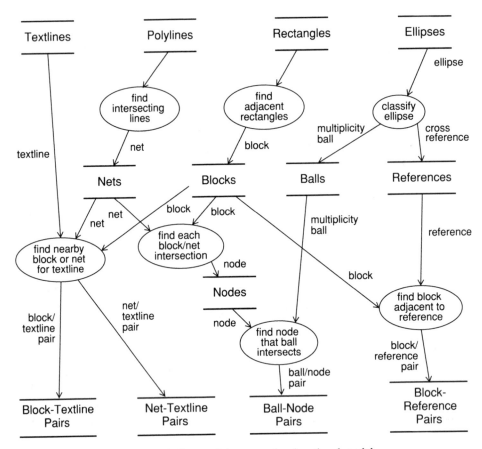

**Figure 18.8** Connectivity extraction functional model

more functional model processes. Recall that during analysis we do not specify algorithms but specify the effects of processes.

In Figure 18.8, groups of contiguous rectangles are recognized as blocks. Groups of intersecting lines are recognized as nets. Each block and net intersection is found and stored as a node. Ellipses are classified into multiplicity balls or sheet cross references. Each multiplicity ball is associated with a node; each reference is associated with a block. Each textline is bound to its nearest block or net.

### 18.3.4 Connection Object Model

The connection model, summarized in Figure 18.9, bridges the geometry model and the internal meta model. Classes that are shaded are carried forward from the geometry model. The connection model regards an object diagram as a topology, a collection of blocks connected with nets. Blocks and nets have attached geometry and text.

The *Block*, *Net*, and *Node* classes form the core of the connectivity model. Each block has a name; each net has a name. A node corresponds to exactly one block and one net. Each block may have many nodes; each net may have many nodes. A node may be connected to a ball or a diamond. A net may be connected to a triangle. A block may have several cross reference circles pointing to other pages. Both blocks and nets have text.

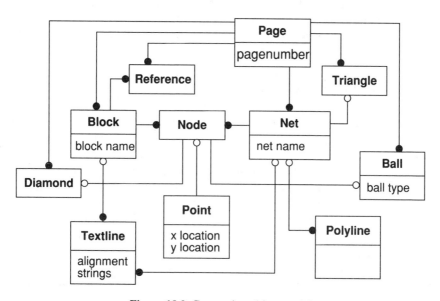

**Figure 18.9** Connection object model

The connection model for our lawn mower example contains the following objects:

- 3 blocks named *Lawn-mower*, *Blade*, and *Engine*,
- 2 nets named *Lawn-mower#Blade* and *Lawn-mower#Engine*,
- 4 nodes,
- 2 diamonds each associated with a node, and
- 2 solid balls each associated with a node.

The *Lawn-mower* block is associated with two textlines: *mower-number* and *mower-width*. Similar associations occur for *Blade* and *Engine*.

### 18.3.5 Abstract BOM Entities

The third pass raises the level of abstraction. The graphical symbols in a BOM diagram have more meaning than their mere shape. A block denotes a class; a net represents a generalization or association. Pass 3 coalesces cross references to classes, verifies uniqueness of

names, and classifies relationship types. Pass 3 applies hard coded rules for mapping relationships to tables (see Chapter 17). The second and third passes correspond to semantic
analysis in a conventional programming language compiler.

The functional model for this pass is complicated by extensive error checking. Much of
this error checking derives from using a general purpose graphics editor to construct the input object diagrams. In general, the user can make many diagramming errors, such as dangling association lines, duplicate class names, and class blocks without a name. The *Object
Diagram Compiler* also checks for errors peculiar to BOM generation. The Pass 3 functional
model is too large and complex to display here.

### 18.3.6  Internal Meta Object Model

Figure 18.10 summarizes the internal meta model that captures the meaning of BOM diagrams. A BOM database has many class and association tables. Each class table has many
attributes. An attribute may be a role or a nonrole attribute. Nonrole attributes belong to exactly one class or association table. Role attributes appear in many class and association tables. Role attributes connect together the various tables. A class associates with all blocks
that refer to it. Each relationship associates with one net.

A BOM database also has many relationships. Each relationship is either a generalization or an association. Association may be further refined into aggregation. Each generalization has one role attribute that denotes the superclass and many role attributes that denote the
subclasses. (We did not need multiple inheritance for our BOM applications.) A discriminator indicates which subclass pertains to each superclass instance. Since BOM generation
only uses binary associations, each association has exactly two role attributes. An association may have zero or more nonrole attributes.

The internal meta model for our lawn mower example contains the following objects:

- 3 class tables named *Lawn-mower*, *Blade*, and *Engine*,

- 0 association tables. (Our hard coded rules bury both associations in the *lawn-
  mower* example. See Section 18.4.),

- 3 role attributes: *mower-number*, *blade-number*, and *engine-number*,

- 5 nonrole attributes,

- 2 aggregations (Both associations are aggregations.), and

- 0 generalizations, and 0 link values.

### 18.3.7  Generate Database Commands

The fourth and final pass transforms the internal meta model into the database meta model.
This process is simple because the internal meta model is similar to the database meta model.
The last pass is analogous to code generation in a conventional programming language com-
piler and produces the desired output of DBMS commands.

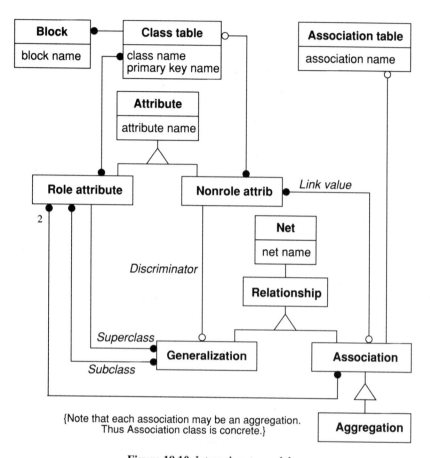

**Figure 18.10** Internal meta model

## 18.4 SYSTEM DESIGN

The choice of system archifecture for the *Object Diagram Compiler* was straightforward and directly follows from the overall functional model in Figure 18.6. We chose to implement the program as a batch transformation as discussed in Chapter 9.

The *Object Diagram Compiler* consists of a sequence of passes that transform between layers. We chose a closed architecture where each layer can only access the objects in itself and the immediate preceding layer. The advantage of a closed architecture is increased information hiding which simplifies debugging, extension, and porting. In general, the disadvantage of a closed architecture (relative to an open architecture) is loss of efficiency. For the *Object Diagram Compiler*, efficiency is good because of the careful design of each pass. Our object models show these linkages between object models as shaded rectangles. Thus *Class table* in the internal meta model refers to *Block* in the connection model.

Each pass of the *Object Diagram Compiler* completes in full before proceeding to the next pass. This is because there is little locality of reference in our BOM diagrams. For example, a *Lawn mower* class on Sheet 1 can refer to a *Blade* class on Sheet 27. In contrast most programming language code has more locality, and compiler processes can operate with some degree of parallelism. For ordinary compilers, once enough characters have been read to recognize a lexical token, the token can be passed to semantic analysis; semantic analysis need not wait for completion of lexical analysis.

The *Object Diagram Compiler* manages all data in memory. Input is a file; output is a file. There is no need to make intermediate data visible outside the program. Since the program has a closed architecture, we considered deallocating objects from earlier passes that are no longer needed to recover memory space. We did not deallocate objects because of the extra logic required and fear of dangling pointer bugs. (The language used to implement the *Object Diagram Compiler* does not have garbage collection.) Memory consumption has not caused us any problems to date.

Implementation of control is not an issue. The *Object Diagram Compiler* is a batch program. The user has no interaction with the program after starting it; there is no interactive debugger. All error messages are printed to a file. Once again, our approach was dictated by simplicity. It was simpler not to provide an interactive debugger; the batch approach has worked well in practice.

## 18.5  OBJECT DESIGN

Most of the work remaining after analysis was to implement associations, prepare pseudocode, and then write actual code. The process of writing pseudocode uncovered several analysis flaws. We revised the analysis as needed. Design was a straightforward application of object-oriented programming and mostly a matter of adding detail.

### 18.5.1  Functional Models

In this problem, as in many batch transformations, functional dependencies can be expressed as an acyclic directed graph among data stores containing sets of objects. Each data store contains all the objects of a given class, such as *Rectangles* and *Nodes,* or all the links of a given association, such as *Ball-Node Pairs.* The data flow diagram can be constructed by examining each class and association in the output model and determining the input classes and associations that it depends on.

In many cases the final algorithm can be written down directly without actually drawing a data flow diagram. We found that a "marking" approach aids formulation of functional algorithms. A mark represents a class, association, or attribute that has been computed at a given point in the algorithm. First all input classes and associations are marked on the object diagram. Then all classes and associations in subsequent stages of the batch transformation are examined. Pseudocode for each attribute and association is written in terms of previously marked classes and associations, and the corresponding output attribute or association is marked. When all the attributes of a class are marked, then the entire class is marked. When the entire output object model is marked, the functional algorithm is complete. This marking technique works because the dependencies form a partial order.

In Figure 18.8, *Blocks* can be computed from *Rectangles*. *Balls* can be computed from *Ellipses*. *Nets* can be computed from *Polylines*. *Nodes* can be computed from *Nets* and *Blocks*. After these computations, *Ball-Node Pairs* can be computed from *Balls* and *Nodes*. We did not actually draw the data flow diagram because the functional algorithm is so directly derivable from the object model.

The first pass (parse graphics editor language) reads the ASCII file that contains a BOM diagram and loads the geometry model. We used UNIX compiler generation tools for this pass to improve our productivity. This pass required little design effort and no pseudocode.

The second pass (extract connectivity) scans the geometry model and produces the connection model. Most of our design effort for this pass was concerned with devising graph traversal algorithms. As an example, Section 18.5.3 describes our algorithm for finding connections.

The third pass (abstract BOM entities) scans the connection model and generates the internal meta model. Like the second pass, most of the design effort for this pass concerned choice of algorithms.

The fourth pass (generate database commands) scans the internal meta model and writes DBMS commands to a file. All generalizations are implemented with distinct superclass and subclass tables. Some associations are represented by distinct tables; others are captured through buried foreign keys. (See Chapter 17.) Hard coded rules in the *Object Diagram Compiler* determine how to implement each association.

## 18.5.2 Intermediate Object Models

An important design decision was the choice of programming language. Based on past favorable experience, we decided to use an in-house object-oriented programming language called DSM [Shah-89]. DSM's class library provided us with several convenient choices for handling associations. DSM can implement associations with foreign keys, sets, arrays, tables, and a built-in generic association type. Our choice of technique was determined by the type of access required. We frequently used foreign keys and arrays. For example, Figure 18.11 shows a common way of implementing a one-to-many association.

A *Polygon* object may access points through the array of points stored in the *points* attribute. A *Point* object may access a polygon through the *parent* attribute. Since points may belong to exactly one of several different types of objects, the data type of parent is "object." "Object" indicates that the value is an object but does not specify the class.

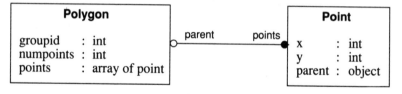

**Figure 18.11** Implementation of a one-to-many association

The internal meta model captures the intended meaning of object diagrams. Initially, this model was similar to Figure 18.10. However, much of the internal meta model was not needed for implementation, so we simplified it during design. In the end, the internal meta model was a simple mapping of blocks and nets into classes and relationships, as shown in Figure 18.12.

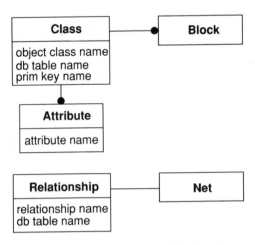

**Figure 18.12** Internal meta object model

The structure of the database meta model is similar to Figure 18.10. We hand converted the database meta model into database tables to bootstrap the system. The *Object Diagram Compiler* was only intended to compile BOM diagrams, thus it cannot compile itself.

### 18.5.3 Connectivity Algorithm

A commonly occurring theme in the *Object Diagram Compiler* is determining connections. Lines connect to rectangles, ellipses, and each other. Text is contained in rectangles and is adjacent to lines. Rectangles are adjacent to each other. During design we observed that each of these separate problems could be reduced to a special case of a more general problem: Find the intersection of a bounding box with a bag of points.

For each page and element type, we construct bags of points as follows. (A bag is the same as a mathematical set, except it may have duplicates.) For each rectangle, we add the four corner points to the rectangle bag; each corner point is an object that contains a pointer to its parent rectangle. Each line adds two point objects to the line bag; a line of text adds one point object to the text bag; and similarly for other graphical primitives. Then for example, we find all rectangles intersecting a line by constructing a bounding box around the line and checking the intersection of the bounding box with the rectangle bag of points.

We used a doubly sorted dictionary to efficiently search a bag of points for intersections with a bounding box. Each bag of points is first sorted on the x-coordinate and then on the y-coordinate. Figure 18.13 shows an object model of our point access structure. Three important operations are: Insert a point, delete a point, and find points.

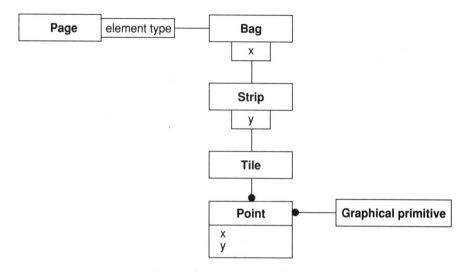

**Figure 18.13** Object model of point access structure

To insert a point, first find the strip to which the point belongs. Try for an exact match on the x-coordinate in the qualified association between *Bag* and *Strip*. If none is found, create a new strip and add it to the association. Next, find the tile to which the point belongs by trying for an exact match on the y-coordinate in the qualified association between *Strip* and *Tile*. If none is found, create a new tile. Finally, associate the point with the tile.

Tiles are not of uniform size. Figure 18.14 has twelve points, seven strips, and seventeen tiles. (Each tile has a point at the lower left hand corner; when points coincide, one tile corresponds to multiple points.) A tile is merely a useful abstraction for organizing points in a search space for efficient interval searches.

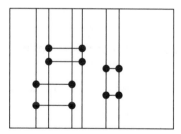

**Figure 18.14** Strips and tiles for rectangle bag of points

Deletion is similar, except tiles and strips are deleted as they become empty.

Searching starts with the x-values of the bounding box. We implemented a special operation on the qualified association that returns all strips between the minimum and maximum values. Then, we queried the y-qualified association to determine all tiles in the strip between the y-values of the bounding box. Finally, all points associated with the tiles were added to the collection of points found. We convert the collection of points into a set of graphical primitives by traversing the association between point and graphical primitive.

We had several reasons for constructing a general purpose connectivity routine. First of all, we expected that finding connections would be a common operation, and we wanted efficiency. The naive algorithm of checking all possible combinations of elements on a page yields an execution time proportional to the square of the number of elements. In contrast, our algorithm is linear with the number of elements and connections. (Our problems have a limited number of connections, so in practice the order of the execution time was effectively reduced from $n^2$ to n, where n is the number of elements.) Our algorithm has the disadvantage of added complexity; thus we wanted to design a general purpose routine once and reuse it for all the special cases: Line intersect line, line intersect rectangle, and so forth.

## 18.6 IMPLEMENTATION

We implemented the *Object Diagram Compiler* with the DSM language. (DSM is an inhouse object-oriented programming language that is implemented on top of C.) The final code was 13,000 lines long. It took one person three months to develop the diagram compiler. Six weeks were consumed by analysis and design and six weeks by coding and debugging. About twenty bugs were found, each of which took only a few minutes to find and correct.

The compiler is presently being used for several BOM generation applications. One application has a current input of more than 100 classes and 150 associations yielding a graphics editor file with over 13,000 lines. The compiler runs fast, compiling 5,000 lines per minute. This was a pleasant surprise because we initially feared that using an object-oriented language might degrade performance. The *Object Diagram Compiler* fully satisfied its requirements. Our success with the compiler has motivated work on more comprehensive software to support the OMT methodology.

## 18.7 LESSONS LEARNED

We draw the following conclusions from our experiences in developing the *Object Diagram Compiler*.

- Stick to the object-association paradigm and avoid the temptation to use stacks, pointers, and other data structures. In most cases, the use of associations eliminates the need for complex data structures.

- Use of a limited number of paradigms and a rich library of container classes greatly cut the number of bugs and increased our software development productivity.

- When making enhancements, don't just patch the design, rethink the analysis. Wherever we violated this rule, we wasted time and made errors. Think through the consequences of your "enhancement" deeply and not superficially.

- Batch software is much easier to write than interactive software; batch software does not need to contend with user interface and dialogue considerations.

## 18.8 CHAPTER SUMMARY

The *Object Diagram Compiler* accepts as input a textual description of an object diagram. The compiler produces DBMS commands that can be executed to load data dictionary tables. We call this program a compiler because it must not only transform its input, but it must also detect errors. A general purpose graphics editor provides no inherent support for object diagramming, so the compiler must detect many error conditions.

We chose a multipass architecture with intermediate object models; each pass gradually raises the level of abstraction. Pass 1 recognizes that the ASCII characters in the input file denote graphical primitives. Pass 2 detects graphical connectivity. Pass 3 abstracts a graphic picture into an object model. The fourth and final pass converts the internal format of the *Object Diagram Compiler* into that required by the application data dictionary tables.

Both the object and functional models were important for the *Object Diagram Compiler*, as there is much data to handle and substantial processing to convert the data from pass to pass. The dynamic model was relatively unimportant because the compiler is batch software and has no user interaction.

The design and implementation of the *Object Diagram Compiler* proceeded rapidly and were simply a matter of detail. The most significant tasks were to implement associations, prepare pseudocode, write the actual code, and then debug. Probably, our most important design decision was choosing the DSM object-oriented programming language. DSM has a rich class library that simplifies programming. We also decided to use UNIX compiler generation tools to parse the input. The *Object Diagram Compiler* completely satisfied its requirements. The compiler had excellent performance, despite the lax requirement in this area.

## BIBLIOGRAPHIC NOTES

The first pass in our *Object Diagram Compiler* was implemented with UNIX compiler construction tools. [Schreiner-85] describes how to use these tools. [Aho-79] describes the theoretical basis of compiler design. [Shah-89] describes the DSM language that was used to implement the *Object Diagram Compiler*. [Blaha-90] describes the larger BOM configuration generation application that was briefly summarized in Section 18.1.

## REFERENCES

[Aho-79] A.V. Aho, J.D. Ullman. *Principles of Compiler Design, Third Edition*. Reading, Mass.: Addison-Wesley, 1979.

[Blaha-90] M.R. Blaha, W.J. Premerlani, A.R. Bender, R.M. Salemme, M.M. Kornfein, C.K. Harkins. Bill-of-Material Configuration Generation. *Sixth International Conference on Data Engineering*, February 5-9, 1990, Los Angeles, CA.

[Schreiner-85] Axel T. Schreiner, H. George Friedman. *Introduction to Compiler Construction with UNIX*. Englewood Cliffs, New Jersey: Prentice Hall, 1985.

[Shah-89] Ashwin Shah, James Rumbaugh, Jung Hamel, Renee Borsari. DSM: an object-relationship modeling language. *OOPSLA'89* as *ACM SIGPLAN 24*, 11 (Nov. 1989), 191-210.

## EXERCISES

**18.1**  (3) An object model compiler that supports a subset of the OMT notation uses the meta model in Figure E18.1. The compiler reads object models and generates instances of classes and associations (objects and links). Which of the following constructs does the meta model support: object classes, methods, object attributes, generalization, aggregation, binary association, ternary association, link attributes, qualified associations, role names, association names? If a construct requires something that is missing from the meta model, the construct is not supported.

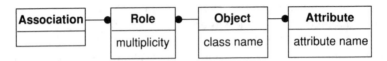

**Figure E18.1** Meta model for an object model compiler

**18.2**  (5) Figure E18.2 is an input to the compiler described in exercise 18.1. The output of the compiler can be thought of as an instance diagram. A partially completed instance diagram corresponding to Figure E18.2 is shown in Figure E18.3. The links are correct, but some names and values are missing. Fill them in.

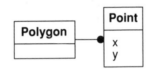

**Figure E18.2** Compiler input object model

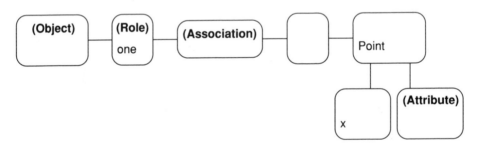

**Figure E18.3** Partially completed compiler output instance diagram

**18.3**  (7) The meta model itself is fair game as input to the compiler. Figure E18.4 is the corresponding partially completed output instance diagram. The links are correct. Finish filling in names and values.

**18.4**  (9) Extend the meta model from Figure E18.1 to include generalization and aggregation relationships as well as relationship names. Make sure the meta model itself is valid input for the compiler.

**18.5**  (9) Prepare an instance diagram for the output of the compiler using the object diagram you prepared for the previous exercise as input.

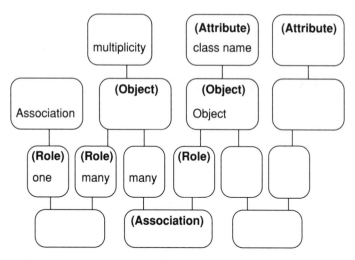

**Figure E18.4** Partially completed compiler output instance diagram

# 19

## Computer Animation

Computer animation systems create sequences of images, which when shown one after the other, create the illusion of motion. Computer animation systems require an extensible design so that new applications and new graphics hardware can be easily added.

This chapter describes a three-dimensional computer animation system. The system, *OSCAR*, the *O*bject-oriented *SC*ene Animato*R*, produces high quality film and video sequences of the results of scientific and engineering calculations and experiments. *OSCAR* automates the creation, control, and management of 3-D computer-generated animation sequences. Using an object-oriented script language as its user interface, *OSCAR* controls analysis, modeling, rendering, display, and filming. Interfaces have been developed for scientific analysis programs in the areas of molecular modeling, robotics, mechanisms analysis, and fluid mechanics. The object-oriented design has produced a system that lends itself to interfacing with existing and future applications.

The *OSCAR* application demonstrates how an object-oriented design can be successfully implemented with a non-object-oriented language. *OSCAR* is written in C using an object-oriented development environment that includes macros and run-time support for inheritance, instancing, and message passing. *OSCAR* includes an interpreter that permits users to create instances from the animation classes in the system and to control these instances by sending messages. Computer animation systems have a dynamic simulation architecture as discussed in Chapter 9.

## 19.1 BACKGROUND

*OSCAR* is the result of research, started in 1984, on the application of object-oriented technology to industrial applications. Because we expected computer graphics systems to increase performance dramatically throughout the 1980s, we proposed developing a 3-D computer graphics animation system that would allow scientists and engineers to study the results of their experiments and analyses. At the time, no C-based object-oriented systems were generally available, so we developed our own object-oriented interpreter to support the animation research. This interpreter, called *LYMB*, includes a run-time library for creating objects and communicating with them using commands and run-time message passing. The interpreter has no dependencies on computer animation; animation knowledge is held with the animation-specific classes.

### 19.1.1 The Animation Process

*OSCAR* simulates the steps in the traditional, manual animation process. As in all disciplines, animation has its own terminology. We briefly describe the animation process, defining enough jargon for the reader to understand the *OSCAR* system.

The user of a computer animation system acts as the producer, writer, and director of the final animation sequence. This sequence may be played back on a computer graphics terminal or recorded onto movie film or video tape. The producer manages the overall film production, keeping schedules, assigning tasks, and organizing resources. The writer creates a script based on the requirements of the customer. The director controls the animation, positioning the props, actors, cameras, and lights.

The animation process proceeds as follows:

1. *Story.* The writer, working with a customer, develops a narrative story that describes the actors and their roles, including their appearance, dialog, and actions. Writing is an artistic process and is difficult to assist with the computer. The actors may include inanimate objects.

2. *Story board.* A story board is a graphic synopsis of the animation, illustrating the appearance of the animation and the flow of the story. The story board contains a representative drawing for each major point in the story. The art director normally produces the story board.

3. *Script.* The script contains the detailed positioning and movement of the actors, cameras, and lights in the animation. Some computer animation systems provide scripting languages. Since the script may change over the course of production, a good language allows the script to be easily modified when minor animation changes are required.

4. *Simulations.* Experiments and simulations often provide the motions of the animation for scientific applications. Scientists and engineers familiar with the application domain set up and execute these simulations. Simulations can be computation-intensive.

5. *Models*. Each prop and actor in an animation must have a geometric model that describes its appearance. This model is translated, during the rendering process, from a mathematical description into a portion of a 2-D image.

6. *Preview*. Before committing the animation sequence to film, a fast preview of the animation helps establish critical timing and the overall look of the final product. Producing high quality film output is usually costly, so changes to the simulation should be made as early as possible.

7. *Render*. Rendering produces shaded images for later display by applying algorithms to the geometric model, surface properties, and lighting. The render operation corresponds to assembling a single frame of a conventional animation. Rendering realistic effects such as multiple light sources, texture, shadows, translucency, and refraction can be computation-intensive.

8. *Recording*. After rendering, the images are recorded on either film or video, one frame at a time.

A typical animation application is three-dimensional molecular modeling. First a batch simulation is run on a supercomputer to compute the position of each atom in a vibrating molecule over a period of time. The actors are the atoms in the molecules and their chemical bonds. The animator prepares a script viewing the molecule from interesting angles. Rapid previewing is essential because it is hard to choose the right viewing angles without seeing the results. The final animation is run at full resolution, and a film is produced. Actually exposing a film of several minutes' duration can take a full day of computer time.

## 19.2 PROBLEM STATEMENT

The goal of the graphics animation system is to provide an automated system for the efficient creation, control, and management of 3-D computer generated animation sequences. The system provides facilities to record animation sequences on 16mm film or video. The system also provides interfaces between diverse simulation, modeling, and rendering systems. Realizing that the application of computer animation is broad, the system must adapt to new applications with a minimal amount of new software.

The following requirements were derived from knowledge of the conventional movie making process and the scientific and engineering analysis process. The movie animation metaphor used is that of stop-frame animation. In a stop-frame animation system, frames are recorded one at a time. All participants in the animation are changed slightly and another frame is exposed.

The user input consists of text files that contain animation scripts. Scripts can reference a library of complex actions, as well as define new actions. The scripting language serves as a base for animation description and documentation of an animation.

Each animation consists of one or more scenes. Within a given scene, the script can control any participant in the animation including actors, cameras, and lights. Control is provided through lists of actions that the director groups into cues. Cues are active for a user-specified duration and specify actions applied to objects in the animation. Any valid statement in the animation language can be an action. For example, an actor might be told to move at a constant velocity during the scene. Each scene specifies the renderer that produces its frame images.

Actors are the active participants in the animation. They have shape, position, orientation, and appearance properties, such as color and texture. For example, in a planetary exploration animation, actors would include planets, rings, satellites, rockets, stars, and the sun. The specification of actor motions must be flexible enough to allow rotations and scaling about arbitrary axes and origins. The visibility of individual actors must also be controllable. Often, it is useful to group actors together, so the system must provide a mechanism to allow actors to be collected and controlled enmasse.

The geometry of an actor is kept in a geometric model. Models range from rigid motions of simple geometric shapes to complicated deformations of complex objects. Since modeling is a complicated and tedious task, the system must be able to use models that already exist. Also, users may have invested large amounts of training in the use of specific modelers. Modelers should quickly produce low-resolution models during previewing so that the computation time to produce a high-resolution model is only be required for the detailed film.

All animation is viewed through a camera. Multiple cameras can exist, but only one is active in a scene at one time. The user can place the camera in the environment and control its aim and orientation. Different camera movement effects like panning, zooming, and tracking are required.

Multiple lights can be used to illuminate the animation. Lights can be turned on and off and their intensity can be controlled. Lights also have geometry—spherical, cylindrical, point, or flood.

Engineers and scientists who use the system will rely on their own analysis programs to provide much of the physics of the animation. Therefore, the animation system must provide a way to interface to these external programs. These programs should not be modified just to interface with the animation system, so the interface burden must be borne by the animation system.

The system must provide a facility to track completion of frames and where they reside. A frame is one image in an animation sequence. A frame can be built from one rendered frame or a combination of rendered frames. A post-production capability allows the user to recall frames, combine them with other frames, and manipulate them on a recoding device.

It is too time consuming to specify the incremental motion of each actor in an animation for each frame, so the system must provide a way to move objects along easily specified paths. Keyframing is an animation technique that lets an animator specify complex motion by giving a few key frames and letting a junior animator fill in the intervening frames. A computerized animation system should have a keyframing capability in which the system interpolates the animation.

## 19.3 ANALYSIS

### 19.3.1 Object Model

Now, following the analysis steps in Chapter 8, we extract objects from the requirements and our knowledge of computer animation and computer graphics. Notice that the terminology from the problem statement is used in the object model. Many of the properties we specify for the objects come from our intuitive feeling for what an object should look like and how it should behave.

*Identifying Object Classes*

We start by listing candidate object classes:

- actor
- camera
- light
- scene
- cue
- renderer
- sequence
- frame

We follow four classes through analysis: actors, cues, renderers, and scenes.

- *Actors* are the participants in our animation. Our actors can represent a variety of objects we wish to model, so we have try to determine what properties are important to all actors, regardless of the application. In a finite element analysis, an actor could be an element mesh of a turbine blade. For molecular modeling, both atoms and bonds are actors.

- *Cues* control the actors, cameras, and lights in the animation. Cues are temporal objects, changing the state of the animation with time. Each cue is a series of events. For example, a cue might tell a ball to start rolling across the room or pan a camera across the stage. Any time dependent action can be affected by a cue.

- *Renderers* produce the individual frames in the animation. Rendering is still an active research area in computer graphics, so we must take care not to restrict ourselves to a particular renderer, such as scan line, ray trace, radiosity, or wire frame. The challenge is to characterize the properties of renderers that we expect all renderers to have. *Renderer* is an abstract class meant to be overridden by subclasses.

- *Scenes* control the animation process, bringing together cues and renderers. They usually describe a coherent set of actions within the animation.

*Identifying Associations and Attributes*

Here we define associations and attributes in the model:

- Each *actor* has a model that describes its geometry. Modeling is an active research area, and there is no one modeling technique that can be used in all situations. Also, the requirements state that existing modelers have to be supported, so *Model* is an open-ended abstract class.

  Actors also have position, orientation, color, and visibility. An actor's orientation is with respect to some origin. We group positional properties, such as translate, rotate, and scale, under a general 3-D transform. Actors also have light transmission properties which we break out as a separate object as new variations may be invented.

- *Cues* are time sensitive. Each cue has a time interval during which it is active. Usually, the user wants to do something special when an interval is entered and when it is exited. We call actions that should be executed at the start of the interval *start actions* and those that should be executed when the interval expires *end actions*. While a cue is active, it executes *tick actions* at the time resolution of its enclosing scene.

- *Renderers* need to know what actors, cameras, and lights are in a given scene so that they can create images. A user may not want to render every frame of an animation and should be able to specify a rendering resolution. The user also must be able to specify a spatial resolution that tells the renderer how big an image to create and where that image lies in the camera's view space. Graphics people call this spatial resolution the *viewport* of a rendering. The background color of the rendered image is also a property of renderers.

- A *scene* must know what cues and renderers are required to create the animation sequence. Like a cue, a scene also has starting and ending actions that perform initialization and termination.

### Identifying Operations

Most classes in the *OSCAR* animation system have interesting operations.

- *Actors.* We certainly will want to *translate*, *rotate*, and turn an actor *on* and *off*.

- *Cues.* We invoke a cue with a *tick* operation that includes the current time within the scene. The cue performs all its tick actions.

- *Renderers.* A *render* operation causes a renderer to create one frame of animation.

- *Scenes.* A *start* operation begins a scene's execution. The scene in turn steps through its time interval, invoking cues and rendering frames.

### Identifying Inheritance

Scenes and cues both have time intervals during which they are active, as well as start, tick, and end actions. We group *Scene* and *Cue* under the abstract superclass *Sequencer*. Scenes also have a clock and a time resolution; cues do not need these attributes as they are driven by scenes.

Lights, cameras, and actors all have position, orientation, and graphical transformation operations which we group under the abstract superclass *Transformable object*.

Figure 19.1 shows the final object model for the *OSCAR* system.

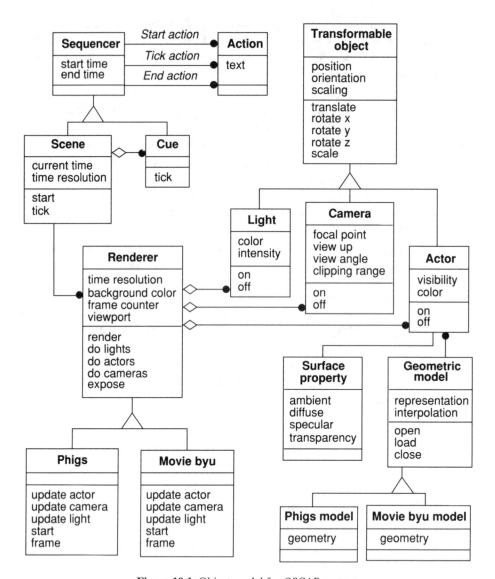

**Figure 19.1** Object model for *OSCAR* system

## 19.3.2 Dynamic Model

The dynamics of an animation are specified by a scene, which encapsulates a series of user-defined events. Figure 19.2 and Figure 19.3 show the dynamic model for *Scene* and *Cue*. A scene repeatedly enters the *tick* state, each time incrementing the current time and sending *tick* events to its cues and *render* events to its renderers. A cue is similar, but it receives tick events from the scene.

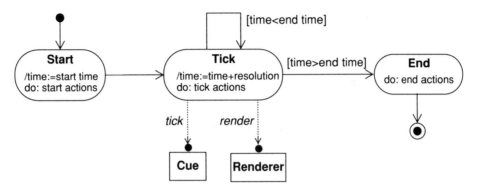

**Figure 19.2** State model for *Scene*

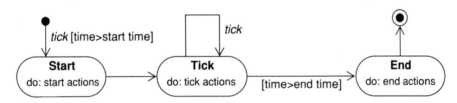

**Figure 19.3** State model for *Cue*

### 19.3.3 Functional Model

The most computation-intensive functional model is that for the renderer. A functional model for a renderer is shown in Figure 19.4.

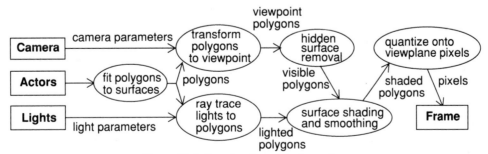

**Figure 19.4** Functional model of a renderer

## 19.4 SYSTEM DESIGN

### 19.4.1 Subsystems

The system architecture groups objects in the system according to the steps in the animation process. The anthropomorphic flavor of the model descriptions helps to maintain the correspondence with the animation process. Figure 19.5 shows the architecture of the animation system.

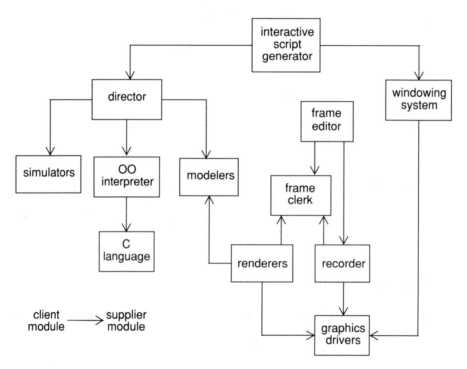

**Figure 19.5**  Architecture of *OSCAR* system

The interactive script generator permits the user to generate scripts using a graphical interface. With the script generator, the user can position cameras, lights, and objects interactively. Other script generators provide easy specification of complex camera and actor movements. The script generator is built on the director and the windowing system.

The director controls the animation using a variety of predefined tools. The director reads a script, prepared by the user or a script generator, and sends messages to objects in the animation. The director is built on the interactive OO interpreter, modelers, and simulators. By implementing a powerful, easy-to-use interpreter and a library of useful animation operations, we avoid the need to provide a special animation language.

Simulators are the external analysis programs. Typically, simulators are run separately from the animation process. They provide the physics for the animation sequences. Often, a simulator controls a complete animation, with *OSCAR* doing little more than positioning a camera and turning on a light.

Modelers create the geometries for actors. They are loosely related to renderers, since some renderers can only process models from specific modelers. Often the models are made from polygons, but the system must be able to handle other modeling primitives.

Frame editor objects do post-production editing, combining frames and creating special effects like wipes, dissolves, and fades.

A frame clerk tracks where each frame came from and where it is stored. It is a data store accessed by other modules.

Renderers take actor, camera, and light information to produce a single frame of animation. External renderers run in batch mode, producing their images from command files created by *OSCAR*. Other renderers are built within the animation system itself, but all renderers respond to the same protocol.

Recorder objects take finished frames and commit them to film or video. They also respond to a specific recording protocol, converting these messages into device-specific control functions.

### 19.4.2 Concurrency and Control

*OSCAR* is run as a sequential, batch job, so concurrency is not an issue, nor is allocation of tasks to processors. Control is implemented procedurally by explicitly sending messages to objects within iterative loops simulating scenes.

### 19.4.3 Data Formats

Scripts are written as sequences of operations in the OO interpreter language, rather than in any special format. The format of the frame clerk must be given, but we omit it here. The format of the simulators, modelers, and renderers is specified by their suppliers and is beyond our control, so we must accept them as they are.

### 19.4.4 Trade-offs

The director and the interpretive language must be easy to use and flexible, but they will not consume much run time, as most of the execution time is spent in predefined simulators, modelers, and renderers. Thus we chose to make the interpretive language highly symbolic. Operations are encoded as text strings which are interpreted at run time using an explicit search of the class hierarchy for methods. Operands are passed using variable-length argument lists and text keywords for flexibility. Set-up operations use several levels of indirection for flexibility. We also incorporated several debugging aids. The efficiency of the director is less than 50% but does not matter because the director consumes a small portion of the overall *OSCAR* execution time.

## 19.5  OBJECT DESIGN

During object design, we begin to shift our focus from the external requirements to the computer implementation. We extend the object models we derived during analysis to include associations and attributes that objects require for internal processing. Most of the design, however, is a simple and direct implementation of the analysis model.

### 19.5.1  Actors

To retain the state of an actor's position and orientation, we introduce a new class: the *Matrix*. *Camera* and *Light* also implement much of their behavior with *Matrix*. Each instance of *Matrix* is a 4-by-4 transformation matrix that captures the geometry of a *Transformable object* and provides an efficient basis for implementing motion. Translate, rotate, and scale are simply special cases of matrix multiplications on the 4-by-4 matrix. Successive transformations can be combined by multiplying their respective matrices. Each *Transformable object* delegates its behavior to a *Matrix* object.

### 19.5.2  Cues

The only external operation on a cue is *tick*. The operation is a direct implementation of the dynamic model:

1.  If clock has just entered the active interval for a cue, execute *start actions*.
2.  If clock is within the active interval for a cue, execute *tick actions*.
3.  If clock has just left the active interval for a cue, execute *end actions*.

This simple algorithm gives the animation system control over any object in the system. The power comes from the ability to use any statement in the language as an action. Later, in some examples, we show how the cue appears to the user.

### 19.5.3  Scenes

The only external operation on a scene is *start,* which steps through a scene as follows:

1.  Execute *start actions*.
2.  Set *current time* to *start time*.

As long as *current time* is less than *end time*:

3.  Increment *current time* by *resolution*.
4.  Execute scene *tick* actions.
5.  Send *tick* operation to each cue in the scene.
6.  Send *render* operation to each renderer in the scene.

Once the scene's *current time* exceeds its *end time:*

7.  Execute scene *end actions*.

## 19.5.4 Renderers

In the *Renderer* class, the *render* operation is the only complicated external operation. *OSCAR* supports many renderers, but all rendering is controlled by a uniform protocol. The render protocol determines whether a frame should be rendered, based on the renderers *time resolution* property. Then it positions the cameras, lights, and actors; the frame is built; and an *expose* operation requested. Finally, the time of the render operation is noted and the frame counter incremented. An abstract class, called *Renderer*, executes the rendering protocol. Specific renderers are subclasses of this abstract class and must implement any operations not implemented by the abstract class (noted as subclass responsibility).

The render protocol is as follows:

*Render operation*

1. If the frame counter is not a multiple of the rendering time resolution, just increment the frame counter and return.

2. If this is the first frame to render, perform the *start* operation (subclass responsibility).

3. Perform *cameras* operation.

4. Perform *lights* operation.

5. Perform *actors* operation.

6. Perform *frame* operation (subclass responsibility).

7. Perform *expose* operation.

8. Update render time.

9. Increment frame counter.

*Operations for Cameras, Lights, and Actors*

These operations check their list of objects to see if any have been changed since the last render operation. For each changed object, they perform *update_camera*, *update_light*, or *update_actor* operations with the object name as an argument. Unmodified objects use the image from the previous frame. It is necessary to store the current image for each object as an optimization to avoid recomputation.

Next we describe the subclass responsibility operations for a typical renderer called Phigs+. Phigs+ is a graphics standard for three-dimensional displays that have a hierarchical display structure.

1. *Start:* If the system is not initialized, open it, create a workstation, and set its update mode to deferred.

2. *Update_camera* queries the named camera for its viewing parameters and converts the *OSCAR* camera parameters into Phigs+ parameters to form a view orientation matrix. It inserts this matrix into the workstations view table.

3. *Update_light* calculates the light direction vector by asking the named light for its focal point and position. It also gets the color of the light and stores the direction and color in the light table for the workstation.

4.  *Update_actor* checks to see whether its model has changed since the named actor has
    changed. If the model has changed, it applies a load operation to the model. If this actor
    is not in a Phigs+ actor group, the actor is added to the group and a segment is opened.
    Then update_actor queries the status of the actor's position, color, orientation, and cre-
    ates the appropriate structure elements. Finally, the segment is closed and posted to the
    workstation.

5.  *Frame* sets the background for the workstation, and tells the workstation to render all
    segments.

These five operations are all that are required to add a new renderer to the system. Each operation performs one task that does not interact with the other tasks. The order of the operations is enforced by the abstract renderer class.

## 19.6 IMPLEMENTATION

*OSCAR* is implemented using an object-oriented interpreter based on the C language. The
interpreter implements creation of classes and objects, single inheritance, and operations
coded as text strings. Its syntax is similar to Smalltalk, with some extensions. The user interface consists of a parser that interprets operations of the form:

>   *object_name message_sequence*

A message sequence consists of messages with optional arguments. The suffix of the message determines whether a message requires arguments. The following suffixes illustrate
message semantics:

>   ?    requests the value of an instance variable
>
>   =    sets an instance variable
>
>   :    has arguments but does not set an instance variable
>
>   @   defines an index
>
>   +, -, /, and * terminate arithmetic operations

Messages to one object can be concatenated on a statement. A typical statement is:

```
Actor new: aBox position=(0,5,0)
        rotate_x:30 color=(1,0,1) on!;
```

*Actor* is a class that responds to the *new:* message by creating an instance of itself with the
name *aBox*. Classes, when they receive *new:* messages, return a pointer to the new instance
that will receive the rest of the messages in the statement. This new actor receives the *posi-
tion=* message, causing its position instance variable to be set to (0,5,0). The remaining messages rotate *aBox* 30 degrees about its x axis, set its color to magenta (red=1, green=0,
blue=1), and turn it on.

    The system's knowledge of the problem domain, here computer animation, is kept with-
in the classes and not in the language.

### 19.6.1 Sample Animation

A simple animation illustrates the power of the animation system and the language. This short animation shows a bouncing ball that starts at rest and moves along a path that simulates gravity. Here, we do not use an accurate scientific simulation of gravity but rather use a sine curve to simulate the motion.

First we need an actor for the ball. We start it at (0,0,0), make it red, and give it a model called ball_model.

```
actor new: ball position=(0,0,0)
        color=(1,0,0) model= ball_model;
```

Now we need a modeler to describe the physical model of the ball. For this example, we use a Phigs+ modeling primitive for a sphere.

```
Phigs_sphere new: ball_model radius=.5;
```

Phigs_sphere is a predefined class that creates a Phigs+ compatible representation of a sphere.

An *OSCAR* camera is similar to a physical camera. We give it a position, a focal point, an up direction, angle for the lens (view angle), and turn it on.

```
camera new: camera_1 position=(10,0,80) focal_point=(10,0,0)
        view_up=(0,1,0) view_angle=30 on!;
```

We also need lights to illuminate the scene. We place a light at the camera with the following statement:

```
light new: light_1 position=[camera_1 position?]
        focal_point=[camera_1 focal_point?] intensity=.8 on!;
```

Here we used a message sequence with square brackets to take the results of one message, *position?*, to use as an argument for another, *position=*. This powerful construct is used throughout computer animation. Even though the light object does not know about cameras, the parser provides a simple mechanism to communicate state information from one object to another.

Now we create a renderer, an object that will take the actors, cameras, and lights and create one frame of animation.

```
Phigs new: aRenderer lights=light_1 cameras=camera_1
        actors=ball;
```

Next we define the cue that controls the motion of the ball. In this animation, the ball will bounce once in six seconds. Although there are many ways to do this, we use half a sine curve to simulate the effects of gravity. To make the action more interesting we add a bit of horizontal motion. The cue will start at time 0 and last for 6 seconds.

```
cue new: bounce
        start_time=0 end_time=6
        start_actions="scalar new: x; scalar new: y;"
        tick_actions=("x = 20 / 6 * [bounce time?];",
        "y = 30 * [bounce time?] sin! * 10;",
        "ball position= [x ?], [y ?], 0);");
```

*Scalar* is a scalar number class. The message "=" sets the scalar instance's *value*, while the message "/" divides the current value by its argument. Likewise, the *sin!* message changes the scalar's current value to the sine of its value. To get the value of the scalar, we send a "?" message. Here, using our simple message passing parser, we have added an arithmetic capability to the animation system. Remember, a cue sends messages to the parser whenever the cue receives a message and the time is within the cue's start and end times.

The last part of our script defines the scene.

```
scene new: scene_1
       start_actions= "! Scene 1 Starts"
       renderers=aRenderer cues=bounce
       end_actions="!Scene 1 Complete"
```

The scene starts when it receives a *start!* message and runs until its clock reaches its duration.

```
scene_1 start!;
```

An interesting variation of the script places the camera's focal point at the ball's position, a "follow the bouncing ball" effect. This will keep the ball in the center of the frame. To appreciate this, we should place a few balls of varying size around on the floor of the room, which we add as follows:

```
actor new: room model=room_model;
actor new: ball1 model=ball_model position=(5,2,0)
       scale=(.5,.5,.5);
actor new: ball2 model=ball_model position=(5,7,0)
       scale=(.2,.2,.2);
actor new: ball3 model=ball_model position=(3,5,0)
       scale=(1.7,1.7,1.7);
aRenderer actors+ (room, ball1, ball2, ball3);
```

The *follow* cue keeps the camera's focal point on the ball:

```
cue new: follow duration=[bounce duration]
       tick_actions="aCamera focal_point=[aBall position?];"
```

Then we add this cue to the scene:

```
scene_1 cues+ follow time=0 start!;
```

Animations often evolve this way: one cue at a time. We might get more sophisticated and simulate the ball squashing against the floor by changing its z scale factor. Another cue might pan the camera around the room while the ball bounces.

## 19.7 LESSONS LEARNED

*OSCAR* made its first film in December of 1984 when it consisted of twenty five classes including actors, cameras, lights, cues, and renderers. Since its initial implementation, *OSCAR* has grown to contain over ninety classes, fifty eight of which are subclasses of the original classes. Thus over half the classes share code with other classes.

During this project, we made several observations:

- Applying object modeling to animation produces a natural user interface with terminology that is familiar to experts in the application domain.

- The abstraction step of the design is critical and requires the most effort.

- The object-oriented approach partitions a complex system into manageable pieces.

- The system is less fragile than others we have written. We make changes and additions without fear of breaking *OSCAR*.

## 19.8 CHAPTER SUMMARY

*OSCAR* is a three-dimensional computer animation system which produces high quality film and video sequences of the results of scientific calculations and experiments. *OSCAR* is extensible and able to accommodate new applications and advances in graphics technology. *OSCAR* was designed using the object-oriented paradigm and implemented in the C language. The jargon used in constructing *OSCAR* mimics that used in the traditional, manual animation process: scene, cue, light, camera, and actor. Since the structure of *OSCAR* parallels the application domain, the resulting software is straightforward to use and understand. *OSCAR* adopts the "stop-frame" metaphor. Each frame is constructed and recorded one at a time; the resulting frames are played rapidly in succession to create the illusion of motion.

The object, dynamic, and functional models are all significant for *OSCAR*. However, most of *OSCAR*'s development effort dealt not with the static data structure but with designing and programming various operations. *OSCAR*'s architecture closely follows that of the object model; most classes in *OSCAR* are autonomous and correspond to entities in the real world. To a large extent, the object design phase just added detail to the analysis models. Nevertheless there was some conversion of application concepts to computer concepts, such as the introduction of class *Matrix* to implement *Camera* and *Light* behavior.

## BIBLIOGRAPHIC NOTES

Computer animation is an active research area in the computer graphics community. [Laybourne-78] describes the conventional animation process including topics on stop-frame animation, cartoon animation, and Disney animation. [Magnenat-Thalmann-85] describes the animation process and several computer animation systems. The ACM Special Interest Group on Computer Graphics, SIGGRAPH, holds an annual technical conference on computer graphics and publishes proceedings each year in the summer. [Rogers-85] describes various rendering algorithms. [Weinstock-86] shows how to do computer animation on personal computers. [Hayward-84] defines common computer animation terminology and techniques. [Gaskill-85] describes techniques that help make a good movie, whether it is computer generated or shot in your back yard with a portable video camera.

## REFERENCES

[Gaskill-85] A. L. Gaskill, D. A. Englander. *How to Shoot a Movie and Video Story*. Dobbs Ferry, New York: Morgan and Morgan, 1985.

[Hayward-84] S. Hayward. *Computers for Animation*. Boston, Mass.: Focal Press, 1984.

[Laybourne-78] K. Laybourne. *The Animation Book*. New York: Crown, 1978.

[Lorensen-89] W.E. Lorensen, B. Yamrom. Object-Oriented computer animation. *Proceedings of IEEE NAECON*, Dayton, Ohio, May 1989, Volume 2, 588-595.

[Magnenat-Thalmann-85] N. Magnenat-Thalmann, D. Thalmann. *Computer Animation: Theory and Practice*. Berlin: Springer Verlag, 1985.

[Rogers-85] D.F. Rogers. *Procedural Elements for Computer Graphics*. New York: McGraw-Hill, 1985.

[Weinstock-86] N. Weinstock. *Computer Animation*. Reading, Mass.: Addison-Wesley, 1986.

## EXERCISES

**19.1** (7) Discuss the feasibility of using the object-oriented approach to extend *OSCAR* to the following applications. In each case, extend the object model and describe any operations that you add.

    a. A system to add color to existing black and white movies. Input to the system is a digitized movie. The user colors objects in selected frames and the system colors the same objects in other frames.

    b. A display for a flight simulator for training pilots. The system displays the view from the cockpit of an airplane based on the position and orientation of the plane and a landscape database.

    c. A video games display system. The system displays a background and several moving objects under the control of the game.

**19.2** (4) Identify the actors in the following animation domains:

    a. Depiction of structure and transformations of molecules during chemical interactions. Molecules are represented by ball and stick figures, where colored balls represent atoms.

    b. Animated television network logos, shown on television during station breaks. Combining the best of art and computer science, these animations are visually pleasing.

    c. Analysis of mechanisms. Mechanical components, such as gears, cams, and pistons are modeled in motion.

**19.3** (5) Describe how *OSCAR* could be used to simulate the glider described in exercise 12.2.

**19.4** (4) Compare the design of *OSCAR* with that of the system described in chapter 18. Be sure to discuss the differences in use of methods, global/local scope of operations, system architecture, and relative importance of object modeling, functional modeling, and dynamic modeling.

**19.5** (7) Using the syntax defined in this chapter, animate a scene in which you are viewing a bowling alley from the perspective of a bug sitting at the bottom of a finger hole in a bowling ball as it rolls down an alley.

# 20

# Electrical Distribution Design System

A computer-aided design (CAD) tool is a software system specifically designed to automate all or part of a design activity. CAD tools typically have an interactive user interface and are graphics intensive. CAD tools are currently used in applications such as drafting, chemical process design, mechanical design and analysis, HVAC (heating, ventilation, and air conditioning), integrated circuit chip design, printed circuit board layout, and piping and instrumentation design.

This chapter describes the *One-LI*ne diagram *E*ditor (OLIE), a CAD tool for designing electrical power distribution systems. The system permits an engineer to lay out a power distribution system as a network of components connected by buses and circuits. The editor is controlled by fixed menus, pop-up menus, and direct input to the diagram.

As with most user interface applications, OLIE is dominated by the dynamic model. The object model is also significant, but the functional model is relatively unimportant. The most difficult aspect of developing OLIE was the requirement to integrate with several existing subsystems: a graphics system, a database manager, and a menu system. These subsystems had various quirks, flaws, and performance overheads, which OLIE had to overcome in order to provide lively and natural user interaction. OLIE illustrates the interactive interface architecture described in Chapter 9.

## 20.1 BACKGROUND

A "one-line diagram" [Russell-78] is a schematic drawing of an electrical power system that uses a concise, standard notation accepted by all power engineers. One-line diagrams get their name from the fact that only one phase of a three phase system is shown. Standard symbols are used to represent components of a power system, such as transformers, circuit breakers, generators, fuses, and switches [ANSI-75]. Circuits and buses connect the standard symbols. The distinction between circuits and buses is based on electrical voltage drop. Circuits are connections with measurable voltage drop (especially if there is a short circuit on the power system) and are typically implemented with wires, cables, or transmission lines. Buses are connections with no appreciable voltage drop and are usually implemented with large cross section aluminum, copper bars, or pipes.

A sample portion of a one-line diagram is shown in Figure 20.1. Two high voltage (138 KV) buses are shown. Arrows at the top of the diagram indicate sources of power, such as a utility. Arrows at the bottom indicate loads. Circuit breakers are shown as squares; transformers are indicated by zig-zag lines. The small solid dots distinguish connecting lines from overlapping lines. Four separate sources are connected to the two high voltage buses through nine circuit breakers. By selecting which circuit breakers are open and which ones are closed, the power system operator can configure the power supply to the three transformers in several ways. This would allow one bus to be disconnected during construction of additional circuits, for example. The loads on transformer 1 and transformer 2 can be served by either transformer by closing the breaker that connects the two secondary buses.

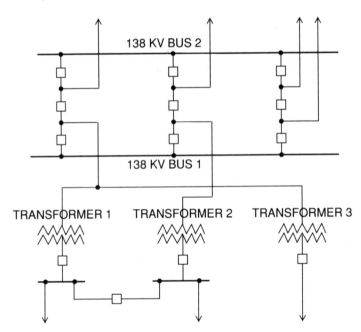

**Figure 20.1** Sample one-line diagram

The motivation for developing OLIE derives from recent advances in computing technology. Engineers of various disciplines would like to replace the old analysis software developed twenty years ago that operates in batch mode and requires that input be submitted as card images. A more natural approach to specifying a simulation is to draw a diagram on the screen and annotate the drawing with desired design conditions. This new approach permits menu driven interaction and possibly interaction with the simulation program during its execution. For example, an engineer can check on the convergence of a simulation or change design conditions as a computation proceeds.

## 20.2 PROBLEM STATEMENT

Several sources were used to determine functional requirements, including marketing studies, customer requests, examination of other graphics editors, and the experience of the OLIE software designer as an electric power engineer. Marketing studies envisioned that OLIE would integrate with other computer-aided design and engineering software tools used in architecture, engineering, and construction (AEC) applications through common project databases, as shown in Figure 20.2.

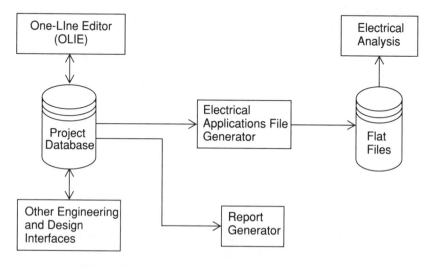

**Figure 20.2** Integration of OLIE with other applications

### 20.2.1 Functional Requirements

OLIE must store its data in a database to be managed by a database management system (DBMS). At first, this may seem to be an improper "requirement" and appear to be a possible decision that could result from analysis of the "true" requirements. However, the OLIE software is not intended to be an end in itself but merely one of a suite of tools that electrical power engineers would use to perform their work. Thus OLIE must interface to other power engineering programs. The requirements analysis for this larger system lead to the conclusion that OLIE must use a database.

By definition, OLIE must provide basic commands for editing one-line diagrams, such as create, pan, zoom, drag, move, copy, pick, and put. OLIE must have a lively response so that it does not interrupt the user's train of thought. The user interface must be natural to engineers who are not computer experts.

OLIE must permit data to be shared among users, application programs, and projects. The system must permit portions of a design to be locked for periods of extended work. These extended duration locks permit work that may last for days or weeks, in contrast to the ordinary database transactions that complete in a matter of seconds. A typical OLIE user has several active projects at a time; multiple engineers may work on each project. Libraries of information, such as drawing symbols, span many projects.

OLIE must recover from storage media failures, computer failures, and software errors. The software must be portable to other hardware, operating systems, and software subsystems, including new graphics hardware. OLIE must be extensible to include new functions and new application programs and be easily maintained. Engineers must be able to generate reports about a power distribution system in several formats.

### 20.2.2 Architectural Requirements

Management required that OLIE be built on several in-house software packages:

- a graphics system for creating, selecting, and editing symbols, text, and straight lines,
- an interface for inserting, deleting, updating, and querying the database,
- a user interface system for displaying forms and menus and recognizing user input, and
- an in-house object-oriented programming language.

## 20.3 ANALYSIS

### 20.3.1 Object Model

The object model comprises five modules: packaging, electrical properties, geometry, grouping, and connectivity. The packaging module contains the high level structure for a project: A project consists of multiple one-line diagram drawings, each of which is further organized into one or more sheets. The electrical properties module defines attributes for each electrical component. Geometry describes the appearance of electrical items on the screen. Grouping describes the construction of composite items from simple items. The connectivity module captures the correspondence between a diagram and an electrical network.

The actual modules have much detail that is not shown; here we just show the basic structure. We have shaded classes that are shared between modules.

*Packaging Module*

The packaging module (Figure 20.3) hierarchically organizes data for user access. The class OLIE *root* has a single instance that provides a context for library and project names. A customer may have one or more projects active at the same time, each identified by project name. Within each project there are several drawings, each qualified by a drawing name. A drawing name is unique within a project but may be reused in other projects. A drawing has multiple sheets that are also named.

There may be several symbol and macro libraries. Each project is assigned one symbol library and one macro library. A symbol is an icon that has meaning within the context of a one-line diagram; thus for instance, parallel zig-zag lines denote a transformer. A macro is a user defined grouping of symbols, buses, and circuits. A macro or a symbol is qualified by

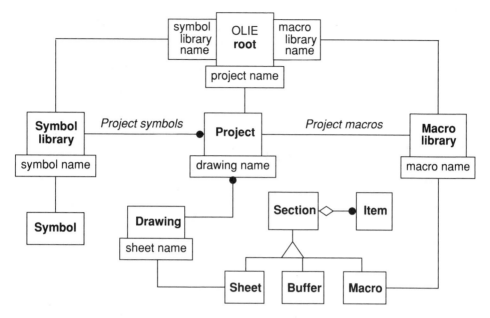

**Figure 20.3** Packaging module

name within its library, so the same name may be used in several different libraries. A library may be used in several projects.

A section is a rectangular region of a one-line diagram containing a collection of items, such as symbols, buses, and circuits. A section is the smallest unit of access control to a diagram, as different sections can be edited by different engineers concurrently. Sheets, buffers, and macros are all sections. A sheet is the lowest level in the project hierarchy containing a portion of a one-line diagram. A buffer contains a portion of a one-line diagram involved in an editing operation. Since sheets, buffers, and composites all contain the same type of items, generalizing them into a section permits code reuse.

*Electrical Properties Module*

The electrical properties module (Figure 20.4) defines electrical properties for components in a power distribution system. The purpose of this module is to define attributes of classes; this module contains no associations. Circuits come in two varieties, cables (underground) and transmission lines (above ground), each inheriting common attributes from circuit. Bus segments have simple structure. Units come in many different varieties, such as transformers and circuit breakers. The attributes in this module do not appear on the one-line diagram; their values are entered by the engineer on pop-up forms.

*Geometry Module*

The geometry module (Figure 20.5) describes the layout of a one-line diagram on the screen. Circuits and bus segments, collectively called path items, are drawn as polylines (connected line segments) with user set width. Units are represented with arbitrary symbols chosen from

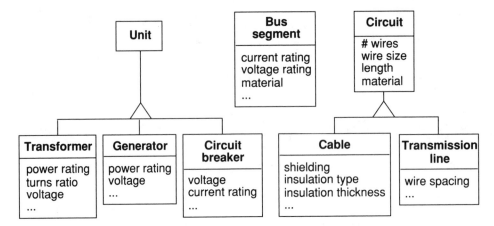

**Figure 20.4** Electrical properties module

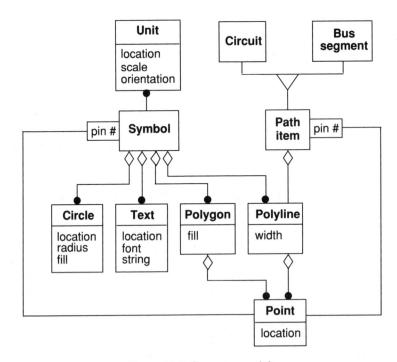

**Figure 20.5** Geometry module

the symbol library. Each symbol is constructed from geometrical shapes. Each symbol has a fixed number of predefined connection points, or pins, which can be connected to pins of other symbols on the diagram. Each path item has two pins, one at each end of the polyline.

Once two pins are connected, they remain connected as the items are moved on the screen; the diagram is adjusted as necessary to maintain the connection.

*Grouping Module*

OLIE supports two types of grouping of items, equipment and bus sets (Figure 20.6). Equipment is a group of electrical components purchased as a single unit, generally in a metal cabinet, and is shown on a one-line diagram as a dashed rectangle enclosing the corresponding units, circuits, and buses. A bus set is a group of bus segments in a one-line diagram that constitute a single physical unit. Equipment and bus sets are similar in that each is a set of one or more items. Items may belong to at most one set.

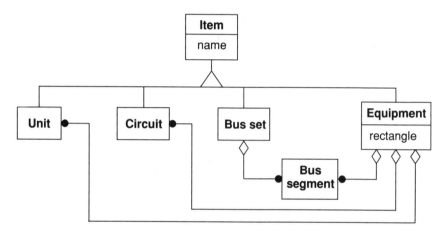

**Figure 20.6** Grouping module

*Connectivity Module*

The connectivity module (Figure 20.7) relates the physical connections in the diagram to the electrical connections in the power system. The one-line diagram editor and electrical analysis programs each have a slightly different view of a power system. The editor regards a one-line diagram as consisting of an interconnected network of symbols, buses, and circuits. Editing operations such as move, copy, and cut must quickly determine broken connections and buses and circuits that are stretched or compressed. Electrical analysis programs view a power system as an electrical circuit: a branch and equipotential representation, similar to

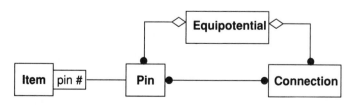

**Figure 20.7** Connectivity module

an edge-vertex graph. A branch is a two port circuit element that relates electrical current through the branch to the voltage difference across the branch. Ports of branches are connected together in an equipotential. All ports connected in an equipotential are at the same voltage. The sum of the currents entering an equipotential is zero.

The mapping from symbols, buses, and circuits in one-line diagrams to branches and equipotentials as an equivalent electrical circuit is not trivial. A simple example is shown in Figure 20.8. With the circuit breakers closed, the two buses are equipotential.

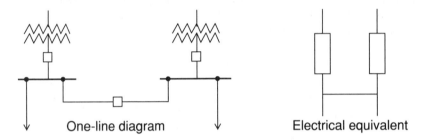

**Figure 20.8**  Mapping a one-line diagram to an electrical equivalent circuit

One complication is the naming of branches and equipotentials. In order to interpret the results of analysis programs, it is necessary to uniquely identify branches and equipotentials. At first glance it would seem that this could be done by simply naming symbols, circuits, and buses. However, several complications arise. The electrical model of a symbol depends on what it represents. Some symbols, such as transformers and circuits, represent circuit branches, while others, such as switches and buses, represent connections. The user could inadvertently assign more than one name to an equipotential, by naming the buses on either side of a switch, as shown in Figure 20.9.

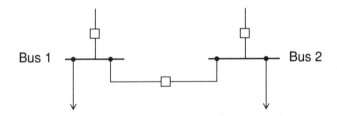

**Figure 20.9**  Ambiguity in assignment of names to buses

Ideally, OLIE should check the uniqueness of names in the electrical model any time a name is created in the one-line diagram. At the worst, there should be a graceful way of correcting the situation when the input files for the electrical applications are created.

In the geometry module in Figure 20.5, symbols, bus segments, and circuits have pins for making connections. Pins that are electrically joined together are associated with a common connection. Equipotentials, pins, and connections map between the representation of the one-line diagram as symbols, buses, and circuits and the branches and nodes. Branches are not explicitly shown in the model, because they are easy to determine.

## 20.3.2 Dynamic Model

Since OLIE is an interactive editor, the dynamic model and the user interface are essentially the same thing. After revisions to the object model became infrequent, we began designing the user interface. We examined other graphic editors and selected the features with the best "look and feel." We grouped user interactions by function, such as display control, editing, traversing the project hierarchy, and so on, and developed scenarios.

Then we designed menus and specified mouse behavior. The left mouse button selects items from the diagram or commands from fixed menus. The middle button extends selections. The right button select commands from pop-up menus. Sometimes, selecting a menu item would raise another menu. The depth of menu nesting was limited to three, as we felt that deep nesting would be confusing to users.

We culled the scenarios for atomic operations, such as select, move, copy, delete, mirror, and display text. We constructed dynamic models for each operation, some of which are discussed below.

### Adding Bus Segments and Circuits

The user creates a series of alternating horizontal and vertical line segments with a series of mouse operations. OLIE automatically connects to symbols and other circuits or buses. Figure 20.10 shows the dynamic model for adding bus segments and circuits. The two differ slightly because bus segments can "dangle" without being connected to anything, while each circuit runs between a pair of pins.

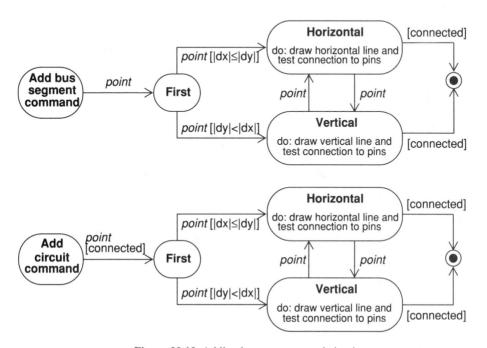

**Figure 20.10** Adding bus segments and circuits

*Adding Items*

Items can be symbols or macros. They are identified by name from the library, followed by a location at which the image of the item is drawn on the diagram as shown in Figure 20.11. Multiple copies of a symbol can be added by clicking on a series of points. The user must indicate when to stop adding items by choosing *done*.

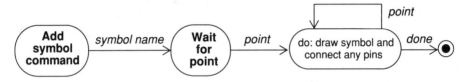

**Figure 20.11** Adding symbols

*Selection of Geometry*

In Figure 20.12, buses, circuits, symbols, and text are selected individually or in groups for further operations. The left mouse button starts a new selection while the middle button adds items to an existing selection. If either button is pressed and released, then an item (if any) near the mouse point is selected. If either button is pressed, held, slid, and released, all items (if any) enclosed in the rectangle between the down point and up point are selected. The details of press-hold-slide-release are not shown on the dynamic model. Such details belong to the model of the graphics driver that captures mouse events. Instead, the diagram shows *left* and *left region* as distinct logical events.

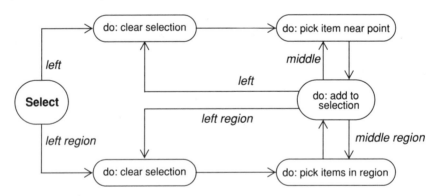

**Figure 20.12** Selecting items

## 20.3.3 Functional Model

The functional model for the OLIE system is shown in Figure 20.13. As with many interactive editors, the functions in the system are mostly trivial, since the purpose of the system is to interact with the user to build data structures. It is not useful to prepare lower-level data flow diagrams for the editor or project control. The electrical analysis is the only significant part of the functional model. Electrical analysis is performed by external stand-alone programs, so their internal functional models are generally inaccessible (it is useful to prepare a list of the inputs to each one, however). The extract connectivity process is the only part of the analysis that is part of the OLIE system proper.

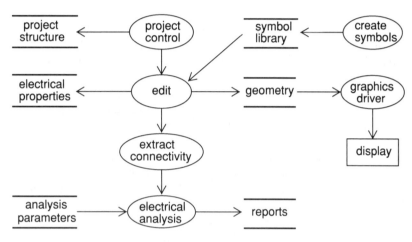

**Figure 20.13** Functional model of OLIE system

*Connectivity Extraction*

Most of the effort in preparing input files for application programs derives from converting symbols, buses, circuits, pins, and connections to branches and equipotentials as shown in Figure 20.14. The conversion algorithm starts by assigning an equipotential to each pin. All pins of a given bus are assigned the same equipotential, which is given the same name as the bus. Symbol and circuit pins are given their own unnamed equipotentials. The next step is to scan all connections, merging the set of equipotentials for each connection into one equipotential. The name given to the merged equipotential depends on how many names are being merged. If there are no names, the merged equipotential is not given a name. If there is exactly one name, the merged equipotential is given that name. If there are several names, the merged equipotential is given one of the names, and a warning is issued.

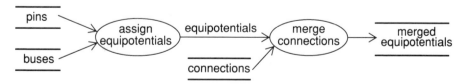

**Figure 20.14** Connectivity extraction

## 20.4 SYSTEM DESIGN

We feared that it would not be possible to simultaneously satisfy the requirements that we store one-line diagrams in a database, support data sharing, and provide a fast, lively user interface. We considered the possibility of OLIE directly interacting with the database, but benchmark testing revealed that response would be too slow to support a lively user interface.

A related problem was that of database synchronization and rollback. The graphics subsystem stored its data in flat files apart from the database. This raised issues of how to synchronize the flat files with the database, taking into account the problem of database rollback.

We considered several system architectures. The final solution, shown in Figure 20.15, used a database shadowing subsystem [Premerlani-90]. The shadowing subsystem intercepts all database operations and converts them into memory operations when possible, accessing the relational database at limited intervals. The shadowing system requires that chunks of data must be checked out of the database, manipulated at memory speed, and then checked into the database again. In this application, database checkout is not a handicap because it is undesirable to allow two engineers to edit the same part of the design simultaneously.

Operations access stored data through the shadowing module. Since the relational database maintains concurrency control, each OLIE execution can operate as a single-user program without having to worry about concurrency.

Operations access the graphics display through the graphics subsystem, which displays the one-line diagram and stores graphical information in flat files. The editing module main-

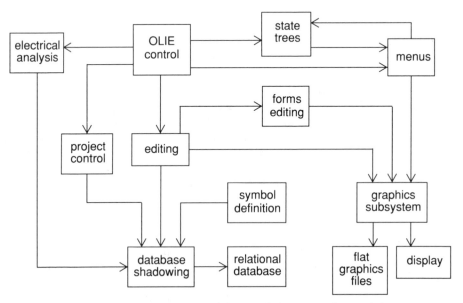

Arrows show dependence of client module on supplier module.

**Figure 20.15** Architecture of OLIE system

tains the consistency of the database and the flat files. Graphical information is stored redundantly in the database and the flat files to boost performance. Normally, the graphics system stores graphical information in the flat files and the shadowing system stores graphical and other information in the database. In the event that the information in the flat files becomes inconsistent with the database, the shadowing system rebuilds the flat files through the graphics system.

We were willing to trade-off additional memory and storage space for performance and functionality. Users of this system require high-performance workstations anyway, so this trade-off is reasonable.

The names in a diagram must be unique. We decided to defer checking uniqueness of names until the user is done editing. Incremental checking of names would have greatly complicated the concurrency constraints among multiple users, and a survey of users showed that they were satisfied with deferred checking.

Database checkout also permits OLIE to support the notion of a *long transaction*, that is a transaction that lasts for days or weeks, in contrast to the usual database activity that transpires in a matter of seconds. An engineer's work may be internally inconsistent during a long transaction; thus engineers can freely pursue their work and at the same time OLIE can satisfy database integrity requirements.

Our implementation of control adopts the event driven paradigm and is based on an explicit state diagram organized into a tree, called a *state tree* (see Chapter 5 and Section 20.5). All input events cause state transitions within the tree. Menus are enabled and disabled by the state tree control; in turn, user menu selections generate input events interpreted by the control. Transitions in the tree force the execution of actions, such as cut, paste, and move. We implemented control with state trees, instead of Harel's statecharts (we regard statecharts as a superior approach) for historical reasons. We had an implementation of state trees available in-house; OLIE was developed before we became aware of Harel's work.

## 20.5 OBJECT DESIGN

Object design was straightforward, given the analysis and architecture decisions. The graphics, database, state tree, menuing, forms editing, and electrical analysis subsystems were all predefined. The main work with these subsystems was to properly set up input parameters. Considerable effort went into the layout of menus, forms, and item attributes, but we will not reproduce the details here. The bulk of the work involved the editor: the high-level interactive flow of control (policy) and the low-level operations (implementation).

### 20.5.1 State Tree Control

Because of the importance of the user interface, we paid particular attention to the dynamic model. We used a variation of the state-event model called a state tree to control the user interface. (See Chapter 5.) State trees are a technique for organizing states into trees and attaching events to tree nodes to share common structure and behavior, permitting a layered decomposition of control structures and the elimination of redundant information. Events attached to states specify how events are interpreted and can be inherited by substates, just like attributes and operations on object classes. Entry and exit actions attached to states specify the effect of entering and leaving a state. Because states are organized into a tree, a substate cannot be entered without its superstate being entered so that the entry (and exit) actions are inherited as well.

A state tree is equivalent to a Harel state diagram in which subtrees are nested states within the superstate representing a tree node. The entry and exit actions on the tree nodes are equivalent to entry and exit actions on the nested state contours.

State trees naturally support a menu driven interface. Each menu entry causes a transition to a given state. Any menu entry can be selected in any state because the exit actions of the current state allow it to be cleaned up regardless of the user command.

The state tree used in OLIE consists of two separate trees: a main tree and an auxiliary tree. The main tree contains states normally encountered during user interaction. All main states are mutually exclusive; the user can only execute one main command at a time. The auxiliary tree handles user interrupts without losing the context of the main tree. For example, OLIE has pan and zoom commands that can be picked at any time, even in the middle of other operations. Pan and zoom commands retain control until the user exits from them, at which time control returns to the main tree.

One feature of state trees that OLIE exploited is that menu organization does not have to reflect the state structure. This eliminates the problem frequently encountered in other approaches in which a series of "quit" or "exit" commands are needed in changing context.

### 20.5.2 Main Tree

A portion of OLIE's main tree is shown in Figure 20.16. The tree is organized according to command functionality with subdivisions within each kind of command.

Only some states are shown. When the program starts, it enters the *Initialize* state, which displays the fixed menus, performs initialization, and transfers control to the *Select sheet* state, which allows the user to select an initial sheet for editing. *Utilities* substates create reports, composites, plots, or the files needed by electrical analysis programs. *Add geometry* substates create items in one-line diagrams. The *Exit* state queries the user to save any changes that have been made. The exit command can be picked by the user at any time, because any command in progress is cleaned up by the exit functions on the state tree path from the current state to the *Exit* state. *Layout* substates perform editing operations such as pick, put, move, and copy. *Annotate* substates pop-up text forms to enter electrical parameter values.

### 20.5.3 Auxiliary Tree

The auxiliary tree, shown in Figure 20.17, contains states for commands that can interrupt other commands. *Pan-zoom* is used for changing the viewpoint of the one-line diagram. *Display control* changes display options such as the visibility of a grid or text. *Select geometry* provides control for selecting elements of the one-line diagram. *Orient-scale* is used to change the orientation or size of selected elements.

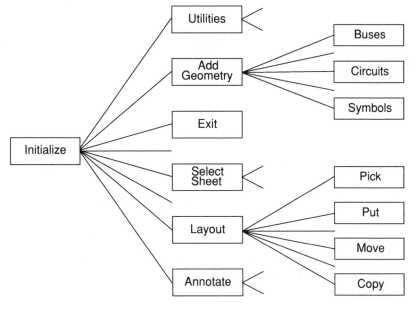

**Figure 20.16** Main state tree

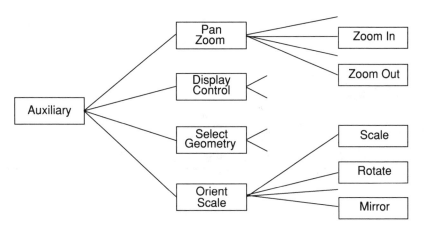

**Figure 20.17** Auxiliary state tree

### 20.5.4 Low-level Operations

Objects were implemented directly from the analysis model in an object-oriented language using association objects to directly implement associations. The same objects are stored in memory and in the database (the shadowing subsystem uses memory to cache the database), so the objects were not optimized because it is important to keep the mapping clean. Most operations were implemented directly from the dynamic model. A direct mapping from the analysis to design is common for interactive editors, which usually consist of a loose collection of operations that act directly on the object model. During requirements analysis it is important to try to avoid dependencies in the order in which user commands can be issued, so that a direct mapping from analysis to design is possible.

## 20.6 IMPLEMENTATION

It was not always clear how the subsystems would interact. Each subsystem was intended to be a software productivity tool that encapsulated commonly found operations. OLIE was the first application to use all of them at once. Paradoxically, the more software tools we had, the more trouble we encountered. The problem was that although each subsystem was easy enough to use by itself, it often had resource requirements, usage constraints, or philosophy of operation that conflicted with the other subsystems. For example, there was overlap between the graphics subsystem, the menuing subsystem, and the state-tree subsystem. In order for each subsystem to work as originally designed, each needed exclusive access to user input-output. We modified all three subsystems to work together. Such difficulties are hard to avoid when external constraints are imposed on the architecture and implementation.

OLIE contained around 100,000 lines of code. We estimate that the object-oriented approach reduced design and implementation time by about a person-year. The resulting system was easy to maintain. Object modeling helped us solve many of the problems we encountered. State trees simplified our modeling of the user interface.

## 20.7 LESSONS LEARNED

Some of our observations based on the OLIE project are:

- Systems are enhanced until they become unwieldy, at which point they should be scrapped. (Some of the subsystems that we were required to use were dinosaur programs that should have been rewritten long ago.)

- It is possible to have too much of a good thing with regard to software productivity tools.

- Interactive software is much more difficult to develop than non-interactive software. We have found that we tend to underestimate the work involved.

- Relational databases are too slow for naive use with an interactive CAD/CAM system. However, by hiding the relational database within an object-oriented language with a shadowing scheme, we found a workable solution.

- There is a large gap between the vision of software and the reality of development.

## 20.8 CHAPTER SUMMARY

OLIE is a computer-aided design (CAD) tool for designing electrical power distribution systems. OLIE supports drawing of one-line diagrams which are the standard notation accepted by power engineers. One-line diagrams are two dimensional diagrams that show connections between electrical devices. The primary objectives in developing OLIE were to provide a polished user interface and to capture the content of a one-line diagram in a database so that the information could be used for other purposes. The OLIE software development effort was hobbled by political decisions that we use certain software subsystems, even when these subsystems were poor technical solutions.

OLIE has a rich object model, since there are many electrical components to specify and all the data must be stored in a database. The dynamic model also was significant because of the importance of a polished user interface. The functional model was unimportant for OLIE. The system design for OLIE was largely determined by the requirement that we build on several subsystems. Object design and implementation were straightforward for this application.

## BIBLIOGRAPHIC NOTES

Although power system technology is mature, advances continue to be made, particularly with respect to the use of computers, that are well documented in the IEEE Transactions on PAS. A comprehensive, although somewhat dated, summary of power systems is given by [Westinghouse-64]. This excellent reference is revised from time to time. A more recent treatment of power systems is given by [Russell-78]. A complete summary of the symbols used in one-line diagrams is contained in [ANSI-75]. The shadowing technique used in OLIE to boost the performance of the database interface is described in more detail in [Premerlani-90].

## REFERENCES

[ANSI-75] American National Standard ANSI Y32.2-1975, Canadian Standard CSA Z99-1975 or IEEE Standard IEEE Std 315-1975. *Graphic Symbols for Electrical and Electronics Diagrams.*

[Premerlani-90] W.J. Premerlani, M.R. Blaha, J.E. Rumbaugh, T.A. Varwig. An object-oriented relational database. *Communications of the ACM 33,* 11 (November 1990), 99-109.

[Russell-78] B. Don Russell and Marion E. Council. *Power System Control and Protection.* New York: Academic Press, 1978.

[Westinghouse-64] Central Station Engineers of the Westinghouse Electric Corporation, *Electrical Transmission and Distribution Reference Book*, East Pittsburgh, Pennsylvania, 1964.

## EXERCISES

**20.1** (8) Relational database operations (insert, delete, update) in OLIE are buffered in memory with a checkout/check-in scheme. When a user wishes to edit a sheet, OLIE locks the sheet and reads all records from the database belonging to the sheet. Each record is converted into an object instance in memory and tagged with a state that is used to determine what should be done to update the database when the user saves editing changes or checks the sheet back in. As the user edits the sheet, OLIE updates the tags. Possible states are *Same, Different, Not Inserted Yet*, and *Not Deleted Yet*. *Same* indicates that the object instance in memory contains the same data as the record in the database. *Different* means the instance has different data than the corresponding record. *Not Inserted Yet* indicates the instance is due to be inserted into the database. *Not Deleted Yet* means the instance is due for deletion from the database. When objects are copied from the database, they are placed in the *Same* state and remain in that state unless they are updated or deleted. Newly created objects are in the *Not Inserted Yet* state. Objects that need to be deleted are placed in the *Not Deleted Yet* state. Each time an object is accessed, its new state is determined from the operation and the old state. The operations are *insert*(new data), *delete*(object), *update*(object), *save*(set of objects), and *load*(portion of database). Some operations may undo others. For example, an insertion can be elided with a subsequent deletion.

Figure E20.1 is a partially completed state diagram for updating tags. Initial and final states are missing as well as activities, actions, events, and so forth. (Refer to Chapter 5 for a discussion of initial and final states, which in this case are used to allocate and deallocate memory used for objects.) Complete the diagram. Be sure to show what needs to be done for a save operation. Some helpful hints: objects in the *Same* state do not require any action during a *save* operation, since the data in memory is the same as that in the database. Certain operations are illegal on objects in certain states and need not be shown. An *update* operation on an object in the *Not Inserted Yet* state leaves it in the same state, since the database does not yet know about the object. The only legal operation on an object in the *Not Deleted Yet* state is *save*, which requires the corresponding record in the database to be deleted and the object to be terminated.

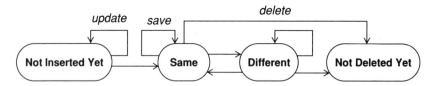

**Figure E20.1** Partially completed state diagram for a system to buffer database operations by shadowing records with object instances

**20.2** (7) A commonly occurring problem in the design of graphical diagram editors which preserve connectivity is that of detecting bridging networks. For example, if some symbols in a network are moved, some lines in the network may require adjustment to accommodate the relative displacement between symbols that are being moved and those which are not. Three ways of modeling connectivity are shown in Figure E20.2, Figure E20.3, and Figure E20.4. In each case, networks may connect many symbols, and symbols may be connected to many networks. A given network may be connected several times to a given symbol, and more than one network may be connected to a symbol at the same place. In Figure E20.2, the object class, *Port*, is the place on a symbol where a connection is made or the end of a branch of a network where it is connected to a symbol. Figure E20.3 shows the result of eliminating the *Port* class. A connection is the attachment point of a network to a symbol. Figure E20.4 is a further simplification.

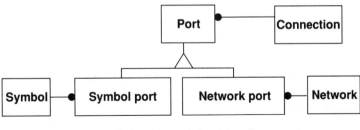

**Figure E20.2** Connectivity object diagram

**Figure E20.3** Connectivity object diagram

**Figure E20.4** Connectivity object diagram

For each diagram, describe how you would accomplish the following operations. If an operation cannot be carried out using one of the diagrams, explain why not.
a. Two sets of symbols are given, a set of all symbols and a set of symbols that have been selected for a moving, cutting, or copying. The output of the operation will be three sets that partition the set of all networks: The set of networks that are connected only to selected symbols, the set of networks that are connected only to unselected symbols, and the set of bridging networks that are connected to both selected and unselected symbols.
b. Given a symbol, find any networks that form more than one connection with the symbol.
c. Given a network, find all symbols that are connected to it.
d. Make a copy of a set of selected symbols. Also copy networks which are connected entirely to symbols which are selected. Ignore bridging networks.
e. Determine all symbols that are connected directly or indirectly to a given set of symbols (transitive closure).

**20.3** (6) The dilemma of how to make copies frequently arises in the design of graphics editors. Methods can be broadly categorized into shallow copy and deep copy. Shallow copy methods simply create a reference to the object(s) being copied. Deep copy involves copying the contents of the object(s) being copied, including any objects(s) that it refers to. The choice depends on the application. For each of the following copy operations, discuss the relative merits of the two approaches:
a. Copy of a library object, such as symbols or macros, into a sheet (see Figure 20.3).
b. Copy of sheet from an old project into a new one. After the sheet is copied, it will be edited. Editing changes to the new sheet should not affect the old sheet.
c. Copy of selected *item*s from one place on a sheet to another.

**20.4**   (5) Modify the state trees in Figure 20.16 and Figure 20.17 so that the pick, put, move, and copy operations can be performed at any time, including in the middle of adding geometry to a sheet.

**20.5**   (6) Prepare a list of types of diagrams in which connectivity is important, such as electrical schematics, data flow diagrams, and decision trees. Include as many as you can think of from a wide range of disciplines. Discuss similarities and differences in connectivity rules. For example, are networks binary or n-ary? Are edges directed or undirected? Are connections allowed anywhere on symbols? Does the location of a connection on a symbol convey any meaning? May networks be connected directly to other networks? Can networks be connected together? Does it make any sense to allow ends of networks to be unconnected? Are there any restrictions concerning how many networks may be connected at the same point?

**20.6**   (7) The system described in this chapter was built on top of 6 existing software subsystems: a relational database, an object-oriented language with a container class library, a windowing system, a menuing system, a graphics system, and a C run-time library. The object-oriented language was a C preprocessor. For various reasons, none of the subsystems could be modified in any way. Several problems arose because the subsystems were developed independently. Discuss workarounds for each problem:

a.  Name clashes. During software development, the linker frequently complained about multiply defined symbols caused by the same name being used in two or more of the subsystem libraries, including the C run-time library.

b.  Preprocessor incompatibilities. Some subsystems used preprocessor constructs that were illegal for the other preprocessors.

c.  Memory allocation. Each subsystem used dynamic memory allocation. There were several different strategies used. Some of them did not check to see if memory was actually allocated successfully, resulting in memory fault errors.

d.  Interrupt processing. Some subsystems performed input/output synchronously, others asynchronously. Two subsystems intercepted keyboard interrupts.

**20.7**   (7) Repeat the previous exercise, this time assuming that you have a free hand to change any of the subsystems.

# Appendix A

## OMT Graphical Notation

All of the graphical notations that are used to build the object model, dynamic model, and functional model have been summarized on the inside covers of the book. Those four pages should be useful as a quick reference while constructing or reading diagrams. We caution you not to simply give those four pages to a novice and expect that person to understand them. To understand the concepts being represented, refer to the chapters of Part 1. To learn how to apply the notation and concepts within the software development life cycle, the chapters in Part 2 should be consulted. If you find you need to review any of the concepts represented graphically here, use the index to locate the explanation in the book.

With the exception of the label for each construct and a few descriptive comments, all of the diagram elements, text names, and punctuation symbols shown are intended to be part of the notation itself. The names in these diagrams (such as *Class*, *attribute-1*, *operation*, and *event-2*) have been chosen to indicate what kind of element they are examples of. You may wish to modify the syntax of names and the declarations of attributes and signatures to make them consistent with the syntax of your implementation language.

Most of the items shown are optional, especially during early stages of modeling. Even in design, it is unwise to overspecify by including names and notations that are not needed. For example, when an association is labeled by its role names, it is usually not necessary to give the association itself a name. We have not indicated which elements are optional because we wanted to show only the actual OMT notation wherever possible, without obscuring it with an additional meta-notation.

Similarly, there are a few constructs that you may never need to use. We have placed the more important constructs toward the top of each page. In most of our work we use only about one third of the notation, but the additional constructs are occasionally necessary.

# Appendix B

## Glossary

**abstract class** a class that cannot have direct instances but whose descendants can have instances.

**abstract operation** an operation defined but not implemented by an abstract class. The operation must be implemented by all concrete descendent classes.

**abstraction** a mental facility that permits humans to view real-world problems with varying degrees of detail depending on the current context of the problem.

**action** (in dynamic modeling) an instantaneous operation. Actions are associated with events and are usually formal in nature.

**activity** (in dynamic modeling) an operation that takes time to complete. Activities are associated with states and represent real-world accomplishments.

**actor object** (in a DFD) an active object that drives the data flow graph by producing or consuming values.

**aggregation** a special form of association, between a whole and its parts, in which the whole is composed of the parts.

**analysis** a stage in the development cycle in which a real-world problem is examined to understand its requirements without planning the implementation.

**ancestor class** a class that is a direct or indirect superclass of a given class.

**architecture** the overall structure of a system, including its partitioning into subsystems and their allocation to tasks and processors.

**assertion** a statement about some condition or relationship that can be either true or false at the time that it is tested. (Contrast with *constraint* and *invariant*.)

**association** a relationship among instances of two or more classes describing a group of links with common structure and common semantics.

**attribute** a named property of a class describing a data value held by each object of the class.

**automatic transition** (in dynamic modeling) an unlabeled transition that automatically fires when the activity associated with the source state is completed.

**batch transformation** a sequential input-to-output transformation, in which inputs are supplied at the start and the goal is to compute an answer; there is no ongoing interaction with the outside world. (Contrast with *continuous transformation*.)

**cached data** data that is redundant because it can be derived from other data.

**call-by-reference** a language mechanism that passes arguments to a procedure by passing the address of each argument rather than its value. (Contrast with *call-by-value*.)

**call-by-value** a language mechanism that passes arguments to a procedure by passing a copy of the data values. If an argument is modified, the new value will not take effect outside of the subroutine that modifies it. (Contrast with *call-by-reference*.)

**candidate key** a minimal set of attributes that uniquely identifies an instance or link.

**class** a description of a group of objects with similar properties, common behavior, common relationships, and common semantics.

**class attribute** an attribute whose value is common to a class of objects rather than a value peculiar to each instance.

**class descriptor** an object representing a class itself, containing a list of attributes and methods as well as the values of any class attributes. Class descriptors are implemented in some, but not all, languages. A class descriptor is an instance of a *metaclass*.

**class diagram** an object diagram that describes classes as a schema, pattern, or template for many possible instances of data. (Contrast with *instance diagram*.)

**class operation** an operation on a class, rather than on instances of the class. An instance creation operation is a common example.

**class variable** (in Smalltalk) an attribute of a class descriptor object; a *class attribute*.

**classification** a grouping of objects with the same data structure and behavior.

**client** a system component that calls upon the services provided by another component. The component providing the service is a *supplier*.

**coherence** a property of an entity, such as a class, an operation, or a module, such that it is organized on a consistent plan and all its parts fit together toward a common goal.

**conceptual schema** (in a relational database) a design from the perspective of an entire enterprise.

**concrete class** a class that can have direct instances.

**concurrent** two or more tasks, activities, or events whose execution may overlap in time.

**condition** (in dynamic modeling) a Boolean function of object values valid over an interval of time.

**constraint** a functional relationship between objects, classes, attributes, links, and associations; a statement about some condition or relationship that must be maintained as true. (Contrast with *assertion* and *invariant*.)

**constructor** (in C++) an operation that initializes a newly created instance of a class. (Contrast with *destructor*.)

**container class** a class of *container objects*. Examples include sets, arrays, dictionaries, and associations.

**container object** an object that stores a collection of other objects and provides various operations to access or iterate over its contents.

**continuous transformation** a system in which the outputs actively depend on changing inputs and must be periodically updated. (Contrast with *batch transformation*.)

**contour** (in a state diagram) picture of a state that can contain substates. The contour for a state totally encloses the contours of its substates.

**control** the aspect of a system that describes the sequences of operations that occur in response to stimuli.

**control flow** (in a DFD) a Boolean value that affects whether a process is executed.

**database** a permanent, self-descriptive repository of data that is managed by a DBMS.

**database management system (DBMS)** a computer program that manages a permanent, self-descriptive repository of data.

**data dictionary** a textual description of each class, its associations, attributes, and operations.

**data flow** (in a DFD) the connection between the output of one object or process and the input to another.

**data flow diagram** a graphical representation of the functional model, showing dependencies between values and the computation of output values from input values without regard for when or if the functions are executed.

**data store** (in a DFD) a passive object that stores data for later access.

**DBMS** (acronym) *database management system*.

**delegation** an implementation mechanism in which an object, responding to an operation on itself, forwards the operation to another object; (in object-oriented languages) a mechanism in which methods may be attached directly to instances and where the method resolution is performed by searching a chain of instance pointers, rather than by searching a class hierarchy.

**derived association** an association that is defined in terms of other associations.

**derived attribute** an attribute that is computed from other attributes.

**descendent class** a class that is a direct or indirect subclass of a given class.

**destructor**  (in C++) an operation that cleans up an existing instance of a class that is no longer needed. (Contrast with *constructor*.)

**DFD**  (acronym) *data flow diagram.*

**dictionary**  a class of container object that maps a value of one type into a value of another type, possibly the same type; a lookup table. Mathematically, a discrete function from a domain to a range.

**direct instance**  an object that is an instance of a class but not an instance of any subclass of the class.

**discriminator**  an attribute of enumeration type that indicates which property of a class is being abstracted by a particular generalization.

**domain**  (in a database) the set of legal values for an attribute in a database; (mathematics) the set over which a function or relation is defined.

**dynamic binding**  a form of method resolution that associates a method with an operation at run time, depending on the class of one or more target objects.

**dynamic model**  a description of aspects of a system concerned with control, including time, sequencing of operations, and interaction of objects.

**dynamic simulation**  a system that models or tracks objects in the real world.

**encapsulation**  a modeling and implementation technique that separates the external aspects of an object from the internal, implementation details of the object (also called *information hiding*).

**entity-relationship (ER) diagram**  a graphical representation that shows entities and the relationships between them.

**entity integrity**  (in a relational database) a property of a database such that each table has exactly one primary key.

**event**  (in dynamic modeling) something that happens instantaneously at a point in time.

**event attribute**  data values conveyed by an event from one object to another.

**event trace**  a diagram that shows the sender and receiver of events and the sequence of events.

**extensibility**  a property of software such that new kinds of objects or functionality can be added to it with little or no modification to existing code.

**extension**  (in generalization) the addition of new features by a subclass.

**external schema**  (in a relational database) a design from the perspective of a single application.

**feature**  either an attribute or an operation of a class.

**fire**  (in dynamic modeling) to cause a transition to occur.

**first normal form**  (in a relational database) a property of a schema such that an attribute cannot contain a repeating group.

**fixed aggregate** an aggregate with a predefined number and types of components. (Contrast with *variable aggregate*.)

**foreign key** (in a relational database) a primary key of one table that is embedded in another (or the same) table.

**functional model** description of aspects of a system that transform values using functions, mappings, constraints, and functional dependencies.

**garbage collection** a language mechanism for automatically deallocating data structures which can no longer be accessed and are therefore not needed.

**generalization** the relationship between a class and one or more refined or specialized versions of it.

**generics** (see *parameterized classes*)

**guard condition** (in dynamic modeling) a Boolean expression that must be true in order for a transition to occur.

**guarded transition** (in dynamic modeling) a transition that fires only if a guard condition is true.

**hybrid object-oriented language** a language that has both object-oriented types (classes) and non-object-oriented types (primitive types).

**identity** a distinguishing characteristic of an object that denotes a separate existence of the object even though the object may have the same data values as another object.

**implementation** a stage in the development cycle in which a design is realized in an executable form, such as a programming language or hardware.

**implementation method** (style) a method that implements specific computations on fully-specified arguments, but does not make context-dependent decisions. (Contrast with *policy method*.)

**index** a data structure that maps one or more attribute values into the objects or database table rows that hold the values, usually for optimization purposes.

**indirect instance** an object that is an instance of a class and also an instance of a subclass of the class.

**information hiding** (see *encapsulation*)

**inherently concurrent** two objects that can receive events at the same time without interacting.

**inheritance** an object-oriented mechanism that permits classes to share attributes and operations based on a relationship, usually generalization.

**instance** an object described by a class.

**instance diagram** an object diagram that describes how a particular set of object instances relate to each other. (Contrast with *class diagram*.)

**instance variable** (in Smalltalk) an attribute.

**instantiation** the process of creating instances from classes.

**integrity** (in a relational database: see *entity integrity* and *referential integrity*)

**interactive interface** a system that is dominated by interactions between the system and agents, such as humans, devices, or other programs.

**internal schema** (in a relational database) the actual code required to implement the conceptual schema.

**invariant** a statement about some condition or relationship that must always be true. (Contrast with *assertion* and *constraint*.)

**iterator** a language construct that controls iteration over a range of values or a collection of objects.

**join class** (in multiple inheritance) a class with more than one superclass.

**lambda transition** (see *automatic transition*)

**layer** a subsystem that provides multiple services, all of which are at the same level of abstraction, built on subsystems at a lower level of abstraction. (Contrast with *partition*.)

**leaf class** a class with no subclasses. It must be a concrete class.

**link** an instance of an association; a physical or conceptual connection between objects.

**link attribute** a named data value held by each link in an association.

**message** (in Smalltalk) invocation of an operation on an object, comprising an operation name and a list of argument values.

**metaclass** a class describing other classes.

**metadata** data that describes other data.

**method** the implementation of an operation for a specific class.

**method caching** an optimization of method searching in which the address of a method is found the first time an operation is applied to an object of a class and then stored in a table attached to the class.

**method resolution** (in a programming language) the process of matching an operation on an object to the method appropriate to the object's class.

**methodology** (in software engineering) a process for the organized production of software using a collection of predefined techniques and notational conventions.

**model** an abstraction of something for the purpose of understanding it before building it.

**module** a coherent subset of a system containing a tightly bound group of classes and their relationships.

**multiple inheritance** a type of inheritance that permits a class to have more than one superclass and to inherit features from all ancestors.

**multiplicity** the number of instances of one class that may relate to a single instance of an associated class.

**normal form**  (in a relational database) a set of rules that reduce consistency problems from table updates.

**null**  (in a relational database) a special value that denotes an attribute value which is unknown or not applicable for a given row.

**object**  a concept, abstraction, or thing with crisp boundaries and meanings for the problem at hand; an instance of a class.

**object design**  a stage of the development cycle during which the implementation of each class, association, attribute, and operation is determined.

**object diagram**  a graphical representation of the object model showing relationships, attributes, and operations. (See *instance diagram* and *class diagram*, which are the usual special cases. However, models with metadata do not permit such a dichotomy.)

**object model**  a description of the structure of the objects in a system including their identity, relationships to other objects, attributes, and operations.

**Object Modeling Technique**  an object-oriented development methodology that uses object, dynamic, and functional models throughout the development life cycle. Abbreviated *OMT*.

**object-oriented**  a software development strategy that organizes software as a collection of objects that contain both data structure and behavior. Abbreviated *OO*.

**object-oriented development**  a software development technique that uses objects as a basis for analysis, design, and implementation.

**object-oriented programming language**  a language that supports objects (combining identity, data, and operations), method resolution, and inheritance.

**OMT**  (acronym) *Object Modeling Technique*.

**OO**  (acronym) *object-oriented*.

**OO-DBMS**  (acronym) *object-oriented database management system*.

**OOPL**  (acronym) *object-oriented programming language*.

**operation**  a function or transformation that may be applied to objects in a class.

**origin class**  the topmost class that defines an attribute or operation.

**overloading**  (in a language) binding the same name to multiple operations whose signatures differ in number or types of arguments. A call to an overloaded operation is resolved at compile time based on the types of the calling arguments.

**override**  to define a method for an operation that replaces an inherited method for the same operation.

**package**  (in a programming language such as Ada) a syntactic block with a well-defined interface used to control visibility of its contents.

**parameterized classes** a template for creating real classes that may differ in well-defined ways as specified by parameters at the time of creation. The parameters are often data types or classes, but may include other attributes, such as the size of a collection. (Also called *generic classes*.)

**partition** a subsystem that provides a particular kind of service. A partition may itself be built from lower level subsystems. (Contrast with *layer*.)

**peer** two or more system components that are mutually interdependent for services. (Contrast with *client* and *supplier*.)

**persistent data** data that outlasts the execution of a particular program.

**pointer** an attribute in one object that contains an explicit reference to another object. Pointers are implementation constructs corresponding to associations.

**policy** the making of context-dependent decisions.

**policy method** (style) a method that makes context-dependent decisions, switches control among other methods, combines and parameterizes calls to lower-level methods, and checks for status and error, but which calls on other methods for detailed computations. (Contrast with *implementation method*.)

**polymorphism** takes on many forms; the property that an operation may behave differently on different classes.

**postcondition** a condition that the operation itself agrees to achieve.

**precondition** a condition that the caller of an operation agrees to satisfy.

**primary key** (in a relational database) a combination of one or more attributes whose value unambiguously locates each row in a table.

**private** (referring to an attribute or operation of a class) accessible by methods of the current class only. (Contrast with *public*.)

**process** (in a DFD) something that transforms data values.

**programming-in-the-large** the creation of large, complex programs with teams of programmers.

**propagation** the automatic application of an operation to selected objects in a network when the operation is applied to some starting object in the network.

**protected** (referring to an attribute or operation of a class in C++) accessible by methods of any descendent of the current class. (Contrast with *public* and *private*.)

**protocol** specification of the semantics of an operation, including its signature, a description of the function performed by the operation, and any preconditions or postconditions.

**public** (referring to an attribute or operation of a class) accessible by methods of any class. (Contrast with *private*.)

**qualified association**  an association that relates two classes and a qualifier; a binary association in which the first part is a composite comprising a class and a qualifier, and the second part is a class.

**qualifier**  an attribute of an object that distinguishes among the set of objects at the "many" end of an association.

**query operation**  an operation that returns or computes a value without modifying any objects.

**range**  (mathematics) the set over which the results of a function are defined.

**real-time system**  an interactive system for which time constraints on actions are particularly tight or in which the slightest timing failure cannot be tolerated.

**recursive aggregate**  an aggregate that contains, directly or indirectly, an instance of the same kind of aggregate.

**referential integrity**  (in a relational database) a property of a database such that each foreign key is consistent with its corresponding primary key.

**reflective**  a property of a system such that it can examine its own structure dynamically and reason about its own state.

**relation**  (mathematics) a set of tuples, usually from a list of specified domains; (relational database) a table in the database.

**relational database**  a database managed by a relational DBMS.

**relational DBMS**  a computer program that provides an abstraction of relational tables to the user. It must provide three kinds of functionality: present data in the form of tables, provide operators for manipulating the tables, and support integrity rules on tables.

**restriction**  (in generalization) a constraint that a subclass places on the value of an attribute contained in a superclass.

**robust**  a property of software such that it does not fail catastrophically when some of its design assumptions are violated.

**role**  one end of an association.

**role name**  a name that uniquely identifies one end of an association.

**scenario**  (in dynamic modeling) a sequence of events that occur during one particular execution of a system.

**schema**  the structure or template of the data in a database.

**second normal form**  (in a relational database) property of a schema such that it is in first normal form and each row has a primary key.

**self**  (in Smalltalk) the default name of the target object of a method. (Corresponds to *this* in C++ and *Current* in Eiffel.)

**service**  a group of related functions (or operations) that work together to provide a functional capability.

**sheet** (in an object model) the mechanism for breaking large object models into a series of pages.

**signature** (for an attribute) the attribute's type; (for an operation) the number and types of its arguments and the type of its result.

**single inheritance** a type of inheritance in which a class may have only a single superclass.

**specialization** the creation of subclasses from a superclass by refining the superclass.

**SQL** a standard language for interacting with relational DBMS.

**state** the values of the attributes and links of an object at a particular time.

**state diagram** a directed graph in which nodes represent system states and arcs represent transitions between states.

**strong typing** a property of a programming language such that the type of each variable must be declared. (Contrast with *weak typing*.)

**structure chart** a tree-shaped graph in which the nodes represent procedures and the arcs represent caller/callee relationships.

**subclass** (in generalization) a refined version of another class, the superclass. An instance of the subclass is also an instance of the superclass.

**subsystem** a major component of a system organized around some coherent theme. A system may be divided into subsystems using either *partitions* or *layers*.

**superclass** (in generalization) a more abstract version of another class, the subclass.

**supplier** a system component that provides a service to another component. The component requesting the service is a *client*.

**system** an organized collection of components that interact.

**system design** the first stage of design, during which high-level decisions are made about the overall structure of the system, its architecture, and the strategies used to implement the system.

**system development life cycle** the process of creating a hardware/software system from its conception, through analysis, design, implementation, testing, and maintenance.

**table** (in a relational database) an organization of data that has a specific number of columns and an arbitrary number of rows. Often called a relation.

**ternary association** an association between three classes.

**third normal form** (in a relational database) property of a schema such that it is in second normal form and each nonprimary-key field depends on the primary key.

**this** (in C++) the default name of the target object of a method. (Corresponds to *self* in Smalltalk and *Current* in Eiffel.)

**thread of control** a single path of execution through a program, a dynamic model, or some other representation of control flow.

**transaction manager**  a database system whose main function is to store and access information.

**transition**  a change of state caused by an event.

**triggering**  (see *propagation*)

**tuple**  an ordered list of data values.

**type**  a set of objects or values with similar behavior, usually expressed by the operations defined on the type, without regard for the potential implementation of the type. A type is a semantic property.

**variable aggregate**  an aggregate with a finite number of levels but a varying number of parts. (Contrast with *fixed aggregate*.)

**view**  (in a relational database) a virtual table that is derived from one or more underlying tables.

**virtual**  something that has conceptual but not actual existence; (in C++) an operation that can be overridden by a descendent class.

**weak typing**  a property of a programming language such that the type of each variable need not be declared. (Contrast with *strong typing*.)

**wrapper**  a class or operation that encapsulates a call to library routines or some other code that is being reused.

# Answers to Selected Exercises

Criteria for selecting exercises to be answered include: exercises with short answers in the core chapters; exercises that extend chapters by introducing new material; key exercises in a series of questions; answers that clarify subtle or difficult points; and prototypes for real problems that are commonly encountered. Most exercises have multiple correct answers so the answers given here should be used as a guide and not as a test of correctness.

**1.5b.** Criminal investigations use combinations of photographs, fingerprinting, bloodtyping, DNA analysis, and dental records to identify people, living and/or deceased, who are involved in, or the subject of, a criminal investigation.

**d.** Telephone numbers are adequate for identifying almost any telephone in the world. In general a telephone number consists of a country code plus a province, city, or area code, plus a local number plus an optional extension number. Businesses may have their own telephone systems with other conventions. Depending on the relative location of the telephone that you are calling, parts of the number may be implied and can be left out, but extra access digits may be required to call outside the local region. In North America local calls require 7 digits. Long distance calls use an access digit (0 or 1) + area code (3 digits) + local number (7 digits). Dialing Paris requires an access code (011) + country code (33) + city code (1) + local number (8 digits). The access code is not part of the identifier. Dialing is an example of navigation, not identity.

**g.** One way that employees are given restricted, after-hours access to a company is through the use of a special, electronically-readable card. Of course, if an employee loses a card and does not report it, someone who finds it could use it for unauthorized entry. Another approach is a picture ID which requires inspection by a guard.

**1.8a.** These are all devices that enhance vision in some way. With the exception of the scanning electron microscope, all the devices listed work by reflecting or refracting light. Eyeglasses and binoculars are designed for use with two eyes, the rest of the objects on the list are designed for use with one eye. Telescopes, bomb sights, and binoculars are used to view things far away. A microscope is used to magnify something that is very small. Eyeglasses may enlarge or reduce, depending on whether the prescription is for a near-sighted or a far-sighted person. Some other classes that could be included in this list are optical microscopes, cameras, and magnifying glasses.

**b.** Pipes, check valves, faucets, filters, and pressure gauges are all plumbing supplies with certain temperature and pressure ratings. Compatibility with various types of fluids is also a consideration. Check valves and faucets may be used to control flow. With the exception of the pressure gauge, all of the items listed have two ends and have a pressure-flow characteristic for a given fluid. All of the items are passive. Some other classes include pumps, tanks, and connectors.

**f.** Square root, exponential, sine, and cosine are all functions of a single variable. Both real and complex definitions are commonly used. As real functions, each maps a real input to a real output. As a real function, square root is defined only for nonnegative numbers. As complex functions, each maps a complex input to a complex output.

**2.3a.** For a Trans-Atlantic cable, resistance to saltwater is the main consideration. The cable must lie unmaintained at the bottom of the ocean for a long time. The ratio of strength/weight is important to avoid breakage while the cable is being installed. Cost is an important economic factor.

**c.** Weight is important for wire that is to be used in the electrical system of an airplane, because it affects the total weight of the plane. Toughness of the insulation is important to resist chafing due to vibration. Resistance of the insulation to fire is also important to avoid starting or feeding electrical fires in flight.

**3.2** A class diagram is shown in Figure A3.2. The smallest number of points required to construct a polygon is three. One way to express the fact that points are in a sequence is to indicate that the association is ordered. The multiplicity of the association depends on how points are identified. If a point is identified by its location, then points are shared and the association is many-to-many. On the other hand, if each point belongs to exactly one polygon, as shown in the diagram, then several points may have the same coordinates. The difference between the two situations is clarified in the next answer.

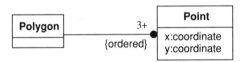

**Figure A3.2** Class diagram for polygon and points

**3.3a.** An instance diagram for two triangles with a common side in which a point belongs to exactly one polygon is shown in Figure A3.3a.

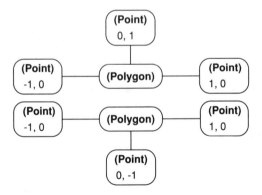

**Figure A3.3a** Instance diagram where each point belongs to exactly one polygon

**b.** An instance diagram for two triangles with a common side in which points may be shared is shown in Figure A3.3b.

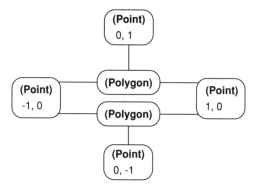

**Figure A3.3b** Instance diagram where each point can belong to multiple polygons

**3.8a.** An instance diagram for the expression *(X+Y/2)/(X/3+Y)* is shown in Figure A3.8a. The object diagram in the exercise is actually a metamodel for binary expressions. Parentheses are required for an infix representation but are not needed in the metamodel. There are other representations, such as postfix, in which parentheses also are not needed. For example, the same expression becomes *X Y 2 / + X 3 / Y + /* in a postfix representation.

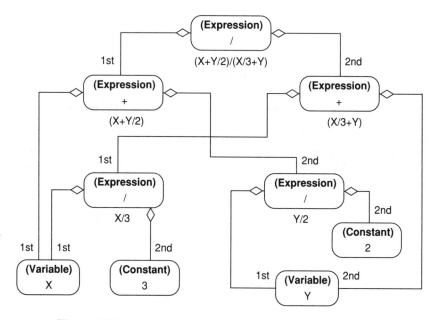

**Figure A3.8a** Instance diagram for the expression (X+Y/2)/(X/3+Y)

The diagram in this exercise contains recursion. Expressions are formed from terms which themselves may be expressions. Very complex expressions may be represented leading to complex instance diagrams.

Figure E3.6 indicates that terms may be shared by expressions. The situation is analogous to sharing of points discussed in exercise 3.3. If the direction of the links in the corresponding instance diagrams are taken into account, then instance diagrams are directed acyclic graphs.

The instance diagram shown in Figure A3.8a treats *Term* as an abstract class, since only direct instances of the classes *Expression*, *Variable*, and *Constant* are shown.

The partial expressions in the instance diagram are shown for clarity. To save space, *1st* and *2nd* have been substituted for the role names *first operand* and *second operand*. In reading the instance diagram, remember that the role names are on the *Term* end of the associations.

**b.** The extensions to not share terms and to handle unary minus are shown in Figure A3.8b. Note that because of the possibility of a unary operator, the multiplicity of the second operand is zero-one. Also the diagram does not express very well the fact that every term must belong to exactly one expression. The diagram could be further improved by replacing the two associations between *Term* and *Expression* with a single, qualified association with the qualifier *operand*. This would result in a multiplicity of exactly one on the *Expression* end of the association. Several other variations are possible.

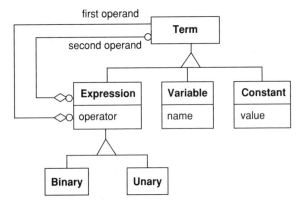

**Figure A3.8b** Extended class diagram for simple arithmetic expressions

**3.22** An object diagram for the dining philosopher's problem is shown in Figure A3.22. The one-to-one associations describe the relative locations of philosophers and forks. The *In use* association describes who is using which forks. Other representations are possible, depending on your viewpoint. An instance diagram may help you better understand this problem.

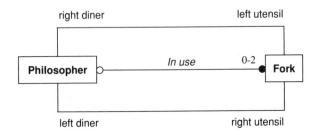

**Figure A3.22** Object diagram for the dining philosopher problem

**3.23**   This is an important exercise, because graphs occur in many applications. Several variations are possible, depending on your viewpoint. Figure A3.23a accurately represents undirected graphs as described in the exercise. Although not quite as accurate, your answer could omit the class *Undirected graph*.

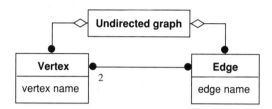

**Figure A3.23a**  Object diagram for undirected graphs

We have found it useful for some graph related queries to elevate the association between vertices and edges to the status of an object class as shown in Figure A3.23b.

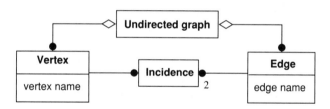

**Figure A3.23b**  Object diagram for undirected graphs in which the incidence between vertices and edges is treated as an object class

**3.26**   One object diagram describing directed graphs is shown in Figure A3.26a. The distinction between the two ends of an edge is accomplished with a qualified association. Values of the qualifier *end* are *from* and *to*.

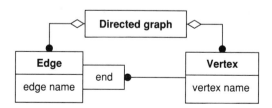

**Figure A3.26a**  Object diagram for directed graphs using a qualified association

Figure A3.26b shows another representation of directed graphs. The distinction between the two ends of an edge is accomplished with separate associations for the two ends of an edge.

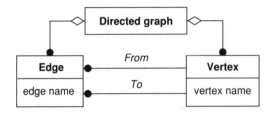

**Figure A3.26b** Object diagram for directed graphs using two associations

The advantage of the qualified association is that only one association must be queried to find one or both vertices that a given edge is connected to. If the qualifier is not specified, both vertices can be found. By specifying *from* or *to* for the *end* qualifier, the vertex that is connected to an edge at the given *end* can be found.

The advantage of using two separate associations is that the need to manage enumerated values for the qualifier *end* is eliminated.

**3.28** An object diagram for car loans in which pointers are replaced with relationships is shown in Figure A3.28.

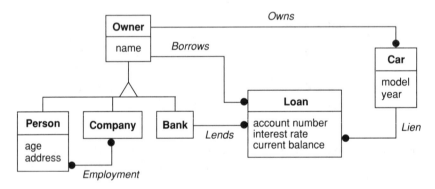

**Figure A3.28** Proper object model for car loans

In this form, the arguably artificial restriction that a person have no more than three employers has been eliminated. Note that in this model an owner can own several cars. A car can have several loans against it. Banks loan money to persons, companies, and other banks.

**4.2** The object diagram in Figure A4.2 abstracts the classes *Buffer, Selection*, and *Sheet* into the superclass *Collection*. Overall, this revision is recommended. Using the generalization relationship promotes code reuse because many operations apply equally well to the subclasses. Six aggregation relationships in the original diagram, which shared similar characteristics, have been reduced to two. Finally, the constraint that each *Box* and *Link* should belong to exactly one *Buffer, Selection,* or *Sheet* has been captured by the structure of the diagram.

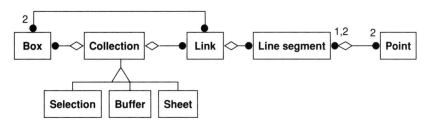

**Figure A4.2** Abstraction of the classes *Selection*, *Buffer*, and *Sheet* into the class *Collection*

**4.4** An object diagram for a graphical document editor is shown in Figure A4.4. The requirement that a *Group* contains 2 or more *Drawing object*s is expressed as a multiplicity of 2+ on *Drawing object* in its aggregation relationship with *Group*. The fact that a *Drawing object* need not be in a *Group* is expressed by the zero-one multiplicity.

It is possible to revise this diagram to make a *Circle* a special case of an *Ellipse* and to make a *Square* a special case of a *Rectangle*.

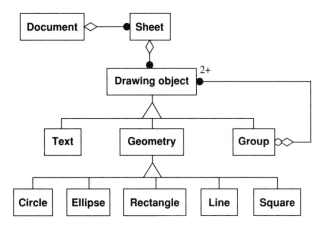

**Figure A4.4** Object diagram for a graphical document editor that supports grouping

**4.8**    An object diagram showing the relationships among several classes of electrical machines is shown in Figure A4.8. We have included attributes that were not requested.

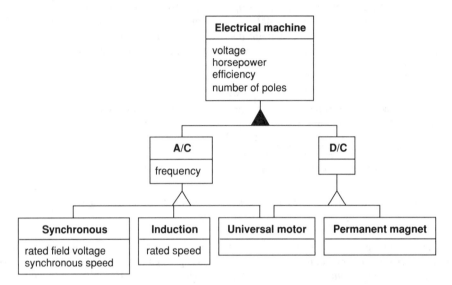

**Figure A4.8**  Partial taxonomy for electrical machines

**4.9**    One way to eliminate the multiple inheritance in to convert the overlapping combination of classes into a class of its own as shown in Figure A4.9.

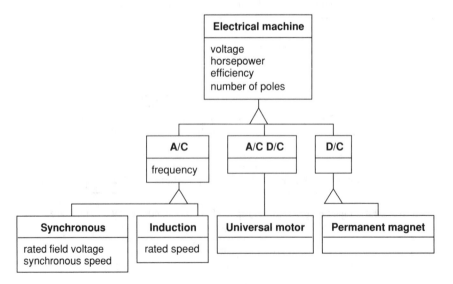

**Figure A4.9**  Elimination of multiple inheritance

**4.10**  The object diagram in Figure A4.10 is a metamodel of the following subset of the OMT notation: object classes, attributes, and binary associations.

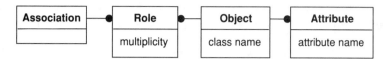

**Figure A4.10** Metamodel for a subset of the OMT notation

**4.13** The object diagram given in the exercise does support multiple inheritance. If an instance of *Object class* is a subclass in more than one generalization relationship, there is an instance of *Generalization role*, with *role type* equal to *subclass* for each generalization relationship.

**4.14** To find the superclass of a generalization using the metamodel given in the exercise, first query the association between *Generalization* and *Generalization role* to get a set of all roles of the given instance of *Generalization*. Then sequentially search this set of instances of *Generalization role* to find the one with *role type* equal to *superclass*. (Hopefully only one instance will be found with *role type* equal to *superclass*, which is a constraint that is not enforced by the model.) Finally, scan the association between *Generalization role* and *Object class* to get the superclass.

One possible revision which simplifies superclass lookup is shown in Figure A4.14a. To find the superclass of a generalization, first query the association between *Generalization* and *Superclass role*. Then query the association between *Superclass role* and *Object class* to find the corresponding instance of *Object class*.

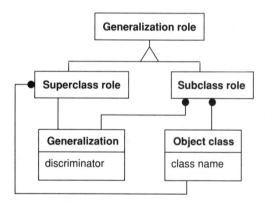

**Figure A4.14a** Metamodel of generalization relationships with separate subclass and superclass roles

Another metamodel of generalization which supports multiple inheritance is shown in Figure A4.14b. To find the superclass of a generalization using this metamodel, simply query the *Superclass* association.

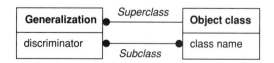

**Figure A4.14b** Simplified metamodel of generalization relationships

We do not imply that the metamodel in Figure A4.14b is the best model of generalization, only that it simplifies the query given in the exercise. The choice of which model to use will depend on other factors as well.

**5.3**    The state diagram for the control of the headlight and wheels of an electric train is shown in Figure A5.3. The event *power off-on* is the sequence of the two events *power off* followed by *power on*. Strictly speaking, there should four more unlabeled states in the state diagram for the wheels that we have eliminated by introducing the event *power off-on*.

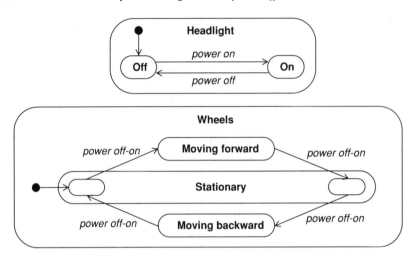

**Figure A5.3**  State diagram for the control of an electric train

The inspiration for this exercise was an actual electromechanical control which contained a wheel with contacts. Each time the power was pulsed a solenoid driven ratchet advanced the wheel one quarter of a turn. The stationary state allowed the train to be stopped with power still applied to the track. If the train was running forward before you shut it off and put it away, it would be stationary the next time you turned it on.

The control also had a switch to disable it that left the control in whatever state it was in when it was shut off. You might want to modify the diagram to add this feature. You also might prepare a state diagram with 8 states, showing how the control works if separate events *power on* and *power off* are used instead of *power off-on*.

**5.5**    A state diagram for a simple digital watch is shown in Figure A5.5. We assume that pressing a button is an event and that we may ignore the release of a button. We use *A* in the diagram to refer to pressing the A button and *B* to refer to pressing the B button.

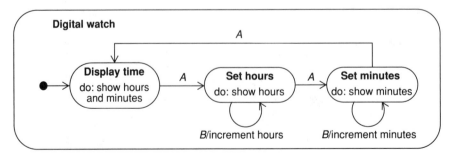

**Figure A5.5**  State diagram for a simple digital watch

**5.10** The completed state diagram for the motor control described in the exercise is shown in Figure A5.10.

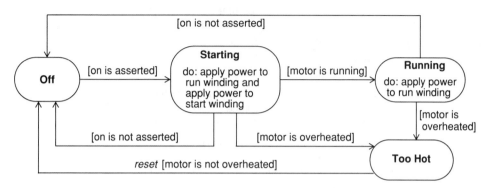

**Figure A5.10** State diagram for a simple motor control

**5.20** This exercise demonstrates that even simple state diagrams can lead to complex behavior. A state diagram that will explain the scenario given in the exercise is shown in Figure A5.20. A *change* event occurs whenever the candle is taken out of its holder or whenever it is put back. The condition *at north* is satisfied whenever the bookcase is behind the wall. The condition *at north, east, south, or west* is satisfied whenever the bookcase is facing front, back, or to the side.

When you first discovered the bookcase, it was in the *Stopped* state pointing south. When your friend removed the candle, a *change* event drove the bookcase into the *Rotating* state. When the bookcase was pointing north, the condition *at north* put the bookcase back into the *Stopped* state. When your friend reinserted the candle, another *change* event put the bookcase into the *Rotating* state until it again pointed north. Pulling the candle out generated another *change* event and would have caused the bookcase to rotate a full turn if you had not blocked it with your body. Forcing the bookcase back is outside the scope of the control and does not have to be explained.

When you put the candle back again another *change* event was generated, putting the bookcase into the *Rotating* state once again. Taking the candle back out resulted in yet another *change* event, putting the bookcase into the *Stopping* state. After 1/4 turn, the condition *at north, east, south or west* was satisfied, putting the bookcase into the *Stopped* state.

What you should have done at first to gain entry was to take the candle out and quickly put it back before the bookcase completed 1/4 turn.

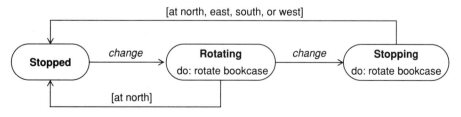

**Figure A5.20** State diagram for the control of the entrance to a secret passageway

**6.4**   Figure A6.4 contains the data flow diagram for computing cylinder geometry.

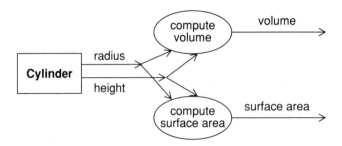

**Figure A6.4**  Data flow diagram for computing cylinder volume and surface area

Some different ways to compute volume and surface area for a cylinder are:

- *A formula*. Volume = $\pi r^2 h$. Surface area = $2\pi rh$. (r=radius, h=height)
- *A lookup table*. Volume and surface area are listed for standard values of radius and height.
- *Numerical methods*. Calculate volume and surface area from differential equations.

**6.5**   Figure A6.5 shows the data flow diagram for computing the mean for a sequence of input values.

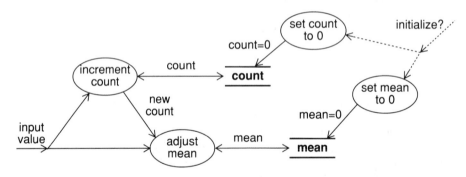

*adjust mean* process

(Note: n+1=new count, $x_n=n^{th}$ input value, $\bar{x}_n$=average after n values)

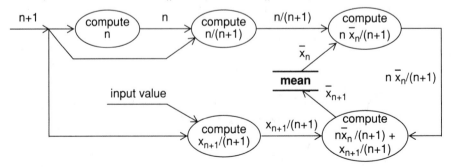

**Figure A6.5**  Data flow diagram for computing mean of a sequence of values

**6.7a.** Using conditional statements, the algorithm for T(x) can be expressed as:

```
if (x > -3) and (x ≤ -2) then T = 3+x
else if (x ≤ -1) then T = -x-1
else if (x ≤ 0) then T = 1+x
else if (x ≤ 1) then T = 1-x
else if (x ≤ 2) then T = x-1
else if (x ≤ 3) then T = 3-x
end if
```

The above pseudo code can be simplified to the following.

```
t = (x mod 2) - 1

if (t<0) then T = -t
else T = t
end if
```

**c.** The data flow diagram for T(x) in Figure A6.7 only uses functions and arithmetic.

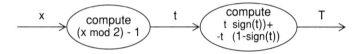

**Figure A6.7** Data flow diagram for *T(x)*

**6.10a.** absolute value: if $x \geq 0$ then $|x| = x$, else $|x| = -x$

**b.** trigonometric sine: $\sin \theta = y/r$

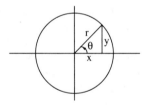

**Figure A6.10** Definition of trigonometric sine

**c.** natural logarithm: $\ln(x) = \int_1^x (1/t)\, dt$

**d.** square root: $y = \text{sqrt}(x)$ such that $x = y * y$

**6.11a.** pseudo code for absolute value

```
if x ≥ 0 then return x
else return -x
end if
```

**b, c, d.** Two ways of implementing trigonometric sine, natural logarithm, and square root are by power series and fixed point iteration.

Mathematics can be used to derive an infinite power series $(a_0 x^0 + a_1 x^1 + a_2 x^2 + ...)$ that is equivalent to the desired function. The function can then be approximated by evaluating the first portion of the power series and truncating the remainder. The sine, logarithm, and square root functions have an infinite number of power series; a desirable power series would converge quickly for the arguments of interest and bound the maximum error. Before computing a power series, the argument value is usually normalized to lie within a standard range. Thus for instance, the following property can be used to transform the sine argument to an equivalent argument that lies in the range of 0° to 360°

```
sin (θ) = sin (θ mod 360°)
```

One could normalize the argument of the sin function even further by recognizing that

```
sin (θ) = - sin (θ - 180°)
```

and thus transform the sin argument to lie in the range of 0° to 180°.

Another way of implementing these functions is by fixed point iteration: Guess an initial value and then repeatedly apply an identity formula, until you are close enough to the correct answer. For example, an initial estimate of y = sqrt(x) is y = (1+x)/2; in fact this is a very good estimate of the square root for values of x close to 1. A new value of x can be computed with the following formula:

```
yₙ₊₁ = (yₙ + x/yₙ) / 2
```

**8.1**   Do not worry if your answers do not exactly match ours since you had to make assumptions about the functional specifications. The point of the exercise is to make you think about the examples in terms of the three aspects of modeling.

**a.** Functional modeling, object modeling, and dynamic modeling, in that order, are important for a bridge playing program because good algorithms are needed to yield intelligent playing. The game involves a great deal of strategy. Close attention to inheritance and method design can result in significant code reuse. The interface is not complicated, so the dynamic model is simple and could be omitted.

**c.** The order of importance of aspects of modeling for a car cruise control is dynamic modeling, object modeling, and functional modeling. Because this is a control application you can expect the dynamic model to be important. There is a need to thoroughly understand scenarios and protocols for interaction. The functional model is simple because there are not many calculations.

**e.** For a spelling checker the order of importance of aspects of modeling is object modeling, functional modeling, dynamic modeling. Object modeling is important because of the need to store a great deal of data and to able to access it quickly. Functional modeling is important because an efficient algorithm is needed to check spelling quickly. The dynamic model is simple because the user interface is simple. All that is needed is to give the user a chance to correct each misspelled word that is found.

**8.8a.** We assume there is exactly one instance of the class *Selection*. Declare an error if there is not exactly one instance. Ascend the class hierarchy to the class *Collection*. Scan the association between the classes *Collection* and *Box* to obtain a set of boxes. Scan the association between the classes *Collection* and *Link* to obtain a set of links.

**c.** We assume that *boxes* is a global variable that contains a set. Initialize *boxes* to be empty. To determine all boxes that are linked directly or indirectly to a given box, call the following recursive procedure with the given box as the argument:

```
Retrieve_boxes(given_box)
      Retrieve set of links associated with given_box
    for each link
      for each box associated with the link
        if box is not in boxes then
          Add box to boxes
          Retrieve_boxes(box)
        end if
      end for each box
    end for each link
```

**e.** Take advantage of the fact that a link is associated with exactly 2 boxes. If *given_box* and *given_link* are not associated then declare an error. Otherwise place the 2 boxes associated with *given_link* into a set and delete *given_box* from the set.

**g.** We assume that *selection* is a global variable that contains an instance of *Selection*. We assume that *bridges* is a global variable in which the set of bridging links is to be placed.

```
Ascend the class hierarchy from the class Selection to the
      class Collection for the instance selection.
Scan the association to the class Box to obtain a set of all
      boxes in the selection.
Initialize bridges to be an empty set.
for each box in the set.
      for each link associated with the box.
          Get the box on the other end of the link,
            using the answer to part e).
          if the box on the other end is not in the selection.
            Add the link to bridges.
          end if
      end for each link
end for each box
```

**8.9**     There is more than one way of satisfying the given queries. Some readers may find Figure E8.3 easier to understand than Figure E8.2 and will consequently arrive at simpler queries by using it. Others may find the reverse to be true. However, the two are nearly equivalent from the point of view of the given queries. For some of the queries Figure E8.3 requires an extra step. The reader may find that one of the approaches has advantages during implementation in a particular language (or database) depending on the features of the language.

**8.16**   The following candidate classes are really attributes or redundant attributes:

   address, age, average score, child's name, date, difficulty factor, net score, team name

The following are redundant:

   child, contestant, individual, person, registrant

These are vague or irrelevant:

   back, card, conclusion, corner, individual prize, leg, pool, prize, team prize, try, water ballet

The following are implementation details:

   file of team member data, list of scheduled meets, number, group

These candidates are really operations:

compute average, register

The astute reader will notice some of the candidate classes that are not eliminated here do not appear in Figure E8.4. That is because Figure E8.4 is only a partially completed object diagram.

**8.19a.** Scan the association between the classes *Team* and *Competitor* using the given team to get the set of its members.

  **c.** There are several ways to find the net score of a competitor for a given figure at a given meet. One way is the following:

Find the set of all events held at the given meet from the association between *Meet* and *Event*. Find the set of all events associated with the given figure. Intersect the two sets. Given the way that meets are conducted, there should be exactly one event in the intersection. Use a similar process using the event and competitor as input to find the trial for the competitor in that event. The net score is contained in the trial.

  **e.** Use the association between *Meet* and *Event* to find all events held at the given meet. Use the association between *Event* and *Trial* to find all trials of all events at the given meet. Use the association between *Competitor* and *Trial* to find all trials by the given competitor. Intersect the set of all trials of all events at the given meet with the set of all trials by the given competitor. The result is the set of all trials by the given competitor at the given meet. Compute the average score from net scores of the trials by the given competitor at the given meet.

  **g.** The object diagram in Figure E8.4 does not support this query very well. Find all meets in the given season. From all meets find all events in the given season. From all events find all trials in the given season. For each trial merge the associated competitor into the answer set.

**8.23** The 2 teams were the Dolphins and the Whales. The 4 competitors were Heather Martin, Elissa Martin, Cathy Lewis, and Christine Brown. Stations were set up on the northwest and southeast corners of the pool with three judges each. The 4 events were the Ballet Leg, the Dolphin, the Front Pike Somersault, and the Back Pike Somersault. Heather was number 3. In this scenario we assume that there is a personal computer at each station. There are other possible scenarios, depending on the system architecture. When Heather approached the station to try the Ballet Leg the computer operator called her number as it appeared on the display. When Heather verified her number the operator confirmed it with the computer which was then ready to accept scores. After Heather performed the Ballet Leg the 3 judges held up the scores 3.8, 3.6, and 3.7. A scorekeeper read the scores. As they were read the computer operator entered them into the computer. Another scorekeeper wrote them down and checked the numbers on the computer display after they were entered. In this case the operator made a mistake and the judges were asked to repeat the scores. When everyone was satisfied the operator verified the scores and the computer stored them in a database.

When all of the events were over a batch program was run to merge the data from the two stations into a single database. Then another batch program was run to convert the raw scores into net scores for each trial, to compute the overall scores for each competitor, to sort the competitors by overall score, and to print out the results. The print outs included an ordered listing of the winners and summary sheets for each competitor. The summary sheet for each competitor included raw scores, degree of difficulty, and net scores for each event.

**8.26**   A partial shopping list of operations is shown in Figure A8.26.

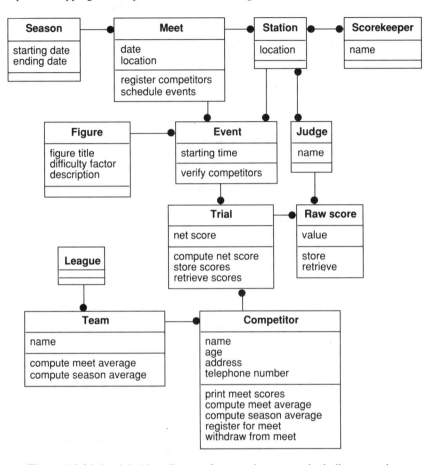

**Figure A8.26**   Partial object diagram for a scoring system including operations

**8.28**   The revised diagrams are shown in Figures A8.28a-A8.28d. Note that Figure A8.28a could be simplified by combining *Appointment* and *Date-time* and treating *Date-time* as an attribute. Figure A8.28d could be simplified by combining *Edge* and *Incidence*. In general a ternary association can always be converted into a class. Some thought may be required to get the multiplicities right.

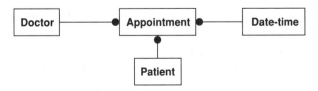

**Figure A8.28a**   Object diagram for appointments

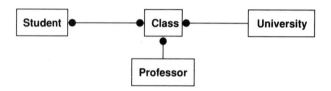

**Figure A8.28b** Object diagram for classes

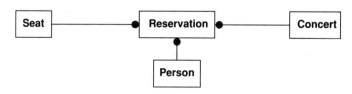

**Figure A8.28c** Object diagram for reservations

**Figure A8.28d** Object diagram for graphs

**8.33a.** Candidate keys are *Flight + Seat* and *Flight + Person*.
  **b.** The only candidate key is *Flight + Seat*.

**9.6** Figure A9.6 shows one possible partitioning.

| command processing | | | | | | |
|---|---|---|---|---|---|---|
| user interface | construct expression | | | | file interface | |
| line semantics | apply operation | substitute | rationalize | evaluate | save | load |
| line syntax | | | | | | |
| operating system | | | | | | |

**Figure A9.6** Block diagram for an interactive polynomial symbolic manipulation system

**9.7** A single program provides faster detection and correction of errors and eliminates the need to implement an interface between two programs. With a single program, any errors that the system detects in the process of converting the object diagram to a database schema can be quickly communicated to the user for correction. Also, the editing and the conversion portions of the program can share the same data, eliminating the need for an interface such as a file to transfer the object diagram from one program to another.

Splitting the functionality into two programs reduces memory requirements and decouples program development. The total memory requirement of a single program would be approximately equal to the sum of the requirements of two separate programs. Since both programs are likely to use a great deal of memory, performance problems could arise if they are combined. Using two separate programs also simplifies program development. The two programs can be developed independently, so that changes made in one are less likely to impact the other. Also, two programs are easier to debug than one monolithic program. If the interface between the two programs is well defined, problems in the overall system can be quickly identified within one program or the other.

**9.11**  The reader should note that this problem does not give an exhaustive list of solutions.

**a.** *Do not worry about it at all. Reset all data every time the system is turned on.* This is the cheapest, simplest approach. It is relatively easy to program, since all that is needed is an initialization routine on power up to allow the user to enter parameters. However, this approach cannot be taken for systems which must provide continuous service or which must not lose data during power loss.

**c.** *Keep critical information on a magnetic disk drive. Periodically make full and/or incremental copies on magnetic tape.* This approach is moderately expensive and bulky. In the event of a power failure, the system stops running. An operating system is required to cope with the disk and tape drive. A operator is required to manage the tapes, which would preclude applications where unattended operation is required.

**e.** *Use a special memory component.* This approach is relatively cheap and is automatic. However, the system cannot run when power is off. Some restrictions may apply such as a limit on the number of times data can be saved or on the amount of data that can be saved. A program may be required to save important parameters as power is failing.

**9.12a.** *Four function pocket calculator.* Do not worry about permanent data storage at all. All of the other options are too expensive to consider. This type of calculator sells for a few dollars and is typically used to balance checkbooks. Memory requirements are on the order of 10 bytes.

**c.** *System clock for a personal computer.* Only a few bytes are required, but the clock must continue to run with the main power off. Battery backup is an inexpensive solution. Clock circuits can be designed that will run for 5 years from a battery.

**e.** *Digital control and thermal protection unit for a motor.* On the order of 10 to 100 bytes are needed. This application is sensitive to price. An uninterruptable power supply is too expensive to consider. Tape and disk drives are too fragile for the harsh environment of the application. Use a combination of switches, special memory components, and battery backup. Switches are a good way to enter parameters, since an interface is required anyway. Special memory components can store computed data. A battery can be used to continue operation with power removed but presents a maintenance problem in this application. We would question this requirement, seeking alternatives such as assuming that the motor is hot when it is first turned on or using a sensor to measure the temperature of the motor.

**9.13a.** A description of the diagram, assuming that tabs, spaces, and line feeds are ignored, is:

```
(DIAGRAM
     (CLASS
       (NAME "Polygon"))
     (CLASS
       (NAME "Point")
       (ATTRIBUTE "x")
       (ATTRIBUTE "y"))
     (ASSOCIATION
       (ROLE (NAME "Polygon") ONE)
       (ROLE (NAME "Point") MANY)))
```

**9.14** The hardware approach is fastest, but incurs the cost of the hardware. The software approach is cheapest and most flexible, but may not be fast enough. Use the software approach whenever it is fast enough. General purpose systems favor the software approach, because of its flexibility. Special purpose systems can usually integrate the added circuitry with other hardware.

Actually, there is another approach, firmware, that may be used in hardware architectures. Typically, in this approach a hardware controller calculates the CRC under the direction of a microcoded program that is stored in a permanent memory that is totally invisible externally. We will count this approach as hardware.

**a.** Use a hardware approach for a floppy disk controller. Flexibility is not needed, since a floppy disk controller is a special purpose system. Speed is needed because of the high data rate.

**c.** Use hardware to check memory. This is an example of a very specific application, where the function can probably be integrated with the circuitry in the memory chips. The data rate is very high.

**e.** Use a software approach to validate an account number. The data rate is very low. The system handling the account number is probably running on a general purpose computer.

**10.5** Figure A10.5 enforces a constraint that is missing in Figure E10.1: Each boundary corresponds to exactly one ellipse or rectangle. One measure of the quality of an object diagram is how well its structure captures constraints.

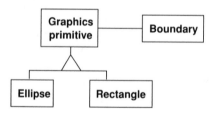

**Figure A10.5** Improved object diagram for part of a CAD system

**10.11** A derived association supports direct traversal from *Page* to *Line*. In general derived entities present a trade-off: They speed execution of certain queries but incur an update cost to keep the redundant data consistent with the base data.

The line-page association is derived by composing the line-column and column-page associations. Since it is present for optimization, it would probably be traversed only from lines to pages and could therefore be implemented as a pointer attribute within class *Line*.

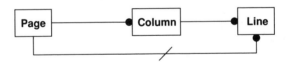

**Figure A10.11** Object diagram for a newspaper with a derived association

**10.12** Type *Rank* is an enumeration of {Ace, King, Queen, 10, 9, 8, 7, 6, 5, 4, 3, 2}. The ranks are ordered but the order varies from game to game (some games rank the ace highest, some lowest). Depending on the games to be supported, the enumeration could be ordered or unordered. If the enumeration is unordered, then an ordering function must be provided for rank values in a particular game. It would be possible to implement a rank value as an integer. Type *Suit* is an enumeration of {Spade, Club, Heart, Diamond}. For many games, suits are unordered; the order of suits varies in other games, so an ordering function on suit values is probably best. Suit and rank could also be implemented as objects rather than pure values, given the complexity of the ordering functions and other peculiarities of real card games.

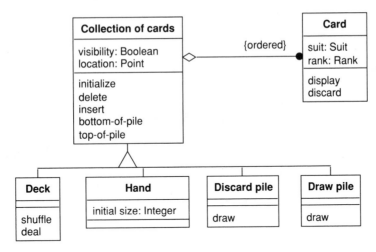

**Figure A10.12** Portion of an object diagram for a card playing program

**10.19** The code listed below sketches out a solution. This code lacks internal assertions that would normally be included to check the correctness of the metadata. For example, error code should be included to handle the case where the role is a subclass and the relationship is not Generalization. In code that interacts with users or external data sources, it is usually a good idea to add an error check as an else clause for conditionals that "must be true."

```
trace_inheritance_path (class1, class2): Path
{
      path := new Path of Class;
      // try to find a path from class1 as descendent of class 2
      classx := class1;
      while classx is not null do:
        add classx to front of path;
        if classx = class2 then return path;
        classx := classx.get_superclass
      // try to find a path from class2 as descendent of class 1
      path.clear;
      classx := class2;
      while classx is not null do:
        add classx to front of path;
        if classx = class1 then return path;
        classx := classx.get_superclass
      // the two classes are not directly related
      // return an empty path
      path.clear
      return path
}

Class::get_superclass : Class
{
      for each role in self.connection do:
        if the role is a Subclass then:
          relationship := role.relationship;
          if relationship is a Generalization then:
            other_roles := relationship.end;
            for each other_role in other_roles do:
              if other_role is a Superclass then:
                return other_role.class
}
```

**10.22** Political party membership is not an inherent property of a voter but a changeable association. The revised model better represents voters with no party affiliation and permits changes in party membership. If voters could belong to more than one party, then the multiplicity could easily be changed. Parties are instances of class *Political party* and need not be explicitly listed in the model; new parties can be added without changing the model and attributes can be attached to parties.

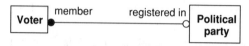

**Figure A10.22** Improved object diagram for representing voter membership in a political party

**10.24** The left figure shows an index on points using a doubly-qualified association. The association is sorted first on the *x* qualifier and then on the *y* qualifier. Because the index is an optimization, it contains redundant information also stored in the point objects. The right figure shows the same diagram using singly-qualified associations. We had to introduce a dummy class *Strip* to represent all points having a given x-coordinate. The second model would be easier to implement on most systems because a data structure for a single sort key is more likely to be available. The actual implementation could use B-trees, linked lists, or arrays to represent the association.

**Figure A10.24** Object diagram for fast two-dimensional searching

The code listed below specifies search, add, and delete methods.

```
PointCollection::search (region: Rectangle): Set of Point
{
        make a new empty set of points;
        scan the x values in the association until x ≥ region.xmin;
        while the x qualifier ≤ region.xmax do:
          scan the y values for the x value until y ≥ region.ymin;
          while the y qualifier ≤ region.ymax do:
            add (x,y) to the set of points;
            advance to the next y value;
          advance to the next x value;
        return the set of points;
}

PointCollection::add (point: Point)
{
        scan the x values in the association until x ≥ point.x;
        if x = point.x then
          scan the y values for the x value until y ≥ point.y
        insert the point into the association;
}

PointCollection::delete (point: Point)
{
        scan the x values in the association until x ≥ point.x;
        if x = point.x then
          scan the y values for the x value until y ≥ point.y
          if y = point.y then
            for each collection point with the current x,y value:
              if collection point = point, delete it and return
        return error, point not found
}
```

Note that the scan operation should be implemented by a binary search to achieve logarithmic rather than linear times. A scan falls through to the next statement if it runs out of values.

**10.27** Pseudo code for a garage door opener is listed below.

```
<closed>       wait for depress event
<opening>      start opening door
               wait for door open event
<open>         wait for depress event
<closing>      start closing door
               wait for either depress or door closed event:
                  if depress event then goto opening
                  if door closed event then goto closed
```

Don't be afraid to use gotos! They have a legitimate use in representing exceptional flow of control, such as exceptions and interrupts.

**14.3a.** This is an example of poor programming style. The assumption that the arguments are legal and the functions called are well behaved will cause trouble during program test and integration. The following statements will cause the program to crash if the argument to *strlen* is zero:

```
root_length = strlen(root_name);
suffix_length = strlen(suffix);
```

The following statement will assign zero to *sheet_name* if the program runs out of memory, causing a program crash during the call to *strcpy* later in the function:

```
sheet_name = malloc(root_length + suffix_length + 1);
```

The following statements will cause the program to crash if any of the arguments are zero:

```
sheet_name = strcpy(sheet_name, root_name);
sheet_name = strcat(sheet_name, suffix);
```

If *sheet_type* is invalid the switch statement will fall through leaving *sheet* without an assigned value. Also, it is possible that the call to *vert_sheet_new* or the call to *horiz_sheet_new* could return zero for some reason. Either condition would make it possible for the following statement to crash:

```
sheet->name = sheet_name;
```

**15.5a.** An interpreter provides a convenient way to quickly find out how a subroutine in a library behaves, bypassing the edit, compile, link, and execute cycle encountered in compiled languages. Some languages have both a compiler and an interpreter. The interpreter is used for rapid program development and the compiler is used to produce an efficient final version of the program.

**b.** A system builders is recommended to avoid this kind of error. It assures that all of the required steps and only the required steps are executed to rebuild an application after you modify one or more source files. Otherwise you are faced with the choice of rebuilding everything, which is time consuming, or trying to remember which steps are affected by your changes, which is error prone.

**c.** A symbolic debugger is a convenient tool for diagnosing this type of problem. It allows you to run your program until the fault condition occurs and then see the line where the fault is occurring as well as the values of program variables. This particular problem is likely to show up in the function described in Exercise 14.3. It appears that the program is running out of memory.

**d.** A change control system is an excellent way of coordinating a team software project.

**e.** A system builder solves this problem.

**f.** Some languages provide a solution to this problem. In C, for example, there is a #line construct that a preprocessor could insert into its output to point to a line in another file.

**15.6a.** Because of tight memory requirements a text segment should be deallocated when it is no longer needed. The problem is to develop a uniform policy that determines when segments are no longer needed. Classes and methods provide a convenient framework for a solution. One set of guidelines is to place the responsibility for memory reclamation with the methods which modify text segments. Access to text segments outside of the object which owns them should be read only. Temporary text segments should be deallocated as soon as possible.

One way to combine text segments follows:

```
Determine the size of the segments that are to be combined.
Allocate enough memory for the result.
Copy the original text segments into the allocated memory.
Deallocate the memory assigned to the original text segments.
```

**b.** For a multipass compiler it is a good strategy to simply let the operating system allocate a large amount of virtual memory. The amount of memory needed depends on the size of the source code being compiled. Because programs are partitioned into modest sized modules it is possible to place a reasonable upper bound on the amount of memory needed.

**c.** You cannot let the operating system allocate a large amount of virtual memory and forget about garbage collection in systems that run indefinitely. Eventually all memory will be consumed. Memory must be deallocated when objects are no longer referenced.

**d.** The first approach, deallocating memory within the subroutine that allocated it in the first place, guarantees that memory is reclaimed without burdening other routines with the responsibility of determining when a block of memory is no longer needed. However, doing so complicates recursive procedures.

**17.14** Object diagram for Figure E17.9.

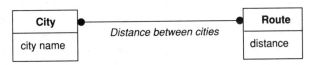

**Figure A17.14** Object diagram for distance between cities

**17.15** The following SQL code determines the distance between two cities for Figure E17.9.

```
select distance
from   Route, City C1, City C2,
       Distance-between-cities D1, Distance-between-cities D2
where  D1.route-ID = D2.route-ID and
       D1.route-ID = Route.route-ID and
       D1.city-ID = C1.city-ID and
       D2.city-ID = C2.city-ID and
       C1.city-name = :given-name1 and
       C2.city-name = :given-name2;
```

**17.16** Object diagram for Figure E17.10.

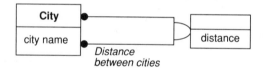

**Figure A17.16** Object diagram for distance between cities

**17.17** The following SQL code determines the distance between two cities for Figure E17.10.

```
select  distance
from    City C1, City C2, Distance-between-cities D
where   D.city1-ID = C1.city-ID and
        D.city2-ID = C2.city-ID and
        C1.city-name = :given-name1 and
        C2.city-name = :given-name2;
```

**17.18** We make the following observations about Figure A17.14 and Figure A17.16.

- Figure A17.16 is awkward because of the symmetry between city1 and city2. Either data must be stored twice with waste of storage, update time, and possible integrity problems, or special application logic must enforce an arbitrary constraint.

- Figure A17.14 has an additional table.

All in all, Figure A17.14 is a much better approach. With a self association it is frequently helpful to promote the association to a class in order to break the symmetry.

**20.3** Shallow copy methods use less space than deep copy methods. Subsequent changes to the original are automatically inherited by a shallow copy. A deep copy is independent of the original.

**a.** For library objects a shallow copy has the advantage of saving a great deal of space since it is likely there will be many copies of the original. We assume there are two types of applications that will access library objects. A librarian will have read and write access to the original. All other applications will have read only access. With a shallow copy a change in the original is automatically reflected in the copies. This may be desirable in some applications and undesirable in others. A danger of the shallow copy is that a mistake while using the librarian program could have disastrous results.

**b.** Because changes in the new sheet should not affect the old sheet a deep copy must be used.

**c.** Either a shallow copy or a deep copy is suitable for copying selected items from one place on a sheet to another, depending on the desired behavior. Use a shallow copy if the copies should inherit changes made to the original. Use a deep copy if it is desired to change the copies independently.

# Index

# Dynamic Model Notation

**Event causes Transition between States:**

**Event with Attribute:**

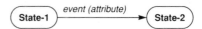

**Initial and Final States:**

**Action on a Transition:**

**Guarded Transition:**

**Output Event on a Transition:**

**Actions and Activity while in a State:**

| State Name |
| --- |
| *entry* / entry-action |
| do: activity-A |
| *event-1* / action-1 |
| ... |
| *exit* / exit-action |

**Sending an event to another object:**

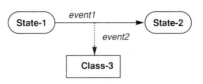

**State Generalization (Nesting):**

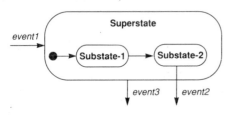

**Concurrent Subdiagrams:**

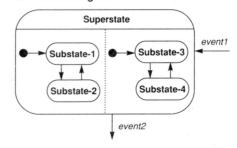

**Splitting of control:**          **Synchronization of control:**

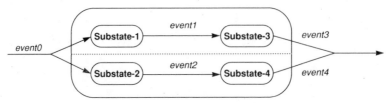

# Functional Model Notation

**Process:**

**Data Flow between Processes:**

**Data Store or File Object:**

**Data Flow that Results in a Data Store:**

**Actor Objects (as Source or Sink of Data):**

**Control Flow:**

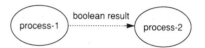

**Access of Data Store Value:**

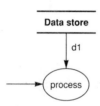

**Update of Data Store Value:**

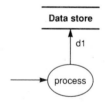

**Access and Update of Data Store Value:**

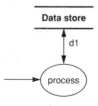

**Composition of Data Value:**

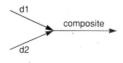

**Duplication of Data Value:**

**Decomposition of Data Value:**

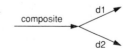